CASES IN ORGANIZATIONS:
BEHAVIOR, STRUCTURE, PROCESSES

BERNARD J. WHITE — The University of Michigan
JOHN H. STAMM ———— Babson College
LAWRENCE W. FOSTER — Michigan State University

1976

BUSINESS PUBLICATIONS INC.
DALLAS, TEXAS

PREFACE

The use of cases in the study of organizations is a long-standing practice. Indeed, it is so well-accepted that a detailed review of the many advantages of the case method need not be recounted in detail here.[1] We are certain that users of this book will soon discover for themselves that case analysis complements the study of theory by demonstrating the descriptive and predictive power of valid theory as well as the inevitable limitations of any theory. In that sense, the casebook serves as an excellent supplement to textbooks such as Organizations: Behavior, Structure, Processes[2], whose basic arrangement this volume parallels. In addition, it will become apparent that case discussions challenge students and teacher to learn from each other through creative reinterpretation of their own experiences as well as through engagement in productive conflict over the many issues which will inevitably arise.

However, these and other familiar benefits of the case method do not accrue automatically. Essential conditions for an effective case discussion include a willingness to share experiences, openness to learning through personal change and growth, and an acceptance of the risks which such learning always entails. We have found that a classroom climate characterized by trust and confidence among students and teacher encourages the taking of such risks, and is conducive to a free-wheeling expression and exchange of ideas and viewpoints upon which learning through the case method depends. While an effective discussion may well be heated and aggressive, it is an underlying attitude by the participants of personal trust and intellectual acceptance of each other which insures that potentially unproductive conflicts are in fact a constructive learning experience.

We have attempted in selecting cases for this volume to generate a good "mix" in terms of length, complexity, subject matter, and perhaps most important, situational and organizational setting. The cases in each section tend, of course, to highlight issues relevant to the subject of that section: effectiveness, behavior, structure, processes, organizational change. However, the cases do represent an effort to raise these issues in a variety of settings. We believe this is appropriate for two reasons. First, we concur with the position taken by many organizational theorists that organizations as social inventions share enough characteristics in common that whatever their specific makeup or function (profit-making, governmental, voluntary, nonprofit), they can be studied generically as organizations. The inclusion of cases from a variety of settings requires the student to make the all-important transition from general theories to many diverse applications.

Second, we have found that students in courses where these cases might be used have an increasingly wide range of interests and career objectives. The majority, to be sure, may well continue to work in large business organizations. But there is growing interest in the management of governmental and educational, of nonprofit and voluntary organizations. In addition, analysis of cases from varied settings has simply proven to be inherently more interesting that the traditional steady diet of cases from business organizations alone. We believe that users of this book will find cases such as Blare General Hospital, Midlandia (state government), Atlanta Police Department, Spaulding University, Aspen County High School, and the United Methodist Church add some unique dimensions of learning to the many excellent business cases and will be very well received by students.

The organization of the book reflects a theoretical approach to the study of organizations which is experiencing growing acceptance. Part I, Organizational Effectiveness, deals with the ever-present problem of evaluating organizational performance. What criteria should be employed? What is the relevant time span for performance appraisal? Whose interests shall be served? Part II raises issues of individual motivation, group phenomena, and leadership which together constitute the major elements of Behavior within Organizations.

The cases in Part III focus on the Structure of Organizations. Structural considerations, those involving relatively fixed relationships among tasks, the prescribed roles of people, and the formal division of lines of authority and communications, are today again being recognized as critical factors in explaining organizational behavior and performance. Communications and decision making, two important Processes within Organizations, are the subject matter of the cases in Part IV.

---

[1]For an introduction to the use of the case method, see "A Note to the Student: On the Use of Cases," page xi.

[2]J. Gibson, J. Ivancevich, and J. Donnelly, Organizations: Behavior, Structure, Processes (rev. ed.; Dallas: Business Publications, Inc., 1976).

All of the above topics--evaluation of organizational effectiveness, behavior, structure, and processes--converge in the cases in Parts V and VI. Part V, The Climate and Development of Organizations, is concerned first with the emerging concept of organizational climate, the totality of organizational properties which influence the way in which members perform their job, and the degree of satisfaction they experience in doing so. Second, the cases in Part V demonstrate several techniques for changing or developing organizations and raise important questions which must be dealt with by the manager who initiates a change effort, the consultant who directs it, and the individuals who participate in it. Finally, Part VI presents four Integrative Cases which challenge students to approach relatively unstructured presentations of facts and impressions about organizational situations and to identify the nature, causes, and possible solutions of organizational problems. Both the skills of analysis and the body of theory and research findings which the student has incorporated into his own approach to organizational problems must be brought to bear in tackling these four cases.

We wish to thank the many individuals who, either as authors or as representatives of organizations, granted permission for cases to appear in this book. (Their names appear on pages v-vi.) The cases which are included represent our judgment in selection, and we take pleasure in the knowledge that their publication here will allow many more students than ever before to learn about and explore the fascinating complexities of organizations through them.

January 1976

Bernard J. White
John H. Stamm
Lawrence W. Foster

CREDITS

Individuals and organizations make a substantial investment of effort and resources in the development of case materials. The contributors to this book, by making that investment, will enrich the education of the many students who will use their cases. The authors take this opportunity to recognize, acknowledge, and thank the following contributors:

Professor Garret L. Bergen, Graduate School of Management, Northwestern University, for "THE CORONET INSURANCE COMPANY."

Professor Edward L. Christensen, School of Business, Brigham Young University, for "BELLEFONTE RUBBER WORKS."

Professor Joel Corman, Suffolk University, for "THE NAHOC COMPANY" and "THE U.S. POST OFFICE AT NEWTON, MASSACHUSETTS."

Professor Jack T. Dobson, School of Business, The Florida State University, for UNITED METHODIST CHURCH."

Professor Margaret Fenn, School of Business Administration, University of Washington, for "A CASE OF DISCRIMINATION?" and "DICK SPENCER."

Professor Wendell French, School of Business Administration, University of Washington, for "PLASTICS INTERNATIONAL LTD." (A) through (E).

Professor David Hawkins and Professor Thomas Raymond, Graduate School of Business Administration, Harvard University, and the Law Enforcement Assistance Administration, U.S. Department of Justice, for "ATLANTA POLICE DEPARTMENT" (D) and (E). The cases were prepared for the Management Institute of Police Chiefs with funds provided under a grant supported under the Law Enforcement Act of 1965. These cases do not necessarily reflect the views of the Department of Justice. Permission granted by Mr. Jack A. Nadal, Attorney-Advisor, Law Enforcement Assistance Administration, U.S. Department of Justice, Washington, D.C.

Dean John W. Hennessey, Jr., Amos Tuck School of Business Administration, Dartmouth College, for "SAVEMORE FOOD STORES 5116."

Professor Herbert G. Hicks, Louisiana State University, and the Southern Case Research Association, for "FISHER MANUFACTURING COMPANY."

Professor James C. Hodgetts, Memphis State University, for "COHACK MANUFACTURING CORPORATION."

Professor David R. Kenerson, University of South Florida, for "JACK DOBBINS' PROBLEM."

Professor Charles R. Klasson, University of Iowa, for "BLARE GENERAL HOSPITAL."

Professor H. R. Knudson, School of Business Administration, University of Washington, for "CENTER CITY ENGINEERING" and "CONVERSATION WITH A SUPERVISOR" (A) and (B). Permission granted by Professor Knudson and Holt, Rinehart & Winston, Inc. which holds a copyright on the cases appearing in Knudson, H., Human Elements in Administration (New York: Holt, Rinehart & Winston, 1963).

Professor Thomas Kubicek and Professor Harold Shaffer, School of Business, Sir George Williams University, for "ECONOMY FASHIONS LIMITED." Permission granted by Professor Kubicek.

Dean Harold Lazarus, School of Business, Hofstra University, for "ANALYSIS OF ERRORS MADE BY A MANAGER."

Dr. Harry Levinson and the Harvard Business Review, for "BOB LYONS" (A) and (B). Dr. Levinson wrote and published the material in "BOB LYONS," Emotional Health in the World of Work (New York: Harper & Row, 1964) and in "What Killed Bob Lyons?" Harvard Business Review, January-

February 1963, pp. 127-43. It is presented here with the permission of Dr. Levinson, President of The Levinson Institute, Cambridge, Massachusetts, and with the permission of the Harvard Business Review.

Dr. Jay Hall, President and Chairman of the Board of Telemetrics International, developed and holds the copyright on the "LOST ON THE MOON" exercise. More information on the exercise and related topics is available from: Telemetrics International, P.O. Box 1850, Conroe, Texas 77301, Tel. 713-756-1185. Permission granted by Mr. David Bollahite for Dr. Hall.

Mr. Walter Milne, School of Industrial Management, Massachusetts Institute of Technology, for "ANDERSON MANUFACTURING AND DEVELOPMENT COMPANY." The case was prepared by Mr. Milne under the direction of Professors A. H. Ruberstein and H. A. Shepard.

Professor Richard B. Peterson, School of Business Administration, University of Washington, for "CONNORS FREIGHT LINES."

Professor Robert F. Pethia and Professor Burnard H. Sord, College of Business Administration, The University of Texas at Austin, for "MODERN FOODS, INCORPORATED."

Professor William J. Reddin, The University of New Brunswick, for "MAX WHITE--RESPONSES IN A T-GROUP," based upon a T-group conducted by the author.

Professor Jack L. Rettig, School of Business Administration, Oregon State University, for "SOUTHERN BANK."

Professor John J. Sherwood, Krannert Graduate School of Industrial Administration, Purdue University, for "SPAULDING UNIVERSITY: THE EDUCATION OF PETER TOPPING," Parts I and II.

Professor Fred E. Schuster, Florida Atlantic University, for "WATERTITE-FLORIDA COMPANY," (A) and (B).

Professor Harold R. Smith, College of Business Administration, University of Georgia, for "THE BOSS IS THE BOSS."

Mr. Graeme M. Taylor, Vice President, Management Analysis Center, Washington, D.C., for "MIDLANDIA."

Professor Sherman Tingey, School of Business Administration, Arizona State University, for "ASPEN COUNTY HIGH SCHOOL."

Professor Robert A. Ullrich, Graduate School of Management, Vanderbilt University, for "THE PRICE OF AMBITION." Professor Ullrich is the copyright holder; work used by permission.

Professor Ralph Westfall, Graduate School of Management, Northwestern University, for "HENRY RESEARCH CORPORATION."

Professor Samuel M. Willson, School of Business Administration, Temple University, for "NEW-COMER-WILSON HOSPITAL."

The University of Western Ontario, Graduate School of Business Administration, for "NATIONAL PAINT PRODUCTS, INC."

Professor Thomas W. Zimmerer, Florida Atlantic University, for "OCEAN ELECTRONICS, INC."

TABLE OF CONTENTS

Page

PART V. THE CLIMATE AND DEVELOPMENT OF ORGANIZATIONS

PART VI. INTEGRATIVE CASES

NOTE

The cases in this book are intended to provide a basis for analysis and discussion, and not to illustrate either correct or incorrect handling of organizational and administrative problems.

A NOTE TO THE STUDENT: ON THE USE OF CASES

There is no better way to learn to use cases than to use cases. So we encourage you to dig right in; however, keeping a few tips in mind may help you along.

In Preparation:

--The key to your learning and to good performance in case discussions is preparation. Indeed, while a high degree of preparation is not enough to insure a productive case discussion, it certainly is an essential condition for one.

--In your preparation we suggest:

(1) reading through the case one time to get an overview of the situation and a sense of the problem areas, if any. (Remember that in some cases there may be no pressing problems. The same skills are required to recognize and understand the causes of normal as well as of abnormal organizational functioning.) Then,
(2) go back and undertake a systematic diagnosis of the organizational situation described. Note (in writing!) specific problems and possible causes, and jot down the facts and observations you are citing as supporting evidence.

--Remember that cases are tools. We have designed this book to encourage you to use them as such. Underlining key points, making notes in the margins, etc., will aid you in your preparation and serve to jog your memory during case discussions.

--Once you are satisfied with your diagnosis, decide on your objectives in attempting to resolve any problems you have identified. Then generate a number of alternative solutions and evaluate each in terms of the objectives you have established. Don't be afraid to be creative in developing solutions. Remember that the implementation of any solution will have "unintended consequences." Try to anticipate as many of these as possible, and consider them in your evaluation of alternatives.

--If possible, discuss your analysis of the case with others prior to the class discussion, unless instructed not to do so. Participation in an established study group is a tried-and-true method of improving your performance in class discussion and increasing your learning from the case. The give and take of a small, informal group is difficult to replicate in the larger class.

During the Case Discussion:

--Get involved. More perhaps than in any other educational setting, the members of a case discussion are dependent on each other for learning. Members of the class who sit back and decline to participate, whether out of shyness or smugness or for whatever reason, are essentially parasites. Not only do they learn only from the efforts of others, but they detract from the potential performance of the group as a whole.

--Value the contributions of others. One can learn from the erroneous analyses and conclusions which are inevitably presented from time to time as well as from the occasional flashes of genuine insight which will also occur. It is the feeling of each class member that his or her contribution is appreciated and valued--even if its content is contested and debated--which facilitates the free flow of ideas essential to a good case discussion.

--Trust your own experiences. Draw on them to illustrate points you attempt to make and to interpret material from the case. But equally important, be prepared to learn from your experiences by being open to reinterpreting them in light of new insights gained in the case analysis and discussion.

--Your values inevitably influence the way you perceive and interpret situations and problems, and they bias your preference for certain solutions over others. In the case discussion, the most which can be asked of you, and the least you should do, is to attempt to make your values explicit to yourself and to others. There is no need to hide or deny them; try to discover them.

--Many times you will feel that the case simply offers too little information for you to do your analysis. We suggest that it would be wise for both you and the class to adopt a rule prohibiting the statement, "There isn't enough information" as a rationale for the early termination of your analysis. Instead, at a minimum, define precisely what information you feel you lack, and consider how you would go about obtaining that information. It is worth remembering that decision makers are almost always forced to make decisions with what they feel is very inadequate information. Indeed, experienced administrators often fault cases for providing the student with more information than they ordinarily have in "real life."

--Don't be satisfied with shallow analysis or pat answers, your own or those of your classmates or teacher. Digging deeper and stretching your thinking is usually rewarding. Contrary to standard economic principles, the marginal benefits of additional analysis of a case often begin to increase again long after they seem to be permanently decreasing.

--The cases provide an excellent opportunity to test your understanding of various concepts and theories introduced in your text and in other readings. Equally important, they allow you to test the usefulness and validity of those concepts and theories. Where, on the basis of your analysis, there appear to be ambiguities in the concepts or gaps in the theories, don't hesitate to point these out. All concepts and theories have some power and certain limitations; it is only in attempting to use them to explain real situations that both their power and limitations become clear.

As you gain experience in analyzing and discussing cases you will undoubtedly develop your own *modus operandi* which may well depart in a number of ways from some of the above suggestions. So much the better. However, we believe that the above points represent a useful starting point, and that some of the conditions--a high level of preparation, involvement, mutual trust and respect among group members--are essential to a productive case discussion.

One final word. Prepare to enjoy the experiences to come! A genuinely new insight, a creative solution to a problem, the challenging of a heretofore unchallenged assumption are all memorable moments in a case discussion and genuine "highs" in an academic career. They are moments which richly repay the work required to experience them.

PART I

ORGANIZATIONAL EFFECTIVENESS

INTRODUCTION

Imagine walking into a room and observing a group of fifteen or twenty people engaged in a heated discussion. Out of the general uproar, you catch the following comments:

"I'm delighted with the company. Profits have been increasing at the rate of 18 percent per year for the last four years, and so have my dividends. That's an effective organization!"

"It's sure a lousy place to work--and I ought to know! Sure, the pay is good, no gripe there. But the big shots watch every move, jump on you if anything goes wrong. And another thing...".

"That company deserves the title "good neighbor." One of its plants is less than a mile from my home--right in the neighborhood. Not only have they spent money to clean up the foul odors that used to come from the stacks, but they also make a real effort to hire people from the neighborhood."

"As a member of management, I'm concerned. It's true that we've had a good earnings record for several years, and that we are considered socially responsible, but that may all be a part of past glory. Demand for our products is slipping in the face of necessary price increases, competitors are introducing low-cost substitutes, and we don't seem to have the research and development capacity to adapt to these changing conditions. Frankly, we seem to be a less and less effective organization, and I'm wondering if our future prosperity, if not our survival, isn't in jeopardy."

The individuals making these comments all are talking about the same company. Question: Is the company under discussion an effective organization?

In its simplest sense, organizational effectiveness refers to how well an organization achieves specified objectives, or measures up against specified performance criteria. This definition should immediately help to answer the question raised above. The comments we have heard would suggest that the company is effective on certain criteria: increasing profits and dividends, providing employment to people in its immediate neighborhood, and not contaminating the physical environment. There is also evidence that it is not effective against other criteria: providing a positive working environment for employees, contributing to a high level of job satisfaction, and adapting to changes in its market, an essential condition for continued prosperity and possibly for survival.

Thus, the response to the apparently unambiguous question, "Is the company an effective organization?" cannot be an unambiguous "yes" or "no." This example illustrates a central feature of the effectiveness concept. Organizations can and do pursue numerous objectives, or stated differently, there are numerous potential criteria against which to judge organizational performance. An organization will frequently do well in pursuit of certain objectives and against certain criteria, and poorly in pursuit of other objectives and against other criteria. Can an organization therefore be simultaneously effective and ineffective? The answer, of course, is yes.

Out of the numerous potential organizational objectives and effectiveness criteria which might be used in measuring organizational effectiveness, which are most relevant? While it is true that some objectives and criteria vary from organization to organization and over time, students of organizations have fortunately identified several which appear to be nearly universal, applicable to all types of organizations at all times. A particularly useful way of looking at these universal objectives and criteria is offered by Gibson, Ivancevich, and Donnelly[1] as follows:

Criteria of effectiveness and time:

(TIME)	Short run	Intermediate	Long run
	←———	———	———→
(CRITERIA)	Production Efficiency Satisfaction	Adaptiveness Development	Survival

[1] J. Gibson, J. Ivancevich, and J. Donnelly, Organizations: Behavior, Structure, Processes (rev. ed., 1976).

The meaning of this diagram is straightforward, but most important. Given a desire by its members that their organization should survive, survival then becomes the ultimate or long-run objective and effectiveness criterion for any organization. Two conditions, adaptation and development are essential conditions for organizational survival,[2] and thus constitute over the intermediate term key objectives and effectiveness criteria. And, since the organization will not even have the opportunity to adapt in the absence of the ability to produce a product or service efficiently and the ability to maintain a level of member satisfaction high enough to motivate continued contributions of effort from those members, production, efficiency, and member satisfaction constitute universal, and essential short-run objectives and criteria for organizational effectiveness.

Beyond these universal measures of effectiveness about which there is general agreement, however, one can only offer guidelines on how to go about identifying additional relevant objectives and criteria. It would appear, and it is probably true, that virtually every group which interacts with an organization (employees, managers, shareholders, government agencies, suppliers, customers, etc.) has its own set of criteria, with related priorities, by which to judge the effectiveness of the organization. Thus, it is always appropriate to ask in an analysis of situations like those presented in the cases in this section, the following questions:

> What are the most relevant effectiveness criteria? Why? Who is imposing them on the organization? What power do they have to enforce their demands? Which objectives can be simultaneously pursued? Which appear to be in conflict? How might the conflict among objectives be resolved? Which criteria must be satisfied? How can effectiveness against each of the relevant criteria be measured?

What will become evident as you attempt to answer these questions is that, contrary to popular belief, organizations do not exist for a single purpose. Organizations do not exist either solely to provide a product or service, or solely to make a profit. Hospitals do not exist solely to treat patients. Universities do not exist solely to educate students. (Indeed, it might very well be fairer to say that hospitals, for example, exist to provide employment for people who like to earn income, do research, serve others, interact with each other, display their mastery of skills, etc., and that caring for patients is the means to achieving those and other ends.) The hard evidence in support of these statements is that if these organizations engaged solely in a single-minded pursuit of the objectives mentioned, without regard for efficiency, for member satisfaction, and for adaptation and development, they surely would not survive. Even assuming agreement on the central objective of an organization (which seldom exists), numerous subobjectives must simultaneously be pursued if an organization is to prosper. For example, organizations must, as noted above, provide employment opportunities which are satisfying enough to attract and retain competent personnel, and they must maintain relationships with their critical environment favorable enough to permit the organization to function.

What specific objectives the organization must achieve, what specific criteria it must measure up to, will vary from organization to organization and from time period to time period. For example, many U.S. corporations have been asked and required in recent years to reduce their pollution of the physical environment, to produce safer consumer products, to employ greater numbers of minority group members, and most recently, to reduce their consumption of energy. These all represent newly-imposed objectives for the organizations to work toward achieving and new criteria of organizational effectiveness against which their performance can be measured. Failure to achieve any of these and numerous other objectives will result over time in reduced ability to achieve the organization's central objective and over the long term can lead to threats to organizational survival.

Thus, in a very real sense, the most important job of an organization's managers is to determine, through careful analysis, which objectives the organization will pursue through the use of its scarce resources. Stated differently, managers must decide to which effectiveness criteria they will respond and which they will ignore. The purpose of the cases which follow is to give you the opportunity, or perhaps motivate you, to the difficult task of asking the critical questions which underlie that decision.

ECONOMY FASHIONS, LIMITED

When Joe Smart, president of Economy Fashions, Limited, engaged the consulting firm of Fleischman and Katz, Incorporated, to review the organizational and management effectiveness of Economy Fashions, Limited, he believed that they would assure him that he was perfectly capable of controlling Economy Fashions which he considered as easy as holding a paper tiger. However, after the first meeting between Fleischman and his chief executives, Smart had the uncomfortable feeling that he was holding a real tiger by the tail. Yet, looking back at his career in Economy Fashions, he had no idea how the tiger evolved and, more perplexing, what he should do about the beast, or more precisely, the predicament in which he now found himself.

Economy Fashions, Limited were manufacturers of inexpensive men's ready-to-wear and made-to-measure suits, sports wear, and young men's clothing with a 1968 sales volume of approximately eight million dollars. The company was founded by Joe's father, Harry, who had come to Canada from England in 1910 and opened an exclusive tailoring shop in Montreal. Harry soon developed a growing clientele as he had been trained by one of London's master tailors and his pleasing personality and English gentlemens' gentleman manner were easy to take by his customers. Soon he enlarged his premises and engaged one, then two, then three assistants.

Because Harry felt that he was working in a limited market he began to make made-to-measure suits for the more exclusive retailers in Montreal. These merchants were so pleased with Harry's tailoring expertise that they asked him to experiment with ready-made suits. Because of his training, he had to sell these suits at higher prices than most manufacturers, but as they contained excellent workmanship and styling, they were eagerly bought by his Montreal accounts. This encouraged him to give up his tailoring shop and go into the manufacturing of made-to-measure and ready-made suits for exclusive retail stores both inside and outside of Montreal.

However, in a few years he realized that the better suit market was limited and he looked for broader areas in which he could expand. He soon realized that mass merchandising was the answer, and so he completely altered his production to turn out made-to-measure and ready-to-wear suits that could be sold in the bargain basements of Canada's largest department stores and in low-end men's wear chains. Again he was successful for no matter how inexpensive he made his suits, they still contained a touch of his early training, and so they appeared so rapidly that he was forced to separate his production and rented space for his made-to-measure factory in another building.

In 1934 he saw the coming market for sportswear and decided to manufacture separate trousers, sports jackets, and ski wear at a third factory. Again because he gave these garments the unique touch of the master tailor, he was successful even though they were sold to Canadians in the lower income brackets.

Harry's only son, Joe, had always liked the clothing business and even as a young lad he spent all his spare time doing odd jobs around the factories. In this way he learned how to lay out cloth, pack suits, work the pressing machines, etc., and, during his senior high school year, he began to wait on the trade. When he went to college he studied commerce and spent his vacations on the road with the salesmen. In each city that he visited, he talked to as many retailers as he could and from these interviews suggested to his dad a number of ways he thought his father could make Economy Fashion lines more attractive to retailers. Harry listened to his son with a smile but accepted very few of Joe's proposals. However, this never discouraged Joe as he decided that when he was president, he would inaugurate the ideas which he thought would improve Economy Fashions.

When Joe received his B. Comm. he decided that rather than continue college for his master's degree, he would enrol in a designing school in New York and then work for a few years in various men's clothing factories in the States. Then he planned to settle down and make his career in Economy Fashions. Harry was pleased with Joe's interest in Economy Fashions and proud of his academic and business accomplishments and, after Joe's experiences in New York, Harry offered him a sales territory. Joe accepted and spent the next five years on the road; then he moved into his dad's office as vice-president in charge of production and marketing. By this time Harry had begun to think of retiring and so made arrangements for Joe to buy him out. Shortly after the purchase arrangement had been concluded, Harry suffered a heart attack. When he recovered he turned the presidency of Economy Fashions over to Joe and retired to Florida.

It was soon apparent that Joe had inherited his father's tailoring genius and that his academic and practical experiences would make him a much more successful manufacturer than his dad, for the business prospered at a phenomenal rate. As Joe was an avid reader of trade and business papers, he became aware of the potential benefits of developing a specialized factory for young men's clothes and sportswear. After much thought, he decided to organize a separate division for this segment of the Canadian population. This entailed renting a fourth factory site but it proved as successful a venture as his made-to-measure, ready-to-wear, and sportswear divisions.

However, as Joe passed his middle forties he began to find it increasingly difficult to complete a day's work. He was fairly energetic in the morning but immediately after lunch his strength would ebb and he quickly reached a point where he ceased to function as he knew he must if he were to continue to run a successful business. He began to suffer from headaches, indigestion, and insomnia, and finally became sufficiently worried about his health to consult his physician. The doctor assured him that his health was good, but that he was suffering from too much business pressure. "Try taking things easy," the doctor said. "Go away on a leisurely holiday and, when you are rested, think about ways to organize your work so that you can take care of the business but still have time to relax and enjoy life."

Joe took the doctor's advice and, for the first time in his life, went to a small resort village where he knew no one and where life was conducted in a leisurely manner. At first Joe had trouble adjusting to the slow pace of the villagers, but eventually he began to accept their leisurely pace and this permitted him to think about Economy Fashions objectively.

To help him examine how the company was operating, he drew up an organizational chart (Figure 1, p. 14). Although this chart gave the impression that Economy Fashions was highly decentralized, Joe knew that he and only he made decisions at all levels. These could be as minor as purchasing another desk for the office or as important as finding the money to finance his operations, finalize style designs, or make changes in manufacturing techniques. He now realized that if he were to take the doctor's advice he would have to make the chart come true by really delegating authority to his executives and then letting them run the company. "I'll be the coach and my executives will be the team," Joe thought. "And in this way we will all work together for the betterment of Economy Fashions."

When he examined the chart more closely, he noticed that he had only one executive at the head office. This was Phil Samson, a smart young C.A. he had hired away from a competitor two years ago because he had heard that Samson was a good systems man and, at the time, Joe felt that systems organization was what he needed most. But although he gave Phil a good salary and the grandiose title of vice president--finance, Joe soon reduced Phil's real function to that of office manager. Before Joe left on his enforced vacation, he had heard rumors that Phil was very unhappy and was looking for another position.

Joe decided that when he got back, he would elevate Phil to controller as well as vice president --finance and let him look after that end of the business. Moreover, he would hire another bright young man, make him assistant general manager, and let him take care of such detailed work as minor analyses, interpretation of data, and so on. This would allow Joe to relax more frequently and still enable him to visit his factories and a certain number of his retail accounts. This was something he had wanted to do for a long time but had never managed because he was either too busy or too tired.

He recalled interviewing a Pierre Laurie who had an M.B.A. from Harvard and some experience in the needle trade. Laurie had claimed that he wanted a bigger challenge than his present position could give him. Joe decided he would hire Laurie when he got back and was pleased with this arrangement because he knew that Samson was about 35, and he thought Laurie was close to 30. Thus he would be a coach to a smart, educated, young head-office team which was something he could boast about when he socialized with his competitors.

The "Coach and Team Syndrome" Concept

When he looked at the organization chart (the plant manager level), Joe Smart was not happy. All the managers except Steve Brown, who was in his late thirties and whom he hired when he went into young men's fashions, were close to or in their sixties and had spent over twenty years with the company. Joe realized that the three older men had always been told what to do by his father and that he had continued with this practice when he took over. Could the four plant managers adjust to a real decentralized structure? Well he had no alternative. For his own good and that of the company, he had to break down its functions into natural segments and permit the top executive of each one to run his own show. Joe and his head-office staff would act as advisors--like a head coach and his two assistants.

When Joe returned to his office, he hired young Laurie and within the week called Laurie and Samson into his office for a consultation. This consisted of an outline of his ideas for decentralization which he called his "coach-and-team syndrome" and said he wanted to put it into effect immediately. He was surprised when both young men cautioned a go-slow implementation policy and suggested that he should first test his ideas. Here he was the oldest in the group, and he was pushing the youngsters instead of vice versa. Joe felt proud of his new-found youth and vigor and dismissed his staff suggestions with "As far as I know, all progress in history is a result of trial and error."

Two weeks after this meeting and without further consultation with his head-office staff or the plant managers, Joe issued a memorandum that introduced his new organizational philosophy. Each plant was to be restructured as a separate division of Economy Fashions, and the present managers of each plant would be elevated to the position of product divisional manager. The memo suggested that all executives below divisional manager refer to the revised organizational chart to check on their status (Figure 2, page 14).

This part of the memorandum concluded with

> ...we are satisfied that an organization on these lines will make the most effective use of the company resources. Furthermore, it will increase our potential to arrive at the best technical solutions aimed at the most valuable markets without incurring the duplication of expense by separate companies.

The memorandum then went on to explain that the divisional managers were to become responsible for all of their factory operations and that these would be judged on the "return-on-capital-employed concept" that had been suggested to Joe by Phil Samson shortly after Samson began to work for Economy Fashions. According to Mr. Samson's formula, the following items were to be included in arriving at the amount of capital employed:

1. Fixed plant less depreciation.
2. Total divisional volume of sales less the profit margin. (This included a portion of the head office overhead and current depreciation.)
3. Divisional inventories (raw materials, supplies and finished product).

Each division would become responsible for formulating its own budget which would then become part of the overall master plan. Divisional budgets were to be prepared by each divisional accountant, who was also responsible for the production of financial and cost statement which were to show two sets of figures: the current month and the total-to-date. As these reports were considered an essential tool of planning and control, all projections of sales were to cover a period of 15 months. At the end of each quarter, the current budget was to be adjusted to the actual figure, and then a new three months' projection was to be added. The memorandum produced a sample of how the revolving type of budget would look.

	ACTUAL	BUDGETED	TENTATIVE
At the beginning of the year	Oct.-Nov.-Dec.	Jan.-Feb.-Mar.	April thru Dec.
End of first quarter	Jan.-Feb.-Mar.	Apr.-May-June	July thru March
End of second quarter	Apr.-May-June	July-Aug.-Sept.	Oct. thru Jan.

As far as expenses were concerned, divisional managers were allowed to spend a thousand dollars without authorization. However, this did not include personal expenses which were to be approved by the corporate controller nor did it encompass capital expenditures which were considered to be those items whose original costs were a hundred dollars or more and whose life extended over a one-year period. This included office furniture, equipment, plant machinery, etc.

Joe's memo produced considerable dismay among the newly designated divisional managers and their executives, and a foreboding awareness of the difficulties to come on the part of Laurie and Samson. It did not take long for interoffice memos to move from the divisions to the head office and back again. For example, Steve Brown writes Phil Samson:

> Dear Mr. Samson:
>
> It seems clear to me that for the purposes of which we are speaking, the investment should be the assets employed by the Division minus the liabilities. To exclude the outstanding payables is, in my opinion, to deny that this form of financing is of importance to the operation. A rescheduling of our invoice paying only a short time ago served to free a very large sum of money for other purposes, and we feel that this phase of the business should not be overlooked. Also, it strikes me that monthly comparisons at the head-office level would not be worthwhile. This, of course, is entirely your own affair. But I would suggest that a quarterly review of the divisional performance may be more meaningful.
>
> Steve Brown

> Dear Mr. Brown:
>
> Your memo re: the use of the investment base minus the liabilities might have merit when considering the company as a whole. However, for divisional purposes I like to think that all assets used, rather than equity, constitutes the base upon which return is calculated. The rate of return should be determined from the standpoint of the user rather than the supplier of capital.
>
> Furthermore, I would like to comment on your discussion with Mr. Joe Smart re: the head-office overhead. I would not be disturbed with some bookkeeping inequalities of this nature. I do not think that intention is to equate the different divisions. Since we cannot make the marketing conditions as fairly comparable as possible, I fail to see your concern about such differences of bookkeeping nature. For ultimately each division's performance will be compared against its own target, i.e.: the budget. The success or failure in meeting the target will then be equated and evaluated.
>
> Phil Samson

The divisional managers continued to attack Samson's return-on-capital-employed concept. Mr. Alfie Knobel, manager, Ready-to-Wear Division, pointed out that the return-on-capital-employed concept should be replaced by the "return-on-net-worth concept." Mr. Samson rejected this suggestion as impractical and continued to insist that divisional operating reports based on his concept be in his office not later than the seventh day of the following month. He would then review the results of each division with the president, and if they indicated a serious departure from the budget, the divisional manager would be called in to explain the cause of the variances.

However, since the divisional managers continued to disagree with Mr. Samson on the return-on-capital-employed concept, divisional reports were often delayed. Jack Jones, the plant accountant in Mr. Knobel's division, strongly objected to Samson's concept and with the connivance of his divisional manager persisted in including certain adjustments in his monthly report which the controller was not ready to accept. This resulted in the correction and revision of several other reports and, thus, all the budgets were delayed. Phil Samson became very annoyed at Jack Jones and complained to the president that Jones was not qualified to do the job. Joe was inclined to believe Phil as for some time now he had had little use for divisional managers and other executives who, in his opinion, did not use modern management techniques and therefore did not know where they were going. Thus when Joe was on one of his usual plant visits to the ready-to-wear division, he asked Mr. Jones why he came to work at 10:00 a.m. instead of 9:00 a.m. The accountant replied that "My wife was visiting her relatives and unfortunately took the alarm clock with her. Being alone I slept in."

Later on when Mr. Smart asked for the amount of the net divisional contribution for the current month, Jones was somewhat indecisive. Angered by the accountant's apparent incompetency, Mr. Smart suggested that there was not much future for Jones in the company and that he might perhaps be better off if he looked for another position. When Mr. Knobel returned from out-of-town the following day and read Mr. Smart's memo regarding the dismissal of Mr. Jones he became very annoyed and immediately contacted the president. Smart assured Mr. Knobel that he had nothing to worry about as the Personnel Department had a number of first-class applicants for the position of accountant for the Ready-to-Wear Division and that any of these would do a better job than Jones.

As noted by the above, Mr. Smart was extremely active, and now he considered that he was not only head coach but the boss as well. He felt that he had to make every effort to visit each division and give the executives in charge all the help and consultation that his time permitted. Every morning, Joe toured one plant or another and talked to various supervisors and department heads, always stressing the point that he was just one of them; that in his company nobody should be afraid to talk to the boss because "here there was no boss, just one team with the same goal." Whether it was production, quality control, or choosing the right shades of fabrics, Joe was always ready to advise; for as he constantly reminded his team "he had had considerable experience in these lines." His afternoons were spent at the head office except when he would remember the doctor's advice and force himself to stay away from the office and pretend to relax.

Although the reports for the first quarter of 1968 indicated that it would be a good year for all lines of Economy Fashions, Limited, both in terms of sales and profits, Mr. Smart felt a vague persistent uneasiness about the company's operations. In particular, he could not understand why Steve Brown had resigned as plant manager of the Young Men's Division and taken a less responsible position with a smaller salary with a competing company. Brown's resignation not only reinforced Joe's feeling that his managers seemed antagonistic to the various proposals that he made, but it triggered a decision to engage a firm of management consultants to assess the effectiveness of Economy Fashions' organizational structure. The following is a transcript of the first of several meetings held by Mr. Arthur Fleischman of Fleischman and Katz, Inc., and the Economy Fashions' management group that met to review the organizational and management effectiveness of Economy Fashions, Limited.

WAY HE PICKED PEOPLE.

Plant is out control

- VIOLENT CHG - IMPLEMENTATION POOR

- POOR Communication

- Decentralized but didn't operate as Div. Mgr.

- STRUCTURE O.K.

Do.

- LISTEN TO DIVISION Mgrs.

- Budget - Explain & Train for DIV. INVOLVEMENT

- Insist on Measures

Highlights of the Transcript of a Meeting of the
Executive Committee of Economy Fashions, Limited
held in the Board Room of the Company
on July 31st, 1968

Present: Messrs. Smart, Parker, Elliott, Knobel, Samson, and Fleischman

Smart: Gentlemen, thanks to your concerted effort we are in the happy position of being a company which, I feel, and the records indicate, is going places. But going places presents problems and I have asked you to attend this meeting so that we can have a frank and open discussion of these problems. I am sure that by now you have all met Mr. Fleischman whom I have retained to study our organization and to advise us on any possible improvements. At this point, I would like to ask Mr. Fleischman to take the Chair and come right to the point, Mr. Fleischman.

Fleischman: Gentlemen, this is the first of a series of meetings which I would like to utilize for a twofold purpose:

First, I would like to review our investigations of your operations in order to make sure we have a clear picture of how you are managing your company, and the problems you are facing.

Second, I would like to start considering some of these issues in terms of their implications for your business. I would like to open this discussion with a question which I feel is indicative of the kind of problems you now face.

Why did Steve Brown leave?

Parker: If I may?

Fleischman: By all means.

Parker: Steve and I had a good relationship, and we still meet occasionally. I posed some questions to him and he told me that he quit because of two things. Firstly, he saw no prospects for advancement shortly after Mr. Laurie joined the company, and secondly because he was fed up with heavy responsibilities but no freedom to manage.

Smart: How could he say that? With increasing sales, all our managerial jobs have been getting bigger and bigger, with salaries none of our competitors can match. Furthermore, ever since we decentralized, Steve commanded far more authority and responsibility than he had ever done before. For all practical purposes he was running his own business. If this isn't freedom to manage, I do not know what is. I cannot see what Laurie had to do with Steve.

Parker: Assistant General Manager is a higher position than that of Division Manager. Steve is extremely ambitious, and with his experience and degree in Business he felt he was well qualified for the Assistant General Manager position. No doubt he saw it as a stepping stone to the position of General Manager.

Smart: General Manager?

But Laurie was not hired with that end in mind--and I never even thought of him as part of my executive committee. His main job was to help me with paper work analysis, interpretation of data, and so on. I am sure Steve would not have liked that kind of work or not being on my executive team.

Fleischman: This seems to me to be a typical case of lack of communication. Normally, the title of Assistant General Manager conveys line relationship. If Mr. Laurie's position is that of a staff employee, don't you think it should be so designated?

Knobel: I would like to come back to Bob's remark (points to Parker) regarding the assumption of "heavy responsibilities but no freedom to manage." I believe that the financial setup we have here is nothing but vaguely defined cost centers in a centralized company. Yet, our performance, even our competence, is measured with data over which we have little or no control. On one hand, Joe insists on autonomous divisions; on the other he comes to my plant and fires my employees in my absence without my knowledge or approval. Would you call this freedom to manage?

Samson: If you are referring to Jack Jones, then I would answer. It was I who insisted to Joe that Jones should be fired. You know very well, Alfie, that he was not qualified to do that particular job. I am sure Joe saved you the embarrassment of having to fire him yourself.

Knobel: Phil, was Jones working for you, or was he working for me? If he was working for me, then I was responsible for both his reports and their content. He reported what I told him to report, so any confusion in his reports could be a reflection on the deficiency of your system.

Smart: Don't tell me that you are still sulking over the Jones' case. We have discussed it too often, I don't want to hear about it again.

Knobel: Well you asked for a frank discussion. I have mentioned only one of the many causes why people are beginning to be dissatisfied around here. There are others. For instance, I do not believe that my performance can be measured by costs over which I have no control, such as apportioning the head office costs to divisions on the basis of divisional contribution to total sales. Neither do I believe in the formula of performance appraisal through return on capital employed.

Elliott: I'd say Alfie is right. I find that some of my best men are becoming dissatisfied in spite of my trying hard to prevent it. You must realize that as the company gets bigger, its becoming more unwieldy, and I believe that unless we stop and consolidate what we are now operating, Economy Fashions may get out of control before we realize it.

Smart: Well, this is exactly why we're here and what I am trying to do. To keep everything under control. With my experience I can assist with various operating problems. At the same time, my mixing with the people promotes an informal atmosphere. I do not want to stifle their initiative by governing them with an iron hand.

Elliott: I don't agree!

Smart: What do you mean?

Elliott: Well, your frequent visits to our plants, whatever the intention, are undermining our authority in the divisions. Instead of discussing operating problems with us, you go directly to our subordinates saying that, in fact, there is no boss in this company. For this reason, if my employees have a problem, they ignore me and wait for your next visit to approach you with it.

Smart: But the trend today is away from the structured organization. The team spirit facilitates a better environment and of course helps to build a better worker morale.

Elliott: Do you feel that it is proper to go around the authority of your divisional managers rather than channeling everything through them? You know, with your attitude you may either encourage talebearing, or the divisional supervisors might acquire the habit of leaning on you as a crutch instead of trying to think for themselves.

Smart: I think that group participation rather than a strict superior versus subordinate relationship is highly stimulating and productive.

Fleischman: Your intention is a good one, Mr. Smart. However, do your regular visits to the plants get the desired results? In my experience I have come across two different practices. One, that the top manager should be concerned solely with strategic functions; the other, that both operating and strategic functions are his domain. Both of these seem to be correct. However, their applicability usually varies with the size of the company and the kind of its particular environment.

Samson: I have a feeling that we are wasting our time on trivial things, while neglecting bigger issues, such better communication, problems of reporting, control, etc.

Fleischman: I thought you were proud of your budgetary control system?

Samson: Well, it is true that we have a better system than a number of our competitors; however, there are still deficiencies in it which need correcting.

Fleischman: Why do you think your reports are late?

Parker: I'll answer that! Because the division managers don't believe in them. There is not only a lack of planning, but today we are told to do this, and tomorrow to do that. It looks like our only objective is opportunistic exploitation of changing situations regardless of the long-range consequences. Our accountants are overworked because of constant "crash programs" for the head office. I believe that with a little more planning and organizing, all this "extinguishing of business bushfires" could be avoided.

Smart: Our planning must be adaptable to fast movement. You mustn't forget that this is a constantly changing industry. If we miss an opportunity, it will never come back.

Samson: And under these circumstances, it takes time to establish smoothly running procedures.

Knobel: I agree, but it is not what we do not do here that is worrying us; rather it is what we do and how we are doing it. For instance, there is no doubt that control over expenditures must be maintained. But, I cannot see the practicality of the present limits. Don't you think that all such controls should be built into the divisional budget for which we are responsible, rather than deprive us of the opportunity to buy most of the things we need to operate?

Samson: Ours is a pretty common procedure which is followed by the best companies, and while theoretically in decentralized operations the budgets should control both the capital and expense expenditures, in practice, some of the best-managed companies are keeping a grip on the purse strings, regardless of the amounts budgeted. Further, our formula of the return-on-capital-employed is a valuable management appraisal tool. Do you know of any better?

Fleischman: Although this is a good way to check on the overall company performance, there may be some doubt how equitable it would be for use in divisions like yours. Furthermore, I would call it a method of control rather than an appraisal system.

Elliott: Do I understand you right, Phil, that you are seeking even more control, when I feel that the conflict here results from the fact that the head office controls all purchases, all salaries above common labor, and that most of our designs emanate from the head office? In fact, everything except production seems to be controlled by the head office.

Smart: I never made a secret about it. Our company is centralized for control purposes and decentralized for operating purposes. Under our system many items are budgeted, but must be reapproved by top management at the time actual expenditures are to be made. This procedure could be credited for our excellent cash position.

Fleischman: Well gentlemen we've made a good start. We have aired several issues. We are all aware of the fact that a lack of tight control over expenditures could run you out of house and home. However, there are other issues equally important we have not touched on yet. For example, how is your organizational structure to be built? Is it at present a typical staff and line organization or is it a functional one? Further, should the functions and the locus of accountability of the plant accountant, the purchasing agent, and the designer be more clearly defined than at present? Maybe we should even determine whether there is any need for job descriptions, or manpower planning, including the retirement age for executives and other personnel. All these areas are serious considerations in a company like yours. I would therefore like you to think about these and other problems which must be solved if we want to formulate a more viable organizational structure for Economy Fashions than it has at present.

Thank you, gentlemen, for coming, and this meeting is now adjourned.

Figure 1
ECONOMY FASHIONS, LIMITED
Management Organizational Chart

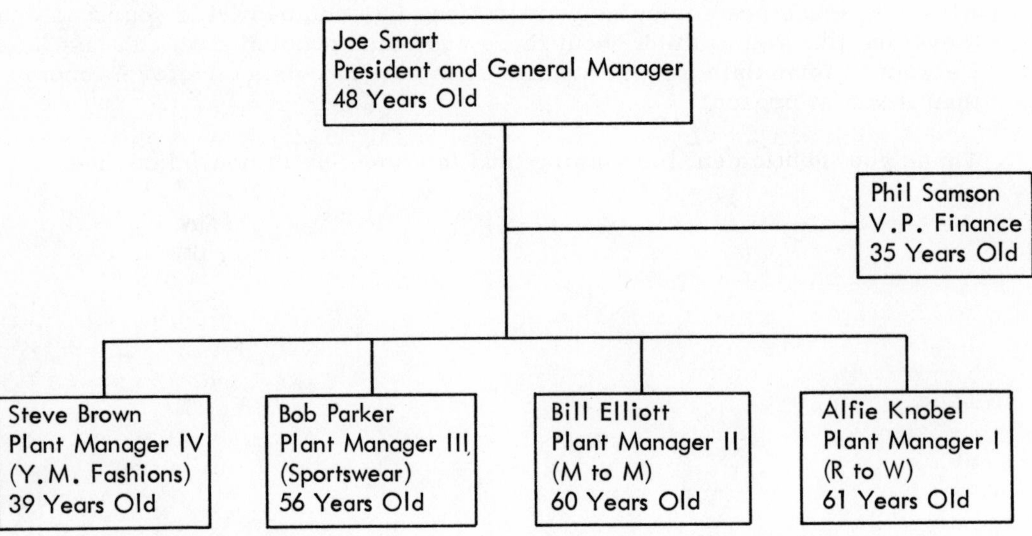

Issued: January 1, 1967

Figure 2
ECONOMY FASHIONS, LIMITED
Complete Organizational Chart

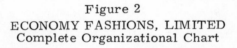

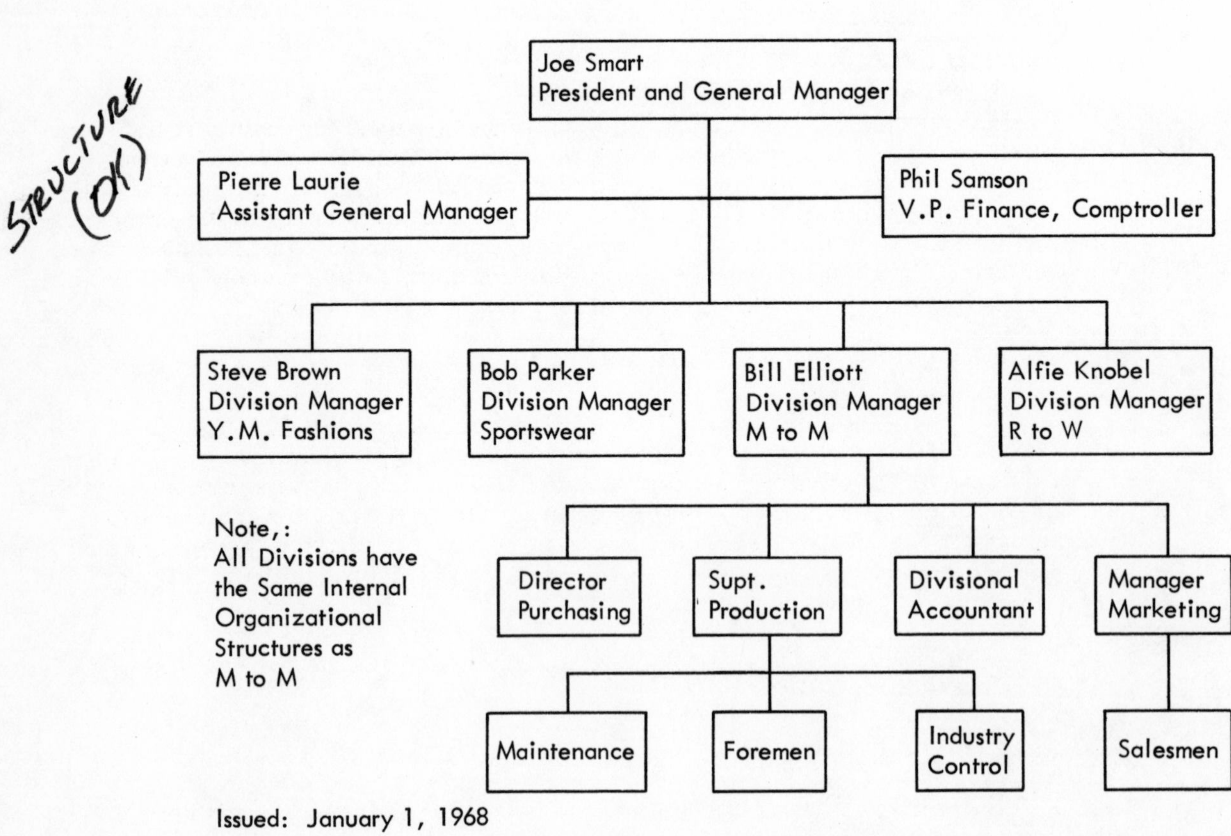

Issued: January 1, 1968

OCEAN ELECTRONICS, INC.

In June of 1967 Ralph Roberts graduated from Florida Atlantic University with a Master's degree in ocean engineering. Ralph was not the typical June graduate; at age 36 he had spent 12 years in the United States Navy. During those 12 years Ralph had learned a great deal about naval electronics. The more he studied electronics the more ideas he had about ways to improve existing equipment. With little opportunity to have his ideas studied, Ralph made an important decision; he left the Navy and, with the aid of his G.I. benefits, entered the University of California at Santa Barbara to major in ocean engineering. His academic record was spotty. His science, engineering, and math courses all showed outstanding performance, yet his studies in the social sciences and humanities were never more than average, and often below average.

Upon graduation from the University of California at Santa Barbara, Roberts looked to continue his education and came to the newly founded Florida Atlantic University in Boca Ratan, Florida. The location had been responsible for the formation of an excellent department of ocean engineering. Ralph's record in his major allowed him to be accepted, and his record at Florida Atlantic University was much above average. His faculty viewed Ralph as an outstanding student. His knowledge of practical ocean engineering, gained through his years in the Navy, lent much to his research projects. It was during his research for his Master's thesis that Ralph made some interesting findings. The result of these findings were the basis of a series of ocean electronics sounding instruments whose accuracy were of a magnitude three times more accurate than existing equipment. Encouraged by his professors, upon graduation Ralph sought financial assistance to establish a production facility to gain the rewards of his research. He believed that much of the profits could be diverted into the development of an ocean research company to allow Ralph to continue his work.

Jim Stanton was contacted in May of 1967 by the chairman of the Ocean Engineering Department about forming a corporation to support the work of Ralph Roberts. Stanton talked to Roberts, asking him what he wanted in terms of selling the new electronics process. Roberts commented that, "I want freedom to do research and a company which will encourage my research by plowing back profits into the firm." Stanton and two Miami associates formed Ocean Electronics, Inc., giving Ralph Roberts 20 percent ownership for his patents and put up a total of $1,400,000.

Stanton stated that, "We thought we saw a good investment, and we put up the needed money. It will be financially rewarding to all involved."

Jim Stanton:
(to interviewer) My associates, David Rubin and Tim O'Leary, and I wanted to invest in a company which could take advantage of the rising market for specialized electronics. Ralph has some patents which we felt provided the nucleus for forming a mutually profitable business venture. We gave Ralph 20 percent ownership in the company which, in 1969, netted him $15,000 in dividends, plus his salary of $10,000 a year. Our prediction for 1970 indicates that his share of distributed earnings will be in the neighborhood of $26,000. That's not a bad neighborhood, is it?

Interviewer: No, I guess not. What was your role in the early formation of the company and its management?

Jim: When Ike Lawson, the chairman of the Ocean Engineering Department at Florida Atlantic University, called me and told me of Ralph, I made an appointment to visit the campus and meet with both Ike and Ralph. At the meeting I was impressed with the capabilities Ralph had shown in his work and told him that I would see if capital could be raised. I subsequently met with David Rubin and Tim O'Leary and they agreed to join in the venture.

Now, as far as management, I am chairman of the board and, in the early stages, was active in its management.

Interviewer: What do you mean, active?

Jim: Well, Ralph was busy making operational the new inventions, so I hired both Ron Able, the manager of sales, and Herb Schultz, the production manager.

Interviewer:	Was Ralph ever involved with these decisions?
Jim:	Yes, he concurred on all decisions. He was president of the company but, as I said, involved at that time with our technical problems.

The Other Executives (See Table 1, page 19.)

Manager of Production, Herb Schultz, Age 47

Herb had been hired in December of 1967 by Jim Stanton. Herb had been the assistant manager of production of a medium-sized electronics firm located in the southwest United States.

Interviewer:	Why did you come with a new firm? Ocean Engineering was just being established and its future was not secured.
Herb:	Well, I like this business. Production is a real challenge. Before, I was the assistant manager; I want to be the top man.
Interviewer:	Are you happy you made the change?
Herb:	You bet. I came here and started from scratch. I have ordered all our production equipment, installed it, designed the work layout, hired and trained the men; in general, I feel its my area.
Interviewer:	What is the work force in your production area?
Herb:	At present we have two other engineers and 15 technicians. We have grown from just myself and no one has ever been layed off. In fact, only two men have left the shop, and both had offers we just couldn't match. They left with our best wishes for success. I think we have a very compatible work group. We have never failed to meet a production schedule. Each technician respects his fellow workers and this respect breeds cooperation.
Interviewer:	Does Ralph ever interfere with your operation?
Herb:	In the last six months Ralph has been causing us a few headaches. He [Ralph] never really cared how we assembled the instruments. He did worry about quality --he always has--and so have I. My men are proud of our quality. Because of the nature of electronic instruments of this type, we inspect each before shipment. Lately he has been making all sorts of ridiculous requests. Two months ago he wanted us to stop assembly of one line so that he could alter the model to include some new improvement he had just developed. Well, it took all Ron Able and I could do to convince him that it would be better to include the changes on next year's line. The cost to redesign and alter our assembly processes in mid-production seemed to have no impact on his opinion.
Interviewer:	Can you still work with Ralph?
Herb:	If Ralph would only go back to the way it was; he does the research and I assemble the instruments.

Manager of Sales, Ron Able, Age 37

Ron also came to the company when it was being formed. Ron had been in the ocean instruments industry with a major producer and was hired because of his proven selling ability. He had many major Washington contacts, which had given him the reputation of being the top man in the field when it came to Government contracts.

Interviewer:	What brought you to Ocean Electronics, Inc.?

Ron: Money. I thought that Ocean Electronics was going to be a winner. The new technology that Ralph was developing was going to set the pace in the future. It is easy to sell the best, and Ralph Roberts had the patents for the next generation of ocean instruments.

Interviewer: How successful has Ocean Electronics, Inc., been?

Ron: Very successful, I believe; and what's more, this is only the beginning. From what I see around the industry, we have the finest electronic ocean instruments in the world. The established firms are really sitting up and taking notice of our products. In fact, I will predict that the 1970 sales will be at $1,400,000, and that 1971 will approach $3,000,000.

Interviewer: How would you describe the customer relations of Ocean Electronics, Inc.?

Ron: To be truthful, spotty.

Interviewer: Can you explain further?

Ron: Many of the sales we make are to governmental agencies, primarily the Department of Defense. They have very exacting standards, and if you wish to compete for a contract, you had better have a product which matches their specs. To this point we are great; the technical specialists of the Department of Defense evaluate our product and make a recommendation that it be purchased over its competitors; then, since we are still small and new, we are investigated as to ability to comply with the contract. In other words, will we be able to do what we said we could? These personnel are not technical types in general. On occasion, Ralph has given these men a tough time. Not by design, but Ralph is just not too aware of how to handle these visitors.

Interviewer: What specifically did he do?

Ron: On a number of occasions while we were entertaining visitors, Ralph would begin on his favorite conversation: his research and his electronic instruments. When most of the visitors showed no technical knowledge of the workings of the product or the nature of his research, Ralph would put them down and just leave, seldom even a good-bye.

Interviewer: Has this happened with civilian clients as well?

Ron: Yes, it has. Most people don't mind eccentrics, but they prefer polite ones.

By June of 1970, Ocean Electronics, Inc., was two and one-half years old and was a financial success. (See Figure 1, page 19.)

Company facilities had been expanding and in 1970 the physical plant comprised two buildings located in an industrial park in Pompano Beach, Florida. One building, the largest, was now used exclusively for production. It had originally served as the entire facility until the recent completion of the office building and research laboratory. The research laboratory had been designed by Ralph and included the finest in modern electronic equipment. The company also owned two boats, which were used as test beds for new equipment and for the personal use of the executives.

Tom Clayton, the executive vice-president, had been hired in 1969 by the board of directors to oversee the general operations of the company. Ralph had not really been opposed to Tom's being hired because he felt that this would take a lot of troublesome problems off his back.

Ralph:
(to interviewer) I just didn't realize that business had so many time-consuming problems. In research, you work at one problem until it's solved. This day-to-day business stuff was really getting to me. Last year Jim Stanton brought up to the Board of Directors the idea of hiring an executive vice-president. Jim said he knew of someone with excellent qualifications who would administer the day-to-day business problems and coordinate with the functional area (sales and production).

Interviewer: What was your reaction to his suggestion?

Ralph: Well, in 1967 when we started, everything was great. I worked on perfecting my inventions and packaging them in a size that fits the needs of boat and ship owners. Each product, though identical in theory, differed in its application, depending on the size of the ship. For instance, an ocean-going freighter is not as limited as to size and weight as a 30-foot pleasure boat. The 30-foot pleasure boat, on the other hand, won't need the range and accuracy of the ocean-going freighter. Then there are the military uses that completely differ again. Anyway, while I was getting all those technical problems solved, Jim Stanton brought together Ron Able and Herb Schultz. He knows about business, and if he said they were qualified it was all right with me; besides, I was really busy.

Interviewer: What happened after you perfected the product?

Ralph: When I was satisfied with the product, we began production and started our sales campaign. About this time Jim Stanton let me take over the reins. By mid-1968 we were showing a profit and the outlook was very promising. Ron and Herb were in almost every day about one thing or another. Delivery schedules, production runs, pricing policies, discounts; it was all new to me. What worried me most was our lack of research. I didn't have the time to get any research done. From the middle of 1968 until we hired Tom Clayton was a miserable time for me. I felt a little lost sometimes. I guess Ron and Herb saw this, and they tried to help. When Tom came, it got me back where I wanted to be.

On a warm July afternoon, Ralph was speaking to Tom Clayton about the proposed cut in the research budget.

Ralph: I don't understand the stockholders; we must do research to prosper. It was my research that got this whole thing started.

Tom: Ralph, look at their side. They put up over a million dollars to get this company going and they want to get a return on their investment.

Ralph: [Interrupts] Return, hell, they want to milk it dry.

Tom: Now that's not so. You own 20 percent of the company yourself. And, besides, the proposed budget for research for 1970 was $110,000 and all of it is yours. That was more than a 45 percent increase over last year.

Ralph: But I am on to something, and we need to buy the equipment now. You don't turn research ideas on and off like water from a faucet.

Tom: We understand that, but there are other things to consider.

Ralph: [Interrupting] You and your bastard costs. I'm going back to the lab.

(Ralph leaves.)

Table 1
OCEAN ELECTRONICS, INC.
Income Statement

	1/1/68	12/31/68	1/1/69	12/31/69	1/1/70	6/30/70
Sales (Net)		$345,000.00		$671,000.00		$584,000.00
Less Expenses						
Administrative	$ 29,000.00		$ 44,000.00		$ 38,000.00	
Operating	160,000.00		361,000.00		261,000.00	
Research	25,000.00	314,000.00	75,000.00	480,000.00	101,000.00	380,000.00
Net Profit		$ 31,000.00		$191,000.00		$204,000.00
Dividends		-0-		75,000.00		

Figure 1
OCEAN ELECTRONICS, INC.
Organizational Chart

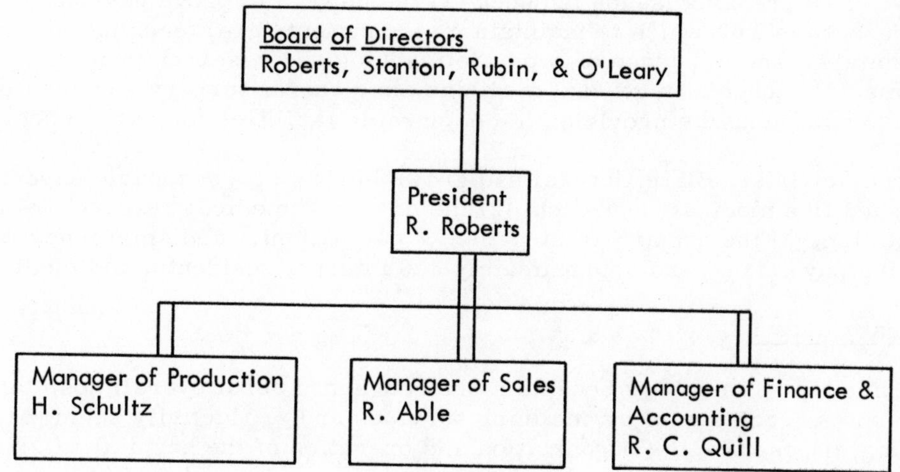

BLARE GENERAL HOSPITAL

In 1864, Blare General Hospital, one of the first municipal hospitals in this country, opened its facilities which consisted of four buildings erected at a cost of $350,000. The original 100-bed, in-patient hospital was built as authorized in 1858 as a facility for the temporary care of indigent and medically indigent persons who needed hospital care. The Acts (authority to develop the hospital) of 1858 stated:

> The City . . . hereby is authorized to erect, establish, and maintain a hospital for the reception of persons who by misfortune or poverty may require relief during temporary sickness.

Through its first 25 years of operation, the hospital continued to pursue its original mission of furnishing proper care to the medically indigent. At the turn of the century, Blare General Hospital assumed a new and leading responsibility in the development of medical care through a program of medical research and education. This decision, a major one, placed tremendous and new demands upon human and nonhuman resources of the hospital. Physical facilities were then expanded, additional staff acquired, and the work of advancing medical frontiers initiated. It was necessary for the hospital to make a number of organizational affiliations, both formal and informal, with the two major medical schools located in the city. During the following three decades Blare General pioneered in the use and development of many advancements in medical science.

From 1932 through 1958, with its existing programs of medical care for patients, medical research, and educational internship for medical doctors and nurses, Blare General was gradually besieged with a growing but common number of problems which then confronted similar aging urban general hospitals. Two pressing issues included (1) the need to improve physical facilities, and (2) the shortage of resources with which to maintain major patient care, teaching, and research programs of the hospitals. The existence of separate teaching and research programs conducted by faculties of two medical schools in general medicine and general surgery services created special sorts of problems concerning the provision of comparable facilities for each school.

By 1958, a century later, Blare General had grown beyond all reasonable expectations in terms of (1) its established fine medical reputation, (2) the desire of medical researchers and interns to work at the institution, (3) the quantity of in-patient,[1] out-patient,[2] and emergency care, and (4) the staff of 400 visiting physicians, and approximately 300 interns, residents, and medical fellows.

<u>Board of Trustees' Concern</u>

In 1953, the five Board members became more concerned about overall hospital operations. Rising operating costs accompanied by declining services and productivity seemed to reflect the need for improving, if possible, the organization and operation of the hospital. During the 1956-1958 period, the above trends continued. Total and net expenditures of the hospital had continued to increase. Along with this occurrence, employee turnover edged upward, absenteeism climbed above the average for similar institutions, morale appeared to be low, and considerable difficulty existed for recruiting competent, nonprofessional help. With three-fourths of total annual expenditures allocated to wages and salaries, the Board expressed a sense of urgency regarding an immediate improvement in hospital operations. For several years (1956-1958), the Board of Trustees openly recognized that clear objectives did not exist for the hospital. This led to questions such as the following: (1) What responsibility does the city have for providing patient care, teaching, and research in a city hospital? (2) Is the original character of the hospital appropriate now or should it be formally changed? (3) How can the administration of the hospital be improved?

To answer these questions, in 1958 the Board of Trustees decided to hire a management consulting firm to study the overall structure and operation of the hospital. The basic purpose of this study was to reorganize the hospital so as to achieve a management organization capable of increasing revenues and decreasing costs. An annual net savings to the taxpayers of $3.5 to $4.0 million as related to the existing budget structure at that time was the overall financial goal sought. After extensive interviews with various consulting firms, a company was retained to conduct the desired

---

[1]In-patient refers to all individuals admitted to hospital for medical and/or surgical treatment.
[2]Out-patient refers to all individuals treated at the hospital but not admitted to the hospital

management study of the hospital. Based upon findings of this study, the Board planned to act objectively incorporating, insofar as their judgment saw fit, the recommendations of the consulting firm. The following information consists of factual and judgmental data obtained either during interviews or as a result of examining records and reports prepared by hospital staff. To insure its accuracy, information collected for analytical purposes was checked by hospital personnel. Close to 200 supervisors and nonsupervisory personnel of the hospital were interviewed during this study which revealed in part the following information:

Operating Characteristics of Hospital: 1940-1958

From 1940 to 1958, the amount of patient service had declined steadily along with constantly rising operating costs.

Patient Service Statistics. Gross hospital admissions (out- and in-patients) declined from 44,875 in 1940 to 32,885 in 1945, a decline of about 37 percent. Also, the total number of patient days of service provided declined from approximately 511,000 in 1945 to 390,170 in 1958, a reduction of 23.6 percent, and the average census of in-patients declined from 1,400 in 1940 to 1,023 in 1958. Hospital officials attributed these declines in hospital service to several factors including:

(1) General advance in the prosperity of citizens of the community.
(2) Marked increase in coverage of persons by health insurance plans.
(3) Inadequacy of the physical facilities both as to accommodations for private patients and condition of the patient care facilities available.

Growth of Expenditures. Total operating expenditures for the hospital increased from approximately $3.2 million in 1940 to about $14.8 million in 1958--about 362 percent. Operating expenses excluded capital budget items which were provided solely from bond issues of the city. A comparative analysis of expenditures by function for 1940 and 1958 revealed the following information:

Expense Classifications	1940 ($3,148,000)	1958 ($14,800,000)
Administration	9.1%	7.1%
General services (1)	37.2	29.6
Plant (2)	10.2	7.7
Professional care of patients (3)	43.5	55.6
Total	100.0%	100.0%

(1) Includes functions such as dietary, housekeeping, laundry, etc.
(2) Includes functions such as heating, lighting, maintenance, etc.
(3) Includes physicians' salaries, nursing, medical, and surgical equipment, etc.

Costs per Patient Day. An analysis of costs per patient day of service rendered showed a constant upward trend with pronounced increases during the 1956-1958 period. Costs jumped from $5.59 in 1940 to $36.54 in 1958. Of this increase, the largest portion represented salary and wage costs which in 1940 amounted to 63.9 percent of expenditures; in 1958 it was 75.7 percent.

Changes in Staff. During the 1950-1958 period, the number of hospital employees increased constantly from 2,837 to 3,266. Also, during this same period the actual number of employees always remained significantly below those officially authorized. In 1958, Blare General operated without its full quota of authorized personnel even though many service departments were overstaffed while critical vacancies existed in a number of technical areas. Hospital officials attributed this increase in personnel strength to two major factors: 1) advent of five-day, 40-hour week for employees (had previously worked 45-50 hours a week), and 2) reduction in the amount of service provided by student nurses.

Revenues. Of the $14.8 million operating expenses incurred during 1958, the hospital generated only $3,692,648. Sources of this revenue included group insurance (31.4 percent), old-age assistance (24.2 percent), public welfare, city and state (14.0 percent), veterans' services (8.0 percent), self-paying patients (7.6 percent), disability assistance (6.5 percent), aid to dependent children (6.0 percent), all others (2.3 percent).

Physical Plant. The entire hospital facility in 1958 consisted of 35 major and several minor buildings situated on a 14-acre site in the middle of an old, low-income district of the metropolitan city of approximately two million persons. Of this number, 21 buildings were built before 1925. Because of its age, inadequacy, and lack of periodic maintenance, the entire hospital pavilion-type complex was a depressing and dingy sight. Because of this fact, and its location, hospital officials found it difficult to recruit personnel, expecially nurses who had reasons to be concerned about their personal safety to and from work.

Administrative activities were located in 13 separate buildings which were not all interconnected by the maze of underground passageways. Fifty different nursing wards (20 beds each) were similarly located in many different buildings. Some wards included supporting facilities such as treatment areas, nursing stations, medication and utility rooms, which were considered inadequate. Ward personnel also dispensed food to patients. All food was transported in bulk to each ward on separate carts from the central kitchen. Dishes were cleaned in a kitchen located at the end of each ward unit.

Surgical facilities were located in three buildings, radiology services in seven buildings, and service laboratories in 10 buildings. All the diagnostic and laboratory facilities were used for both in-patient and out-patient service.

Administration of Hospital

Under the immediate direction of the mayor of the city, the hospital Board of Trustees was responsible for the management and operation of Blare General Hospital as shown in Figure 1. The Superintendent, in turn, was responsible for providing staffwork to the Board, and, in accordance with policies established by the Board, for directly managing all phases of hospital operations.

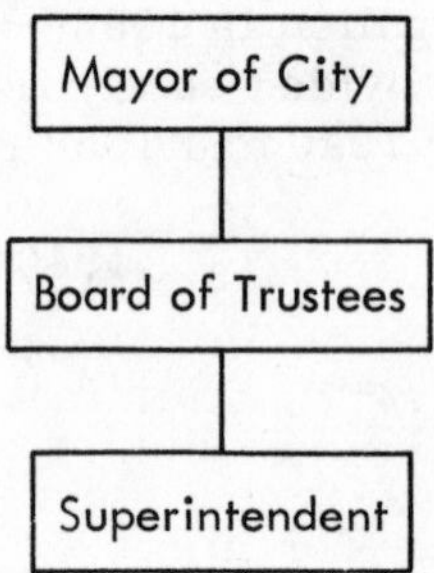

Figure 1. Top management of Blare General Hospital, May 1959.

Board of Trustees. The Trustees were not a completely independent Board since their mandate was to operate the hospital "for the city." Behind all policy decisions and day-to-day administrative matters were (1) statutory and ordinance requirements of a municipal government, (2) Act of 1880 which incorporated the Trustees, and (3) Rules and Regulations of Trustees.

The Board as authorized in the Act of 1880 consisted of five members. Each Trustee was appointed by the Mayor for a five-year term, on a rotating basis, so that one new Trustee would be appointed and confirmed each year. The Mayor had the power to remove from office any Trustee and the hospital superintendent for any reason. Annually, the Board selected a president. Powers of the Board included the right to make rules and regulations relative to the operation of the hospital, to its employees, and to fix and enforce penalties for violation of these directives. All directives were subject to amendment by City Council and needed to be framed within existing city statutes applicable to the hospital. Most of the "Rules and Regulations of Trustees" concerned assignment of duties of certain employees and similar items. The most recent document of "Rules and Regulations" published in 1924 along with its addenda was considered to be largely outdated, ignored, and of little value to hospital operations in 1959.

Meeting twice monthly, a majority of the Board constituted a quorum. Standing board committees included: Rules, Supplies, Finance, Service, Building and Grounds, Library, Heating, Lighting and Ambulance Service, and Medical Department and Training School. These committees met infrequently because of the two regular Board meetings held each month. Rarely did these committees contemplate future problems or issues of the hospital or make major policy decisions. Usually committee matters were discussed and handled at regular board meetings. Since 1957, a Joint Conference Committee functioned to improve communications and to provide a joint review of medico-administrative matters between the medical staff and administrative staff.

Usually, the superintendent prepared and presented matters to the Board for its consideration and action. In fact, the Board had come to rely heavily upon the judgment of the Superintendent regarding the quality of patient care offered by Blare General. Because of city statutes, Trustees were forced to spend much time approving contracts and expenditure of funds. As well, a considerable amount of Trustee time was consumed with reviewing minor administrative matters such as conducting hearings (according to city statute) for employee disciplinary and discharge hearings. Individual Trustees commented that more than half their time was spent on trivia and less than 20 percent on major policy matters. A review of 281 agenda items showed that a majority of Board time concerned routine administrative practices and requests of the medical staff. Some Board members felt they did not have sufficient time to review materials before a decision would be required.

Hospital Superintendent. Responsible directly to the Board, the Superintendent (a physician) was personally held responsible for all activities performed within the hospital. His duties were specified in the "Rules and Regulations" of the Board and included the following partial list:

--He shall have charge of all patients admitted to the hospital until attended to by physician or surgeon to whom assigned.
--He shall, together with Director of Nursing and one member of senior staff, plan and control the method of instruction of the School of Nursing.
--He shall see that there is no waste or carelessness in any department and shall report to the Trustees omissions of duty, or disorderly conduct, on the part of any officers, appointees, and employees.
--He shall make no purchases exceeding the amount of $100 or of any unusual nature without sanc, tion of the Trustees or of one of the Board committees.
--He shall submit to the Trustees all bills ready for payment at regular meetings, twice monthly.
--He shall receive all applications for admissions to the hospital and shall admit such persons as in his opinion are proper cases for treatment.

The above list indicates a few of the many duties specified for the Superintendent position in the "Rules and Regulations of Trustees." The incumbent who held this position had no job security since his employment could be terminated at any time by the Mayor. No recourse was available to a person discharged in this manner.

Organization of Hospital

Figure 2 shows a chart of the main organization structure and administrative reporting relationships within the hospital as of March 1959. This chart contains position titles for each of the individuals and/or groups which participate in the management of the hospital and who report to the superintendent or one of his principal assistants. Deans of the medical schools appointed all chiefs of staff, the Mayor appointed all major nonmedical administrators, and minor supervisory positions were controlled by Civil Service Regulations.

Administratively, Blare General was organized around six functionally defined areas. Each administrative head had responsibility for directing and conducting all activities within his or her area. The major areas consisted of:

--Administrative and Control Services
--Professional Medical Services
--Nursing Services
--Other Professional Services
--General Services
--Plant Services

Administrative and Control Services. These services related to planning, coordination, personnel administration, and management controls. Specific activities included financial planning, budgeting, control over income, patient account management, accounting, property control, and expenditure control. Supervisors and others who performed administrative and control functions included personnel in the Office of Superintendent, Assistant Superintendent, Executive Officer, Finance Officer, Personnel Officer, Executive Secretary, Chief Clerk, Chief Payroll Clerk, Statistician, Supervisor, and Admitting Clerk.

Personnel in the Superintendent's office assisted him directly by providing clerical assistance. Two administrative assistants performed staff studies as directed and were assigned limited supervisory jobs.

Figure 2
BLARE GENERAL HOSPITAL
Organization Chart

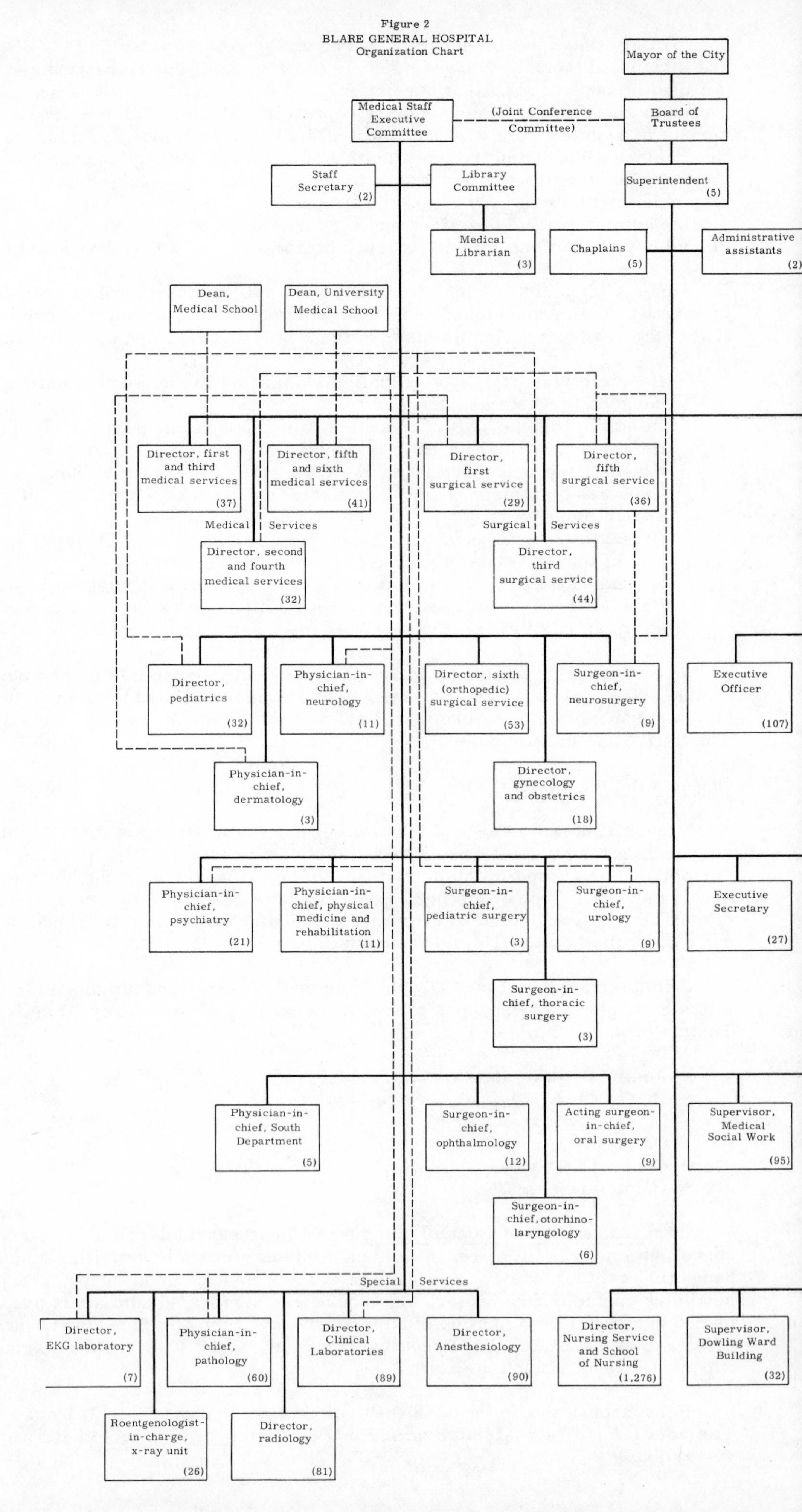

March, 1959

Legend:

(a) These positions are occupied by one person.
(b) Also is responsible for plant operation and maintenance of the Langston hospital and sanitorium divisions.
(c) These laboratories have dual supervision.

Note:

The number of authorized positions in each organizational unit is indicated in parenthesis in each position title box.

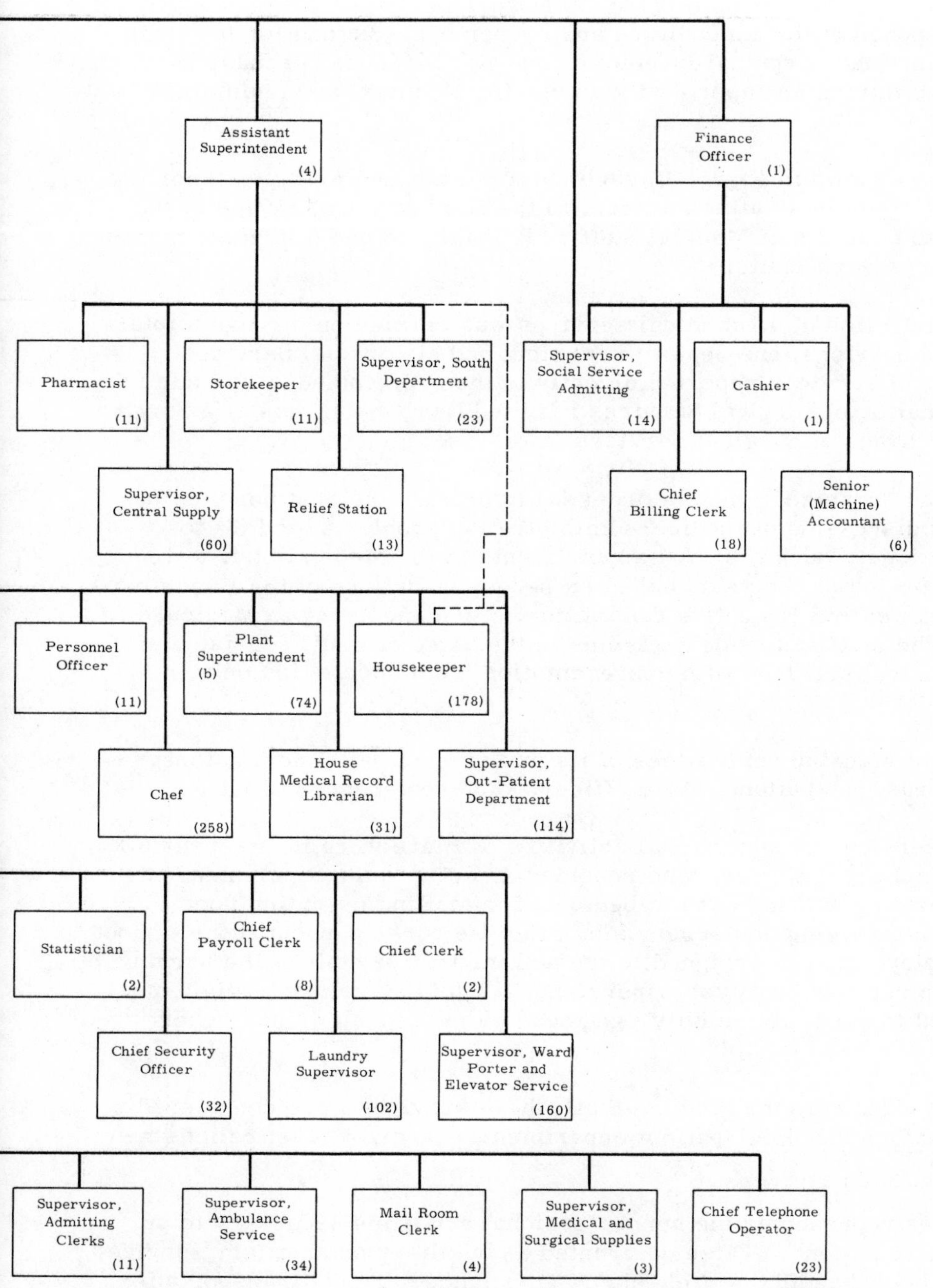

An Assistant Superintendent supervised six employees, as shown in Figure 2, and administered the resident and intern Medical Staff. He also approved purchase requisitions, requests for maintenance and repair work, and similar accounts.

The Executive Officer, together with six other physicians, took charge of the hospital in the absence of the Superintendent and/or Assistant Superintendent. In addition, he had responsibility for supervising five individuals as listed in Figure 2.

The Finance Officer had responsibility for revenue and income operations and the direct supervision of four employees. He directed the preparation of regular and special reports relating to payment to outside agencies and was responsible for all income control operations.

The Personnel Officer was responsible for liaison with the Civil Service agency, maintaining personnel records, maintaining position control, and for processing all forms relating to the employment, transfer, promotion, and discharge of employees.

The Executive Secretary was responsible for expenditure and proper records and for preparing reports of expenditures. He also maintained perpetual inventory records, screened purchase requests and prepared purchase requisitions, examined and approved invoices for payment, and maintained records of payments.

Professional Medical Services. As shown in Figure 2, each chief of staff had multiple reporting relationships: to the Superintendent for administrative matters, to the Executive Committee of the Medical Staff for matters pretaining to business of Medical Staff, and usually to one of the two medical schools for specific teaching and research matters.

As shown in Figure 2, the administration of all medical services was carried on through a total of eight Medical Services, 12 Surgical Services, one Separate Service, and six Special Services. Each of these 27 administrative heads of services reported directly to the Superintendent for administrative matters. Informally, coordination of Surgical Services resulted from the efforts of a Surgical Advisory Board composed of selected heads of Surgical Services.

The Medical Staff organization had organized itself in order (1) to provide the best possible patient care, (2) to provide a means for discussion of medico-administrative problems, and (3) to provide education and maintain educational standards. All appointments to the Medical Staff were made by the Board of Trustees for a period of one year, based on recommendations of the Executive Committee of Medical Staff. (Members of this Executive Committee, which according to Medical Staff Bylaws carried out business of the staff and made decisions in the name of staff, consisted of administrative heads of the major medical services with representation from specialties only on a rotating basis.)

The Medical Staff maintained eight standing committees of its own (executive, tumor, autopsy and tissue, ether prize, medical records, out-patient, house officer, joint-conference).

Nursing Services. The nursing service and educational activities of Blare were the responsibility of the Director, Nursing Service and School of Nursing who reported directly to the Superintendent. Major nursing service concerned providing nursing care at bedside, for staffing operating rooms, delivery rooms, and nurseries and for providing and supervising graduate nurse personnel throughout the hospital. As of May 1959, 67 employees were assigned to the administrative staff of the nursing office of which 49 assumed leadership responsibility for supervising 1,208 full- and part-time employees whose services were required to staff this activity. Of these 49 personnel, 48 had reporting relationships with the Director.

Other Professional Services. In addition to the Medical Staff, these services were considered a part of the "patient care" concept and included out-patient department, pharmacy, east relief station, and medical social work.

General Services. These services represented the nonprofessional activities necessary to operate the hospital and to provide care to patients. Often designated as auxiliary or ancillary services, they included the following: dietary, housekeeping, storekeeping, ambulance service, transportation of patients and materials, laundry, security, mail room, telephone, medical records, and elevator operation. Of these 13 supervisors, 11 report to the Superintendent and two to the Assistant Superintendent.

Plant Services. All plant services were provided under the directive of the Plant Superintendent, including repair and maintenance, renovation and operation of the power plant.

Administrative Relationships

Inability of supervisors to see some officer with authority to make decisions and to take action constituted one of the prime complaints of supervisory personnel in the hospital. Practically all supervisors, medical and administrative, stated that it was necessary to get certain decisions from the hospital Superintendent who was almost impossible to see. Moreover, many supervisors were frustrated because of additional time delays and lack of action once administrative decisions were made. Frequently, months would pass before any effort was made to implement agreed-upon decisions.

Management Reports. Department supervisors were not required to submit regular reports about their respective operations and performance to the Superintendent. Nor did they receive regular information from the Superintendent regarding hospital operations. However, many departments did prepare daily, weekly, monthly, and annual reports about their operations. These, for the most part, did not reflect departmental performance effectively since no standards or controls over the amount of work produced by different departments existed. It was therefore impossible to compare the number of assigned personnel to some standard (for example, pounds of laundry cleaned per man-hour) to determine whether personnel were being utilized effectively.

Each month the Finance Officer prepared a report for top management which contained the following data:

(1) Balance Sheet
(2) Analyses of accrued charges
(3) Accrued revenue by service
(4) Summary of cash revenues
(5) Free work and allowances
(6) Statement of cash receipts
(7) Statement of unencumbered balances
(8) Expenditure statement by program (research)
(9) Distribution of expenses by assignment code (not separate administrative units).

The statistician maintained detailed records about patient days, admissions, discharges, deaths, births, and other similar information for the Annual Report of the Board.

As of December 30, 1958, receivables were estimated at approximately $14 million. If payment was not received from a released patient, the account was maintained as an open receivable indefinitely. During the 1951-1959 period, an estimated 81,200 unpaid accounts existed.

Budgeting. The Executive Secretary was responsible for preparing the budget. Early in August, he would request each department to estimate its expenditures and submit them the following month. Upon review of department requests and previous years' expenditures, a budget was prepared by the Executive Secretary, submitted to the Superintendent who, in turn, requested Board approval prior to forwarding it to City Hall. Figure 3, "Chart of Accounts for Budgetary Accounting" shows 20 expense accounts for which balances were reported monthly. Since they were not broken down by organizational units, no one department head was held responsible for his expenditures in any individual expense account. No means existed to insure that expenditures were contained within budgeted appropriations. In 1958, eight of 20 accounts were overexpended as well as the total for the hospital. Through the years no attempt was made to establish standard costs where appropriate and feasible to do so.

Although department heads prepared and submitted annual budget requests, they were not informed of their approved budget and were not provided with regular expenditure reports so they might participate in control over expenditures.

Number	Category
20	Permanent Employees
21	Temporary Employees
22	Overtime
31	Communications
32	Light, Heat, and Power
36	Repair and Maintenance of Building
37	Repairs and Servicing of Equipment
38	Transportation of Persons
39	Miscellaneous Contractual Services
40	Automotive Supplies and Materials
42	Food Services
43	Heating Supplies and Materials
44	Household Supplies and Materials
45	Medical, Dental, and Hospital Supplies
46	Office Supplies
49	Miscellaneous Supplies
59	Office Furniture
66	Miscellaneous Equipment
69	Miscellaneous Current Charges
801	Installation, Alteration, and Repairs

Figure 3. Chart of accounts for budgetary accounting at Blare General Hospital.

Personnel Administration

Of the 3,456 employees authorized as of April 1959, only 3,181 had been hired. From 1940 to 1958, the hospital had never hired the full number of personnel authorized. To perform his job in procuring and maintaining the hospital work force, the Personnel Officer was authorized a staff of 10 but actually only had seven on the payroll. (During the 1957-1959 period, three Personnel Officers had resigned their position.) The personnel staff spent most of their time processing forms involving appointments, transfers, terminations, and related personnel actions, and reflecting these changes on permanent records. The Personnel Officer would sign as many as 15,000 personnel actions annually. All appointments to positions were conducted in accordance with Civil Service statutes for all employees except physicians and graduate nurses. While reliable statistical data on employee turnover, sick leave, and absenteeism and related types of performance indicators were not available, the Personnel Officer estimated turnover to be 20-27 percent. For a one-month period, an analysis of absenteeism revealed an 8 percent rate which was twice that of similar institutions.

Morale and Productivity. Morale was considered to be generally low throughout the nonprofessional ranks in the hospital. Productivity correspondingly was low. Many employees failed to report for work on time and regularly left their jobs early. Frequently, employees failed to obey orders of their superiors and were not disciplined. Oftentimes employees could not be accounted for during their shift and could not be found. And many employees were found idle, standing around with no apparent supervision.

Orientation and Training. The hospital had no formal orientation or training program for any of its employees. No employee handbook existed to communicate hospital personnel policies and practices. What orientation existed was provided by supervisors once a new employee arrived on the scene. What went on then varied greatly among departments. Training normally consisted solely of acquainting the employee with tasks to perform and of limited supervision to insure that tasks were performed in proper manner. All employees were permitted to visit the Personnel Office at any time to get answers to questions about their job.

Compensation. Except for professional employees (who frequently were paid from three different sources) employees received automatic advancements in grade at specified time intervals within their job-range classification once having been removed from a six-month probationary employment period. Little opportunity existed for the hospital to recognize and reward excellent work. No performance rating or appraisal plan was used. Incremental increases were merely subject to satisfactory performance and good attendance. As a result, many employees performed only to the extent that they could hold down their jobs. There was no employee counseling program or labor contract with the employees.

Exercise

EFFECTIVENESS CRITERIA FOR THE CLASS AS AN ORGANIZATION

Objective

The objective of this exercise is for the members of your class to come to agreement on a statement of the criteria against which they wish to evaluate, near the end of the term, the effectiveness of the class as an organization. On some criteria, there may be universal or near universal agreement. On others, there may be conflict, and only one or a few members may hold these criteria. All criteria, however, should be listed and defined in the statement and note should be made of the degree of support for each.

In addition, the class should explore two other issues:

(1) Which criteria may be satisfied simultaneously and which criteria are clearly or potentially in conflict (i.e., satisfying one will or may prevent or detract from satisfaction of the other(s)?)
(2) What class variables (e.g., teacher's expertise or supportiveness, quality of exams, student abilities and experience, physical environment, grading policies, etc.) do you feel will be most important in satisfying each criterion of class effectiveness you have identified?

Instructions

Your instructor will provide specific directions for the procedure you are to follow in pursuing the objectives stated above, since the best procedure will vary according to class size and time available. Whatever the procedure, you may find the following statement to be a helpful starting point in your thinking on effectiveness criteria for the class:

> The important criterion in education (and in the management of organizations) is what is LEARNED and not what is TAUGHT. Consistent with this approach, the accomplishment of a course can be measured in terms of what students learned (which grades may not reflect) and not what the instructor taught, since these may not coincide. What is meaningful to each individual is the manner in which he has benefited as a function of his own role in the course.[1]

The final result of the class effort should be a statement (1) listing the criteria identified and noting the degree of support for each; (2) summarizing probable conflict and nonconflict between and among the criteria; and (3) discussing possible relationships among class variables and the various effectiveness criteria.

NOTE: Retain this statement for possible use in doing the exercise at the end of Part IV entitled "Survey Feedback in the Classroom."

[1]The authors wish to acknowledge Professor J. B. Ritchie of Brigham Young University who has refined this thought-provoking statement over a number of years.

PART II

BEHAVIOR WITHIN ORGANIZATIONS

Individual Behavior

Group Behavior

Leadership

INTRODUCTION

A critical function of the manager is motivating and directing the behavior of other members of the organization toward the completion of certain tasks and the achievement of certain goals. Managers have long recognized that insights into why individuals behave the way they do and into what needs they are trying to satisfy through their work and their affiliation with an organization, can increase managerial effectiveness in performing the motivation/direction further. In addition, it is clear both from practical observations, as well as from research, that the groups in which an individual finds himself can contribute to or detract from his overall satisfaction and his job performance. And finally, the elusive but central managerial function of providing leadership within the organization has become increasingly recognized as primarily a behavioral phenomenon--a complex interaction between a manager and his subordinates. This section will briefly discuss each of these topics--individual and group behavior, and leadership--and the cases in this section offer situations in which to explore them as they actually occur.

Individual Behavior

While there are many types of individual behavior, the concern of managers is obviously with that which is motivated or goal-directed. Perhaps more than anything else it is this concern of managers and the promised insights into individual motivation by behavioral scientists which has provided the most durable link between the two groups. Starting from the basic premise that motivation is essentially a process by which the individual attempts to satisfy certain needs by engaging in various behaviors, one can quickly identify several major contributions of behavioral scientists to managerial thinking and practice.

A more complete picture of the motivation process is offered by expectancy theory, a simplified form of which is presented in the following model:

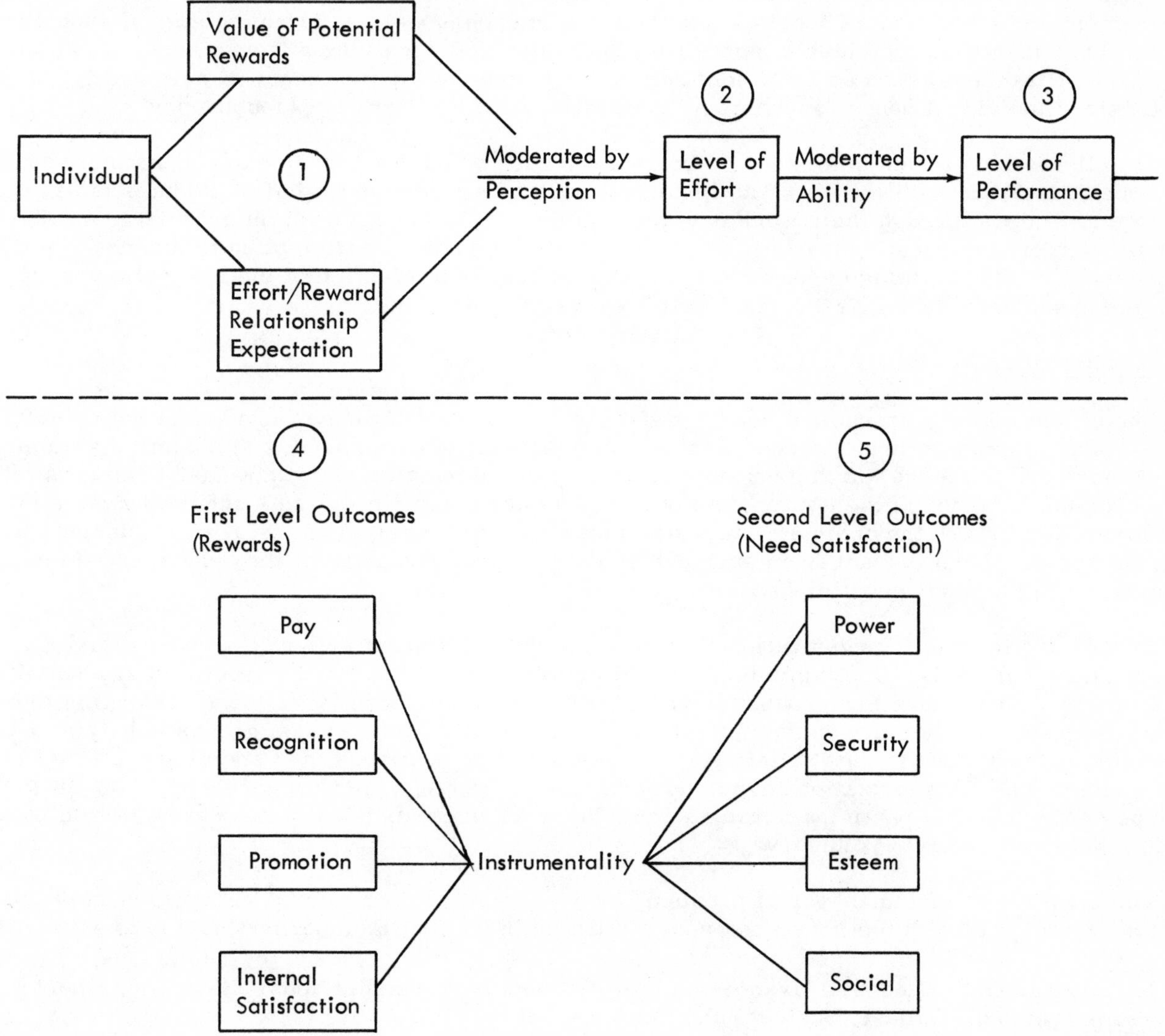

The Motivation Process. A simple model of the basic motivation process described on the preceding page is the following:[1]

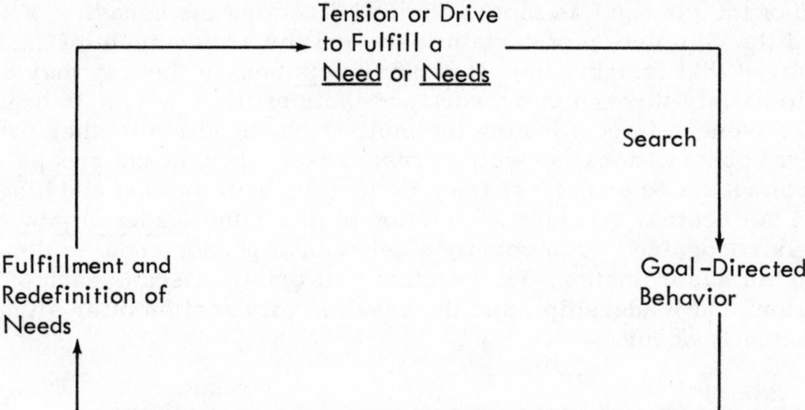

It should be clear from the first diagram that one of the driving forces in the motivation process is the degree to which the individual values certain rewards or second level outcomes--or stated differently, what needs are operating at what strength to motivate the individual's behavior. Several well-known need theories of motivation (also known as "content theories") address precisely this question.

Content Theories of Motivation. While full descriptions are readily available elsewhere, it is worth noting here some of the major content theories of motivation which hypothesize specific categories of needs that motivate individual behavior. One major level of thought is encompassed by Maslow's "hierarchy of needs," McGregor's "Theory X and Theory Y," and Herzberg's "hygiene-motivator" theory. Other researchers like McClelland have focused on individuals' needs for power, achievement and affiliation. Theorists interested in interpersonal and group relations, such as Schultz, have identified individuals' needs for expressing and receiving affection, control, and inclusion. And still others, such as Levinson, relying on a comprehensive theory of personality, have hypothesized individual needs for mastery, maturation, and ministration (dependency).

This list is only a sample of need or content theories which attempt to explain the motivating forces behind individual behavior. The important point of agreement is that individuals attempt to satisfy many needs through their work and through their relationship with an organization. Clearly, identification of the operative needs is an excellent starting point in attempting to diagnose motivational issues in the following cases and in actual practice. Examination of the motivation process, using the expectancy model, is a logical next step.

Group Behavior

One of the primary sources of need satisfaction in organizational settings is the individual's affiliation with various groups. Indeed, managers seldom fail to be amazed (and sometimes dismayed) by the enormous influence which groups, employing only informal, nonorganizational rewards, can exert over the behavior of members. The objective of harnessing group influences to motivate individual behavior toward the achievement of organizational tasks and goals, or at least insuring that these influences do not detract from such achievement, underlies much of the behavioral sciences' contribution to the study of group behavior.

Groups are formed in organizations to serve two quite different primary purposes, and may be categorized accordingly. One type is the formal or work group. The other type is the informal or social group. While some few groups may be characterized as "pure types," i.e., belonging to only one category or the other, it can realistically be argued that in most cases, groups belong to both categories, in that work groups satisfy some social needs of members, and social groups may perform some tasks. Categorization should be performed on the basis of the group's primary purpose, and perhaps on the fact that participation in a particular work group is usually mandatory, while participation in a social group is voluntary.

The most perplexing managerial problem is posed by formal or work groups which in practice overlap a great deal with the social category. For it is here that members' behavior is subject to

[1] Adapted from J. Gibson, J. Ivancevich, and J. Donnelly, *Organizations: Behavior, Structure, Processes* (rev. ed.; Dallas: Business Publications, Inc., 1976).

powerful, and sometimes conflicting, sources of influence. A useful model for understanding group behavior in such situations consists of the related concepts of background factors, required behaviors, emergent behaviors, and individual and group outcomes (productivity, satisfaction, group cohesiveness, etc.).

If one assumes, as most theories of motivation would suggest, that individuals join organizations to satisfy multiple needs, it should be clear that the nature of the work, itself, the direct rewards from it, and formal, job-related interactions with others, will satisfy only a subset of those needs, and some of those only partially. Stated differently, the interaction of the background factors (individual needs and abilities plus the nature of work, physical setup, etc.) and the required behaviors of the job, required tasks, interactions, etc., will result in a given level of productivity and individual satisfaction. The effort of the individual to satisfy needs not at all or only partially satisfied through required behaviors will result in what might be called emergent behavior, such as nonwork-related interpersonal interactions (to satisfy social needs). These emergent behaviors are a cause of the formation of informal social groups, and subsequently take place in a group context. Emergent behaviors obviously have a positive impact on individual satisfaction and on group cohesiveness. Their impact on productivity can be both direct and indirect, positive and negative, depending on group norms and attitudes of group members toward their jobs, their supervisor, department, and organization. It should be clear, therefore, that emergent behaviors must be managed with the same care as required behaviors, in that their impact on productivity and satisfaction may be equally potent, if less direct and less viable.

Group behavior in organizations potentially involves numerous issues beyond the scope of this discussion: morale, status, cohesiveness, internal norms and control, roles, communication, inter- and intragroup conflict, competition, and so on. Analyses of cases dealing with group behavior will illustrate many of these issues. And perhaps the most critical insight to be gained is the important effects of groups (and thus of the management of groups) on many criteria of organizational effectiveness.

Leadership

Leadership is one of the most complex, elusive, and yet critical, functions of management. There is little question about what a successful leader does. He effectively influences the behavior of followers toward the completion of group tasks and the achievement of group goals. (Needless to say, the selection of those tasks and goals is also heavily influenced by the leader.) In addition, it is generally agreed that a successful leader must exercise his influence without generating excessive resistance on the part of his followers.

Thus, the perplexing question in the area of leadership is not what a successful leader does, but rather, how he does it. Early efforts to answer that question focused on the personality or character traits common to effective leaders, such as physical energy, intelligence, and friendliness. The assumption that traits lead to effective leadership had at least two important implications. It suggested that if those traits could be determined then leaders could be identified by trait measurement, and it also suggested that since such traits are "inborn," leadership training would probably be of little value. However, the trait approach has been discarded in recent years since, as our experts put it, "Fifty years of study have failed to produce one personality trait or set of qualities that can be used to discriminate between leaders and non-leaders."[2]

Our understanding of leadership today is based on the belief that it is primarily a behavioral phenomenon (an influence/interaction process) and a situational phenomenon. These two assumptions result in the important insight that the most effective leadership behavior may vary from situation to situation. One implication is that while leaders may be selected on the basis of their preferred behavior or behavioral adaptability, selection should not be done in the absence of an understanding of the nature of the leadership situation. A second implication is that training, to the extent it results in behavior change or greater behavior flexibility, can result in increased leadership effectiveness.

What are the potential dimensions of effective leader behavior? Studies in recent years have repeatedly pointed to two: a task, or "production" orientation, and a relationship, or "people" orientation. While these dimensions appear under a variety of terms, they fortunately make good intuitive sense in terms of the way leadership was defined earlier. If a leader must influence, then he or she must be concerned with the personal needs of the followers as individuals and with their interactions

---

[2]Jennings, E., "The Anatomy of Leadership," Management of Personnel Quarterly I, No. 1 (August 1964).

(the relationships, or people, orientation). But because followers also must be influenced toward goal achievement, or task accomplishment, the leader also must be concerned with assuring that the group knows its job and knows how to accomplish it. Thus, the two major dimensions.

The important and still perplexing question under study at present is, what "mix" of these two dimensions should characterize a leader's behavior in any particular situation? Researchers such as Fiedler have begun to provide some answers (for example, that the most appropriate behavior will center on the "favorableness" of the situation to the leader), but the picture of the relevant contingencies is only beginning to emerge, and its complexity promises to present a problem in making the finds useful to leaders.

In summary, in your analysis of cases where leadership appears to be an issue, you should attempt first to diagnose the problem in terms of at least the two major dimensions of leadership behavior identified above, and then second, to apply whatever contingency theory and research you have studied. But third, and most important, do not hesitate to suggest additional dimensions of leader behavior which you think may be important and to identify situational factors you think may be relevant in prescribing a solution to the leadership problem. A manager must follow essentially the same trial-and-error procedure, and while you will be unable actually to implement your suggestions, they will undoubtedly be amply tested in the discussion by your instructor and the class.

BOB LYONS (A)

Those who knew Bob Lyons thought extremely well of him. He was a highly successful executive who held an important position in a large company. As his superiors saw him, he was aggressive, with a knack for getting things done through other people. He worked hard and set a vigorous pace. He drove himself relentlessly. In less than ten years with his company, he had moved through several positions of responsibility.

Lyons had always been a good athlete. He was proud of his skill in swimming, hunting, golf, and tennis. In his college days he had lettered in football and baseball. On weekends he preferred to undertake rebuilding and repairing projects around the house, or to hunt, interspersing other sports for a change of pace. He was usually engaged, it seemed, in hard, physical work.

His life was not all work, however. He was active in his church and in the Boy Scouts. His wife delighted in entertaining and in being with other people, so their social life was a round of many parties and social activities. They shared much of their life with their three children.

Early in the spring of his ninth year with the company, Bob Lyons spoke with the vice president to whom he reported. "Things are a little quiet around here," he said. "Most of the big projects are over. The new building is finished, and we have a lot of things on the ball which four years ago were all fouled up. I don't like this idea of just riding a desk and looking out the window. I like action."

About a month later, Lyons was assigned additional responsibilities. He rushed into them with his usual vigor. Once again he seemed to be buoyant and cheerful. After six months on the assignment, Lyons had the project rolling smoothly. Again he spoke to his vice president, reporting that he was out of projects. The vice president, pleased with Lyons' performance, told him that he had earned the right to do a little dreaming and planning; and furthermore, dreaming and planning were a necessary part of the position he now held, toward which he had aspired for so long. Bob Lyons listened as his boss spoke, but it was plain to the vice president that the answer did not satisfy him.

About three months after this meeting, the vice president began to notice that replies to his memos and inquires were not coming back from Lyons with their usual rapidity. He noticed also that Lyons was developing a tendency to put things off, a most unusual behavior pattern for him. He observed that Lyons became easily angered and disturbed over minor difficulties which previously had not irritated him at all.

Bob Lyons then became involved in a conflict with two other executives over a policy issue. Such conflicts were not unusual in the organization since, inevitably, there were varying points of view on many issues. The conflict was not a personal one, but it did require intervention from higher management before a solution could be reached. In the process of resolving the conflict, Lyons' point of view prevailed on some questions, but not on others.

A few weeks after this conflict had been resolved, Lyons went to the vice president's office. He wanted to have a long, private talk, he said. His first words were, "I'm losing my grip. The old steam is gone. I've had diarrhea for four weeks and several times in the past three weeks I've lost my breakfast. I'm worried, and yet I don't know what about. I feel that some people have lost confidence in me."

He talked with his boss for an hour and a half. The vice president recounted his achievements in the company to reassure him. He then asked if Lyons thought he should see a doctor. Lyons agreed that he should and, in the presence of the vice president, called his family doctor for an appointment. By this time the vice president was very much concerned. He called Mrs. Lyons and arranged to meet her for lunch the next day. She reported that, in addition to his other symptoms, her husband had difficulty sleeping. She was relieved that the vice president had called her, because she was beginning to become worried and had herself planned to call the vice president. Both were now alarmed.

BOB LYONS (B)

The vice president and Lyons' wife decided that they should get Lyons into a hospital rather than wait for the doctor's appointment which was still a week off.

The next day Lyons was taken to the hospital. Meanwhile, with Mrs. Lyons' permission, the vice president reported to the family doctor Lyons' recent job behavior and the nature of their conversations. When the vice president had finished, the doctor concluded, "All he needs is a good rest. We don't want to tell him that it may be mental or nervous." The vice president replied that he didn't know what the cause was, but he knew Lyons needed help quickly.

During five days in the hospital, Lyons was subjected to extensive laboratory tests. The vice president visited him daily. Lyons seemed to welcome the rest and sedation at night. He said he was eating and sleeping much better. He talked about company problems, though he did not speak spontaneously without encouragement. While Lyons was out of the room, another executive who shared his hospital room confided to the vice president that he was worried about Lyons. "He seems to be so morose and depressed that I'm afraid he's losing his mind," the executive said.

By this time the president of the company, who had been kept informed, was also becoming concerned. He had talked to a psychiatrist and planned to talk to Lyons about psychiatric treatment if his doctor did not suggest it. Meanwhile, Lyons was discharged from the hospital as being without physical illness, and his doctor recommended a vacation. Lyons then remained at home for several days where he was again visited by the vice president. He and his wife took a trip to visit friends. He was then ready to come back to work, but the president suggested that he take another week off. The president also suggested that they visit together when Lyons returned.

BOB LYONS (C)

A few days later, the president telephoned Lyons' home. Mrs. Lyons could not find him to answer the telephone. After 15 minutes she still had not found him and called the vice president about her concern. By the time the vice president arrived at the home, the police were already there. Bob Lyons had committed suicide.

THE NAHOC COMPANY

"I do not understand how this place can operate at all, let alone make a profit," remarked John to a co-worker. "The place goes against everything I have read and studied in my textbooks. I have been on both sides of the fence while working here, and I wish someone would inform the management about what is going on."

John's co-worker heartily agreed with him. Although he was not a graduate school student, he had two years of college accounting before leaving to work full time.

John continued on, "As a worker, I really should not be complaining. Although the pay is below average the company has made up for it in many other ways."

Bob, John's co-worker, just mumbled at this. "How have they been good to you? Most of us full-time workers feel that we have been getting a raw deal here for a long time."

John said, "I have been working here for two-and-a-half years, both part-time and full-time, during which time they have allowed me and a number of other part-time employees to set our own working hours. Even when I went into the Navy they allowed me to work part-time while my ship was in the shipyard for repairs. I have also worked here on summer vacations and school recesses. All of the part-time employees have received the annual Christmas and Thanksgiving company turkeys along with the Christmas and July bonuses. Of course, it is not as large as the full-time workers, but it does make up part of the difference between working here and at another factory."

Bob remarked again, "Where else could you get a boss that's a drunk most of the time? Only here it is tolerated."

The men, realizing that it was fifteen minutes after the lunch period supposedly had ended, got up and slowly made their way back to their respective jobs.

Fred Tinberry, the company's senior chemist with a Ph.D. in Chemistry, had been sitting near the testing laboratory's door and happened to overhear the men's conversation. During his two years' employment at the company he had started to realize that not everything was working smoothly and satisfactorily. He sat back in his chair and began to go over in his mind the facts that he knew about the company.

The Nahoc Company has been in business for over thirty-five years. It was started by Mr. Nahoc, a man who never completed high school, but who saw the need for adhesive tapes and coated products for the industrial market. He borrowed a small amount of money, rented a barn, and went into business for himself. It was just after the depression and business was slow. He had three or four steady employees and at slack periods they would all sit down and play cards while waiting for business. There were many weeks when Mr. Nahoc could not take $5.00 for his own salary. With the increasing tension as World War II approached, business picked up significantly. They received government subcontracts for coated products that were to be used in rubber life rafts and airplane self-sealing gas tanks. Business has prospered and has grown ever since. Although Mr. Nahoc has had neither college nor professional training he has a very high mechanical aptitude and has designed and built most of the machines in the factory.

Mr. Nahoc has stated over and over that if the men do not like the working conditions or pay they could leave any time and new employees would be hired. However, Fred Tinberry and the rest of the Nahoc management realize that times have changed since the depression, and labor is hard to get, even bad workers. The men up until two years ago (1967) were paid $1.80 an hour. The rate was the same for those just joining the firm and for the 20-year veteran workers. Christmas and July bonuses were given, but the men had been finding it extremely difficult to live on $72.00 ($1.80 p/h) per week. The living expenses did not occur just in July or December but all year-round. The bonuses ranged from $1,000 to $3,000 yearly. Mr. Nahoc, under great pressure from the workers, finally agreed to raise the weekly pay to $2.00 per hour last year. Ninety percent of the men were married and had two or more children. Even with the raise it was hard for them, if not impossible to live on $80.00 a week (after taxes $65.00) and manage between bonus times.

The men's morale and production decreased. The men found an answer by working overtime. Business had been very good and they were allowed to work as much overtime as they wanted. Fred, over a week's time, observed the amount of time actually spent on production and the time spent for breaks, etc. Only during the nine-to-five workday did he observe the men. He estimated the rest from secondhand reports. (See (Figure 1.)

The men would not work this schedule every night but would follow it two or three times a week. The unauthorized breaks were allowed simply because no one ever stopped them. When the management was not present before nine and after five, the men probably worked only 50 percent of the time.

Mr. Nahoc realized that wastefulness was occurring, but he rationalized that the extra money spent on wages for overtime was better than giving the men more hourly pay. Also, the overtime pay was used as a deductible and lowered Nahoc's taxes. However, the men, fearing reprisals, rushed the production they did do and, more common than not, produced substandard materials. This caused a number of Nahoc's large customers to look for other suppliers or to make Nahoc reimburse them for the poor material. At first, this action by Nahoc's customers did not hurt sales since there were many customers to replace the lost ones, but as word spread, sales of various products declined. In addition to the poor workmanship, there was widespread evidence of falsified punch-in and punch-outs. A member of one department would come in and punch the others in, and another member would stay late and punch them out. Other men working on their own would go home for supper if they lived nearby and then come back to the factory to punch out. This was not widely organized but was becoming more popular with the men.

Fred also began to think about the statement Bob made about the "drunk boss." This had bothered him, as it had everyone else in the company, but he did not know what to do. In fact, most of the poor management at the firm could be attributed to the "drunk boss," who happened to be Mark Nahoc, Mr. Nahoc's nephew. Mr. Nahoc was childless and treated Mark like a son. After a year of college Mark gave up studying chemistry to come to work for his uncle. He had been working there for fourteen years and was actually second in command of the whole firm (see Figure 2), although he concentrated most of his effort on one of the subsidiaries of Nahoc Company (Division B). The subsidiary is located in the same building as the Nahoc Company. They make rubber rolls for the machine tool industry. Mark was in the habit of using the company's expense accounts very liberally. He was an avid golfer and belonged to one of the better clubs in Boston. He charged both the membership and the bar bill to his company expense accounts. Numerous times he would come back to work after playing golf drunk and full of trouble. However, he would go out to lunch with customers or the other chemist only to return three hours later drunk. Most of the time he would have to be driven back by the customer or the chemist. This happened two or three times a week. Fred heard from some of the men that Mark usually had the smell of liquor on his breath even in the morning. Fred had known Mark's parents and they both had died as a consequence of alcoholism.

Alcohol, itself, is not necessarily bad, but it had an adverse effect on Mark's personality. He was normally a meek person and, in order not to cause any trouble, would usually give in to the men's wishes. For instance, he had approved their coming in at one in the morning and working until nine (eight hours). They usually came in, started a machine, and slept the rest of the time. When drinking, Mark's courage would be built up and he would go about the factory changing things to his way of thinking. This caused confusion and the next morning things would be changed again by Mark's uncle. The men were getting fed up and in some cases were doing only what they felt like doing. They were beginning to ignore and disrespect Mark. This caused morale problems since when Mr. Nahoc was at his Florida home or away from the factory no decisions could be made or implemented. Because of Mark's drinking, the rubber roll company was losing customers; his expense account was also helping to put the company in the "red."

What Fred feared most was the future. Mr. Nahoc had merged an outside subsidiary with his own company and had been in the process of moving them into the plant. After a few days at the plant, the new men and a number of the other men realized how much Mark's men were getting away with. They began to behave in the same way; they were leaving early after payday and going to the local tavern. The men also were becoming more disenchanted with the long hours they had to put in to make a livable weekly wage.

Early in November a baseball banquet was held for those members who belonged to the baseball pool. Mark, although not a member of the pool, went to the banquet. Most of the fellows said he was drunk before he even got there. He became very loud and insisted on talking company business with the men. The men simply wanted to relax, forget work, and enjoy the floor show. The police officer on duty had to quiet down Mark a number of times so others could watch the floor show. The same thing happened at the bowling banquet and bowling matches, and as a direct result of Mark's actions bowling was discontinued. The same thing has now happened to the baseball club; they also have disbanded. While Mark was drunk he had promised to see his uncle about a raise for the men. When the men found that he did not remember his promise they became even more disenchanted.

Fred knew things were getting worse. A week ago he had to change the code numbers on the machines in order to ensure that the men were stamping the proper code and their own names on the adhesive tape being sent out. There had been many complaints and one customer threatened to retract his business. This would mean the loss of one of the company's biggest profit sources. The labor situation was getting even worse. Some of the men had stayed out of work and then came in to borrow part of their bonuses. After getting an okay from Mark they would not show up for a few days as they had the extra bonus money to live on. Meanwhile production had fallen even further behind.

Fred knew he was caught in the middle. If everything kept up the way it was going, the company could and would suffer more financial setbacks. He knew the men were discontented and that a number of them were threatening to quit if their pay was not increased. Fred had seen Mr. Nahoc talking to Mark when he was in a drunken state, so he knew that he was aware that Mark had been drunk on the job a number of times. However, Fred did not know whether Mr. Nahoc understood the full extent of the problems caused by Mark's drinking.

Fred then heard Mark talking loudly to some of the men, saying that he did not want any more mistakes or they would be fired. Fred thought, "He is drunk again."

A.M.	6:00	Start Friday and Saturday
	7:00	Start Monday-Thursday
	8:00	Coffee break allowance 15 minutes but was more like 30 to 45 minutes
	9:00	
	10:00	Mid-morning break 15-20 minutes--unauthorized
	11:00	
P.M.	12:00	Lunch (punch out) half hour but runs 45 minutes to punch-in time (end work Saturday at 12:00)
	12:30	
	1:00	
	2:00	
	3:00	Break--unauthorized--20 to 30 minutes
	3:30	End of day--overtime
	4:00	
	5:00	Break for half hour supper--punched in lasted 30 to 90 minutes
	6:00	
	7:00	
	7:30	Punched out if still there or someone else punched them out.
	8:00	
	8:30	

Certain other time variations occurred. Some of them are described in the case.

Figure 1. The average workweek for a Nahoc Company employee varied between forty and sixty hours.

Figure 2

Organizational Chain of Command Chart for the Nahoc Company

Closed Family Owner Corporation

Board of Directors - Officers (the same)

Plant Operations - Mr. Nahoc (owner)

Plant Manager - Mr. Mark Nahoc

Office --Manager
--Accountant
--Inventory Control Clerk
--Telephone Operator and Typist
Laboratory --Chemist
--Assistant Chemist
Cloth Room and - Operator Table A (Foreman)
Receiving - Storage - Operator Table B
Mill Room and - Foreman
Churn --Operator Mill A
--Operator Mill B
--Operator Mill C
--Operator Calender
--Operator Dunking Machine
--Helper
Coating --Operator Spreader A (Foreman)
--Operator Spreader B
--Operator Spreader C
--Operator Spreader D
--Operator Roll Coater
Cutting and Shipping - Foreman - Shipper
--Operator Cameron Machine
--Helper
--Operator Automatic Cutting Machine
--Helper
Rewind - Tape - Operator - Foreman
Tape Machines - Foreman
--Operator Machine A
--Operator Machine B
--Operator Machine C
--Operator Machine D
--Operator Machine E
--Operator Spider
--Operator Rewind Machine
Division A - Manager
--Foreman
--Shipper (Receiving)
Division B - Salesman
--Roll Maker A (foreman)
--Roll Maker B
--Roll Stripper A
--Roll Stripper B
--Truck Driver
Maintenance - Machinist
--Fireman (boiler)

This chart has been set up according to the stepwise order of production. The departments are all rated equally and any department that is needed in making a decision on a certain problem would be contacted through the foreman by Mr. Nahoc or Mark Nahoc.

THE U.S. POST OFFICE AT NEWTON, MASSACHUSETTS

My name is Ned Weinerman, and I would like to relate to you some of the experiences that I encountered during the summer of 1966 while I was working on my summer job at a United States Post Office branch in Newton, Massachusetts. Before I describe these experiences let me first describe to you how I came across this job and what I had to do in order to work.

Around January of 1966, the Post Office Department issued a bulletin stating that they were accepting applications for temporary work during the summer either working as a letter carrier during the day or working as a mail sorter at the Post Office Annex in downtown Boston, Massachusetts, at night. This notice was posted at the school I attended then--the University of Massachusetts in Boston--and I assume at other colleges and universities throughout the nation. The only requirements for acceptance of the application were that the applicant had to have a high school diploma and that he (or she for that matter) had to be at least eighteen years of age on or before a certain date, which escapes me at the moment, and that we had to take a qualifying examination.

In the month of February, all of the applicants were contacted by mail telling them that on one of the Saturdays of that month a qualifying test would be given in order to select among the applicants. Naturally, I went for that test and found all it required was the following of directions by matching columns of numbers seeing whether they were the same or whether they were different. The test required no great intellectual ability; however, strict attention to the test material was imperative and speed (the number of items that could be done in the alloted time limit) counted too. Thus what the test was trying to do was to find the quickest and most accurate persons from among the applicants in order to fill the open positions.

I scored very high on the exam and was called about the beginning of June to again come to the Post Office building if I was still interested in the job. I appeared, and they gave me a list of post offices that had requested for summer help. The closest to my house was the post office in Newton Center in Newton, Massachusetts.

Although Newton has just about any racial or ethnic group that can be found in the Boston area, the area which the Newton Center Post Office services is largely populated with people who have a Jewish background (this is also a reason why I chose this post office instead of some of the others which were just as close to my house). Another point worth mentioning about Newton is that it is an upper-middle to upper-class suburban community. Also, another point which may or may not influence this report is that the residents of this town are considered by many to be "snobs."

Now that I have described the community in which the post office is situated and serves, let me describe what my duties and actions as a mail carrier consisted of. The job can be broken down into two parts. The first part deals with duties that occur within the post office building, the second with duties that occur on the route in the course of delivering the mail.

The first part, as I said, involved work within the post office building. What this consisted of was reporting to work from Monday thru Friday (Saturdays we had off while the permanent help had one weekday off) in the building anywhere from 8:00 - 8:30 a.m. What we did during this period was to set up our mail routes.

Setting up a mail route is not very hard, but after doing it for about fifteen to twenty minutes it becomes boring. The process consists of taking letters and postcards that previously have been broken down as being in your route and putting them in the correct slots they belong to which represent addresses of families and homes that you will later deliver to. Needless to say, each route (and there are twenty-four of them(has a different desk. After the letters and postcards had been sorted into their propert slots, the next step was to sort the magazines and other large matter into various piles and then to set these piles in the order in which you would do the route.

This job as I said was not very hard to learn; however, it did take practice to master the setup so that you did not have to take much time looking for the slot to match the letter addresses. The second part of this job was to pull the route down in the order it was to be delivered and then to tie it up and put it in bags which were delivered by trucks to the green boxes that you commonly see on the streets. Since we were temporary mailmen it was our job to fill in for the regular mailmen who were on vacation. As a result, we usually would be on a route for a period of anywhere from two to three weeks. I cannot speak for the other temporary help at the Newton Center Post Office, but for me it took about a week to learn the scheme efficiently enough so that I could have my route pulled down in about the same time that the regulars had their routes pulled down and by the end of the second week on any route, I was able to have my route all pulled down and ready to go on the trucks while some of the regulars were in the process of pulling down their routes.

Even though I finished getting my route down around 7:30, by post office regulations it was not possible for us to leave the post office building until 8:00 a.m. The reason for this, I was told, was that we might possibly disturb some of the people we were delivering to if we arrived too early in the morning. Because I (and usually the other temporary helpers) finished early, the superintendent, Dan Weinbaum, would come over and ask us to do various other jobs such as filing or filling out reports which, before the summer began and we arrived, he formerly designated to the permament carriers who would finish pulling down their routes early. To the permanent letter carriers, I learned, doing these jobs were considered honors; however, they frequently made many errors, and because of this Mr. Weinbaum preferred us college students to do this work.

Let me now describe the relationships that I and the other temporary help had with the permanent letter carriers. These men were all of middle age to just around retirement age (35-65). None of the men seemed exceptionally bright to me, and also, as far as I could see, none of the men had any ambition whatsoever. My conclusion is that these men were there just to do a job and did not really show any interest or pride in the job. Another thing that I seemed to detect was a hostility to the people they were delivering to. The area of Newton that the post office served, as I said, was inhabited by upper-middle to upper-class Jewish residents living in beautiful (my opinion) one-family houses. The letter carriers seemed to me to resent the Jews for all they had, and in the post office I sometimes overheard some of the familiar antisemetic stereotypes mentioned. Another point worth mentioning at this time is that most of the letter carriers were of Irish or Italian origin and rented apartments rather than owned their own homes, so I believe jealousy came very easily.

As far as my friendships with the regulars were concerned, they were just on a very casual, superficial basis. In the morning, we said the familiar "good morning, how are you?" routine and more or less left it at that. The only time that we ever really talked to any great extent was when I was first learning a route and Mr. Weinbaum would delegate one of these men to help me or one of the other temps out in pulling down the route for us and telling us how to walk the route. This was learned in a matter of a few days, and then we could proceed on our own.

The other temps had basically the same relationship with the regulars as I did. As a matter of fact, it seemed that the letter carriers split into four close groups (there were twenty-four regular carriers) and then us three temporary carriers constituted another close group, and about the only real friend that we had in the post office was the superintendent Dan Weinbaum. Throughout the summer he constantly advised us how to do things, and usually he sat with us and just talked to us while we were having coffee at about 7:00 in the morning when the coffee truck came around. During these breaks he would ask us how the job was going, about general things, and about how we should continue with our educations for the best jobs. He was the only one who told us this out of all the men who worked at the post office. I think the reason for this was that he was a college graduate himself, while the others in the post office just had high school educations, and they were not education-oriented. Here, I would like to add that when he did not sit with us he would drink his coffee alone in his office while working at the same time.

The last part of the job I would like to relate is my job of delivering the mail to the houses. This job was by far much more easy than the job of sorting in the post office, if you consider the attention that had to be given to the two parts of the job. All this part required was for you to walk around from house to house and deliver the sorted mail. It goes without saying that the ease of this second job depended upon how accurately you sorted in the first part because if you made too many mistakes in either sorting or pulling down the route, you ended up in an area of Newton with the wrong mail. But as I said earlier, the job of sorting and pulling down was not very difficult so this problem never arose except for a few missorted letters that occurred every so often.

One thing that very substantially made a noticeable difference between my performance and the performance of the regular carriers was the amount of time that it took me to do the route. Because of their ages (35-64) and my age (18) there was no question about who could do the route faster. On top of this (and I do not mean to brag), in high school I was one of the top distance runners in my league, so I was able to keep up a very fast pace of delivering mail for the entire route. As a matter of fact doing the route became a game with me in that everyday I tried to better my previous day's time on how long it took me to do the route. Another reason why I tried to cut the route time down was that we (all the mailmen) were alloted until 2:00 p.m. (from 8:00 a.m.) to do the route, so we would not have to return to the office until 2:00. This meant that the less time it took us to do the route the more time we could have to ourselves.

There was one experience I had that got a few mailmen mad. It came about because of the fact that at the time I was going out with a girl who lived on another carrier's route in our post office. After I finished doing the route I always used to go over to her house and relax until 2:00. Usually I arrived after her mailman had delivered to her street, but this one time I finished my route very early and arrived at her house before he had gotten there. When he came to her house he noticed my car sitting in her driveway, and as he put the mail in her box he saw me having lunch and yelled hello to me and just walked away. Later during the day back in the post office I passed by him and he gave me a dirty look. I believe that most of the men went slowly because home was too far for them to go to, and the women would not let them relax in their homes at all so they were in no hurry to finish.

Another thing I did that go some of the mailmen mad was when they came back from vacation the first day, some of the women or girls would be waiting for me to come (I had made quite a few friends on the routes I delivered) so that they could give me a snack or a drink. What made it so strange was that the regular mailmen on these routes very rarely, if ever, saw these people, and when they did see them on their first day back, all they asked them was where I was and to say hello to me from them. This the mailmen did; however, rather reluctantly.

All and all, I can say that I had a very enjoyable summer delivering mail. Although I did not make too many friends with my coworkers, I did meet a number of very nice girls, some of whom I still go out with or at least keep in tough with.

PROBLEM: The problem that has occurred within the post office is that of hostility and resentment by the regular full-time carriers to the summer employment and the personalities of the college students that were hired to substitute for the vacationing regulars. This is most evident in the separateness between the regular carriers and the temporary helpers. This hostility, however, has not resulted in a falloff of efficiency within the post office.

CONNORS FREIGHT LINES

Connors Freight Lines is a large, interstate trucking concern servicing the north, central, and western states. Its head office is in Fargo, North Dakota, and it has forty-three terminals, with Chicago at one extreme and Los Angeles at the other. The La Crosse, Wisconsin, terminal has been in existence for sixty of the company's seventy-five years and enjoys a fair reputation competitively.

The technical organization of the La Crosse plant consists of a fleet of twenty-seven pickup trucks, ten town-tractors, two fork-lifts, and a cart line hookup track to facilitate loading. This branch is housed at a typical freight terminal which is superior to most other trucking firms, from the technical standpoint, although considered only "adequate" from the standpoint of its social organization. Since the plant is located well away from the business district, most drivers and dock workers bring their lunches, and a small lunchroom is provided for their convenience, where they can also buy coffee or milk. This lunchroom is furnished with long tables and benches, measures approximately 15' x 20' and will comfortably seat about twenty-five workers.

The formal organization of the company, which employs approximately 180 people, consists of the terminal manager, Ralph Preston, and his assistant terminal manager, Jason Hobbs. Figure 1 shows the complete organizational structure (see page 48).

Although the company appears successful enough in solving its external problems, the high rate of absenteeism, the generally low morale among the truckers, and their relatively short tenure of employment are puzzling internal problems that have vexed management for the past several years. The truck drivers at Connors are strongly union-oriented which results in feelings of mixed loyalties. To some extent, therefore, an undercurrent of conflict is felt in this area by the company as well as by the workers.

It is part of the company's policy to select its supervisors from the ranks of the drivers. This assures them of men who are experienced with the specific job and its problems. In theory, at least, this also rewards the employee with the advancement from a job at worker-level to a position within the organization. Upon becoming a supervisor, the employee is no longer a union member, so works overtime without any pay and forfeits his seniority standing. The new supervisor is now salaried, with his base income slightly higher than that which he had earned as a driver on straight time. He no longer wears work clothes as his job is considered a "clean" one, and it would seem that some increase in prestige should also accompany this advancement.

Workers of supervisory caliber at Connors have not been too plentiful among the ranks of truck drivers, and the high rate of turnover aggrevates this further. The drivers fall mainly into three categories: (1) family men in their 30s and 40s who are settled in their job and, because of various circumstances, have decided to make a career of it; (2) young fellows in their twenties who have a few years of college and must earn money in order to continue toward a degree; and (3) young fellows for whom it is simply "a job," and who in time will probably make up the bulk of the first group or drift on to other employment elsewhere.

Chuck Fletcher would belong in the second of these categories. At 25, he had three years of college but was still uncertain about his field of interest so decided to work awhile, keep his eyes open, and do some thinking. Son of parents who were both college graduates, he was well above average in intelligence. Other truckers on his shift both liked and respected him, as did the members of management that had come to know him. He had worked for Connors for two years, spending half his shift on the dock, loading, and the other half as a driver.

Because of the nature of the freighting business, there is a great need for overtime help, since prompt movement of freight is a large part of the "product" which the company sells. Chuck maintained a good attitude about this added work load which was lightened somewhat by his paychecks, reflecting the regular union demand for overtime pay. Not all workers showed as good an attitude toward this overtime work even with the added pay, and several among the top 5 percent in seniority who were given a choice as to overtime work, flatly refused any work other than the regular 8-hour shift, regardless of compensation.

There is a fairly intricate technique involved in the correct loading of trucks and trailers so that the weight is kept under the maximum allowed in highway regulations and is distributed evenly and correctly. The more fragile or perishable items must be given special attention and the merchandise loaded with logic in respect to the order of its being unloaded at the delivery point. Chuck caught on

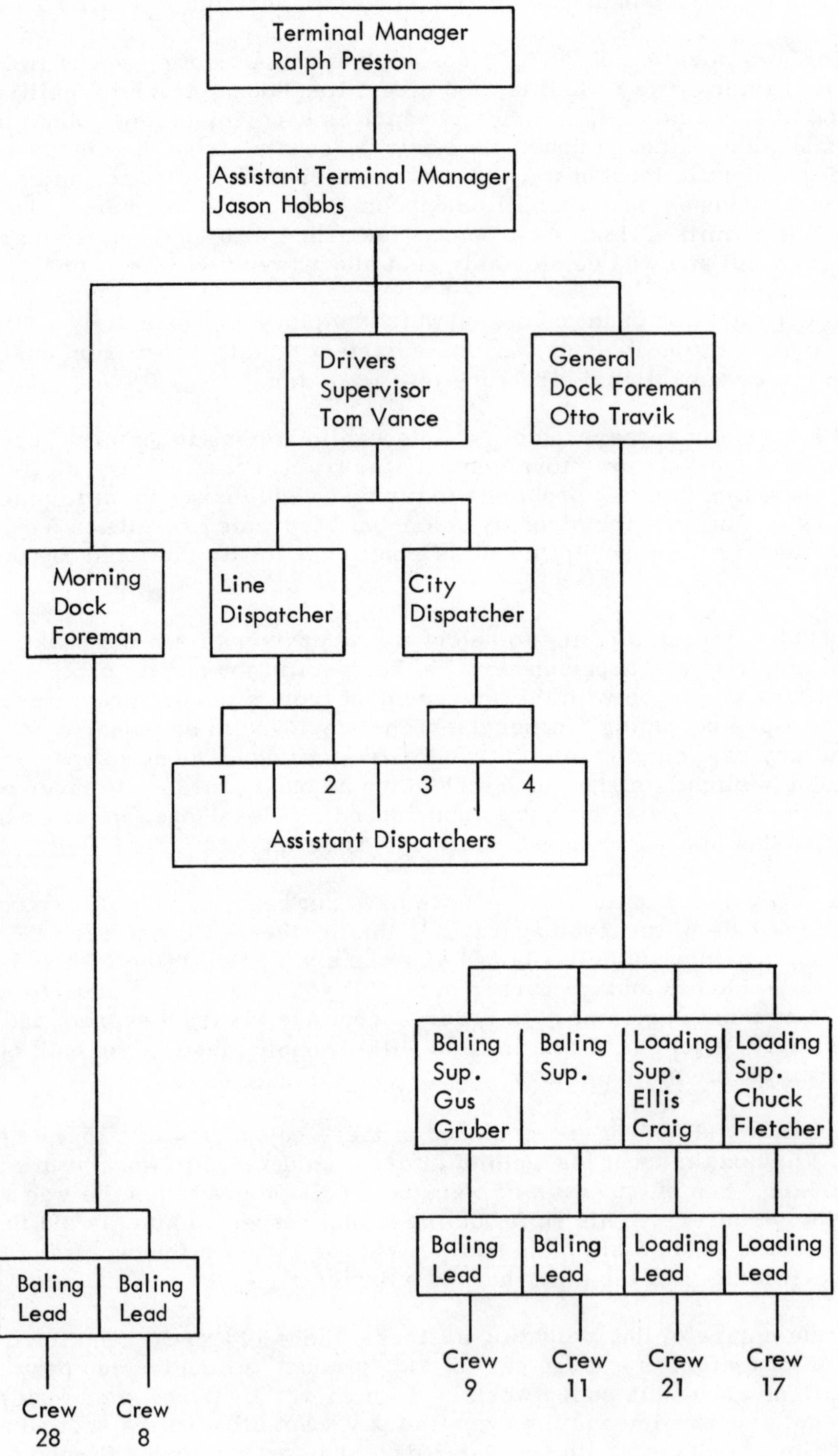

Figure 1. Organizational structure of Connors Freight Lines.

quickly to these loading techniques and soon attracted the attention of the dock foreman, Otto Travik. In a conversation with Chuck's loading supervisor, Ellis Craig, Travik suggested that Craig "keep his eye on" Chuck, with the idea of possibly bringing him into management in the future when an opening might occur within the organization. Craig, who was aware of Chuck's ability to get along well with other workers and knew him as a hard worker, agreed that he was "worth watching."

In January 1966, at one of the regular Wednesday morning staff meetings, Hobbs, the assistant terminal manager, mentioned that a sales job would soon open up, and that they planned to move Al Johnson into this spot. Johnson's move to Sales would then leave a supervisor's job open on the loading dock. Preston, the terminal manager, asked for suggestions as to who might best fill this spot. Thomas Vance, the drivers' supervisor, suggested Ford Wheeler, who had been working on day shift, was thirty-five years old, and a former school teacher. Preston agreed that Wheeler was a good prospect, but Travik and Craig suggested they consider Chuck Fletcher for the position. Qualifications of both men were then compared and discussed and the decision left open, pending more thought on the two candidates, and the actual job opening.

At about this time, Craig said to Fletcher one day:

> "I know you like the shift you're on, but would you consider cancelling your bid on it and taking the St. Paul loading job that's driving me crazy? I know the late night shift is a crummy one, but this would be the chance you've wanted to learn to drive the heavy-duty trucks. Vance is our official qualifier, and he's on that shift, so I'm sure by coming to work early you could qualify inside of a month. I'll help expedite the whole thing if you'll help me out on this. After all, the annual bids come up in five months, so if you don't like the job, you can always re-bid. And keep this under your hat--there's going to be a supervisor's job open before too long, and if you make good on this job I think your chances for it would be excellent."

Chuck thought about the St. Paul loading job. He didn't like the night shift, and the job was an expecially "dirty" one, but he took it for two reasons: he had been hoping for a chance at supervision, and he also had wanted time to learn to drive the heavy-duty rigs both for the increased pay diesel drivers drew and also because it offered him a challenge.

At a staff meeting in June, 1966, after other articles of business were out of the way, the conversation ran something like this:

Preston: There is now a definite need for a new supervisor, and I hope you have all been keeping this situation in mind and giving it earnest thought. What are your suggestions?

Vance: I still think Ford Wheeler is your boy.

Preston: Yes, I've been seriously considering him. Checked into his background from his job application and I was really quite impressed. Do the rest of the workers respect him? Would they work for him?

Craig: I don't feel he has any of the workers' respect! For one thing he's lazy, and we'll be setting the poor example that all you have to do to get ahead in the organization is do nothing. On the other hand, there's Fletcher who really is liked by the other workers, and respected too. In the time he has worked for me he has shown himself a hard worker, often doing more than is required. For a couple of months he's been coming to work an hour early to practice driving heavy-duty trucks on his own time and hoping to get qualified--and by the way, Vance, he's been ready for his test for some time--he shows a great desire to do a thorough job and accepts more than his share of responsibility. To me, this adds up to material for a good company man.

Vance: Hell! He's a union boy straight down the line. Don't you remember how he initiated two valid grievances against us last year? There has even been some talk of his being named shop steward. But Wheeler, now, has a college degree as a school teacher. He can hardly wait to shake loose from the union.

Preston remembered seeing Fletcher many times, and in all kinds of weather, out practicing driving the diesel rig in the loading zones before his shift time. In checking over Fletcher's job application he found it almost as good as Wheeler's, considering the differences in their ages.

After some further discussion Preston decided in favor of Fletcher. The supervisory position was offered to him on the usual 90-day provision which would allow either him or the company to terminate the arrangement at the end of that time, with no loss of status or seniority on his part. After a few days of consideration, Fletcher accepted the new assignment and went to work as supervisor of the same crew with which he had been working previously.

Preston gave Fletcher a short "welcoming" talk before his first day in the new job, and in it he covered three main points. He first suggested that Fletcher try to be tactful in his initiation of ideas, maybe even to the point of making his cooperating supervisors sometime think that the idea came from them. Secondly, he stressed the importance of demanding respect from his crew. "If the occasion demands a reprimand, see that it's done in some private place where others can't see or hear you. Otherwise you both lose face. It must be kept private between you and your man." That led to the third point, that of not being too familiar with the workers on your crew. "It's not really any of our business what you do off the job, but it'd be best if you don't hobnob with your men," Preston had said.

Soon afterwards, at Craig's invitation, Fletcher joined the bowling team of which both Preston and Vance were members. He and Craig, with whom he had always had a good relationship, were becoming close friends since he had been made supervisor. They'd usually go somewhere for a couple of beers together on the nights after bowling.

One night Fletcher was off on his game. After some ribbing from Vance and Preston, he mentioned to Craig how tired he was from so much overtime, "tired and disgusted" was the way he put it. He told Craig that earlier that day he had overheard Preston "chewing out old Gus Gruber" down in the steel bay, and the incident had both embarrassed and disappointed Fletcher. Craig, at that time, was planning a vacation to the East Coast with his family and invited Fletcher to come with them. Chuck said he knew he needed a rest and a change of scenery, but he was short of funds. Last year he had gone up to Canada with some of the men from his crew, but that was when he was getting paid for overtime.

Craig previously had included Fletcher on a couple of family outings and at one time, when the men were alone, they got to talking shop as usual. Fletcher seemed discouraged about the attitude of his crew. "We have always gotten along so well before, but now there's no more kidding. No one hardly cracks a smile and I keep getting jibes like 'Gettin' rich on your overtime, Chuck?' or 'How do you like your new raise by now?'

Part of his interest in taking the supervising job was that he hoped he'd find ways of easing the obvious friction between management and labor, and this development was really discouraging.

The weekly staff meetings, which were attended by all management personnel, were the occasions when affairs concerning the company's technical and social organization and welfare were brought up for discussion. A variety of issues were constantly being introduced, listened to, considered and many were acted upon promptly. At the third staff meeting Chuck himself made the suggestion that the company might see fit to supply work aprons to the workers, adding that these were not expensive items when bought in quantity, and that the gesture of goodwill on the part of the company might help to improve the rather poor relations between it and the workers. This suggestion was listened to but not acted upon.

Another suggestion was made by Fletcher within the next few weeks: that of switching of lunchrooms between the workers and supervisors. The lunchroom reserved for the twelve supervisors was twice the size of the one into which forty-five drivers were crowded at peak times to have their lunches, and this necessitated several of them sitting on the floor or standing to eat. This suggestion, too, was not acted upon, although Craig and Travik both thought it was "worth considering."

Within a short space of time, however, the company was gratified by the outcome of two other suggestions which Fletcher made in work operations. One of these resulted in substantial savings to the company, and the second, in a greater profit. The first was accomplished by Fletcher's simplifying of a certain loading procedure and organizing it in such a way that two men from another crew, ordinarily required for extra help at this time, were no longer needed. Dispensing with this usual short-handing of the second crew enabled it to finish its own loading on schedule, resulting in more efficient moving of freight on the two jobs and less need for overtime on both.

At about this time, two company officials from Fargo were visiting the terminal and Preston took them on a tour of the docks. As they passed the loading area, Fletcher looked up and nodded. Farther on, as they circled the dock, one of the officials said, "Where is this new supervisor, Fletcher, that you've mentioned a few times lately?"

Preston replied, "Oh, he's the fellow in the red shirt we just passed down there at the north end. I'll introduce him to you at coffee break if he comes up."

The second instance in which Fletcher's suggestion worked to the company's advantage took place toward the end of the ninety-day trial period. It was not presented at the staff meeting but to Hobbs in person one day when he happened to be out on the dock as Fletcher came on shift. Fletcher's attitude, which had always been friendly and respectful, seemed to have changed in recent weeks, and Hobbs, who had become confident that Fletcher was proving to be good supervisory material, was a little puzzled by his apparently growing coolness.

Hobbs: Good morning, Fletcher.

Fletcher: Good morning, Mr. Hobbs. May I speak to you a minute when you have the time?

Hobbs: Sure. Right now is as good a time as any.

Fletcher: It's about the St. Paul run. While I was on the St. Paul-loading job I realized that on the last schedule to St. Paul at night there was always more freight moving from La Crosse to St. Paul than returned from St. Paul to La Crosse. We'd always need a 'double' heading east and then always have to haul back one 'empty.'

A college friend of mine is the son of a truck farmer over east of the Mississippi, and I was talking to him the other day. I think we could arrange for a full load of produce to be picked up near Winona. Then we'd have a full paying load in both directions.

I've already said something to Vance about it yesterday but didn't hear anything from him so thought I'd let you know. The arrangements could be made easily. I'll give you the farmer's name, if you're interested. It's all up to you, of course.

Hobbs thought Fletcher seemed a bit abrupt, but the suggestion pleased and impressed him as it did Preston when he was told about it later in the day.

On Thursday of the last week of the ninety-day trial period, Fletcher came into the office of the assistant manager and told Hobbs that he was going to exercise his option and ask to be returned to worker status the following Monday.

Hobbs was surprised by this unexpected turn of events, but said, "Well, we'll live up to our side of the bargain. I'm sure Mr. Preston will want to hear your reasons for this decision, though. He has some free time at two o'clock. Could you come in and see him then?"

In Preston's office later:

Preston: What's this I hear about your request to be returned to your old job as trucker?

Fletcher: Yes, I've decided to hang it up. The long hours are getting me down.

Preston: Well, you knew what the hours were like when you took the job. Aren't they the same ones you worked as a driver?

Fletcher: Yes. Well, I thought perhaps I could expedite a few things and maybe shorten them a little, I guess.

Preston: Well, are you sure you gave this "expediting" your best efforts?

Fletcher: Yes, sir I did. Until I got to the point where I felt I was knocking my head against a stone wall.

Preston: Are you sure it's the long hours, or are there some other reasons?

Fletcher: Well, the money and the shift, coupled with the long hours.

Preston: Well, we think you were doing a fine job, and we are already taking steps in these areas you're dissatisfied with. In two weeks we hope to add one new supervisor and possibly two to cut down hours worked by the supervisors.

Fletcher: Well, that would make it a lot easier all right. . . .

Preston: And there will be an opening in Dispatch in the not-too-distant future that would be a day-shift job rather than a night one.

Fletcher: That would be a real improvement. . . .

Preston: So that just leaves the problem of money. How much more would you say you'd need to make it worth your while to stay on?

Fletcher: A hundred dollars a month, sir.

Preston: Hmmm, well, I think we can probably make some kind of arrangements that will make you more contented. I'll check with the head office and let you know on Monday.

Fletcher: All right. Fine. You can let me know.

After Fletcher left his office, Preston said to Hobbs, "I think the head office will go for an eighty-five dollar raise anyway, and that will probably be enough to hold Fletcher here. Put a note in his locker-box stating we will meet his demands, but don't state a definite amount of money. I have to talk to the head office first."

Hobbs: That's still a lot of money. Do you realize that would make him the sixth highest paid man in this terminal? He'll be jumping over eight men.

Preston: Fletcher has already saved the company more than he'll make in a year on that produce haul alone, and he has come up with quite a number of ideas that have helped us out. He's a thinking boy and that's the kind we need. He has a bright future and I want to keep him with us.

The Monday morning mail contained the following note addressed to Preston:

Dear Mr. Preston:

Please accept this notice of my resignation from the company, to be effective in two weeks.

I have thought it over carefully and this is the only possible solution.

Thank you for your generous offer, even though I cannot accept it.

Sincerely,

Charles S. Fletcher

1) Peer Pressure
2) Identified w/worker
DISLIKED CHEWING out to worker
3) LOST Pay in Overtime
4) DID Not enjoy assoc w/ Mgt
5) Company Not responsive to His Goal Help HRL?

1) TRAINING IN SUPV.
2) TRAINING AND I.D. W/Co
3) More SOCIAL W/SUPV.
4) Other Benefits To offset Loss in Pay

ANDERSON MANUFACTURING AND DEVELOPMENT CO.

"Ham" Wilson looked at the public relations man across his desk with irritation. Then, with his characteristic self-control in dealing with company colonels, he surpressed the quick words that were at his tongue.

It had been a rough morning--a morning of hard, disciplined argument over promotional copy for the new compacting machine. While Ham had become visibly upset and impatient to end the session, the PR man kept smiling, stubbornly fighting it out one point at a time. Ham disliked him intensely.

Although Anderson Manufacturing and Development had not had a PR man long, this guy was surely making up for lost time. Little by little he had taken under his wing everything that had anything to do with business development and promotion. He was young--somewhere in his early thirties, maybe four or five years older than Ham himself--and in spite of his smiling driving assurance, technically ignorant. He didn't even understand what was basically new in the compactor, Ham thought with resentment.

Ham was proud of his compactor. He had directed its development from the beginning. The original concept had been tossed to him as a kind of challenge by his boss, the chief engineer, and Ham had given it long hours of exploratory thought and work on his own. And then he had become excited about it, sold it hard, and management had bought it. They had given him a tight budget and time schedule, and he had made it. He felt damn good about that machine.

"You keep approaching this copy in the wrong way, Ham," the PR man was saying.

"This is aimed at the guys who are holding the money bags and you keep criticizing everything as though we were writing a technical report. I don't want to misrepresent your baby, believe me, but I'm trying to sell it. We've put a lot of money into its development, and we're going to put a lot more into its promotion. Now we've got to sell it. I need good copy. Everybody upstairs wants good copy."

Ham was tempted to tell him what everybody upstairs could do, but checked himself again. He stared blankly at the copy, convinced that he was still right: it stunk. Worse, it seemed to border on dishonesty in some of its implications.

"What I would like to do," Ham finally said to PR, "is to have a chance to talk to the boss before we make a final decision on this. I don't want to let it go through as it stands on my own say-so."

"OK, Ham," said PR, "but remember that I have to get final copy to the printer by the end of the week. I think what we've got right now is all right," he added, "but I certainly wouldn't want to see it watered down anymore."

PR left as he had come--smiling, self-sufficient, and with hearty good words.

What a joker, Ham thought to himself. He wondered how a guy like that could live with himself, how he could do Anderson Manufacturing any real good. Apparently he did--at any rate he sat upstairs in a big room in executive row.

By way of contrast, Ham looked around his own little cubby. His battered desk and chair, and one visitor's chair, all but filled it. "The Conference Room" the boys called it. He laughed, and then lost his laugh when a knock at the door reminded him that he had asked Holden to see him as soon as PR had left.

Bill Holden came in, easy and relaxed as always, and slouched into the chair at Ham's desk. He was a bright, young D.Sc. whom Ham himself had hired. But there were times when he wished he hadn't--and this was one of the times.

"Bill," Ham began, "I've just had a rough time with PR and I'm not going to beat around the bush. When your test results weren't in last Friday, you promised me--quite literally promised me--that we'd have 'em first thing this morning. And we don't have 'em. We practically rescheduled the whole program so that you could do some additional work with the physics group, and now you haven't made the new schedule. What are we going to do about it?"

"I know I promised to have them today, Ham," said Holden, "and believe me, I was shooting for it. The physics group work just took more time than I had expected. We're on some pretty fundamental stuff, and Dr. Maul asked me to do some library work on it. The whole thing just ran beyond our original expectations."

"Bill," snapped Ham, "your attitude confuses me; honestly, it does. I don't doubt that the physics group is doing important work, but you knew damn well that you were assigned part-time to my B project. And you know that when I juggled the schedule, I was doing it to give you a break--you, personally. I never should have done it, but you practically pleaded with me and promised that you would come through on schedule. What do you think we're doing here anyway?"

Ham was flushed and angry, but Holden let it roll off easily.

"I suppose we're doing a lot of different things," Holden said in a tone that seemed half apology, half challenge. "The Chief was talking to me just the other day about the importance of the physics group work and about what a vital part I could play in it. You know it's pretty fundamental stuff, and frankly, that's why it appealed to me. It's well related to my previous experience--some of my doctoral work. I thought that's why you rearranged the schedule."

"Bill," said Ham, "you're talking nonsense and you know it. If all my men felt the way you do about the job, about fitting their work into the pattern, why the whole lab would fall apart."

"Well the whole thing seemed reasonable to me," said Holden. "After all, we're working for the same boss and good results in one place ought to be just as good as good results in another."

"Bill," said Ham in a rising voice, "you know damn well that's not so. Honestly, you're talking as though you were still a school boy and it didn't matter what you did--as though you didn't have responsibility to anyone else."

"But I've done good work," said Holden.

"I know it, and everybody knows it," interrupted Ham. "You've been here what--two, three years? During that time you've had more good ideas than anybody else on the lot. You're a good man, and the Chief has given you a pretty free rein. That's why I can't understand this. You try to run your affairs like a one-man band, but this lab is not being run the way you think it is."

Holden just kept looking at Ham.

"Everybody seems to think I've been doing OK," Holden repeated defensively. "I've always tried to do my best."

"Sure you have," said Ham, "but you run around this place as though we were subsidizing the Royal Academy. You know we're not subsidizing anything--we're organized to make money, and in order to make money we've got to push the stuff out the door. It matters a hell of a lot to me whether we do or not, because if we don't it means my neck."

Ham looked at Holden and Holden looked at the floor and there was a long silence.

Ham liked Holden, but he was also a little envious of him, for Holden had the big degree. He also had brains. In fact, he had been good for the lab, Ham had to admit, even though he never worried much about meeting a schedule.

But, hell, he said to himself as Holden looked up, I have to worry about a schedule even if Bill would rather be doing other things. Sometimes, he thought, I'd rather be doing other things myself.

"Bill," said Ham, finally cutting into the long silence, "I'm sorry I lost my temper. I've never blown my stack like this before. I was wrong in doing it now."

"I'm sorry too, Ham," said Holden. "You make me feel as though I've let you down personally. You've been very decent with me, and I certainly didn't mean to let you down. If you want me to finish off the test runs. . . ."

"No, no need," interrupted Ham, a little wearily.

"When I didn't have the final figures this morning, I took what you'd already done and passed it on to Porter. He's got one of his boys finishing it out. The Chief expected a report before this, but he hasn't been pressing me for it."

Ham doodled for a minute on his scratch pad, and then went on:

"This is no life and death matter as you well know, Bill, and I'm sorry I acted as though it were. The point is not so much that you fouled up this schedule, but that you've fouled up for still another time. Anybody can understand missing once in a while, but it never seems to bother you that you have a reputation for never worrying about time. It would bother me. Every time I miss a schedule it bothers me."

Ham doodled again.

"You certainly know the things I've been saying are right, Bill," he said. "I think we should forget it for now, but let's understand that something's got to be done. I'll speak to the Chief as soon as I can, and we'll see what's to be done."

Holden backed out awkwardly, muttering apologies. As soon as he had left, Ham picked up the phone and called the Chief. The conversation was brief: Ham had a couple of problems he'd like to talk about; could he see the Chief sometime soon? "Sure" was the response--in about an hour--for lunch. Fine; done.

At lunch, the Chief characteristically opened right up with a hearty "What's on your mind, Ham?" He asked it with a smile--a big, genuine, ready smile.

"Well, Chief, I had kind of a bad morning."

"I heard about it," said the Chief.

Ham didn't conceal his surprise. So PR had run to see the Chief, Ham thought. PR had tried to load the dice. That was a lousy trick.

"From PR?" Ham asked.

"No," said the Chief, looking hard at Ham, "from Bill Holden. He was in to see me right after he left your office. He told me the whole story. And as a matter of fact, Ham, there's a part of the story you don't know: Holden's being assigned to Doc Maul's group as part of a general reorganization that's been approved by the Board."

Ham started, and he listened uneasily as the Chief began to explain. The reorganization was to involve the whole works. The lab was to be split into three groups. The Chief was to have overall charge, but the company was going to appoint an assistant chief engineer who would be responsible for some 40 engineers and as many nonprofessionals. Doc Maul was going to direct a smaller group on some of the more fundamental work. This was going to be a low-pressure group.

"Maul's group may not work out at all," the Chief went on, "but we're going to give it a try. It won't be much different from the way the physics group has operated anyway.

"This is where Holden fits in. He's to be a research associate--which, as you know, is a new title with us--Maul's right-hand man. Holden knows about this, and he's happy about it. I think one of the reasons he stopped into my office today was to check on whether you knew it and, of course, you didn't.

"What happened was that Maul jumped the gun in telling Holden what his duties were to be, and Holden jumped the gun in acting like a research associate. He realizes that and he's sorry."

The Chief looked at Ham with an apologetic smile.

"I was going to tell you all this at the end of the week, Ham, after the Executive Committee had formally approved our plans. But let's forget Holden and get right down to brass tacks. Let's see what this is going to mean on our side of things."

Ham's uneasiness increased as the Chief went over things in more detail.

Maul was to become Head Scientist, he said. The Chief himself was to pick up two assistants. One of the two was to have the title, Assistant Chief Engineer. He would work in parallel with the Chief and have charge of about a third of the groups. The other new appointment was to be Assistant to the Chief Engineer--a kind of leg man for the Chief.

"Now how do you fit into all this, Ham?" the Chief asked rhetorically. Ham took a big bite of pie and gestured his curiosity.

"We have discussed this whole thing pretty thoroughly," the Chief went on, "and we've looked at all the men we've got, and we've talked to some from outside in an exploratory way. After looking and talking, we're well decided we want you to be Assistant Chief Engineer."

Ham grinned. This felt good. Here he'd been working his fanny off and up to now, he thought, there hadn't been any gold stars on his report card. This really felt good.

"Actually, Ham," the Chief was saying, "you've been doing a big part of this job already. You know our procedures and you've proved you can keep on top of things. Whatever may have happened this morning I'd read as just a bad day. The record shows you work well with the men and keep them happy and push the stuff out."

Ham thought to himself that this was right. He had been doing part of this job all along. It had started nearly two years ago when Maul was out sick and the Chief began to dump things in his lap. And when Maul came back, the lab started to grow and the Chief kept handing him things. There was no formal pattern--it was one of these things that had just developed.

Still, there had been plenty of time to participate in project work, too. Ham thought of the compactor. He had lived with that thing night and day. And that had been a good part of the setup as it was. Whenever something had come along that he had wanted to jump into, the Chief had always said to go ahead. And he had jumped into the compactor with both feet. That's the only way to do, Ham thought, when you really want to get something done.

The Chief was now talking specifics about the new job.

It would mean a substantial raise--about 15 percent. Better still, it would mean participation in the bonus plan. It would mean a big new office. And it would mean a lot of little things: a private secretary, a membership in the executives' club, office expenses for journals and magazines-- a whole new potful of the niceties of life.

Ham had an inpulse to jump and shake the Chief's hand and to rush out and call his wife, who had taken the youngsters on a two weeks' trip to her mother's. But the impulse was only a quick flash. It passed and was replaced by something like fear. This wasn't something Ham wanted to jump into --not just like that anyway.

As the Chief went through the slow, deliberate ritual of filling and lighting his pipe, Ham expressed his thanks for being considered for the position. But while he said the right things fully and fluently, he thought of reasons for delaying his decision.

He thought of the reports, the judgments, the budgets, the people. He thought of sweating out one project, while you were worrying about the next. And strangely enough, he thought of PR.

He thought of PR because there was a guy he never wanted to be, a guy who was a kind of Mr. Management Merry-Go-Round in person. He wondered briefly if some day PR would wake up and realize he'd been running his whole life without ever catching up to anything. He wondered if some day after it was too late PR would wish he hadn't run so hard and so fast.

There was a pause during which the Chief looked searchingly at Ham.

"You're thinking this is a pretty big decision, Ham?" the Chief asked.

Ham nodded. "A very big decision," he said with emphasis.

"I agree," said the Chief, "and naturally no one wants you to make a snap judgment about it. The vice president told me to tell you to take your time. Personally, I want you to take a good hard look at it.

"We both know," the Chief added, "that you did a whale of a fine job with the compactor, and it may be that that's the kind of thing you ought to stick with, that that's the kind of thing you really want. You've got to balance that equation for yourself, Ham. I emphasize this because if you do take the new appointment--and it's got a lot to offer--you ought to realize that you'll be completely away from the bench.

"When you sold me on the compactor," the Chief went on, "we arranged things so that you could see it through yourself. That wouldn't be likely to happen again. Of course, you'll sit on top of these things, and you'll take pride in these accomplishments, but in a different way--an entirely different way."

The Chief stopped talking and scratched a match to relight his pipe. Ham stirred his second cup of coffee.

"I understand what you're saying all right," said Ham, "and, believe me, I have very mixed feelings about it. I'm tempted by the new job--naturally--and I feel very flattered by the offer. But I do know that I like the purely technical side of things. And I know that if I took the new job, I'd want to keep up in my field."

The Chief smiled at Ham as he waited for him to go on.

"I've enjoyed the courses I've been taking at the Institute," Ham continued, "and I'm satisfied that they've done me a lot of good. If I took this appointment, I'd keep working for my degree--just as I have been--one course at a time. And I'd probably sit in on some seminars. In fact I'd try to keep up technically in every way I could."

The Chief smiled again and then spoke quickly and earnestly:

"You can sell yourself on that line of argument pretty easily, Ham," said the Chief, "because it makes so much good sense on the face of it. But I'll give you long odds that it won't work that way. I don't want to be discouraging, but the older you get the harder it gets. It's hard to find the time--even harder to find the energy.

"Believe me," added the Chief with a wry smile, "I know. I went through it myself."

Ham thought about this. He thought of how little he really knew about the Chief. He did know now he had been a top turbine man. And he knew the Chief had once won the Stalworthy medal "for outstanding contributions to turbine development." Not much of a medal, maybe, Ham thought, but still a medal--a symbol of achievement and recognition. Yet the Chief had traded this away for a stock-bonus deal with the Anderson company. Ham wondered if he had any regrets. He wished he knew.

"The fact is," Ham heard himself saying a little apologetically, "I'd rather thought that this year I might have a go at the degree on a half-time basis. You remember that we talked about this last year, and you said then that the company would sponsor me."

"I did say that, Ham," replied the Chief, "and I'm sure that we can still do it, if that's what you want."

"Well, I'm not sure at all," said Ham, "but I have a tentative program worked out, and I've lined up a thesis."

"If this is what you want, Ham," returned the Chief, "I'd be the first to say Godspeed. My only advice would be to encourage you to pick a good thesis project. There are a lot of awfully facile theses written in that department, and I wouldn't want to see you fall into that kind of trap."

"As a matter of fact," Ham answered quickly, "I've got a pretty exciting project in prospect. Werner wants me to work with him, and you know his work. This could mean a lot for me professionally. There's no denying I would like that. I think anybody would."

"Ham," said the Chief quietly, "I understand your feelings perfectly, and I won't try to dissuade you if that's what you really want. You've got some good projects under your belt here, and a good job with Werner would never hurt you."

The Chief paused and brushed a few tobacco crumbs from the tablecloth to the floor.

"If I decide to finish up the degree on a half-time basis," Ham asked, "will I prejudice my chances here at the lab?"

"Ham, you know better than that, I hope," replied the Chief. "I'm with you either way. And as far as the people upstairs go, forget it. There's no problem there."

The Chief brushed at a last elusive crumb of tobacco.

"No, you won't prejudice your future, Ham," he added, "but it will be a different kind of future."

The Chief looked at Ham for a minute. Then he knocked his pipe on the ashtray and looked at his watch. The lunch was over.

*****

When Ham returned to his desk he sat down with the uneasy feeling that he hadn't been demonstrative enough in thanking the Chief for the opportunity he'd been offered. But he was interrupted by an unexpected call from Jack Masters, an old classmate and a fraternity brother of Ham's at the Institute. Jack was in town on business and their brief, hearty conversation quickly closed with arrangements for dinner at Ham's club.

As Ham cradled the phone, he let his mind savor past memories. He was glad Jack was in town, he decided. Jack was a real solid citizen. It would be good to see him.

During the next two hours Ham tried to put some final changes into his annual report, which was due next week. It was not until long past mid-afternoon that he became aware that only his hands were busy with the papers in front of him. His mind was still churning with confusion over the decision that lay ahead. With a gesture of disgust, he pushed the papers to the back of his desk and left the office. Without real purpose, he walked the length of A wing until he stopped at the cell where George Porter was finishing up the tests that Holden should have done. Porter and one of his technicians were running things with a quiet easy competency. Ham liked George--everybody did.

"How are things going?" Ham called. Porter grinned, and held up a finger asking him to wait a minute. Ham waved an OK.

Ham never thought about George Porter much, but he thought about him now as he waited. He thought about him because he suddenly realized that Porter wasn't so very much different from him. Of course he was twenty years older, but he had the same kind of background, the same kind of education. And Porter, Ham thought to himself, was a guy in a well-worn groove. For the first time, this realization worried him.

Back before the war, George Porter and one of the founders of Anderson company had run a little one-horse shop. And there Porter had helped develop one of the basic patents that had brought Anderson Manufacturing into being. But Porter had never grown away from the first project. Not that he didn't keep improving it, for he did. Just last month, for instance, he had finished making changes that would let it be tied in with a computer-controlled line. A new series of Air Force contract orders had already come in on that development. That's the way Porter's baby was: high-quality and custom-built, and the military kept it well fed.

"Just about winding up, Ham," said Porter, coming out of the open cell. "It all went very easily, no troubles at all. The data looks good."

Ham took the clipboard and scanned the data, plotting them mentally against the earlier runs. "They do look good," he said.

Porter pleased, turned back to his technician. "They look good, Al," he shouted, and the technician grinned.

Ham thrust his hands into his pockets and leaned back against the wall as Porter and the technician kept feeding in the adjustments on the last run. Ham thought about Porter some more. He thought about how helpful Porter had been to him when he first joined the lab. Ham had been in Porter's group then, and they had been quite close for a while.

Ham recalled his first visit to Porter's home. Porter lived in the country and he farmed a little. It wasn't much of a farm, Ham supposed: a couple of hundred chickens, a cow, a small garden. He remembered how impressed he'd been that first night that everything they'd eaten--from the very tasty salad to the peach dessert--had been grown right there. Ham hadn't seen much of the Porters recently, for Ham's wife ran their social life and she didn't care for the Porters. He was sorry, for he rather liked George and his raw-boned, easy-going wife.

Porter came out of the test cell and took the clipboard from Ham to record the data on the final run.

Funny, Porter's doing this job himself, Ham thought. After all, the tests were routine enough and a couple of technicians could have handled the job if company policy hadn't required that an engineer be present. But Porter could have covered this requisite by having one of his young engineers do the job. Yet he didn't, for that's the way Porter was--he never passed anything on to anybody else. He would worry, he once told Ham, that it wasn't being done right if he wasn't out there on the job. As Ham thought about this, he concluded that any worries Porter had were mighty little worries.

When the last run was completed, Ham took the clipboard again and looked at the final readings. They were right on the button.

"We'll all get the Anderson A of Approval for this one," Ham said, and Porter and the technician laughed at this reference to a standing company joke. Ham surprised himself by laughing, too.

"Flip you fellows for a coke," he said, "odd man pays." Porter laughed again.

"You know, Ham," he said, "that's probably the thousandth time you've tried to match me for a coke, and I've never taken you up on it. Not today, either."

Ham smiled, threw back a friendly insult, and then added that the cokes were on him. While Ham was getting them, Porter and the technician shut down the machine. Then they all lounged back on the bench beside the test cell, drank their cokes, and talked. They talked trivia, and Ham didn't say much. But Porter and the technician talked easily, sharing a rough kind of camaraderie.

Ham finished his bottle first, exchanged pleasantries with the two men, and walked on down the wing. As he turned the corner to his office, he looked back to see Porter and the technician closing down for the day. Although he couldn't tell for sure, he thought Porter was whistling. Ham watched him for a minute, and then almost imperceptibly shrugged his shoulders and walked slowly back to his office.

* * * * *

Ham met Jack Masters that evening in the lobby of the Engineer's Club. They exchange quick greetings and went directly to the bar. It was a solid, comfortable bar, a good place to talk.

Over the first drink, Masters carried the conversation He renewed old times, talked about new prospects. Masters was a good talker, and Ham enjoyed listening to him. He hadn't changed much, Ham thought, except that he was a little heavier, a little less volatile.

Masters was with National Company and had been in their New York office for nearly two years. He talked objectively and happily about his job. It seemed like a good deal, and Ham said so two or three times.

"Believe me, Ham," Masters kept saying in self-depreciation, "I'm nobody in the company."

Over the second drink, Ham edged the talk around to his own prospects. Masters was immediately interested. He asked the right questions and drew out the right details. He understood Ham's doubts quickly enough and as quickly dismissed them.

"Hell, Ham," he said, as they went in to dinner, "you don't have a problem, you have an opportunity. You've been doing part of this job already and you like it--well enough--that ought to be all you need. I had to cut a lot of bait before I got this kind of bite."

"What do you mean, you 'had to cut bait'?" Ham asked. He was curious. And he was more than curious, for he was searching eagerly for any patterns of experience he might be able to match against his own.

Masters explained that after he'd been in National's Dallas operation for nearly three years, he began to have an almost panicky fear that he was stagnating. His jobs had become routine, and so had his raises. Masters had decided right then, as he put it, to fight his way out of the corner he was in. He did it by broadening himself technically. He did it by very deliberately avoiding getting stuck in the same kind of job too many times. He did it by smelling out every opportunity that was in the wind.

The break had come when his boss, an assistant to the chief engineer, went overseas to set up a new production facility in the Near East. This man's going left a kind of administrative vacuum which the company decided not to fill. But Masters flew into it and picked up every responsibility he could. He made himself a kind of communications center. And when the assistant's leave was extended, Masters was appointed acting assistant in Dallas. Then, before the first man returned, he was transferred to Jersey and then to New York.

"Well, your story's something like mine in some ways," said Ham, "only I didn't consciously try to bring anything off the way you did."

"That may be," said Masters, "but I think we all do this kind of thinking, whether it's conscious or not. Personally, I like to plan things out quite deliberately, for then you have more control over them. That just seems like a matter of good sense to me."

"What you're saying," said Ham with a laugh, "makes me feel a little like a country boy who's somehow getting along only because he's luckier than he ought to be. You're arguing that a guy has to be an opportunist to get ahead."

"Nothing opportunistic about it at all," Masters interrupted. "It's rather a question of creating opportunity, and certainly a question of taking opportunity whenever it comes along. Take this new job of yours--if you don't take it, somebody else will. That's the way I look at things."

"Maybe I'm just quibbling," said Ham, "so let's say I'm ready to buy your argument. This is not what really bothers me anyway. What bothers me is how do you know you ought to get out of technical work; how do you convince yourself that you ought to throw it all away?"

Masters explained it very readily in terms of money and in terms of status. He told Ham that he had analyzed National Company as thoroughly as though he were going to invest a couple of million dollars in it. This was only good sense, he said, for there he was investing his whole life in it. And his analysis showed that all the glory in National Company went to the guys in the management seats --all the glory, all the money, and all the status. He also discovered that more than half the top men in National had come up out of research and development in the first place, and so he decided that the odds were all in favor of his trying the same thing.

"Right now," Masters said, as though clinching the argument, "I'm making half again as much as the guys who came into the lab with me and stayed there. And I'm more flexible," he added. "I can do more things, and I'm worth more to the company."

Ham bristled a bit at this. The implication was that the man on the bench was some inferior kind of character, and he found himself resenting it. The argument also was clearly something of a personal challenge.

"All this may have been pretty clear-cut in your case, Jack," said Ham, "but I don't think it is in mine. You're with a big outfit--maybe that's where I should be, but I'm not--and I've got to look at my own situation. You fellows at National talk about millions the way we talk about thousands.

"Let's say I look at this thing pragmatically," Ham went on, "and I would agree with you that maybe this has been in my thinking all along. From a practical standpoint, I would say that you can afford to be secure and happy about your choice because your company is fat. If I were with National I might feel the same way. You don't have to worry about finding your next job."

"You don't mean that," said Masters. "You know darn well that if I didn't do my job today, I'd be out on my can tomorrow. We're not running a philanthropy any more than you are."

"No, that's not what I mean," Ham rejoined. "What I mean is that you're insulated from all the wear and tear that affects a guy like me. You're not going to mess your job, and you're not going out on your can. But I might."

Ham was wound up now.

"When the Chief talked to me today, Jack," he said, "he quoted a lot of figures about the progress of the company. But I'll be frank with you--we run on government contracts--we couldn't keep our shop open six months without the military."

Ham disclosed that one of his own projects had had a prospective government contract cut right out from under it, and some of the engineers had been let go. Ham worried that this might happen to the whole kit and caboodle. Then what would happen to the little guy low down on the management ladder, he asked?

"Would I go to you, to National Company, and say won't you please take me on? Would I say, I'm a helluva good man even though I haven't any patents to prove it. Would I say, I'm loyal and I need the work, and if you take me on you'll never regret it?"

Ham was talking at Masters now rather than to him. He wasn't stopping for answers.

"The way I see it," he argued, "if I stick to the technical part of R&D, I've got money in the bank. I'm negotiable. I can go to anybody in the industry, and I can say here's what I've got, and here's what I've done and they can see it right away."

Ham stopped to sign the dinner checks and to order a second cup of coffee. He looked across at Masters again and apologized for his rush of words. He slowed himself down.

Maybe some of these arguments were pretty tenuous, he agreed, but there were other things. There was the plain and simple joy of accomplishment in good project work, for instance.

Ham had written Masters about the compactor, and now he was speaking feelingly about it. That was the kind of thing a guy had to immerse himself in and that was one of the joys he was talking about. If you went into administration full time you kissed that sort of thing goodby. And you lost something pretty substantial.

Ham let Masters chew over this point, while they finished their coffee. Then they went out to the reading room, where they sat in a couple of comfortable chairs and flicked their cigarette ashes into the fireplace.

After a while Ham said: "Jack, I've been thinking pretty seriously about going back for my doctorate on a half-time basis. The company will sponsor me, and Professor Werner wants me to do my thesis under him."

"Well," said Masters, "I remember that you wrote me about a year ago to say that you were thinking about it. I wrote back and urged you to forget it, and I thought you had given it up."

Masters blew a few smoke rings and thoughtfully watched them flatten out and lose their shape.

"If you go back on half-time schedule, will you use your compactor for a thesis?" he asked Ham.

"No, I can't," said Ham, "the machine isn't really mine. I guess I didn't tell you that."

Ham explained that a friend of Bill Holden's--a local man--had come up with the basic concept. Holden had brought him around to see the Chief as a kind of personal favor.

"But believe me," Ham added quickly, "there was plenty wrong with that machine when we first saw it. The inventor didn't have a sound idea of the basic processes involved. In fact, the odds on this thing's paying off looked so slim that nobody really wanted to touch it. But then I came up with a process that made it look better, and we worked like hell on it, and now we've got something that's really good."

Masters took a last drag on his cigarette and flipped it into the fireplace.

"Suppose you do go back for this degree of yours on a half-time basis," he asked Ham, "what's going to come of it?"

"Why, just what I've been saying," said Ham. "In the first place I think it's a good move, just from a practical point of view."

"I don't," Masters countered. "I think you're kidding yourself. Look at this guy Holden, for example. He's already at where you're only going to be. And all the time you're sweating out the earn-while-you-learn routine, he'll be jogging along piling up points. And then when you come back full-time and give it the old college try to catch up, you'll find that all the heroes have already been made."

"Well, maybe you're right," laughed Ham, "but why couldn't I look around just the way you did, only from an R&D point of view? I might just look around for the spot where the R&D man is well off, and then I'd aim for that and try to hit it."

"You won't find it," said Masters with emphasis. "I laugh at this because I think of our annual report in which we say solemn things about basic R&D being the prime mover of everything that comes down the pike, and we publicly pat its little head and sing hymns of praise. And I'm telling you--off the record and as a friend--that all of this is hypocritical as hell. It's like a bad scenario with half the lines stolen from 'The Life of Louis Pasteur.' I don't know who we think we're kidding--unless it's all the sweet old ladies who own most of our stock."

"That's pretty typical of some high-powered wheel in public relations," Ham laughed. And he laughed again recalling his morning meeting with PR over the promotional piece on the compactor.

"And maybe," Ham added with a smile, "This is a pretty good 'for instance' for my argument that by and large you'll find more honest substance in lab work than anywhere else on the lot."

"I won't argue that you won't find mutton-heads in management," said Masters, "but you know darn well that you find them in the lab, too."

Ham nodded his agreement.

"You take the guys on the bench," Masters went on, "and you can pick among them qualitatively. And you know that on any team you've got a few hands with damn good brains in them. But you know, also, that you've got some other good brains seeing things through. It's not just the turn of the wheel that sends one group up and another group down. There are guys seeing things through all along the line. And some of them take plenty of risks."

Ham thought that this was right, too. He had bought a risk, he thought, when he had sold the Chief on the compactor. They had looked at him and said, "OK, it's your baby." It was a money-down, win-or-lose proposition; luckily he'd won.

In contrast, Ham thought of Holden and Holden's new appointment. This was a different kind of deal. The company would carry Holden as a kind of overhead. It was like a sweeps ticket; maybe they'd get their money back and maybe they wouldn't. The whole psychology of the thing was different.

Ham also thought of the pleasure he'd found in "seeing things through" for some of the men and some of the projects the Chief had assigned to him. There was a sense of accomplishment in this, too, he thought.

"Jack," Ham finally said, "I haven't been trying to give you an argument to deny what you might call the joys of management. I've tasted some of them, and I've found that I liked them. It's just that I have very mixed feelings, and I've been trying to see it from all sides.

"And you know," he added after a pause, "I honestly feel that I'm almost ready to decide to take the job."

Masters looked at Ham and smiled broadly with sheer delight.

"Ham," he said, "that's the most sensible thing your befuddled old brain has produced tonight. Let's have a nightcap on it before you lose it."

As they had their nightcap, they talked about their families and they made vague arrangements about getting together again "soon." When they had finished, Ham drove Masters back to his hotel. They were tired, and they rode most of the way in silence. It was not until Masters shook hands on leaving that he returned again to Ham's decision.

"Ham," he said, "Maybe I've got more faith in your company than you have, but I think it's a comer. And I think in this new job you've got a helluva fine opportunity to grow with it. Frankly, I think you'd be a sucker to do anything else. Do yourself a favor and take the job."

"Jack, I'm almost ready to think I will," said Ham, as he waved goodby. And maybe I will, he thought as he drove the long fifteen miles to Cooperstown. He was glad he had seen Jack, he decided, as he turned into his drive. It had been good to talk with him.

The next morning at the plant Ham sat for a long time with his annual report again. And again he stared idly at the pages, thinking and worrying, especially worrying. He wished that he could avoid the decision altogether, that the Chief or somebody else would come up with some inevitabilities as to why it could go only one way or another.

As Ham sat worrying, his mail arrived. It provided something of a diversion, and he was grateful for its coming. He spotted, among the usual run of internal mail, a letter from the Society. He read it with mounting disbelief, and then read it again to make sure. There was no mistaking what it said: his paper on the compactor had won the Society's annual George Peabody Award for the best paper of the year by a young engineer. In stiff, formal phrases the letter sent congratulations from the president of the Society and outlined the Awards Night program at which the Peabody Medal would be presented.

Ham grinned, and the grin grew into a big bubble of elation. Quickly he tucked the letter in his pocket and hurried down the wing to see the Chief. The Chief was in, and he shared Ham's delight as he offered hearty congratulations. He also called the vice president with the news while Ham was still in the office. Ham could hear the vice president's voice gather enthusiasm and begin to dominate the conversation. He couldn't make out the words, but the sounds were friendly.

"He says that you're to make the Society's schedule," said the Chief as he hung up, "and that your wife is to go with you, if she can. And he wants you to take any extra time you may need on either side of the meeting--all at company expense, of course."

Ham felt good. It was nice to have these guys in your corner.

"You're not to let the new job make the slightest bit of difference in planning your schedule around this award," the Chief added.

Ham's bubble burst. There was no escaping the thing.

"He also says," the Chief went on, "that he would like to have an answer by the twenty-seventh, if possible. Now that they've made up their minds to move on this, they want to go ahead as quickly as possible."

Ham felt a sudden emptiness in his stomach. "Sure, Chief," he said, "by the twenty-seventh. I ought to have an answer all right, I've already given it a lot of thought."

"And Ham," said the Chief, smiling, "one last thing: be sure to get in touch with PR on this award so that we can exploit it as fully as possible for the company."

Ham nodded and said he would. He added a few words of personal thanks to the Chief and left. He wanted to get back to his office as quickly as possible. He wanted to come to grips with this thing. He wanted to get it settled.

As he hurried past the physics lab, he saw Holden--cup of coffee in hand--sitting at one of the tables, talking animatedly with Dr. Maul. As Ham neared his own cubby, he saw Porter lounging near the door, waiting for him with the formal report on yesterday's run. And as Ham drew nearer, he could hear that Porter was whistling.

JACK DOBBINS' PROBLEM

Jack Dobbins left the vice president's office feeling elated as well as concerned about the new responsibilities he was about to assume. Ralph Barnes, State College's vice president and comptroller, had just told Jack of the Executive Committee's decision to appoint him Superintendent of Buildings. Jack was concerned because Mr. Barnes had gone into considerably more detail about the many management and morale problems among the College's custodial workers and their supervisors than in any previous interviews.

The Situation

State College was located in a suburban area just outside of a major southern metropolitan area. It was one of several universities run by the state and was less than 10 years old. In this short time it had grown rapidly to 9,500 students, the majority of whom lived off campus and commuted to school each day.

The Superintendent's major function was to plan, organize, direct and control the activities of about 80 employees and supervisors involved in keeping all college buildings (except for dormitories) in clean and orderly condition. There were 10 major buildings ranging in size from 24,000 square feet to 137,000 square feet. Total square footage under the jurisdiction of the Superintendent amounted to 1,025,000. This space included classrooms, faculty offices, administration and library buildings, student center, etc.

Of the 80 employees in the department, 16 were women, 64 were men, including the 4 supervisors who reported to the Superintendent. Starting wages for maids had just been raised to $2,580 per year from $2,300. By some quirk of the state's budgeting system, starting wages for male janitors had just been lowered to $2,700 per year from $2,900. Employees could receive only one raise per year, usually on July 1st at the beginning of the fiscal year. It was within the Superintendent's authority to grant raises up to a maximum of 10 percent the first year, 7 1/2 percent the second year, and 5 percent the third year. In order to qualify for the maximum, however, employees had to receive a rating of "outstanding." The workweek was 40 hours. Vacation leave of 10 working days was allowed while sick leave was accrued at the rate of one day per month to a maximum of thirty days. Group life and health insurance was availably by payroll deduction at employee expense. State employees were not covered under Social Security but did participate in the state retirement system under which both the State and the employee contributed. The total budget for the department amounted to about $280,000, with $250,000 for wages and salaries and $30,000 for supplies and materials.

Turnover among employees was unusually high. In July and August of 1967, turnover amounted to 15 percent and 20 percent. Typically in this type of work in universities, turnover runs 100 percent per year. The majority of employees held down other full-time jobs outside of the College.

Departmental Work Organization

There was no organization chart for the department, but Jack Dobbins felt it would look pretty much as the chart that follows:

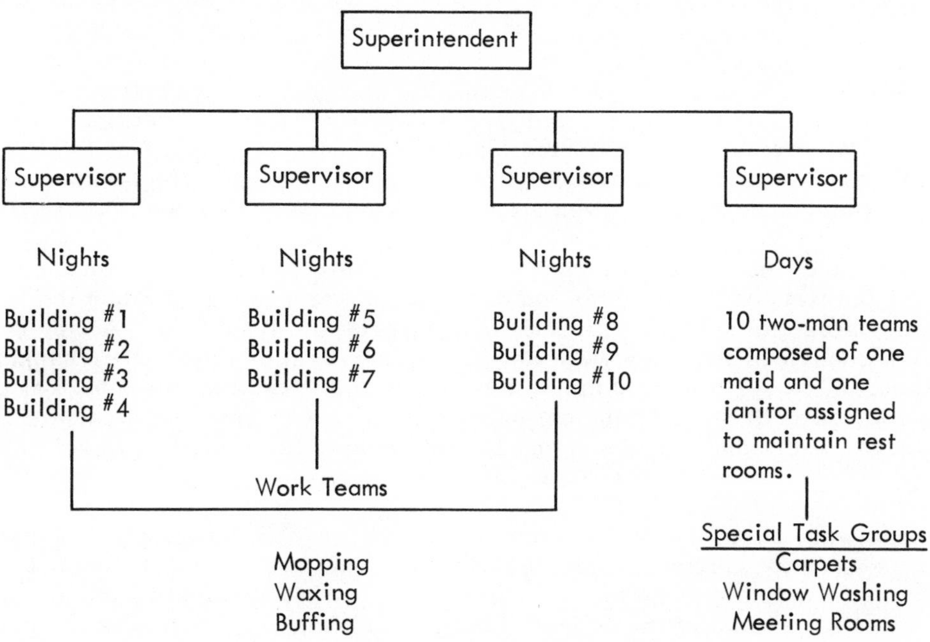

Work was organized on the basis of special tasks. Although supervisors were assigned responsibility for different buildings, work was specialized into floor mopping crews, followed up by waxing and buffing crews. Supervisors decided when particular floors were mopped, waxed, and buffed and coordinated and scheduled the different crews in proper sequence. The day crews worked largely on restroom detail in all buildings with special groups assigned for carpet cleaning, window washing, and straightening and cleaning up meeting rooms before and after meetings.

Jack Dobbins' Background

Jack Dobbins was a retired military man with 20 years' service in various posts as management analyst and operations and training officer. On resigning from the military, he had enrolled as a student in the College of Business Administration in order to earn a degree in management and business administration. At 45 he was looking forward to a new career in a new environment in a field where he felt his experience, knowledge, and training could be most effectively used.

During the last hour and one-half in his talk with Mr. Barnes, he had learned much about the current problems of the department. Harry Kraft, the man he was replacing, had come to State College when the first students were admitted. He was about 50 years old, of limited education, and with a varied background as foreman or supervisor in construction firms. When the College was small with only a few buildings and few employees, he was reasonably successful. However, four months previously, Harry had fired one of the supervisors with rather disastrous results. Rank and file employees were indignant and had sent a petition all the way to the state capital in an attempt to get Harry's decision reversed. Some were threatening not to come to work. Morale was low, turnover high, and top officials of the College, as well as the department itself, were being deluged with complaints about the lack of good housekeeping in all buildings. Toilets were not adequately serviced, classrooms and offices frequently went untouched for a week at a time.

Although Jack was concerned, he was not dismayed because he felt strongly that his recent exposure to a wide variety of management courses would make it relatively easy to show substantial improvements in this department, even despite the fact that no raises could be given to any employees before the next fiscal year 11 months away.

NATIONAL PAINT PRODUCTS, INC.

National Paint Products, Inc. manufactured a wide line of paints which were sold across Canada. The company's manufacturing operations as well as its main warehousing and distribution operations were all located in a small Ontario town in which National Paint was by far the largest employer.

After being packed in cartons, the finished products were transported by conveyor belts from the manufacturing plant to the warehousing and shipping area (Figure 1). Between 1953 and 1963 the company's sales volume increased fivefold with corresponding consequences for the warehousing and shipping operations.

In October, 1961, responsibility for the warehousing and shipping operations was transferred from the Manufacturing Division to the Service Division. As part of this reorganization, Mr. David Brown was appointed Warehousing and Shipping Manager, reporting to Mr. Gordon Ewen, Manager of distribution (Figure 2). Mr. Brown, who was transferred from the manufacturing plant, had had previous warehousing experience, but Mr. Ewen's previous experience had been primarily in marketing.

Both Dave Brown and Gord Ewen believed that there was considerable room for improvement in the department. At the time of the transfer the department was averaging 3,800 lbs. per man-hour. There was no supervision on the night shift and, in the words of Mr. Ewen: "At any time workers were observed, it was obvious that they were not producing anywhere near their capabilities. Many times they were observed taking 15 to 20 minutes between coffee breaks for a smoke or a rest period. They would leave for coffee break 10 minutes prior to the correct time and stop working 20 minutes prior to shift change." Consequently, Ewen and Brown decided to take steps to get "a fair day's work for a fair day's pay."

Altogether there were about 58 full-time employees in the Warehousing and Shipping Department. Two basic activities were carried out by the department. The first was to transport loaded pallets from the conveyor belts to the storage areas. The second was to assemble and ship customers' orders. About one third by volume of these orders consisted of full pallet orders for particular products. Such orders were relatively simple to handle since they could be moved directly from the storage area to the designated shipping point. The remaining two thirds of customer orders were made up of mixed lines. Filling these orders was the job of Section 92, the Pick-up Section, consisting of about 15 men per shift. The pick-up men, or pickers, were required to assemble customer orders for a variety of products and container sizes. These men were equipped with mechanized handlifts, and they traveled to the appropriate pick-up racks or fast-moving items area making up customers' orders. Each order was assembled on pallets and, after being completed, was brought to the checking area where the checker verified that the correct products and quantities had been assembled. During the busy season (May to September) temporary help was sometimes hired to augment the regular work force. Some of these men found picking difficult and failed to produce much above 2,500 lbs. per man-hour. In such cases they were either released or put on mechanically paced jobs like conveyor belt unloading. Moreover, during periods of heavy layoffs, when plant-wide seniority took effect, senior employees from other departments sometimes displaced the regular pickers. Some of these men also found picking difficult.

At the beginning of the shift, each picker was given a set of customer orders by the scheduler. The scheduler was usually an assistant foreman, and he sat in one corner of a small office situated next to the order checking area (Figure 2). When a picker had filled his orders, he returned to the office wicket to get another batch of orders from the scheduler. Customers' orders varied considerably in time and ease of assembly, depending upon the quantities and varieties of products ordered. The scheduler was supposed to apportion the easy and more difficult orders equally among the workers, and to aid in this task he kept a tally sheet on which the orders assigned to each picker were recorded as the shift progressed. The completed tally sheets were forwarded daily to the Industrial Engineering Department. Some schedulers claimed that pick-up men often complained about unfair allocation of orders.

One step taken by Ewen and Brown to increase productivity was to increase first-line supervision. Two assistant foremen were assigned to each shift on a rotational basis. One of these men was required to work "on the floor" overseeing the entire warehousing and shipping operation, while the other spent his time "in the corner" doing the scheduling. Several personnel changes within the supervisory staff also were made. In June, 1962, Bob Hackett and Ross Wilson were promoted from lead hands to assistant foreman, and in January, 1963, Hal Jones and Mike Prior also were brought out of the bargaining unit and made assistant foremen. Of these four men, only two, Hal Jones and Mike Prior, had previous work experience as pickers, and only Hal Jones had been a picker for any length of service.

Another change that was implemented, on the 7th of May, 1962, was the introduction of two balanced shifts in the Warehousing and Shipping Department. Before this, one third of the department had worked on nights and two thirds had worked on days. The night shift was changed every two weeks and thus each worker could normally expect to spend two weeks out of every six on nights. With the introduction of the balanced shift, workers were required to spend two weeks on days and two weeks on nights and there was very little personnel transfer between shifts. At the time of the change, there was a lot of "beefing" among the men about the increase in night work, but this gradually diminished as they became used to the new arrangement.

One consequence of the switch to equalized shifts was improved utilization of departmental equipment. Under the previous system, the department generally had been forced to borrow a fork lift from another department on the day shift, while on the night shift there had been a surplus of equipment. Since the change to balanced shifts, however, the department had standby equipment available on both shifts. Departmental management was quite pleased with this improvement and, in addition, complaints from the workers about equipment holdups decreased considerably.

In June, 1962, a further change was made in departmental operations. Prior to that time the department had been using an allowed minute system to rate worker performance. Under this system, which had been installed by an outside consultant in 1957, each carton size, type of move, etc., was assigned an allowed minute standard upon the basis of work measurement studies, and a worker's performance rating was calculated using these standard data. Although Mr. Ewen thought that the allowed minute system was a good one, he decided to discard it because "employees were using the allowed minute system to 'time' their work load. They could have a 45 performance rating in 5 1/2 hours and do little or nothing the balance of the shift. A 45, in the minds of a handful, was all the effort they and the rest of the department were going to produce in spite of anything we might do." Consequently, it was decided to change to a pounds per man-hour measure of performance. From information supplied by Industrial Engineering, Mr. Ewen knew that over the period November, 1957, to May, 1962, average output in the department had been at a 45.8 allowed-minutes performance rating per hour. Industrial Engineering further informed him that this represented an average output of 3,820 lbs. per man-hour. Before deciding on a reasonable standard for the pick-up section under the pounds per man-hour system, Ewen visited several other companies with comparable shipping operations. These visits convinced him that 5,000 lbs. per man-hour constituted a reasonable average performance for the pickers. Thus, on the 28th of June, 1962, he called together all the departmental employees to introduce the pounds per man-hour system. Mr. Ewen's remarks at this meeting were as follows:

> It was just 9 months ago that the responsibility of the Warehousing operations was changed to the Service Division with Mr. Brown in charge.
>
> Some changes have been made to improve the efficiency of the operations. The plans we are going to tell you about now will be another step in instituting a good operation in the Shipping Department, particularly in the order assembly area. We cannot continue to expect other departments in the plant to carry this department.
>
> The Sales Division is continuing to make bigger and better sales, and the Marketing Division is continually coming up with better plans to move larger quantities of merchandise. There is no doubt in my mind that, if you gentlemen owned or managed a business, you would want the most efficient and compatible operation possible in every area of the business.
>
> To set everyone straight from the beginning, it should be pointed out that any changes that have been made up to the present time have been supported 100 percent by top management. Dave Brown is working hand in hand with management with the aim of obtaining a fair day's work for a fair day's pay.
>
> It has been heard from certain quarters that Dave Brown has been placing a lot of pressure on members of this department. You think there was pressure on you--there also was pressure on Dave from top management to get the department operating properly.
>
> It was not our desire to start a "Get Tough Policy" or tighten the strings. Your work habits made this necessary. What other course is open when employees leave early for break periods, take more than a reasonable amount of time off between break periods and leave early for lunch and before the end of the shift?
>
> From these observations and from time study records that have been made from time to time, it was obvious that, particularly in the assembly area of the department, a fair day's work was not being produced.

To bear out our own observations that we were not obtaining a fair day's work and to be sure that what we expected was not unreasonable, we made a visit to other warehouses in the provinces of Ontario and Quebec. After visiting these operations and comparing them to our own, we confirmed that our production is poor. So that we will all know exactly where we stand and exactly what is required for a fair day's work, we are going to, in the future, speak in a language that everyone understands. That is, pounds, rather than allowed minutes. We have established a fair day's work at 5,000 lbs. per man-hour in the pick-up area, 4,600 lbs. per man-hour in the flat carloading area, and 11,000 lbs. per man-hour in pallet carloading. These figures were, as mentioned, arrived at after careful consideration.

It should be pointed out that in nearly every instance our own warehousing facilities, layout, and equipment is as good as, or better than, the warehouses visited. Our aisles are wider and less congested and we have a fewer number of products to handle. In addition, in most of the warehouses visited, the orders were much more difficult to assemble than ours, in that they consist of a wider range of products with fewer cartons per product. The warehouses visited included: Superior Paints, Acme Products, Consolidated Products, Everwear Paints, and All Purpose Products.

Here are the performances for these warehouses, which are not in order of the names given, but are the actual production figures:

5,600 lbs. per man-hour
5,040 lbs. per man-hour
5,300 lbs. per man-hour
5,000 lbs. per man-hour and
5,600 lbs. per man-hour

From the foregoing, you can see that we are not expecting anything unreasonable or anything that is not easily attainable. We have every reason to believe that you men are as capable of doing a fair day's work in this operation as employees in these other locations visited who are working under handicaps not encountered in our operation.

As mentioned, these figures should be easily attainable, and those who want to do a day's work will fit into the operations. Those who would sooner put in time by talking and taking it easy and keeping others from producing, will have to get into line. We cannot continue to have every member of the department slow his efforts down because of a handful who are not willing to give a fair day's work for a fair day's pay.

We know this plan will be welcomed by the majority. Mr. Brown and your supervisors will be getting together with each one of you individually or in smaller groups and explain any details that are not clear.

We do not plan to dwell on the past, and we feel sure you men will welcome this opportunity to build a competent and compatible department.

Despite the introduction of the 5,000 lbs. per man-hour standard in the pick-up section, output continued to fall far short of the standard (Table 1.) Over the next few months Dave Brown spoke to each man individually, some on numerous occasions, in an attempt to increase production. Average output per man-hour rose somewhat, but it still fell far short of management's expectations. Brown became more and more convinced that there were about half a dozen "radicals" in the pick-up section who were deliberately keeping production down and forcing others to do likewise. Matters finally came to a head in November, 1962, when Brown and Ewen decided to transfer two men, Carr and Brandt, from the shipping department to the material handling department. These men had been two of the lowest performers in the pick-up section.

The employees reacted strongly to the transfer action and on Friday, the 23rd of November, the workers in both the Warehousing and Shipping and the Materials Handling Department staged a sitdown. The sitdown lasted almost two hours before union officials persuaded the men to return to work. Feelings in the whole plant ran high, and there was talk of a general strike, but union officials, including the Canadian director of the union who came to the plant, urged the workers not to take action into their own hands but to give the local's executive full power to take whatever action it deemed necessary. A special meeting was held, and this course of action was endorsed by a vote of the general membership.

Over the next few weeks a series of meetings took place between union and company representatives. The union maintained that the two employees had been transferred as a threat to the other workers in the pick-up section. The union argued that the company had used the introduction of the pound per man-hour system as a device to force a 30 percent speedup in the shipping department.

The union further claimed that the transfer had violated departmental seniority rights and that the company's action had united all plant employees behind whatever steps the union might take. The union said that the best solution to the problem would be for the company to reinstate Carr and Brandt, or at least to give them a fair trial period in their old department. For its part, the company maintained that the transfer of Carr and Brandt was not the real issue; it was a symptom of a more deep-rooted issue--namely, the unwillingness of a group of employees in the shipping department to give a fair day's work for a fair day's pay. Insofar as Carr and Brandt were concerned, the company stated that it thought that the two men had tried their best but could not do the work. Consequently, rather than discipline these men, the company had transferred them to the materials handling department where there was work suited to their capabilities such as unloading the conveyor belts. The company also stated that the 5,000 lb. standard was a fair one and challenged the union to put up money for a study by some third party to determine the fairness of the standard. The company further pointed out that under the contract, no employee is wedded to any job or department; job security means job security with National Paint and not with any specific department or area. The company stated that the union should accept some responsibility for solving the problems of the shipping department and should not let mob psychology prevail among the employees. The company further said that it would not accept the union's proposal of a reinstatement or trial period for Carr and Brandt in the shipping department. The company did state, however, that the employees presently in the department were capable of performing their work satisfactorily and would not be transferred.

The subject of Dave Brown's frequent personal visits with the men in an attempt to increase production was also raised in the union-management discussions. The union stated that employees were being spoken to regardless of their performance, whether satisfactory or not, and as a result, "the employees are developing an attitude of indifference because of this constant visitation." The company countered by stating that it was management's prerogative to speak to employees as it saw fit and "day-by-day visits with employees by supervision is imperative to assist the overall operation of the department. Each employee is judged by his performance over a long haul and not by an individual day." Furthermore, "employees who are doing a good job are not being talked to continually."

Normally, Mr. Brown saw Mr. Ewen daily to talk over the operations of the department. As a rule no one else was present unless a specific point came up which required that someone else be called in to provide information, etc. Mr. Brown's office was located right in the warehouse and shipping area (see Figure 1), while Mr. Ewen's office was located above the warehouse in a block of executive offices.

Mr. Brown held regular weekly meetings with the assistant foremen from both shipping and materials handling to talk over the general operations of the department. Occasionally, if there were particular problems in the shipping operation, he would hold a special meeting with Hackett, Wilson, Jones, and Prior.

Mr. Brown believed that the four new assistant foremen in the shipping area needed experience in disciplining workers. Consequently, he initiated the practice of having the assistant foremen come to his office individually from time to time to admonish workers who were performing unsatisfactorily.

In September, 1963, Jack Morris, a case writer from the Business School of the University of Western Ontario, visited the warehousing and shipping department of National Paint at the invitation of Mr. Ewen. Output in the pick-up section was still falling far short of management's expectations and Ewen was pondering what new steps he might take to rectify the problem. In the course of his visit to the department, Morris talked with the supervisory personnel to obtain their views on the situation. The following conversation took place between Morris and Hal Jones, an assistant foreman in the department.

Morris: Hal, what do you think about the problem in the pick-up area that everyone seems to be talking about?

Jones: The way I see it, the whole thing started in 1957 when the company brought in an expert, Mr. Craven, to set up the allowed minute system. Before that time everybody just did a good day's work and didn't worry about how much he was producing. I know because I've been with this department for ten years. Of course, sales have gone up tremendously since I've been here, and that creates some problems, but still I blame the allowed minute system. That guy Craven may have had a lot of education, but he sure didn't know men. You know what he said about the system? He said, "If we set the standard at a 45, it will be easy to reach, and the men are going to break their necks to beat it." Well you can be sure it didn't turn out that way. They started to post weekly performances for everybody on the bulletin board, and the guys had it figured that a 45 was what should be produced. Anybody who did more got talked to but good. I never bucked them too much when I was picking, but any day that picking was good I would do a 51 or a 52 without much sweat.

Morris: What about the pounds system, what do you think of the 5,000 lbs. per man-hour standard?

Jones: Well, if you want my opinion, I think the standard should be retimed. Mind you, I know that guys are pacing themselves. In fact, there are some men on my shift that I would bet you I could tell within two hundred pounds per hour either way how much they will pick today.

Morris: Do you try to do something about it?

Jones: One thing for sure is that giving them hell doesn't help much. Mr. Brown tries that, but it doesn't do much good. They're pretty cagey and you can't pin too much on them. After a while, they get a laugh out of getting hell. If I'm caught in a jam and have to get out a lot of orders, like last Friday for instance, I just put it up to them and say look guys we've got to get a lot of stuff out today. Usually most of them will pitch right in, but, mind you, I couldn't pull that on them every day.

Morris: What about the sitdown last November, were you involved in that?

Jones: Well, as a matter of fact, it was not on my shift, so all I could tell you would be hearsay, and you know hearsay is no good. I can tell you, though that it was not the first sitdown we've had. We had one soon after the allowed minute system came in. I know about that one because when the general manager came over to find out what the trouble was, all the other guys clammed up, and I had to be the spokesman.

Morris: What was the trouble?

Jones: Well, it was the foreman we had then, Len Cox. When he first started out he was real buddy-buddy, but then he began to crack the whip. The worst part of it, though, was he played favorites. When he brought in the night shift there were two or three guys who never got nights. I told the general manager all this, and he promised action within 24 hours. We got it, too! They transferred Cox out of there in no time and made Mr. Bruce, his assistant, the new foreman.

Morris: Do the men in the department get together much outside of work?

Jones: Oh yeah, a lot of them belong to the same lodges and so on, but I honestly don't believe that they bother talking about work much.

When Jack Morris asked Mr. Ewen about the previous sitdown in the warehousing and shipping department the latter laughed and said "So you heard about that. I guess last November they thought they would do the same thing to Brown and me as they did to Cox. You see, we made one mistake. We had had Carr in before the transfer and told him that if his work did not improve he would be subject to disciplinary action. That was all they needed."

Morris also talked with Bob Hackett and Ross Wilson to find out their views about the situation. These two men had been assistant foremen in the department since June, 1962. Neither of them had ever actually worked as pickers; Hackett had previously worked for some time in the materials handling department and had considerable experience with conveyor belt operations, while Wilson, although he had spent some years as a lead hand doing the scheduling in the warehousing and shipping department, had never done the pick-up job. Excerpts from interviews held individually with these two men follow:

Morris: Do you think there are some people in the pick-up section who are slowing down production?

Hackett: That's a hard question to answer. People are all so different that it's difficult to know what to think or do.

Morris: You find that you feel kind of helpless?

Hackett: Yes, that's it. I feel kind of helpless about this whole thing.

Morris: Do you prefer to be on the floor or in the corner scheduling?

Hackett: I like it better on the floor. That's where you have to do some planning.

Morris: You're working on the floor tonight, aren't you? What will you do?

Hackett: I usually try to walk around the warehouse at least once. This is our busy season right now, so I also help out at the belts between 5:30 and 7:30 to cover them between shifts. I also have to make sure that everything is going right in Warehousing and Shipping.

* * * * *

Morris: Ross, what do you think about the 5,000 lbs. per man-hour standard in the pick-up area?

Wilson: It's hard to say. For instance, the pickers now have to tie the top of each pallet with twine. This wasn't so when the 5,000 lbs. standard came in.

Morris: Have you done anything about it?

Wilson: Yes, I saw Mr. Brown and he promised to have Industrial Engineering look into it.

Morris: When you are in the corner scheduling do you get many complaints about unfairness?

Wilson: Sometimes they beef, but I have the day's tally sheet right there to show them.

Morris: What do you think the real problem is?

Wilson: I don't know, it may be partly my fault. I'm pretty inexperienced as a supervisor.

Morris: What about Mr. Brown, does he help you?

Wilson: Oh yeah, if there is any trouble he'll speak to the men. He doesn't stand for any nonsense and he wants to run an efficient department.

The case writer also interviewed Mike Prior who had been promoted from lead hand to assistant foreman in January, 1963. Prior had been in the Warehousing and Shipping Department since 1953, and during that time he had done most jobs in the department including some time as a picker.

Morris: Mike, what do you think is the problem with the pick-up section? Some people I've talked to think it may be the 5,000 lb. standard. What do you think?

Prior: It's not the standard, they could make that if they wanted to. Why we've got an old gentleman, Walter Janos, who is almost 60 years old, and he regularly turns out close to standard. The trouble is that there is a group of young bucks who've been in this department for 6 to 8 years and they think they run the show. They won't let anyone produce more than they think he should.

Morris: What about Walter Janos? You say that he produced close to the 5,000 lbs.

Prior: They don't bother him too much. Walter and a couple of the other foreign-speaking fellows keep to themselves pretty much. They don't play cards with the other guys at lunch hour or anything like that. Even so, they get after Walter now and then and his production will drop off for a couple of days, but then it goes right back up. He is the kind of guy that hates to be idle. In fact, many times he'll come up to me or the other schedulers and say "give me an order but don't mark it down on my performance record."

Morris: Who get credited for the order?

Prior: Nobody, we just push it through.

Morris: What about yourself when you were working as a picker, did they get after you?

Prior: You're darn right they did. It was real bad when they used to post everybody's performance rating under the old minute system. If you went above a 45 the guys would tell you about it real quick. I'm only a little guy as you can see (laughs) and I've got a wife and family to feed, so I did what they said pretty well. When management brought in the pounds system they stopped posting everybody's performance, but it didn't make too much difference. Mr. Brown said production wasn't any secret, and he issued little black books to everybody, and nearly all the guys keep their books real accurate. They use them to argue with the guy working in the corner to prove that he is being unfair.

Morris: What about working in the corner, do you like it?

Prior: Well, to tell the truth it keeps you on your toes. I've done the job for several years. Long before I was a foreman I used to work in the corner as a lead hand. It was even tougher then because you had to keep the company happy, but you also had to make sure that the guys didn't take you for a squealer. I'll tell you about a rough thing that happened to me one time. There is a guy in this department, John Diemen, who is a real troublemaker. Well this night I was in the corner and he goofed off and went for a sleep in the back of the warehouse. I didn't say anything, but soon the shipper he was working with began to complain about orders piling up. I didn't know what to do, and there was no foreman on the night shift in those days. Finally, I got hold of the union steward. I was lucky because he was a very religious fellow and I knew he wouldn't tell a lie for anyone. Well the two of us walked over to the back of the warehouse, and there was Diemen stretched out on a bench. So the union steward shook him till he got up. We decided not to say anything, but a couple of days later the foreman asked me if it was true about Diemen sleeping on the job. I wasn't going to lie so I told him the whole story. He also went and asked the steward and the steward said he didn't know if the man was sleeping, but he did know he was lying there with his eyes closed. So they had Diemen into the office, and I figured they would send him home for a few days. His story was that he had had his lunch and had lain down to rest for a few minutes and didn't realize what time it was until we came over. That was so much hogwash. When he woke him up lunch break had been over for an hour. But you know what? They didn't send him home, they said they would give him a last chance. That guy had had more than enough last chances.

Morris: What about now that you are supervising on the floor as well as working in the corner, do you run into this kind of problem?

Prior: Well, Hal Jones and I have only been working on the floor every other shift for the last six weeks or so. Before that we always took the corner and Bob Hackett or Ross Wilson ran the floor. I like the floor, though, because I think it is more of a challenge than the corner. Mr. Brown decided that Hal and me should learn the floor job, and he told us that we will continue to alternate with Bob and Ross on the floor so that we can get the experience. I don't know how it will work out because Mr. Brown sometimes changes his mind, but then every man is entitled to do that. It's funny, but the first time I worked on the floor this guy Diemen tried to get smart. It was on the night shift and the men were supposed to work until 4:30 in the morning. One night I saw Diemen goofing off at 4 o'clock so I asked him where he was going and he told me to mind my own business. I told him that I was not talking as Mike Prior but as the National Paint Company, and it sure as hell was my business. Then he said he was punching out and going home.

Morris: Can the men punch out whenever they want to?

Prior: Yes, but they're supposed to have a good excuse and, of course, they don't take home as much pay.

Morris: So what happened about Diemen?

Prior: I told him to punch out and go home. Well, about 4:20 I went to the lunchroom and there were a bunch of the men playing cards, including Diemen. I asked him why he hadn't gone home and he told me it was none of my business now, because he had punched out. There wasn't really much I could do because he had. However, this matter of playing cards had also been becoming a problem, so I decided to lay the law down. The guys had started to drift off at five or ten minutes after four to play cards until quitting time. They really were taking advantage of the company, because they are allowed to stop work at about 4:20 anyway to wash up on company time. So I told them that the next night I would be in the lunchroom at 4:20 and any men I caught in there could expect to be sent home for a few days. When I left the room I could hear them cursing me up and down, but none of them came up early the next night. It seems that the only way to handle some of these guys is to get tough with them. They seem to think that the union will protect them whatever they do and that management can't do anything to them. Why take this matter of helping out on the belt between 5:30 and 7:30 during the busy season. When Bob Hackett started to go over and help out, they tried to make an issue out of it because he drove a fork lift. One morning I was in the corner and the shop steward came in and said he wanted to use the phone to lodge a complaint with the chief steward. I asked him what I had done that he wanted to beef about, and he said he wasn't complaining about me but about supervision doing labor in the belt department. Well, he phoned the chief steward, but the chief steward told him he was wasting his time because it was right in the contract that supervision could help to cover in between shifts during the busy season. I could have told him that, but he wouldn't have listened to me.

Morris: What about the sitdown last November; did you take part in it?

Prior: No, I was lucky, it was my day off. As a matter of fact, I had arranged to come up that afternoon to the warehouse to meet Mr. Brown and go over to the hospital with him to see one of the fellows who was out sick. Well, when I arrived there was this big commotion and Mr. Ewen and Mr. Brown were running around all over. I decided that was no place for me so I beat it out of there as fast as I could. I can tell you, though, that I believe Carr and Brandt were the fall guys, especially Brandt. He had worked as a janitor for some years and he really took an interest in keeping the department clean. But then management said that everyone in the department had to learn to do all the jobs there were. So they put Brandt on picking, and he really tried but it was too much for him. The thing that I don't see is that there are guys in the department right now who have never picked, but they don't put them on it.

During a discussion with the case writer, Mr. Ewen observed that since becoming an assistant foreman, Mike Prior had tried to be tough with the men, whereas while a worker he had been one of the average output producers.

In conversation with Mr. Brown, Morris learned that in the latter's opinion there were "five or six radicals in the department who won't produce and who slow everyone else down, too." When asked to name these men Brown listed Hutton, Singer, Birchall, Savage, and Smithson. He also stated that Hutton was the ringleader who stayed in the background, while Singer was the man who was used by Hutton and the others to see just how far they could push management. Morris also asked Brown if he knew whether these men got together socially off the job. Brown replied, "I don't. This is a small town, however, and I suppose they do to some extent." When Mr. Ewen was shown Brown's list of troublemakers he added another name, that of D. Vanclief.

Personal data on the departmental supervisors and the regular workers in the pick-up section were available to Mr. Ewen from company records.

During his second visit to the department, Morris was told by Gord Ewen that one person whom he might find it useful to interview would be Bill Swan. (Responsible for space requirements. See Figure 2.) Ewen pointed out that Swan was a real "old timer" having been with the company for over 40 years. Ewen observed, "If Bill Swan wants to open up I'm sure he could tell you a lot of things."

Morris talked with Mr. Swan and the gist of his comments were as follows:

Swan: I've been with National Paint for 43 years, in fact, there are only one or two men still active who have been here longer. I'm not directly involved in the problem in the shipping department but I know they are having real difficulties, and they've tried everything. They tried reorganizing the department, changing supervisors, and so on, but nothing seems to work. If you ask me, the problem is the young men these days. That bunch in shipping don't seem to care about anything. Why should they, though, with all these baby bonuses, unemployment benefits, and what not that they have these days? In my day we worked on piece work, and we had to turn out a good day's work. We knew that if we didn't, there were ten men at the door waiting for our jobs. Nowadays, with unions the men think they can get away with anything. I know, I've talked to most of them. They don't seem to realize

> that if they act up too much the company has the power to shut down this plant and move elsewhere, and then where would this small town be? Mind you, there are some good men in the department, and I know that these men are resentful of management because they were visited one by one just like the bad actors. I think that was a mistake, but then it's really none of my business.

Toward the end of Jack Morris' second visit to the department, Mr. Ewen told Morris that provided he could get the backing of the manager of personnel, he was thinking of recommending the adoption of an incentive system in the warehousing and shipping department. While this would require a retiming of the standards, he envisaged that 5,000 lbs. per man-hour would remain as the base rate, but there would be graduated bonuses for those who produced more than this on the average.

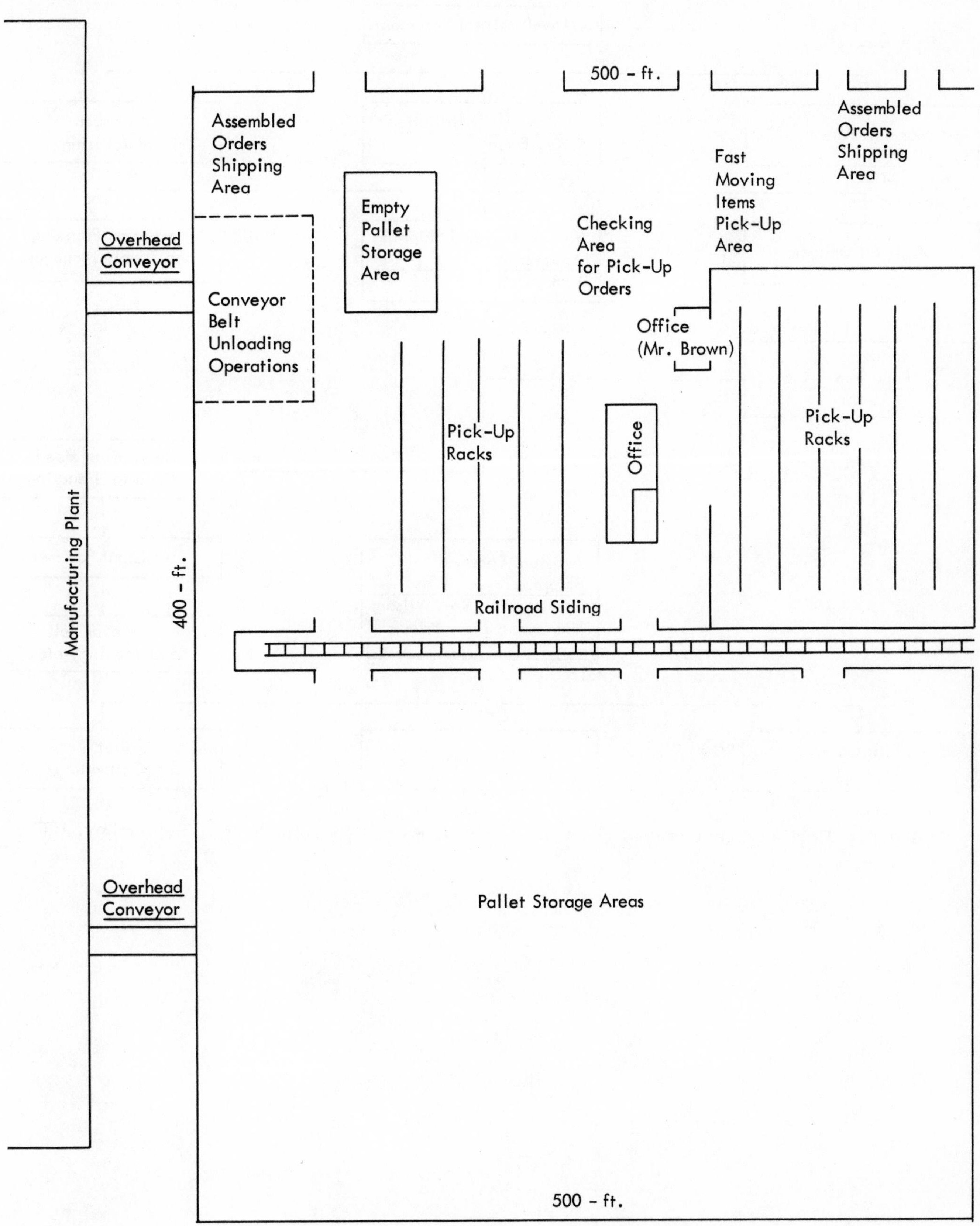

Figure 1. Warehousing and Shipping Department layout for National Paint Products, Inc.

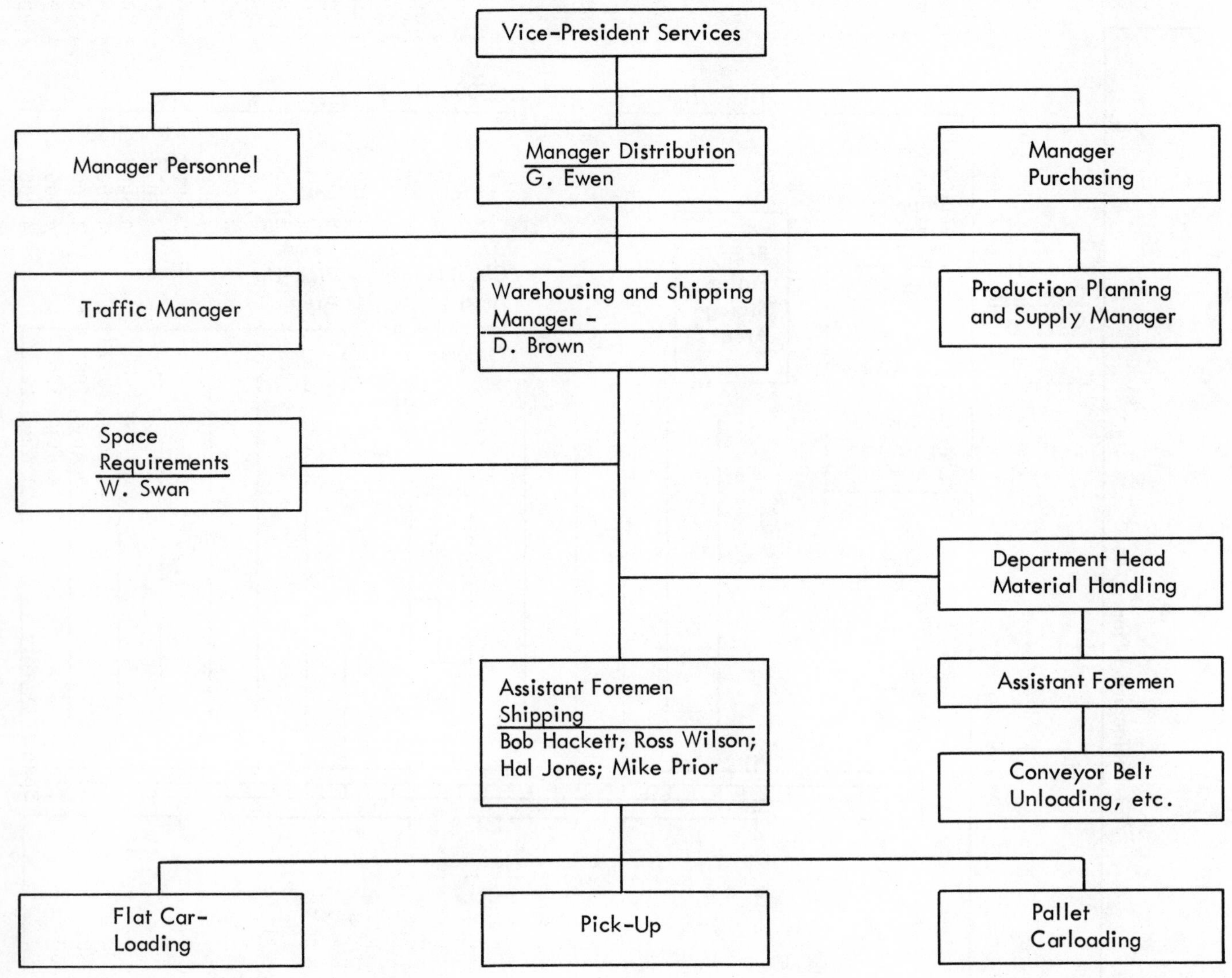

Figure 2. Partial organizational chart for National Paint Productions, Inc., September, 1963.

Table 1

NATIONAL PAINT PRODUCTS

Pick-up Section-Output per Man-hour (May 1962-September 1963)

Week Ending	Average Output[1] (lbs. per man-hour)	Range[2] (lbs. per man-hour)	Remarks	Week Ending	Average Output	Range
2 May, 1962	3,858	4,587-3,502		5 Dec., 1962	4,000	5,000-2,200
9 May, 1962	3,611	4,503-2,251	Shifts Equalized effective 7 May.	12 Dec., 1962	4,000	4,600-2,800
				19 Dec., 1962	4,300	4,700-3,900
				26 Dec., 1962	4,250	4,700-4,000
16 May, 1962	3,169	3,836-2,502		2 Jan., 1963	4,200	4,900-3,700
23 May, 1962	3,452	4,336-2,835		9 Jan., 1963	4,350	4,900-4,000
30 May, 1962	3,169	4,253-2,251		16 Jan., 1963	4,300	5,000-3,900
6 June, 1962	3,336	3,919-2,585		23 Jan., 1963	4,400	6,800-2,700
13 June, 1962	3,419	3,753-2,919		30 Jan., 1963	4,200	5,300-2,800
20 June, 1962	3,436	3,836-2,251		6 Feb., 1963	4,200	4,700-2,800
27 June, 1962	3,619	3,919-2,502		13 Feb., 1963	4,450	5,000-3,400
4 July, 1962	3,960	5,000-2,600	Pounds per man-hour performance rating introduced Effective 29 June	20 Feb., 1963	4,300	4,800-3,900
				27 Feb., 1963	4,100	5,200-2,800
				6 Mar., 1963	4,000	4,900-2,700
				13 Mar., 1963	4,000	5,200-2,700
				20 Mar., 1963	4,100	4,600-4,100
11 July, 1962	4,350	4,700-2,900		27 Mar., 1963	4,100	4,900-3,200
18 July, 1962	4,000	4,700-2,900		3 Apr., 1963	4,100	4,500-3,500
25 July, 1962	4,200	5,000-2,900		10 Apr., 1963	4,200	4,700-3,700
1 Aug., 1962	4,250	4,800-3,000		17 Apr., 1963	4,250	4,800-3,400
8 Aug., 1962	4,270	5,100-2,900		24 Apr., 1963	4,300	4,900-3,400
15 Aug., 1962	4,450	5,800-3,100		1 May, 1963	4.400	4,800-3,900
22 Aug., 1962	4,200	4,800-3,400		8 May, 1963	4,300	5,000-3,700
29 Aug., 1962	4,250	4,800-3,200		15 May, 1963	4,300	4,900-3,200
5 Sept., 1962	4,300	5,200-2,900		22 May, 1963	4,300	4,800-4,000
12 Sept., 1962	4,500	5,000-3,800	Special Quality Discount Campaign on a fast-moving item[3]	29 May, 1963	4,300	4,700-4,000
				5 June, 1963	4,300	5,000-3,800
				12 June, 1963	4,100	4,900-2,200
				19 June, 1963	4,200	4,900-2,800
19 Sept., 1962	4,200	4,800-3,100		26 June, 1963	4,100	5,200-2,800
26 Sept., 1962	4,230	4,700-3,500		3 July, 1963	4,000	4,500-2,700
3 Oct., 1962	4,400	4,900-3,900		10 July, 1963	3,900	5,000-2,200
10 Oct., 1962	4,200	5,000-3,500		17 July, 1963	4,000	5,100-2,700
17 Oct., 1962	4,348	4,900-3,500		24 July, 1963	4,000	5,200-3,300
24 Oct., 1962	4,350	5,300-3,300		31 July, 1963	4,100	4,800-3,500
31 Oct., 1962	4,220	4,800-3,400		7 Aug., 1963	4,100	4,800-3,800
7 Nov., 1962	4,320	5,000-3,500		14 Aug., 1963	4,100	4,700-3,500
14 Nov., 1962	4,500	5,100-3,900	Special Quality	21 Aug., 1963	4,200	4,800-3,200

Table 1 (continued)

NATIONAL PAINT PRODUCTS

Pick-up Section-Output per Man-hour (May 1962-September 1963)

Week Ending	Average Output[1] (lbs. per man-hour	Range[2] (lbs. per man-hour)	Remarks	Week Ending	Average Output	Range
			Discount Campaign on a fast-moving item[3]	28 Aug., 1963	4,100	5,000-3,800
				4 Sept., 1963	4,100	4,900-3,500
				11 Sept., 1963	4,100	4,700-2,700
21 Nov., 1962	4,300	5,100-3,800				
28 Nov., 1962	4,240	4,800-3,500	Sitdown staged in shipping and material handling departments on 23 Nov.			

[1]Performance converted from allowed minute system for period 2 May to 27 June.

[2]Range exclude individuals who worked less than 10 hours in a particular week.

[3]During this period the company shipped special quantity discount orders on a fast-moving item. In effect, it meant that the pickers could rapidly assemble large quantities of a single product from the fast-moving items area located close to the order checking point (Exhibit 1).

THE BOSS IS THE BOSS

My company is located in a large southern city. It has two almost completely separate divisions, one of which is called the City Sales or Local Division. This is the end of our operation for which I am responsible. The General Manager, my boss, is Jim Smathers.

I was just about to open a new Suburban Branch three or four years ago when this series of incidents took place. My choice for manager of the new branch had pretty much narrowed down to Bob Jordan as the man I thought most qualified for this post, although Bob did not know the lightning was so near to striking in his back yard. Bob had been with us some seven years, had done about everything that had to be done on the City Sales side of the business at one time or another, had handled every responsibility he had been given in a top-notch manner, and was, in my opinion, ready to move up.

Against this backdrop you can imagine my surprise when I had the following conversation with Jim at lunch one day.

"By the way, Jim, we will have possession of the Bayview Branch Building in another two weeks, and I'd like to go over with you the progress that has been made toward opening."

"Good! I'm glad you brought that up, I've been meaning to get with you about that."

"Well, I've completed the layout plan for the bin arrangement, and have enough carpenters lined up to do the inside panels. The electricians are set to do the wiring whenever we say the word."

"Actually, Fred, what I had in mind primarily was the question of who ought to be put in charge out there."

"It's just about come down to Bob Jordan for my money. He's not the most senior man available, as you know, but he has been pretty well through the mill with us, and every department head he's ever worked for gives him a very high rating. And in all my contacts with him he has had the very best work attitude."

"Does Bob know this?"

"No, I haven't said anything to him yet--though two of his former department heads have mentioned to me that he is the right man for this spot."

"Well, Fred, I'm not going to say you've got to do this, but I'd like to see Bill Grayson put in charge out at Bayview. There is, of course, no question of Bill's ability, his background is the best you can find, and as you know we are rushing his training for more responsible jobs. In a few years Bill will be a key man with us, and this will be a stepping stone to bigger things up the line for him."

I tell you I was stunned there for a minute. Bill had been brought into the organization about 14 months ago specifically to train for a managerial post with us--this arrangement no doubt having something to do with the fact that Bill's father (head of a large equipment company in the city) and Jim were very good friends. Undoubtedly he was management material, and I knew nothing whatever about him that would suggest he wouldn't make a first-rate branch manager some day. In fact I didn't really know very much about him at all, since he had never worked in the Local Division; I knew his connection with Jim (everybody knew that he was the "fair-haired boy" of Number One), the plan to push him along as fast as possible, that he had been married and had one child, but that his wife had obtained a divorce, and I had heard that on a couple of occasions since he came with us he had been seen downtown at night heavily under the influence. But I would never in the world have thought of Bill in terms of the job that was opening up now.

My response to Jim's suggestion was this: "I agree with you up to a point, but I feel we would be doing Bill an injustice. As you know this work is pretty technical, and it has been our experience that a man needs to be around about five years before he can be put on his own. Bill has been with us only a little over a year, and he's had no Local Division experience at all."

Jim didn't push me any farther just then. He just told me to think it over and we'd get back together in a couple of days.

And we did. He brought it up almost the very next chance we had to sit down and talk.

"I'm sure you've given the new branch manager's job some more thought. What have you decided?"

"Well, I'm still not sold on Bill. You've got to remember we've never tried anything like this before. And we've also got to think about the men like Bob Jordan who feel that they are ready for a promotion. It'd be pretty tough explaining to these men why Bill got the nod and they didn't. Besides, this isn't the last promotion there'll be around here. We'll probably be opening up another branch every year for a number of years. Why not let Bill get some experience in City Sales and give him a branch managership in a year or two?"

But Jim didn't take any of this very seriously. "I'm still not going to order you to do this. However, I do want you to remember that there are two kinds of employees--managers and workers. Bill is definitely management material and should have this store as further training toward this goal."

I told Jim I would sleep on it and let him know tomorrow morning.

1) List Pos Neg of Both

Bob

Pos	Neg
Experience	Maybe Too Detail
Moral of Others	Not Mgt.
Liked in Open Div.	Worker Rather Mgt
	Decide
	End of Road??

Jim

Pos	Neg
Mgt Mtl	Unknown in Div.
Future Use to Comp	Drunkness

IF Equal Go W/Boss

IF Better over all Go W. Boss

IF Still Not as Good - Can Spec

Tell Why. Don't go with Boss

Give Him Option of Demanding Though

DICK SPENCER

After the usual banter when old friends meet for cocktails, the conversation between a couple of University professors and Dick Spencer, a former student who was now a successful businessman, turned to Dick's life as a vice-president of a large manufacturing firm.

"I've made a lot of mistakes, most of which I could live with, but this one series of incidents was so frustrating that I could have cried at the time," Dick said in response to a question. "I really have to laugh at how ridiculous it is now, but at the time I blew my cork."

Spencer was plant manager of Modrow Company, a Canadian branch of the Tri-American Corporation. Tri-American was a major producer of primary aluminum with integrated operations ranging from the mining of bauxite through the processing to fabrication of aluminum into a variety of products. The company also made and sold refractories and industrial chemicals. The parent company had wholly-owned subsidiaries in five separate United States locations and had foreign affiliates in 15 different countries.

Tri-American mined bauxite in the Jamaican West Indies and shipped the raw material by commercial vessels to two plants in Louisiana where it was processed into alumina. The alumina was then shipped to reduction plants in one of three locations for conversion into primary aluminum. Most of the primary aluminum was then moved to the companies' fabricating plants for further processing. Fabricated aluminum items included sheet, flat, coil, and corrugated products; siding; and roofing.

Tri-American employed approximately 22,000 employees in the total organization. The company was governed by a board of directors which included the chairman, vice-chairman, president, and twelve vice-presidents. However, each of the subsidiaries and branches functioned as independent units. The board set general policy, which was then interpreted and applied by the various plant managers. In a sense, the various plants competed with one another as though they were independent companies. This decentralization in organizational structure increased the freedom and authority of the plant managers, but increased the pressure for profitability.

The Modrow branch was located in a boarder town in Canada. The total work force in Modrow was 1,000. This Canadian subsidiary was primarily a fabricating unit. Its main products were foil and building products such as roofing and siding. Aluminum products were gaining in importance in architectural plans, and increased sales were predicted for this branch. Its location and its stable work force were the most important advantages it possessed.

In anticipation of estimated increases in building product sales, Modrow had recently completed a modernization and expansion project. At the same time, their research and art departments combined talents in developing a series of twelve new patterns of siding which were being introduced to the market. Modernization and pattern development had been costly undertakings, but the expected return on investment made the project feasible. However, the plant manager, who was a Tri-American vice-president, had instituted a campaign to cut expenses wherever possible. In his introductory notice of the campaign, he emphasized that cost reduction would be the personal aim of every employee at Modrow.

Salesman: The plant manager of Modrow, Dick Spencer, was an American who had been transferred to this Canadian branch two years previously, after the start of the modernization plan. Dick had been with the Tri-American Company for 14 years, and his progress within the organization was considered spectacular by those who knew him well. Dick had received a Master's degree in Business Administration from a well-known university at the age of 22. Upon graduation he had accepted a job as salesman for Tri-American. During his first year as a salesman, he succeeded in landing a single, large contract which put him near the top of the sales-volume leaders. In discussing his phenomenal rise in the sales volume, several of his fellow salesmen concluded that his looks, charm, and ability on the golf course contributed as much to his success as his knowledge of the business or his ability to sell the products.

The second year of his sales career, he continued to set a fast pace. Although his record set difficult goals for the other salesmen, he was considered a "regular guy" by them, and both he and they seemed to enjoy the few occasions when they socialized. However, by the end of the second year of constant travelling and selling, Dick began to experience some doubt about his future.

His constant involvement in business affairs disrupted his marital life, and his wife divorced him during the second year with Tri-American. Dick resented her action at first, but gradually seemed to recognize that his career at present depended on his freedom to travel unencumbered. During that second year, he ranged far and wide in his sales territory, and successfully closed several large contracts. None of them was as large as his first year's major sale, but in total volume he again was well up near the top of salesmen for the year. Dick's name became well known in the corporate headquarters, and he was spoken of as "the boy to watch."

Dick had met the president of Tri-American during his first year as a salesman at a company conference. After three days of golfing and socializing they developed a relaxed camaraderie considered unusual by those who observed the developing friendship. Although their contacts were infrequent after the conference, their easy relationship seemed to blossom the few times they did meet. Dick's friends kidded him about his ability to make use of his new friendship to promote himself in the company, but Dick brushed aside their jibes and insisted that he'd make it on his own abilities, not someone's coattail.

By the time he was 25, Dick began to suspect that he did not look forward to a life as a salesman for the rest of his career. He talked about his unrest with his friends, and they suggested that he groom himself for sales manager. "You won't make the kind of money you're making from commissions," he was told, "but you will have a foot in the door from an administrative standpoint, and you won't have to travel quite as much as you do now." Dick took their suggestions lightly, and continued to sell the product, but was aware that he felt dissatisfied and did not seem to get the satisfaction out of his job that he had once enjoyed.

By the end of his third year with the company Dick was convinced that he wanted a change in direction. As usual, he and the president spent quite a bit of time on the golf course during the annual company sales conference. After their match one day, the president kidded Dick about his game. The conversation drifted back to business, and the president, who seemed to be in a jovial mood, started to kid Dick about his sales ability. In a joking way, he implied that anyone could sell a product as good as Tri-American's, but that it took real "guts and know-how" to make the products. The conversation drifted to other things, but this remark stuck with Dick.

Sometime later, Dick approached the president formally with a request for a transfer out of the sales division. The president was surprised and hesitant about this change in career direction for Dick. He recognized the superior sales ability that Dick seemed to possess, but was unsure that Dick was willing or able to assume responsibilities in any other division of the organization. Dick sensed the hesitancy, but continued to push his request. He later remarked that it seemed that the initial hesitancy of the president convinced Dick that he needed an opportunity to prove himself in a field other than sales.

<u>Trouble Shooter</u>: Dick was finally transferred back to the home office of the organization and indoctrinated into productive and administrative roles in the company as a special assistant to the senior vice-president of production. As a special assistant, Dick was assigned several trouble-shooting jobs. He acquitted himself well in this role, but in the process succeeded in gaining a reputation as a ruthless head hunter among the branches where he had performed a series of amputations. His reputation as an amiable, genial, easy-going guy from the sales department was the antithesis of the reputation of a cold, calculating head hunter which he earned in his trouble-shooting role. The vice-president, who was Dick's boss, was aware of the reputation which Dick had earned but was pleased with the results that were obtained. The faltering departments that Dick had worked in seemed to bloom with new life and energy after Dick's recommended amputations. As a result, the vice-president began to sing Dick's praises, and the president began to accept Dick in his new role in the company.

<u>Management Responsibility</u>: About three years after Dick's switch from sales, he was given an assignment as assistant plant manager of an English branch of the company. Dick, who had remarried, moved his wife and family to London, and they attempted to adapt to their new routine. The plant manager was English, as were most of the other employees. Dick and his family were accepted with reservations into the community life as well as into the plant life. The difference between British and American philosophy and performance within the plant was marked for Dick who was imbued with modern managerial concepts and methods. Dick's directives from headquarters were to update and upgrade performance in this branch. However, his power and authority were less than those of his superior, so he constantly found himself in the position of having to soft pedal or withhold suggestions that he would have liked to make, or innovations that he would have liked to introduce. After a frustra-

ting year and a half, Dick was suddenly made plant manager of an old British company which had just been purchased by Tri-American. He left his first English assignment with mixed feelings and moved from London to Birmingham.

As the new plant manager, Dick operated much as he had in his trouble-shooting job for the first couple of years of his change from sales to administration. Training and reeducation programs were instituted for all supervisors and managers who survived the initial purge. Methods were studied and simplified or redesigned whenever possible, and new attention was directed toward production which better met the needs of the sales organization. A strong controller helped to straighten out the profit picture through stringent cost control; and, by the end of the third year, the company showed a small profit for the first time in many years. Because he felt that this battle was won, Dick requested transfer back to the United States. This request was partially granted when nine months later he was awarded a junior vice-president title, and was made manager of a subsidiary Canadian plant, Modrow.

Modrow Manager: Prior to Dick's appointment as plant manager at Modrow, extensive plans for plant expansion and improvement had been approved and started. Although he had not been in on the original discussions and plans, he inherited all the problems that accompany large-scale changes in any organization. Construction was slower in completion than originally planned, equipment arrived before the building was finished, employees were upset about the extent of change expected in their work routines with the installation of additional machinery and, in general, morale was at a low ebb.

Various versions of Dick's former activities had preceded him, and on his arrival he was viewed with dubious eyes. The first few months after his arrival were spent in a frenzy of catching up. This entailed constant conferences and meetings, volumes of reading of past reports, becoming acquainted with the civic leaders of the area, and a plethora of dispatches to and from the home office. Costs continued to climb unabated.

By the end of his first year at Modrow, the building program had been completed, although behind schedule, the new equipment had been installed, and some revamping of cost procedures had been incorporated. The financial picture at this time showed a substantial loss, but since it had been budgeted as a loss, this was not surprising. All managers of the various divisions had worked closely with their supervisors and accountants in planning the budget for the following year, and Dick began to emphasize his personal interest in cost reduction.

As he worked through his first year as plant manager, Dick developed the habit of strolling around the organization. He was apt to leave his office and appear anywhere on the plant floor, in the design offices, at the desk of a purchasing agent or accountant, in the plant cafeteria rather than the executive dining room, or wherever there was activity concerned with Modrow. During his strolls he looked, listened, and became acquainted. If he observed activities which he wanted to talk about, or heard remarks that gave him clues to future action, he did not reveal these at the time. Rather he had a nod, a wave, a smile, for the people near him, but a mental note to talk to his supervisors, managers, and foremen in the future. At first his presence disturbed those who noted him coming and going, but after several exposures to him without any noticeable effect, the workers came to accept his presence and continue their usual activities. Supervisors, managers, and foremen, however, did not feel as comfortable when they saw him in the area.

Their feelings were aptly expressed by the manager of the siding department one day when he was talking to one of his foremen: "I wish to hell he'd stay up in the front office where he belongs. Whoever heard of a plant manager who had time to wander around the plant all the time. Why doesn't he tend to his paper work and let us tend to our business?"

"Don't let him get you down," joked the foreman. "Nothing ever comes of his visits. Maybe he's just lonesome and looking for a friend. You know how these Americans are."

"Well, you may feel that nothing ever comes of his visits, but I don't. I've been called into his office three separate times within the last two months. The heat must really be on from the head office. You know these conferences we have every month where he reviews our financial progress, our building progress, our design progress, etc.? Well, we're not really progressing as fast as we should be. If you ask me we're in for continuing trouble."

In recalling his first year at Modrow, Dick had felt constantly pressured and badgered. He always sensed that the Canadians he worked with resented his presence since he was brought in over the heads of the operating staff. At the same time he felt this subtle resistance from his Canadian work force, he believed that the president and his friends in the home office were constantly on the alert, waiting for Dick to prove himself or fall flat on his face. Because of the constant pressures and demands of the work, he had literally dumped his family into a new community and had withdrawn into the plant. In the process, he built up a wall of resistance toward the demands of his wife and children who, in turn, felt as though he was abandoning them.

During the course of the conversation with his University friends, he began to recall a series of incidents that probably had resulted from the conflicting pressures. When describing some of these incidents, he continued to emphasize the fact that his attempt to be relaxed and casual had backfired. Laughingly, Dick said, "As you know, both human relations and accounting were my weakest subjects during the Master's program, and yet they are two fields I felt I needed the most at Modrow at this time." He described some of the cost procedures that he would have liked to incorporate. However, without the support and knowledge furnished by his former controller, he busied himself with details that were unnecessary. One day, as he describes it, he overheard a conversation between two of the accounting staff members with whom he had been working very closely. One of them commented to the other, "For a guy who's a vice-president, he sure spends a lot of time breathing down our necks. Why doesn't he simply tell us the kind of systems he would like to try, and let us do the experimenting and work out the budget?" Without commenting on the conversation he overheard, Dick then described himself as attempting to spend less time and be less directive in the accounting department.

Another incident he described which apparently had real meaning for him was one in which he had called a staff conference with his top-level managers. They had been going "hammer and tongs" for better than a hour in his private office, and in the process of heated conversation had loosened ties, taken off coats, and really rolled up their sleeves. Dick himself had slipped out of his shoes. In the midst of this, his secretary reminded him of an appointment with public officials. Dick had rapidly finished up his conference with his managers, straightened his tie, donned his coat, and had wandered out into the main office in his stocking feet.

Dick fully described several incidents when he had disappointed, frustrated, or confused his wife and family by forgetting birthdays, appointments, dinner engagements, etc. He seemed to be describing a pattern of behavior which resulted from continuing pressure and frustration. He was setting the scene to describe his baffling and humiliating position in the siding department. In looking back and recalling his activities during this first year, Dick commented on the fact that his frequent wanderings throughout the plant had resulted in a nodding acquaintance with the workers, but probably had also resulted in foremen and supervisors spending more time getting ready for his visits and reading meaning into them afterwards than attending to their specific duties. His attempts to know in detail the accounting procedures being used required long hours of concentration and detailed conversations with the accounting staff, which were time-consuming and very frustrating for him, as well as for them. His lack of attention to his family life resulted in continued pressure from both wife and family.

The Siding Department Incident: Siding was the product which had been budgeted as a large profit item of Modrow. Aluminum siding was gaining in popularity among both architects and builders, because of its possibilities in both decorative and practical uses. Panel sheets of siding were shipped in standard sizes on order; large sheets of the coated siding were cut to specifications in the trim department, packed, and shipped. The trim shop was located near the loading platforms, and Dick often cut through the trim shop on his wanderings through the plant. On one of his frequent trips through the area, he suddenly became aware of the fact that several workers responsible for the disposal function were spending countless hours at high-speed saws cutting scraps into specified lengths to fit into scrap barrels. The narrow bands of scrap which resulted from the trim process varied in length from 7 to 27 feet and had to be reduced in size to fit into the disposal barrels. Dick, in his concentration on cost reduction, picked up one of the thin strips, bent it several times and filled it into the barrel. He tried this with another piece, and it bent very easily. After assuring himself that bending was possible, he walked over to a worker at the saw and asked why he was using the saw when material could easily be bent and fitted into the barrels, resulting in saving time and equipment. The worker's response was, "We've never done it that way, sir. We've always cut it."

Following his plan of not commenting or discussing matters on the floor, but distressed by the reply, Dick returned to his office and asked the manager of the siding department if he could speak to the foreman of the scrap division. The manager said, "Of course, I'll send him up to you in just a minute."

After a short time, the foreman, very agitated at being called to the plant manager's office, appeared. Dick began questioning him about the scrap disposal process and received the standard answer: "We've always done it that way." Dick then proceeded to review cost-cutting objectives. He talked about the pliability of the strips of scrap. He called for a few pieces of scrap to demonstrate the ease with which it could be bent, and ended what he thought was a satisfactory conversation by requesting the foreman to order heavy-duty gloves for his workers and use the bending process for a trial period of two weeks to check the cost saving possible.

The foreman listened throughout most of this hour's conference, offered several reasons why it wouldn't work, raised some questions about the record-keeping process for cost purposes, and finally left the office with the forced agreement to try the suggested new method of bending, rather than cutting, for disposal. Although he was immersed in many other problems, his request was forcibly brought home one day as he cut through the scrap area. The workers were using power saws to cut scraps. He called the manager of the siding department and questioned him about the process. The manager explained that each foreman was responsible for his own processes, and since Dick had already talked to the foreman, perhaps he had better talk to him again. When the foreman arrived, Dick began to question him. He received a series of excuses, and some explanations of the kinds of problems they were meeting by attempting to bend the scrap material. "I don't care what the problems are," Dick nearly shouted, "when I request a cost-reduction program instituted, I want to see it carried through."

Dick was furious. When the foreman left, he phoned the maintenance department and ordered the removal of the power saws from the scrap area immediately. A short time later the foreman of the scrap department knocked on Dick's door reporting his astonishment at having maintenance men step into his area and physically remove the saws. Dick reminded the foreman of his request for a trial at cost reduction to no avail, and ended the conversation by saying that the power saws were gone and would not be returned, and the foreman had damned well better learn to get along without them. After a stormy exit by the foreman, Dick congratulated himself on having solved a problem and turned his attention to other matters.

A few days later Dick cut through the trim department and literally stopped to stare. As he described it, he was completely nonplussed to discover gloved workmen using hand shears to cut each piece of scrap.

1) Did Not Generate Desire in individual.

His Characteristics

A) Insecurity
B) Mistrust - Employees
c) Did No Use Proper Channels
Except - Commands
- No Even Then
D) attitude Solve Problem Himself
E) Let Emotions Rule actions Decisions

2) Should have Set Objectives Passed On. Line.

CONVERSATION WITH A SUPERVISOR (A)

(At the close of an executive development session conducted by the author, one of the participants expressed an interest in relating a "case" in which he was personally involved. An appointment was made, and the following conversation took place.)

Supervisor: "I've taken the time to look up some information on Frank, the guy I'd mentioned to you. He's not stupid--in fact, he has a B.A. degree from Northern University. Graduated in 1921, when he was about twenty-four. Prior to working for us, he had several jobs as a salesman, which may have contributed to his major problem now, drinking."

Researcher: "Drinking?"

Supervisor: "Yes. He is 63 years old, and he's been with the company nineteen years. He is a wino. Ninety-three percent of the time he is drunk--but you can't tell. He has been a drunk for so long that you can't even tell when he's been drinking any more. He doesn't stagger or look drunk, and it's not obvious that he is. But if you work with him at all, you know it; you can smell the liquor, for one thing.

He doesn't get in any trouble because he is under no direct supervision. He works on second shift, and we don't see him except for a few minutes at the start of his shift. But there's no supervisor on that shift. In fact, if there is one, he's it. He's the lead man."

Researcher: "Lead man?"

Supervisor: "Informal leader. Not formally recognized as supervision on the chart, but the guy in charge of the workers. Usually, a lead man works directly under a supervisor, but not in this case.

"One of the basic problems here is that we can't prove that he drinks on the job. He has never been seen to take a drink. We've run checks, even using the security guards on occasion, but no one has ever been able to find his bottle. But we know he drinks! He's as drunk at the end of the shift as he is at the beginning."

Researcher: "And this affects his work?"

Supervisor: "His work is satisfactory, but not for a lead man. He works--he's there at least --but not of the caliber of a lead man. He does not lead at all. He has fallen asleep many times, but has never been caught by a supervisor. His people have seen it, though.

"The men under him and others he works with don't like him at all, because they are unable to communicate with him or talk with him. He is very aloof from the rest of the people--very quiet. The people who work for him really hate his guts.

"With a year and a half to work before he retires after working nineteen years with the company, it creates a problem as to whether to fire him right now or let him stay until he is sixty-five."

Researcher: "You'd like to fire him?"

Supervisor: "Sure, but another major problem is with the union. Under the union deal--he's a member--in which they do the bargaining with the company, it is almost impossible to fire him without building up a big case. And you won't find that here (tapping employee's personnel file). Otherwise, I'd fire him in a minute.

"The main fault lies with the supervisors. Frank should have been fired years ago. But they just kept passing him on to the next guy, and he became progressively worse, until now he is a confirmed alcoholic."

"Look at this garbage in his folder. (Supervisor reads the following from employee's evaluation reports in personnel folder.) "Frank is very cooperative and has good attendance." "Very dependable, works well with assigned personnel, and respected by personnel of associated departments." "Very dependable, cooperative, and a good attitude." "Very good attendance and prompt handling of problems is appreciated."

"Supervisors are worse than employees. They mother this guy along for nineteen years and his folder doesn't even mention the problem--that he's such a lush that he's no good to us."

Researcher: "Have you taken any steps to . . . ?"

Supervisor: "I've put several memos in his folder about his drinking since he's worked for me. This doesn't win any popularity contests for me, either, I'll tell you, but you have to do this kind of thing.

"The big boss agrees with me. We say 'fire him.' But M. J., the personnel director, doesn't think so. He's the soft-hearted type. One of his supervisors should have taken the bull by the horns and had enough courage to have done something about him.

"If he were fired now, he would still keep his vested rights in the pension plan. When he reaches sixty-five, he'll still be able to collect all he has vested in the plan."

Researcher: "Would this be the same as full retirement?"

Supervisor: "No, but he'd get along. I fired the guy who was Frank's last supervisor. He also had about nineteen years with the company, but he was a poor supervisor. This guy had worked for Frank years ago, and I guess he figured he was obligated to him. But he didn't belong to the union, and it was easy to fire him. Who can a supervisor complain to?

"Too many supervisors are soft-hearted. If a person is not doing his job they find some reason to feel sorry for him, especially if they have been friends on the job.

"It's awfully hard to let a man go on working as he has been--drinking, not doing his job for nineteen years--and let him get away with it, then all of a sudden in one week crack down and fire him."

Researcher: "You said he was unsatisfactory as a lead man. Would he be a satisfactory employee if he didn't have lead responsibilities?"

Supervisor: "He might possibly be demoted and moved to first shift. There he would be under direct supervision, and they could watch him in an effort to build up a strong case against him. But this is not the answer. The damage has already been done. He is too old. What actually is happening is that he is retired at full pay.

"Ninety-nine percent of the trouble is when supervisors let themselves become fond of their people and feel obligated not to let them go when they aren't doing a good job. What should have been done is to have watched him and kept a record of any rules broken--anything not done right--by now we'd have a good case against him. But nobody kept those kind of records on him (leafing through personnel folder). Except for the fact that he has always been forgetful about punching in. He even has been suspended for this several times.

"A good supervisor has to be mean--a real S.O.B. A good supervisor is just that. He has to know where to draw the line, just as a professor in school can't become attached to the pupils or he might just as well not be a teacher."

CONVERSATION WITH A SUPERVISOR (B)

Several months after the information in Part A of this case had been obtained, Martin Johnson, the personnel director referred to in Part A, volunteered the following information.

"Say, I thought you might be interested to know what happened in that situation you talked about with Dave Blackwell [the supervisor in Part A] last summer.

"After a lot of consideration, we put Frank on the first shift and watched him pretty carefully. We found nothing at all to substantiate that he was a booze hound, so we gave up on it. He was always there and he always did his job. We had no indication at all that he wasn't performing as he should be. Incidentally, Dave is still convinced he is a drunk. Now Frank's back on the second shift and on his old job and seems to be doing fine. We did make some changes, however, that provide for more supervision on the second shift by staggering the hours of some of our day-shift supervisors, so at least a part of the night-shift time is covered.

"The interesting thing about this, though, is that we did find out how the whole thing came about. It was a woman. A gal by the name of Elma, who has been with us for a long time. Now we want to get rid of her. I knew her in the other division before the reorganization, and she's been nothing but a troublemaker. She has good job knowledge, but then she ought to have because she's been with the company so long. We inherited her with the reorganization a few years back. She came with the function and there's nothing that we could do about it. But she's always been a troublemaker. She has a sense of pride of the worst type, if you know what I mean. She competes by cutting others down. For example, she is always calling the head of the plant security at home complaining about things that have happened to her--or that she thinks have happened to her. The 'Joe Smith is always swearing at me' kind of thing. She also tells the head of security of things that other people are doing that she considers bad. He's talked with me about her several times. Unfortunately, she's the shop steward, which, of necessity, requires that we handle her case with a great deal of discretion. Dave is now trying to 'surplus'[1] her, but I'm afraid that could turn into a long-drawn-out affair.

"She got rid of the former shop steward by getting the Union officers and members aroused. The chap who was steward before she took the position was a former production worker who had lost an arm in an accident on the job. It was sort of understood that he would always have a job with the company, and he could work effectively in this particular section with his physical handicap. He was the kind of guy who was oriented toward the top. He wanted to be a focal point and have things funneled through him. As a result of this, he was very useful to the supervisors in the section because, in a sense, he could do part of their jobs for them. He was interested in the company and its welfare and provided a good informal channel of communication for information which the supervisors might not have been able to get by themselves.

"Well, Elma didn't like this at all. She got a lot of people in the section excited about the fact that the union steward was only interested in management and management problems and took management's side in all situations. It was almost a case of inciting to riot, and it wasn't too long before she had a lot of the people thinking that a new steward would be in the best interests of the employees. At the next election, she was chosen steward. Her timing on this maneuver was excellent. She really played it like an old-line politician.

"Well, I certainly won't fight Dave's attempts to try and get her 'surplused.' But this is going to be a hard thing to do. She's in a category that would be very difficult to get declared 'unessential to operations' and even if we did, with her seniority it would be hard to get her moved out of the area entirely, as she would have first call on similar jobs that might open up.

"I think there are some better ways to handle this situation. Maybe we can use the same type of tactics on Elma that she herself uses. For example, we've got a lot of new people in that section. One chap has had a great number of personal problems in the recent past. He's had ten or twelve garnishments on his wages as the result of his recent divorce. During the proceedings he acted as his own lawyer, and you can imagine what kind of settlement he got. His wife has since remarried. Well, the upshot of this whole thing is that we've stuck by this man and tried to do all that we could for him during his period of personal trouble. As a result, I think that he has a feeling of real appreciation for us and for the way he's been treated. I think our best bet to get rid of Elma would be to plant some ideas in this guy's head. He's pretty well liked among the other workers, and if we

---

[1]Have her job declared unessential.

could get him to raise some questions, such as 'Shouldn't the job of steward really be held by somebody on the first shift?' 'Shouldn't the job be rotated?' 'Shouldn't some of the newer people get a chance at the job?' etc., maybe we could get the same kind of end result that Elma got before. At least get her out of the steward's position, if not out altogether.

"I favor this approach and think we could work it successfully, but it would take some planning on our part. I think it's either something like this or live with the situation in the hope that she'll voluntarily ask for a transfer."

CENTER CITY ENGINEERING DEPARTMENT

The Engineering Department of Center City employed approximately 1,000 people, all of whom worked under the provisions of the Civil Service System. Of these employees, about 100 worked in the Design Division. Parker Nolton, an Associate Engineer, had been employed in the Design Division for 19 years and was known personally by virtually everyone in the division, if not in Center City itself. Nolton had held the position of Associate Engineer for seven years on a provisional basis only, for he had never been able to pass the required civil service examinations to gain permanent appointment to this grade, although he had taken them often. Many of his co-workers felt that his lack of formal engineering education prevented him from passing the examinations, but Nolton felt that his failures were the result of his tendency to "tighten up" when taking an examination. Off the job, Nolton was extremely active in civic affairs and city-sponsored recreational programs. During the past year, for example, he had been president of the High School Parent Teacher's Association, captain of the bowling team sponsored by the Engineering Department in the Municipal Bowling League, and a member of the Managing Committee of the Center City Little League.

As Center City grew and the activities of the Engineering Department expanded to keep pace with this growth, younger men were hired into the Department in relatively large numbers. Among those hired were Ralph Boyer and Doug Worth. Both of these young men were graduate engineers, and had accepted the positions with the Engineering Department after fulfilling their military obligations. Ralph Boyer had been an officer in the Army Corps of Engineers. In order to give the new men opportunities to achieve permanent status in the Civil Service System, examinations were scheduled with greater frequency than they had been in the past. Nolton's performance on the examinations continued to be unsatisfactory. The new men, however, passed the exams for successively higher positions with flying colors. Ralph Boyer in particular experienced marked success in these examinations and advanced rapidly. Three years after his initial employment, he was in charge of a design group within the Design Division. Parker Nolton, in the meantime, had been shifted from the position of a project engineer to that of the purchase order coordinator. The position of purchase order coordinator was more limited in scope than that of a project engineer, although the responsibilities of the position were great. He continued to be classified as an Associate Engineer, however.

Ralph Boyer continued his successful career and soon qualified for the position of Senior Engineer. A new administrative group that had been created to meet the problems that arose in the Design Division because of the expanding activities of the Engineering Department was placed under his direction. Doug Worth, too, was successful in his examinations and was shortly promoted to the grade of Associate Engineer and transferred into the administrative group headed by Ralph Boyer.

One of the functions under the new administrative group was that of purchase order coordination. This relationship required that Parker Nolton report to Ralph Boyer. Nolton, however, chose to ignore the new organizational structure and dealt directly with the Chief Engineer, an arrangement which received the latter's tacit approval. Nolton was given a semiprivate office and the services of a Junior Engineer to assist him in his activities. His assistant, John Palmer, soon requested a transfer on the grounds that he had nothing to do, and there was no need for anyone in this position. Nolton, on the other hand, always appeared to be extremely busy and was continually requesting additional manpower and assistance to help him with the coordination of purchase orders.

Some four months after the organizational changes noted above had taken place, the Chief Engineer left the company and his replacement, Stan Matson, was appointed from within the division. Matson was the logical successor to the position; his appointment came as no surprise and was well received by all the employees. His appointment was shortly followed by the assignment of Ralph Boyer to a special position which took him completely out of the Design Division. Doug Worth was assigned to the position thus vacated, Supervisior of the Administrative Group, and consequently inherited the supervision of Parker Nolton's activities. This assignment, initially made on a provisional basis, was soon made permanent when Worth passed the required examinations and was awarded the grade of Senior Engineer. Doug Worth had never worked closely with Parker Nolton but had been on cordial terms with him since his arrival in the Engineering Department. He had had contact with Nolton in several recreational activities in which they both had participated.

During the months which followed, Parker Nolton continued his direct reporting relationship with the Chief Engineer, now in the person of Stan Matson, and never consulted or advised Doug Worth regarding the progress of his activities as purchase order coordinator. His former assistant, John Palmer, had been transferred and had been replaced by an engineering aide. Both the aide and Nolton appeared to be busy most of the time, and Nolton was still requesting more manpower for his activity through formal channels. When occasions arose which required that Doug Worth check on Nolton's activities, he was always forced to go to Nolton's office for information. Nolton always claimed to be too busy to leave his own office. During the conversations which occurred when Worth visited Nolton, Nolton frequently gave the impression that he regarded Worth's activities and interest as superfluous. Several times he suggested that in future situations Worth just send the inquiring party directly to him if questions arose about his activities. He often made the comment that he knew everyone in the department, and often it was better to handle many situations informally rather than through channels.

Doug Worth was concerned with Nolton's attitude, for he did not feel that he could effectively carry out his responsibilities as Supervisor of the Administrative Group if he did not know the current status of activities in all of the functions under his control. Consequently, he attempted to gain more cooperation from Nolton by approaching the subject at times when the two men were engaged in common off-hours recreational activities. These attempts were uniformly unsuccessful. Nolton always quickly brought the conversation around to the standing of the bowling team, the progress of the P.T.A., or any other unrelated subject close at hand.

After several attempts to talk with Nolton in a friendly way off the job, Worth concluded that the situation as it currently stood was intolerable. While he realized he must do something, Worth felt he understood Nolton's attitude and reactions and was sympathetic. After all, Nolton had been in the department for years and had been relatively successful. He knew all the "ropes" and had many friends. Worth reflected that it must be a blow to a man like Nolton to have to report to young, relatively inexperienced men. Worth had faced similar problems during his military career, when he had more experienced men many years his senior under his command. After much thought, he decided his best approach would be to appeal to Nolton in a very direct manner for a greater degree of cooperation. Thus, Worth approached Nolton on the job and suggested that they have a talk in his private office where they would not be disturbed by all the activity in Nolton's office. Nolton protested that he could not take time away from his duties. Worth was firm, however, and Nolton reluctantly agreed to come to Worth's office, protesting all the way that he really could not spare the time.

During his opening remarks to what Worth had planned as a sympathetic discussion of the situation, Worth referred to "the normal relationship between a man and his superior." Nolton's reaction was violent. He stated that he didn't regard any young upstart as a "superior," especially his. He told Worth to run his own office and to let him, Nolton, run his. He concluded by stating "if you haven't anything more to say, I would like to get back to my office where important work is being neglected." Worth, realizing that nothing more could be accomplished in the atmosphere which prevailed, watched in silence as Nolton left.

Doug Worth subsequently reported his latest conversation with Nolton to Stan Matson, the Chief Engineer. He also related the events which had led to this conversation. In concluding his remarks, he stated that he could no longer take responsibility for Nolton's actions, because Nolton would neither accept his guidance, nor advise him of the state of his work. Matson's reply to this last statement was "yes, I know." This was the only comment Matson made during the interview, although he listened intently to Worth's analysis of the situation.

At the next meeting of the Supervisory Staff of which Worth was a member but Nolton was not, Worth proposed that Nolton be transferred to the position of Design Drafting Engineer, in effect a demotion. As Worth was explaining the reasons for his proposed action regarding Nolton, one of the other members of the Supervisory Staff interrupted to proclaim very heatedly that Nolton was "one of the pillars of the entire Engineering Department," and that he would be violently opposed to the demotion of "so fine a man." Following this interruption, a very heated, emotional discussion ensued concerning the desirability of demoting Nolton.

During this discussion Stan Matson remained silent; yet he reflected that he probably should take some action during the meeting regarding the Nolton situation.

BELLEFONTE RUBBER WORKS

Works manager Bill Dalton looked pensively at the heavy raindrops as they beat against the glass sections of the window in his corner office at the Bellefonte Rubber plant. It suddenly occurred to Bill that in his four years as manager at the plant, he had never before allowed himself the luxury of watching the raindrops splash against the plant windows. He had been too busy with internal plant problems.

He thought to himself: "When it rains, it really pours at Bellefonte." Then he turned his back on the July cloudburst and looked at the letter of resignation on his desk. It was signed by Jack Fletcher, one of the day foremen. Jack had worked at the plant seven years--the last four years as a foreman of the Belt Department. Because of his apparent progress, Jack was promoted to a day foreman about a year ago on Bill's recommendation. Jack seemed to appreciate the prestige of his new position and the straight day shift, even though he was on call at the plant 24 hours a day if trouble developed in the Belt Department. However, Jack's attitude had changed considerably the last few months. Jack's problems on the floor had become more serious as well as more frequent.

The first sign of serious trouble in the Belt Department after Jack became day foreman developed in the weeks preceding December 31, 1962. The inventory at the end of the year showed a terrific shortage in the Belt Department where Jack assumed a consistent profit was being made. Jack became very antagonistic toward the Accounting Department head whose records showed that the materials and labor input in the Belt Department, when balanced against the value of the Belt Department's output, left a shortage of over $45,000 for 1962.

Jack refused to believe that the Accounting Department's monthly book inventory of work in process gave a true picture of his operation. (See Figure 1.) Even though he was no statistician, Jack could see where the materials drawn and the labor cost had deviated from the desired norm. He had tightened down on his crew's use of rubber and fabric drawn for belt making after July; and, as a result, the department approached the norm or a full accounting of the raw materials requisitioned in August and September. The chart did indicate this all right. He also had checked carefully the direct and indirect labor time card reports of his men during the same period. The chart reflected a favorable trend toward the desired norm during August and September. Then, after September, the amount of materials actually accounted for in belts produced dropped off, and the labor time going into the belts increased even though the actual belt footage produced did not increase.

It was the first week in January, 1963, that Bill Dalton had a long talk with Jack about the need for operating the Belt Department as if it were a separate business in downtown Bellefonte. Bill pointed out the difficulty of staying in business very long with raw materials being drawn for work in process only to have large amounts ending up as waste in the city dump. Didn't Jack think a foreman ought to hold his crew responsible for unusual and increasing material wastage?

Perhaps a bigger drain on the profit anticipated in the Belt Department was because of the way Jack was failing to control the time reported by his crew. Bill had insisted there was no point in arguing with the Accounting Department about the reliability of its reports on the belt operation. Jack was told that if he approved unreliable, inaccurate information on the time cards, he was likely to get back an unreliable, inaccurate summary of the month's operation. It was clear enough to Jack what Bill was trying to tell him.

Jack's men were paid a base rate plus an incentive for so many items produced above a minimum set by a time-and-motion study. Time spent on directly producing belts was charged and paid as "direct labor." In case of a breakdown or other direct work stoppage, the men would go to work cleaning up, getting supplies, or doing other maintenance chores. Time spent in such "nonproductive" work was charged and paid as "indirect labor."

The record of so much direct or indirect labor time was submitted to the foreman at the end of the shift by each man. The foreman, who supposedly was aware of any direct labor interruptions which occurred during the shift, would verify the time card claim by initialing it. The reporting of time appeared to operate on the honor system, especially if the foreman gave the impression of blinking at or being oblivious to a "doctored" time card.

It was simple enough for a man to claim two hours of indirect labor, and claim--if questioned by the foreman--that he had trouble for that long. Yet during that two hours he could have been turning out belt footage for which he would receive incentive pay, also. It didn't take long for a workman to accumulate an hour of indirect labor through an ordinary day by reporting material shortages or work stoppages for a few short intervals.

Jack understood clearly what Bill meant, because Jack had passed out some pretty fat paychecks to members of his crew on payday. He had seen some of the men on a base pay of $40 a week come out with a $45 bonus! If a belt department had 60 employees doing this, the labor cost charged against the belt footage produced mounted up fast.

Actually, Jack had not given too much thought to the fudging on time cards which he signed daily. He didn't think of this practice as really cheating anybody, and he was sure most of his men didn't look at it as a dishonest practice. It was "just one of those things."

At the conclusion of their talk, Jack told Bill that the Belt Department would push both the materials and labor charges back into normal operating position. During the month of January, Jack made good on his promise of improvement, although the department still had a long pull ahead. Then suddenly, at the end of February, the Belt Department made its poorest production record in 14 months.

Bill, who had been anxiously watching this plant trouble spot, maneuvered Jack into his office for a chat. The foreman half anticipated what was coming. In fact, he didn't wait for Bill to ask him about his family or about Jack's plans for a trip to Pittsburgh to see his son who was a freshman at Carnegie Tech. Jack came right to the point of issue by saying: "I know what's on your mind, Bill; but before you start boring into me about competition and profits, I want to tell you something."

"Good enough, Jack," Bill agreed, "why don't you tell me what's on your mind?"

A deep sigh escaped Jack as he settled down in his chair and wondered momentarily where he should begin. "Have you ever seriously considered the pressures that I face every day out on that floor?" Jack began. Bill nodded understandingly and Jack, feeling encouraged, continued. "You know, I'm the fall guy for everything that goes wrong in the Belt Department. Not one man in my crew is faced with taking initiative to improve our operation. Not one of them will make the most trivial decision. I guess the union won't let them. Brother, when I was working on the line years ago--before the union came along--we felt responsible. Where is the pressure today? On the worker? Oh no! Right on the back of a foreman whose hands are tied more often than they are free to clean house out there.

"At our foremen's training sessions on Wednesdays, Bill, you have stressed the importance of the service departments (see Figure 2) to production. Without doubt you are right or you wouldn't keep them on the payroll. But they never have produced a single foot of belt that ever went out of this plant. Am I right?"

Bill nodded in partial agreement. "Yes, in a way. But, I think you will agree that if, for example, the Planning Department failed to provide you with specifications; if the Laboratory didn't test and control the quality of your product; if Purchasing didn't supply you with needed materials; and if Selling didn't find an outlet for your belts--you just wouldn't be able to go it alone, Jack. Isn't that right?"

"Well, yes, in a way; but that isn't what I meant," Jack replied. "These services, like Accounting which is always making reports on our costs and output, are never under pressure. Their work--I guess they work--is specialized. Every contact I have with them turns out be be pressure on me, not on them. For example, the engineer is much better paid than I am; yet he has fewer problems. He works mostly with things, not people. If he has any headaches, I fail to see them. Most of these service people have quiet, clean, unhurried jobs. Don't they?"

Bill shook his head. "Sometimes we don't see all the pressures that are focused on the other fellow. They do wear different clothes than the men on the production line. However, I'm sure you wouldn't want them to try to do their work in a noisy place or on a greasy table. What are you suggesting that I do about this, Jack?"

"Well, I'm not suggesting anything. I'm only saying that a foreman has the toughest job in this plant. From the time I get a production order until I meet the time schedule that comes with it I'm on the spot. I must keep a variety of belts moving along those lines. I'm responsible for costs, waste, supplies, quality control, stoppages, breakdowns, maintenance. You name it; I seem to have it. Then I can't step on anyone's toes. I'm supposed to maintain discipline, and yet I have to be a good guy. My time schedules stay the same even though some joker doesn't show up for work. All the time I have quality control, the inspector, the shop steward, and the accounting guy with the sharp pencil on my back. How about my morale? Who gives a damn about Jack Fletcher or how he feels?"

"You're right in general, Jack," Bill responded, "but you are an important person in this whole operation. If this were not so, you wouldn't be the focal point of these pressures. You are the catalyst in this process. Although you are in the middle of it all, you have to keep everything under control. In fact, Jack, if we didn't feel these pressures in this competitive industry, we wouldn't be around long. These pressures aren't mean, or vindictive, or intended by anyone. They are a sign we are sensitive to potential trouble, and we ought to recognize them for what they are worth in our productive efforts."

Jack looked thoughtfully out of the window for a moment. Then he ventured: "You make this sound better than I feel about it. I don't know what a catalyst is, unless he is a guy with a thick skin and a thick head. Now you take last week. My paycheck was $437.50 for the month. I put in about ten hours a day five days a week, not to mention three Saturdays, for that check. When I handed out the check to the crew that works for me, I noticed that about a dozen of the men made something over $500. A foreman must have a thick skull all right to stay here after every shift for an hour or two signing time cards, checking other things, and helping the next foreman get under way. I can't leave the minute the whistle blows like the hourly men do. In fact, if they have serious trouble in the Belt Department on the next shift, I might be called out here in the middle of the night, just because I'm day foreman. Do you think this setup is fair to a foreman, Bill?"

Bill shifted uneasily in his chair. He knew this was a tough one to explain. "I can honestly say I think you are worth more to this operation than one of those men who got a bigger paycheck than you did last month. But I also believe that your envelope didn't contain something you get in addition--something which goes only to a man in your position. If you should become sick, Jack, as you were two years ago, we carry you on the payroll, and we are glad to do it. We are not able to do that for your crew. If you need an afternoon off to take your family to Lewistown or your wife to a doctor, you need only suggest this to me. Moreover, you have been recognized by your men as a leader. I know they have confidence in you. People in Bellefonte respect you because of your position here at the plant. This prestige means something to your family, believe me. I might ask you, Jack, how many of those twelve who had a larger paycheck than you, fully earned it? We can't account for their excess time in the inventory. I'm not so sure many of them were entitled to a larger check than you received."

Jack sat studying his safety helmet for a brief time. Then he stood up. "Thanks anyway, Bill," he said. "If it's all right with you, I'll give this thing another try. I better get back on the floor."

"Thanks for the chat, Jack. I know you can put the Belt Department back in the black, if anyone can," Bill said as he opened the door and gave Jack a parting pat on the back.

Bill had been pleased to observe that, during June and July, the Belt Department made obvious improvement in its operation. (See Figure 1.) Jack was apparently getting on top of all those pressures that had laid him low a couple of months ago. Then, out of the clear blue sky comes Jack's letter of resignation. The letter was brief:

Dear Bill:

This thing isn't getting any better. It may be even worse. I guess I want out. Can you use me in the Maintenance Department where they were short-handed this week?

Jack

Here was a chance to move someone else into the position of day foreman in the Belt Department. Bill wasn't certain whom he could confidently move into that position. He wasn't at all sure he wanted to let Jack step down, although he knew Jack was having a struggle. But this could be said about nearly every one of the other ten foremen at Bellefonte Rubber Works.

Bill felt he understood the situation faced by his foremen--especially the day foreman on the lead-off shift. He had followed a policy of placing the night-shift foremen on the day shift. This gave them some experience with the larger crews, the ringing telephones, and the full impact of contacts with the service departments as well as customers. After two weeks of this, the foremen were usually happy to get back on the night shifts. There was good reason for Bill's paying the day foreman a little more money each month, which he did.

No one knew better than Bill that good foremen were scarce. A good foreman had to be many things. He had to be a diplomat, a disciplinarian, a counselor, an instructor, an example to his men, an engineer, a repairman, a lawyer, an inspector, a judge, a manager, a psychologist. While wearing all these hats, he had better arrange to be making a profit in his department. Bill just didn't keep this kind of man on reserve. In fact, if a foreman possessed a fair capability in these desirable areas, he was usually promoted to a higher position in management.

As Bill mentally scanned his roster of eleven foremen and those he considered potential foremen, he was not inspired. Yet, he would argue with anyone that his eleven foremen compared favorably with those in any other plant in his company. Still, each of his foremen had specific weaknesses and certain strengths. At the moment he could think of three men who had indicated an interest in becoming day foremen at the Bellefonte plant. They were Sam Craven, Chuck Weatherby, and George Maitland.

Sam Craven had been a foreman twenty years ago for Sharon Rubber Products in Sharon, Pennsylvania. Although he had been fairly young at the time, Sam had established himself at the Sharon plant as a foreman who made things move. His crews turned out the items on schedule or else. He didn't spare himself, and he developed a reputation for not sparing his men. One of Bill's older friends told him that he had worked for Sam at Sharon. This friend confirmed the fact that Sam had an enviable record for output, but he had no friends among his crew. Bill was reminded, too, that Sam worked in a place where the plant was not unionized.

When Sam came to see Bill about possible openings at the Bellefonte plant, the former had expressed an interest in working as a foreman. This meeting had taken place last December. Sam had recently been retired from the U.S. Army as a master sergeant. According to his discharge, Sam had entered the Army soon after leaving his job as foreman at Sharon Rubber Products. The earlier part of his Army career had been spent in the infantry. The last twelve years Sam had been attached to a number of different finance-disbursing units.

Chuck Weatherby had been working for the past eleven years at the Bellefonte Rubber Works. During the last six years he had been a foreman on the night shift. Bill felt that Chuck leaned rather heavily on the day foreman whenever a problem of any consequence came along in his department. Moreover, he had only 35 men on his shift whereas the Belt Department typically had over 75 men on a day crew.

The men on Chuck's shift seemed to like him all right. At times Bill felt he had to practically force Chuck to use the tools and techniques available to a foreman. During the years, Chuck had attended all the training sessions that had been sponsored for the plant foremen on Wednesday afternoons. It was debatable how effective these sessions had been in upgrading his performance.

Bill recalled that it was on Chuck's shift that a costly mistake had been made on a large ore conveyor belt. The specifications had called for a belt 48" wide, 3/4" thick, 1,000' long, 6 plys of cotton-nylon fabric, and a heavy rubber compound all around. The belt, which had to be out in three weeks, was contracted for $14,000. By mistake, Chuck had started the belt through with five, instead of six, plys of fabric. By the time the error was picked up, valuable time had been lost and an enormous waste had occurred. Chuck had blamed the error on "scheduling in" the custom order when his shift had a four-week backlog of other belts.

About two months ago, Chuck had mentioned that he was interested in the day shift and asked Bill to keep him in mind. Chuck said he could use the money that went with handling the larger crew on the day shift.

The third person who had expressed an interest in becoming a day foreman was a college graduate by the name of George Maitland. George, who was married and about 25 years of age, had majored in psychology at Pennsylvania State University. He had worked at the Bellefonte plant for the past three years. In fact, it was the only job he had even held other than part-time summer work in a grocery chain store.

The foremen under whom George had worked were unanimous in classifying him as a very reliable and effective employee. However, this opinion was qualified in each instance by some reference to the fact that George was good in spite of his college education.

George had taken an interest in problems of the foreman. Occasionally, he had asked them questions about their work. Some of the foremen answered his questions; others let him feel he was getting a bit too "nosey." George did appear to show a great deal of insight into the forces that constantly impinged upon the individual foreman. They didn't know, however, that George was taking courses in foreman training in an extension program at Penn State.

Bill knew that George was taking classes in production control, labor laws, and human relations. One of the professors at Penn State had mentioned the fact to Bill during a Rotary luncheon some time ago. Later Bill had asked George about his evening courses and his plans for the future. It was during the ensuing conversation that George expressed a desire to get into management--the sooner the better. George had some ready answers, too, for plant problems that had bothered Bill and his foremen for a long time. It was clear, this young man didn't lack confidence.

Could it be that Jack Fletcher, whose resignation Bill held in his hand, would want to reconsider? Bill looked again at the promising record of the last two months. Then his eyes settled upon the dismal record of the preceding months. Whatever he did, Bill would have to act promptly. He needed a day foreman to manage the Belt Department, the basic producing unit at Bellefonte Rubber Works.

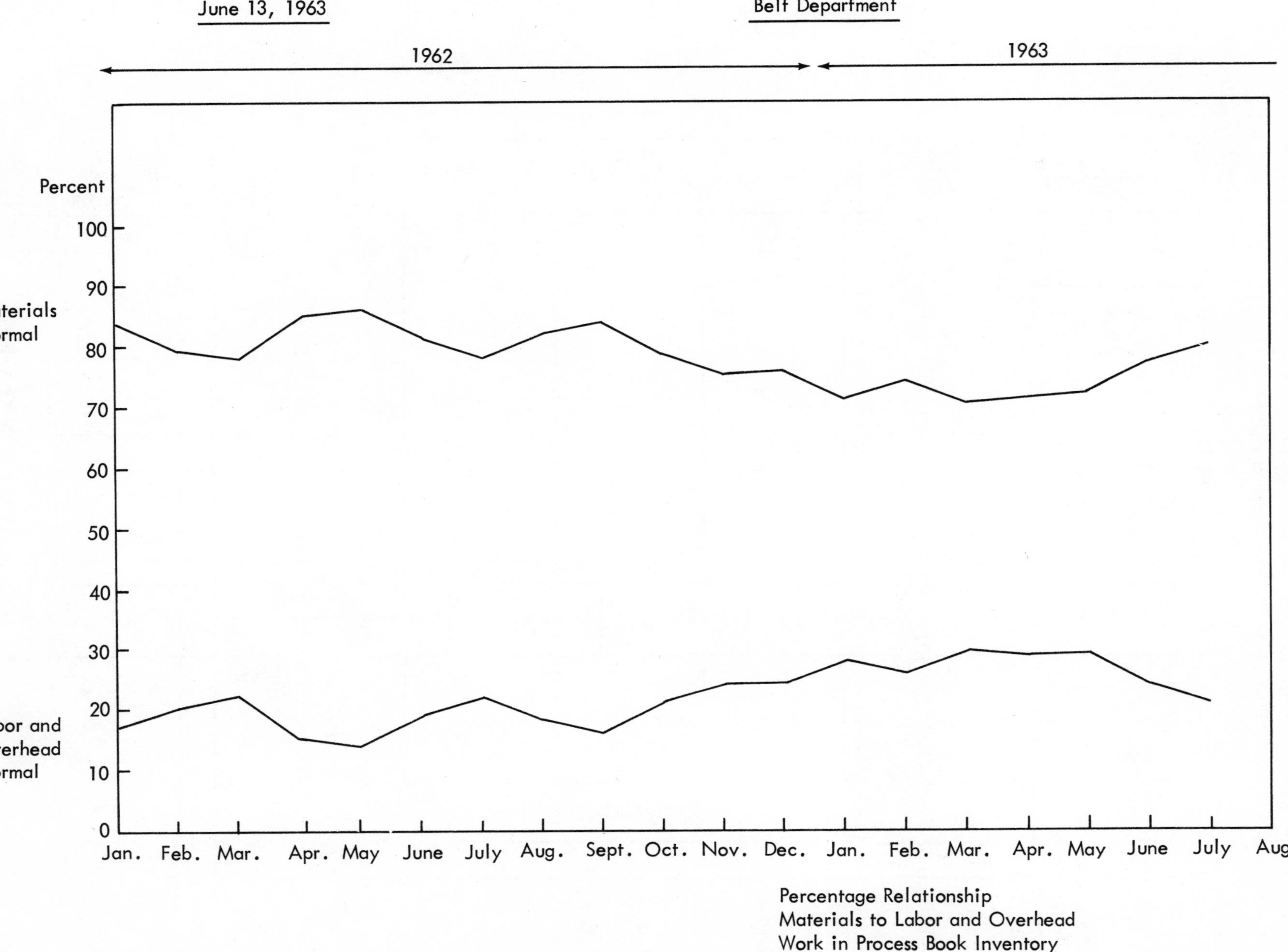

Figure 1. Average monthly materials, labor, and overhead outlays at Bellefonte Rubber Works.

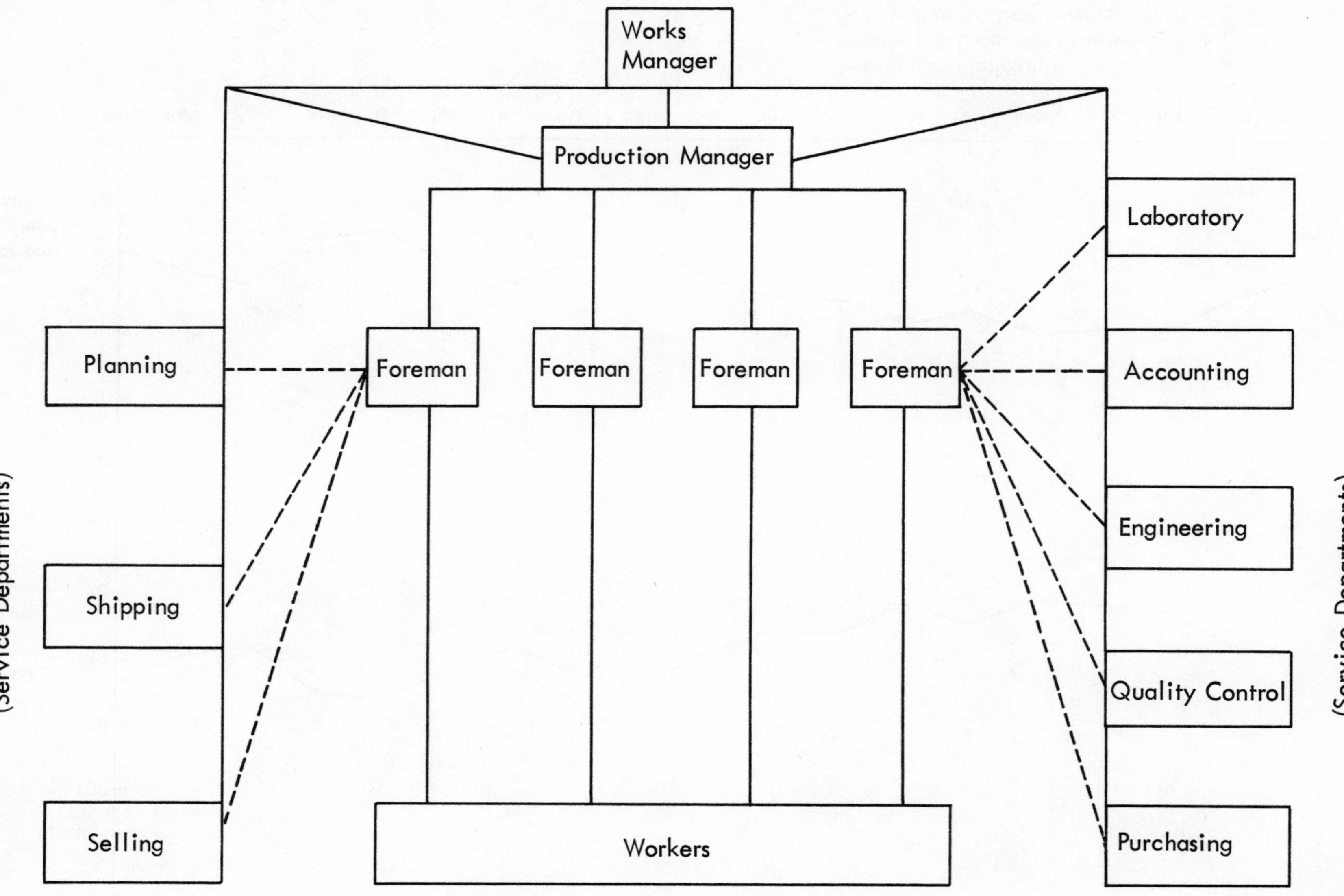

Figure 2. Plant organization at Bellefonte Rubber Works.

Exercise

MOTIVATING PURPOSEFUL BEHAVIOR

Introduction

Organizations depend for their prosperity and survival upon the achievement of goals through the accomplishment of a variety of tasks. The management of these institutions must be concerned with purposeful behavior--the achievement of results. The primary task of managers might be said to be the realization of results through the purposeful behavior of others (subordinates). Motivation and its relationship to purposeful behavior is an important part of the management function and is the subject of this exercise.

Instructions

The class is to select two members for this exercise, one who will assume the role of the manager, the other the role of the subordinate. The subordinate is to leave the classroom in order that the manager and members of the class can select and set up a task for the subordinate to complete. This is to be a physical task, neither too easy nor too difficult. Your instructor will provide some examples. Once the task has been decided and arranged, agreement must be reached on what will constitute a reward, and what will constitute a punishment (a bell and the clap of a hand are examples). A reasonable time limit for task completion should also be specified. The subordinate is then asked to return to the classroom, and following the brief instructions to the subordinate discussed below, the manager attempts to have the task completed as well as possible in the shortest possible time.

The subordinate is told only the following: (1) that the manager may use no oral communications; (2) what constitutes reward and punishment, and to respond accordingly; and (3) that he is to perform some physical task.

Before, during, and after the exercise, members of the class should complete the appropriate portions of the form which follows these instructions.

The instructor may wish to repeat the exercise with the class selecting a new manager and subordinate, and a new task.

Discussion

Your instructor will lead you in a discussion exploring the implications of this exercise. Some questions to think about include the following:

(1) With respect to the management problem of motivating subordinates toward purposeful behaviors, what conclusions can you draw from this exercise?

(2) What conditions must be satisfied to generate the desired purposeful behaviors in subordinates?

(3) The ringing of a bell is obviously an inadequate reward for most people, and the clapping of hands is an ineffective punishment. What rewards and punishments are available to the typical manager for use in motivating purposeful behavior in modern organizations? How effective is each? What is the proper mix between the use of rewards and punishments? What light do various theories of motivation in organizations cast on these questions?

Motivating Purposeful Behavior:

Evaluation Form

TASK: SUPERIOR:
SUBORDINATE:

REWARDS (NUMBER OF TIMES USED):

PUNISHMENTS (NUMBER OF TIMES USED):

TIME REQUIRED FOR TASK COMPLETION: ________minutes or (check)
________maximum allowed (task not completed)

PERFORMANCE EVALUATION (QUANTITY AND QUALITY OF WORK PERFORMED):

High Performance/----0----0----0----0----0----0----0----0----/ Low Performance
1 2 3 4 5 6 7 8 9 10

What factors contributed to task completion?

1.

2.

3.

4.

What factors detracted from task completion?

1.

2.

3.

4.

PART III

STRUCTURE OF ORGANIZATIONS

INTRODUCTION

The structure of an organization refers to the prescribed and relatively fixed relationships that exist among jobs or positions in an organization. Structure therefore dictates much of the individual behavior and group relationships in which people engage in the organizational setting. In addition, the study of structure is important because of growing evidence that the appropriateness of an organization's structure to its particular tasks and environment can have a major impact on various criteria of organizational effectiveness.

Management decisions on four major questions determine an organization's structure:

(1) To what extent should the total task of the organization be divided into job specialties?
(2) According to what bases should these jobs be combined into groups which report to a common supervisor?
(3) What is the appropriate size of each of these groups?
(4) How much authority should be delegated to each of the jobs and groups of jobs?

The four questions refer, respectively, to the issues of division of labor, departmentalization, span of control, and delegation.

Management's answers to each of the above questions can range across the continua shown below:

Elements of Structure

Division of Labor

Specialized ←——————————→ Generalized

Departmentalization

Homogeneous ←——————————→ Heterogeneous

Span of Control

Narrow ←——————————→ Wide

Delegation of Authority

Centralized ←——————————→ Decentralized

It is easy to see that an organization designed according to the characteristics of the far left side of the continua would differ dramatically, both in its appearance on an organization chart and as "a place to work," from one designed according to the characteristics on the right. Management decisions on these design issues clearly are critical.

Before turning to some guidelines which managers can use in making these decisions (and which may prove useful in your analysis of the cases in this section), let us provide some additional comments on the four basic structural characteristics.

Division of Labor. A major advantage of organized effort is that specialties can be created. The advantages of specialized effort has been long recognized by economists, and the development of a society relates directly to the development of specialized manpower and organizations. Organizations utilize division of labor in two general ways, vertical and horizontal.

The vertical dimension is reflected in the existence of chains of command. These chains represent different levels of management as distinct from different functions or the horizontal dimension. In general, a specific job can be distinguished from other jobs in terms of specific assigned authority (vertical dimension) and specific assigned tasks (horizontal dimension). The vertical dimension relates to delegation of authority, while the horizontal dimension relates more specifically to division of labor as usually connoted.

Two concepts are particularly useful in analyzing the horizontal dimension of a job: range and depth. Range refers to the number of tasks a job occupant is expected to perform. Packaging machine operators, bookkeepers, and anesthesiologists can be expected to perform fewer specific tasks than repairmen, nurses, and university department chairmen. Job depth, however, refers to the amount of discretion which the job occupant has in the selection of means to perform the tasks and the sequence in which the tasks will be performed. An assembly line worker has less depth than a mechanic, the bookkeeper has less depth than the anesthesiologist. The managerial decision is to strike the appropriate balance between depth and range.

Departmentalization. Jobs are grouped together and assigned for supervision to a single superior. The major issue is the basis on which jobs are grouped. The literature on organization design identifies a number of bases including functional, territorial, product, customer, and project.

Functional departmentalization refers to grouping jobs according to the common functions of the organization. Thus a business firm has production, marketing, finance, accounting, and personnel departments. The common sense argument for functional departments is that specialists should be grouped together to deal with the function for which they are trained. This basis tends to create highly homogeneous groups with the often-found disadvantage that the specialists may emphasize departmental objectives at the expense of organizational objectives.

Territorial departmentalization is the basis for assigning jobs according to location. Salesmen are often coordinated by managers of particular territories because of the difficulty that would be experienced by central headquarter management. The potential disadvantage is that practices and procedures may be inconsistent from territory to territory due to geographic and customer differences.

Product departmentalization is often used in organizations which provide diverse products or services. The policy of General Motors which groups jobs into Buick, Cadillac, Chevrolet, Pontiac, and Oldsmobile divisions is illustrative of product departmentalization. The argument for the basis is that a manager should be given all the authority and resources necessary to develop, produce, and market his product. A similar basis is used in health agencies which group jobs around specific disease entities such as tuberculosis and venereal disease control programs. This basis results in a relatively more heterogeneous group of jobs and, consequently, greater coordinative difficulties for the manager.

Customer departmentalization places jobs which focus on needs of specific customers in the same department. Governmental agencies such as labor departments, child welfare, Indian bureaus, and the like are based upon services delivered to a specific clientele. Business firms distinguish between industrial, commercial, and final consumer customers in the organization of sales forces. The logic is that the basis for specialization should be the needs and demands of a special class of customers; the result is a heterogeneous grouping of technical and scientific skills.

Project departmentalization is used most often by organizations which produce large and unique outputs, such as aircraft and aerospace firms. In such organizations the task of designing and developing a new product is assigned to a manager who obtains experts from the functional departments of the firm. These experts, engineers, accountants, production specialists, and scientists are assigned to the project manager on a temporary basis. Once the project is completed, the experts return to their permanent assignment. Project departmentalization is much like product departmentalization except for the temporary nature of the arrangement.

In reality, organizations uses a variety of departmentalization bases. The highest managerial levels may be product-based and the next levels functional-based. The decision involves selecting the appropriate basis at each level and for each group on a particular level.

Span of control. The size of a department is limited by the number of subordinates a supervisor can effectively manage. Generally, a manager can coordinate a larger number of jobs if they are narrow in range and depth, similar, and in close proximity. The span of control of a foreman in an assembly plant is wider than that of the director of a research laboratory. Some organizations such as Lockheed Missiles and Space Company have attempted to determine an index of factors which affect optimum span of control. Generally, however, the decision is based upon managerial judgment.

Delegation of authority. The extent to which managers are delegated the decision to use resources without consent by their managers is a measure of authority. Some organizations retain authority at the highest levels in the organization, others decentralize authority to lower levels. It should be recognized that authority is delegated in all organizations, it is a matter of degree rather than either-or. Whenever a job occupant is expected to perform a task (his "responsibility"), he must, of necessity, use resources. The extent to which he has discretion over the use of resources is a measure of authority.

The extent to which authority is decentralized depends upon a number of factors. Three of the more important are organizational size, effective controls, and managerial capability. The larger the organization, the more centralized it will be, simply because top management cannot oversee the entire operation. The more effective are control mechanisms such as accounting, production, and personnel data, the greater the potential decentralization. To delegate authority, the manager must be able to account for its use, and accountability requires control information. Finally, some managers are more capable than others and can be entrusted with greater authority.

Thus, the concept of organization structure is seen to consist of four major characteristics. The combination of these characteristics results in the creation of relatively stable relationships within which organizational processes and behavior occur. The design of the structure, that is, the combination of division of labor, departmentalization bases, spans of control, and delegation is the consequence of managerial decisions. These decisions can be guided by recent theories of organizational design.

Current design theory suggests that there is no single organizational structure which is best in all situations. Rather, contemporary theory and practice indicate that a situational, or contingency, approach is the correct view. Earlier theory and practice seemed to prescribe first that a classical bureaucratic design and, later, that a more informal participative model were, in turn, universally optimal.

The classical bureaucratic design can, in general, be described by organizational characteristics on the far left side of the earlier continua of "Elements of Structure": a high degree of specialization, homogeneous departments, narrow spans of control, and centralized authority. The more informal, participative model can generally be described by the characteristics on the far right side of the continua: a low degree of specialization, heterogeneous departments, wide spans of control, and decentralized authority. Though the two designs differ in all major respects, proponents of each claimed them to be optimal for all situations. The contemporary view is to consider either extreme, or some modification of each, to be optimal, depending on the unique situation.

The key situational variable to be considered in organizational design decisions appears to be the nature of the relevant task and environment. Evidence suggests that as tasks tend toward uncertainty and the environment tends toward instability and rapid change, a less formal, participative structure is more appropriate. Conversely, where tasks are more certain and the relevant environment is relatively more stable, a bureaucratic structure is likely to be more effective. This generalization holds true in part because informal, participative organizations appear to be more adaptable to changing environmental demands than rigid bureaucracies.

An important additional consideration in organizational design is this: within any given organization, the tasks of different departments or functional areas may differ considerably in certainty, and their environments may differ significantly in their degree of stability and rate of change. This implies that an organization may contain some departments with a more bureaucratic structure, and others with a more informal, participative structure. Where this is the case, coordination among departments is likely to be especially difficult. Bureaucratic organizations and departments can be coordinated by rules, procedures, and detailed plans; informal, participative structures must be coordinated by mechanisms like integrative teams, multichannel communications, and mutual adjustment. When both types of structures coexist within the same organizational entity, a combination of both types of integrative techniques must be employed.

Clearly, the application of situational organizational design logic is challenging and complex. Managerial judgment is required and a careful diagnosis of situational variables is essential. The cases in this section offer you the opportunity to sharpen your diagnostic and organizational design skills.

HENRY RESEARCH CORPORATION

The Henry Research Corporation produced an extensive line of nondestructive testing equipment for use in a wide variety of manufacturing, maintenance, and repair functions in industry. The expressed policy of the company was not to sell a testing instrument as such but to sell a means whereby a customer solved a problem. It had always been difficult to coordinate the company's Marketing Department and its Research and Engineering Department because of the technical nature of the testing instruments manufactured and the necessity of constantly developing new instruments and modifying existing ones to suit individual customers' needs. The importance of proper coordination between these departments was emphasized by a problem brought about by the introduction by Henry Research in 1954 of a completely new line of testing equipment generally described as "electronic" testing equipment. By 1958 it was obvious that this new line of equipment had not lived up to sales expectations. Research, engineering, and sales expenses devoted to the line in 1957 alone amounted to $420,000 while total sales of electronic equipment were only $358,000 in the same year. In 1957, sales of all electronic testing equipment comprised approximately 3 percent of Henry Research's total sales volume. Table 1 shows sales of electronic testing equipment by year. Despite the poor results to date, the management was convinced electronic equipment had a large potential.

Table 1

Shipments of Electronics Equipment by Year

Year	Sales
1954	$228,000
1955	232,000
1956	262,000
1957	358,000
1st half of 1958	278,000

Henry Research Corporation was founded in 1929 by Mr. V. M. Danby, a physicist and consulting engineer who developed a magnetic dust inspection method which conclusively located cracks in oil well pipe. The company grew rapidly, and company officials pointed with pride to the fact that it furnished testing instruments to practically every manufacturing industry. Many products, ranging from aircraft to shotguns, had to be tested during manufacture and overhaul to locate any breaks or weak points which might endanger the life or property of the purchaser. Henry Research furnished a nondestructive economical test for this purpose. Other processes of inspection were developed for use with newer metals such as aluminum, magnesium, bronze, tungsten carbide, and even certain ceramics and glass.

Through the years as the company had grown, the sales personnel or field engineers had had the responsibility for recognizing their customers' needs for inspection as their customers developed new products. It was the responsibility of the sales engineers to advise their respective branch and regional sales managers of new problems existing in customers' plants. These needs were discussed with the Marketing Vice President and Technical Coordinator, who appraised the needs and passed them on to Research and Engineering. In passing a problem from the field on to R & E, it was often difficult for the Marketing Vice President to appraise the importance of the new development on which a customer might be working. Many times a customer's enthusiasm for a new or modified type of testing instrument would have no relationship to possible future demands for such an instrument, even though R & E could develop a satisfactory answer for the particular customer's problem.

A typically difficult field was that of aircraft manufacturing. As air speeds became more intense with many planes approaching or exceeding the speed of sound, the need for testing engines and airframe parts became more critical. Often the Henry Research field engineers were urged by their customers to develop testing methods and instruments for assemblies or parts which might only be in the developmental stage, and at such a stage even aircraft manufacturers could not tell whether contracts would be obtained in volume enough to support development of new testing instruments.

As a result of the difficulty of estimating sales potential for possible new testing methods, the amount of emphasis given to new projects by the Marketing Department in passing them to Research and Engineering depended to a large degree on the "seat of the pants" judgment of the Marketing Vice President or the Technical Coordinator. This, in turn, was influenced by the ability of the sales engineers to "sell" the idea to their superiors.

Another difficulty often encountered in coordination between Marketing and Research and Engineering was that, after a problem had been passed to R & E, priority might be determined by R & E's interest in the problem or by whether it felt it would have a reasonable chance of coming up with a solution quickly and easily. In other situations R & E might approach a problem "on its own," without having received any specific indication from the Marketing Department as to the potential market for the potential product or testing method.

In the early 1950s the company's Research Department was attracted to the new "electronic" testing equipment as a potentially profitable, related field. This method of testing, known as eddy current testing, had been developed by Dr. Foerster, Reutlingen, Germany, and was relatively unknown in the United States. According to Dr. Foerster, this method had been researched for a period of some twenty years and was by 1950 in use commercially in numerous industrial plants in Germany. The principles of this electronic type of testing were based upon the measurement of the impendence and phase relationships of electric current passing through coils. The amount of impendence depended upon the physical properties of the material being tested. Such testing instruments, it was claimed, could not only locate defects, both surface and subsurface, with ease, but could detect variations in diameter, grade, tensile strength, and hardness. The obvious relationship of eddy current testing to the company's line and the description of its potential led the company to enter into a patent and licensing agreement with Dr. Foerster whereby his equipment could be distributed by Henry Research in the United States.

Henry Research generally dominated the magnetic testing field, so there was not much pressure to develop new testing methods in a hurry so as to beat competitors. The management did not wish, however, to give other firms too much of an opportunity to develop. The electronic testing field was different; there were more competitors and Henry Research was less well established. If the company delayed in developing an electronic testing method for a new product, there was a real risk that a competitor would beat them to it.

Initially, numerous types of Dr. Foerster's instruments were imported, and a research team was set up to determine what products could be tested by the new instruments and what modifications would have to be made to make them commercially applicable for use by industrial plants in the United States. It was not long before the conclusion was reached that, although basic theoretical work had progressed in Europe for over twenty years, most of the testing instruments as imported were not suitable for commercial distribution to any of the company's customers.

Modifications were made and much field work was done by the Research and Edatest Engineering Department, which proceeded energetically with the problems of making the Edatest line which included all eddy current type of instruments applicable to customers' needs. The problems involved were so complex that about three fourths of all R & E personnel were soon involved, leaving only about one fourth to work on other company problems. In addition, a special Electronic Sales Group of three men was organized to work with customers in adapting Edatest testing methods to their problems.

Henry Research was organized in three principal departments, namely, Marketing, Production and Finance, and Research and Engineering. An abbreviated organization chart as of the time of the introduction and development of the Edatest line is shown in Figure 1.

The Marketing Department was responsible for all sales and was divided into three regions: eastern, central, and western. Each region was in charge of a regional sales manager. Under each region were two or three branches out of which the salesmen, called field engineers, worked. A total of 27 field engineers worked out of the seven branches. Each branch manager was responsible for the field engineers in his branch and for at least one and in some cases as many as four commercial inspection plants.

A field engineer was a typically well-trained technical man whose salary ranged between $8,000 and $15,000 per year. He necessarily had to have a great deal of technical knowledge to appraise a particular customer's problem and determine whether Henry Research had a type of testing equipment which would suitably solve the problem or whether he should call on Research and Engineering for help in developing a new or modified type of equipment to solve the customer's problem.

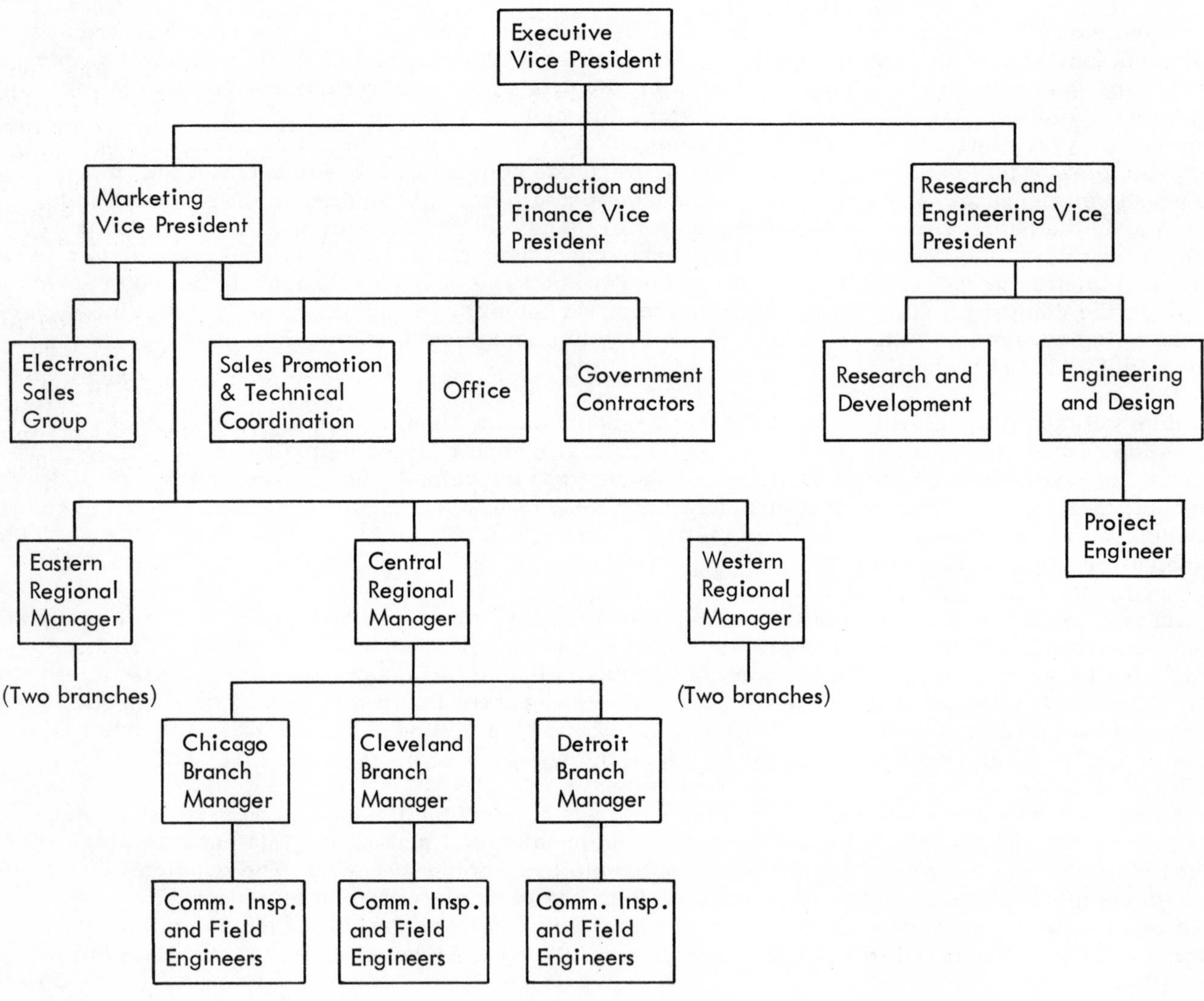

Figure 1. Henry Research Organization during introduction and development of Edatest Line of electronic testing instruments.

Officials of Henry Research believed that the problem confronting the company concerning the large expenditure for sales and research and developmental expense and relatively small sales of Edatest equipment was not only important in itself, but was indicative of the fact that better coordination between marketing and research and development was needed. The company by the very nature of its products had always been heavily research-oriented,and the history of its new products had been that a great deal of money had to be expended developing a new or modified method of testing to suit a customer's need before sales volume of any magnitude could be developed.

It was felt that, in the case of the development of the electronic line of testing instruments, too much of the impetus had come from Research and Development and not enough from Marketing. The special Electronic Sales Group which had been set up to survey customers' needs for electronic testing equipment had worked in somewhat of an "ivory tower" atmosphere and had not sought the opinions of the field engineers (general salesmen) or kept them advised of details of developments. This situation apparently had tended to make the field engineers less interested in the new line of electronic equipment. The salesmen concentrated on the older lines of equipment for which a demand was established and with which they were acquainted.

It was decided that organizational changes were necessary to correct the situation which had been highlighted by the electronic equipment experience. Figure 2 shows an abbreviated organizational chart incorporating the principal changes which management decided were needed to develop better coordination between Marketing and Research and Engineering. Principal changes in the Marketing Department were the establishment of a Market Research Department, the transferring of electronic technical coordination from Sales Promotion to a separate section under Research and Engineering, and the elimination of the special Electronics Sales Group.

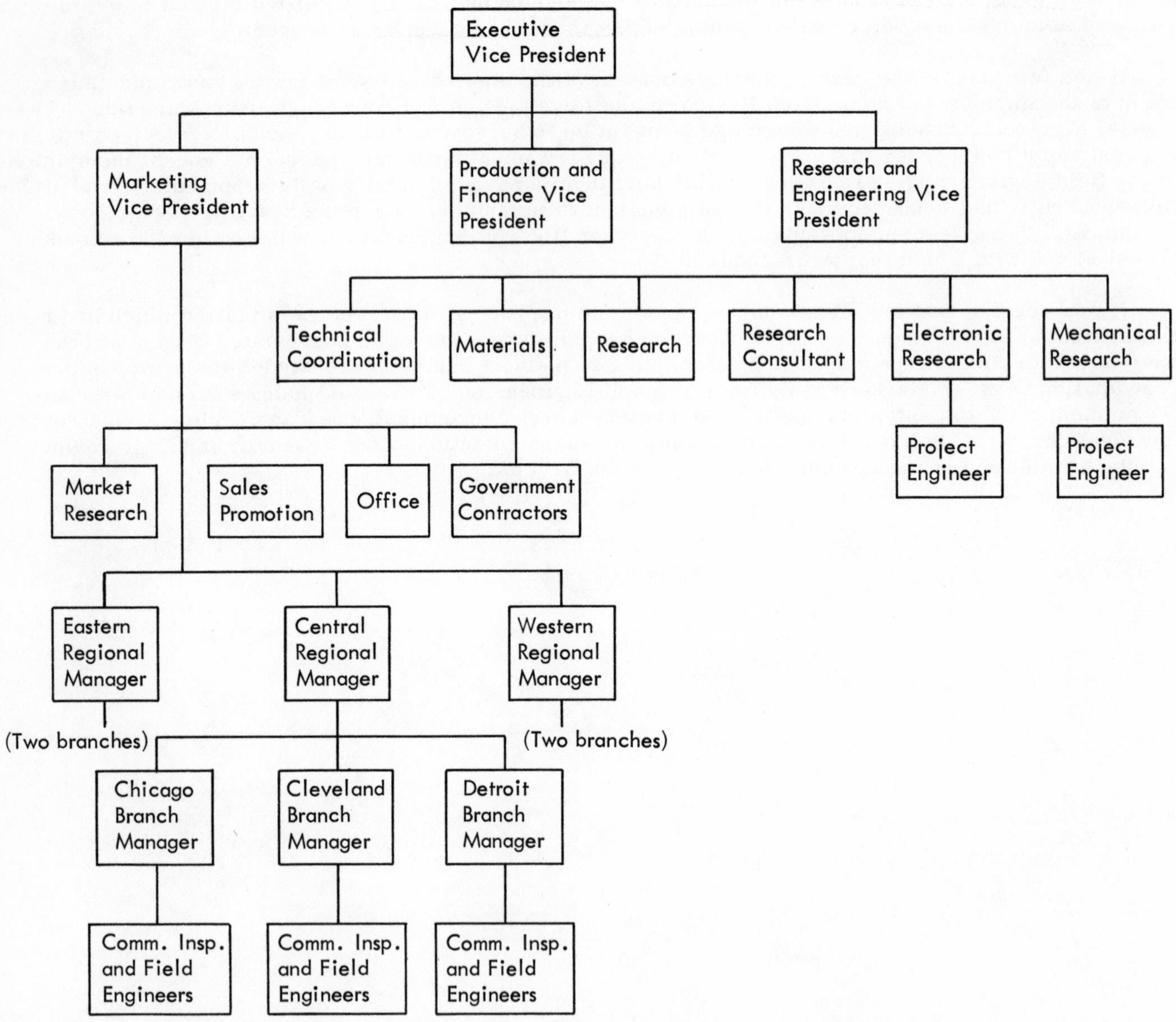

Figure 2. Henry Research Organization reflecting principal changes to affect better coordination between Marketing and Research and Engineering.

Special provision was made for better liaison between Marketing and Research and Engineering concerning the new electronic lines by the creation of three new positions known as Regional Electronic Specialists. Their position in the organizational setup is indicated in Figure 3.

The duties of the Technical Coordinator did not change in the reorganization, but were made into a full-time job and transferred to the Research and Engineering Division. The Technical Coordinator was to maintain records of all applications, successful and unsuccessful, of the company's electronic testing methods; furnish information on these applications and furnish all other pertinent technical data to the field engineers, the regional electronic specialists, the sales promotion manager, and the regional and branch managers; pass information from the field on customer problems and testing applications to the technical departments in the Research and Engineering Division; and pass requests for research from the field to the proper technical department, following research developments, and passing results back to the field.

Regional electronic specialists would set up testing laboratories in each sales region to work on customer problems. If they developed a successful testing method for a given problem, they were to report this to the Technical Coordinator, who would inform both the Marketing and the Research and Engineering Divisions.

It was expected that the new organization would function as follows: if a field engineer (salesman) found a testing problem which Henry Research had solved before, he would attempt to sell the company's testing method to the potential customer. If the field engineer did not know the proper testing method, and if he thought the problem required magnetic testing methods, he would report it to his branch manager. If the field engineer thought electronic testing methods were appropriate, he would report the problem to the regional electronic specialist, who would attempt to solve it by work in his laboratory or at the customer's plant. If the field electronic specialist could not solve the problem, he and the field engineer would report the problem to the branch manager, from where it would be handled in the same manner as magnetic testing problems.

Problems forwarded to branch managers were passed on to the regional managers who would attempt to estimate the following:

1. Were Henry Research testing methods applicable to the problem?
2. How large was the potential sales volume for Henry Research?
3. What was the probability of technical success in solving the problem?
4. What was the probable cost of technical development?

If his estimates of the above questions were favorable, the regional manager passed the problem to the Marketing Research Department for a more formal estimate of the sales potential. This report was then submitted to the Marketing Vice President who sent it to Research and Engineering.

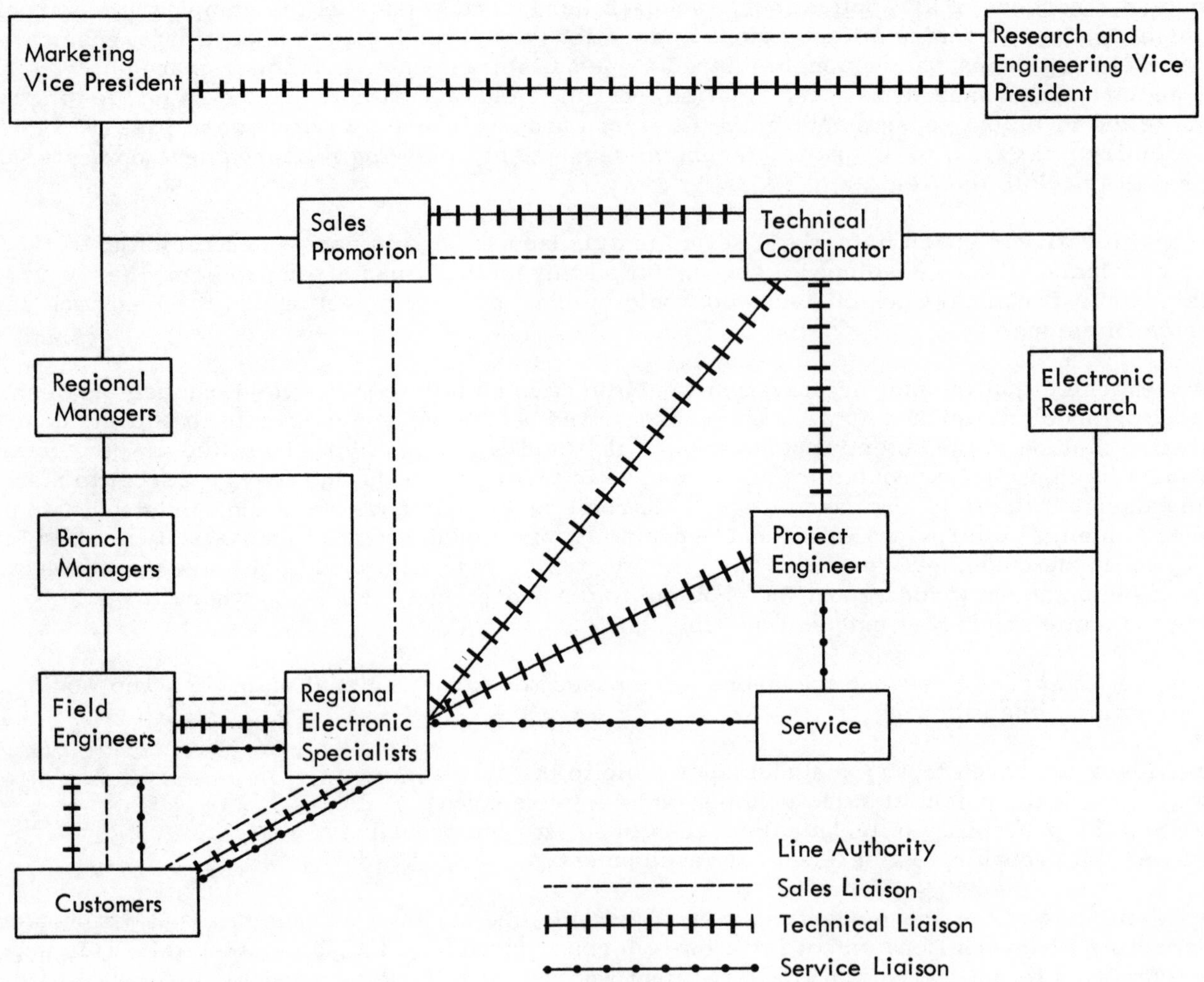

Figure 3. Henry Research Corporation Sales-Engineering-liaison for the new electronics line.

ATLANTA POLICE DEPARTMENT (D)

The function of the Atlanta Police Department is to protect the life and property of the citizens and visitors to Atlanta. To achieve this goal we must effectively prevent crimes, make arrests and carry out the other related aspects of police work.

The 1965 Crime Commission report clearly demonstrated there was a clear relationship between the incidence of crime and poverty in Atlanta. Some of the Commission's recommendations flowing from this analysis would, in my opinion, clearly put the Police Department in the welfare business. Personally, I have always believed welfare and police work should be separate activities. However, the mayor has told me to implement the Commission's recommendations related to <u>crime prevention</u>. He also told me to do it within my present manning and budget limits.

Chief Jenkins (early 1966)

In early 1966, Herbert Jenkins, Chief of Police, Atlanta, was faced with two questions: What changes should I make in my organization structure so as to satisfy the Commission's recommendations? In addition, what other changes in my organizational structure should I consider making?

Figure 1 presents the organization chart and manning table of the Atlanta Police Department.

CRIME COMMISSION RECOMMENDATIONS

The following are excerpts from the recommendations presented by the Atlanta Crime Commission in late 1965:

a. <u>The Atlanta Youth Council</u>

There is a serious need to focus the city's resources on the problem of preventing and controlling juvenile delinquency. We therefore recommend that the Atlanta Youth Council be created as an official agency for this purpose. Membership would include the Superintendent of the Atlanta Public Schools, the head of the Parks Department, the Chief of Police, a full-time executive director, a lay chairman, and six lay members, for a total membership of eleven. . . .

The primary responsibility of this Council would be to formulate and implement a community program of delinquency prevention and control and to be certain that all available public and private resources are fully used in such a program. It also would work with the public, private, and religious agencies devoted in whole or in part to delinquency prevention and coordinate the activities of these agencies to the extent desirable. Finally, it would collect, correlate, and disseminate information, statistics, and data on the subject of juvenile delinquency and make this information available to all agencies which might benefit from it.

b. <u>Day Care</u>

Day care services must be provided on a much more extensive basis by the city or some other governmental agency. . .The Youth Council should address itself at once to this problem.

c. <u>The Family Unit</u>

The principal cause of delinquency is the improper rearing of children. . .This, too, should be a concern of the Youth Council.

d. <u>Police Department</u>
(1) Manpower and Pay

The manpower and pay of the Atlanta Police Department are both presently at a dangerously low level. In order to attain the required manpower and pay levels, the budget of the Police Department must be substantially increased. . . .

(1) Advancement

Policemen must be made secure in their jobs by an appropriate type of merit system. . .A cadet school for qualified high school graduates should be created, and there should be continued police training for recruit and veteran alike.

(2) Modernization

The Police Department itself needs considerable modernization. The department should use all modern developments and law enforcement techniques, including such crime-fighting equipment as computers.

(3) Police Department Study

The Police Department should be studied thoroughly by an independent professional agency to determine its present capabilities and its needs for the immediate future. This study should evaluate and estimate Atlanta's police requirements; it should appraise its organizational structure, personnel, equipment, and promotion system. On the basis of this study, there should be proposed a detailed plan of improvement to give the city and its citizens a modern police organization second to none.

(4) Police in Low-income Areas

There is a serious lack of understanding between residents of low-income areas and the police. All available means should be utilized to inform every citizen of the fact that the police serve not only to arrest and punish the law breaker, but also to protect the average citizen in his day-to-day life. The Atlanta Police Department should send police counsellors into problem areas to hold meetings and generally to inform the public of the protective role of the police. Neighborhood committees, comprised of a policeman trained in social problems and local leaders, should be formed to discuss the community problems and assist the work of the police in problem areas. Existing independent neighborhood civic associations also should be utilized and a police counsellor stationed in each Economic Opportunity Atlanta neighborhood center.

e. Parks

One of Atlanta's most serious problems with regard to juvenile delinquency and crime is that the most congested areas of the city have the least recreation facilities. . .Parks should be built in congested high crime areas of the city. Trained supervisory personnel must be provided. Equipment should be modern. . .More park police should be provided so that Atlanta's people can enjoy their parks. Community centers should be kept open longer during the week and on weekends, particularly during the summer.

f. Atlanta Municipal Court

The Commission is disturbed by indications that the Municipal Court is taking upon itself the responsibility of disposing of many cases which actually involve serious offenses not within that court's jurisdiction. . .The Municipal Court should be thoroughly studied to make sure it is doing a proper job.

g. Care of the Alcoholic

[. . .alcoholic offenders] should be identified and a concerted effort should be made to remedy their addiction, thus eliminating the expense of their continued apprehension by the police, their imprisonment, and their trial before the Municipal Court. . .The Commission feels that this responsibility should belong to the City of Atlanta.

h. Atlanta Public Schools

Aside from the family, the schools have the greatest opportunity to mold young lives in a useful and law-abiding pattern.

A crash program of remedial education is badly needed. . .Chronic absenteeism among unsupervised children in low-income areas must receive immediate attention. If the school cannot meet these needs, the Welfare Department and the Police Department must assume an increased burden.

The school system also should increase its vocational education program and add a job-placement service for all the students who do not finish high school or who are not going on to college. In addition the schools can provide a valuable service in identifying at an early age children with delinquent tendencies and make a concerted effort to straighten them out. Finally, adequate attention must be devoted to emotionally disturbed and mentally retarded children.

i. Organized Crime

The Commission has found that organized crime exists in Atlanta on a local basis. . .More members of the Atlanta Police Department should be trained to deal with the problems of organized crime. All law enforcement agencies in the Atlanta area must constantly be on the alert for encroachments of organized crime on a local or national basis.

j. Community Associations

Local independent community associations are a healthy development. The city should encourage these organizations by making available to them facilities for meeting places and perhaps some educational facilities whenever needed. These associations are stabilizing institutions which help to revitalize neighborhoods. They should be encouraged in every possible way. . . .

(The Crime Commission report also included recommendations involving the county, state, federal government, and citizen's role in crime prevention.)

RECENT HISTORY

Herbert T. Jenkins was elected Chief of Police on February 2, 1947. He inaugurated a permanent recruit school. New types of radio equipment were purchased. The officers were given a much deserved day off each week. The headquarters building was redecorated to make working conditions better. The Detective Department was reorganized by division into robbery, larceny, burglary, homicide, vice, and miscellaneous squads. A wrecker was purchased to impound cars illegally parked, and a parking lot for these impounded cars was built.

In 1948 tradition was broken when eight Negro policemen were hired. They were originally restricted to arresting only those of their own race, but later this restriction was removed and they were made full officers.

In 1950 the first part-time school traffic policewomen were sworn in and given special training. Thirty-two white women were employed for crossings at white schools, and eight colored women were hired for work at Negro schools.

In 1951 the entire Police Department was reorganized into four divisions. These were Services, Uniform, Traffic, and Detective. Training and Detention were made separate divisions later. There was a superintendent in charge of each division. A line-up was also established in the Detective Division.

In 1952 parking meters were installed. The Fulton County Police Department was absorbed into the Atlanta Police Department, and police protection was extended to parts of the county, outside the city, that formerly had depended on the county police.

Major crimes in the city decreased by over 7 percent in 1955. This was the first major decrease in crime in Atlanta since World War II.

Space problems were severely felt in 1956 and several departments had to be moved from headquarters. These problems were relieved in 1959 with the completion of a new headquarters building.

In 1958 there was a rise in racial and religious agitation. A Jewish temple was bombed and attacks against persons grew in frequency. The Negro civil rights and racial problem also became more significant.

A corps of dogs to aid police officers was organized in 1959. It was called the K-9 Corps and was composed of German Shepherds and a Doberman Pinscher.

Racial problems continued to grow in 1960. The public schools were desegregated in 1961. Chief Jenkins had sent trusted officers to other racially troubled spots in the nation to observe the situation. "Fortunately," Chief Jenkins later said, "we were able to at least avoid the mistakes of others." Accordingly, while the Mayor and the Superintendent of Schools prepared the people for the coming of integration, Chief Jenkins prepared the police. As a result, Atlanta was spared many of the racial troubles experienced by other southern cities.

Table 1 presents the City of Atlanta's 1966 Police Budget.

PRESENT ORGANIZATION STRUCTURE

In early 1966, the Atlanta Police Department consisted of six divisions, each headed by a superintendent reporting to Chief Jenkins. The six divisions were: Service, Detective, Traffic, Uniform, Detention, and Training.

Service Division

The Service Division, under the command of Superintendent Beerman, is responsible for all of the administrative aspects of the department. Superintendent Beerman joined the department in 1934 and was named Superintendent in 1960.

Specifically the division is charged with the compilation of criminal records (including the FBI reports), the transmitting and receiving of radio communications, and the telephone switchboard. The Division also is responsible for all monies received by the department as well as the departments inventories, purchases, and maintenance.

The Service Division consists of the Crime Report Bureau, including Missing Persons Bureau, the Tabulation Room, and Communications. In addition, the division includes the Custodian's Office, Arsenal, and Maintenance Crew.

Detective Division

The Detective Division is headed by Superintendent Clinton Chafin. Superintendent Chafin joined the department in 1947 and was named Superintendent of the Detective Division in 1964.

The Detective Division is charged with the prevention of crime, the investigation of criminal offenses, the detection and arrest of criminals, and the recovery of stolen or lost property. The Division consists of nine squads: Auto, Burglary, Homicide, Larceny, Robbery, Vice (includes Narcotic Investigations), Fugitive, Juvenile, and Lottery. In addition, the Division includes the identification Bureau and the General and Criminal Investigation Bureaus.

The most recent additions to the Detective Division are the Juvenile, Security, and Fugitive Squads.

The Juvenile Squad was formed in 1960 following rapid increase in the number of juveniles involved in illegal acts. The squad investigates cases where children under 17 years of age are involved and assists other detective squads (when needed) to investigate crimes by juveniles. The Division also works with the Juvenile Court authorities in the prevention of crime and rehabilitation of wayward children.

Sergeant Spears, who joined the department in 1947, heads the Juvenile Squad. Reporting to Sergeant Spears are three persons.

The Security Squad consists of six men and was formed in 1961. It operates under direct orders from the Chief of Police and the Superintendent of Detectives. The squad is charged with maintaining a constant check on the activities of subversive groups as well as keeping a check on any section of the city where racial tension exists or may start. The squad also is responsible for the safety of any visiting dignitaries (which involves working closely with other governmental agencies), investigating bombings, investigating internal problems that may arise within the Department, and any other special assignments given by the Chief.

Lieutenant Maurice Redding heads the Security Squad. Lieutenant Redding is 32 years old. He joined the department eight years earlier as a uniformed officer patrolling a footbeat.

The Fugitive Squad was created in 1963. This squad specialized in the apprehension and prosecution of fugitives from penitentiary and justice. Lieutenant Barnes heads this squad of eight men from Atlanta plus six from other local jurisdictions.

Traffic Division

The Traffic Division promotes street and highway safety and the enforcement of vehicular traffic laws and regulations. In addition, the division is charged with handling large crowds who attend sports events, conventions, parades, circuses, and funerals. The Traffic Division consists of the following groups: Motorcycle, Accident Investigation, Foot Traffic, Parking Control Radar Speed Control, and Helicopter Traffic Control. The Division also includes School Policewomen, School Patrols, and the police wrecker.

Superintendent James L. Moseley heads the Traffic Division. He joined the department in 1937 and was named Superintendent in 1964.

According to Chief Jenkins, if the Traffic Division can keep the number of fatalities low, the other traffic accident statistics will be reduced also. In pursuit of this goal, Chief Jenkins and Superintendent Moseley meet weekly to discuss the current and projected traffic situation with representatives of the city, county, and state government agencies responsible for highways, the Atlanta Safety Council, and several prominent citizens.

Uniform Division

The Uniform Division is charged with the protection of life and property, the prevention of crime, the detection and arrest of offenders, and the preservation of the public peace. Superintendent I. G. Cowan is the commanding officer. He joined the department in 1934 and was named superintendent in 1951. Superintendent Cowan's division consists of the following squads and bureaus: Radio Patrol; Motorcycle (nontraffic); K-9 Corps; Unincorporated Detail (see below); and Foot Patrols.

The Atlanta Police Department furnishes, through the Uniform Division, services to the unincorporated area of Fulton County under a contract between the City of Atlanta and Fulton County. The personnel and equipment comprising the Unincorporated Detail includes 2 captains; 1 lieutenant; 30 patrolmen; 8 patrol cars; 11 school traffic policewomen; and 4 motorcycles.

Detention Division

The Detention Division was established in 1963. Previously it was part of the service division. According to Chief Jenkins, during the racial problems of the early 1960s, 300 to 400 persons might be jailed at any one time. This created numerous problems which he believed could best be handled by a separate division.

Superintendent J. F. Brown heads the Detention Division, which is responsible for the operations of the detention building adjoining the headquarters building and the detention ward at the Grady Hospital, a large downtown public hospital. During 1965 about 85,000 people were processed by the Detention Division.

Superintendent Brown joined the department in 1939 and was named superintendent in 1951.

Training Division

The Training Division was created in 1964. Formerly it was part of the service division. The Training Division is responsible for police training and the investigation of applicants seeking to join the department. The division's commanding officer is Superintendent J. L. Tuggle. He joined the force in 1935 and was appointed as Superintendent in 1958.

The division's principal training activity is a six-week school for new recruits conducted at least three times a year. Between 30 and 45 people attend each session, which is set up along the same lines as the FBI's National Academy. Each session usually includes several officers from other departments, such as the airport or park police. These officers attend free of charge.

Other training activities include bimonthly discussions by each squad of the training keys prepared by the International Association of Chiefs of Police. These meetings are conducted by lieutenants and sergeants for the men in their squads. Periodically, written examinations are given to all officers. The questions are picked at random from the training keys. These papers are graded and the results recorded in each officer's personnel file. Table 2 presents the topic outline for a typical six-week training session.

Watch System

The Police Department operates on the watch system. The watches are:

Hours	Watch	Division	Hours	Division
11 p.m. - 7 a.m.	Morning Watch	Traffic Division	12 p.m. - 8 a.m.	Uniform & Detective
7 a.m. - 3 p.m.	Day Watch		8 a.m. - 4 p.m.	
3 p.m. - 11 p.m.	Night Watch		4 p.m. - 12 p.m.	
10 a.m. - 6 p.m.	Traffic Watch (intersection control)			
8-9 a.m. & 2-4 p.m.	School Patrol			
8 a.m. - 4 p.m.	Office Personnel			

The morning, day, and night watches comprise the 24-hour patrol duty. The traffic watch handles downtown traffic direction at crossings. The school patrol consists of part-time policewomen and some full-time officers who direct traffic and pedestrians at schools. Office personnel handles administrative work.

Each watch is covered by a captain from either the Uniform or Traffic Divisions, depending upon which one happened to be on duty at the time. "In this way," Chief Jenkins said, "I am able to have a superior officer responsible for whatever happens during the watch."

Districts

For patrol duty purposes, the City of Atlanta is divided into four districts. Either six or seven two-man patrol cars are assigned to each district during each watch. These cars are in constant radio communication with the central radio room located in the police headquarters building. Chief Jenkins referred to these patrol cars as his "mobile precincts." He believed it would take between 20 and 30 percent more funds to operate his department if it were organized on a precinct basis.

Jenkins' Interview

Chief Jenkins spoke on a number of topics with the case writer. He said:

> When I became chief in 1947 there were three areas where I wanted to take action. First, I wanted to improve the training of police officers. I realized a number of officers did not fully realize what was demanded or expected of them. Second, I wanted to strengthen the moral courage and integrity of the department. While it is not always manifest, police officers are always under scrutiny and open to accusation. It appeared to me a number of officers were overly fearful of making mistakes or being falsely accused. I set out to correct this situation through training and clear-cut policies. Third, I felt our housekeeping at headquarters was poor. Most of our "customers" are from the slums. I believed improved facilities and housekeeping would set an example for them to follow as well as lift the spirits of the force. Accordingly, I worked toward getting a new building and strengthening the training department. Over the years we have achieved these objectives.

Chief Jenkins discussed several changes he had made in the formal organization.

> At the time I took over as chief, the service office operated out of the chief's office. In line with my desire to delegate authority, I created the Service Division and moved to the service and other divisions many of the management tasks formerly carried on by the Chief's office. In the process I also abolished the two Deputy Chief of Police positions. Now, in my absence, the Superintendent of the Service Division acts as Chief.

Within the immediate future I may make several changes in the organization. For example, our shifts end at 8 a.m., 4 p.m. and 12 p.m.; 8 a.m. and 4 p.m. are both high traffic movement periods. This is the time that the police need to be out in the field. Perhaps, the shift should end at some other time. I'm opposed to change for the sake of change, but if there's a good reason for change, and I think we're ready for it--I'll change.

Chief Jenkins also spoke about the type of man he wanted in the department. Table 3 presents a recruitment brochure for the Atlanta Police Force.

Our personnel department will accept applicants only if our training division says that in their opinion the applicant will make a good policeman. Once the applicant is accepted and joins the force, he is assigned a counselor who is either a lieutenant or sergeant. The men are encouraged to discuss with their counselor their problems. Also, we have squad meetings periodically to discuss the things on the mens' minds. I've told the counselors that if I get any reports of misconduct involving their advisees, I want to see the counselor. I want results.

We accept only about 3 percent to 4 percent of the applicants who take the patrolman's examination. I'm not interested in a man who is simply looking for a job. . . Unless he has the ability to train and discipline himself and the ambition to be a police officer, I'm not really interested in him.

Most of our recruits come through the family connections of those already in the department. . . Unfortunately, with our low salary scale we are having increasing trouble finding acceptable applicants and holding young officers. The Crime Commission and the Mayor appreciate this problem, and both have recommended police salary increases. However, other city departments are opposed to the police being singled out for a pay increase --so we are still waiting for the increase.

Chief Jenkins also referred to the Crime Commission report:

Now, the Crime Commission has recommended we get more involved in crime prevention activities. The Mayor has told me to follow up these recommendations, but not to go over my budget allocation. In a sense our 6 p.m. detail has functioned as our crime prevention detail. Moreover, the Commission report seems to be calling for more than the normal concept of a policeman's function. How should I organize for crime prevention? How many men should I assign to this task? What kind of men should they be? What are some of the things these men should be doing? What characteristics should the head of the crime prevention activity possess? These are all questions I must resolve quickly?

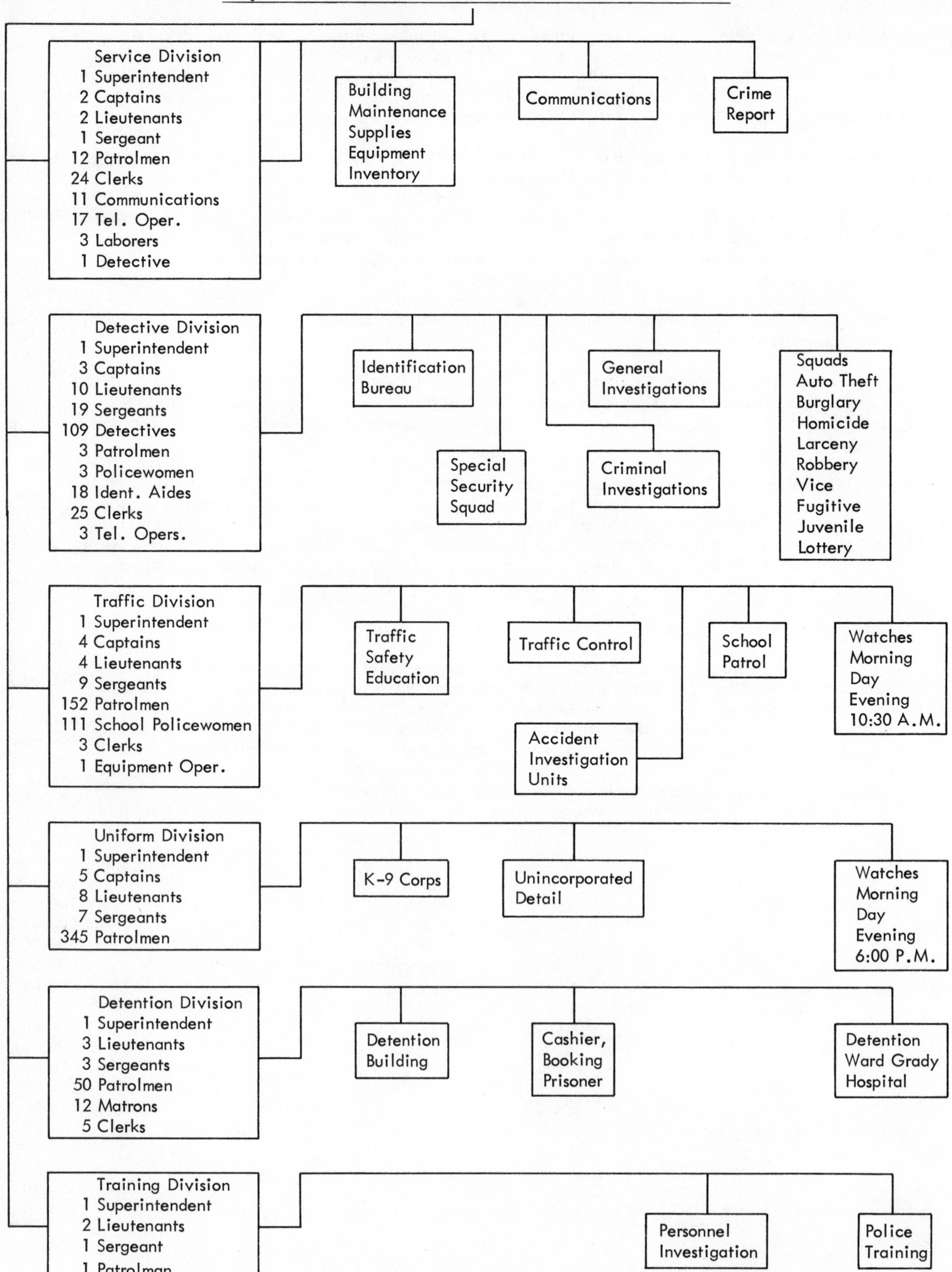

Figure 1. Organizational Chart for the Atlanta Police Department.

Table 1

ATLANTA POLICE DEPARTMENT (D)
GENERAL FUND

1966 Budget Appropriations
Department of POLICE

		Expenditures 1964	Expenditures 1965	Appropriations 1966
CURRENT EXPENSES				
A	Personal Services	$4,312,452.44	$4,852,810.44	$5,356,098.00
B	Contractual Services	468,926.21	496,994.29	524,930.00
C	Materials and Supplies	122,605.47	142,204.71	146,500.00
D	Fixed Charges	70,798.43	87,086.09	90,045.00
	TOTAL CURRENT EXPENSES	$4,974,782.55	$5,579,095.53	$6,117,573.00
CAPITAL OUTLAYS				
E	Land	----	----	----
F	Structures and Improvements	----	----	----
G	Equipment	$ 91,172.36	$ 252,851.71	$ 250,000.00
	TOTAL CAPITAL OUTLAYS	$ 91,172.36	$ 252,851.71	$ 250,000.00
	GRAND TOTAL	$5,065,954.91	$5,831,947.24	$6,637,573.00

ACCOUNT NUMBER	TITLE OF ACCOUNT	1964	1965	1966
G-32-62				
(G) 570	Purchase of Equipment	$ 91,172.36	$ 252,851.71	$ 250,000.00
(B) 700	Laundry Service	1,001.55	1,156.46	1,500.00
(B) 711	Lights and Power	22,128.88	21,967.82	22.000.00
(B) 714	Fuel	8,563.21	7,841.13	10,000.00
(D) 730	Membership Fees	27.50	27.50	45.00
(A) 731	Special Investigation Fund	47.76	416.52	2,500.00
(B) 733	Service Contracts	6,834.07	6,664.69	8,080.00
(B) 733-1	Metropol Service Contracts	----	----	26,100.00
(B) 760	Postage	2,366.57	2,669.19	3,000.00
(B) 768	Service to Motor Equipment	376,133.50	407,926.24	400,000.00
(C) 770	Office Supplies and Expense	3,064.42	4,374.94	6,000.00
(C) 771	Operating Supplies	30,906.14	31,902.94	32,500.00
(C) 771-1	Operating Supplies, Training School.	2,584.38	2,997.74	3,000.00
(C) 771-2	Uniforms	79,000.00	96,710.58	98,000.00
(C) 771-3	Photographic Supplies	7,050.53	6,218.50	7,000.00
(B) 773	Operation of K-9 Corps	9,347.61	8,036.11	10,000.00
(A) 730	Salaries, Overtime	42,808.00	43,219.00	45,000.00
(D) 810	Rental	70,770.93	87,058.59	90,000.00
(B) 812	General Building Repairs	7,660.51	3,623.13	8,000.00
(B) 813	Repairs to Burglar Alarm System	989.18	1,727.85	2,000.00
(B) 814	Radio Maintenance	5,437.07	4,225.01	6,500.00
(A) 830	Salaries	4,185,182.01	4,715,274.28	5,201,333.00
(A) 830-1	Salaries, Part-Time Policewomen	80,136.00	90,865.75	104,765.00
(B) 866	Telephone Service, Burglar Alarm	28,258.95	30,980.40	27,500.00
(B) 867	Telegraph Expense	205.11	176.27	250.00
(A) 868	Special Training	4,278.67	3,034.89	2,500.00
TOTAL - DEPARTMENT OF POLICE		$4,065,954.91	$5,831,947.24	$6,367,573.00

Table 2

ATLANTA POLICE DEPARTMENT (D)

INTRODUCTION	HOURS	INSTRUCTOR
Six-Week Training Sessions Syllabus		
ORIENTATION	1	Chief H. T. Jenkins
NOTE TAKING, READING, AND STUDY HABITS	1	Supt. J. F. Brown
COURSE OPERATION	1	Supt. J. L. Tuggle
COURSE I:		
BASIC FUNCTIONS OF POLICE		
1. Organization-Atlanta Police Department	1	Lt. D. H. Riley
2. Desirable qualities for modern police officer	1	Capt. W. L. Duncan
3. History of policing	1	Lt. S. L. Salvent
4. Operation of detective bureau	1	Supt. C. Chafin
5. Operation of identification bureau	1	Capt. R. E. Hulsey
6. Rules and regulations	12	Lt. D. H. Riley
7. First aid	12	Pt. C. V. Forrester
8. Gymnasium	15	Lt. R. M. Lane
9. Care of police equipment	1	Sgt. C. L. Herring
10. Civil defense	1	Gen. William Woodward
11. Complaints	1	Supt. J. F. Brown
12. Police brutality	1	Supt. J. L. Tuggle
13. Special investigators responsibilities	1	Capt. E. O. Mullen
14. Juveniles	1	Sgt. M. J. Spears Det. E. W. Felder
15. Courtesy, discipline, and deportment	1	Lt. H. Baugh
16. Public relations	1	Mr. K. McCartney
17. Radio procedure	1	Mr. J. P. Born
18. Bribery	1	Supt. J. L. Tuggle
19. Care of prisoners	1	Supt. J. F. Brown
20. Uniform crime report system	1	Lt. C. W. Blackwell
21. Constitution and Bill of Rights	1	FBI
22. Semantics	1	Capt. M. A. Hornsby
23. Patrol methods	1	Capt. A. C. Roberts
24. Copy book and subpoena	1	Sgt. H. M. Kersey
COURSE II:		
LEGAL AND INVESTIGATIVE		
1. City ordinances	21	Lt. D. H. Riley
2. State law	13	Lt. R. M. Lane
3. Narcotics investigation	2	Sgt. J. C. McIntyre
4. Lottery investigation	1	Sgt. W. W. Gable
5. Larceny and pawn shops	1	Lt. C. J. Strickland
6. Forgery and bad checks	1	Capt. W. L. Duncan
7. Court procedure	1	Supt. J. L. Mosley
8. Mechanics of arrest	1	Lt. R. M. Lane
9. Auto larcency	1	Lt. A. L. Posey
10. Handling abnormal people	1	Dr. T. Malone
11. Arrest, searches and seizure	6	Pt. C. V. Forrester
12. Robbery investigation	2	Lt. G. H. Christian
13. Bookmaking and vice	1	Lt. C. J. Strickland
14. Case preparation, preserving evidence	1	Fulton Co. Sol. Gen. Louis R. Slaton, Jr.
15. Arson investigation	2	Atlanta Fire Dept.
16. Homicide investigation, rape, and sex crimes	2	Capt. R. E. Little

Table 2 (continued)

	Hours	Instructor
17. Report writing	7	Lt. C. W. Blackwell
18. Conducting interviews	2	Capt. R. E. Little
19. Scientific crime detection	1	FBI
20. Federal law	1	FBI
21. Civil rights investigation	1	FBI
22. Conducting interviews (practical work)	1	Capt. R. E. Little
23. Burglary investigation	2	Lt. N. W. Flanagan
24. Introduction to traffic	2	Capt. J. T. Marler
COURSE III:		
TRAFFIC		
1. Traffic ordinances	11	Capt. M A. Hornsby
2. Enforcement tactics	1	Supt. J. L. Mosley
3. Abnormal people	1	Dr. T. Malone
4. Rules of evidence	14	Lt. R. M. Lane
5. Accident investigation	12	Capt. J. T. Marler
6. Photography	3	Mr. Curtis Luke
7. Traffic films	5	School Staff
8. Why drivers violate	2	Lt. L. A. Pendergrass
9. Speed and skid marks	2	Lt. L. A. Pendergrass
10. Patrol techniques	2	Lt. L. A. Pendergrass
11. Intersection control	2	Capt. J. T. Marler
12. Intersection control (practical exp.)	4	Capt. J. T. Marler
13. Records and accident reports	6	Capt. M. A. Hornsby
14. Responsibilities of a police officer	1	Lt. L. A. Pendergrass
15. Traffic engineering	2	Mr. Karl Bevins Traffic Engineer
16. Writing the citation	1	Lt. L. A. Pendergrass
17. Georgia Highway Patrol	1	Capt. E. Mink
18. Mock accident	4	School Staff
19. Enforcement in accidents	3	Lt. L. A. Pendergrass
20. Mock trial (in court room)	2	School Staff
21. State traffic laws	2	Judge Bynum
22. Measurements and diagrams	3	Lt. L. A. Pendergrass
23. Class speech participation	2	School Staff
24. Detecting violations	2	Lt. L. A. Pendergrass
25. Stopping and approaching vehicles	2	Lt. L. A. Pendergrass
26. Officer-violator relationship	2	Lt. L. A. Pendergrass
27. Psychological factors related to traffic	2	Capt. J. T. Marler
28. Selective enforcement	4	Lt. L. A. Pendergrass
COURSE IV:		
1. Firearms training on pistol range	48	School Staff

Table 3

ATLANTA POLICE DEPARTMENT (D)
RECRUITMENT PROCEDURE

MINIMUM REQUIREMENTS

AGE LIMITS: 20-34. Applicants must have reached their 20th birthday by the closing date for receipt of applications, but must not have passed their 35th birthday by the date of appointment.

CITIZENSHIP: Applicants must be citizens of the United States, unless no qualified U.S. citizens are available.

MEDICAL STANDARDS: An exacting physical examination by the City's examining Physician is required (at no expense to applicants). Any serious defect will disqualify. Minimum height 5' 7" with proportionate weight required. 20-50 natural vision, corrected to no less than 20-30. Normal color vision.

DRIVER'S LICENSE: Possession of a valid driver's license is required.

CHARACTER: Statements made on the application will be verified. The detection of false information will result in disqualification. Fingerprints will be taken and will be checked with local, state, and federal police records. Credit, personal, and employment investigations will be made.

VETERANS are required to present an honorable discharge, which entitles them to 5 points added to their combined passing grades if they entered service prior to July 1, 1955. Disabled veterans presenting a letter from the Veterans Administration dated within the past 6 months showing proof of a service-connected disability are given 10 points. Any discharge other than "HONORABLE" will reject.

SERVE WITH PRIDE!

ATLANTA POLICE DEPARTMENT

YOUNG MEN 20-34

HONEST
INTELLIGENT
WILLING TO LEARN

NO OTHER REQUIREMENTS!

S402 - S497

ASK YOURSELF. . . .

The Examination for Patrolman Consists of -

(1) a written examination to test your learning ability - 70%

(2) a medical examination

(3) a physical agility test (running, chinning, etc.) to see whether or not you are physically capable of performing the duties of a patrolman.

Should I Be a Policeman?

YES! If you are interested in protecting life and property, preventing crime, and playing a leading part in the community.

YES! If you understand the need for laws and respect the men who enforce them.

Table 3 (continued)

(4) a personal investigation--All applicants are fingerprinted and a careful investigation of each man is made.

(5) and an oral examination to determine if an individual has the personality and interests necessary for the position of patrolman. 30%

TOTAL 100%

Do I Have to Be a Resident of Atlanta?

NO! You should live within easy driving distance of the City, but you do not have to live inside the City limits.

How about Military Status?

PAID MILITARY LEAVE! If you are ordered into service, you have two weeks' pay to take with you and a guaranteed place when you return. Your salary increases continue while you are in service.

What about Reserve Obligations?

NO PROBLEM! All reservists and National Guardsmen are allowed two weeks' military leave each year WITH PAY in addition to their regular vacation.

Can I Get Life Insurance?

YES! You may apply for group insurance in amounts ranging from $1,000 to $10,000 at a cost to you of 70 cents per month per $1,000 of coverage. Your family is protected from the beginning of your employment.

How about Hospitalization Insurance?

GROUP insurance is available for you and your family at minimal cost. Both life and hospitalization insurance may be continued at the SAME RATES after you retire.

What Do I Have to Know to Be a Policeman?

You need no special experience or special education. You will receive five weeks of intensive training at Atlanta's modern Police Academy. You will be paid while in training.

Will I Have to Buy Equipment?

NO! Your uniforms and all necessary equipment except a belt and holster will be furnished.

Will I Have Long Hours?

NO! You will work 8 hours a day, five days one week and six days the next.

How Much Vacation Will I Receive?

20 DAYS! after the first year on the force.

When Will I Get a Raise?

EVERY YEAR for the first five years. Additional increases for longevity are given after ten, fifteen, and twenty years, even if you have not been promoted.

What if I Get Sick?

30 DAYS' sick leave is allowed each year for ordinary illness. If you are injured in line of duty, time lost is not charged to sick leave.

Is there a Pension Plan?

YES! A very good one. With 25 years service, you may retire at age 55 with full benefits, or at age 50 with reduced benefits. The Peace Officers' Association offers additional pension benefits in which you may participate. If you want another job after retirement, your work in law enforcement will probably make it easy to get one.

What Are Some of the Other Advantages?

While in uniform, you may ride public transit free. You have the use of the modern Police gymnasium including steam room, sun lamps, and other equipment. You know that you are a member of one of the best law enforcement agencies in the nation.

MIDLANDIA

Role and Organizational Location of the Central Staff Unit in a State's PPB System

In the summer of 1968, Governor Hardy of the state of Midlandia met with his chief advisors to consider a Task Force proposal outlining organizational arrangements for initiating a statewide PPB system, and particularly, for the carrying on of the central staff functions within such a system.

Governor Hardy had been elected in 1967 for a 4-year term after a campaign in which he promised a program of social and economic development and a "businesslike" and efficient management of all state activities. He was convinced that a statewide PPB system--and the ensuing analytical activities for which it sets the framework--offered the best hope of meeting a Governor's requirements for the fullest possible information to guide and support his policy and priority decisions. Furthermore, he believed that it would be politically useful to him to have had an effective PPB system in operation for a substantial period before running for reelection. He had announced that he would make an early decision on the central staff organization for the effort.

In addition to the members of his ad hoc Task Force, there were present at the meeting in the Governor's office, the Treasurer (also state Comptroller), the Attorney General, and the Dean of the School of Public Administration at the State University.

THE TASK FORCE

Soon after his inauguration the Governor had assigned one of his chief executive assistants, Mr. Edward Arnold, to make a preliminary exploration of the possible ways of installing a PPB system. Mr. Arnold reported to the Governor his tentative conclusions, as follows:

1. No existing department or agency then contained the capabilities necessary for full implementation of a PPB system and, further, it would be neither feasible nor desirable to seek to establish a fully centralized PPB operation;

2. It would be essential, however, to set up some central analysis unit to be responsible for introduction of the new concepts and procedures, for preparation and issuance of guidelines and instructional materials to participating departments and agencies, and to play a generally coordinating role;

3. The continuing organizational arrangements should be generally acceptable throughout the Executive Branch and to independent agencies (e.g., the state university complex) and should be such as to provide close links to staff agencies, strengthen departmental planning, encourage communication and analysis across organizational lines, and make effective use of the information and analytical skills developed in the several departments; and

4. The two executive branch agencies with the most staff strength for PPB activities were the Department of Planning and Economic Development (PED) and the Office of Budget and Finance (OBF), but because of this very fact, there had been instances of serious rivalry in recent years.

Convinced that if the system was to have practical usefulness, the administrative framework must combine the necessary technical skills with maximum acceptability to and participation by other agencies, the Governor appointed an ad hoc Task Force on Organization for Central Direction of the State PPB System. Mr. Arnold was named chairman. The other members were: the Commissioners of Budget and Finance, Administration, Planning and Economic Development, Transportation, Agriculture, Labor, Education, and Health and Social Services.

Charge to the Task Force. In general, the Task Force was directed by the Governor to make recommendations for a continuing administrative framework for the statewide PPB operation, and for the general operating procedures necessary therefor. Specifically, it was asked to recommend an appropriate organizational location for the central program analysis unit and to outline the major components of the functions appropriate to such a central unit.

In developing its recommendations, and particularly its recommendations on the organizational location of the central analysis unit, the Task Force was asked to give special consideration to the importance of such factors as (a) close ties between the agencies and activities that need to be involved; (b) responsiveness to emerging public needs; (c) balance among the various kinds of expertise required; and (d) clear delineation of relationships between the "staff" functions and responsibilities of the central unit and the functional operating responsibilities of the "line" departments and agencies.

STATE GOVERNMENT IN MIDLANDIA

The executive branch of the Midlandia state government consists of the Executive Office of the Governor, with a small professional staff immediately responsible to the Governor, and about 20 major administrative departments, each headed by a Commissioner. These include a Department of Administration, the Office of Budget and Finance, and a Department of Planning and Economic Development; the remaining departments have program responsibilities in such fields as health, welfare, education, labor, commerce and industry, taxation, transportation, highways, etc. (see chart, Appendix A).

The Commissioners heading most of these departments are appointed by the Governor. The Commissioner of Education, the Commissioner of Labor, the Secretary of State, the Attorney General, and the Treasurer (also Comptroller) are elected. The Governor has broad statutory authorities for the reorganization of and transfer of functions among the "staff" departments and agencies, but no equivalent authority for the functional "line" departments.

In addition, there is an Interdepartmental Committee for State Planning, established under executive order in a previous administration, and composed of the Commissioners who head staff departments and Commissioners of selected functional agencies. This Interdepartmental Committee has not been staffed adequately and, even at its most active, it tended to function as a sort of subcommittee of the Governor's cabinet. Historically, it has been used chiefly as a channel for the settling of immediate issues by negotiation and compromise, rather than a mechanism for the formulation and proposal of long-range objectives and major governmental policies.

Midlandia is an "executive budget" jurisdiction. The Governor is assisted in his review of departmental budget requests by both the Department of Budget and Finance and the Department of Administration, with review by the latter focussing particularly on proposed staffing patterns and capital expenditures.

THE TASK FORCE PROPOSAL

The major recommendations of the ad hoc Task Force on Organization for Central Direction of the State PPB System were:

1. The Interdepartmental Committee for State Planning should be abolished and replaced by a new staff unit (established by Executive Order) to be known as the Office of Program Planning and Coordination (OPPC).
2. The new Office should be located organizationally in the Department of Administration.
3. The Director of the Office of Program Planning and Coordination should be appointed by the Governor, although he would report administratively to the Commissioner of Administration.
4. The new Office, and the whole PPB effort, would be assisted by an Advisory Committee, which should be chaired by an executive assistant to the Governor, and composed of the Director of Office of Budget and Finance, the Commissioner of Planning and Economic Development, and such other Department heads and outside experts as the Governor might select.

The Task Force proposed four major components within the new "Office" (probably at the "Division" level).

1. Central Research and Statistics--to be responsible for the compilation of the data base for the PPB effort, the consolidation and standardization of statistical activities within the state, promotion of comparibility with the statistical activities of other states and the federal government agencies, and guidance on data processing, etc.
2. Program Analysis and Evaluation--to be responsible for initial design of the statewide program structure, preparation of guidelines and instructions for participating departments and agencies, guidance and technical assistance for program analysis activities carried out by other agencies, performance of special analyses as desirable (e.g., new policy issues, in-depth analyses of interdepartmental scope or special technical difficulty, etc.), general review and assistance in con-

nection with departmental PPB activities and program proposals, and preparation of the tentative multiyear program and financial plan and other materials useful for providing an "overview" of the composite of program decisions.

3. Federal-State Program Coordination--to be responsible for keeping abreast of existing and proposed federal program and planning aids, and the requirements and policies governing their availability, and for assisting state and local agencies and appropriate private organizations and agencies to qualify for and make maximum effective use of the federal aids relevant to their programs and objectives.
4. Local and Urban Assistance--to be responsible for making available to cities and localities information, data, and technical assistance as the capabilities of the new Office permit, and to act as a liaison between cities and localities and the OPPC and other state agencies that could so assist them.

REPORT OF THE MEETING IN THE GOVERNOR'S OFFICE

Explanation of the Task Force Proposal--Mr. Arnold presented the proposal of the Task Force (using the Chart attached as Appendix B). As a backdrop for the discussion, he outlined the principal guidelines adopted by the Task Force to aid them in the formulation of their proposal. These were:

1. The primary objective of the system is to produce an orderly and digestible package of relevant information--needs, options and their evaluation, available resources, and potential federal aids --at the decision-making level, whether at the Governor's Office, departmental, city, county, multicounty, or development district level. The organizational pattern must therefore provide for both horizontal and vertical inputs, communication, and coordination.
2. Overall state goals and priorities are the context within which departmental programming must be carried out. This overall framework will be essentially a political choice of policy direction, representing a synthesis of the long-range goals and the more immediate and specialized objectives posed by the complex of comprehensive development and functional planning activities.
3. Only "staff" and advisory and assistance functions should be lodged in the central office. The program-operating functions should be lodged in the line agencies and departments, and those agencies and departments should have an active part in the planning and programming for those operations.
4. The necessary information base can best be assured by a central operation that combines statistical clearing-house and liaison functions with responsibilities for coordinating statistical efforts within the state and for assistance in the development of additional basic information as needed.
5. Shortages of skilled, analytical personnel make it clear that the central office operations will have to be quite selective--at least in the early stages. Thus, the guiding policy will have to be one of deploying central office strength where most needed, e.g., for in-depth analyses of the most emergent issues, or to buttress (and train) departmental analytic staff whose skills are most in need of supplementation at any given time.

Mr. Arnold next summarized the Task Force's view of the role of the new Office of Program Planning and Coordination as embracing two major types of functions:

1. Staff functions for the Governor--review, analysis, and appraisal of policy issues and departmental submissions and proposals, and preparation of materials needed to provide an overview of the composite program plans and their financial implications (the basic program structure and the multiyear program and financial plan).
2. General supervision, guidance, and technical assistance--for the full range of PPB activities carried on by other state departments and agencies (and local jurisdictions) and maintenance of an adequate data base for use as background information by all participating agencies.

This rather limited role for the central staff unit, with broad and active participation by other staff and line agencies, was the pattern chosen by the Task Force, Mr. Arnold said, for two main reasons: (a) it would permit maximum use of scarce analytical skills wherever located organizationally, and (b) participation by the agencies concerned in program development would promote acceptability of the new procedures, develop analytical skills for future program planning, and encourage program coordination. Moreover, the Task Force was of the view that even with comparatively dispersed responsibilities, the Governor's power of appointment for most department heads, buttressed by his reorganizational authorities, would provide sufficient leverage to gain widespread compliance with centrally-issued guidelines--particularly since his very strong interest in a successful PPB effort was well known.

On the question of placement of the new Office, Mr. Arnold said there had been more diversity of views among the Task Force members than on any other issue. Organizational location within the Department of Administration represented a compromise solution. It provided a more "neutral" setting for the new PPB effort as compared to placement within either of the two other departments that were the chief contenders for it--the Office of Budget and Finance and the Department of Planning and Economic Development. It was generally agreed that a completely independent office--even if placed in the immediate office of the Governor--would require a greater build up of supporting staff and services than a new unit added to an established organization. Appointment of the Director by the Governor and the presence of one of the Governor's immediate aides on the Advisory Committee were considered effective safeguards against possible absorption of the new Office into existing bureaucratic routines.

Important additional considerations were the personal qualifications and the keen interest of the present Commissioner of Administration. Theoretical considerations aside, most members of the Task Force seemed to feel that the chances for a successful collaborative effort in the inauguration of a PPB system, and the establishment of good working relationships, would be enhanced by his experience and his sympathetic support of the new Office.

SUMMARY OF DISCUSSION

Following Mr. Arnold's explanatory statement, the Governor asked for comment from each of those present. He was, he said, favorably impressed by the carefully worked-out Task Force proposal, andhe intended to make his decision within the week. He wished, however, to have before him the views of those agencies most importantly involved in the new PPB effort, particularly with regard to: (a) organizational placement of the new central staff unit; and (b) which of the component functions of the PPB system, or which phases of the initial developmental effort, should be given heavy emphasis in the early stages of implementation. He was seeking practical guidance on how best to get ahead with the job of giving the state an effective means for pulling together the capabilities and the information needed for sound executive decision making.

The responses of the officials present are summarized below.

Commissioner of Administration--In the interests of orderly administration, it appears desirable to have long-range planning functions separate from the central PPB effort. The problem is to find a workable solution that will permit both kinds of planning to make a significant contribution to state government. He outlined the reasoning which had led him to this conclusion roughly as follows:

1. Planners generally (including PPB central staff and departmental staff) perform two main functions:
   (a) They provide factual information and documentation in an effort to influence and improve decision making. They do not make decisions.
   (b) They help the executive to foresee emerging problems and issues, propose solutions, prepare reports and studies for the executive's use and for the use of other staff and policy-shaping agencies, and review proposals for program development.
2. It would be most difficult for a division of an operating agency to assume many of these responsibilities, particularly responsibilities for assisting in the coordination of the planning of all other departments. It would lack the necessary authority over its fellow agencies; and its claims to objectivity would always be suspect, since it would be part of another operating agency which has its own particular mission.
3. A central PPB staff unit, for similar reasons, really ought to be located in the Governor's immediate office, or at least in a staff agency that had no substantive responsibilities. It must be prepared to deal with program issues as they come up, and to give guidance on priorities and budget development to all operating agencies.
4. The "long-range, comprehensive planning" effort, in the sense of studies of the future and setting ultimate goals, is distinguishable from the PPB effort that needs to go on continuously, on an across-the-board basis and on a much more pragmatic level, as a decision-making tool that can be applied to specific and immediate, as well as multiyear and somewhat more general, issues. So, the issue of the location of the long-range planning function is a different issue from that under discussion.
5. To locate both the comprehensive planning activities and the PPB system's central staff unit in the same agency would tend to blur and confuse the distinction between the two types of "plans," and the distinct kinds of efforts and the very different assumptions and considerations that go into their development.

The long-range planners certainly will have a most important contribution to make to the PPB activities--both by way of inputs and by way of technical assistance at all stages. Their main function, however, is that of long-range exploration of potentials and the proposal of major routes to be followed toward the realization of those potentials. He does not believe this function will be advanced by involvement in the hard, immediate realities of analyzing program choices, though overall state planning goals that have been approved by the Governor will have a major influence on the pattern of program development and on the development of the state's capital improvemen program.

Moreover, the PED Department, which has the long-range goal-setting function, has, in addition, substantive responsibilities for economic development, conservation of natural resources, and the promotion of business and industry.

6. This line of reasoning leaves as placement possibilities for the new office: the Executive Office of the Governor, or one of the other two major staff agencies--the Budget Office or his own Department of Administration. Unless it is feasible to set the unit up in the Governor's Office, the Department of Administration would offer one distinct advantage--there would be less likelihood that the new activities would be taken for granted as simply a new type of budgeting procedure. A "nonfiscal" organizational setting might help to promote understanding and acceptance of the broader concepts underlying PPB activities.

Director of Budget and Finance--With one major exception, he said he found himself in pretty close agreement with everything the Commissioner of Administration had just said. The exception is that he believes it is highly important to integrate the functions of program planning and budget making.

On the location issue, he believes there is considerable advantage in a "prestige-of-location" factor. Being part of the Executive Office would provide considerable muscle; an agency on an equal footing with other line agencies is likely to find it difficult to carry out such central office functions. A budget office occupies such a central staff position almost by definition.

PPB central office activities are, in essence, an extension of the central budget examination functions with emphasis on program purposes.

Budgeting has long been used as an analytical tool; it needs to become a tool for synthesis. One way to accomplish this would be to shift from a line-item budget toward program budget preparation. Planning ought to be an integral part of the everyday operations of all agencies of government. Therefore, there should be strong guidance for the line agency program planners. The traditional budget cycle could be adapted: (1) to include regular annual submission of future consequences of program plans; (2) to provide time for critical analysis and evaluation of agency program plans; and (3) to encourage preparation of the annual executive budget on the basis of a full understanding of total projected program requirements.

Wherever there has been greatest success in the coordination of functional plans, there has been strong involvement of the budget-making process. Preparation of the executive budget is the most powerful tool in the executive office. In this state, even the State University's budget is a part of the executive budget presented by the Governor, as are the statewide programs earning federal matching grants, e.g., the welfare and medical assistance programs, and construction projects in the capital expenditure program that are aided by federal grants. So, whatever the decision on location, he will make a strenuous effort to work out these functional relationships to the budget processes.

Commissioner of Planning and Economic Development--He would be strongly opposed to any organizational location that tended to continue the present overemphasis on budgetary procedures for implementation of policy decisions. Many decisions in relation to action programs do not have explicit budget implications. Furthermore, the linkage to comprehensive planning would be likely to be greatly weakened by location of the PPB central staff in the Budget Office unless there were conscious and continued efforts to coordinate with the state planning agency and to distinguish the planning and coordinating functions from cost control and budget management. Also, the staff relationship to the Governor's Office should be made very clear.

His preference is that the central PPB activities and the long-range planning functions both be lodged in the Department of Planning and Economic Development, and carried on with the aid of an Interdepartmental Committee. The major points urged in support of this position were:

1. The arrangement would increase departmental interest in internal planning activities, and would bring to bear the views of the various advisory groups which now assist most of the departments. It allows for the establishment of working subcommittees to give detailed consideration to particular problems and issues, e.g., a long-range capital improvements program would go through review and discussion from a number of angles.
2. State departments are already realizing the need for internal planning processes and are getting aid from this department. The aim of the department is to assist each line agency to work out a major development program, and to obtain full-time, competent staff planners who will work on a day-to-day basis in developing departmental reports and programs.
3. In general, if the planning role is soundly conceived and well understood, the precise location in the executive staff arm is of relatively minor importance. The Department of Planning and Economic Development believes that role to be one of acting as a service agency to all of state government--all departments, the Governor's Office, and cities and localities.
4. The planning unit is, and the PPB activities unit would be, kept separate from the economic and industrial promotion activities and would not get involved in the details of those operations. Their real function is to develop planning processes throughout government, to take a long-range look at the needs of the state, and to analyze and evaluate various approaches as means of meeting those needs.

Dean of the School of Public Administration--Asked if he might raise the point here that the "planning component in PPB activities is not really the same as the "planning" function in comprehensive planning as just described by the Commissioner of PED--aid to planning staff development in all state activities and in the delineation of long-range developmental goals.

As he understood it, he said, the "plan" of a PPB system is an orderly summary of the decisions taken arrayed by objective-oriented categories. It embraces all--and deals in turn with each--of the programs and activities directed toward the achievement of the state's agreed-on objectives. These objectives may be--and frequently are--stated in terms of publicly provided consumer goods and services. Program relationships between measures addressed to different objectives are not routinely dealt with as a part of the PPB system's procedures. The PPB system should, of course, when staff and time permit, try to identify program interactions for selected key issues and problems. For emergent program issues, time and dollars may have to be made available for analytical work on a crash basis.

By contrast, "planning" in a comprehensive planning program does focus on long-range goals and the interactions of programs in relation to those goals, and tries to gauge their developmental impact in terms of such things as enhanced income and higher levels of employment for state residents, better land-use patterns, more adequate public facilities, new industries, population distribution, transportation and highway systems, etc. This question of long-range program interaction seems implicit in what the Commissioner of PED has said about working with departments to improve and coordinate their internal functional planning efforts. But there was also the implication that he did not expect his planners to be involved in providing day-to-day service to the Governor's office on immediate issues as they arise. This continuing concern with the short-range, immediate program choices within the framework of current resource constraints is the essence of the PPB system's promise, i.e., when fully operational, it will provide the basis for making a better choice among the options offered at any particular point in time. (To do this, it will, of course, have to take into account the future implications of those options.)

Commissioner of Planning and Economic Development--Said he was not sure of the best way to reply to these last remarks, but there were several points he would like to make in response. First, long-range planning must be made an integral part of the policy formulation mechanism of state government; it must have direct communication with the Governor's Office and have strong linkages with budgeting, management, and program innovation functions. Economic development is only one dimension of comprehensive planning, but it must be carried on in relation to more specific functional planning at the departmental level in order to be truly effective.

Second, he would agree that the question of organizational location is largely a practical one of "what will work best," but the PPB system in operation should further the utilization of comprehensive planning as a framework for functional planning, and its implementation through budgeting and program direction.

Third, he cannot agree that the "planning" process in long-range planning is really distinct from the "planning" component in a PPB system. The latter is simply a more immediate application of the same techniques on a short-range basis in the light of current resource constraints. These annual or multiyear resource allocation issues should be framed and resolved in the context of overall development goals. The department has been doing in-depth analysis on a selective basis with the collaboration of the functional agencies concerned, and, after all, the new office also will have to be selective about its initial undertakings wherever it is located.

Fourth, cost effectiveness should not be the central concern of the new analytical efforts, but rather program and policy issues--which involve many intangibles. Moreover, he doesn't believe in the reality of the distinction between public provision of immediate consumer goods and services as program objectives in a PPB system, and the long-run payoffs from public investment as the focus or objectives of a comprehensive planning effort. Frequently, these turn out to be opposite sides of the same coin.

Mr. Arnold--Pointed out here that there cannot really be one "best" solution; the three crucial staff agencies all have their own important parts to play. What we are really trying to do is to establish both vertical and horizontal channels of free-flowing information, comment, technical aids, and expertise in functional program areas as well as in processes. That being so, it seems appropriate to remind the group that the Task Force discussions brought out a couple of pretty generally accepted conclusions; (1) strong linkages and willing cooperation are of more importance than formal organizational arrangements; and (2) an interdepartmental advisory group (to replace the old Interdepartmental Committee for State Planning) could be of enormous assistance in working out and maintaining such linkages.

Overall comprehensive planning procedures and functions seem to him distinguishable from the more immediate, analytical efforts and the marshalling of current factual materials required of a PPB effort. For one thing, comprehensive or long-range planning efforts are oriented toward future development and desirable goals without necessary regard to current resource constraints that set bounds for annual, even multiyear, program decisions. But longer range planning efforts offer possibilities for important inputs into a PPB system. Some of the examples of such inputs that were discussed in the Task Force meetings were: projections of public service requirements; forecasting of long-term manpower trends; formulation and carrying out of econometric models for the state; and development of matrices of industrial inputs and outputs and of companion matrices of public facility and land use interrelations.

His own view is that the most important consideration is not to permit the new staff unit and its activities to be submerged in any present operation or set of procedures. It needs high visibility, dynamic leadership, and a "prestige" location. If it were not for the advantages to be gained from existing interdepartmental relationships and lines of communication, and the logistical support that can be afforded by a going organization, these considerations would point to location in the Governor's immediate office. He believes, however, that with care and determination both kinds of advantages can be realized--prestige and separate identity as well as strong logistical support. The Governor's appointment of the Director would provide additional leverage.

Dean of the School of Public Administration--On the whole, he believes the Task Force has produced an eminently workable proposal. His one major disagreement with the proposed arrangement is that, for a number of reasons--most of which have already been mentioned--he would very much prefer a completely independent Office of Program Planning and Coordination attached only to the Governor's Executive Office. Failing that, he thought the right organizational choice had been made.

Like Mr. Arnold, his main concern if the proposed placement within the Department of Administration is followed would be that departmental responsibility for the new PPB activities be kept to a minimum--that the arrangement be essentially one of "housing" the new unit and supplying supporting staff and services. He recognizes that additional strengths may be gained from being a part of a strong-going department, particularly if a tight budget situation should operate to hold the new unit down to pretty skeletal staffing. For one thing, more funds might be devoted to professional salaries if some costs of clerical and administrative staff and services could be absorbed by the "host" department. There could be intangible gains too. For example, academically-oriented specialists and consultants who were working on technical PPB activities might more quickly and easily acquire the "governmental" and public administration orientation they will need. Another incidental gain could flow from location in this particular department which is responsible for personnel system and employee training, since recruitment and staff development are bound to be urgent concerns of the new effort.

His first choice, however, would still be for an independent unit in the Executive Office of the Governor. Most of the reasons for this strong preference can be summarized in the concept that a PPB system is in essence an improved tool for executive leadership and decision making. The Task Force recognized this principle in classifying the functions of such a unit as (a) staff service to the Governor, and (b) guidance to the whole of the executive branch.

The Governor--Intervened here to say he was most appreciative of the straightforward way in which comments had been addressed to the practical realities of working out a viable administrative arrangement for this new activity. Such an attitude augured well for the willing collaboration such an effort would require. Most of the main considerations bearing on the issues of organizational placement seemed to have been pretty well outlined by now, and he would like to hear an expression of views on the second set of questions he had posed at the beginning of the discussion; i.e., what should be the main thrust of the initial effort?

Mr. Arnold--Suggested that it might be useful to start off this part of the discussion with a quick summary of the Task Force's preliminary conclusions on the major initial steps for instituting a PPB system. They had blocked out the following activities for intensive attention by the new unit in the early stages of the effort:

1. Tentative identification and formulation of governmental objectives and broad program categories for the statewide "program structure."
2. Preparation and issuance of guidelines, instructions, and operating procedures for participating agencies--covering both further refinement of the subcategories of the program structure and preparation of materials for the tentative multiyear program and financial plan.
3. Identification of major issues facing the state government in the near future which should be given priority for program analysis effort on a selective basis, and an early identification of the data requirements for these efforts.
4. Identify (with the help of agency heads) appropriate personnel for participation in PPBS activities and arrange for their orientation and training.

The Task Force realized, of course, that these are not one-time tasks, but they felt that they should be given strong emphasis from the beginning, even though resources might have to be spread pretty thinly. The general view was, he thought--and he would be glad to have this corrected or amplified by the individual members of the group present--that this list represented key components of the new way of looking at program development issues and resource allocations and, therefore, they all ought to be given prominence from the very beginning. Ultimately, the value of the system would lie in the way it was used. Effective participation was more likely to be gained if agency and department heads (and participating staff) were given a clear picture at the outset of the scope of the effort and the relationships between their agencies and the central unit.

Commissioner of Planning and Economic Development--His greatest concern is that we may be overselling the idea that it is possible to do a PPB system cheaply--in terms of both time and dollars. For one thing, we need a greatly improved information base; for another, we will require a substantial buildup of qualified personnel. Therefore, he believes the two most crucial activities for the early years are training and improvement of the data base. Adequate staffing--for both the central unit and the line agencies--will be a major problem for a long time to come.

For the immediate future, it should be possible to put together a team that possesses the necessary combination of skills for blocking out the materials needed to launch the PPB effort--the tentative program structure, the first instructions and guidelines, etc.--if some staff is drafted from program agencies and some outside consultants are used.

But the long-run effectiveness of the system will depend on development of the necessary internal capabilities, and each department should have the staff capabilities for producing the department's functional plan, developing its program recommendations, making the necessary reports, and participating in program analyses that involve its program responsibilities. The same also should be said for its data collection responsibilities when those are clarified and assigned.

Dean of the School of Public Administration--He certainly agrees that adequate staffing will be a major--and really troublesome--problem for the central unit and for most agencies. It also will be a continuing problem. He is inclined to think, however, that other activities should not be held in abeyance during a "tooling-up" period in which crash training programs would be carried on. For one thing, it will be important to publicize the PPB system concepts, and that means that all its major components and implications need to be seen in relation to each other. In order to work effectively, the system will have to be widely understood and accepted sympathetically. It seems we all are in agreement with that.

Secondly, there are some kinds of training that can be begun fairly soon and will be accomplished within a comparatively brief period. For people who have been through these short training programs, it will be important to have an opportunity to use their new skills and techniques. There is danger of losing momentum if we do not do as much as we can as soon as we can.

For example, some jurisdictions have begun to use the "Issue Paper," or some similar document, as a starting point for their PPB efforts. In essence, the Issue Paper is an initial blocking out of the salient characteristics of some significant governmental issue. It identifies the then apparent options with some appraisal of them, and makes recommendations for appropriate program analysis--or even immediate program proposals when the situation demands quick action, with suggestions of evaluation efforts that should follow. This kind of activity can be much more than a transitional step toward the substantive work of a PPB system; it affords an opportunity for training staff in analytical skills, and it can have substantial value for the illumination of immediate policy issues.

There are a number of things that can be done to build up the capacity of present staff, especially those with a fairly wide background of public service. For example, two kinds of programs might be organized in the early months:

1. Orientation programs for agency heads and key staff, to gain the necessary understanding of the purposes and uses of the new system and assure staff support for its application.
2. Intensive in-service training programs for selected staff members who will be working directly on PPB materials and instructions.

The University might be helpful in connection with the design of programs of these types, as well as by providing direct consultation for special aspects of the PPB effort, and by doing a little recruitment among our graduate students. There also are a number of course offerings at the University and at other institutions, as well as specialized PPB-oriented training programs under federal government and other auspices that should be explored as resources for staff development and training.

Commissioner of Administration--His views had been so well presented by the Dean that he had very little to add except that he was particularly pleased by the prospect of active collaboration by the University, both in the development of training opportunities and as a resource for the whole PPB effort.

Director of Budget and Finance--He was in general agreement with the Task Force list of activities for early and intensive attention. He would be the last to argue that budget making was not highly important for both analytical purposes and for program development as well--particularly when tentative resource allocations are displayed over a period of time, as in one of the key processes of the PPB system. He thought, however, that current budget-making procedures could stand for the time being, while the basic framework was being hammered out.

He would put heavy priority on development of the basic program structure and a uniform format for agency response as subcategories are developed to represent program activities. Clearly, it is also extremely important to begin immediately on orientation and in-service training of appropriate personnel in all agencies. University assistance with this would be highly advantageous, but he would hope that it also would expand its offerings of more formal training programs.

At the risk of repetition, he would like to urge again that budgetary procedures be brought more closely into line with program structures and with the format of the multiyear program and financial plans, as soon as there is a fairly firm framework to work with. Otherwise, we would be neglecting an important opportunity to gain more rational consideration of public expenditure issues.

MIDLANDIA

Appendix A

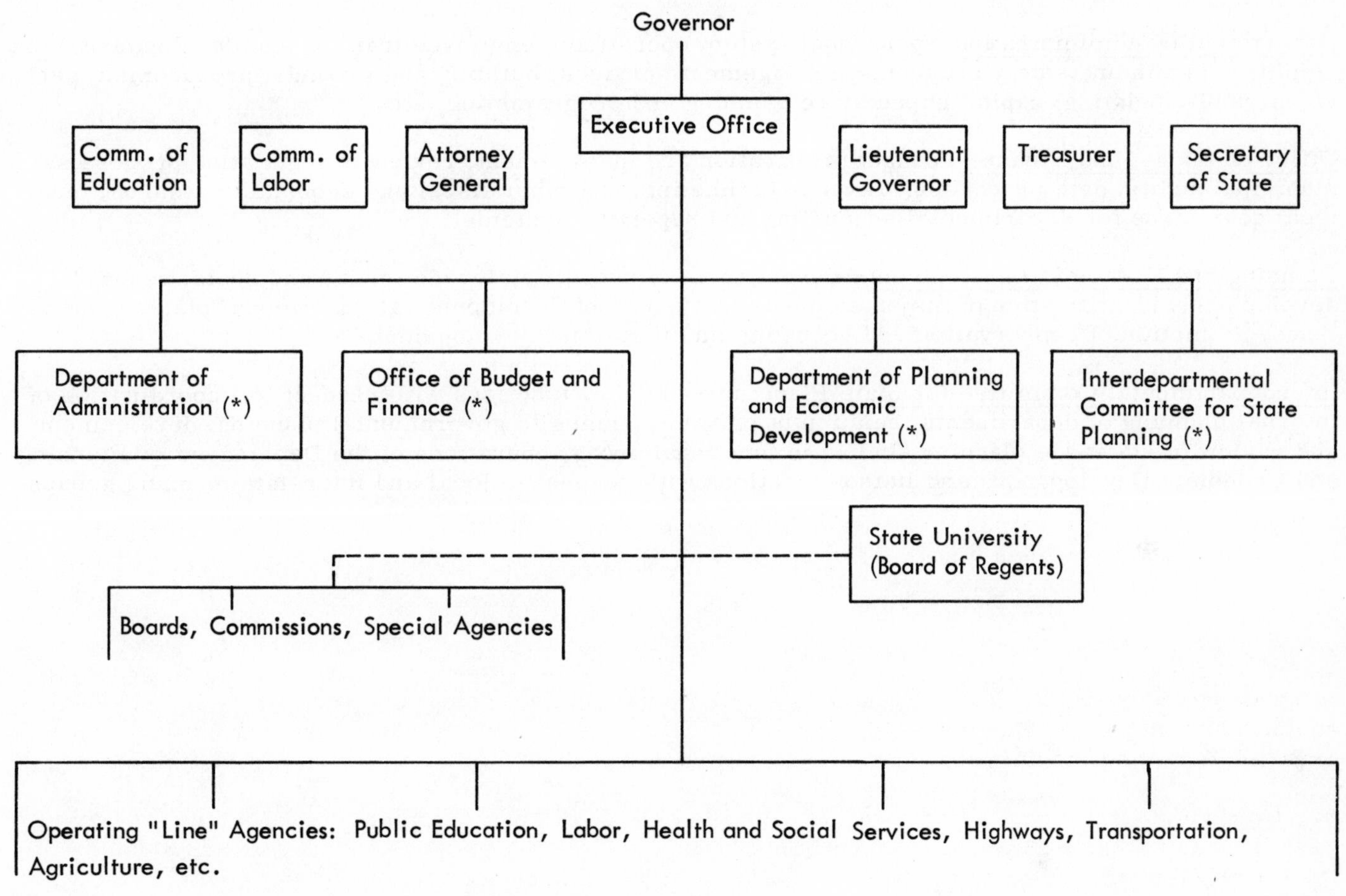

(*) Outline of principle functions in footnote.

Footnote to Appendix A

(*) Functions of the principal departments with direct staff relationships to the Governor:

Department of Administration--personnel system operations, employee training and development, employee health and safety programs, management services, building and grounds, procurement services, public printing, capital expenditure planning and programming, etc.

Office of Budget and Finance--budget preparation and management, review of legislative proposals, municipal audits, data processing, revenue estimating, and other fiscal and economic research, technical assistance for departmental accounting and reporting systems.

Planning and Economic Development--development of overall statewide issues and goals, resource development, identification of major elements in support of developmental goals, local planning assistance, promotion of conservation and economic and industrial development.

Interdepartmental Committee for State Planning--advisory functions with respect to: coordination of internal planning of departments, relation of private planning to governmental planning, development and review of statewide planning studies in functional areas, operations of the Department of Planning and Economic Development; and liaison functions with respect to local and interstate planning groups.

MIDLANDIA

Appendix B

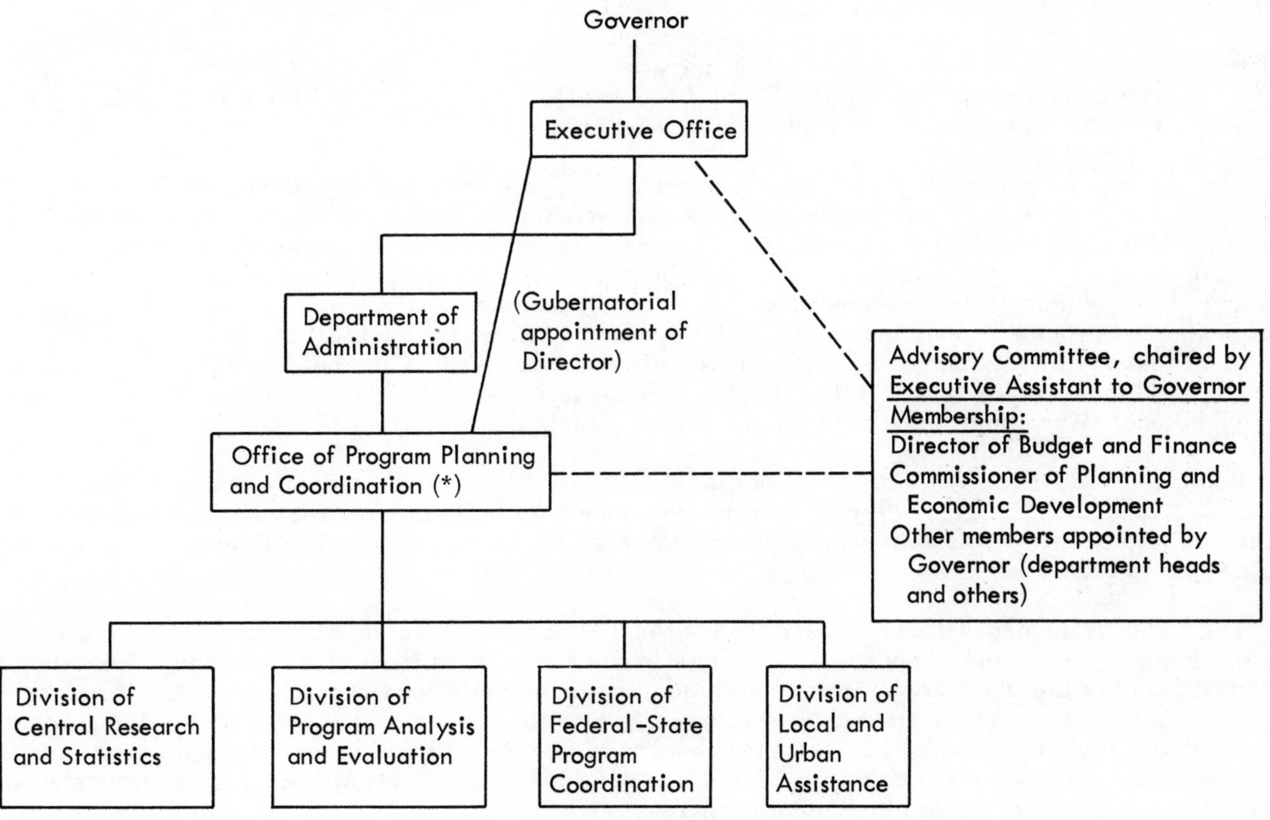

(*) Functions:

1. Review and staff functions for the Governor.
2. Guidance, direction, technical assistance--information services for line departments and agencies and other jurisdictions (general or special) within the state.
3. Basic research, statistical work (economic, demographic and fiscal, trends, projections, etc.), and clearing house and liaison functions.

A CASE OF DISCRIMINATION?

On June 17, 1963, John Trenton, an engineer in research and development, dropped by the Technical Recruitment Office in the Industrial Relations Department of Cromwell's Semiconductor Division. John's younger brother, Lincoln or Linc as he was called, was soon to be discharged from the U.S. Navy. The young man had completed two years of electrical engineering at the University of Nebraska. In 1959 he had left the University because of marginal grades and had joined the Navy. His career in naval electronics had been successful. Young Linc wanted to be considered for a technician's job at Cromwell when he was released from the service in July.

The personnel specialist, Bob Morsey, scanned the application. It appeared to be excellent. Bob remarked that there were a number of openings for technicians within the division and that the young man should fit right in. Bob thumbed through his requisition book which contained a listing of all approved openings within the division. From this book Bob extracted the names of all the supervisors who had noted job specifications approximating Linc's presumed qualifications. One of the supervisors was Dale Hunter. John asked that Dale's name be skipped. John felt his brother didn't have a prayer in that area. As John noted, "Dale has a great group. One of the best in the plant. However, every person working for him. . .all of them. . .are Druids. My brother isn't a Druid and isn't likely to become one. Why waste time having Dale review Linc's qualifications?"

Bob expressed disbelief. Any form of discrimination was against company policy. Could a supervisor have practiced religious discrimination long enough to build up a group without being detected? It seemed impossible. Was John wrong or was Personnel, like the husband in French comedies, simply the last to know?

The Cromwell Corporation had been founded in 1928 in Los Angeles, California. Originally it had marketed a small line of consumer products in the electronics field. The founder, Alexander Buchanan, was of the old school. He was domineering, autocratic, and charismatic. Gruff and outspoken, this first generation American was known to practice both religious and racial discrimination quite unabashedly. In addition, Mr. Buchanan was very conservative in his business dealings and in his political espousals. A frequently repeated company joke stated that Mr. Buchanan distrusted Calvin Coolidge because of Cal's left-wing tendencies.

During the depression years, the company not only survived but prospered in a minor way. Cromwell was able to obtain several large and annually renewed contracts from the automobile industry. As the company slowly grew, the president's political conservatism became more evident. He was violently antiunion. His theory of business management might be best described as benevolent despotism. Authority and responsibility rested solely in his hands and were delegated downward as sparingly as possible. Communication was a one-way process from top downward. As the same time the Cromwell Corporation became noted for its solicitude for the employees' welfare. No one knew whether this solicitude stemmed from a genuine regard for the employees or whether it was simply a ploy to deter the unions. Regardless, working conditions for clerical and blue-collar workers were excellent. The six divisions of the company, all located in the Los Angeles area, were physically bright and cheerful, pay was standard for the area or above, all normal fringe benefits were included in the employment package, the company sponsored innumerable activities including athletic events, hobby clubs, sweetheart dances. In addition, the company instituted an excellent profit-sharing plan in which all of the employees shared equally in the company's good fortune.

The company prospered and grew in a modest way from 1928 through 1939. In 1939, Alexander Buchanan hired Dr. Donald Haler, a remarkable combination of scientist-inventor-administrator-businessman. Largely because of Dr. Haler's inventive genius and business acumen, Cromwell was able to market several products of immense value to the military. During the years 1940 through 1945, the company expanded enormously. Throughout the war years the practice of racial and religious discrimination diminished noticeably, because of the shortage of labor.

After World War II the company switched back to its consumer lines and continued to expand in a highly profitable manner. In 1947, the aging president promoted himself to Chairman of the Board and was replaced by his youthful son William, or Bill, aged 37. Bill was intelligent, diligent, capable. Totally unlike his father, Bill was a calm and careful administrator. He was an organization man. Bill was not, however, without humor and often attributed his rapid rise in the company to "a good mind, a darn good education, and being the owner's son." He was both respected and liked.

Two events of importance occurred in 1948. Cromwell entered the TV field which was to prove a major success. In the same year, Dr. Haler left the company. His leaving was without prejudice on either side. He simply no longer cared to live in the Los Angeles area. He had been offered a Full Professorship at the University of New Mexico in Albuquerque and had accepted. He remarked that he was exchanging the glories of business leadership for the glories of New Mexico's clear air. Even after leaving the corporation, Dr. Haler continued as a consultant on an irregular basis. In 1954, the founder and Chairman of the Board, Alexander Buchanan, died.

In 1956, Cromwell determined to enter the semiconductor business. The board of directors realized that an entrance into this new and largely untried field of electronics would require a large outlay of capital and would constitute a major gamble. Under the circumstances it was only logical for the still youthful president to turn once more to Dr. Haler. Dr. Haler was intrigued by the challenge and accepted with only one proviso. Dr. Haler would rejoin the company as director of the Semiconductor Division, provided the division was physically located in either Carlsbad or Albuquerque, New Mexico. The corporation agreed. It was a case of the mountain coming to Mohammed. With the establishment of the Albuquerque division, all racial and religious discriminations were abolished in theory. Perhaps to expiate old sins, President William Buchanan and Executive Vice President Donald Haler exerted every effort to eradicate all remnants of the old hiring inequities.

From 1956 to 1959, the Semiconductor Division, then the smallest of Cromwell's eleven divisions, struggled along. In 1959, however, several major scientific breakthroughs occurred. Business increased rapidly and the work force increased from approximately 860 in 1959 to over 5,000 in 1963.

After John Trenton had left the personnel office, Bob contemplated his next move. The accusation seemed too absurd to be true. Dale Hunter did not seem the type to discriminate on such an overt and continuing basis. Bob knew Dale both professionally and personally. He and Dale belonged to the same Naval Reserve unit and often drove back and forth from Reserve meetings in the same car-pool. Bob knew for a fact that Dale was a Druid. In spite of the improbability of John's accusation, Bob felt he should check it out.

Dale Hunter was an electrical engineer, age 37. He was Section Leader of the Tablo Final Test Quality Control Group. "Tablo" was the trade name for the fastest selling transistor or semiconductor then manufactured by the division. It was often referred to as the "bread and butter line" since it provided the profits for the expensive research and development work being undertaken by the division. The Tablo transistors were manufactured in the Tablo Production Department. The Tablo Production Final Test Group, a part of the Tablo Production Department, conducted the first quality control check. This group was under the supervision of Foreman Harry Turner. Here thirty-four young ladies fed the transistors into the automatic testers. The Tablo Final Test Quality Control Group under Dale Hunter worked with Harry Turner and his girls. They were not, however, in the same departments, since Dale's group was part of quality control. An organizational structure such as this placed a strain on both Harry and Dale and on the members of their respective groups. It was essential that rapport exist between the groups and that they cooperate with one another and coordinate their activities.

The Tablo Final Test Quality Control Group had three principal responsibilities:

a. To check semiconductors failing in the quality control test to determine, where possible, the reasons for failure.
b. To maintain the electronic transistor testers.
c. To schedule testing in such a manner that rush orders would receive priority.

Within the Tablo Final Test Quality Control Group, Bob found that Dale had sixteen men and a clerk-steno. Two of the men were foremen and the rest were technicians who ranged from labor grade 23-technician trainee to labor grade 30-engineering-aide. (See Table 1 and Figure 1.)

Bob obtained the personnel records of all seventeen people reporting directly to Section Leader Hunter. Normally, it is difficult to ascertain an employee's religion from this personnel folder. This is not true in the case of Druids. First of all, their names tend to be standardized with such names as Grant, Brent, and Lee very popular. Secondly, Druids are concentrated heavily in one state with a fairly heavy sprinkling in nearby states. Thirdly, certain schools are run by the Druidic religion. Rarely does a non-Druid attend. Fourthly, young Druids are in the habit of going on "missions" for their church between their 18th and 20th years. Fifthly, Druids, a very closely knit group, frequently list a high-ranking member of their church as a reference.

Within 30 minutes Jerry had determined that all seventeen of the personnel reporting to Dale Hunter were in fact Druids. There wasn't a shadow of a doubt in any case. Of the seventeen, thirteen had noted "missionary work" on their applications. Of the remaining four, all had listed a member of the church hierarchy as a reference and had placed "Druidic church work" after the question "outside interests."

Such religious discrimination directly countervened Section 7.1 of the Industrial Relations Manual of the Cromwell company. Section 7 of this Industrial Relations Manual is devoted to "Hiring Practices." The first subsection, 7.1, states that there will be no discrimination based on race, religion, creed, or national origin.

Dale Hunter could not possibly have built an organization of seventeen people, all his co-religionists, by accident. Bob wondered how this violation of company policy had been achieved without the Technical Recruitment Office becoming suspicious. Bob believed that this could have been done only after careful planning by Dale. Within the Technical Recruitment Office there were three personnel specialists including Bob himself, two secretaries and a file girl. (See Figure 2.) Each specialist was responsible for all of the open requisitions. There was no breakdown of responsibility assigning openings, within specific areas, to certain personnel specialists. While most of the candidates were initially contacted by Technical Recruitment through advertising or employment agencies, a number of technicians were "walk-ins." A "walk-in" candidate simply walked in the door and requested an interview. Sometimes he asked for a specific personnel interviewer and sometimes he had been asked to come in by a supervisor with an opening. Looking over the hiring dates of the 17 people in the Tablo Final Test Quality Control Group, Bob realized that they had been hired over a period of forty-four months. Without exception they had been "walk-in" candidates. Without exception they had been referred to a specific personnel specialist by someone in the Tablo Final Test Quality Control Group, but never by Mr. Hunter himself. Interestingly, they had staggered their referrals so that Mr. Mark Thompson, personnel specialist, saw one, Mr. Clark Brose, personnel specialist, saw the next, and Bob Morsey saw the third. The fourth candidate, of course, was seen by Mr. Thompson and so on. Since the hiring had been scattered throughout the Technical Recruitment Office, no one personnel specialist was aware of the hiring pattern established by Mr. Hunter. There could be no doubt that discriminatory hiring practices had been practiced for several years. Personnel was indeed the last to know!

It was obvious that the situation could not be ignored. Bob discussed the problem with Carl Younger, the Director of Industrial Relations. Carl was, of course, disturbed. He was also perplexed. He first asked how Dale had been able to accomplish this coup without detection. Bob explained his theory to Carl, and Carl accepted it as probable if not definite. In addition, Carl was genuinely curious as to why no one had ever complained about such an obvious breach of corporate policy.

As a first step it was agreed that Bob should make discreet inquiries throughout the various final test groups in Quality Control and in those areas of Tablo Production which had close and frequent contact with Dale Hunter's group. Since this was a situation which necessitated discretion, Carl suggested that Bob utilize the grapevine and personal friends rather than a "through channels" frontal attack.

Bob first contacted Joe Roget, a young engineer in charge of the Silicon Control Rectifier Final Test Quality Control Group. Joe was a peer of Dale's and knew him well. His group worked along side Dale's although in a different product area. Joe was a close personal friend of Bob's and expressed amazement that personnel was unaware of Dale's hiring policy. It seemed that everyone knew and always had known that Dale hired only Druids. Joe happily volunteered the information that Dale's group was exceptionally able. The men were very hard working, dependable, and exhibited an astonishing degree of cooperation with one another and with the personnel of the Tablo Production Department. Ruefully Joe admitted that his own group did not begin to come up to the standards established by Dale's.

Second, Bob checked with Charles Galliger, the Director of the Tablo Production Department. (See Figure 3.) Upon inquiry, Charles expressed amusement that personnel did not know of Dale's hiring policy. Charles' opinion of personnel was none too high, and he was overtly delighted that once again someone had "pulled the wool over personnel's eyes." Charles was able to offer little positive information. He did state, however, that he rarely had any reason to complain about the activities of Dale Hunter's group. He felt very fortunate in having this particular group within quality control doing his final test work.

Next, Bob had a long chat with Harry Turner, foreman of the Tablo Production Department girls who worked in the Tablo Production Final Test area. Harry also was aware of Dale's hiring policy. At the outset he was visibly irritated that anyone in Personnel should see fit to investigate Dale. Harry believed that Dale's final test group was far and away the best final test group not only in Cromwell but in the semiconductor industry. Harry stated that all of the men were dependable, hard working, and cooperative. More than anything else Harry appreciated the fact that they did not swear and kept their hands off his girls. Harry stated emphatically that he did not care what their religious beliefs were. So long as they had clean mouths and did not bother the girls he did not care if they painted themselves green and worshipped the Himalayan mountains. Toward the end of the interview, Harry's irritability evaporated. Harry expressed the opinion that no one had ever reported Dale's group to Personnel simply because most people regarded his group as superior. Under the circumstances, why rock the boat?

There was little or no doubt in Bob's mind regarding the excellence of Dale's group. However, he felt it wise to check and double check. A thorough investigation of company records revealed that not one grievance had ever been filed by any member of Dale Hunter's group. The tardiness record was the lowest of any final test group in Quality Control and the second lowest in the entire plant. Interestingly, the only group with a better tardiness record was the plant guards. Since the guards were in charge of the accumulation of tardiness records, their own performance was somewhat suspect. In terms of absenteeism, Dale's group was in the lowest tenth percentile. While good, this record was not outstanding. Bob later confirmed that some minimal absenteeism was authorized by Dale so that the members of his group might attend to certain "church work."

The next step was obviously a confrontation with Dale Hunter himself. Bob did not anticipate this meeting with relish. He felt certain Dale would either deny any duplicity or, realizing that a denial was pointless, resort to histrionics. The actual meeting was amusing in retrospect. Dale readily acknowledged that he hired only Druids. In addition, he confirmed Bob's suspicion that the hiring had been planned well in advance with the stated purpose of fooling Technical Recruitment. There was no evidence whatsoever of chagrin. Far from feeling a sense of guilt, Dale felt an evident pride in his accomplishment and was more than happy to discuss it.

Dale volunteered the information that most of his recruits had come either from the central Druidic employment agency in Los Angeles or from Duridic bishops in the towns throughout New Mexico. Before even coming to the plant, a Druidic candidate would be interviewed away from the plant by Dale and his foremen. If they considered the candidate acceptable, the man was unofficially hired. The man was instructed to come into the plant and to ask for a specific personnel specialist.

Dale had every reason to be proud of the record his group had established. He felt they were personable, technically competent, and cooperative not only amongst themselves but with the Tablo Production Final Test Group. Dale further pointed out that his men felt more comfortable in a homogeneous group since they were not subject to ridicule by non-Druids, that the temptation to proselyte was minimized, that there was no smoking or drinking of any stimuli, and no foul language. Dale stated, somewhat smugly, that his was one of the few groups in the entire plant where a "decent man" could work without any feeling of regret or estrangement.

Amazingly, Dale hotly denied that he was in any way discriminating against non-Druids. Repeatedly, Dale stated that he, a Druid, hired only Druids and would not object if other supervisors adopted similar practices. Dale also pointed out that he had never once refused to interview a worthy candidate recommended by Technical Recruitment. Bob interjected that such a courtesy interview was akin to whipping a dead horse since Dale had no intention of hiring any of these non-Druid referees. Dale retorted that this was correct. However, he made it an ironclad rule always to refer worthy non-Druid candidates to other supervisors who had openings. Dale not only referred these candidates but followed up the referrals and made it a point to help, where possible, in the placement. With a sly grin Dale displayed a list of twenty-three candidates, all non-Druids, whom he had helped to place in other areas. He volunteered to give this list to Bob and Bob accepted. The interview ended on a note of cordiality. Dale seemed happy to discuss his achievement. Bob was baffled by Dale's intransigence regarding the question of religious discrimination.

Painstakingly Bob checked out every one of the twenty-three non-Druids whom Dale had allegedly helped to place. Each was personally contacted and each confirmed that Dale had indeed interviewed him in depth. In addition, each had been shown around the Tablo Final Test Quality Control area, introduced to the personnel, and shown every courtesy. None was aware at the time why he was not hired to work in Dale's group. Each of the twenty-three, however, knew that Dale had been instrumental in placing him elsewhere in the Division. Many came to realize, at a later date, that they had been discriminated against because of religion. None displayed any concern or resentment. After all, each had come looking for a job and had found one. Why "get shook"?

In spite of this, it seemed obvious that Dale was practicing what appeared to Bob to be an overt and vicious form of discrimination. At Carl Younger's suggestion, Bob's investigation was written up in detail. Carl, Dale, and Bob had a formal meeting three weeks to a day after John Trenton had first reported discrimination in Dale's hiring practices. Dale's conduct at this meeting was similar to his first discussion with Bob. He readily admitted that he hired only Druids, felt no chagrin for doing so, and calmly denied any discrimination in his hiring practices.

When it became apparent that Dale had no intention of modifying his discriminatory hiring practices, Carl reluctantly informed him that the matter would have to be referred to Dale's superior, Dick Stangle, the head of Final Test Quality Control Engineering. Dale stated quite frankly that he felt this matter would be ironed out with Dick. Carl was quick to point out that in all probability, Dick would wish to refer this matter to George Nattell, the Manager of Quality Control. George was noted for his long, black cigar and short fuse. Carl elaborated upon possible disastrous consequences for Dale should this matter reach George. After several moments of reflection, Dale stated that he would not change his hiring policies and that if George wished to take drastic action, that was his privilege.

The next morning Bob's report was submitted to Dick Stangle. Realizing the seriousness of the situation, Dick referred the matter to George Nattell's attention that same day. Immediately after reading this report, George scheduled a meeting with Dick Stangle and Dale Hunter. Neither Carl nor Bob was present. Dick Stangle, however, told Carl that Dale had remained intransigent with regard to his discriminatory hiring practices, had refused to admit that he was in any way in the wrong, and had refused to change his modus operandi. Dick had frankly considered Dale's attitude incredible.

EPILOGUE

Within the next five working days, George had transferred 50 percent of Dale's personnel to other areas in Quality Control. He had stripped Dale of all authority to interview and hire. While Dale remained as section leader of the Tablo Final Test Quality Control Group, he was no longer able to submit any personnel actions such as promotions, pay increases, or reclassifications without the co-signature of Dick. In the three months that followed all but two of the Druids still remaining in Dale's group were transferred out and non-Druids either hired from outside or transferred into Dale's group from within the plant.

Several weeks after the "explosion," Bob had coffee with George. A volatile man, George was still upset. In George's opinion, Dale's single greatest mistake was repeating his belief that every supervisor should have the privilege of hiring people and only people of his own faith. As George said, "I took him at his word. I am his supervisor, and by God I'm no Druid."

Table 1

TABLO FINAL TEST QUALITY CONTROL GROUP

Name	Personnel Specialist	Grade	Classification	Age	Salary	Hire Date
Dale Hunter	No record	51	Section Leader Engineer, Class A	37	$212 wk	9/59
Nair Shay	Clerical	23	Clerk-steno	22	76 wk	Transfer "in"
Rick Tarcon	No record	30	(Foreman) Engr. Aide	45	167 wk	10/59
Lee Bradford	Clark Brose	27	Tech Cl "A"	33	132 wk	12/60
Brent Leavitt	Bob Morsey	26	Tech Cl "B"	29	127 wk	5/61
Johnnie Freestone	Mark Thompson	25	Tech Cl "C"	24	112 wk	10/61
Lee Sayner	Bob Morsey	24	Tech Cl "D"	24	96 wk	12/61
Grant Garlick	Bob Morsey	24	Tech Cl "D"	23	92 wk	9/62
Bob Olason		23	Tech Trainee	22	80 wk	Transfer "in"
Tom Tremond	Clark Brose	23	Tech Trainee	21	72 wk	11/62
Brent Johnston	Bob Morsey	28	(Foreman) Sr. Tech.	27	150 wk	9/60
Grant Smith	Mark Thompson	27	Tech Cl "A"	36	134 wk	2/61
Grant Dunn	Clark Brose	25	Tech Cl "C"	25	117 wk	8/61
Taft Benson	Clark Brose	24	Tech Cl "D"	23	96 wk	3/62
Trevor Kilgore	Mark Thompson	24	Tech Cl "D"	23	95 wk	6/62
Gary Holbert		23	Tech Trainee	21	83 wk	Transfer "in"
Mike Toomey	Mark Thompson	23	Tech Trainee	21	81 wk	2/63
Lionel Dickson	Bob Morsey	23	Tech Trainee	20	72 wk	5/63

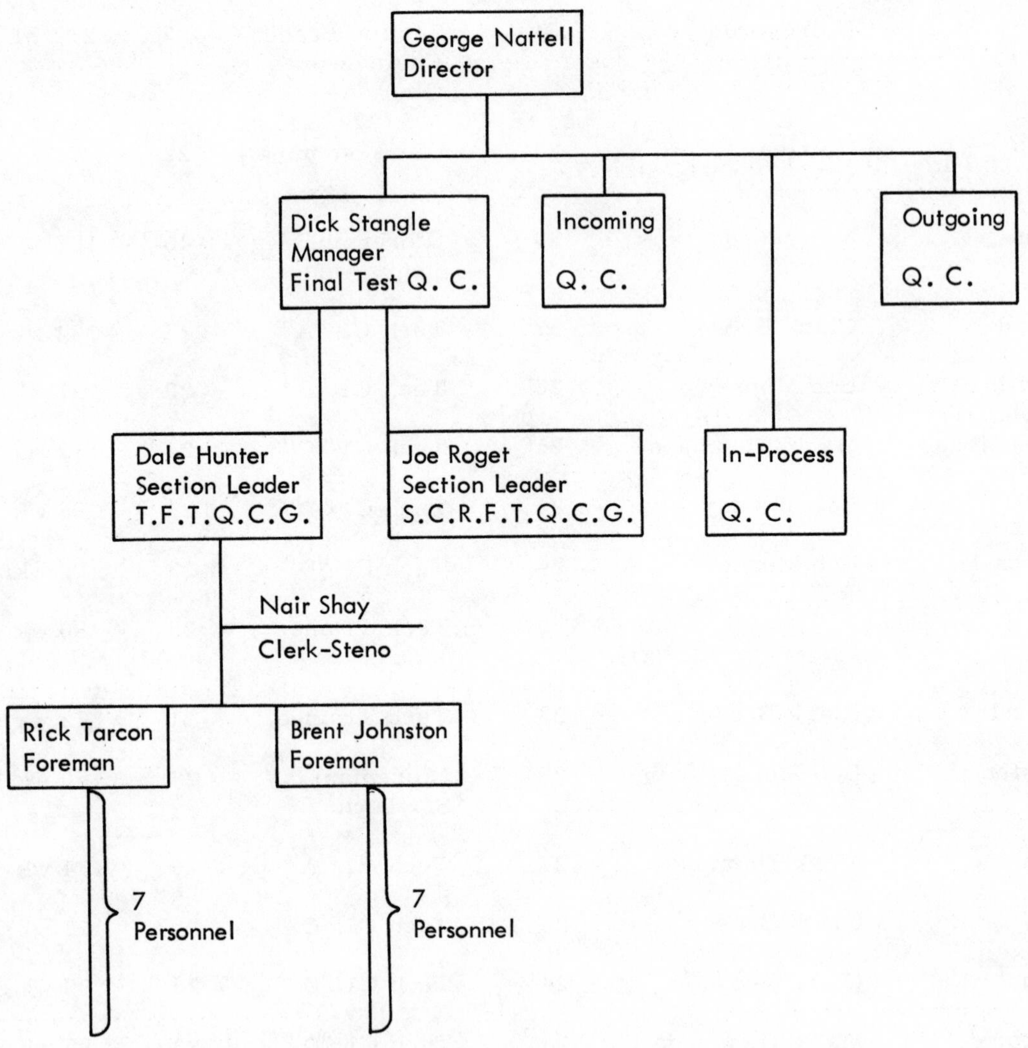

Figure 1. Organization of the Quality Control Department, Cromwell Semiconductor Products Division.

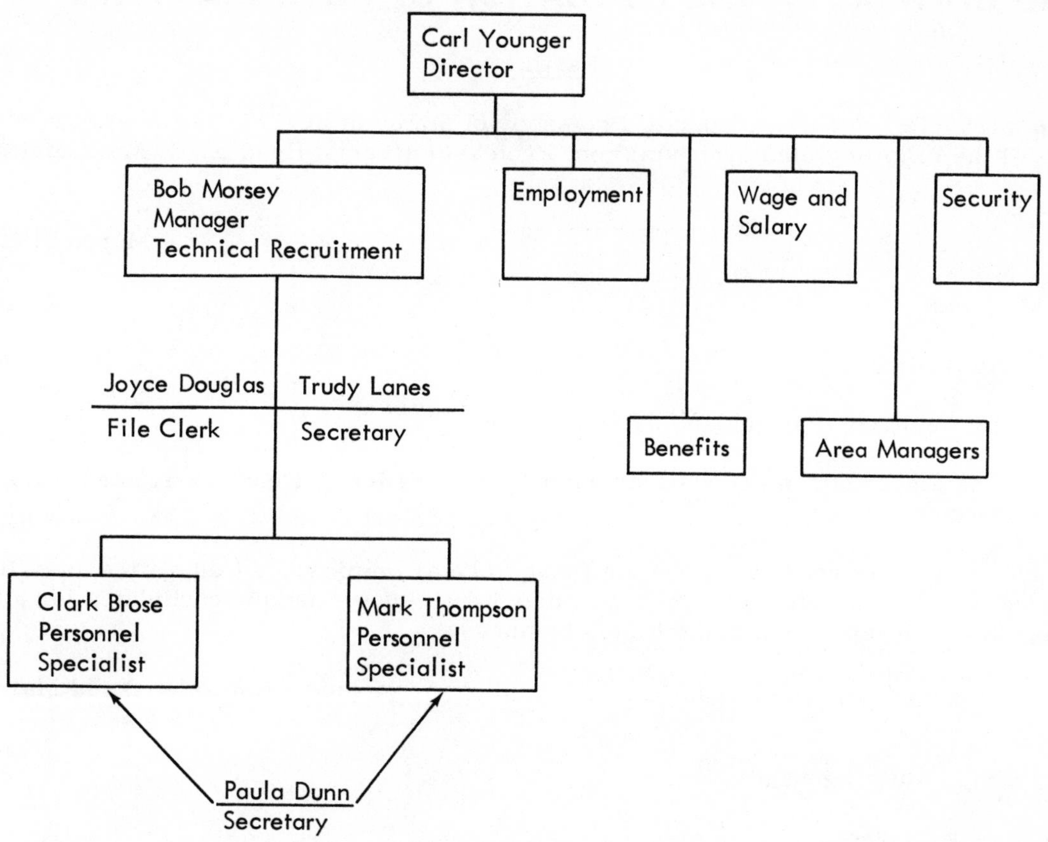

Figure 2. Organization of the Human Relations Department, Cromwell Semiconductor Products Division.

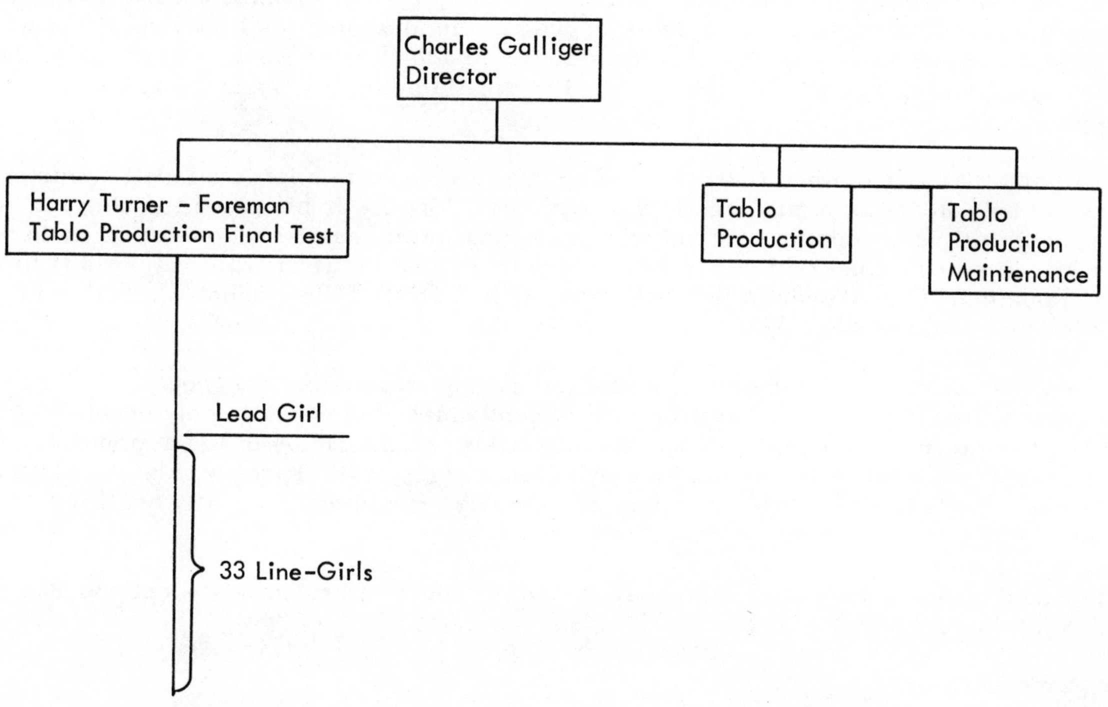

Figure 3. Organization of the Tablo Production Department, Cromwell Semiconductor Products Division.

SPAULDING UNIVERSITY: THE EDUCATION OF PETER TOPPING

Part I

On March 9, 1966, Dr. Adams, Associate Professor of Mathematical Statistics at Spaulding University, received the following memorandum from Professor Harris, Head of the Mathematics Department:

March 8, 1966

TO: Mark Adams

FROM: Oscar B. Harris

SUBJECT: Admission of Topping and related issues

Enclosed is a copy of a memorandum which I have mailed to Dean Goodwin and other interested persons.

You are relieved of your duties on our Departmental Admissions Committee as of this date. Please return any materials which you may have concerning any candidates for admission or other aspects of the committee's business.

Professor Harris enclosed a carbon copy of the following memorandum, also dated March 8.

TO: Dean Wallace W. Goodwin

FROM: Oscar B. Harris

SUBJECT: Attached letter

I am enclosing a copy of a letter received by me from a prospective graduate student.

It should be noted that Dr. Adams has been a member of our departmental admissions committee representing applied mathematics. It was upon his recommendation that Mr. Topping was admitted to study for a Ph.D. degree in the Mathematics Department. It was also upon his recommendation that the decision was made to offer Mr. Topping one of the two National Fellowships which were assigned to the Mathematics Department by the University.

As late as March 1, when I wrote Mr. Topping offering him a National Fellowship, Dr. Adams did not inform us of his negotiations with Mr. Topping or his plans to enter into any negotiations with Mr. Topping. When I was preparing letters on the fellowship, I could not locate Mr. Topping's folder. I called Adams and found that he had it. He returned it to me but, as mentioned above, with no indication that he had offered the student admission in Statistics or an alternative appointment.

Needless to say I find this entire procedure unconscionable on two grounds. First, this seems to be an outrageous pirating of a student which was possible only because of Dr. Adams' position on our committee. Second, his failure to inform us of his action delays our offer of a fellowship to an alternative by at least eight days. In the highly competitive recruitment of graduate students this may prevent our attracting an equally qualified student.

The attached letter to Professor Harris from the prospective graduate student was dated March 5. It reads as follows:

Dear Professor Harris:

Thank you very much for your very generous offer of a National Fellowship. I regret that I am unable to accept it, however. Professor Mark Adams of the Statistics Department has offered me admission to the new doctor's degree program in his department and also a very generous research assistantship offer. He has advised me that the National Fellowship is not applicable to study in statistics, but only in mathematics. Since I have decided to accept Professor Adams' offer, I am unable to accept your offer. I felt I should inform you of this so that you can make the fellowship available to someone else who needs it.

I regret that I will not, after all, be studying in your department, but I will be studying in a very closely allied department and, I understand, I will be taking a number of courses from the Mathematics Department. I appreciate your efforts, and I hope to meet you and other mathematics faculty members next fall when I enroll at Spaulding University.

Sincerely,

Peter C. Topping

Adams had been a member of the faculty of Spaulding University for almost two years. His training and professional credentials were considered excellent, and he came to Spaulding University highly recommended. His former colleagues held high aspirations for him and felt he would make significant contributions to research. They also expected him to take special interest in his students and in the educational goals of the university.

Dr. Adams held an appointment as Associate Professor of Mathematical Statistics in the School of Science. Dr. Adams was also an Associate Professor of Mathematics in the Mathematics Department, which was located in the School of Liberal Arts. Three other professors--James, Stanford, and Thomas--were also faculty members of both these departments. A partial organization chart of Spaulding University is shown in Figure 1.

Dr. Adams had recently been promoted to the rank of Associate Professor. At this time the Faculty Promotions Committee had described him as a successful teacher and scholar, and as a contributing member of the University faculty. Some of the older professors in the Mathematics Department had been against his promotion at this time, speaking of him as "an outspoken and aggressive young man, who should be promoted eventually--perhaps next year--but not at this time." The Head of the Mathematics Department, Professor Oscar Harris, however, had intervened and had recommended that Dr. Adams be promoted. During these deliberations Dean Goodwin commented, "Often I could kiss him because of the contributions he makes and the commitment he has given us--but he is often a problem to a smooth-running organization."[1]

As a part of his duties, Dr. Adams was a member of the Admissions Committee for graduate students in the Mathematics Department, where he represented those faculty whose interests were in applied mathematics. The Admissions Committee operated on a subcommittee basis. Each member of the committee sent applications for graduate study to his colleagues who were interested in the area of mathematics which he represented on the departmental committee. Decisions about admission were made in these subcommittees representing different areas of mathematics. In addition to Adams, the applied mathematicians were the three professors: James, Stanford, and Thomas, who held joint appointments in both Statistics and Mathematics.

[1]Since deliberations about promotions are secret, these discussions were unknown to Adams.

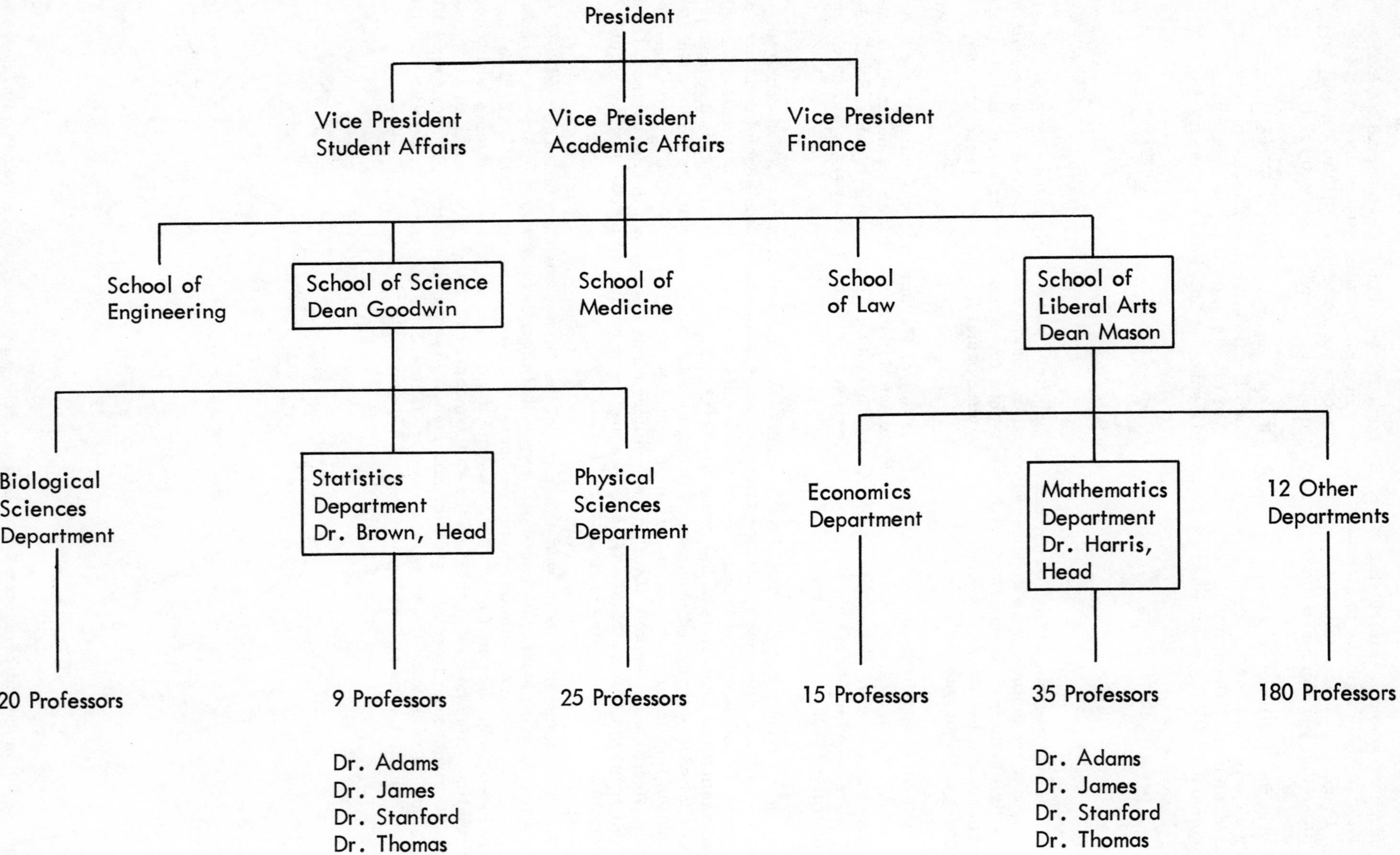

Figure 1. Partial organization chart of Spaulding University.

Dr. Adams also participated in the work of the Admissions Committee for graduate students in the Statistics Department. This was a new department at Spaulding University. It operated on a very informal basis. All professors were members of the Admissions Committee for graduate students. This new department was an attempt to bring together members of different departments to collaborate in initiating a new program of graduate study. Each of the faculty in the Statistics Department was also a member of another department: four were in mathematics, two in physical sciences, two in economics, and one in biological sciences. All of the faculty involved saw this as an exciting new venture in interdisciplinary education.

Professor Adams' first reaction to the memoranda which he received from the Head of the Mathematics Department was one of bewilderment. Upon rereading these memoranda, he felt personally hurt--he saw Dr. Harris' comments as a personal attack upon himself and the ethics of his behavior. Adams became angry and commented, "This is a vicious personal attack." It was not until Adams read the memoranda for a third time that he noticed that the one which he found so offensive was not addressed to him. He had received a carbon copy; the memorandum was addressed to Dean Goodwin. "Poor Wally Goodwin is always getting into some kind of squeeze play between some administrator and me."

At that moment, Dr. Roger Brown, the Head of the Statistics Department, came into Adams' office and told Adams that Dean Goodwin had called and told him about Harris' memoranda. Adams then shared his feelings with Brown, and Brown suggested to Adams that he visit Dean Goodwin of the School of Science before contacting Dr. Harris. Whereupon, Dr. Adams called Dean Goodwin and told him that he was on his way over to see him about the Topping affair.

Dean Goodwin wondered what he should say to Professor Adams. Dean Goodwin liked Dr. Adams and considered him an unusually bright and energetic young mathematical statistician, but a headache to an administrator.

SPAULDING UNIVERSITY: THE EDUCATION OF PETER TOPPING

Part II

Professor Adams began his conversation with Dean Goodwin by saying, "Wally, I'm hurt, offended, and mad!" Adams then suggested that he should first inform the Dean about the facts of the Topping affair, and that he then would like to ask the Dean's advice as to how he should respond to the Head of the Mathematics Department. Dean Goodwin agreed that this seemed to be the best way to proceed, and Adams began with an historical account of the Topping affair:

"I am a member of the Admissions Committee for graduate students in the Mathematics Department, where I represent James, Stanford, Thomas, and myself. Earlier this year this committee decided to award a National Fellowship to one applicant in applied mathematics. Topping's application looked good and we decided to admit him, and to award him the National Fellowship. On February 1st, I informed Professor Harris of the committee's action. On the same day, Professor Harris wrote to Topping informing him that he had been admitted to the Mathematics Department. Now, according to the rules, the National Fellowship could not be offered to Topping until March 1st. And on February 16th, at the weekly luncheon of the Statistics Department, it was suggested that Topping's application to the Mathematics Department looked good and that he might make a good graduate student in statistics. I liked the idea, and that afternoon I wrote Topping a letter which said:

> Since you are interested in applied mathematics, I thought you might be interested in a new program of study which we have in statistics here at Spaulding University. I am enclosing a description of our program of study in statistics. Should you be interested in pursuing this further, please drop me a line.

My title clearly indicated that I was on the faculty of both the Mathematics and Statistics Departments. A week later, I received a letter from Topping indicating that he was "very excited" about the prospects of studying statistics at Spaulding, and he asked if we would consider him for admission as a graduate student in the Statistics Department. I was delighted! I checked out his application from the secretary in the Mathematics Department.

On March 1st, the Statistics Department agreed to admit Topping to study statistics, and we also decided to offer him a research assistantship. James and Thomas participated in this decision.

Incidently, the assistantship which we decided to offer Topping was not as lucrative as the National Fellowship in Mathematics. It does not pay quite as well and is for only one year in contrast to the three-year National Fellowship.

On March 1st Oscar Harris called me and asked me to return Topping's application materials, because he was going to write to Topping and offer him the National Fellowship. At the time, I thought about telling Harris that I was about to telephone Topping and offer him admission and an assistantship in statistics, but I didn't tell him--and the reason I didn't do so was because he sees our new Statistics Department to be in competition with the Mathematics Department. While James, Stanford, Thomas, and myself see this new department as a cooperative adventure, Harris always fails to see that <u>we</u> are members of <u>both</u> groups. He treats us, and especially me, as if we were not even a part of the Mathematics Department.

Given Harris' feelings about statistics, I was afraid that he would not offer Topping the National Fellowship in mathematics if he knew that I was about to call Topping; so I withheld that information. As you know, Harris is very resentful that part of his faculty chose to become involved in the Statistics Department. There are also some other mathematics professors who agree with him. Had Topping been offered fellowships by both departments, and had he chosen statistics, Harris would have lost face in his own eyes. I therefore figured that Harris would avoid this possibility by not entering into competition for a student.

I then called Topping. I introduced myself as a member of the Admissions Committee of both the Mathematics and Statistics Departments, and that I would wear two "hats" in our conversation. First, with my mathematics "hat" on, I said that Oscar Harris was writing him that same afternoon to offer him a National Fellowship for study in mathematics and that, as a mathematician, I hoped he would accept Harris' offer. I then said, speaking with my statistics "hat" on, we were prepared to offer him a research assistantship, and that I hoped he would decide to study statistics. We then discussed the two graduate programs for a while, and I ended the conversation with the statement that, "in any event, I personally hoped he would decide to study at Spaulding University."

I feel very self-righteous about this entire affair, since I feel that I acted in the best interests of Mathematics, Statistics, Spaulding University, and hopefully in the best interests of Peter Topping. I simply offered Topping an alternative, and he chose it. Last year we had a similar incident, but in that case the student chose to study mathematics; therefore, it did not come to the attention of Harris.

"Well, Wally, what do you think?"

DEAN GOODWIN: It seems to me that the only mistake you might have made, or at least the only complaint that Oscar Harris really has, is that you overlooked informing him of your plans on March 1st.

PROF. ADAMS: Okay, I can certainly give him that. I can't tell him that I "neglected" to inform him because of his own competitive feelings--he couldn't take that. But I can surely give him the fact that I neglected to inform him on March 1st that I was about to call Topping.

But how should I respond to Harris at this point? As I see it there are three major alternatives.

Indicently, I spoke with James about this, and he suggested that I use this opportunity to make a fool out of Harris by denying that I contacted Topping. While I admit that the possibility of making Harris look foolish is quite attractive to me at this moment, the long-run consequences of lying would be very difficult to undo.

So realistically, I see three alternatives. First, I could ignore him and his memos. Second, I could counterattack. I see his position as one of attack. Or, finally, I could try and negotiate with him. It seems to me that if I just leave things where they have fallen, this will not help the relations between the Mathematics and Statistics Departments. Our relations have never been very good. I want to be very careful and not let my personal feelings dictate a course of action which would further rupture the relations between these two departments.

What I would really like to do would be to make a cause celebre out of the Topping affair, and demand a public hearing before I turn in my Admissions Committee portfolio. I feel like asking Harris to state his charges before a meeting of the entire faculty of the Mathematics Department, and give me a public forum in which to answer him. Did you notice that his memo to you was also sent to "other interested persons." I really resent his involving you in this affair. I'm sorry that here you are again in another squeeze plan between these two departments. But I cannot let personal satisfaction further disrupt the relations between the two departments. I guess I will go in and see Oscar and see what we can work out together. If I admit that I might have informed him of my plans, I hope that he will see that I acted in the best interests of all concerned.

I hope that he can see two things. First, that there are two sides to this question. Second, and most important, I would like him to see that when he received the letter from Topping, it would have made sense for him to come to me and ask me what the facts were before he began sending memoranda in all directions without knowing what had happened.

DEAN GOODWIN: Mark, I think that if you speak with Oscar Harris you can work this out with him. Let me know what happens.

Later that day, Dr. Adams prepared a memorandum which he intended to carry with him to serve as a basis for discussion in his meeting with Dr. Harris. He brought a draft copy to Dean Goodwin to get his reactions. After reading the draft, the Dean said, "Mark, you're really upset about this aren't you," and suggested that the memo be "toned down" a little. The Dean also suggested that Adams carry the memo with him and say that this is a response which he felt like making but that talking it over with Oscar Harris was probably a better idea. Professor Adams replied, "Yes, that is what I had in mind," and returned to his office to make some alterations in his memorandum to Harris. When he finished, the final draft read as follows:

TO: Oscar Harris

FROM: Mark Adams

SUBJECT: Your Memorandum of March 8

Dear Oscar:

I am very offended by your memorandum:

(1) Your memorandum appears to me to be a deliberate and open act of disrespect. You did not ask me if your allegations were true, but rather you simply sent me a carbon copy of your memorandum to Dean Goodwin and "other interested persons."

(2) You imply that I behaved unethically in my relationship with Mr. Topping. I think that I behaved in the best interests of the Mathematics Department, the Statistics Department, and perhaps most importantly, in the best interests of Spaulding University and of Mr. Topping.

(3) You imply that I have not and cannot behave responsibly as a member of two departments. I think I have done so.

(4) You imply that in the case of Mr. Topping I acted as an individual. In fact, I acted as a representative of the Admissions Committees of the two departments.

In view of the fact that you publicized your feelings through your memorandum, I would like to answer it publicly at the next meeting of the faculty of the Mathematics Department.

Mark

cc: Dean John Mason

After this memorandum had been prepared, Professor Adams called Professor Harris and told him that he was on his way over to see him.

In thinking about his forthcoming conversation with Harris, Adams recalled that his previous contacts with Harris had been infrequent and they had all been rather unpleasant. When they first met, Harris had apparently mistaken Adams for a book salesman and had ignored him in a rather discourteous way. When Harris learned that Adams was a new professor, his attitude appeared to change to one of stern paternalism. It seemed to Adams that these initial attitudes had characterized their relationship--Harris had either ignored Adams or had treated him paternalistically. It was difficult for Adams to cope with both of these attitudes. He was particularly resentful when he was ignored. Harris had, however, offered Adams a full-time position within the Mathematics Department, which he refused.

As he walked toward Professor Harris' office, Professor Adams reflected that he had no specific plan for handling the coming meeting. He wondered how he should use the memorandum he had prepared, or whether he should use it at all.

Exercise

CONSTRUCTING A TOWER

OBJECTIVE

You will be a member of a team competing against other teams to determine which can build the tallest self-supporting structure within the constraints of the following instructions.

INSTRUCTIONS

Each team is to build the tallest self-supporting structure it can, on the floor or on a table as directed by your instructor, using only the materials provided to you. You will have fifteen minutes to plan with your teammates what you will build and how you will build it. During this fifteen minutes, you may handle the building materials, but you may not put any of the pieces together. After the planning session, you will have forty seconds to build the structure. You will be given starting and stopping times by your instructor, and that is all.

Planning Time: 15 minutes
Construction Time: 40 seconds

JUDGING

When it is announced at the end of the construction period that time is up, all building activity must stop immediately. All members of the team are to move at least five feet away from the structure and leave it freestanding. Your instructor will time one minute, at the end of which all standing structures will be eligible for measurement. A member from each team should, at the end of one minute, support the team's structure to insure that it remains standing until it is measured by the instructor. The instructor will announce as the winner of the competition the team with the tallest structure, and then guide you in a discussion exploring your experience.

PART IV

PROCESSES WITHIN ORGANIZATIONS

The Communication Process

The Decision-Making Process

INTRODUCTION

It has been said that if one reduces organizations to their common and most fundamental characteristics what will be found are the related elements of information and decisions. Information can be defined as anything which contributes to reducing uncertainty; "communication" is "the use of words, letters, symbols, or similar means to achieve common or shared information. . ."[1] or stated differently, communication is the effort of two or more parties to achieve a particular level of understanding. "Decision making" is simply the process of choosing from an array of alternatives. Obviously, the effectiveness of decision making is related directly to the quantity and quality of information available to the decision maker, and thus to the communication system of the organization.

Communication

As any management consultant will confirm, the most common organizational problem expressed by managers is, "We have a communications breakdown here." While, in many cases, communications breakdowns are only the visible symptoms of other underlying problems involving motivation, leadership, organizational climate, and so on, it is nonetheless true that communication is usually involved since it is a process which permeates nearly all organizational activities. Communication is the medium by which certain members of an organization attempt to motivate, exert influence over, and lead others, by which a certain type of organizational climate is expressed and perceived, and so on. Clearly problems in these and other areas are inextricably intertwined with the communication process. It is thus imperative, in diagnosing organizational problems, to examine both the medium (communication) and the substantive problem area (motivation, leadership, climate).

A simple model[2] of the communication process is useful in identifying likely points of breakdown or distortion in that process.

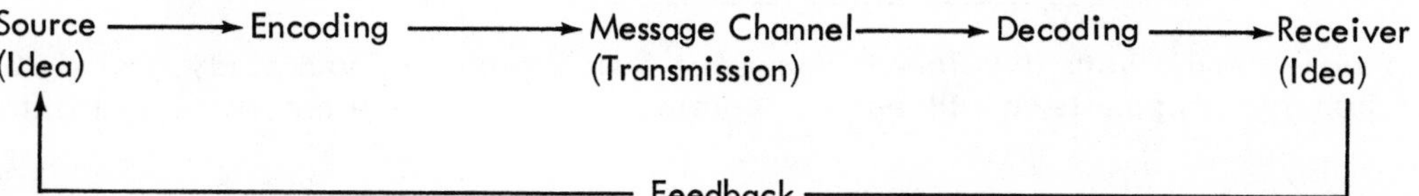

There exists potential for "noise" (breakdown, interference, distortion) in every phase of the communication process described above. Indeed, in an organizational setting, the probability of the sender's idea being received with 100 percent accuracy is remote, given the many organizational conditions which contribute to "noise." These would include:

- --distraction and time pressures (which reduce the time and attention necessary for idea clarification, careful encoding, choice of a channel, and decoding.
- --differences in values and status on the part of sender and receiver (which affect the receiver's evaluation of the meaning of the message, apart from its pure information content); and
- --semantic problems (resulting in sender and receiver attaching different meanings to the same words).

It is clear that the ideal toward which organizational members should work is transmission of maximum information with a minimum of "noise."

Communication takes place at many levels in the organization: between individuals (interpersonal), between work groups or departments, from superiors to subordinates, from subordinates to superiors, from top management to "the organization," etc. In addition, communications may be formal (memoranda, policy statements, bulletin boards, announcements), or informal (word of mouth, "the grapevine"). These individual types of communication and their overall mix will certainly affect the total amount and quantity of communications in an organization.

---

[1]For further discussion see C. Cherry, On Human Communications (New York: Science Editors, 1961), pp. 2-16.

[2]Adapted from J. Gibson, J. Ivancevich, and J. Donnelly, Organizations: Behavior, Structure, Processes (rev. ed.; Dallas: Business Publications, 1976).

Cases in this section will require you to diagnose organizational communications problems, and to suggest appropriate changes to resolve the problems and improve the communication system. A useful starting point in the diagnostic process is the model depicted earlier; examination of each phase in that model in terms of the specific case under study should yield valuable insights as to the sources of problems. With respect to recommendations for resolving these problems, clearly, proposed solutions should follow directly from the problem diagnosis. Gibson, Ivancevich, and Donnelly in their text[3] propose a most useful model incorporating several techniques which can potentially improve message accuracy and clarity:

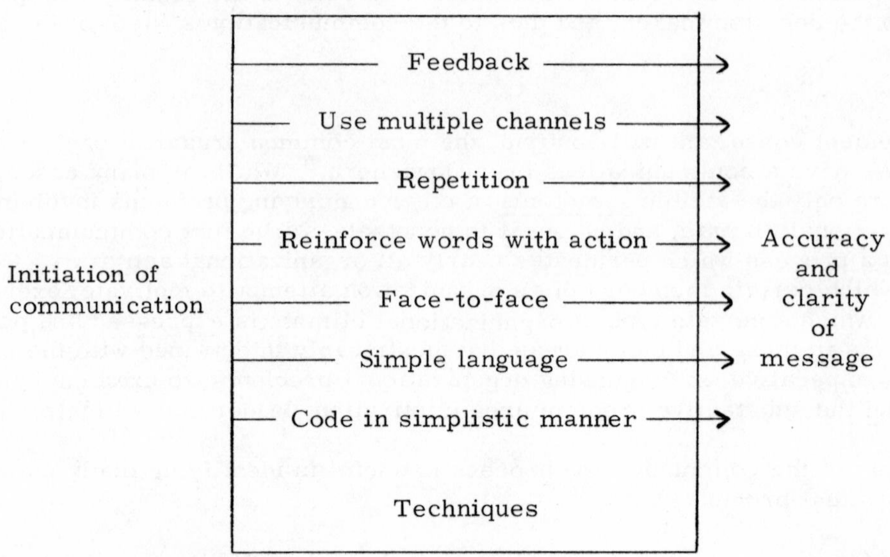

From these techniques and others developed from your own experience and study, you should draw together comprehensive proposals to address the communications problems diagnosed in the following cases.

Decision Making

A decision is simply the selection of a course of action from a range of alternatives. While decision making has been the subject of some of the most complex, sophisticated, and abstract work in the study of organizations, a few relatively simple and straightforward ideas on decisions should prove useful in analyzing the cases and doing the exercises in this section.

While they are seldom made fully explicit, the decision maker always faces an array of alternatives (possible courses of action), and associated with each alternative are a number of potential consequences (outcomes). Following each consequence is another array of alternatives which the decision maker may face in the future, and associated with each is a set of consequences. If projected far into the future, it can be seen that the decision maker faces a long series of alternatives and consequences, alternatives and consequences, the number of each growing rapidly over time:

[3] J. Gibson, J. Ivancevich, and J. Donnelly, Organizations: Behavior, Structure, Processes (rev. ed.; Dallas: Business Publications, Inc., 1976).

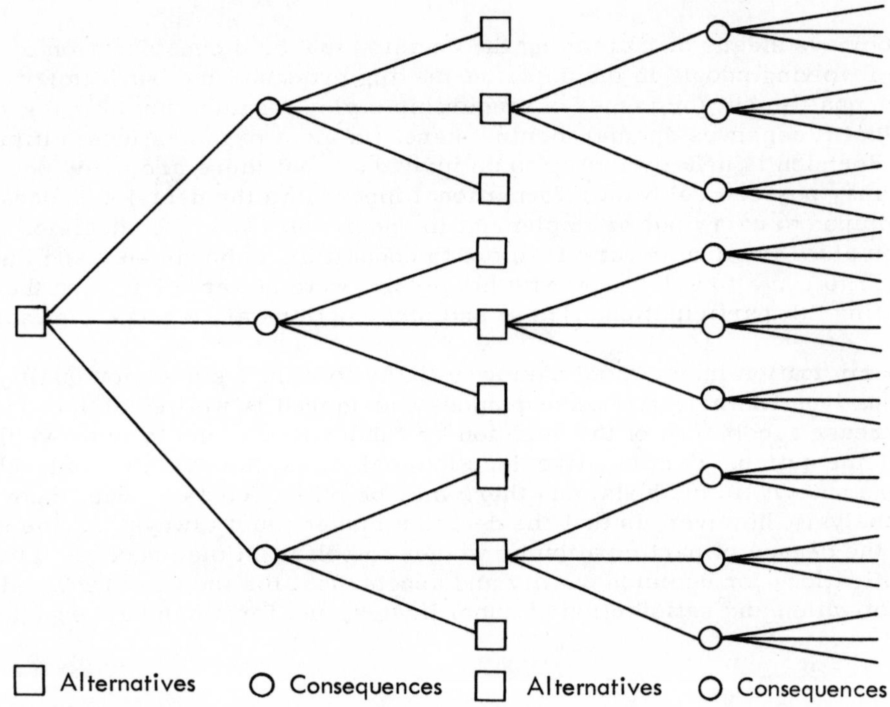

It might be noted that the major distinction between alternatives and consequences is that the choice of the former is within the control of the decision maker, while the occurrence of the latter is beyond his control.

A fully "rational," or the best possible, decision obviously would be one in which the decision maker has complete information--i.e., full knowledge of all the possible alternatives, all the possible and actual consequences, a clear understanding of and consistency in his preferences over time, and so on. The fact that it is not possible for an individual either to know or handle all possible alternatives available to him at any point in time, that consequences occur in the future and cannot be predicted with complete accuracy, and that individuals' preferences are neither always consistent nor unchanging all lead to the realization that decisions are made under conditions of uncertainty, and can therefore never be termed fully "rational."

But, recognition of these limitations on rationality also leads directly to insights on practical ways of improving the quality of decisions. These can be divided into two major categories:

(1) expanding the number of alternatives and potential consequences of which the decision maker is aware; and
(2) improving the quantity and quality of feedback to the decision maker on the actual consequences of his decision.

The logic behind the first recommendation is straightforward: an alternative not even considered clearly cannot be chosen, regardless of its quality, and a consequence not foreseen clearly cannot be sought or avoided in the process of selecting an alternative, regardless of its desirability. The logic behind the second recommendation is more subtle. Since a decision always must be made under conditions of some uncertainty about its consequences, no matter how great the efforts to reduce it, the decision maker essentially must make an "act of faith" in the predicted consequence of his decision: "If I choose this alternative, I believe it will be followed by certain consequences which I wish to avoid." Only one check exists on the accuracy of the decision maker's predictions about consequences: that is information feedback on the actual consequences of his decision. If his predictions were completely accurate (which they seldom are), so much the better. If they were not, he can take corrective action (make new decisions) in an effort to achieve the desired outcome.

There are numerous individual, group, and organizational phenomena which limit the ability and the tendency of decision makers to expand consideration of alternatives and consequences, and other phenomena which distort and limit the informational feedback to the decision maker in the actual consequences of his decision. Identifying these and exploring ways of combating them should constitute a portion of your discussion of the cases and exercises in this section.

However, one obvious means of increasing the decision maker's consideration of alternatives and consequences, i.e., involving people in the decision-making process--has such important implications, not just for decision quality, but for issues of leadership style, organization climate, motivation of subordinates, etc., that it deserves special mention here. In most organizations, ultimate responsibility for making a decision is usually left up to an individual, but there are many people--usually his subordinates--who may possess relevant informational inputs into the decision process, and who will ultimately be called upon to carry out or implement the decision. Thus, the decision maker's choices: to make the decision alone in an autocratic fashion, to consult his subordinates and then make the final decision, to ask them to come to a decision with his holding veto power, or to turn the decision over to them, thus soliciting full participation. These and other options are always available.

That greater participation in decision making is likely to improve decision quality by increasing the number of alternatives and potential consequences considered is well established. Participation also is likely to increase acceptance of the decision by subordinates, and to improve the probability of its effective implementation. Participative decision making is, however, considerably more time-consuming than more autocratic methods, and there may be other "costs." The important point to recognize in case analysis, however, is that the decision maker must always "decide how to decide"--he must determine the degree of participation he wishes to solicit in the process. That choice will have important implications for decision quality and acceptance, for the time required to make the decision, for the motivation and satisfaction of subordinates, and for other key organizational variables.

THE PRICE OF AMBITION

In the fall of 1962 Ted Michod graduated from the Newark College of Engineering as an electrical engineer and went to work for a small but growing computer manufacturing firm in New England. His first position with the company was that of a junior engineer in the Data Processing Systems Division. He worked with twenty other engineers designing primary computer circuits and electromechanical linkages. Basically, his job consisted of designing various electrical and mechanical subsystems to perform logical and arithmetic operations. Most of the time he worked out designs on paper, although, on occasion, Ted actually tried his ideas in the lab.

In June 1964 Ted received a promotion which, along with increase in salary and status, provided him with an opportunity to expand his knowledge of the industry. As an associated engineer in the Programming Systems Division he served as a liaison between his old design group and a systems engineering team which was responsible for the creation of new programming languages. Ted's duties were to make sure that the programming languages being developed were consistent with the design capabilities being incorporated into new computer systems by his old work group. Thus, he was able to relate his previous experience with hardware (circuits) to the creation and design of software (program languages).

After a year in his new position Ted began to feel that, although he was mastering the technical side of the computer industry, he was not being prepared for the managerial responsibilities to which he aspired. It seemed to him that a graduate degree in business administration would greatly improve his chances for promotion in the future. He gave the problem considerable thought and in the fall of 1966 took a two-year educational leave of absence to work on an M.B.A. His decision was based upon what he perceived as a need for managerial development and his observation that his interest had gradually shifted from the technical to the administrative aspects of the industry.

In June 1968 Ted graduated from the university in the top 20 percent of his class. Within two weeks of graduation he was married and back at work with his old company. This time, at his request, he was assigned to the Midwestern Marketing Region as a customer engineer. Ted felt that experience in the field of customer relations together with his previous technical work would greatly increase his worth to the firm and thus his chances for success. For this reason both Ted and his bride viewed their move to the Chicago office as a "step in the right direction."

Once settled in Chicago, Ted reported to the Customer Engineering Manager, John Lucas. Mr. Lucas assigned Michod to the customer education section as an instructor. The section's purpose was to train customer employees in the installation and use of computer systems. Since this was not considered to be a full-time assignment, Ted was given additional duties as the supervisor of a program modification team. This second job consisted of giving technical assistance and direction to a group of four programmer trainees who were modifying existing computer programs to keep them consistent with improved methodology and technology. Both positions required that he report directly to Mr. Lucas. On the average, Ted taught thirty hours a week and devoted fifteen hours to his second job.

As a result of the group's work modifying a set of market forecasting programs, Ted hit upon the idea of using a form of the Markov Process to predict growth in sales of new industrial products.[1] The Markov Process simply views life as a series of probabilities that an event will (or will not) occur given that it has (or has not) taken place in the past. He studied the problem evenings at home and in mid-October proposed his ideas to Mr. Lucas. John Lucas seemed interested in the project but told Ted that he would like to think the matter over for some time.

On November 1, 1968, Ted's program modification team completed its assigned projects and was disbanded. When he reported to John Lucas to be reassigned Michod was instructed to see Wayne Smith, the head of the Computer Installation Department. Mr. Smith, like John Lucas, was the head of a staff department. They enjoyed equal rank within the firm and reported to the same district manager.

---

[1]For a description of forecasting methods which use the Markov Process see the following: Ronald E. Frank, Alfred A. Kuhen, and William F. Massy, Quantitative Techniques in Marketing Analysis (Homewood, Ill.: Richard D. Irwin, Inc.) p. 395.

Mr. Smith outlined Ted's next assignment as follows. Ted would provide technical advice for two junior systems engineers in the installation of small computers and would have limited responsibility for each installation project. The job, at first, would require about ten hours a week of his time. In addition Ted would continue to serve in his present capacity of instructor until the middle of the year. At this time an additional instructor would be transferred to the Midwestern Region, and Ted would be relieved of his teaching responsibilities to devote his entire efforts to the installation department. Until then, however, he would report to Mr. Smith concerning installation problems and to Mr. Lucas for matters involving the education program.

The following day Ted received a note from Mr. Lucas to see him as soon as possible. Upon entering Mr. Lucas' office Ted found himself engaged in the following conversation.

Ted: "You wanted to see me, Mr. Lucas?"

Lucas: "Yes, Ted. Sit down. You know, I liked the proposal you submitted for forecasting with Markov Processes. I'd like you to work up some programs and make it operational. Do you think you could wrap up the job in two months?"

Ted: "Well, I could if I had the time, but as you know I'm still working as an instructor, and I've just taken over an installation team for Wayne Smith."

Lucas: "Yes, I know about that. You'll have some free time on Wayne's project, though. I don't see why you won't be able to fit my project around your other work. It won't take long, will it?"

Ted: "I just don't know. I can make a wild guess at a hundred twenty man-hours. I don't think I'll have the time to tackle it."

Lucas: "Sure you will, Ted. Smith's project won't take all your time. Besides, a hundred twenty hours isn't very much. Why, it's not even two weeks' work."

After leaving Mr. Lucas' office Ted stopped in to see Wayne Smith.

Ted: "Hi. I was just wondering when I should start working for you."

Smith: "Today. Now!" (jokingly)

Ted: "Well, what I mean is, will it be full time at first or will I have some time on my hands?"

Smith: "No. It should be a full ten hours a week right from the start. Why do you ask? Any special reason?"

Ted told Mr. Smith about his conversation with Mr. Lucas and explained that he didn't think he would be able to handle all three projects. Wayne Smith agreed, but felt that there had been some misunderstanding. He told Ted that he would talk to John Lucas that afternoon and that Ted should let the matter "ride" until it had been looked into further.

Ted: "Good. I hope this gets cleared up soon."

Smith: "Don't worry, Ted, we just have our wires crossed. Stop in and see me first thing in the morning."

The next day the following conversation took place between Ted and Mr. Smith.

Smith: "Ted, I saw John Lucas yesterday and I'm not sure I've solved your problem. He said that the project he had in mind wasn't very big, and that you should have plenty of time to get it done."

Ted: "But I told him it would take a hundred twenty hours. Since then I've been worried that my estimate was way too low."

Smith: "Well, you'd better talk with him again. I understood that I was to have you for ten hours a week and believe me you'll need every bit of that time."

Ted saw Mr. Lucas a few hours later and reiterated his commitments and lack of available time. He went on to suggest that he could instruct a new man to carry out the project if that was acceptable to Mr. Lucas.

Lucas: "I don't know who else would be available to do this type of work. . .Look, Ted, just fit it in around your other work. You'll have time to do it. . .Oh, before I forget, see Mary in Personnel on your way out. They need some information for your records. And tell my secretary to come in, will you? I have a stack of letters to get out."

Ted walked down to Personnel wondering how he wound up in the middle of all this. Furthermore, he wondered what he should do next.

1) Get Help (assigned)

2) Make it a project in INSTRUCTING Class
Let Them do it.

3) Don't work overtime.

4) Challenge Jr. Engs. INST. To help

5) Try all above - Don't work
- Set up new Timetable
and give it to Bosses

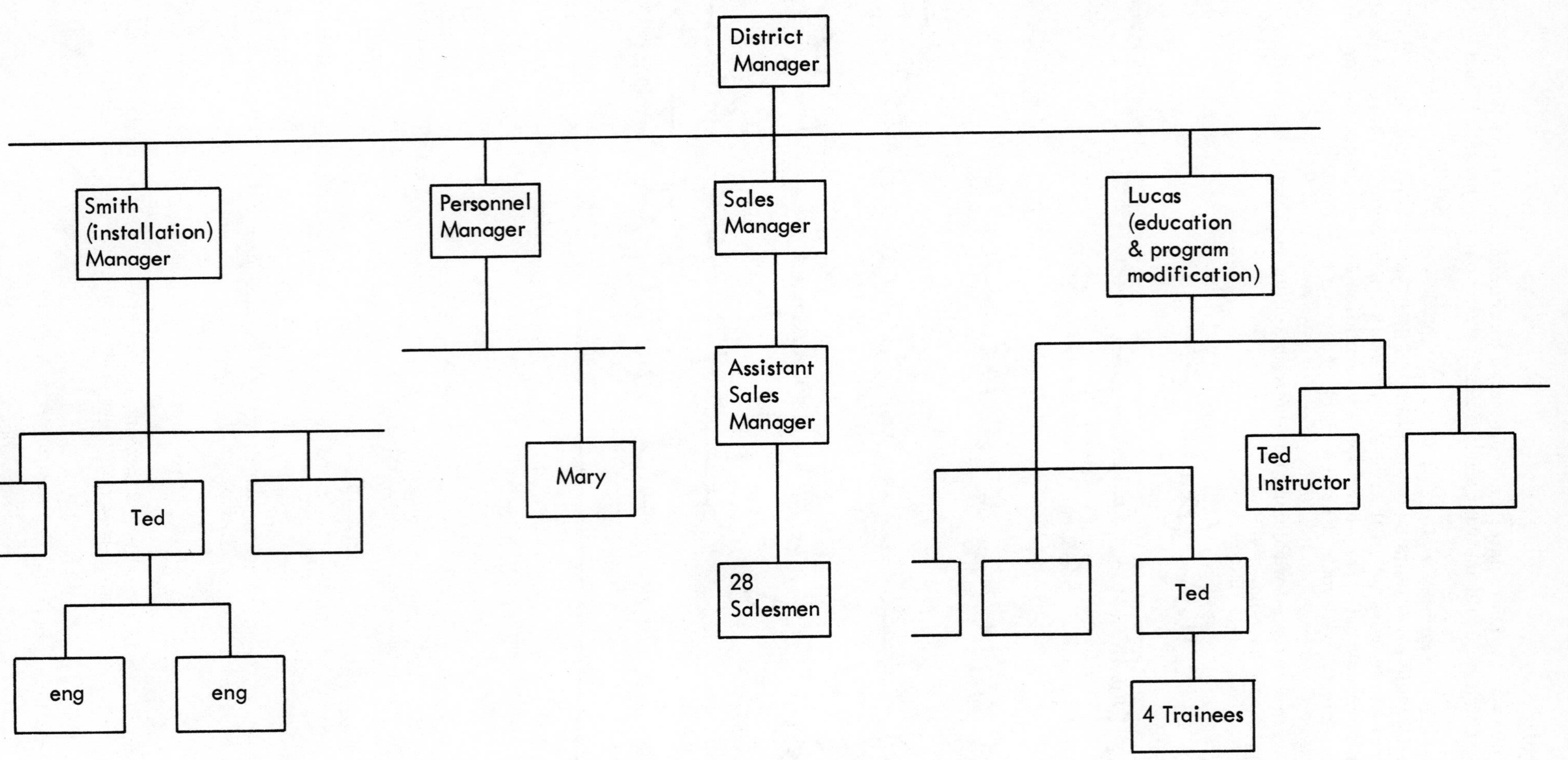

Figure 1. Partial organizational chart for the midwestern marketing region.

SOUTHERN BANK

History and Organization

Southern Bank, established shortly after the Civil War, had developed over the years a distinguished record for prudent, conservative financial service. An independent, single-location bank located in a medium-sized city, it now (1965) employs some 550 persons and is one of the largest institutions of its kind in the area.

The bank is organized into eight divisions: General Administrative; Banking; Investment; Trust Administration; Business Development; Management Consulting; Marketing, and Legal. (See Figure 1.) In addition, there are three service groups: Planning and Personnel, Building and Office Services, and the Controller's Group. There are six levels of management in the bank: President; Division; Group; Department; Section; and Unit.

About 100 of the bank's employees are officers, of whom six are women; another 100 employees are men in various stages of professional banking careers. The remaining 350 employees are women, about 50 of whom are highly trained career specialists. Approximately one half of the female employees are young, unmarried high school graduates. These girls typically remain with the bank for two or three years before leaving to be married or for other reasons.

Since the inauguration of a new president in 1959 and the subsequent employment of a number of "bright young men," the bank has aggressively been exploring new ways of rendering financial services to its customers. This combination of aggressiveness and innovation has proved to be highly successful in promoting the growth and profitability of the bank. The Management Consulting Division, for example, was established to meet a perceived need and has not only become a profitable new service in its own right, but also has served, through its activities, to bring valued new accounts to the bank.

The top management people in Southern Bank believe that if the institution is to continue to grow through aggressiveness and innovation, the ideas and cooperation of all employees at all levels should be solicited and encouraged. In other words, excellent communication is considered by top management to be vital to the successful operation of this dynamic organization. To this end, Mr. Harold Walsh of the Personnel office was designated in 1963 as the coordinator of communications and training. Also to this end, a variety of communication techniques, channels, and devices, described on the following pages, have been adopted.

Officers' Meetings

The President meets formally with the Board of Directors once each month. A day or two after this meeting, the President holds his regular monthly meeting for the bank's officers. In this meeting, the President reports on selected topics from the Board meeting and reviews the monthly financial statements. At the end of this presentation, which usually lasts about 15 minutes, the President asks for and responds to questions from the officers in attendance.[1]

As the conference room is not large enough to accommodate all of the bank's 100 officers at one time, the monthly officers' meetings are held in two sections on successive days, with approximately one half of the officers attending each session.

Each officer is free to decide for himself which of the nonconfidential topics covered in the officers' meetings, if any, will be reported back to his subordinates. Officers typically do not hold group meetings for this purpose.

The officers' meetings are the only regularly scheduled meetings in the bank designed for the purpose of routinely disseminating information.

"COMCOM"

"COMCOM" (popular abbreviation for "Communications Committee") was the brainchild of Alice Davey, an officer in the bank, who suggested her idea to President Libbert at a cocktail party one

---

[1] More will be said later about the sources of these questions.

evening in 1963. Mrs. Davey had been concerned about the discontinuation of the bank's house organ, Southern Messenger, earlier that year, and felt that something was needed to bolster communication to and from the lower levels of the organization. The stated objective of "COMCOM" was to "promote internal understanding of all matters of common concern at all levels throughout the organization."

President Libbert accepted Mrs. Davey's suggestion and announced the establishment of "COMCOM" in White Paper No. 81, dated October 2, 1963. (See Figure 2.) The functions of "COMCOM" were described by the President in White Paper No. 86, dated November 25, 1963. (See Figure 3.)

Each of the eleven members of "COMCOM" is an officer in the bank; all eight divisions are represented on the committee. George Storm and Alice Davey are the co-chairmen. Each "COMCOM" member is expected to solicit questions from employees at all levels in his division for submission to President Libbert for discussion at the monthly officers' meetings. Questions on any topic except grievances and personalities are welcomed.

"COMCOM" members report that they devote perhaps two hours each month to the task of gathering questions. These questions are reviewed at a regular monthly "COMCOM" meeting held one week prior to the officers' meeting. Suitable questions are agreed upon and then forwarded to the President well in advance of the officers' meeting. Typically, about five members attend "COMCOM" meetings.

"COMCOM" presents to the President an average of four questions per month. Most of these questions originate with the "COMCOM" members themselves or from persons in the top three levels of the organization. One of the "COMCOM" co-chairmen stated that perhaps 20 questions per month could be submitted to the President if the members had more time to devote to the task and if "people thought in terms of communications problems."

The President feels that "COMCOM" is working well; the "COMCOM" co-chairmen feel that the committee is reasonably successful in reaching its objectives; the Personnel Manager feels that "COMCOM" is failing to attain its objectives and wonders how it might be made more effective.

Southern Messenger

The Southern Messenger, the bank's unusual house organ, originated in 1946 through spontaneous employee interest. A few employees volunteered to produce the publication on their own time if the bank would provide the necessary supplies and equipment. The paper was started on this basis.

Typewritten, then reproduced by the mimeograph process, the Southern Messenger was primarily a "gossip sheet" published approximately quarterly. Over the years the paper grew until, by early 1963, an issue might consist of as many as 100 single-spaced, typewritten pages.

By this time, however, employee interest in the paper apparently had declined, and when the volunteer editor left the bank for other employment in 1963, Southern Messenger collapsed from the lack of volunteer workers.

Largely through the efforts of Alice Davey and "COMCOM," Southern Messenger was reactivated in September, 1964, as an official house organ.

Southern Messenger is now published bi-monthly, entirely on company time and entirely at company expense. The present editor spends about 40 percent of her time at the editor's job; the remainder of her time is spent at a clerical job in the bank. The paper now runs six 8 1/2" x 11" pages in length; the bank allocates $500 per issue to cover printing, photographic, and other costs. Seven hundred fifty copies of each issue are printed.

The editor has 20 people (including three officers), scattered throughout the bank, who serve as informal reporters. These reporters serve on a voluntary basis and tend to obtain and report news items on an opportunistic, rather than a systematic, basis.

According to the editor, Southern Messenger space allocations run about as follows:

1/3 News about company plans and activities
1/6 Information regarding company policy
1/6 "Profiles of New Employees"

1/12	Gossip and personal items
rest	Crossword and scientific puzzles

The puzzles have proved to be highly popular with the employees, partly because of their intrinsic appeal and partly because of the prizes offered for the best solutions. The winner for each puzzle receives a pair of theater tickets. The crossword puzzles often contain words related to business and banking.

Although Southern Messenger is mailed to each employee at his home, the paper often finds its way back to the bank, where stimulating discussions regarding the puzzles sometimes occur.

Task Force

The Communications Task Force was established in February, 1965, at the suggestion of John Templeton, Vice President and Personnel Manager for the bank. Templeton felt that the Task Force might be more successful than "COMCOM" had been in improving communication to and from personnel in the lower echelons of the bank. The Task Force consists of five nonofficer employees nominated for the part-time assignment by their respective Division heads. Task Force members were notified of their appointments by interoffice memorandum from Mr. Templeton. (See Figure 4.)

The Task Force's basic assignment, as seen by the chairman, Stuart Seaton, is to circulate among and talk with lower level employees to discover questions, problems, and suggestions from the ranks. These items are then cleared by "COMCOM" which may modify but not block them, after which they are passed on to the Management Committee.[2] John Templeton's concept of the Task Force's assignment is presented in Figure 4.

The Task Force, which has now been in existence for five months, had a flurry of meetings immediately following its establishment but has had only one meeting during the past two months because of vacations and the demands of other work. To date, the Task Force has made six suggestions to the Management Committee via "COMCOM."

The Communications Task Force is only one of several task forces presently operating in the bank. Others include the Training, New Services (Marketing), and Trust Administration task forces. Conceptually, each task force is assembled to accomplish a particular, well-defined job and upon completion of that job, or task, it is to be disbanded.

Chairman Seaton indicated that Communications Task Force members spend perhaps one hour per week on this assignment, and that most of the group's suggestions to date have originated from among its members.

When asked what caused him to believe there was a need for a Communications Task Force, the Personnel Manager replied, "There's no feedback around here, particularly from the lower levels. An order, report, or policy change is sent down the line and we wait for questions, or complaints, or some kind of response. What we get back is silence. Absolutely nothing. We find it very difficult to measure the impact of, say, a policy change. It's like shouting down a well and getting no echo. It's eerie."

Asked whether employees complain about poor communication in the bank, the Personnel Manager replied, "No. Oh, there is an occasional comment in the lunch room, but these are not specific and are mentioned in a very casual way. No one appears to be disturbed about it."

The chairman of the Communications Task Force, when asked about the condition of the bank's grapevine, replied, "Healthy."

Suggestion System

Southern Bank's suggestion system has been in continuous operation since its installation in 1952. Suggestion boxes are conveniently located on all floors, with a rack of blank suggestion forms attached to each box.

---

[2]The Management Committee consists of the President and four key Vice Presidents.

Suggestion forms are collected monthly. Over the years the input of employee suggestions has consistently averaged about ten per month. Most of the suggestions come from the Operations Group of the General Administration Division and deal with improving the heavy flow of paper processed by that group.

The suggestions are reviewed and evaluated by a six-man Suggestion Committee, presently comprised of both officers and nonofficers, representing the Trust Division (3 members), the General Administration Division (2 members), and the Investment Division (1 member). An effort has been made to staff the committee with younger people from the lower echelons of the bank in the hope that this might stimulate employee interest in the suggestion system.

Committee members serve staggered two-year terms. When a replacement is needed, the committee meets to discuss individuals who may be interested in and suitable for a Suggestion Committee assignment. The most promising prospect is then contacted, and if he is willing to serve he is added to the committee after the approval of his supervisor is obtained.

When a suggestion is to be evaluated, it is given to the committee member most familiar with the operations of the department from which the suggestion came. This member then discusses the suggestion with the person who made it and with the head of the affected department(s). The member then reports back to the full committee, making a recommendation as to the disposition of the suggestion. The committee ordinarily accepts these recommendations.

If a suggestion is deemed to be practical and useful, the committee's next task is to determine the amount of money appropriate as the suggestion award. The usual award range is from $10 to $50. The criteria used to determine the amount of the award are the estimated amounts of time and/or money saved by the suggestion. The committee often finds it difficult to arrive at the amount of this saving.

Every two months the committee issues a report listing all the suggestions made and the awards given during the preceding period. A copy of this report is placed on each bulletin board in the hope that it will stimulate further suggestions. When an award is given the report indicates the suggestor's name; suggestions receiving no award are listed by number.

The committee's decisions as to whether or not a suggestion is deserving of an award, and the amount of the award, is final. Approximately one third of the suggestions submitted are considered worthy of awards.

Performance Review

Top management at Southern Bank believes that the bank's system of regular performance review provides an excellent opportunity to foster communication between each supervisor, at whatever level he might be, and his subordinates. The private performance review sessions, which deal primarily with the employee's job performance, also provide an opportunity for the employee to talk with his boss about his problems and for superior and subordinate to plan together the employee's future growth and progress.

Performance reviews are held after 90 days for new employees, then annually on the employee's anniversary date.[3] The reviews, which are keyed to the employee's job description, average perhaps 30 minutes in length. The same basic system is used for all employees--from clerks to vice presidents.

A few days before his anniversary date, the employee receives from his supervisor a form notifying him when the review will occur, and inviting him to write on the form any questions that he would like his boss to answer during the review. This form is then returned to the supervisor. It is not uncommon for employees to write questions on these forms which the supervisor considers sensitive and/or difficult to answer. Nevertheless, the supervisor is expected to answer the questions. The form is destroyed after the review session.

---

[3]Reviews may be held more frequently if the supervisor considers this desirable. The Personnel Officer encourages more frequent reviews to facilitate communications.

Supervisors use a checklist form in rating their subordinates and use this form as a basis for the performance review discussion. Items on the checklist include such things as job knowledge, quality of work, effort, dependability, teamwork, communication, and profit-mindedness. The applicability of each item on the form with respect to the employee's particular job is recorded. The supervisor then checks whether the employee's performance "exceeds," "meets," or "falls short" of standard on each item. The resulting profile provides the core of the review discussion.

The supervisor retains the checklist rating form and notifies the personnel office regarding the result of the review in a separate summary report. Most employees receive a pay increase following their annual performance review. The amount of this increase, which usually ranges between 5 percent and 10 percent of present rate, depends upon the supervisor's evaluation of the employee's performance. The typical supervisor in the bank has from eight to ten subordinates to review during the course of a year.[4]

The Personnel Manager believes that many of the performance reviews are too superficial, but wonders how much time and effort a supervisor should spend in reviewing a young, female clerk who may marry and leave the bank next month. He also is concerned about what he believes to be inadequate training in interviewing techniques on the part of some supervisors in the bank. (Supervisors receive nine hours of in-bank training on the performance review system, of which one hour is devoted to interviewing techniques.)

When asked how the nonmanagement people feel about the performance review system, the Personnel Manager said, "We really don't know. There is very little feedback. Occasionally, in an exit interview, a terminating employee will say that his supervisor had not kept him informed as to the adequacy of his performance or about his future potential with the bank."

White Paper

When information on matters of bank-wide interest is to be disseminated, a "White Paper" is used. Each employee receives a personal copy. An average of two White Papers per month are issued. Examples are White Papers No. 81 and 86 (Figures 2 and 3), dealing with the formation of "COMCOM." Other White Papers may deal with such matters as holiday announcements, changing hours of work, etc.

Occasionally a White Paper deals with a policy change. In such cases, supervisors sometimes call their subordinates together to discuss the change and to answer pertinent questions.

[4]It should be noted that not all officers are supervisors, nor are all supervisors officers.

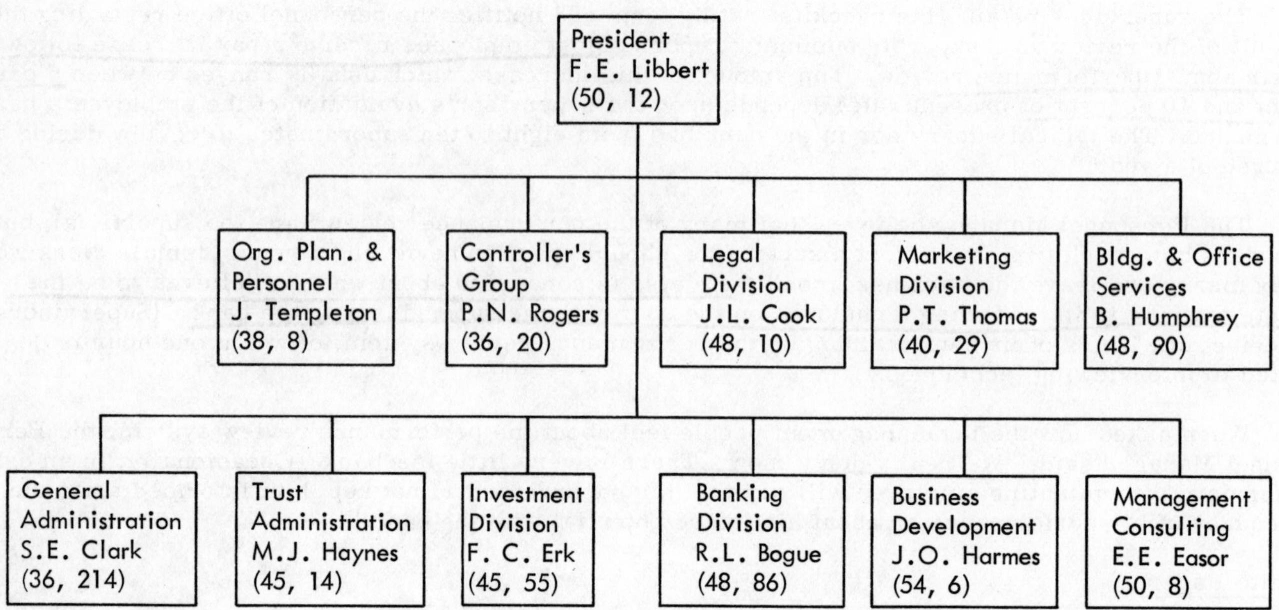

NOTE: Numbers in parentheses indicate manager's age and number of subordinates. For example, Mr. Cook, Head of the Legal Division, is 48 years old and has 10 people in his Division.

Figure 1. Organizational chart for Southern Bank.

No. 81 October 2, 1963

COMMUNICATIONS COMMITTEE

For an extended period of time, I have personally felt that a committee should be established to serve as an organized pipeline for the flow of information throughout the organization. We all like to know "what's going on when it's going on," and I believe that the Communications Committee can provide this type of information for all of us. I have appointed the following to serve on this committee:

George Storm - Co-Chairman
Alice Davey - Co-Chairman
Ronald Brooks
John Cassidy
Norman Euler
Ruth Hobgood
Roy Munford
Elmer Nagel
Jack Phillips
Ed Ralston
George Robinson

The committee is currently in the organizational stage, and when its program for effective internal communications has been established, it will be announced.

(signed)
Frederick E. Libbert

Figure 2. Example of a Southern Bank White Paper.

No. 86 November 25, 1963

COMMUNICATIONS COMMITTEE

Our Communications Committee, which I appointed last month, has recommended several steps to improve our communications program.

The Committee feels strongly, and I agree, that all employees should be informed promptly of what we're doing, why, and how it effects them; and that they should be able to communicate their ideas to top management and get timely answers to their questions and requests.

If you have any questions or ideas you want to pass along, see your supervisor or a bank officer, or use our Suggestion System if it is a formal suggestion you wish to make. And during the formative stages of the new program, members of the Committee will welcome your suggestions, recommendations, and questions.

Members of the Committee are:

George Storm - Co-Chairman
Alice Davey - Co-Chairman
Ronald Brooks
John Cassidy
Norman Euler
Ruth Hobgood
Roy Munford
Elmer Nagel
Jack Phillips
Ed Ralston
George Robinson

(signed)
Frederick E. Libbert

Figure 3. Example of a Southern Bank White Paper.

To: Stuart Seaton

cc: June Hugger — Louis Newton
Benjamin Allen — Byron Edwards

The Management Committee of Southern Bank is interested in the effectiveness of communications within the Company, especially as it affects the ability of supervisors and officers to apply and to interpret to others the policies and procedures of the Company, and to supply information about new developments that should be of interest to all employees.

The Committee requested nominations from Division Heads and selected you to organize and direct the project. You will be assisted in this task force study by the persons listed above as recipients of copies of this memo.

For purposes of this project, "communications" refers to formal and informal exchange of diffusion of information about such matters as:

a. Responsibilities and authorities
b. Policies governing personnel administration
c. Applications of various procedures, such as performance review, purchase requisitions, expense approvals, etc.
d. Information about significant new developments, new personnel, changes in benefit programs
e. Problems in supervision and administration which require the attention of higher levels of management.

To carry out this project, the task force will be expected to:

a. Determine the best way to assess communications; e.g., by interviews, questionnaires to supervisors, etc.
b. Consult with the Chairmen of the Communications Committee, with personnel officers, and with the Supervisory Development Groups, to establish the kinds of possible communications problems that may exist.
c. With the Chairmen of the Communications Committee, meet with the Management Committee to discuss findings.

I shall be available to assist in whatever way seems appropriate to the task force.

(signed) John Templeton
February 1, 1965

Figure 4. Interoffice memo of Southern Bank outlining Communications Committee responsibilities.

FISHER MANUFACTURING COMPANY[1]

In the early spring of 1964, The Fisher Manufacturing Company appeared to be on the verge of greatly increasing its sales and scope of operations. Since its organization by Mr. Leonard Fisher in 1955, the company realized profits from the manufacture and sale of wood-plastic building panels. In 1958, for instance, a profit of approximately $25,000 was earned, in addition to the approximately $15,000 drawings for that year by Mr. Fisher.

Since 1958 reported profits were not as substantial because much time and between $75,000 and $100,000 of funds were applied to research and development and were considered expense items. Nevertheless, profits were shown in every year except 1961, when a loss of approximately $12,000 was incurred. This was in the midst of the development of the largest portion of the new products and manufacturing processes. During this period much of Mr. Fisher's time was devoted to research and development. The erstwhile profitable lines which were the basis of the 1955-58 substantial profits were not emphasized, but rather attention was centered on the development of the new products and new manufacturing processes. During the fiscal year ended June 30, 1963, the firm showed a profit of $17,500, in addition to officers' salaries.

On July 1, 1963, the company moved from the small southern town in which it was located to a larger town, in Mississippi, of nearly 40,000 population. To accommodate this greatly expanded scope of operations, the company was financially reorganized on October 1, 1963. At this time, the old stock was retired, and a new issue of 400,000 shares of $1 par value was authorized. Leonard Fisher was given $200,000 par value of the new stock in exchange for his old stock. It was anticipated that the $200,000 new capital that was authorized would help the firm in realizing growth due to its position of having new products, new and efficient manufacturing processes, a new plant, a new qualified plant manager, and some of the best knowledge and experience in its field.

[1]All names have been disguised.

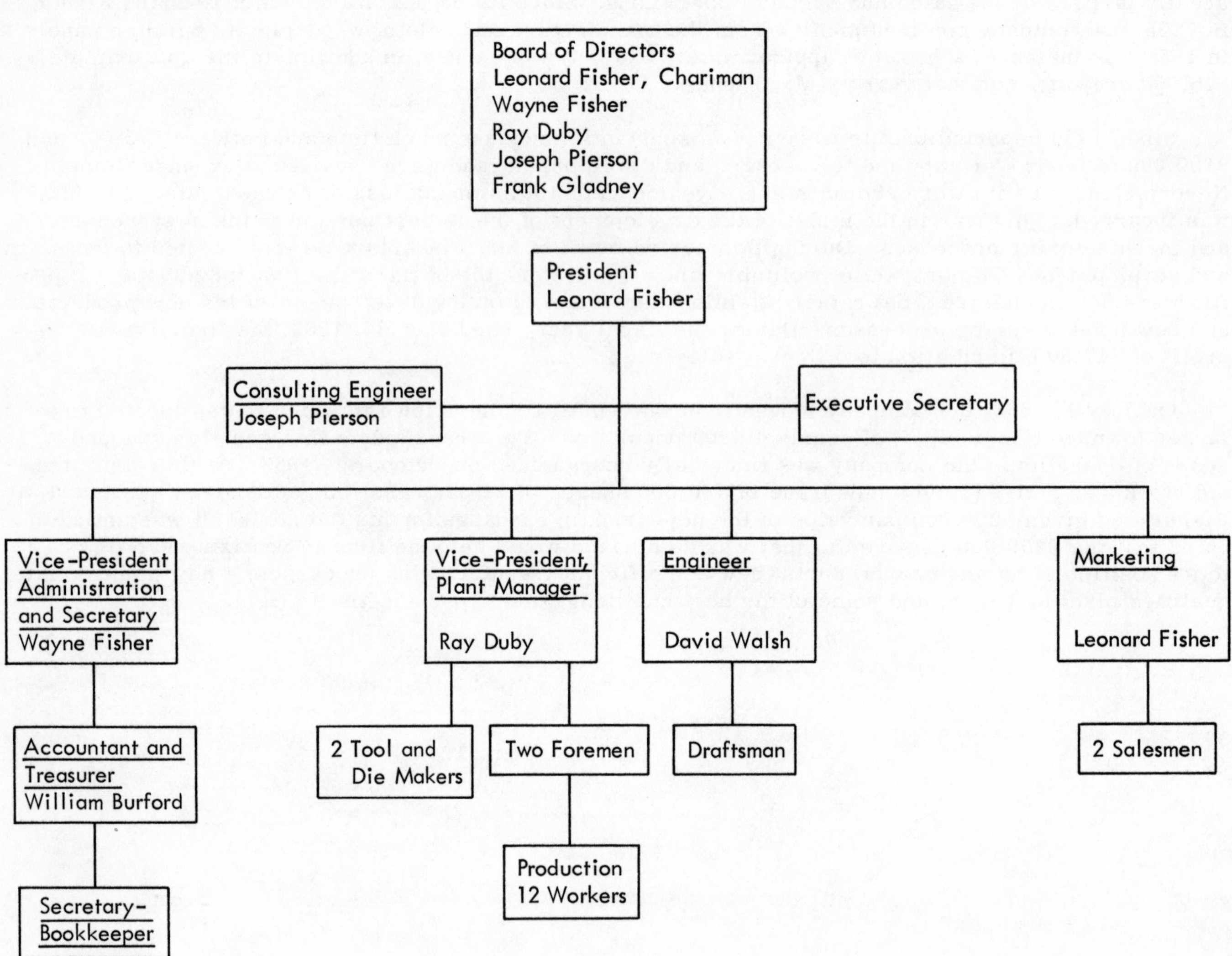

Figure 1. Organization of Fisher Manufacturing Co.

The Organization and the Officers

An organization chart of the company (Figure 1) shows the formal relationships which existed as of January 1, 1964, in accord with the established procedures in the company.

According to company literature, the president was the chief executive officer in the company and had final and complete authority and responsibility for all the operations. However, each manager was to make all practicable decisions in his area because of a policy of decentralized authority. Performance was to be measured primarily by preset goals and with data provided in systematic ways.

The officers were:

Leonard Fisher, founder of the company, Chairman of the Board, and President, age 45, was born near Baton Rouge, Louisiana. After completing high school in Baton Rouge, he worked in various construction jobs in Baton Rouge and New Orleans, with most of this work in the area of insulation. From 1941 to 1945, he served in the United States Army and rose to the rank of Sergeant in Armored Maintenance. During his last year in the Army, Mr. Fisher was in charge of a twelve-man truck maintenance crew.

Leaving the Army in late 1945, Mr. Fisher entered his uncle's hardware and building supply business in central Louisiana. By 1946, his uncle had allowed him to buy into the business, which was experiencing rapid growth in the postwar boom. Although this business enjoyed considerable success and growth, Mr. Fisher decided in 1954 to start his own business for the manufacture of wood-plastic building panels, in which he had become interested as the answer to the demand for sturdy, durable panels that could be easily installed and would have good insulation performance. These panels were made by a technique which combined wood shavings and plastic materials in a molding process to produce panels of varying sizes and widths.

After completing arrangements for his new business, The Fisher Manufacturing Company, Mr. Fisher took the approximately $45,000 which he had accumulated during his association with his uncle and started the new venture. Under Mr. Fisher's careful and constant supervision, the company has grown to its present size. Although not trained formally, Mr. Fisher is recognized as one of the foremost authorities in the nation in insulation panel technology and applications. He has exhibited a high level of proficiency in all areas of the industry. His acceptance as an expert in the industry is reflected in the officer capacities which he holds in two national organizations and the number of addresses he has made to professional groups and other interested parties.

Throughout the growth of the company, Mr. Fisher has personally designed, engineered, and supervised the production of a wide range of the wood-plastic panels and related products.

Wayne Fisher, age 32, Leonard's younger brother, was the Vice-President of Administration and Secretary of the company, a position he had held since joining the firm in the fall of 1959. In this position, Wayne was in charge of personnel, planning and policy, accounting, motivation and incentives, and finance. Leonard's idea was to groom his younger brother to take over the presidency within the next four years, so that he, Leonard, might become a "super salesman" for the company and not be bothered with administrative details, although he would still retain his position as Chairman of the Board.

After graduating from Baton Rouge High School, Wayne attended Louisiana State University, where he received an undergraduate degree in mechanical engineering in 1954. After working for several months as a design engineer for a St. Louis firm, he entered the United States Air Force as an engineering officer. While in the Air Force he supervised up to 175 employees and was in charge of a power plant and other equipment worth approximately $18,000,000.

Resigning from the Air Force in 1957, Wayne entered Graduate School at The University of Texas, where he was awarded a Master in Business Administration degree in August of 1959. While in school in Austin, Wayne was employed part time at The Balcones Research Center, working on government projects.

Ray Duby, Vice-President and Plant Manager, was 29 years old and a native of Natchez, Mississippi. He indicated in his rèsumè that he had attended several different courses in production management, taught in high school and at one of the small Mississippi state colleges. He had also attended several management seminars held at Mississippi State University.

Prior to joining The Fisher Manufacturing Company in the spring of 1963, Ray was employed by Johnson & Johnson, Inc., a metalworking firm located in New Orleans. With this company he was promoted from line foreman to plant superintendent, and was offered the position of plant manager when he advised his superiors of his plans to resign and join Fisher because he felt that his opportunities were greater there. At Johnson & Johnson, Ray had up to 125 men under his supervision, and he was in full charge of all production facilities, buildings, and equipment. He had eight years of training in production cost control and budgetary controls. He also had considerable experience in the engineering of products, and was in charge of tooling and die programs at Johnson & Johnson.

The following quotation is from Ray Duby's resumè which he sent to Leonard Fisher and the other company officers in early 1963.

> In the future, I plan to actively try and work myself out of my present position. I expect to set a good example for my subordinates to do the same, and thus have a rapidly growing organization which will stay ahead of any competition.
>
> My ultimate goal is--the Presidency!

Joseph Pierson, age 54, was a Director and Consulting Engineer for Fisher Manufacturing Company. After receiving his mechanical engineering degree from M.I.T. in Boston, Mr. Pierson was affiliated with several companies in engineering design capacities; then he took a position with Boeing Aircraft in 1942. At Boeing, he was instrumental in designing several significant contributions to the war effort. He ended his career in the aircraft field as an assistant plant superintendent.

After the war he acquired and directed an electric motor manufacturing plant in New Orleans. Since that time he has expanded and consolidated his operations to include multiple-line electrical equipment. Although he still maintains an interest in his business complex, the major part of his time for the next few years will be spent in helping to increase production at Fisher. In his words, "Fisher Manufacturing Company has the greatest potential of any company with which I have ever been affiliated."

David Walsh, Production Engineer for the company, was 39 years old and a native of the town in which the plant is located. He graduated from high school in 1943 and entered one of the small state universities where he studied electrical engineering for two years. Interrupting his education to serve in the United States Navy for two years, he returned to finish his degree in electrical engineering. After graduating, he was employed by an oil company and eventually advanced to a position of heading up an oil exploration crew. This job carried him to many foreign countries and gave him experience in hiring, maintenance of equipment, purchasing, and promoting good foreign relations. In 1959, he left the oil company to be with his family more. His next job as a research engineer with a national manufacturer of windows, doors, and curtain walls carried him to the West Coast and the Middle West operations of the company. He left this company in the fall of 1963 to join Fisher Manufacturing Company because "I felt my new employer had greater growth capacity than the company I was presently with."

William Burford, Accountant and Treasurer, was 32 years of age and a native of Little Rock, Arkansas. After graduating from the University of Arkansas with a Bachelor's degree in Accounting in 1954, he went to work for a national accounting firm in their Dallas office, and was subsequently transferred to their New Orleans office in 1957. In 1960 he joined Fisher Manufacturing Company as their accountant because of the great potential which he felt existed for the company. A statement in his resumè read, "I feel that my past experience will be an asset to the company in many ways, and that both Fisher and I will be able to grow and mature together."

Frank Gladney, a Board member and old friend of Leonard Fisher, had purchased some of the stock of the company when it was organized in 1954. Although he gave advice to the company on occasions about finances, his role in the company was largely passive.

Other employees in the company were:

Sam Clark . . . . assembler
William Cooper . . . . semiautomatic mold
David Cross . . . . die maker
Joe Panzica . . . . assembler
Rick Harrison . . . . semiautomatic mold
Mike Williams . . . . salesman
Jerry Smith . . . . draftsman
Holt Kelley . . . . welder
Bill Davidson . . . . chemical mixer
Manuel Jordan . . . . semiautomatic mold

Joe Burke	carpenter	George Mason	salesman
Tom Patterson	material control	Curtis Hatcher	assembler
Gil Thrasher	toolmaker	Paul Davis	foreman
Sherman Anderson	assembler	Martha Roberts	executive secretary
Ronald Peacock	foreman	Sarah Edwards	secretary bookkeeper

Cooper, Anderson, and Jordan were Negroes and had been with the company longer than those in the other positions.

The Products

The Fisher Manufacturing Company originally produced insulation panels for refrigerated storage units. These panels were made by a patented process, purchased by Leonard Fisher in 1953, that combined wood shavings and plastic foam. However, since 1960 the company had been pushing for expansion into nonrefrigerated building applications, which would include prefabricated convenience stores and service stations. Further, applications of the panels to interior curtain walls were being vigorously investigated. Even though these products constituted a lucrative market, Leonard Fisher has constantly stressed that the company must continue to innovate in order to continue to grow. Therefore, he states that the product line will include anything that the company is able to produce profitably, for to restrict the product line would restrict innovation and opportunity and lead to an early decline in sales when the competition in the present lines becomes intense. The prospectus of the company, as written by Wayne Fisher, stated:

> A policy of the Company is to be market-oriented. The functions of both marketing and production are to satisfy customer needs. More specifically, the function of marketing is not merely to sell what the production function can produce. Both production and marketing are to view themselves in the partnership of creating customer satisfactions.

The major products of the company fell into the classes described below.

Nonrefrigerated Boxes

Nonrefrigerated boxes made from wood-plastic panels were a product that had such excellent insulation qualities that they could replace, for instance, refrigerated trucks used in the distribution of frozen food. The frozen items could simply be placed in the boxes in the morning, and without refrigeration they would stay frozen all day.

The company enjoyed a competitive advantage because of its pioneer production of the panels for the refrigeration industry.

Estimated sales were:

Fiscal Year Ended June 30	Amount
1964	600 boxes at $75 = $ 45,000
1965	2,000 boxes at $75 = $150,000
1966	3,000 boxes at $75 = $225,000

Wood-Plastic Architectural Building Panels

These panels were the key to the company's growth and profits because they were used in some form or another in every one of the company's products. Because of the cost, insulating, and structural advantages over competing products, the situation was generally one where superior products to those presently on the market could be offered at lower prices than present products commanded.

The company had invested very heavily in research, development, and engineering and had developed a manufacturing process superior and less costly than any other known process.

Present production capacity for these panels by the company was easily 5,000,000 sq. ft. of panels per year. If pushed, the present facilities could produce 8,000,000 sq. ft. per year. With the investment of an additional $10,000, production could be increased to 15,000,000 sq. ft. per year.

Productive capacity for these panels appears virtually unlimited. Moreover, since this was a new product, the Company had not yet been able to find the demand limits of the market. Fisher executives strongly felt that in the areas of cold storage plants, refrigerated rooms and boxes, nonrefrigerated boxes, prefabricated buildings and interior curtain walls, the product the company had was superior to competing products and could be sold at lower than competitive prices at a profit.

However, the company could not make accurate estimates of the size of the market for these panels, but it was Leonard's opinion that the market was tremendously large. Very conservatively, he estimated that sales of panels, in addition to those used in their other products described above, would be:

Fiscal Year Ended June 30	Amount
1964	72,000 sq. ft. X $1.00 = $ 72,000
1965	240,000 sq. ft. X $1.00 = $240,000
1966	360,000 sq. ft. X $1.00 = $360,000

After returning from a midwinter vacation-business trip to Trinidad, Leonard started pushing the idea that the company should use its knowledge and product resources to set up an outlet for its panels in the West Indies. He suggested to a Board meeting that since supermarkets were just beginning to develop in the Islands and since low cost, sturdy housing was also in demand, the company could find a profitable and extensive market for its products there. In order to acquaint the local businessmen with the advantages of the panels, he wanted to set up a mango juice processing plant made out of the panels as a model of their various uses. Further, he said the plant itself would be profitable since there would be a ready market for the juice in the States. The Board decided not to take any definite action on Leonard's latest proposal, but to keep the possibilities in mind.

Pre-Fabricated Stores and Service Stations

As another end use of the panels, the company was in a position to supply prefabricated stores and service stations. Like the panel sales, the size of this market was indeterminate, but it estimated from experience in this area that sales would be:

Fiscal Year Ended June 30	Amount
1964	20 stores @ $15,000 = $300,000
1965	40 stores @ $15,000 = $600,000
1966	60 stores @ $15,000 = $900,000

The company felt that the construction of convenience and grocery stores would provide a means of capitalizing on some knowledge of store layout, design, and merchandising in the grocery field. Leonard Fisher was recognized an an authority in all these areas. He had twice addressed the Southern Association of Convenience Stores on these topics. Further, Wayne Fisher had extensive training in this area while in graduate school.

Incidents at Fisher Manufacturing Company

The following incidents took place during the month of March 1964. Because many of the workmen had appeared uneasy with Leonard in an office which had a window looking directly into the plant area, Leonard had moved to an office in a Motor Hotel two blocks from the plant. During March, Leonard traveled on company business a great deal; consequently, with Leonard out of town and in line with Wayne's recent innovation of stressing the need for written communication instead of spoken (he had given out pads with the words DON'T SAY IT--WRITE IT! at the top), several memos appeared which normally might not be written.

Incident

INTEROFFICE CORRESPONDENCE March 3, 1964

To: Leonard

The following quote was interesting to me:

"The test of a good manager is not how good he is at bossing, but how little bossing he has to do because of the training of his men and the organization of their work."

By: Wayne

Incident

INTEROFFICE CORRESPONDENCE March 3, 1964

To: Ray

Subject: Panel Costs

Please get me labor costs for our standard wall panels in the following quantities per month:

100
150
200
250

By: Wayne

Incident

INTEROFFICE CORRESPONDENCE March 5, 1964

To: Ray

Subject: When foremen are sick

I thought I had made it clear that if a foreman is out for some reason that Cooper, Anderson, or Jordan are not to take over. Those men may be able to operate that complex machinery OK, but it just wouldn't look right or be right for them to operate people. With me going out of town tomorrow I don't want this to happen again.

By: Leonard

Incident

William Burford entered Wayne's office late in the afternoon on March 10, and the following conversation took place.

FISHER: "Hi, Bill, what's on your mind?"

BURFORD: "I've got those revised cost statements you wanted. The projections were really off. If Ray doesn't come a little closer, we're going to have to revise all our projections, 'cause it doesn't look like we'll hit anywhere near the sales level we need."

FISHER: "Yea, I know that things aren't going exactly to plan, but with a little bit of luck the adjustments won't be too significant. Besides, we can't do any juggling until Leonard gets back next week."

BURFORD: "True, but we've got another problem that's going to have to be solved right now."

FISHER: "How's that?"

BURFORD: "Well, Martha (Martha Roberts, executive secretary) called her lawyer this afternoon. She blew up when I asked her to clear her desk. You remember Leonard got on a "clean the office up" campaign before he left, and I finally got around to saying something to her. She said that if the company was too cheap to hire a janitor then she wasn't going to do that. And that not only was she not doing the work of an executive secretary, but that she had not seen any executives around this place."

FISHER: "What did you do?"

BURFORD: "I told her that we would try to work something out, but I heard her call some lawyer anyway after I left the office."

FISHER: "What do you think we should do"?

BURFORD: "I don't know. There's really not enough work to keep Martha busy all the time, but I hate to see her leave because Leonard will put Cynthia (Leonard's wife) in there and she'll be just like a spy when he's not around."

FISHER: "Now, Bill, you know that Cynthia won't purposefully be spying on anyone if she comes in."

BURFORD: "Hell, if I don't! Leonard's been complaining about Martha for a month now, and she's a damned good secretary regardless of what he says. Besides, now that he's exiled over at the motel, he just wants someone here that'll tell him everything that happens."

Incident

Martha called in on March 10 and said that she would not be returning to work, and asked that her final check be mailed to her.

Incident

An excerpt from an Air Mail, Special Delivery letter to Wayne from Leonard at a manufacturers' conference in Chicago, dated March 10 and received March 11.

". . .so in the light of the ideas and encouragement I've picked up here, I think that we should move up the time schedule for you to take over the operations and let me concentrate on selling. I think I can begin to build a really top-notch force right away. I showed some of our material to a salesman from Alcoa, and he said we had the hottest building material in the country and he would like to talk to us about joining up. And he wasn't the only one that's showed such enthusiasm."

Incident

INTEROFFICE CORRESPONDENCE March 13, 1964

To: Bill Burford
Subject: Source and Application of Funds Statements

I have not yet received the statements which you promised to have in my office by today at noon. I had planned to work on them over the weekend. Perhaps it has been delayed in getting to me, if so please disregard the following.

I believe it is important that you keep your promises,or at least let the other person know in advance that you can't.

By: Wayne

Incident

The following letter was written to Leonard on March 16. Carbon copies were sent to all members of the Board.

Dear Mr. Fisher:

This is to inform you of my resignation as accountant-office manager of your company.

I am truly sorry to bring this up at a time when we are just getting operations under control, but I feel that public accounting is more promising and suited for me.

I believe that we are able to say that the worst part is over and my resigning now will not affect operations.

I have gained valuable experience with this company during the short while employed, and want to personally congratulate all the men and yourself for the fine efforts and patience extended during this reorganization.

I hope that my resignation will not hinder our relations as professional men, but instead, improve them.

If ever I may be of assistance to you or any employee of your firm, you can be assured that the matter will receive my immediate attention.

Yours very truly,

s/William Burford

Incident

INTEROFFICE CORRESPONDENCE March 19, 1964

To: Leonard
Subject: Bond Issue

A bond issue for us might be a good idea. I have done most of the work already and will discuss it in detail at your house Sunday. I would estimate the cost of a $250,000 issue as follows:

$ 400	Printing
300	Filing fee
500	Selling costs
$1,200	

Of course, I do not think it would be wise for you to spend too much time selling these if you could better spend your time on sales.

By: Wayne

Incident

INTEROFFICE CORRESPONDENCE March 20, 1964

To: Leonard
Subject: Ideas to discuss as soon as we can

I feel that the following ideas are helpful in the present stage of the development of our organization. It seems to me that a thing that we need in the organization is more discipline (not necessarily punishment, now, discipline). And discipline to do the following things:

(1) Planning. Set up goals and objectives in advance and stick to them. (Unless there are very compelling reasons to change.)

(2) Controlling. Comparing what does happen with what was supposed to happen according to the plan. Obviously, no real control can be done without good planning in the first place.

By: Wayne

Incident

On the afternoon of March 20 Wayne went into the plant area to talk to Ray about getting more realistic cost estimates on panels. The conversation eventually got around to the company as a whole.

DUBY: "Frankly, Wayne, I don't think anyone pays any attention to what I have to say around here. I'm not paying my own way and Leonard won't sit down and talk things over with me. If things don't improve, then I'm going to leave this mess."

FISHER: "Ray, it's not all that bad. We're just going through some growing pains that all businesses have to experience when they move from small to large scale operations."

DUBY: "That may be true, but why in the hell won't Leonard let me run the plant like I want to? After all, he hired me to make decisions, and now when he's around he tries to run the whole show. We're on an eternal merry-go-round; we're not moving, not making sales. Every time we get a new product all lined up, it's off on some tangent and the really good ideas are left by the wayside."

FISHER: "OK, simmer down, Ray. Things may not be going very smoothly right now, but a lot of the trouble between you and Leonard can be traced to you. You're competitive with him too much--after all, this just adds fuel to any smoldering fires. And of course he's defensive about this company's operations; he did start the company you know."

DUBY: "Well, you're right of course, but if things don't cool down, then Leonard's going to have a heart attack or something, and I'm going to get out of here but fast."

FISHER: "I promise I'll try to talk to Leonard about all this tension as soon as we get all the other matters taken care of. A lot has piled up while he's been away."

Incident

Going through his desk late on the night of March 21 after returning from his business trip, Leonard found the following on top of a stack of correspondence.

INTEROFFICE CORRESPONDENCE March 20, 1964

To Leonard

I sincerely hope that we'll be able to sit down Sunday and work something out definitely about several problems.

By: Wayne

On Sunday, after discussing Leonard's trip and some minor company problems, Wayne and Leonard had a long discussion about all the recent developments in the company. The following are excerpts from that conversation.

LEONARD: "Well, it just seems like Duby's not panning out as we expected. I think he really sold us a bill of goods, and we believed that he'd produce a helluva lot better than he did. Don't you agree?"

WAYNE: "Yes, but I don't think Ray's to blame alone. We've had an awful lot of tension and disruption in the plant recently, although he really has messed us up on those estimates about the panels."

LEONARD: "Right! I'm going to call him in Monday and find out what his excuse is. I have several people in mind that I know can do his job, and probably all of them can do it better than him! In fact, the more I think about it, the more I know we can get along a lot better without Ray Duby."

WAYNE: "Leonard, at least promise you'll give him a chance to explain. After all, several of his mistakes can be traced to your not bothering to write out a communication and then expecting him to remember a lot of details."

LEONARD: "My failure to write everything out is beside the point. Besides, you know I hate to write things out because of my poor grammar and spelling. After all, I can't have the employees thinking I'm an illiterate. You stick to the memos, Little Brother, and I'll stick to making the big decisions and pushing those sales up."

. . . .

LEONARD: "I'm sold on the idea that we're about to really get moving, and we'll pass up a golden opportunity if we don't go through with that idea of mine about setting up an operation in Trinidad. I want you to go down there with me as soon as we can get a new plant manager and get him squared away."

WAYNE: "I thought we had decided not to do anything about that right now, until we sort of get firmed up in some other areas."

LEONARD: "No, I'm sure this is the best thing right now. The other areas will take care of themselves. We just can't make the mistake of not taking advantage of all those sales waiting for us down there."

WAYNE: "Leonard, don't you think we're jumping around too much? We just get going with one product, in one area, and then before things are really running smoothly, we jump into something else. There's a lot more to being a success than making sales, you know."

LEONARD: "Hell, Wayne, if you can sell enough, you can cover up any managerial mistakes you make along the way--you don't have to go to college to know that. I want those sales. That's what'll make us a big company."

WAYNE: "That may be your idea, but mine is different; and if we don't get some organization and cooperation here, then I'm pulling out. You might have built this company into what it is today, but you damn sure will never get any further with the attitude you have now. And I don't want to worry with it and then have the lid blow off in my face--and that's exactly where we're headed!"

Incident

INTEROFFICE CORRESPONDENCE March 24, 1964

To: Mr. Ray Duby
Subject: Resignation

After our talk yesterday, I'm sure the best thing for you to do is to resign. Your failure to follow orders and the general mess in the plant and the poor estimates all show that you would be better off somewhere else, and we would too.

I expect you to turn your resignation letter in to Wayne by noon tomorrow. He'll give you a check for one week's work. Good luck in finding a new job.

By: Leonard Fisher, President

INTEROFFICE CORRESPONDENCE March 24, 1964

To: Wayne
Subject: Duby's resignation

Ray will never work out no better than he has. I told him to resign by noon Wednesday. Give him a check for one week's wages. Better place an ad in the New Orleans paper for a new man. I'll interview applicants when I get back in town Friday. Sorry I won't be here until then, but am sure you can work things out OK.

By: Leonard

FISHER MANUFACTURING COMPANY
Balance Sheet - December 31, 1963

ASSETS

Current Assets:			
Cash on Hand and in Bank		$ 2,075.91	
Accounts Receivable	$ 50,620.01		
Less: Allowance for Doubtful Accounts	5,010.13	45,609.88	
Notes Receivable		1,451.73	
Inventories		83,071.07	
Prepaid Insurance		1,250.32	
Deposits on Notes Receivable Discounted		13,604.38	
Total Current Assets			$147,063.29
Other Assets:			
Telephone and Utility Deposits			$ 227.50
Fixed Assets:			
Land		$ 10,000.00	
Building	$ 97,114.61		
Machinery and Equipment	77,990.14		
Automobiles and Trucks	14,015.19		
Furniture and Fixtures	5,121.61		
Total Depreciable Assets	$194,241.55		
Accumulated Depreciation	29,881.97	164,359.58	
Total Fixed Assets			$174,359.58
Intangible Assets:			
Goodwill			$ 82,184.16
Total Assets			$403,834.53

LIABILITIES AND STOCKHOLDERS' EQUITY

Current Liabilities:		
Accounts Payable	$ 28,525.98	
Mortgage Payable--Sherman Building Co.	15,000.00	
Federal Income Taxes Payable	2,742.20	
Accrued Payroll and Other Taxes	3,056.37	
Accrued Payroll	1,149.13	
Accrued Expenses--Other	726.41	
Reserve for Warranty on Panels	7,072.75	
		$ 58,272.84

Long-Term Liabilities:

Mortgage Payable--Townson Building Assn.		$ 69,028.74
Total Liabilities		$127,301.58

Stockholders' Equity:

Capital Stock (Note)	$273,100.00	
Surplus Arising from Reevaluation of Fixed Assets .	14,142.88	
Retained Earnings (Deficit)	(10,709.93)	
Total Stockholders' Equity.		276,532.95
Total Liabilities and Stockholders' Equity .		$403,834.53

FISHER MANUFACTURING COMPANY
Statement of Income (Loss)
for the Six-Month Period Ended December 31, 1963

Income:

Sales	$264,367.15	
Less: Sales Returns and Allowances.	5,599.23	
Net Sales		$258,767.92
Cost of Sales.		233,175.08
Gross Profit on Sales		$ 25,592.84

Operating Expenses:

Factory Selling Expenses	$ 10,392.74	
Factory General Expenses.	12,624.64	
Operating Expenses	30,722.73	
Total Operating Expenses		$ 53,740.11
Net Loss from Operations		($ 28,147.27)

Other Income:

Discounts Earned.	$ 2,781.10	
Interest and Carrying Charges	2,108.41	
Miscellaneous	221.94	
Total Other Income		5,111.45
Net Loss before Other Deductions.		($ 23,035.82)

Other Deductions:

Interest		2,536.95
Net Loss for the Period		($ 25,572.77)

FISHER MANUFACTURING COMPANY
Projected Statement of Income
for the Year Ended June 30, 1964
(At June 30, 1963)

		Amount		Percent to Sales
Sales			$838,000.00	100.00%
Cost of Goods Sold:				
Direct Material		$603,600.00		72.01%
Direct Labor		38,100.00		
Factory Overhead:				
Indirect Labor	$16,850.00			
Overtime Premium	10,700.00			
Factory Supplies	11,800.00			
Utilities	1,600.00			
Repair and Upkeep	3,700.00			
Employee Benefits	2,350.00			
Supervision	400.00			
Rent	7,900.00			
Engineering	5,500.00			
Depreciation	8,600.00			
Insurance	2,400.00			
Payroll Taxes	4,250.00			
Superintendent	13,000.00			
Miscellaneous	1,750.00	90,800.00		10.85%
Total Cost of Goods Sold			732,500.00	87.42%
Gross Profit on Sales			$105,500.00	12.85%
Selling Expenses:				
Salesmen's Salaries and Commissions		$ 34,400.00		
Depreciation		300.00		
Insurance		825.00		
Payroll Taxes		625.00		
Salesmens' Traveling Expenses		6,275.00		
Advertising		1,175.00		
Rent		700.00		
Stationery and Printing		175.00		
Telephone		5,600.00		
Delivery Expense		1,500.00		
Miscellaneous		425.00		
Total Selling Expenses			52,000.00	6.20%
Net Profit on Sales			$ 53,500.00	6.38%

	Amount		Percent to Sales
General and Administrative Expenses:			
Salaries	$19,000.00		
Depreciation	300.00		
Insurance	425.00		
Payroll Taxes	1,150.00		
Travel and Entertainment	375.00		
Telephone	1,800.00		
Rent	375.00		
Utilities	100.00		
Repair and Upkeep	400.00		
Employee Benefits	350.00		
Engineering	625.00		
Experiments	375.00		
Professional Fees	8,500.00		
Stationery and Printing	1,025.00		
Miscellaneous	1,000.00		
Total General and Administrative Expenses		$35,800.00	4.27%
Net Income from Operations		17,700.00	2.11%
Other Income:			
Discounts Earned		9,000.00	1.07%
Net Income before Other Deductions		$26,700.00	3.18%
Other Deductions:			
Administrative Services	$ 1,200.00		
Interest	4,500.00		
Total Other Deductions		5,700.00	.68%
Net Income for the Year		$21,000.00	2.50%

FISHER MANUFACTURING COMPANY
Projected Income Statements
for Fiscal Years Ending June 30
(Thousands of Dollars)
(At June 30, 1963)

	1964	1965	1966	1967
Sales	$838	$3,000	$4,500	$5,500
Cost of Goods Sold (80%)	670	2,400	3,600	4,400
Gross Profit on Sales (25%)	168	600	900	1,100
Selling Expense (7.5%)	63	225	338	412
Net Profit on Sales (12.5%)	105	375	562	688
General and Administrative Expense (2.5%)	21	75	112	138
	84	300	450	550
Less Expense for New Plant	61	---	---	---
Net Income before Taxes	24	300	450	550
Taxes	12	150	225	275
Net Profit after Taxes	$ 12	$ 150	$ 225	$ 275

ASPEN COUNTY HIGH SCHOOL

The following is part of a conversation between the Superintendent of Schools and Mr. Don Mason, Aspen County High School Principal, that took place at the regular Wednesday meeting of the Aspen County School District Board of Trustees during the last week of March.

Superintendent: Don, it seems like every time you come to our meeting you've got your hand out for more money. Last month it was money for new band uniforms. Before that you were trying to tell us the athletic teams needed another $2,000 worth of equipment. Now you hit us with this across-the-board raise for your faculty. You know we're working on a very limited budget and we have other demands that must be met, too.

Don Mason: Of course, it costs money to run a school district. I can understand your problems. But remember, the only way we're going to be able to offer good instruction to this community is by having well-qualified teachers on the staff. And good teachers cost money! Besides, remember you promised us last year when we asked for a raise that we'd get it this year, and. . . .

Superintendent: Now, just a minute Don. We never promised you that you'd get a raise this year. We simply said that it was impossible to give you a raise last year because Western Steel had closed down as a result of the strike and the district's income was decreased substantially.

At that time we thought that Western Steel would soon be operating at full steam and that we would have the funds available for a raise this year. As everyone knows only too well, Western still is only operating at about one-third capacity. This means that their payroll is only about one third. Quite a few people have moved from the area to get jobs. Business income is low and some of the shops have closed their doors permanently. We just don't have the money in the General Fund and we probably couldn't pass a special bond issue at this late date anyway.

* * * *

Aspen County School District was a unified district comprised of four elementary schools, two junior high schools, and one high school. The district served the entire population of the county. The major source of income for this small western community was Western Steel. Strikes and slowdowns at Western Steel often had resulted in extreme fluctuations in the population and the financial well-being of the community. As a result of these problems and others, the superintendent and the Board experienced frequent discord with the teachers and administrators on financial matters.

* * * *

At 8:30 a.m. the following Monday, the thirty-seven faculty members and administrators of Aspen High School held their weekly faculty meeting. The meeting was called to order by the vice-principal of the high school, Bob Lane.

Bob Lane: (Vice-Principal) We have a lot of business to cover in our meeting this morning, but first I think it is appropriate that we hear from Don. As most of you know by now, Don went to bat for the faculty against the Board for a salary increase and he wants to bring this item up first so that everyone will understand exactly how things are progressing.

Don Mason: (Principal) I met with the Board last Thursday and asked about that raise they had promised us. They gave the same old excuse of no funds. It looks like we're going to have a tough battle on our hands if we expect to get an across-the-board raise this year. Since their major objection appears to be a lack of funds, the Teachers' Welfare Committee has been working over the weekend on possible ways that the funds can be obtained. They have worked up a couple of alternatives that can be presented. The most attractive one involves not receiving your three summer months' checks in one lump sum in June as some of you have been doing. Phil, why don't you explain just how that is going to work?

Phil, the chairman of the Teachers' Welfare Committee, then explained to the group that approximately one half of the teachers had been exercising the option to receive their three summer checks in a lump sum at the beginning of the summer. If receipt of these checks could be postponed until after June 30, the expense would appear in the next fiscal year. This could be a permanent postponement. If only 75 percent of those now exercising this option were willing to forego this advantage, enough funds would be created to finance the desired salary increases. A hand vote of those who were willing to give up this option indicated that 16 of the 18 teachers involved would probably be able to rearrange their financial affairs to support the proposal.

Don Mason: Thanks very much for your support. I'll present this proposal to the Board this Thursday and see if we can't work something out. Bob and I were talking just yesterday and we both expressed the opinion that we have an excellent staff here at the high school and we think that you deserve a raise in the salary schedule. Besides, Bob and I are on a schedule, too, and we'd benefit from a raise the same as you would. Both "X" County and "Y" County received schedule increases this year and our county is falling behind.

The meeting was turned over to Bob who conducted the remaining business. That same afternoon a group of teachers were discussing the situation in the teachers' lounge after school.

Teacher A: I heard Bill [an English teacher] say that he was going to investigate the possibility of a position at Sacramento if it looked like we weren't going to get a raise this year. Do you think we'll get the raise?

Teacher B: Naw, we probably won't. But I wouldn't leave because of that alone. Money isn't everything. I think the kind of work environment we have here is worth something. Not very often will you find a school where both the principal and vice-principal will stand behind their teachers and support them 100 percent. I think that's one of the reasons Don and Bob are so well liked by the teachers.

Teacher C: I'll agree with that! I'll never forget that incident with Bob Lane when I first came here. You remember that he asked me to be the Lettermen's Club Advisor? None of the coaches wanted the job because it takes a lot of time and the kids are pretty rough to handle. Well, anyway, when he introduced me to the Club members, he said that the administration would stand behind me in whatever I wanted to do as long as I thought it was for the best benefit of the Club.

Later, when I told the Club members that the initiation had to be toned down considerably because of the danger of seriously hurting someone, they stormed right into Bob Lane's office complaining. They figured that since they had to go through all that rough stuff to be initiated, it was only fair for them to "get revenge" against the new members. Boy, it really made me feel good when I found out Bob had told them, "If that's the way your advisor wants it, then that's the way its going to be." It surely made my job a lot easier from then on.

Teacher A: Do you remember that problem I had in the Boys' Cooking Class right at the first of the year?

Teacher B: No, what was that?

Teacher A: Well, it really wasn't a problem. I was nervous since this was my first teaching job. We were supposed to be making cookies. Two boys were laughing and goofing around and somehow they broke a bottle of milk. I was so upset that I sent them to the office. Really it was just an accident, but Don gave the boys a talking to anyway and told them not to goof off in class. I realized afterward that sending them to the office was too strong of a discipline measure, but I was surely glad that Don stuck up for me anyway.

Teacher D: I really think a lot of Don and Bob. Remember last fall when I was teaching that adult evening class in bookkeeping? Dayle [another teacher] and I had gone out for a little deer hunting after school one afternoon. We shot a three-point near the top of Hogback Mountain and it took us a lot longer than we expected to get that deer out. The class I was teaching was supposed to meet at 7:00 and we didn't get back to town until about 7:30. When Don phoned my home about 7:20

and found out that I was still out deer hunting, he said, "I'll tell the students to go ahead and work on their own. He's probably shot a big one and is having difficulty getting it out."

When I got to class 40 minutes late all my students were still there waiting for a deer hunting story. After class I met Don in the hall and he asked just one question: "Did you get your deer?"

The following Thursday at the Board of Trustees' meeting, Principal Don Mason presented the proposal of the Teachers' Welfare Committee in an effort to show the board members where they could get the funds for a salary increase. After considerable discussion of the proposal, the Board said they would take it into consideration but still didn't feel a salary increase would be forthcoming.

At this poing in the meeting, the Board revealed to Don Mason that during the week they had decided to set his salary for the next year at $12,000. They emphasized that he would be receiving $900 increase in addition to the regular yearly increment of $400. They also emphasized that they expected a lot more cooperation from him in the future.

Mason expressed his thanks for the raise but also expressed his opinion that the teachers should also receive a salary schedule increase. He then rose to leave. As he was leaving he heard one member of the Board whisper, "Boy, talk about ungrateful!"

At the next Board meeting, Mason had arranged for members of the Teachers' Welfare Committee to meet before the Board in an effort to convince the board members of the necessity of a salary schedule raise and that the means for the raise were accessible. After the presentation by the committee, the Board said they would consider this information and requested time to verify the data the committee was using. They also expressed their opinion that there was little hope of obtaining raises this year.

Three days later, all the teachers at the high school received notification of a special faculty meeting to be held immediately after school for the purpose of discussing recent events in the negotiations of salary increases.

As some of the teachers met in the hall on the way to the meeting, Teacher G was asked if he knew what was going on. He replied, "I don't know for sure, but Bob Lane said it was 'something big' and for everyone to be sure to attend."

Teacher H: Maybe we're going to get our raise after all!

Teacher G: Not a chance! You know as well as I do the Board isn't going to let Don tell them what they should do. Something else must be in the air.

As Bob Lane, the vice-principal, called the meeting to order, some of the teachers were commenting on the absence of Principal Don Mason.

Bob Lane: I think everyone is here now. We've called this special meeting because we think that you should know exactly what has been going on during the past few days. Apparently Don has pushed the Board a little too hard for salary increases for the teachers. The night before last one of the board members called me at my home around 9:00 and asked me if I could come over to his house. When I arrived, three of the board members were there to greet me. They asked how I liked my job as an administrator in the high school and I told them I really enjoyed my work here. Then they asked me if I would like to be principal of the high school next year with a nice increase in salary. [Several oh's and ah's were heard in the group.] All I could think of was: What about Don? I asked them if Don had quit and they said, "No, but we aren't going to offer him a contract for next year." [Looks of astonishment and surprise appeared on many faces as a few teachers leaned over and whispered to each other.]

When I asked them why they weren't offering Don a contract, they said it was personal and they didn't want to discuss it with anyone. Well, I didn't hesitate to tell them if they didn't offer Don a contract for next year, they needn't offer me one either because I wouldn't sign it. Now I think this is information that you should know. I think Don finds himself in this position because of his efforts to help you teachers. If there is any way that you can support Don in his fight, I certainly think you should, and I know that he would welcome your help.

At this point Bob Lane left the room and Teacher P, the president of the High School Teachers' Association, took over the meeting. The room was filled with loud talk and excitement.

Teacher P: May I have your attention, please! I know that this is quite an unexpected turn of events. It surprised me as much as it did you when Bob explained the situation to me about an hour ago. But you haven't heard the whole story yet. Don met with the Board in a special meeting that was called at Don's request last evening. He specifically requested reasons for his dismissal, but the Board said they did not have to give any reasons for their actions.

Contracts will be offered on the first of May--that's about ten days away. What can we do to help Don?

Teacher D: (jumping up excitedly): Well, I'll tell you one thing! If they fire Don they can find a replacement for me too. I don't want to work for a Board that can fire someone without any reason other than disagreeing with them.

Teacher E: I have no ties here. The main reason I stay is because I like to teach under Don and Bob. If they go, I'll go too, and I'd like to see the rest of you do the same.

The faculty meeting continued for another hour. It was determined by secret ballet that approximately 90 percent of the faculty would be able and willing to support Principal Mason in the following manner: If Don Mason was not offered a contract, the teachers would not sign their contracts. It was also decided that this information should be conveyed to the Board immediately.

On May 1, the teachers received their contracts in sealed envelopes. Also in each mailbox was a mimeographed note saying Don Mason had not received a contract. All contracts were to be returned to the Board of Trustees by May 15.

During the next two weeks the following appeared in the local newspaper:

Dear Editor:

I read in The Daily Times this evening that Mr. Don Mason has requested four times a statement from the school board as to why his contract was not renewed as principal of the Aspen High School.

I do not know much about civil law, but I do know of a moral law that reads: "Do unto others as you wish them to do unto you." Any person who has been employed in a school system whether principal or teacher for a period of years is definitely entitled, as a matter of courtesy, to be given an explanation as to why his contract is not renewed.

I feel this very unjust to the man and the teachers as a whole. No teacher can feel secure under an administration of this caliber. I think the public should demand an explanation. Any innocent member of the school board who sits back and lets this go on is as guilty as the rest.

Sincerely,

A parent

The following letter was signed by approximately one fourth of the 650 students at Aspen High School.

Dear Editor:

What is the school board trying to do by dismissing Mr. Mason without giving any reasons? We feel that Mr. Mason has done an excellent job of building up our high school.

We have been told that better than 90 percent of our teachers have refused to sign their contracts for the coming year. This would result in drastic conditions for our school system. If this happens our school could possibly become a nonaccredited school. This could pose many problems for the seniors planning to attend college.

Parents! Are we the only ones concerned about these problems?

A citizens committee had been formed to investigate the current school "crisis." This committee had requested the investigating services of Dr. Williams, an executive from the State Education Association. A special meeting was held at which Dr. Williams reported his initial findings to the Citizens Committee. The newspaper printed the following as part of the report of that meeting:

> It was stated during the meeting that there has been a complete breakdown of the communications between teachers, administrators, and school board members, thus creating a crisis in the education system. There has been unwillingness on the part of the school board, it was said, to discuss the situations as they arise with the persons involved. In addition. . . .
>
> Dr. Williams stated that he had checked with attorneys on such a problem and he was now certain that a school board has the right to refuse to give new contracts to teachers without having to give an explanation of the refusal. However, to prevent the type of breakdown that now exists here, that person should be called in and an explanation given as to the cause for action.

Five days prior to May 15, the date the contracts had to be returned to the Board, the local paper printed the following in its editorial column:

> This week appears to be the week of decision, for the contracts are supposed to be returned to the school board within five days. The Board is apparently counting upon most of the good teachers signing up by the deadline.
>
> Thinking on the basis of the present situation and eliminating what is already "water under the bridge," there seem to be three things that could happen: (1) the school board could reverse its decision regarding the principal, or (2) the teachers could decide they want their jobs even more than they want victory in this strange fight, or (3) the board and the teachers could remain adamant and the board could attempt to recruit as many new teachers as needed.

ATLANTA POLICE DEPARTMENT (F)

The (F) case in the Atlanta Police Department Case Series deals with information flow for management control and decision-making purposes. The bulk of the case examines the management information flow within the Detective Division. The case raises the question: How might the Detective Division's information flow be improved?

The Atlanta Police Department's basic information flow system consists of a series of daily crime, traffic and cases booked reports, and a monthly tabulation of crime statistics called "Facts." In addition, because all of the departments' offices are located in one building, day-to-day contact between men within a division is possible. Also, the Department is still small enough so that superior officers at as high a level as superintendent are able to find time to read many of the daily activity reports submitted by their subordinates.

Tabulation Department

The punch card tabulation and crime reports group is under the direction of Lieutenant C. Blackwell, who in turn reports to Superintendent Beerman, Services Division. Lieutenant Blackwell told the case writer:

> This department is statistically minded. The problem we face is where to stop. You can become saturated with statistics very quickly if you are not careful. You have to know when you are approaching the point where the potential use of a report does not justify its cost.
>
> By having the crime report group in the Service Department we can be objective about our work. We have a number of double checks in our data collection system to ensure reliability of data. Then, the detectives keep an eye on us. They'll quickly complain if we don't give them credit for an arrest.
>
> We have just started preparing special M.O. files for sex crimes, following a significant increase in these crimes. We have always had such files for burglaries and robberies. The problem we face in putting together these files is a lack of manpower to do the job.
>
> The detailed analysis of crime reports is done in each division. No particular person does it. The job falls to whomever is available. Perhaps, if we continue to grow we may well have to go to something like Chicago's Crime Analysis and Tactical Squad. Also, if we continue to grow we may well have to go to some type of real-time information system.

The tabulation department included three alpha key punchers, one verifier, one sorter, and an IBM 402 tabulator.

Detective Division

In early 1966 the case writer interviewed Superintendent Clinton Chafin, commanding officer, Detective Division. The interview focuses on the nature of the information flowing to Superintendent Chafin for management control and decision-making purposes. According to Superintendent Chafin:

> The key statistic I use to judge my division's effectiveness is the clearance by arrest ratio. This is the ratio between arrests and reports. Fortunately, in recent years this ratio has been fairly high, principally because so many homicide cases involve combatants who are arrested at the scene of the crime or soon thereafter. . . .
>
> Actually, I find the more detailed monthly crime statistics more useful than the daily reports. The monthly statistics are included in "Facts" (see Table 2 for excerpts from "Facts" related to the Detective Division).
>
> "Facts" gives me a fairly complete picture of what is going on by arrests and offenses. It shows the pattern of homicide, for example, by day of the week and hours of the day. It also shows the high crime areas. Crimes by juveniles are listed. . . .These statistics are useful in establishing patterns.
>
> The number one statistic I always look at first in "Facts" is "crimes cleared by arrest." If we fall off here we are really getting into trouble. . . .
>
> In addition to "Facts," which comes out about 13 to 16 days after the end of the month, I receive IBM printouts which give more detailed information. I receive these soon after "Facts" is available. One of these printouts shows the distribution of crimes by streets.

Each street is assigned a code, which the computer prints out along with the crime frequency for the street. I have to have one of my men write in the street names. . . .With this data on crimes by streets I am able to shift my men into the high crime areas. I've thought about using pin maps to present the same data, but I discarded the idea because it would take up manpower I can use better elsewhere. (Figure 1 reproduces part of the IBM printout for February 1966 showing the frequency of residential, night burglaries by streets.)

The second IBM printout I receive shows the arrests by each of my units. This helps me to keep on top of what the men are doing. If a squad or car is making arrests, you know they are doing their job. . . .(Table 3 shows a portion of the IBM printout for February 1966 giving arrest data by units.)

When I look at these reports I ask--"Are the men living up to their potential?" What I look for in particular depends on the squad. I want answers to these questions--"Are the men hustling in their investigations? Are they making arrests? What is their clearance by arrest ratio? What trends are observable?" A copy of these IBM reports on units goes to each squad and a copy is placed on the bulletin board. . . .

Of course, with all the report and arrest data on IBM cards, I can ask for special reports if I need them. . . .

The department is not so big that I can't still read every morning the reports for the previous day. Also, I normally know the details of the major crimes we are investigating.

Periodically, the tabulation department prepares a summary report for the year to date showing comparative major crime statistics. This summary compares the current period with the same period last year. It highlights the percentage change in crime reports and the percentage of crimes cleared by arrest, which is compared in turn with the national average. The major crimes by juveniles is also shown. This report gives me a good picture of how well I am doing. Sometimes I take the figures and compare them to the similar figures prepared by the FBI for cities comparable to Atlanta, say, Dallas and Houston. . . . (Tables 4 and 5 present the crime comparison reports for 1965 and the period January 1 through April 18, 1966.)

Other reports include "The Daily Bulletin," which is placed on the notice board daily. (See Table 2.) This report, among other things, shows the additions to the stolen automobile list.

Then, we have a "line-up" every day at 4 p.m. The shift ending and the shift going on are present. . . .

Since we are a centralized organization--at least in terms of physical facilities--I'm in the office from 8 a.m. to 4 p.m. The public expects me to be here. Of course, on major crimes I go out into the field. Also, I often ride around in a car after regular hours to observe what's going on. . . .

We rely heavily on field supervision. The largest group under one supervisor is 22 men. We have a lieutenant and sergeant for every 10 to 12 men, often less in some squads. The lieutenant is responsible for evaluating his men. He must look at things like the quality of their reports, court testimony, etc. Once monthly I go over these topics with my supervisors at our superior officers' meeting. Then, of course, we have a 5-man investigating group which checks out complaints against officers. Some of these complaints might originate at Chief Jenkins' weekly open meeting with citizens.

Being centralized has an advantage in that we see each other daily. . . .

Every officer in the headquarters has a speaker directly tied into the radio center. I hear every police call made. My automobile also has a radio tied into the switch board . . .

Crime Prevention

In early 1966 the Crime Prevention Bureau was established under the command of Captain M. Redding. [See Atlanta Police Department (E).] Captain Redding reports to Superintendent Chafin.

The case writer spoke to Captain Redding about the type of information he was receiving for management control and decision-making purposes. Some of Captain Redding's comments are presented below:

Crime prevention is a slow process. Some people expect crime to drop overnight, but we have had to learn how to crawl in the crime prevention area before we could walk.

At this stage of the Bureau's history the big problem is to reach people. We want to get to the man on the street as well as the social and civic leaders.

Essentially, my men are on their own, so I need some kind of check sheet to keep up with them. Here are some reports and records I set up to give me an idea of how and what we are doing.

My monthly crime prevention report gives me a picture of our activity level. The report tells me what we are doing in some of our key areas: Helping hardship cases, getting school dropouts back into school, and meeting people. Any special assignment, such as handling the Vine Street demonstration, is noted on the report. [See Atlanta Police Department (E).] Also, as you can see from the report, the men attended a number of meetings outside of normal working hours. Table 6 presents a copy of the Monthly Crime Prevention Activity Report for March 1966.

Here are some of the records I have established. For example, we have a "contact" file. A separate file card is made from each group contacted. The card lists the name, topics covered, attendance, data, place, and the officer's name. As you can see, the men have spoken to a number of different organizations.

Then there is the "information file" which lists "our friends." These are people or groups we have contacted who have expressed a willingness to talk to us if we should call them. The list includes church people, people on the street, committee chairman, etc.

This file is kept by streets and names. It is very useful; for instance, whenever there is trouble in an area we can call these people and talk to them about it. In this way we can get a feel for the situation.

These people are not informers. They are citizens who are interested in their community. We can rely on them.

In this job its hard to measure whether or not you are being successful. One indication we are making progress is the fact we have had to increase our phones from two to five, each phone having five lines. We are open for calls 18 hours a day. People are constantly calling us to talk to children, groups, etc. Other people call in to tell us they are interested in our work. . . .There are no areas in the city where my men need be afraid to enter.

The case writer also spoke to Superintendent Chafin about the problem of measuring "progress" in the area of crime prevention. According to Superintendent Chafin:

Measuring progress in crime prevention is difficult. You never know for sure what would have happened if you had not undertaken the program.

It will take time to evaluate this work. One statistic we can watch is the juvenile crime figures in "Facts." If the ratio of crimes by juveniles to total crimes goes down, it might be one indication the program is working.

Initially, however, the bureau has to enlist the support of the public. We have to convince the public crime prevention is a joint responsibility of the police and citizens. . . .

Table 1

ATLANTA POLICE DEPARTMENT (F)

Daily Crime Report

CRIME REPORT FOR	DATE 4/30/66		
	YEAR	MONTH	DAY
MURDER	33	12	1
RAPE	54	16	2
ROBBERY	177	56	3
ASSAULT	369	111	9
BURGLARY	1636	385	15
RESIDENCE	636	146	6
NON. RES.	1000	239	9
AUTO LARCENY	1008	309	11
LARCENY OVER $50.00			14
SUICIDE			0

CRIME REPORT FOR	DATE 4/30/65		
	YEAR	MONTH	DAY
MURDER	28	8	0
RAPE	46	16	0
ROBBERY	194	48	1
ASSAULT	261	76	2
BURGLARY	1777	423	16
RESIDENCE	888	207	9
NON. RES.	891	216	7
AUTO LARCENY	1391	368	9
LARCENY OVER $50.00			5
SUICIDE			0

Table 2

ATLANTA POLICE DEPARTMENT (F)

EXCERPTS FROM "FACTS," MARCH 1966

Homicides

	THIS MONTH	TO DATE
NO. REPORTS	3	23
UNFOUNDED		2
	3	21
VICTIM		
White male		6
White female		
Non-white male	3	8
Non-white female		7
	3	21
DAY OF WEEK		
Sunday	1	4
Monday		3
Tuesday		3
Wednesday		1
Thursday		2
Friday	1	4
Saturday	1	6
Cleared by arrest	3	23
NUMBER ARRESTED	1	20
NWM kills NWM	2	7
NWM kills NWF		
NWF kills NWM	1	1
NWF kills NWF		1
NWM kills WM		
WM kills WM		5
WM kills WF		
WM kills WF		
WF kills WM		1
NWM kills WF		
WM kills NWM		
WF kills WF		
Unknown		
	3	21

TIME		THIS MONTH	TO DATE
12	12:59		2
1	1:59		1
2	2:59		1
3	3:59		
4	4:59		
5	5:59		
6	6:59		
7	7:59		
8	8:59		
9	9:59		1
10	10:59		
11	11:59	1	2
12	12:59	1	2
2	1:59		
2	2:59		1
3	3:59		
4	4:59		1
5	5:59		1
6	6:59		
7	7:59		2
8	8:59		2
9	9:59		1
10	10:59		2
11	11:59	1	2
Not stated			
		3	21

DISTRICT CRIME COMMITTED		
71		5
72		2
73	1	9
74	2	5
Not stated		
	3	21

Table 2 (continued)
Rape
March 1966

	THIS MONTH	TO DATE
NO. REPORTS	13	44
UNFOUNDED	7	15
ACTUAL REPORTS	6	29
VICTIM		
White female	4	14
Non-white female	2	15
	6	29
DAY OF WEEK		
Sunday	1	2
Monday	1	3
Tuesday		
Wednesday		3
Thursday	2	5
Friday		4
Saturday	2	12
Not stated		
	6	29
CLEARED BY ARREST	3	24
NUMBER ARRESTED	6	36
PERPETRATOR		
Non-white male attacks non-white female	2	15
Non-white male attacks white female	2	8
White male attacks white female	2	6
White male attacks non-white female		
Not stated		
	6	29
Juveniles arrested	1	7

TIME		THIS MONTH	TO DATE
12	12:59	2	4
1	1:59	1	3
2	2:59		2
3	3:59	2	4
4	4:59		1
5	5:59		2
6	6:59		2
7	7:59		
8	8:59		
9	9:59		
10	10:59		1
11	11:59		1
12	12:59		
1	1:59		1
2	2:59		
3	3:59		
4	4:59		1
5	5:59		1
6	6:59		
7	7:59		
8	8:59		1
9	9:59		1
10	10:59	1	3
11	11:59		1
Not stated			
		6	29

DISTRICT CRIME COMMITTED	THIS MONTH	TO DATE
71	3	13
72		
73	2	5
74	1	11
Not stated		
	6	29

Table 2 (continued)
Robbery
March 1966

	THIS MONTH	TO DATE
NO. REPORTS	35	127
UNFOUNDED	5	12
ACTUAL REPORTS	30	115
CLASSIFICATION		
Highway, street alley, etc.	1	10
Commercial House	7	23
Oil Station	5	24
Chain Store	2	10
Residence	5	12
Bank	2	2
Miscellaneous	8	34
	30	115

TIME		THIS MONTH	TO DATE
12	12:59	2	5
1	1:59	2	4
2	2:59		1
3	3:59	1	3
4	4:59		4
5	5:59		3
6	6:59	1	1
7	7:59	1	4
8	8:59		
9	9:59		2
10	10:59		1
11	11:59	1	2
12	12:59		3
1	1:59	2	7
2	2:59		3
3	3:59	2	5
4	4:59	1	3
5	5:59	1	3
6	6:59		5
7	7:59	2	5
8	8:59	3	11
9	9:59	4	12
10	10:59	4	16
11	11:59	3	9
Not stated			3
		30	115

DAY OF WEEK	THIS MONTH	TO DATE
Sunday	2	13
Monday	5	16
Tuesday	2	11
Wednesday	6	16
Thursday	2	7
Friday	9	26
Saturday	4	26
	30	115
REPORTS CLEARED BY ARRESTS	16	50
JUVENILES ARRESTED	2	9
NUMBER ARRESTED	16	61

DISTRICT CRIME COMMITTED	THIS MONTH	TO DATE
71	3	24
72	2	20
73	13	40
74	12	30
Not stated		
	30	115

Table 2 (continued)
Aggravated Assaults
March 1966

	THIS MONTH	TO DATE
NO. REPORTS	102	258
UNFOUNDED	9	22
ACTUAL REPORTS	93	236

DAY OF WEEK		
Sunday	10	27
Monday	5	23
Tuesday	8	21
Wednesday	4	12
Thursday	9	20
Friday	26	52
Saturday	31	81
	93	236

WEAPONS		
Force	6	7
Pistol	24	69
Shotgun	3	9
Rifle	2	5
Ice Pick	2	2
Knife	33	108
Iron pipe		1
Others	6	14
Unknown	17	21
	93	236

CLEARED BY ARRESTS	70	118
NUMBER ARRESTED	88	231
JUVENILES ARRESTED	4	15

CRIME COMMITTED BY		
WM assaults WM	10	25
WM assaults WF	3	5
WM assaults NWM		
WF assaults WM	1	3
NWM assaults WM	2	7
NWM assaults NWM	45	112
NWF assaults NWM	6	25
NWM assaults NWF	15	41
NWM assaults WF		1
WF assaults WF	1	1
WF assaults NWM		
NWF assaults WF		
WF assaults NWF		
NWF assaults WM		
NWF assaults NWF	4	99
Not stated	6	7
	93	315

TIME		THIS MONTH	TO DATE
12	12:59	6	15
1	1:59	3	8
2	2:59	3	15
3	3:59	2	9
4	4:59	1	1
5	5:59	1	1
6	6:59	1	2
7	7:59		1
8	8:59		
9	9:59	2	3
10	10:59		5
11	11:59	2	4
12	12:59	4	7
1	1:59	2	5
2	2:59	3	14
3	3:59	2	6
4	4:59	2	7
5	5:59	3	8
6	6:59	8	14
7	7:59	10	16
8	8:59	8	19
9	9:59	6	16
10	10:59	8	24
11	11:59	12	26
Not stated		4	10
		93	236

DISTRICT CRIME COMMITTED		
71	28	71
72	9	24
73	21	57
74	35	82
Not stated		2
	93	236

Table 2 (continued)
Burglary Reports
March 1966

CLASSIFICATION	THIS MONTH	TO DATE
Residence-night	47	157
Residence-day	113	277
Residence-unknown	20	46
Nonresidence-night	206	617
Nonresidence-day	9	28
Nonresidence-unknown	24	87
	419	1212
NO. UNFOUNDED	38	76

DAY OF WEEK	THIS MONTH	TO DATE
Sunday	44	149
Monday	88	244
Tuesday	62	157
Wednesday	58	157
Thursday	55	153
Friday	56	162
Saturday	56	184
Not stated		6
	419	1212

TYPE PROPERTY STOLEN	THIS MONTH	TO DATE
Currency, notes, etc.	81	280
Jewelry and precious metals	4	33
Furs	5	6
Clothing	13	46
Locally stolen auto		
Miscellaneous	283	706
No loss	419	1212

JUVENILES ARRESTED	THIS MONTH	TO DATE
White	30	64
Colored	42	117
TOTAL	72	181

DISTRICT CRIME COMMITTED	THIS MONTH	TO DATE
71	108	342
72	81	215
73	109	333
74	120	320
Not stated	1	2
	419	1212

HIGH BURGLARY LOCATIONS-RESIDENCE

4 Burglaries--334-425 Chappell Rd. N.W. (2 day - 2 night)
5 Burglaries--3201-3800 Gordon S.W. (2 day - 2 night - 1 unknown)
3 Burglaries--2091-3712 Gordon Rd. (exten.) S.W. (1 day - 1 night - 1 unknown)
3 Burglaries--157-1218 North Ave. N.E. (3 day)
3 Burglaries--101-210 Peachtree St. (1 day - 2 night)
4 Burglaries--551-1610 Ponce de Leon N.E. (3 day - 1 night)
3 Burglaries--3411-4717 Roswell Rd. (2 day - 1 unknown)
3 Burglaries--1425-2125 Simpson N.W. (2 day - 1 night)

NON-RESIDENCE

10 Burglaries--766-2826 Bankhead N.W. (10 night)
3 Burglaries--105-155 Broad S.W. (3 night)
5 Burglaries--226-921 Flat Shoals Ave. (4 night - 1 unknown)
3 Burglaries--472 Fraser S.E. (1 day - 2 night)
3 Burglaries--271-510 Glen Iris Dr. N.E. (3 night)
6 Burglaries--844-3561 Gordon S.W. (6 night)
4 Burglaries--1041-1942 Howell Mill Rd. (4 night)
3 Burglaries--841-1116 Hunter N.W. (3 night)
3 Burglaries--87-323 Luckie N.W. (2 night - 1 unknown)
3 Burglaries--1335-2275 Marietta Blvd. (1 day - 2 night)
6 Burglaries--253-1107 McDaniel S.W. (5 night - 1 unknown)
7 Burglaries--280-1129 Memorial Dr. S.E. (7 night)
3 Burglaries--245-327 Memorial Dr. S.W. (3 night)
5 Burglaries--537-1263 Moreland Ave. S.E. (5 night)
17 Burglaries--14-3455 Peachtree (3 day - 13 night - 1 unknown)
7 Burglaries--98-2581 Piedmont N.E. (3 days - 4 night)
3 Burglaries--128-294 Pine N.E. (1 day - 2 night)
4 Burglaries--552-863 Ponce de Leon (1 day - 3 night)
12 Burglaries--517-1184 Pryor St. S.W. (11 night - 1 unknown)
4 Burglaries--3172-4361 Roswell Rd. (1 day - 2 night - 1 unknown)

Table 2 (continued)
Burglary Reports
March 1966

NON-RESIDENCE

5 Burglaries--440-1617 Simpson N.W. (1 day - 4 night)
5 Burglaries--915-2861 Stewart S. W. (5 night)
3 Burglaries--351-396 Techwood N.W. (3 night)
3 Burglaries--418-533 Whitehall S.W. (1 day - 2 night)

Larceny
March 1966

CLASSIFICATION	THIS MONTH	TO DATE
Pickpocket	18	62
Purse Snatch	21	67
Shoplifting	88	243
From auto (not accessories)	252	715
Auto Accessories	313	948
Bicycles	116	249
From building	271	791
From coin machine	31	78
Others	62	169
	1172	3322
NO. UNFOUNDED	39	141
$50.00 and over	457	1302
Under $50.00	715	2020
	1172	3322
NO. REPORTS CLEARED	281	785
NO. ARRESTED	363	1004

DAY OF WEEK	PICK PKT.	PURSE SNATCH	SHOP LFT.	FROM AUTO	AUTO ACCESS	BIKE	FROM BLDG.	COIN MCH.	OTHERS	TO DATE
Sunday	2			21	45	9	21	3	5	344
Monday	1	2	15	37	38	23	44	3	12	466
Tuesday	1	2	16	30	38	16	45	2	7	415
Wednesday		2	17	55	42	12	28	1	4	434
Thursday	2	3	14	33	44	11	35	6	6	458
Friday	3	5	12	45	48	24	33	7	10	547
Saturday	8	7	14	28	49	17	50	7	13	564
Not stated	1			3	9	4	15	2	5	94
	18	21	88	252	313	116	271	31	62	3322

JUVENILES ARRESTED	THIS MONTH	TO DATE
White	44	89
Colored	144	360
	188	449

DISTRICT CRIME COMMITTED	THIS MONTH	TO DATE
71	213	565
72	221	662
73	485	1398
74	237	654
Not stated	16	43
	1172	3322

Table 2 (continued)
Juvenile Arrests
March 1966

White Males

CHARGE	10 & under	11	12	13	14	15	16	This Month	To Date
Drunk (including D&D)							1	1	1
Disorderly Conduct			3	2	1	10	16	32	75
Curfew and Loitering				1		1	1	3	8
Runaways					5	5	2	12	24
Aggravated Assaults									1
Other Assaults			2	1			1	4	4
Burglary		1	2	8	9	3	6	29	58
Embezzlement and Fraud									
Forgery and Counterfeiting					1		1	2	2
Gambling-Bookmaking									
Lottery									1
Homicide									
Larceny (except auto)	3	3	5	9	6	77	4	37	77
Auto Theft				1	3	55	6	15	36
Liquor Laws									
Vandalism	7	1	1	5	3	11	3	21	36
Drug Laws-Opium etc;									
Marijuana									
Synthetic Narcotics									
Dangerous Drugs									
Offenses against Family and Children									
Prostitution and Vice									
Rape									
Robbery									
Sex Offenses				1			1	2	3
Stolen Property				2	1			3	3
Vagrancy									
Weapons									3
Arson									
All Others							1	1	2
TOTAL	10	5	13	30	29	32	43	162	338

Automobile Thefts
March 1966

	THIS MONTH	TO DATE
(NO. REPORTS)	254	819
UNFOUNDED	84	239
	170	580
OPERATING WITHOUT OWNERS CONSENT	17	64
NO. ARRESTED	76	239
NO. REPORTS CLEARED	58	204
AUTOS STOLEN LOCALLY AND RECOVERED LOCALLY	102	315
AUTOS STOLEN LOCALLY AND RECOVERED BY OTHER JURISDICTIONS	50	152
	152	467
STOLEN ELSEWHERE RECOVERED LOCALLY	13	46

* *

Table 2 (continued)
Automobile Thefts
March 1966

DAY OF WEEK	THIS MONTH	TO DATE
Sunday	23	97
Monday	28	89
Tuesday	40	83
Wednesday	21	73
Thursday	15	62
Friday	16	68
Saturday	27	108
Not stated		
	170	580

JUVENILES ARRESTED	THIS MONTH	TO DATE
White	15	39
Colored	14	40
	29	79

TYPE CAR STOLEN	THIS MONTH	TO DATE
Buick	6	21
Cadillac	2	10
Chevrolet	83	263
Chrysler		2
Corvette	2	9
Dodge	2	6
Ford	37	134
Mercury		4
Rambler	3	3
Oldsmobile	4	18
Plymouth	4	18
Pontiac	10	40
Studebaker		
Thunderbird		2
Others	17	50
	170	580

DISTRICT CRIME COMMITTED	THIS MONTH	TO DATE
71	27	109
72	28	105
73	76	224
74	39	141
Not stated		
	170	580

Table 2 (continued)
General Arrests (Exclusive of Juveniles)
March 1966

CHARGE	THIS MONTH	TO DATE
Murder and Non. Neg. Homicide	1	18
Rape	5	29
Robbery	14	53
Aggravated Assault	84	216
Burglary	87	215
Larceny (except auto)	175	555
Auto Theft	47	160
Other Assaults	105	283
Forgery and Counterfeiting	19	49
Embezzlement and Fraud	16	38
Stolen Property	14	39
Arson	1	66
Weapons	100	267
Prostitution and Vice	32	69
Sex Offenses (except rape and prostitution)	40	90
Offenses against Family and Children	21	51
Narcotics and Drug Laws	28	95
Liquor Laws	96	271
Vagrancy	29	76
Gambling	71	196
Vandalism	32	86
Others	53	158
Drunk	3759	10001
Drunk and Disorderly	548	1618
Disorderly Conduct	1345	4054
TOTAL	6722	18693

ARRESTED BY AGE AND SEX

WHITE--AGE	THIS MONTH	TO DATE	NONWHITE --AGE	THIS MONTH	TO DATE
17	51	135	17	85	258
18	43	140	18	84	248
19	48	156	19	83	222
20	37	107	20	59	182
21	63	156	21	75	199
22	64	185	22	98	259
23	48	157	23	106	273
24	48	129	24	76	235
25-29	277	715	25-29	429	1171
30-34	296	770	30-34	416	1182
35-39	395	1074	35-39	469	1324
40-44	402	1181	40-44	380	1060
45-49	450	1201	45-49	341	927
50-54	312	849	50-54	202	571
55-59	192	517	55-59	164	432
60-64	117	307	60-64	63	204
65 and over	85	207	65 and over	65	199
Not stated	289	787	Not stated	310	965

Table 2 (continued)
Breakdown of General Arrests
March 1966

WHITES	TOTAL ARRESTS	RESIDENT OF CITY	METRO AREA	ELSEWHERE IN STATE	OUT OF STATE	NOT STATED
Males	2910	2003	196	226	105	380
Females	307	210	32	18	9	38
TOTAL	3217	2213	228	244	114	418

% of total arrests 48.2%
69% of white arrests live in city limits.

NONWHITE						
Males	2878	2591	30	21	9	227
Females	627	570	1	1	1	54
TOTAL	3505	3161	31	22	10	281

% of total arrests 51.8%
90.05% of nonwhite arrests live in city limits.

TOTAL	6722	5374	259	266	124	699

TOTAL ARRESTED ON WARRANTS 154.

* *

ARRESTED BY DAY OF WEEK

	SUNDAY	MONDAY	TUESDAY	WEDNESDAY	THURSDAY	FRIDAY	SATURDAY	NOT STATED
White	282	300	493	463	430	539	687	23
Nonwhite	429	279	400	354	387	665	978	13
TOTAL	711	579	893	817	817	1204	1665	36

* *

ARRESTED BY HOUR OF DAY

Mid	12:59	235	1	1:59	296
1	1:59	270	2	2:59	256
2	2:59	230	3	3:59	276
3	3:59	101	4	4:59	225
4	4:59	63	5	5:59	320
5	5:59	52	6	6:59	367
6	6:59	39	7	7:59	430
7	7:59	47	8	8:59	514
8	8:59	63	9	9:59	529
9	9:59	141	10	10:59	574
10	10:59	170	11	11:59	509
11	11:59	250	Not stated		490
12	12:59	275			6722

Burglary - Residence Night			*	*	*
Sixth, N. W.	33	569	1		8200
			1*	*	8200 *
Argone Ave., N. E.	318	769	1		
			1*	*	*
Argone Way, N. E.	320	300	1		182500
			1*	*	182500*
Bakers Ferry Rd., S. W.	613	3722	1		100
			1*	*	100*
Bankhead Ave., N. W.	617	1401	1		20000
			1*	*	20000*
Bolton Rd., N. W.	736	950	1		1800
			1*	*	1800*
Blvd., S. E.	755	228	1		13000
			1*	*	13000*
Blvd. Granada, S. W.	759	2233	1		100
			1*	*	100*
Broadland Rd., N. W.	806	200	1	1	5000
			1*	1*	5000*
Broyles, N. E.	837	484	1		
			1*	*	*
Blanton Rd., N. W.	929	402	1	1	2500
			1*	1*	2500*
Calloway Drive, N. W.	1114	1859	1	1	1400
			1*	1*	1400*
Carver Drive, N. W.	1159	2289	1		5000
			1*	*	5000*
Chappell Rd., N. W.	1197	350	1		33000
			1*	*	33000*
Chestnut, N. W.	1222	395	1		4000
			1*	*	4000*
Dellwood Drive, N. W.	1651	2011	1		7500
			1*	*	7500*
Drummond, S. W.	1708	824	1		
			1*	*	*
Ezzard, S. E.	2036	589	1		40000
			1*	*	40000*

Figure 1. Frequency of crime printout for Atlanta Police Department.

Table 3

ATLANTA POLICE DEPARTMENT (F)
Arrests by Units Report
February 1966

General Arrest

Security	Squad	Car #	Charge	No.		Extra Counts
	71	114	101	1		
	71	114	119	1		
	71	114	152	1		
				3*	*	*
				3*	*	*
Homicide	72	120	331	1		
				1*	*	*
	72	122	101	5		
	72	122	119	5		
	72	122	128	3		
	72	122	128	1		
	72	122	219	1		
	72	122	309	1		
	72	122	311	2		
	72	122	314	3		
	72	122	346	1		
	72	122	358	1		
	72	122	415	1		
	72	122	428	1		
				25*	*	*
	72	123	101	1		
	72	123	380	1		
				2*	*	*
	72	124	118	1		
	72	124	151	2		
	72	124	308	1		
	72	124	311	2		
	72	124	428	1		
	72	124	465	1		
	72	124	466	1		
				9*	*	*
	72	126	101	4		
	72	126	116	1		
	72	126	118	2		
	72	126	119	4		
	72	126	128	7		
	72	126	158	5		
	72	126	157	2		
	72	126	182	2		
	72	126	219	4		
	72	126	228	1		
	72	126	308	4		

Table 4

ATLANTA POLICE DEPARTMENT (F)
January through December, 1965
In Comparison with Same Period, 1964
January 1, 1966

CRIME	1964	1965	PERCENTAGE OF INCREASE OR DECREASE	CLEARED BY ARREST 1964	CLEARED BY ARREST 1965	PERCENTAGE OF CLEAR-UP	NAT'L. AVERAGE	TOTAL ARREST	JUVENILE
Homicide	106	100	-6%	105	98	98%	90%	103	2
Rape	105	115	+10%	75	91	79%	67%	124	12
Robbery	591	417	-29%	298	216	52%	37%	366	51
Assault	1,066	903	-15%	897	801	89%	74%	962	48
Burglary	5,506	4,820	-12%	1,432	1,468	30%	25%	1,506	667
Larceny Over $50	4,010	4,200	+5%	564	601	21%	19%	4,354	1,773
Larceny Under $50	9,088	8,168	-10%	2,156	2,019				
Auto Theft	4,210	2,974	-29%	1,006	1,014	34%	26%	1,031	409
Autos Re-covered	3,035	2,280							

TOTAL CRIMES - 1964 .24,682
TOTAL CRIMES - 1965 .21,697

TOTAL ARRESTS 8,446
TOTAL JUVENILE ARREST 2,962

Decrease of 12% January through December, 1965 in comparison with same period, 1964 counting Larceny under $50 not counting Larceny under $50, decrease 13.2%.

Table 5

ATLANTA POLICE DEPARTMENT (F)
January through March, 1966
in Comparison with Same period, 1965
April 18, 1966

CRIME	1965	1966	PERCENTAGE OF INCREASE OR DECREASE	CLEARED BY ARREST 1965	CLEARED BY ARREST 1966	PERCENTAGE OF CLEAR-UP	NAT'L. AVERAGE	TOTAL ARREST	JUVENILE
Homicide	19	21	+11%	19	23	110%	90%	20	2
Rape	22	29	+32%	21	24	83%	67%	36	7
Robbery	135	115	-15%	73	50	43%	37%	61	9
Assault	172	236	+37%	162	188	80%	74%	231	15
Burglary	1,330	1,212	-9%	471	426	35%	25%	396	181
Larceny Over $50	1,098	1,302	+19%	151	213	24%	19%	1,004	449
Larceny Under $50	2,237	2,020	-10%	514	572				
Auto Theft	928	580	-37%	355	204	35%	26%	239	79
Autos Re-covered	740	467							

TOTAL CRIMES - 1965 5,941
TOTAL CRIMES - 1966 5,515

TOTAL ARRESTS 1,987
TOTAL JUVENILE ARRESTS 742

Decrease of 7.2%, January-March, 1966, in comparison with same period, 1965, counting Larcney under $50. Not counting Larceny under $50, decrease 5.6%.

Bulletin #19-86	Atlanta, Georgia	Tuesday May 3, 1966

ITEM

1 SPECIAL ORDER NO. 390 - May 3, 1966

The following transfers and assignments are effective May 4, 1966:

DAY WATCH TRAFFIC

C. J. Cleveland
B. G. Penrod
R. J. Lawrence
Clyde Chitwood
R. E. Baker
W. R. Herbig
E. C. Mitchell
J. D. Rainwater
J. D. Harp

* * * * * *

In the future, the 10 A.M. Traffic Watch will be known as the 12 O'Clock Traffic Watch and will work from 12 noon to 8 P.M.

Ptl. N. C. Oliver pensioned 3/1/66.

2 SPECIAL NOTICE: NEW FEDERAL WITHHOLDING TAX. Attached to your paycheck Tuesday will be a pre-punched Federal W-4 Withholding Form for you to fill out, sign and return immediately to the General Office. Everyone must fill one out, sign and return no later than May 6, 1966.

Your paycheck will indicate what the proposed increase or decrease will be. If you want the higher amount taken out of your paycheck, place an "S" outside the box indicating total exemptions claimed. Place an "M" outside the box indicating total exemptions if you prefer the decrease, or lesser amount of tax to be withheld.

STOLEN AUTOS ('66 unless otherwise stated)

	CHEVROLETS				
# 3	66-2 door	maroon	1-60469	4144710745	831 Ashland N. E.
# 4	66-2 door	white	1-15732	21847B164885	560 Casanova S. W.
# 5	62 Corvair	light yellow	1-D40164	20927W220411	Ct'land and Harris
# 6	55-2 door	green	2-14893	B55N025203	77 Whiteford S. E.
# 7	54-2 door	black		B54N121306	1001 Smith S. W.
# 8	59-2 door	black	1-J38917	D59A120269	45 Whitehouse Dr.
# 9	55-2 door	black	1-26244	VC55A057851	886 Woodrow St.
#10	54-2 door	green	1-64078	B54J079380	Sunset and Magnolia
#11	49-4 door	green	2-36785	GAA922943	2151 College Ave.
	FORDS				
#12	55-2 door	blue		U5AG143001	749 Hill St. S. E.
#13	52-2 door	black	29-853	A2AT134524	Courtland St.
#14	65 Mustang	yellow		5T07T193060	242 Auburn St.
#15	64-2 door	white	79-J1111	4A66R145484	Willis Rd. Alpharett
#16	59 Station Wagon	white/red	1-R11719	H9AR124959	376 Spring St. N. W.
#17	53-2 door	gold	1-32288	B3AV174453	Wash. Rd. Coll. Pk.
	OTHERS				
#18	66 Cadillac	blue	GA7455 (S.C.)	G6135425	1630 Pinetree St.
#19	60 Pontiac	white	2-J27279	160D172	687 Memorial Dr.
#20	60 Rambler	black	7-D8141	0220969	Pinetree and 11th
#21	56 Plymouth	red/white	7-19367	P29123660	Hurt and Edgewood
#22	55 Buick	white/blue	1-J45178	V8997766	P'mont and Houston
#23	66 Honda	red	C41	CT200137547	1365 Mayson-Turner
#24	61 Pontiac	maroon	PGL187	561A1318	Ormewood & Confed.

Figure 2. Example of an Atlanta Police Department Daily Bulletin.

Figure 2 (continued)

#25	59 Pontiac	red	10-A337 (65)	459A8068	Simpson and Elm
#26	61 Buick	gold	1-A24870 (65)	4G6013186	819 Simpson Rd.
#27	Trailer (20 ft.)	white	1T/D2148		1750 Marietta Blvd.

#28 SPECIAL NOTICE: Summer Uniforms for Patrolmen are ready for delivery at Banner Uniform Co., 35 Pryor St.

HERBERT T. JENKINS, CHIEF OF POLICE

By:

Table 6

ATLANTA POLICE DEPARTMENT (F)
Crime Prevention Report

CRIME PREVENTION BUREAU WEEKLY REPORT	E.O.A. CENTER	NO. HARDSHIP CASES HANDLED AND COMPLETED	NO. DROPOUTS PROCESSED	NO. PEOPLE CONTACTED (OTHERS)	DATE March FROM 2-27 TO 3-26-66 MEETINGS ATTENDED OFF DUTY	SPECIAL ASSIGNMENT	TOTAL
Dalton, H. L.	Nash Washington	1	1	433	0	2	437
Cordell, A. L.	Central City	1	0	209	2	3	215
Harris, A. A.	Northwest Perry Homes	2	30	962	7	0	1,001
Arnold, J. P.	Price Center	0	4	2,017	1	0	2,022
Jackson, V. E.	Mechanics-ville Sum-merhill	0	2	37	0	3	42
Lyons, H.	Mechanics-ville Sum-merhill	0	0	30	0	0	30
GRAND TOTAL		4	37	3,688	10	8	3,747

Exercise

LOST ON THE MOON: A Decision Exercise

OBJECTIVE

After reading the "Situation" below, you will first individually, and then as a member of a team, rank in importance a number of items available for carrying out your mission. Your objective is to come as close as possible to the "best solution" as determined by experts of the National Aeronautics and Space Administration.

INSTRUCTIONS

PHASE I: Read the "Situation" below and the directions which follow it. Then, in Column 2 ("Your Ranks") of the worksheet, assign priorities to the fifteen items listed. Use a pencil since you may wish to change your rankings. Somewhere on the sheet it may be useful to note your logic for each ranking.

TIME: 15 minutes

PHASE II: Your instructor will assign you to a team. Your task is to arrive at a concensus on your rankings. Share your individual solutions and reach a concensus--one ranking for each of the fifteen items that best satisfies all the team members. Thus, by the end of Phase II, all members of the team should have the same set of rankings in Column 4 ("Group Rankings"). Do not change your individual rankings in Column 2.

TIME: 25 minutes

PHASE III: Your instructor will provide you with the "best solution" to the problem, i.e., the set of rankings determined by the NASA experts, along with their reasoning. Each person should note this set of rankings in Column 1 ("NASA's Ranks"). (Note: While it is fun to debate the experts' rankings and their reasoning, don't forget that the objective of the game is to learn more about decision making, not how to survive on the moon!)

EVALUATION

It is time now to see how well you did, individually and as a team. First, find your individual score by taking the absolute difference between Your Rank (Column 2) and NASA's Rank (Column 1), and writing it in the first Error Points column (Column 3). (Thus, for "Box of Matches," if you ranked it 3 and NASA's rank were 8, you would put a 5 in Column 3 next to "Book of Matches." Then total the error points in Column 3, and write the total in the space at the bottom of the column.

Next score your group performance in the same way, this time taking the absolute differences between Group Ranks (Column 4) and NASA's ranks (Column 1), and writing them in the second Error Points column (Column 5). Total the group error points. (Note that all members of the team will have the same Group Error Points.)

Finally, prepare three pieces of information to be submitted to your instructor when he calls on your team:

(1) Average Individual Error Points (the average of the points in the last space in Column 3. One team member should add these figures and divide by the number of team members to get the average).
(2) Group Error Points (the figure at the bottom of Column 5).
(3) Number of team members who had fewer Individual Error Points than the Group Error Points.

Using this information, your instructor will evaluate the results of the exercise and discuss your performance with you. Together, you will then explore the implications of this exercise for the decision-making process.

"LOST ON THE MOON"

The Situation

Your spaceship has just crash-landed on the moon. You were scheduled to rendezvous with a mother ship 200 miles away on the lighted surface of the moon, but the rough landing has ruined your ship and destroyed all the equipment aboard, except for 15 items listed below.

Your crew's survival depends on reaching the mother ship, so you must choose the most critical items available for the 200-mile trip. Your task is to rank the 15 items in terms of their importance for survival. Place number one by the most important item, number two by the second most important, and so on through number 15, the least important.

WORKSHEET ITEMS	1 NASA'S RANKS	2 YOUR RANKS	3 ERROR POINTS	4 GROUP RANKS	5 ERROR POINTS
Box of Matches					
Food Concentrate					
50 ft. of Nylon Rope					
Parachute Silk					
Solar-Powered Portable Heating Unit					
Two .45 Caliber Pistols					
One Case of Dehydrated Pet Milk					
Two 100 Pound Tanks of Oxygen					
Stellar Map (of the Moon's Constellation					
Self-Inflating Life Raft					
Magnetic Compass					
Five Gallons of Water					
Signal Flares					
First-Aid Kit Containing Injection Needles					
Solar-Powered FM Receiver-Transmitter					

TOTAL ERROR POINTS: Individual _______ Group _______

Exercise

AUCTIONING DIMES

INSTRUCTIONS

Your instructor is going to offer you the opportunity to bid for and purchase dimes from him, along with other members of a group. Please bring a good supply of nickels and pennies to class.

The rules are simple. Your instructor will offer to sell ten dimes to your group; each will, of course, go to the highest bidder. Each dime will be auctioned separately. The instructor will designate the person who may start the bidding. The only requirements are that the minimum bid be one cent, and of course the minimum increase in the bidding must be one cent. Each person in the group will in turn have the option of either raising the bid or passing. If a bid is made, and each member of the group in turn passes all the way back to the person holding that bid, the dime is sold for that price.

A scoreboard showing who purchased each dime and for what price should be posted and kept.

EVALUATION

Your instructor will provide specific questions to help you explore the results of this experiment. Your general objective is to attempt to understand the motives of the purchasers of dimes. How "rational" were the purchase prices paid? What is the relationship of the results of this experiment to "real" organizational life?

PART V

THE CLIMATE AND DEVELOPMENT OF ORGANIZATIONS

INTRODUCTION

The cases in this section focus on two relatively new concepts in the study of organizations, namely climate and development, which rest heavily on and draw directly from the other topical areas discussed in previous sections. The two concepts are logically addressed together in that organization development can be viewed as a set of pragmatic behavioral science intervention techniques the objective of which is to change one or more aspects of organizational climate, and thus to increase organizational effectiveness.

Organization Climate

In the introduction to the section on organizational structure, it was suggested that two organizations, each designed according to characteristics from the various structure continua (e.g., division of labor, span of control, nature of departmentalization), would differ not just as abstractions depicted on organizational charts, but as "places to work." Indeed, if one employs these and other structural dimensions, and adds the organization's communication systems and decision-making procedures and the motivational conditions as embodied in leadership styles and reward and control systems, an organizational diagnosis could be undertaken which would reveal a very great deal of information about how it feels to live and work in that organization. In short, one would be measuring some of the many factors which contribute to the organization climate. The concept has been defined as "a set of properties of the work environment, perceived directly or indirectly by the employees who work in this environment, and is assumed to be a major force in influencing their behavior on the job."[1] It should be added that it is the relationship of these job-related behaviors (and attitudes) to various dimensions of organizational effectiveness, like productivity, product or service quality, absenteeism, and turnover, as well as employee satisfaction, which constitutes the critical link between climate and effectiveness.

What are the important dimensions of organizational climate? There is no one exhaustive, agreed-upon set. Indeed, different researchers have identified a discouragingly large number, many unique, some simply labeled differently. A small sample would include: leadership patterns, goal-direction, size and structure of the organization, communication networks, amount of challenge and responsibility, degree and nature of conflict, members' identification with the organization, nature of reward and punishment systems, and so on.

Just as we have pointed out that there is no one "best" leadership style for all situations, so is there no one unique set of organization climate dimensions, or one best value for each of those dimensions. This becomes obvious when one recalls that organizations differ both in the nature of their tasks and the character of the environments they face and, equally important, their members possess differing needs which they bring to the organization unsatisfied to differing degrees. Accordingly, which dimensions of climate are most important to identify, assess, and perhaps change will depend on (1) the particular criteria of effectiveness the manager wishes to improve, and (2) the particular set of situational and personal factors involved.

While behavioral scientists have developed exceedingly useful techniques and instruments for measuring various dimensions of an organization's climate (this is one aspect--the diagnosis phase --of the process called "organization development"), few managers have continuous access to such relatively careful measurement. They must rely, as you will in your case analyses, on their own perceptiveness. As suggested above, they (and you) must ask questions like:

> What is the particular behavioral or attitudinal problem I want to work on here (which effectiveness criteria need improvement?) Which climate dimensions may be involved in causing the problem? How might these dimensions be changed? What characteristics of the situation and individual needs of the people involved should be taken into account in planning and making such a change?

Hopefully, your own study and experience, as well as the discussions in earlier introductory sections of this volume, should help you answer these questions as you apply them to a specific case. As usual, a manager facing a "live" problem would have the opportunity to engage in trial and error to assess the correctness of his analysis. But that "opportunity" is also a risky, potentially high-cost

[1] J. Gibson, J. Ivancevich, and J. Donnelly, Organizations: Behavior, Structure, Processes (rev. ed.; Dallas: Business Publications, Inc., 1976).

method of learning. An important purpose of doing case analyses is to provide you a relatively risk-free opportunity to test your abilities to diagnose climate problems and develop programs of change.

Organizational Development (OD)

There are many competing definitions of "organization development," none of which is totally satisfying. Some are too narrow, focusing on only one technique or objective, while others are too global, projecting the image of a more rational and comprehensive field of activity than in fact exists. Because organization development remains a field defined largely by its practice (as opposed to its theory), the following rather pragmatic definition is offered as relatively accurate:

> Organization development is the process of employing techniques of intervention, measurement, and change developed in the behavioral sciences to diagnose organizational problems and induce prescribed changes at various levels, including individual attitudes, skills, knowledge, and behaviors, and group and organizational processes and structures. These changes are presumed to have an ultimately positive impact on various criteria of organizational effectiveness.

Even this definition bears a slightly optimistic relationship to reality in that by no means all organization development efforts undertake a systematic, individualized diagnosis prior to commencing the attempted change program, nor is careful measurement of results an integral part of all such efforts.

It is not possible to discuss in detail here the many techniques which in total comprise the field of activity called organization development; many newer texts and specialized volumes perform that function quite well. These techniques include the two major lines of development of the OD field, namely sensitivity training or "T-groups," and survey feedback. Other, somewhat more recent techniques include process consultation and comprehensive management-by-objectives programs. (Cases involving applications of all four of these OD techniques are included in this section.) Additional methods include socio-technical systems consultation, "grid" organization development, various forms of leadership training, and many others.

Because OD is such a new and diverse activity, and because it is a field largely defined by its practice, the cases in this section involving OD techniques have three primary objectives: (1) to provide you with a glimpse of what actually happens in various types of OD programs; (2) to offer you the opportunity to critique the OD techniques as they were applied in each case against an "ideal model" of how an OD program should proceed; and (3) to encourage you to raise a number of important questions about the objectives, effectiveness, and values of OD. The remainder of this introduction will expand on these last two points.

Ideal Model. Gibson, Ivancevich, and Donnelly[2] offer an ideal model of the organization development process which serves as a useful "check list" against which to evaluate OD efforts:

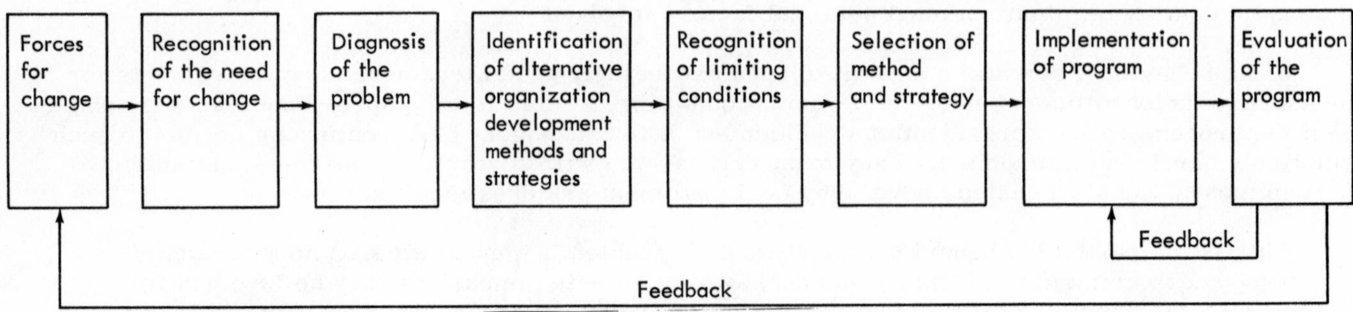

[2] J. Gibson, J. Ivancevich, and J. Donnelly, Organizations: Behavior, Structure, Processes (rev. ed.; Dallas: Business Publications, Inc., 1976).

The model should prove particularly helpful if one focuses on the suggested steps following "recognition in the need for change." The following questions may help to guide your analysis:

(1) Is an adequate diagnosis made of the organizational problem by the consultant, as well as by the manager? Is the diagnosis an intrinsic part of the development program, or is it done separately, prior to selecting the appropriate technique?
(2) Are alternative OD techniques considered, and is the logic for employing the one selected sound? Does the prescription (the selected OD technique) fit the diagnosis (the identified organizational problem)? Are the "limiting conditions" (the attitudes of top managers toward the OD program, the nature of the formal organization, the norms of the organizational culture, etc.) taken into account in selecting the OD technique to be employed?
(3) Is the program implemented skillfully? Does the consultant possess the requisite expertise to use the selected technique effectively?
(4) Is any effort made to evaluate formally, to measure the effectiveness of the OD program? Are before-and-after measures taken to determine whether change attributable to the program has taken place in individuals and/or in the organizational system? Are revised and modified efforts made if these measures suggest a lack of program effectiveness?

Important Questions about Organization Development. The OD cases in this section will hopefully serve as a springboard for you to explore some fundamental questions about organization development. As a relatively young field, it is both exciting and promising, with a great deal of potential already realized. But, not surprisingly, it is also characterized by a number of perplexing questions. For example:

(1) What should be the ultimate goals of an OD program? What criteria of organizational effectiveness should it attempt to improve? Can several or all be improved simultaneously? Are any contradictory?
(2) What should be the intermediate targets of change (the means) in pursuit of those ultimate goals? On what immediate organizational variables should the OD effort work?
(3) Can OD programs be "value-free" as some experts suggest, or does the consultant inevitably impose his values on the client organization? Does the consultant need to make those values (what he thinks an organization "should be") explicit to the members of the organization?
(4) Whose interests should be served by the OD consultant? His presence and activities may very well augment the power and control of some members of the organization and diminish that of others. Should this be a matter of concern?
(5) How can change be measured and attributed to the OD program in a dynamic, "live" organization? Stated differently, how can the critical job of assessing the effectiveness of various OD techniques be done?

These and many other difficult questions deserve careful attention by OD consultants, by managers, and indeed, by all members of organizations who are likely to be touched at some time in the not-too-distant future by the rapidly growing practice of organization development.

SAVEMORE FOOD STORE 5116[1]

The Savemore Corporation is a chain of four hundred retail supermarkets located primarily in the Northeastern section of the United States. Store 5116 employs over fifty persons, all of whom live within suburban Portage, New York, where the store is located.

Wally Shultz served as general manager of store 5116 for six years. Last April he was transferred to another store in the chain. At that time the employees were told by the district manager, Mr. Finnie, that Wally Shultz was being promoted to manage a larger store in another township.

Most of the employees seemed unhappy to lose their old manager. Nearly everyone agreed with the opinion that Shultz was a "good guy to work for." As examples of his desirability as a boss the employees told how Wally had frequently helped the arthritic Negro porter with his floor mopping, how he had shut the store five minutes early each night so that certain employees might catch their busses, of a Christmas party held each year for employees at his own expense, and his general willingness to pitch in. All employees had been on a first-name basis with the manager. About half of them had begun work with the Savemore Corporation when the Portage store was opened.

Wally Shultz was replaced by Clark Raymond. Raymond, about twenty-five years old, was a graduate of an Ivy League college and had been with Savemore a little over one year. After completion of his six-month training program, he served as manager of one of the chain's smaller stores before being advanced to store 5116. In introducting Raymond to the employees, Mr. Finnie stressed his rapid advancement and the profit increase that occurred while Raymond had charge of his last store.

I began my employment in store 5116 early in June. Mr. Raymond was the first person I met in the store, and he impressed me as being more intelligent and efficient than the managers I had worked for in previous summers at other stores. After a brief conversation concerning our respective colleges, he assigned me to a cash register, and I began my duties as a checker and bagger.

In the course of the next month I began to sense that relationships between Raymond and his employees were somewhat strained. This attitude was particularly evident among the older employees of the store, who had worked in store 5116 since its opening. As we all ate our sandwiches together in the cage (an area about twenty feet square in the cellar fenced in by chicken wire, to be used during coffee breaks and lunch hours), I began to question some of the older employees as to why they disliked Mr. Raymond. Laura Morgan, a fellow checker about forty years of age and the mother of two grade-school boys, gave the most specific answers. Her complaints were:

1. Raymond had fired the arthritic Negro porter on the grounds that a porter who "can't mop is no good to the company."
2. Raymond had not employed new help to make up for normal attrition. Because of this, everybody's work load was much heavier than it ever had been before.
3. The new manager made everyone call him "mister. . .he's unfriendly."
4. Raymond didn't pitch in. Wally Shultz had, according to Laura, helped people when they were behind in their work. She said that Shultz had helped her bag on rushed Friday nights when a long line waited at her checkout booth, but "Raymond wouldn't lift a finger if you were dying."
5. Employees were no longer let out early to catch busses. Because of the relative infrequency of this means of transportation, some employees now arrived home up to an hour later.
6. "Young Mr. Know-it-all with his fancy degree. . .takes all the fun out of this place."

Other employees had similar complaints. Gloria, another checker, claimed that, ". . .he sends the company nurse to your home every time you call in sick." Margo, a meat wrapper, remarked "everyone knows how he's having an affair with that new bookkeeper he hired to replace Carol when she quit." Pops Devery, head checker who had been with the chain for over ten years, was perhaps the most vehement of the group. He expressed his views in the following manner: "That new guy's a real louse. . .got a mean streak a mile long. Always trying to cut corners. First it's not enough help, then no overtime, and now, come Saturday mornings, we have to use boxes[2] for the orders 'til

---

[1]At the time of this case, the author, a college student, was employed for the summer as a checker and stockboy in store 5116.

[2]The truck from the company warehouse bringing merchandise for sale and store supplies normally arrived at ten o'clock Saturday mornings. Frequently, the stock of large paper bags would be temporarily depleted. It was then necessary to pack orders in cardboard cartons until the truck was unloaded.

the truck arrives. If it wasn't just a year 'til retirement, I'd leave. Things just aren't what they used to be when Wally was around." The last statement was repeated in different forms by many of the other employees. Hearing all this praise of Wally, I was rather surprised when Mr. Finnie dropped the comment to me one morning that Wally had been demoted for inefficiency, and that no one at store 5116 had been told this. It was important that Mr. Shultz save face, Mr. Finnie told me.

A few days later, on Saturday of the busy weekend preceding the July 4 holiday, store 5116 again ran out of paper bags. However, the delivery truck did not arrive at ten o'clock, and by 10:30 the supply of cardboard cartons was also low. Mr. Raymond put in a hurried call to the warehouse. The men there did not know the whereabouts of the truck but promised to get an emergency supply of bags to us around noon. By eleven o'clock, there were no more containers of any type available, and Mr. Raymond reluctantly locked the doors to all further customers. The twenty checkers and packers remained in their respective booths, chatting among themselves. After a few minutes, Mr. Raymond requested that they all retire to the cellar cage because he had a few words for them. As soon as the group was seated on the wooden benches in the chicken wire enclosed area, Mr. Raymond began to speak, his back to the cellar stairs. In what appeared to be an angered tone, he began, "I'm out for myself first, Savemore second, the customer third, and you last. The inefficiency in this store has amazed me from the moment I arrived here. . . ."

At about this time I noticed Mr. Finnie, the district manager, standing at the head of the cellar stairs. It was not surprising to see him at this time because he usually made three or four unannounced visits to the store each week as part of his regular supervisory procedure. Mr. Raymond, his back turned, had not observed Finnie's entrance.

Mr. Raymond continued, "Contrary to what seems to be the opinion of many of you, the Savemore Corporation is not running a social club here. We're in business for just one thing. . .to make money. One way that we lose money is by closing the store on Saturday morning at eleven o'clock. Another way that we lose money is by using a 60-pound paper bag to do the job of a 20-pound bag. A 60-pound bag costs us over 2 cents apiece; a 20-pound bag costs less than a penny. So when you sell a couple of quarts of milk or a loaf of bread, don't use the big bags. Why do you think we have four different sizes anyway? There's no great intelligence or effort required to pick the right size. So do it. This store wouldn't be closed right now if you'd used your common sense. We started out this week with enough bags to last 'til Monday. . .and they would have lasted 'til Monday if you'd only used your brains. This kind of thing doesn't look good for the store, and it doesn't look good for me. Some of you have been bagging for over five years. . .and you ought'a be able to do it right by now. . ." Mr. Raymond paused and then said, "I trust I've made myself clear on this point."

The cage was silent for a moment, and then Pops Devery, the head checker, spoke up: "Just one thing, Mis-tuh Raymond. Things were running pretty well before you came around. When Wally was here we never ran out'a bags. The customers never complained about overloaded bags or the bottoms falling out before you got here. What're you gonna tell somebody when they ask for a couple of extra bags to use in garbage cans? What're you gonna tell somebody when they want their groceries in a bag, and not a box? You gonna tell them the manager's too damn cheap to give 'em bags? Is that what you're gonna tell 'em? No sir, things were never like this when Wally Shultz was around. We never had to apologize for a cheap manager who didn't order enough then. What'ta you got to say to that, Mis-tuh Raymond?"

Mr. Raymond, his tone more emphatic, began again. "I've got just one thing to say to that, Mr. Devery, and that's this: store 5116 never did much better than break even when Shultz was in charge here. I've shown a profit better than the best he ever hit in six years every week since I've been here. You can check that fact in the book upstairs any time you want. If you don't like the way I'm running things around here, there's nobody begging you to stay. . ."

At this point, Pops Devery interrupted and, looking up the stairs at the district manager, asked, "What about that, Mr. Finnie? You've been around here as long as I have. You told us how Wally got promoted 'cause he was such a good boss. Supposin' you tell this young fellar here what a good manager is really like? How about that, Mr. Finnie?"

A rather surprised Mr. Raymond turned around to look up the stairs at Mr. Finnie. The manager of store 5116 and his checkers and packers waited for Mr. Finnie's answer.

COHACK MANUFACTURING CORPORATION

The Washburn Division of the Cohack Manufacturing Corporation came into existence in August, 1963, when Cohack completed building a new production plant at Crooked Tree, Montana. Crooked Tree is a small town in a rural-resort area approximately 125 miles from Butte, Montana, the home office of Cohack Manufacturing.

The work force had grown to approximately nine hundred employees by July 1, 1969. They were recruited from Crooked Tree and the surrounding ten counties. Almost all new employees were completely without past industrial experience. However, employment standards were high and all persons hired appeared to have considerable potential. With only five exceptions, on July 1, 1969, all production supervisors in the lower three echelons of management had been promoted from within.

Washburn Division had the usual problems of all new plants plus the technological problem of a manufacturing process completely new to industry.

In January, 1966, the plant was organized by the Amalgamated Workers of America after a long and costly strike. Employee-management relations were never recovered. There were numerous changes in top management and union leadership. The union refused to follow the grievance procedure and demanded instant affirmative answers to all problems, the wild cat strike was frequent, lower echelons of management suffered repeated abuses and threats from a limited number of employees, sleeping, loafing, gambling, and even sabotage of production was not unusual. Higher management had, at times, failed to back lower management when it attempted to take disciplinary action.

By the end of 1968 the Washburn Division had forced the Cohack Manufacturing Corporation to the verge of bankruptcy. Early in 1969 the company was able to borrow $4,000,000 on the physical facilities at Washburn, and local top management was again changed. By July, 1969, the technical problems were decreasing, but the human problems remained unchanged.

On July 29, 1969, the president of the company wrote the following letter to all Washburn employees with the hope that it might help to correct the situation:

Cohack Manufacturing Corporation
Butte, Montana
July 29, 1969

TO ALL WASHBURN DIVISION EMPLOYEES:

As you know we have recently made many changes in the top management group at Butte. There also were some changes made at Washburn. These were made because mistakes in the past had taken us to the point of bankruptcy. It was recognized that there were two (2) basic problems. One was the deterioration and lack of proper operating facilities and the other was the small percentage of our employees who were seriously affecting our operating efficiency.

With regard to the first problem, this new management team immediately appropriated approximately four million dollars ($4,000,000) to improve facilities over the next three (3) years. Some improvements already can be seen; others will take time because of engineering and delivery delays.

Concerning the second problem, there are some employees who loaf, sleep, play cards, abuse and threaten our management or just plain don't do the job they are being paid to do. We know, as you do, that no business can operate for long under these conditions. Their actions have caused us to reach the point where our operations are being seriously affected. When this happens the security of everyone is threatened--we will not allow this to continue. Some feel that we were afraid to correct these problems. Nothing could be further from the truth. We honestly believed that since the future of so many employees and their families were at stake we, as management, had to first try persuasion and cooperation before resorting to disciplinary action. This approach has not been successful; in fact, matters have gotten worse.

In the interest of the job security of everyone concerned, we are hereby serving notice that we will no longer tolerate such things as sleeping, loafing, gambling, or game playing on company property, threats or abuse to management, or other interferences which affect production. Our management has the authority to take the necessary corrective measures to stop these practices.

We feel confident that most of our employees will do the job that has to be done. They performed magnificently in our recent production crisis. The only thing which good employees have to worry about is what the few bad ones can do to their job security. We ask for your cooperation in helping us make this a better, safer, more secure place to work. We are doing everything humanly possible and within reason to reach this goal.

C. J. Cohack, President

Where is Back up Plan?

1) Here is what you do when infractions Happen.

2) Was WASHburn Div. Mgt Involved. Should have Comp Pl Mgr. He Should inform,

3) Was action Planned w/ Washburn Mgt & Union?

WATERTITE-FLORIDA COMPANY (A)

In the spring of 1968 Dr. Sidney Harris, Executive Advisor in the management personnel section of the industrial relations division of Watertite-Florida Company, was trying to evaluate the results of the first two years' operation of a management by objectives program that was adopted by the company in 1966.

Background and Growth of the Company

Watertite-Florida Company, in Key West, Florida, one of the five principal divisions of the Watertite Submarine Corporation was primarily engaged in the development of military and commercial submarine vessels and in conducting a variety of scientific research. The Watertite Submarine Corporation had been formed by Jonathan Greenwald and six other young associates in September, 1934.

During the pre- and post-World War II period of the 40s, Watertite experienced a phenomenal growth because of the increased need for military submarine vessels and because of an unprecedented scientific interest in underwater research. In the space of a decade, Watertite's work force expanded from 460 in 1935 to 60,000. By the mid-1960s, from a small, independently owned firm with assets of less than $200,000 in 1934, the Watertite Submarine Corporation had grown into one of the largest corporate enterprises in the United States. Employment was over 70,000.

The Watertite-Florida Company

Watertite Submarine Corporation's rapid expansion and the broadening nature of its business had brought about major revisions in its internal organization in 1954. Watertite had grown in twenty years into an industrial giant, spread from Florida to Mexico and Hawaii. In 1954, under a long-term plan of reorganization and a policy of diversification and decentralization, the corporation established the Watertite-Florida Company as a separate, integrated operating unit.

By 1967, the Watertite Submarine Corporation was divided into five major companies--Watertite-Florida Company, Watertite-Mississippi Company, Watertite-Canada, Ltd., Watertite-Mexico Company, S.A., and Watertite-Hawaii, each with a chief operating officer given the title of president. These semiautonomous companies operated independently from the parent corporation with regard to internal management and personnel policies. (See Figure 1 for an organization chart of the Watertite Submarine Corporation.)

In 1968, the Watertite-Florida Company employed approximately 18,000 people, most of whom worked in Key West or nearby facilities. Employee skills ranged from a large number of scientific and technical Ph.D.s through a sizable group of administrative personnel with advanced degrees in business and related fields down to a surprisingly large number of employees with less-than-high-school education. The latter category of employees arose largely from the fact that the company's greatest period of growth was in the 1940s, when manpower was in very short supply. For the same reason, the average age of employees was high, with many in their 50s. In the decade 1955 to 1965, however, with the increasing requirements of new technologies and diversification, the company added substantial numbers of highly trained technical specialists in their late 20s and 30s, and this category of employees was becoming an ever-growing proportion of the work force.

In 1968, Watertite-Florida programs involved highly technical research and engineering and advanced manufacturing techniques, as well as some comparatively simple and standard "tin bending."

One of the major activities of Watertite-Florida was the construction of the "Argus," the world's fastest underwater vessel. Another program was research to determine man's total needs to live indefinitely in an underwater environment. Conducting marine research for various purposes was still another concern of Watertite-Florida.

One of the most significant industry factors affecting Watertite as well as other companies was the highly competitive nature of the submarine industry. Because productive capacity of the industry has traditionally exceeded demand, it has always been extremely competitive; but Department of Defense changes in contract award and procurement regulations instituted recently have tended to make the industry even more competitive than before. Virtually all production contracts in the submarine industry are awarded by an agency of the government after competitive bidding. More and more contracts are being awarded on a fixed price basis. Clearly, then, in getting business and in making a profit on it, a major management problem is the control and reduction of costs to the lowest point possible. One of the reasons for the company's adopting a management-by-objectives program, no doubt, was the hope it would aid in the overall company cost-reduction effort. Thus, tangible results in terms of increased productivity were certainly one of the goals of the management-by-objectives program.

The Employee Performance and Development Planning Program

Sidney Harris was an Advisor in the management personnel section of the industrial relations division of the Watertite-Florida Company. His primary assignment covered the coordination of all development activities for middle- and top-management executives of the company, including university executive development programs and conferences. In 1966 he was given a special assignment to design and coordinate the installation of an employee performance and development planning program for the entire Watertite-Florida Company. (See Figure 2 for a simplified organization chart for the Watertite-Florida Company and Figure 3 for a partial organization chart for the industrial relations division showing the relationship of the management personnel section to the other functions within the division.)

The management personnel section was responsible for advising all executives of the company on the internal selection and placement of salaried employees. As part of this function, it maintained a computer-operated skill-locator file to help in filling new personnel requirements. In addition, the section operated all company management training courses and coordinated all outside management training activities.

The formal name of the program adopted was the Personal Development Plan. In discussing this program with a case writer from Florida Atlantic University, Sidney Harris commented as follows:

"Management by objectives has been a part of Watertite's philosophy and practice for at least a decade, and it was adopted and made effective many years ago by David S. Eisele, corporate president of Watertite. My assignment was to evolve a performance and development planning procedure which followed the spirit of management by objectives and which might be paraphrased 'performance and development planning by objective,' i.e., the establishment of personal objectives in much the same way that organizational segments have been making organizational objectives for many years.

"Fundamentally, at the very start of the program in 1966, I was probably moved by three things: first, an awareness of McGregor's views on performance appraisal described in 'An Uneasy Look at Performance Appraisal'[1] and a complete sympathy with it; second, a growing awareness that other major corporations, General Electric in particular, were moving in the direction McGregor had indicated; and third, mounting evidence internally here at Watertite that the existing procedures for performance appraisal were inadequate, and that the objectives, to a considerable extent, were not being met.

"The procedures and forms that were in use immediately preceding our present system represented a shot-gun marriage of two procedurally separate matters, namely, performance planning--with which I was concerned--and the appraisal of past performance.

"As experience with those forms and the accompanying procedures accumulated, it became painfully clear that by the time the supervisor and the subordinate had gone through the charade and the implied insults, which seem inseparable from performance appraisal, neither party was in any mood to do a thoughtful or creative job of planning future development. The environment by then had become one of hostility or fantasy, and neither contributes much to what we are getting at. In one of my discussions with the president of the company, I reviewed for him the vast chasm between what we had hoped to do and what we were in fact accomplishing. He indicated an overwhelming interest in performance planning, which is in the future, versus performance appraisal, which is in the past. The former we can do something about. The latter is over and done with--yesterday's toast, if you see what I mean.

"In the two years' experience that we have had with our new program, I feel that remarkable progress has been achieved. But, having come up through the line organization myself, I, of course, have some feeling for, and understanding of, the initial reaction of the staff and management people to the numerous demands of the so-called support functions upon their time.

---

[1] An article by Douglas McGregor, Harvard Business Review 35, No. 3 (May-June, 1957), pp. 89-94.

"I have no doubt that this initial response has been, and still is, the major obstacle to overcome in the introduction of my own or any other system or program. In the face of this obstacle, however, I have considerable feeling and some evidence that the company did a much better job this year than it did the first time around. A good job in this context, of course, would involve the individual's making a significant commitment to himself and to his superior for certain kinds of specific performance during the coming year--performance that is often nonrecurring, usually of a significant, meaningful, and valuable nature to the company as well as to the man's own career development.

"I might add, parenthetically, that we face one other major obstacle in this particular program: a performance planning program is of no use whatever to people who have no intention of performing. Now, while this problem may be found at all ages, it is most serious as men approach the age of retirement. Some of these people seem to have only one thing in mind, and that is holding on until the day of retirement arrives. I have noticed that the more intelligent persons in this category look upon our program with some consternation because they realize that it is an invitation to go beyond the usual, to innovate, to be creative, and to do all sorts of things that, of course, are the opposite of complacency.

"While it is only an untested hypothesis in my mind, I think we can come to terms with these people without destroying their basic point of view. It would seem, for example, that to whatever extent these individuals can be coaxed into committing themselves to even one meaningful, nonrecurring contribution, then we are that much ahead, and it doesn't really destroy their 'don't-rock-the-boat' syndrome. We'll have to work on this problem in a rather subtle way, because it is not good form to separate these people publicly from their colleagues, or to make fools of them, or to imply that their usefulness has come to an end. Obviously, we want quite the opposite, and I should think that this could be done with a little time and effort.

"Meanwhile, the thinking, imaginative person appears to find our new program a fairly rewarding contribution to his way of life. It is an opportunity and a formalized procedure whereby they can commit themselves, in cooperation with their superiors, to significant performance targets. I have a feeling that many people are willing to commit themselves but that industry has forgotten to ask and, indeed, doesn't even want to listen if told. In short, the thinking person approaches this new procedure with a considerable measure of enthusiasm and appears to have little difficulty getting the task accomplished.

"On the other hand, since this is virtually a blank sheet of paper, when placed in the hands of an unimaginative, unthinking individual it undoubtedly represents a terrifying and threatening affair. They have never had this kind of open-endedness and, of course, they are almost totally unable to do anything with it.

"So, there you have some first thoughts about our new program. It is not going to be a complete success for everyone, for it seems destined, primarily, for those who have some intentions of going somewhere. I may be doing the program an injustice, however, because a glance at the form will show you that it can be used for even the most modest improvement targets, such as a bath, a haircut, or a shoe shine. (See Figure 4 for the form titled "Career Planning--A Two-Step Process," with instructions on one side and a work sheet on the other, which was used by participants in the Personal Development Plan.)

"I should add two more comments. First, you will notice I have emphasized that our new approach encompasses total performance planning, not just management development activities in the narrow sense. And I can assure you I emphasize this approach even more strongly in the 30 or 40 training meetings on this subject that I hold annually."

"Finally, I realize I had better clarify my own position vis-à-vis performance appraisal. Having done away with it in such a cavalier fashion, has it ceased to exist at Watertite? The answer is clearly no. It is an inherent and automatic process in a number of selection functions: merit salary increases, promotions, selections for advanced training programs, and so on. Past performance is a very good criterion of future performance, though it is only one of the indicators.

"Moreover, it should be obvious that an appraisal of past performance is implicit but not explicit in the performance planning process, itself. After all, the navigation function requires two points: first, where you want to go, and second, where you are now. As we go through life, none of us achieves all of his goals; but a very healthy and positive action is that of reestablishing targets periodically in the light of what, in fact, has been accomplished at any given point.

"Thus, I would argue that I haven't destroyed the performance appraisal function but, like McGregor, we hope that a good deal of the venom has been removed from it. To whatever extent a formal, recorded appraisal of performance of salaried individuals is to be used at this company, I should like to see it located in the wage and salary area. It seems to me that the very core of their continuous appeals is that salaries should match performance, and so let it be located there. Such a formal appraisal does not exist at the present time.

"The numerous postwar efforts in industry to separate performance appraisal from the merit increases always did appear to be pure hokum. But I hope I'm not making the same mistake, in asking that the performance planning process be removed in time from the usual wreckage left at the scene of the typical performance appraisal. God has not allowed us to learn how to play God. So I retain my jaundiced feelings about the whole affair of performance appraisal."

As indicated in his comments, Sidney Harris introduced the new Individual Development Plan to the division heads individually. Then, a series of meetings was held for each of the divisions. At each meeting, the division head was present along with his immediate subordinates and staff assistants. It was then the responsibility of the division head and his assistants to introduce and implement the program in their particular division.

(Sidney Harris continued:)

"With regard to statistics on participation in the program by divisions, my estimate would be that we regularly obtain about 90 percent coverage from all the divisions. There is a natural gap in the figure because of terminations, transfers, field assignments, et cetera, which result in some people being omitted. But, by and large, I am unaware of any significant failure to do the job requested. The engineering division, however, is only now preparing to utilize our pink sheet (the first copy of the Personal Development Plan form was printed on pink paper and was referred to as the "pink sheet" within the company) in the fashion in which the other divisions have been using it for two years.

"As for a subjective evaluation of the quality of participation, this is another matter entirely. My first reaction, however, is that whatever variation in quality exists, it exists not in terms of one division from another, but rather in terms of one department or one section from another. At the division director level, there is very strict compliance with the letter and, to considerable extent, the spirit of the law; but, as I go deeper and deeper within the salaried organizations, I find great variations in understanding and ability and, perhaps, even honesty of intention in the completion of these performance objectives. Hence, I would have to say the results we get from the pink sheets vary just as naturally as the results one might get from many other assignments. Managers vary in their intelligence and in motivation and in their willingness to accept the concept, and their subordinates usually reflect these virtues or faults.

"With regard to the meetings I hold annually about the pink sheet, these meetings begin in each division director's staff meeting, where I make a one-hour presentation, which includes comments on the quality and quantity of targets, on what approaches seem to be meaningful, and on what kind of target can be measured, on what the philosophy of the whole thing is. And, in general, I review what has been done to date in that division and what opportunities for added usefulness and meaningfulness might be obtained from alternate approaches. The size of each division is quite variable and, therefore, the number of people in these meetings usually varies from perhaps 7 to as many as 25 persons. I then, finally, move down to what might be called the department level and, then, ultimately, to a limited number of sections that have specifically requested my assistance at that level. In total, I probably conduct in January and February of each year about 30 such meetings, give or take 5. There is complete freedom of discussion, my methods are quite informal, and I would be surprised if anyone felt he were at gunpoint when I finished with him. On the other hand, I want to be completely honest. There simply is not time to look each manager in the eye during these meetings and do any kind of careful soul-searching as to whether this man is now, or will possibly in the future be, dragging his feet or goofing off. I must emphasize again that managers in any company vary widely in their total span of ability. As a result, I cannot help but conclude that such variations as we find in the pink sheets are nothing more than the normal variations that are found in any other performance areas.

"I am usually introduced by the senior man in each of these meetings. The cooperation they extend is normally higher than I probably have a right to demand. Continuous emphasis is placed upon the fact that this is their opportunity to commit themselves to something meaningful in their own context and that this is not a phony staff invention or research effort that is a waste of time. How much of that emphasis really sticks I will never know. But, as these things go, it seems increasingly clear that the implementation of this significant change in procedure and philosophy will require about five years before it truly 'sinks in' on the organization as a whole. This is a large body of troops as you know, and it is quite a task to get them all in motion and in step. I believe that reality is far more useful than hope or fond wishes, and I am trying to reflect only the realities of any program of this kind."

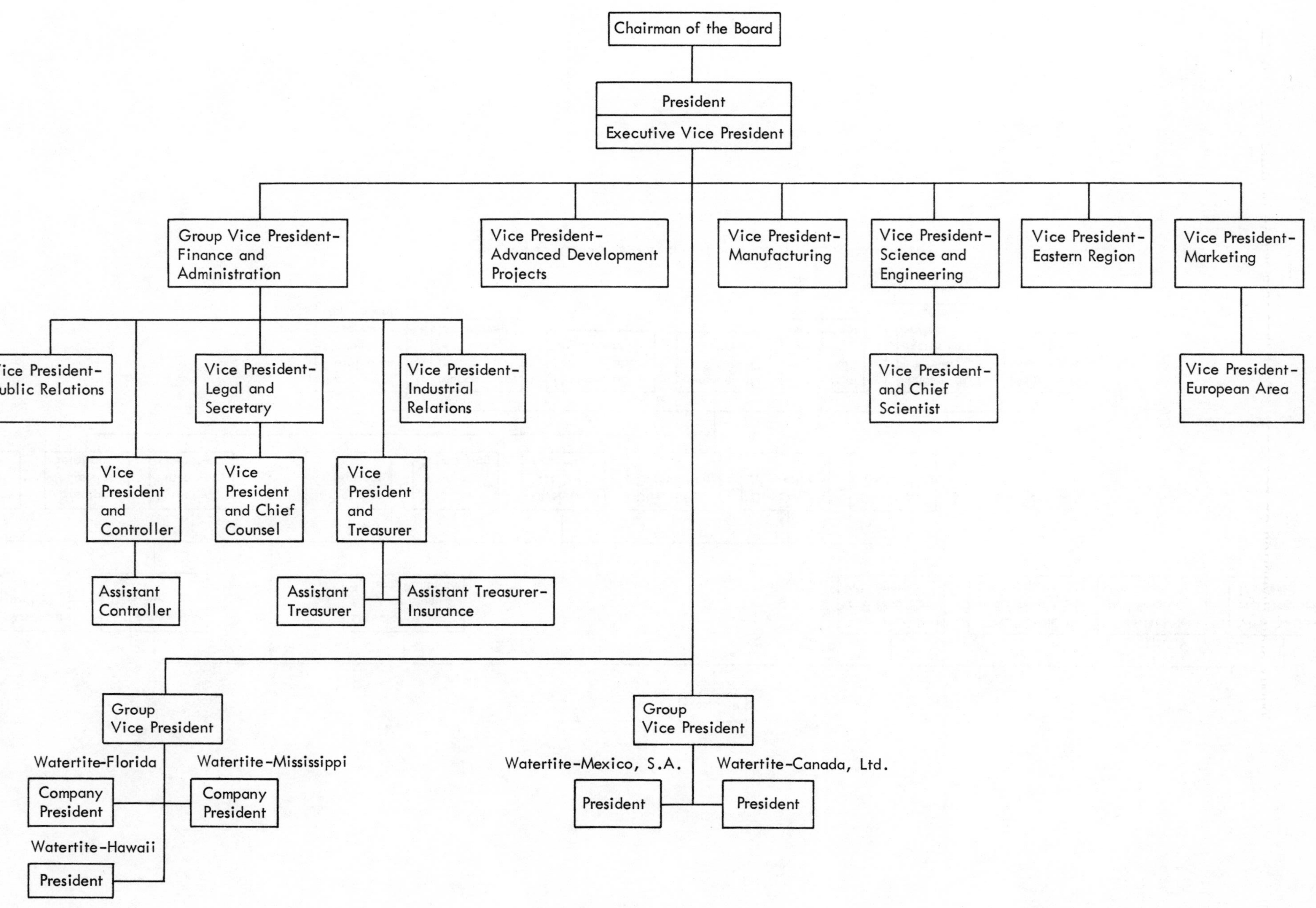

Figure 2. Organization chart for the Watertite Submarine Corporation.

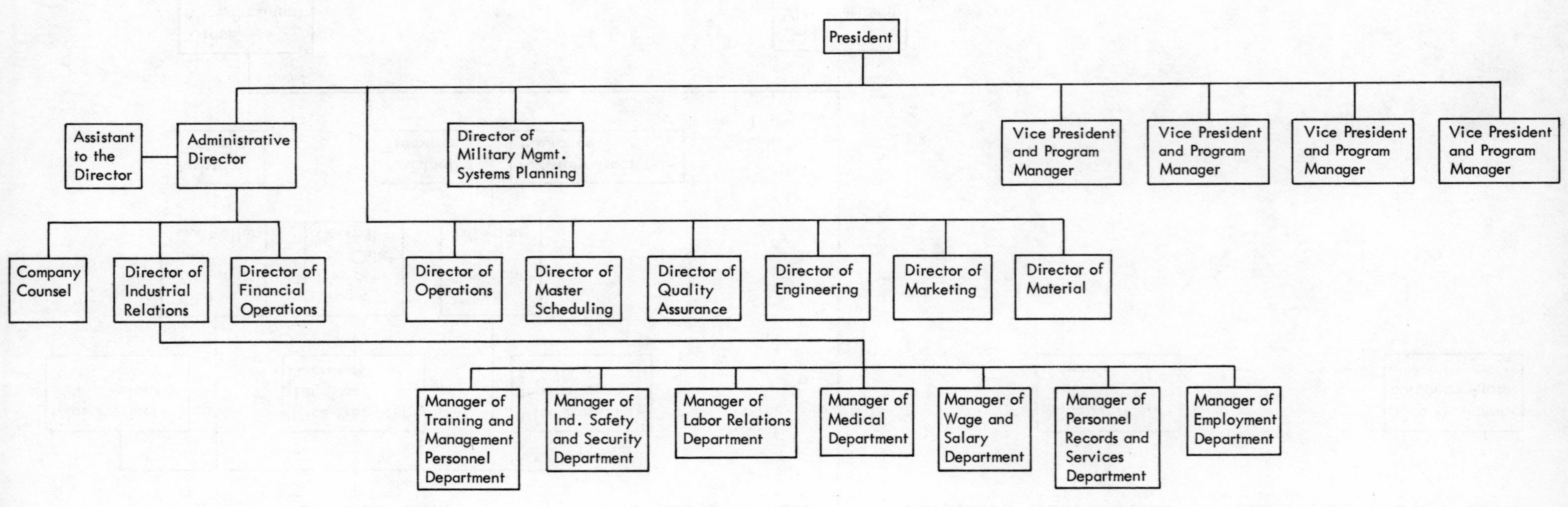

Figure 2. Organization chart for Watertite-Florida Company.

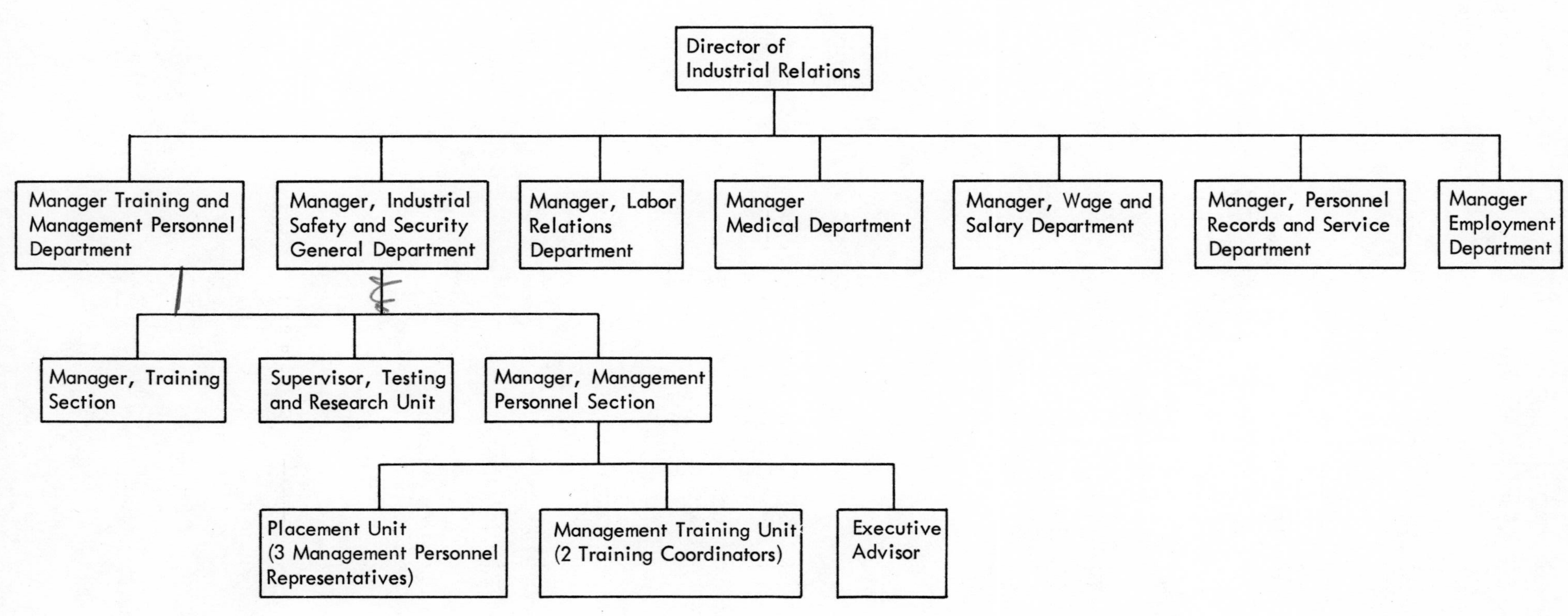

Figure 3. Partial organization chart for the Industrial Relations Division of Watertite-Florida Company.

Annually, each salaried employee, with this superior, is given an opportunity to plan job and related personal development objectives for the coming year. Two separate interviews or discussions are held in order to accomplish this--the first in order to develop a mutual understanding of the individual's major job and development goals.

FIRST INTERVIEW - Job Responsibilities

Prior to this first interview, the superior should detach the "worksheet" copy of this form and make a rough draft in pencil of the top half of the form. Any format may be used, so long as the rough draft clearly emphasizes the principal job responsibilities of this man in this job at this time. In some cases, even the priority of importance can be indicated.

The purpose of the first interview is to review and discuss the rough draft of job responsibilities with the incumbent, making sure than a genuine, mutual understanding of what is important and what is not is obtained.

While this statement of job responsibilities is not "negotiable" in the usual sense, it should only be in rough draft, pencil form at this time, so that additions or revisions can be made during the interview to clarify or emphasize the major points.

At the conclusion of this first interview, the worksheet is given to the incumbent and a date and time is established for the second interview. The superior should suggest, but only suggest, some possible avenues of development which the incumbent might consider in preparing the rough draft, also in pencil, of the other half of the worksheet.

SECOND INTERVIEW - Personal Development Plan

Prior to this second interview, the incumbent should give careful consideration to his job as it has been discussed in order to formulate performance targets--key job goals--for the coming year.

The key job goals and related development activities which he plans to accomplish should take into consideration both the needs of the organization and the personal attributes of the individual.

Since most development occurs on the job, this type of personal development planning usually places greater emphasis upon on-the-job performance targets, but may also inculde formal training goals, professional activities related to the job, or even highly personal study or research activities.

Listing each key performance goal is half of this important step--the other half is to be specific by indicating who is going to do what by when, and how progress can be measured.

The incumbent then takes the completed "rough-drafted" worksheet to the second interview and discusses his tentative plans with his superior. In a manner similar to the first interview, changes may be made in the incumbent's plan as a result of this second discussion, but should be made only if the incumbent genuinely intends to follow his plan.

When agreement is reached at the conclusion of the second interview, both the incumbent and his superior sign the worksheet, which is then used to typewrite an original "Personal Development Plan" with two copies. Distribution will then be made as follows: original to the incumbent, first copy to the immediate superior, and second copy to Management Personnel Section. The worksheet may be retained by the superior or passed on to Division Coordinators.

Experience has indicated that a quarterly review of progress or accomplishment of these goals can be useful to both the incumbent and his superior. Each has a responsibility to the other in this important matter of career development.

Figure 4. Career planning is a two-step process at Watertite-Florida Company.

WATERTITE-FLORIDA COMPANY (A)
PERSONAL DEVELOPMENT PLAN
- WORKSHEET -

Name: ______________________ Clock # ______________________ Date: ____________

Classification ______________________ Dept. ____________

JOB RESPONSIBILITIES: Record the principal responsibilities of the employee's job at this time as mutually understood by the employee and his superior.

PERSONAL DEVELOPMENT PLAN: Record employee's plan to accomplish key job goals and other development activities during the coming year.	MEASUREMENT OF PROGRESS: Indicate target dates for accomplishment of these goals, and how progress is to be measured.

The above items have been discussed and are mutually understood.

Employee: ______________________ Supervisor: ______________________

WATERTITE-FLORIDA COMPANY (B)

In the spring of 1968, Dr. Sidney Harris, executive advisor in the industrial relations division of Watertite-Florida Company, was attempting to evaluate the first two years' operation of a management-by-objectives program. In 1966 Sid Harris had been given the special assignment of designing and coordinating the installation of a MBO program for the entire company. The official name adopted for the program was the "Personal Development Plan." [See the Watertite-Florida Company (A) case for a discussion of the background to the adoption of the program, a description of the program adopted, and a discussion of the means utilized for introducing and implementing the program.]

Sample of Completed Personal Development Plans

In June 1968, as part of his review of the management-by-objectives program, Sid Harris assembled a sample of personal development plans that had been completed by managerial personnel in several divisions of the company. (See Figures 1 through 20 for copies of the completed forms in the sample. Department numbers have been disguised.)

Interviews with Executives

Also as part of his review, Sid Harris held discussions with a number of people in the company about the effectiveness of the program. Three of these people wrote summaries of their comments, which were as follows:

Comments of a Personnel Executive

I am for extending "management by objectives" to the individual. It was the way I operated relative to work assignments. It is the way my boss manages. Each of the people on his staff is responsible for fulfilling certain of the group's objectives. He goes over them with us about quarterly. Of course, we might have other contacts with him on them as we have problems we wish to discuss. This, as a way of managing, simple as it sounds, is, I suspect, still rather foreign to many managers. It is what GE has formalized in a few divisions into what they call "Work Management and Review." It is a way of managing--not a once-a-year form to be filled out.

I think the concept should be taught all managers; I don't think they get enough in actually learning how to manage, in contrast to a lot of interesting, but probably remote from application, stuff. But I think work, planning and review, to be properly introduced, would probably take a six-hour training course, broken up by periods of time, so the trainees could try it out and bring results back to class for discussion.

Most of the valuable development a man gets occurs on the job, usually in terms of the experience he gets. Undoubtedly, a big part of a man's development is up to him, and he can seek out outside activities that will promote his development--courses, Toastmasters training, et cetera. But he cannot transfer himself. He cannot give himself broadening assignments. He cannot send himself to meetings where he would learn. I think this part of development, the manager's side of the coin, is really the most important.

I think all management development activities should be evaluated on the basis of how well they are meeting well-defined objectives. Evaluations should be based on more than conjecture or personal enthusiasm.

In short, let's study this new approach. Let's see how people feel about it--if that is an important criterion of success. Let's see whether it is being carried out in practice as intended? What measures do we have that it's meeting its objective?

There are a number of questions about which we still have inadequate research evidence. Can people learn how to improve performance without some feedbacks on how they did? If a person does not know when he has done poorly or when he has done well, is he as likely to learn? Does he always have within his own knowledge or experience the way in which he can improve? Is he always the best judge of what he should do to improve and advance?

Comments of a Personnel Staff Member

I don't disagree with Sid on any major point concerning his support of the Personal Development Plan procedure. The new pink sheets are an excellent tool for development. It does seem, however, that Sid has omitted one important consideration from his unqualified support of the pink sheets and his nearly unqualified attack upon appraisal: he has omitted consideration of the purpose. The Personal Development Plan procedure is an excellent tool for development, but not any good for some other purposes. For example, it provides no information at all for use in transferring people or promoting them. How do we evaluate for this? The same way we always have: on some manager's opinion, which is certainly not a systematic procedure. I have recently been informed that the pink sheets can be used for evaluating people, but I'm not convinced. I don't think the pink sheets can do any better at appraisal than the appraisal system did at development. And I do think that there is a need for appraisal information.

I happen to believe that salaries should relate to performance--for motivational purposes, of course--so maybe ratings <u>should</u> be done in Wage and Salary. If I thought performance and salary were already related--maybe Sid does, I don't--I wouldn't care if there were any performance appraisals for motivational purposes because the motivational purposes would be being accomplished.

In summary, every program should have a valid purpose. This one does: <u>development</u>. But so does performance appraisal: placement, promotion, motivation, et cetera. Using a program for purposes not in keeping with its major purpose is what is causing the problems, and that is what we <u>should</u> have learned from our experience with the appraisal system. WE MUST KEEP THE PURPOSE IN MIND!

One other point, the present procedure has the same weakness than any other required system has: if the immediate superior does a superficial job of administering it or does not follow up to see if the objectives are completed, his subordinate will quickly come to realize that it is just an exercise. He will recognize that no instrumental relationship exists between it and any meaningful extrinsic award and will thereby be unmotivated by the procedure. He, of course, could still receive intrinsic rewards from accomplishing his goals, but he could have gotten this by carrying out the same procedure for himself without a boss. And it appears to me as though there is some of this superficially with respect to this program in the company at this time. After all, for the boss it is just another time-user. I have received a few isolated comments of the nature of "Oh, that again!" when time came for completion of that form this year.

<u>Comments of a Line Department Manager</u>

Last year we really went all-out on Sid's form in this department. And I feel we wrung everything from it--and more. Many man-hours were dedicated by staff and supervisory persons in introspection, self-assessment, and mutual working out of the prime and secondary tasks and goals, plus joint setting of target dates, criteria of evaluating results, et cetera.

As I say, in 1967, we really got down to brass knuckles. We indulged in oral ricochets, and I got as much constructive assistance from it as I hope the other did. It was a good demonstration of staff-supervisor-manager exchange.

This year I kept in the wings, and it was essentially a staff-supervisor affair.

Certainly not unique to our function are the unplanned tasks and programs that are predictable in their unpredictability, but still louse up any neatly programmed set of tasks and target dates. Another thing: follow-up seems always to be a difficult matter. You set down all of this material, and then it can fall flat on its posterior if you don't follow up.

About all the men in my function are quite vigorous and want to move on up. The number of course-completion documents covering my people would fill a fair-sized cabinet. My guys have been Toastmaster presidents, Company United Crusade representatives, bartenders--all damn fine, base-broadening activities. They're a pretty sassy group and don't buy development just for the kicks of it--they want to know what station the track is running to.

<u>A Director's Instructions on Use of the Personal Development Plan</u>

On January 28, 1968, Sid Harris had received a copy of a xeroxed memo that had been sent with the pink sheets by a division head to five of the managers immediately under his supervision, giving instructions for the use of the Personal Development Plan in his division. The instructions read as follows:

> As stated in referenced IDC [interdepartmental communication referred to in the heading of the memo], the goal for completing the Personal Development Plan for all salaried, nonrepresented employees (except Managers) is set for February 28. We are, of course, most anxious to meet this date and have established certain schedule milestones and guidelines to be followed in the execution of the program.

STEP I - "OBJECTIVES"

This Division is again taking a "Management-by-Objective" approach rather than a review of the functions for which the man is responsible. Therefore, the first step, and preparatory to the first interview, the superior should list those objectives which he expects the subordinate to accomplish within the year ahead, rather than listing his principal responsibilities in the "Job Responsibilities" block of the form.

The determination as to who will fill in the "Objectives" ("Job Responsibilities") portion of the "pink or worksheet" copy of the form and conduct the interviews will be left to the discretion of the cognizant manager; however, this portion should be filled in by the person who actually is responsible for the administrative direction of the incumbent, recommending salary increases, promotions, etc. In no instance should this function be delegated to a staff man.

The "Objectives" block should be filled in (pencil) and the first interviews held with the incumbent on or before February 11, 1968. The date and time for the second interview should be established during the first interview.

STEP II - "PLAN FOR ACHIEVEMENT" AND "MEASUREMENT OF PROGRESS"

The "Personal Development Plan" block of the worksheet actually will reflect the employee's plan for achieving his objectives. The incumbent is to fill in these two portions of the form (pencil) and complete his second interview with the supervisor on or before February 22. At this time, both the supervisor and the incumbent sign the worksheet copy.

STEP III - FINAL REVIEW

Upon completion of the second interview, the worksheet will be reviewed and approved by the second level of supervision--unless the Manager has filled in the job responsibilities portion and conducted interviews, in which case no further review is required. Completion date--on or before February 25.

STEP IV - FINAL TYPING AND DISTRIBUTION

Upon completion of Step III, an original "Personal Development Plan" with two copies will be typed from the worksheet and distribution made as follows on or before February 28, 1968:

Original (pink)	- Incumbent
Second (yellow)	- Supervisor
Third (green)	- Management Personnel Department

The worksheet may be retained by the Manager or the Section Head at the discretion of the Manager.

I believe the enclosed worksheets and final sets of the form will be sufficient to cover your people; however, additional forms may be obtained by calling. . ., Ext. . . .

January 28, 1968

Enclosures

cc: S. Harris
[and list of 35 names]

In June 1968, Sid Harris wondered what conclusions he could draw as to the success and the problems of his program. He also wondered what recommendations he should make regarding the future of the plan and the further implementation of the concept of management by objectives within the Watertite-Florida Company.

NAME: DATE: 2-14-68

CLASSIFICATION: DEPARTMENT MANAGER DEPT.: 200

JOB RESPONSIBILITIES:

Administers operation of the Receiving Inspection Department, which includes two Supervisors, 42 direct hourly personnel, 2 indirect hourly personnel, and 11 direct salaried personnel.

Functions include: Receiving inspection of purchased parts, castings and forgings, machined parts, and raw materials; also functional testing of hydraulic, fuel, electrical instruments, oxygen, pneumatic, electro-mechanical, and other equipments. Functions also include Quality Engineering, covering product analysis, verification testing, supplier acceptance test evaluation, and coordination with other company organizations and with suppliers. The Material Review operation also is under the cognizance of and reports to this department.

PERSONAL DEVELOPMENT PLAN:	MEASUREMENT OF PROGRESS:
1. Maintain zero lost time accident rate.	1. 12-31-68.
2. Beat Cost Reduction target in department by 10 percent. Target is $103,000.	2. Review quarterly targets and stress this in group meetings. 12-31-68.
3. Average at least one accepted Zero Defect from each man in department for 1968.	3. Review quarterly and stress in group meetings. 12-31-68.
4. Set up training program for hourly employees consistent with budget.	4. 2-28-68.
5. Obtain at least one young college graduate for product analysis function. Man must have management potential.	5. 6-13-68.
6. Complete course in "Decision-Making"--evening school.	6. 3-2-68. Certificate to be issued.
7. Take a graduate level management course.	7. 2-10-69. Grade report to be issued.
8. Work out a rotational management development program for myself with Division Manager.	8. 3-28-68.
9. Work out a supervisory vacation replacement plan for maximum personnel development.	9. 2-21-68. Measurement to be accomplished by a written report from each replacement to this office upon completion of assignment.
10. Beat all direct hours and overhead budgets by 5 percent min.	10. Review semimonthly to track. 12-31-68.

Figure 1. Sample Personal Development Plan.

NAME: ____________________ DATE: 2-9-68

CLASSIFICATION: SUPERVISOR DEPT: 200

JOB RESPONSIBILITIES:

Supervises the activities of 17 hourly and 7 salaried employees in the Quality Conformance Testing, Environmental Testing, and Product Analysis of primarily nonelectronic purchased and customer furnished functional items intended for use on operational submarines and as spares. Is responsible for safety, scheduling, budget control, and workmanship in these areas. Contacts customer, supplier, and in-plant representatives with a view toward the resolution of mutual problems concerning the testing and eventual utility of the article.

PERSONAL DEVELOPMENT PLAN:	MEASUREMENT OF PROGRESS:
1. Maintain excellent safety record. Promote safety via regular safety meetings and maximum utility of safety bulletins.	1. Target--Sustaining measure via chart to be reviewed quarterly with Manager.
2. Maintain Zero Defects level under more severe scoring system. Promote Zero Defect in my personnel. Average at least one Zero Defect accepted per man per quarter.	2. Zero Defect Program and via log/chart to be reviewed quarterly.
3. Promote Cost Reduction. Exceed Dept. Cost Reduction quota. Make concerted effort to have "Run of the Mill" Cost Reduction items evaluated and recorded. Especially encourage hourly personnel in Cost Reduction efforts.	3. Cost Reduction Program and via log/chart to be reviewed quarterly. $15,000 per quarter.
4. Re: 2 and 3, investigate and analyze, or cause to be done, at least one FTP per week toward clarification of procedure and intent and less costly or more effective test technique.	4. Track via #3 and #4 and FTCR/Review log/chart. To be reviewed quarterly.
5. Review at least one Q.A. Division J.I. per week and discern Dept. position. To take appropriate action as indicated via instruction or revision request.	5. Begin February 14, 1968. Keep log/chart of progress and action taken. Review quarterly.
6. Obtain Florida State Vocational Teaching Credential.	6. Target July 1968. Measure by presenting for personnel folder log.
7. Re: 6. Establish on-the-job training aimed at raising technical level of lab personnel.	7. Will program one hour per man per month for training--within budget. Will review monthly with department manager.
8. Take at least one job-oriented training class per semester (Supervisory and Technical).	8. Next available. Measure by certificate.
9. Replace Supervisor or Receiving Inspection during his vacation as part of Management Development.	9. August 7, 1968.

Figure 2. Sample Personal Development Plan.

NAME: ______________________ DATE: __________

CLASSIFICATION: CONTRACT ADMINISTRATOR, SR. DEPT: 205

JOB RESPONSIBILITIES:

In 1968 Watertite plans to win the Submarine 2-A Contract.

The objective established for Mr.__________ is to formulate a personal plan which will maximize his contribution to a winning Company effort.

PERSONAL DEVELOPMENT PLAN:	MEASUREMENT OF PROGRESS:
Obtain agreement with SCA (Submarine control agency) as to their Government Property control plan relative to a complete program and coordinate the understanding with Watertite-Florida functional units.	*See note below. 4-1-68 continuing 10-1-68.
Become expert on new contract facilities.	Continuing 4-1-68, 7-1-68, 11-1-68.
In addition to Financial Operations and Master Scheduling's obvious interest in PERT/Cost as a means of Program Control, indicate to the customer an increased and continuing understanding of it by other members of the Management team.	Continuing 2-28-68, 6-1-68.
By way of responding to RFQ's on Ancillary Programs and by indicating adequate performance to the customers on each, contribute to the expanding image of the company.	Continuing.
Represent the Division on the 2-A Contract Data Management Board seeing to it that no contract requirement is overlooked.	
Help to establish the adequacy of the Watertite Data Management plan in the eyes of the customer and contribute to successful II-C performance here in Data Management.	Continuing - Customer Review 7-1-68.
Periodically review with Engineering, Manufacturing, Q.A., and Financial Ops the adequacy of existing Work Orders to determine adequacy of cost accumulation control when the contract is reviewed. Coordinate, as required, with the customer and with Financial Operations.	Reviews: 4-1-68 7-1-68 10-1-68
Complete the UM course of Government Contract Administration with a grade of B or better.	June 15, 1968, grade received.
	*Note: Progress will be measured on or before the dates indicated above through the issuance of an IDC depicting Watertite activity and success in the particular areas where required.

Figure 3. Sample Personal Development Plan.

NAME: DATE: 2-15-68

CLASSIFICATION: QUALITY ASSURANCE ENGINEER, SR. DEPT.: 120

JOB RESPONSIBILITIES:

Perform QA Test Engineering and Planning in support of 2-A contract, oxygen, and accessory drive.

- Establish QA test requirements thru review, evaluation, and analysis of system performance specifications, equipment specifications, designs, reliability requirements, and related reports.
- Recognize potential functional and test problems and initiate corrective action which will contribute to product quality.
- Develop Phase III Test Plans.
- Establish and define Phase V test equipment, manpower, and space requirements.
- Participate in design development and reliability test programs to assure maximum test/performance data and experience is obtained and contributions made.
- Provide technical support to and liaison with Supplier Quality Assurance, M & P, and Inspection Planning; participate in supplier proposal evaluations.
- Approve supplier test procedures and/or evaluate test facilities.

PERSONAL DEVELOPMENT PLAN:	MEASUREMENT OF PROGRESS:
Develop test requirement concepts and technical competence necessary to: 1. Establish QA Test Plans. 2. Participate in supplier proposal evaluations. 3. Establish test equipment, personnel, and laboratory space requirements. 4. Contribute to technical progress of new program. These goals will be accomplished by: Maintaining close liaison contact with pertinent Engineering design groups to keep current with design concepts, anticipating changes, and injecting quality attributes where need exists. Participate in applicable development tests to obtain related test experience. Utilization of performance histories of equipment/systems found in other vessels that have similar environments. Timely review Engineering Test Plans, Test Procedures, Specification and Related Engineering Reports/Data.	1. Complete initial draft of Phase III Test Plan (in support of assigned systems) on or before 8-1-68; up-date test plan bi-monthly. 2. Provide technical support required to evaluate supplier proposals as scheduled (based on current specification release dates, accessory drive components 6-1-6, oxygen system components 7-1-6). 3. Develop test equipment, test personnel, and laboratory space estimate justifications and back-up data--complete initial evaluation of previously established estimates by 3-15-68. Update and revise estimates by 6-1-68. 4. Submit Monthly Technical Progress Report and/or State-of-the-Art items.

Figure 4. Sample Personal Development Plan.

NAME: ______ DATE: 2-15-68

CLASSIFICATION: QUALITY ASSURANCE ENGINEER, SR. DEPT.: 120

JOB RESPONSIBILITIES:

Primary area of responsibility: Quality Engineering functions in Nonmetallics, Hot-Forming. Sealants and Metallics Processing.

Secondary area of responsibility: Quality Engineering functions in Welding.

A. In area of primary responsibility:

1. Plan, layout, and schedule inspection stations and manpower, updating equipment requirements for Phases III, IV, and V.
2. Review and evaluate characteristics of pertinent Manufacturing Process Standards and Engineering designs and specifications coordinating as required with other affected Quality Assurance divisions to discover and resolve quality problems, new inspection equipment or capability requirements and inputs to the Manufacturing Inspection Manual (MIM) or related Inspection Instructions.
3. Monitor production processes and technically evaluate suppliers of nonmetallic raw materials to establish effective, economical inspection controls.
4. Prepare and maintain pertinent MIM and II inputs from analysis and evaluation of II-C tests, test results, development hardware, and Manufacturing Research Information.

B. Support, as required, supplier Quality Control, secondary responsibilities, Quality Engineering and Inspection in solution of related quality problems.

PERSONAL DEVELOPMENT PLAN:	MEASUREMENT OF PROGRESS:
Coordinate with Manufacturing Engineers and Quality Engineering functions for plant layout/inspection equipment to ensure compliance with Material and Process Specifications covering Nonmetallics, Metallics Processing, Hot-Forming, Welding, and Sealants.	Weekly activity report for evaluation by Group Leader that shows actions taken or required to assess and implement program requirements.
Identify Process Specification QA and Manufacturing problem areas and secure timely resolution through Manufacturing Inspection Manual or Job Instructions, new Inspection Equipment, or new Inspection Methods development.	Monthly review of "I" tags in 2-A contract data bank to identify Process Spec. problems and immediate handling of inspection-submitted critical items. Report to be issued monthly to Group Leader for evaluation and submittal to Quality Performance Report.
Contact 2-A Production areas at least once each week for inspection or production problems encountered by Operations or Inspection on in-plant items. Solicit personnel and receiving inspection for quality problems involving suppliers of nonmetallic materials, hot-forming or processing.	
Contribute Process Inspection and Nonmetallic Material and Process inputs to Manufacturing Inspection Manual from analysis and evaluation of Phase II-C Test Programs.	Provide monthly updating write-up for Inspection Instructions to Group Leader.
Prepare Supplier QA survey for each new Process Specification and maintain existing surveys incorporating changes.	Complete within 10 days of specification prerelease review.

Figure 5. Sample Personal Development Plan.

NAME: ______________________________ DATE: March 17, 1968

CLASSIFICATION: PROCUREMENT PLANNING ANALYST DEPT.: 300

JOB RESPONSIBILITIES:

1. Maintain a monthly workload forecast for use in division-wide manpower requirement projection.
2. Analyze inventory activity relationships and develop targets and charts by individual accounts.
3. Audit, periodically, Procurement Planning completed work in Accounts XYZ and AB.
4. Maintain by part number the Buying group code system.
5. Prepare and maintain Procurement Planning Job Instruction and Bulletins.
6. Audit of various lists, surveys, and reports pertinent to Inventory Control.
7. Participate in the development and updating of the Procurement Division annual dollar commitment forecast.
8. Assist planners with problems pertinent to Procurement and interdivisional activity.
9. Provide and maintain a priority program of work distribution through processing of monthly reports.
10. Maintain the military spares tracking operation.
11. Maintain surveillance as required for control of inventory turnover compatible with Management goals.
12. Coordinate discrepancies with Stores, Order Writing, Change Control, and related operations.

PERSONAL DEVELOPMENT PLAN:	MEASUREMENT OF PROGRESS:
1. Analyze, quarterly, material surplus costs to determine cause and recommend corrective action.	1. Each month report to Supervision, June 30, 1968, on recommended corrective action to be implemented.
2. Survey, periodically, Procurement Planning and surplus documents for job instruction conformance.	2. Daily.
3. Review and update existing Procurement Planning Job Instructions.	3. As required by Supervision.
4. Implement and maintain surveillance over processing by priority method.	4. Report progress to Supervisor by June 15, 1968.
5. Update Inventory Turnover Charts, monthly cycle.	5. Each month.
6. Supervise spares tracking operation.	6. Bi-monthly report to Mr. Jones.
7. Take an additional course in personnel relations, as new ones are offered by the company.	7. Progress can be measured by issuance of Completion Certificate--Year End December 1968.
8. Review the ordering and maintenance activity of all forms and stationery supplies to effect economy of operation.	8. Report progress May 1, 1968.

Figure 6. Sample Personal Development Plan.

NAME:	DATE: March, 1968
CLASSIFICATION: CUSTOMER SERVICE REP.--RESEARCH SUBS	DEPT. 300

JOB RESPONSIBILITIES:

Analyze purchased parts and raw material shortage situations in order to determine the cause for such shortages and to implement corrective action. Perform coordination activities between internal organizational units and with suppliers in order to avoid or resolve shortage problems. Prepare and maintain shortage information to reflect shortage status for management and operating units.

PERSONAL DEVELOPMENT PLAN:	MEASUREMENT OF PROGRESS:
Take a course in either Oral or Written Communications to improve abilities along these lines.	By end of December, 1968, as courses are offered.

Figure 7. Sample Personal Development Plan.

NAME: ______________________________ DATE: 3-24-68

CLASSIFICATION: CUSTOMER SERVICE REP.-RESEARCH SUBS DEPT. 210

JOB RESPONSIBILITIES:

Mr.______________ receives inquiries from Watertite customers on problems pertaining to the maintenance, servicing, and operation of research subs. It is his responsibility to code and log incoming correspondence, assign action, and distribute to concerned personnel. Further, he obtains answers by investigation and coordination with appropriate personnel. He composes wires and letters and reviews letters originated in Engineering for completeness and correctness. He visits local customers periodically for technical discussions with their engineering personnel. He also conducts research on many problems including accidents. He meets visiting customers and coordinates interdivision activity as required. He visits with local vendors as required for technical discussions of their products.

PERSONAL DEVELOPMENT PLAN:	MEASUREMENT OF PROGRESS:
1. Plan to acquire a better understanding of loads causing stress corrosion. Combined with a full understanding of thinking behind the design of repairs and preventive measures.	1. With the release of comprehensible information in the form of a corrosion manual and the Field Service Digest, a better source of information is available. Close liaison work with Service Engineering will provide information on design thinking. Measurement of progress is subject to release of this information. Target dates not predictable.
2. I plan to further expand ultrasonic inspection experience, which is part of nondestructive testing. Since contact with operators requires an interpretation of ultrasonic indications and also of X-rays, it is desirable to have a better than average knowledge of nondestructive testing.	2. A gauge of progress in this area is hard to define. Since the only experience that is available is working with operators, the date when the degree of capability of being able to interpret presentations is open. The lack of available equipment and training at the Field Service Lab make education on this subject an impossibility.
3. I plan to keep current on Watertite's development of the 2A Contract. Periodic visits to submarine operators have indicated the requirements to be able to transmit the status of this project. Again, lack of information is noted; often newspaper information is only source of released data.	3. No target dates or measurement of progress is possible under present policy.

Figure 8. Sample Personal Development Plan.

NAME: ______________________________ DATE: 2-25-68

CLASSIFICATION: INTERDIVISIONAL SALES CONTRACT ADMINISTRATOR DEPT. 215

JOB RESPONSIBILITIES:

__________ has been assigned the following objectives for the year:

1. Extend customer contacts to develop closer working relationships. Seek out new areas of work potential.
2. Expand his knowledge of shop practices.
3. Direct special attention and assistance toward achieving the department's Zero Defects and Cost Reduction goals.
4. Participate in 1-A and 2-A negotiations to assure a profitable position for the Florida Company.

PERSONAL DEVELOPMENT PLAN:	MEASUREMENT OF PROGRESS:
1. By tracing back a step, the customer's documents will show the initiating parties. The purchase requests will be started in the areas with earlier knowledge of work load. Those earlier in the procurement sequence contacts will also indicate newer work potential areas.	1. Introduction of new type work into the plant will be the result of this effort.
2. A closer shop follow-up will develop a better working knowledge of shop practices. Inquiries into the troubled spots will show the working problems.	2. Better job knowledge and leadership of discussions will be gained to a measurable extent.
3. If jobs are observed with a critical eye toward improvements and elimination of excessive errors, a closer alignment with the department's goals will be made.	3. Preparation or participation in cost reduction reports and elimination of error will assist the Zero Defects program.
4. A thorough prenegotiation review with representatives of the divisions involved and a proper checking of incurred costs will enable Watertite-Florida to come out with the most profitable position in subsequent negotiations.	4. Increased profit percentage and profit dollar volume will mark the level of effort.

Figure 9. Sample Personal Development Plan.

NAME: ______________________________ DATE: March 3, 1968

CLASSIFICATION: DATA PROCESSING PROGRAMMER DEPT.: 405

JOB RESPONSIBILITIES:

_______________ is responsible for programming and maintaining portions of Data Processing Systems and for the operation of equipment necessary to process such systems in the Advanced Development Projects Organization. Her current assignments are:

1. Scheduling and operation of the ADP computer facility on the day shift. Scheduling jobs and preparing pickups for swing and graveyard shifts.
2. Develop operating procedures and job processing specifications to aid in the operations' function.
3. Program, as required, Data Processing Systems utilizing the latest and most efficient programming language suitable to the specific problem.

PERSONAL DEVELOPMENT PLAN:

1. I plan to maintain a schedule of "360" job-processing requirements which will provide the best possible workload balance.
2. I plan to complete and maintain the "ADP Operations Systems and Procedures Reference Manual."
3. I plan to retain and maintain all working tapes, card files, 557 boards, program decks, tab runs, etc., in clearly labeled repositories in a current status.
4. I plan to become thoroughly adept at operating the System 360 including any and all components which may be added.
5. I plan to work with other members in the Department to convert all existing programs to "360" mode and thus eliminate the need for the compatibility feature.

MEASUREMENT OF PROGRESS:

1. While this is an effort requiring constant adjustment, the initial schedules should be completed by March 1968.
2. This will be complete for all current jobs by April 1968.
3. Currently in operation but requires constant attention and update.
4. A constant process with proficiency measured on a relative basis being the only method of determining progress.
5. Schedule dependent on availability and adaptation of software.

Figure 10. Sample Personal Development Plan.

NAME: ______________________________ DATE: 3-7-68

CLASSIFICATION: STAFF TRAINEE (COMPUTER OPERATOR) DEPT.: 405

JOB RESPONSIBILITIES:

Operate a large scale computer used to process business data for the Watertite-Florida Company.

Responsible for processing Computer work in accordance with detailed program instructions and established schedules.

PERSONAL DEVELOPMENT PLAN:	MEASUREMENT OF PROGRESS:
Learn to operate the RCA 3301 and IBM 360.	Complete by 6-1-68.

Figure 11. Sample Personal Development Plan.

NAME: ______________________________ DATE: 2-22-68

CLASSIFICATION: PROJECT PRICE ESTIMATOR DEPT: 400

JOB RESPONSIBILITIES:

______________ is responsible as Project Estimator to coordinate the RSV Vehicle pricing activities that are required during the Engineering Development Contract. This job includes obtaining information from the divisions and developing the data into the required prices, and developing a procedure to handle this pricing activity.

PERSONAL DEVELOPMENT PLAN:	MEASUREMENT OF PROGRESS:
Achievements that I plan to accomplish during the coming year are listed in their approximate chronological order:	
1. Supply necessary data to the RSV negotiations in Baton Rouge. This includes constant updating of the bulk of material, processing of RFQ's, answering phone inquiries from the negotiators, etc.	1. RSV negotiation support--March 15, 1968.
2. Indoctrinate new personnel on the overall responsibilities of the pricing dept., and train them to fill specific job assignments.	2. Training new personnel--Dec. 31, 1968.
3. Maintain data to support the RSV cost estimates so that such data can be presented for audit upon request.	3. Audit data--March 15, 1968.
4. Maintain coordination between the RSV proposal and the final proposal as resolved by negotiations to insure that the cost effect is included in all changes.	4. Proposal coordination--March 15, 1968.
5. Prepare a data bank on the RSV cost elements that can be used by the pricing dept. to evaluate estimates submitted on future programs.	5. Data Bank--June 1, 1968.
6. Assemble cost data for submittal of a production program target cost proposal.	6. Production Target Cost Proposal--Nov. 1, 1968.

Figure 12. Sample Personal Development Plan.

NAME: ______________________ DATE: March 14, 1968

CLASSIFICATION: PRICE ESTIMATING ANALYST DEPT: 400

JOB RESPONSIBILITIES:

Mr. __________ is responsible for the preparation of price proposals for Model 2-A maintenance trainers, trainer publications, and spare parts. He also prepares price proposals for Engineering changes to the maintenance trainers. He explains, in detail, the content of each proposal to the Project Price Estimator to assist in subsequent submittal to the customer.

PERSONAL DEVELOPMENT PLAN:	MEASUREMENT OF PROGRESS:
1. Enroll in "Introduction to Data Processing" in September 1968 eventual goal being classified as a Programmer.	1. Course complete December 1968.

Figure 13. Sample Personal Development Plan.

NAME: DATE: March 1, 1968

CLASSIFICATION: DEPT: 220

JOB RESPONSIBILITIES:

Prepare Operations Division quotations. This includes:

1. Development of the hours quotation;
2. Development of first article spans and rate spans;
3. Prepare production hours estimates in sufficient detail for scheduling purposes;
4. Prepare production and labor loads which reflect the proposed hours and schedule and their impact upon current firm business manloads;
5. Obtain approvals of the completed quotation to final signature of the Division Director or his designate on or before the due date of the quote. As a member of a major proposal task force, he is responsible for the evaluation of engineering design concepts in terms of cost and schedule data for quotation purposes.

Evaluate the impact of major design changes on Operations Division direct hours and schedules. Prepare historical data records for use as a basis of analysis of future quotations.

PERSONAL DEVELOPMENT PLAN:	MEASUREMENT OF PROGRESS:
Will take a course in statistics.	Enroll by October 31, 1968. Obtain completion by January 31, 1969.

Figure 14. Sample Personal Development Plan.

NAME: _______________ DATE: March 1, 1968

CLASSIFICATION: MANUFACTURING FORECASTER DEPT.: 220

JOB RESPONSIBILITIES:

Prepare Operations division quotations for the 2-A contracts. This includes:

1. Development of the hours quotation;
2. Development of first article spans and rate unit spans;
3. Prepare production hours estimates in sufficient detail for scheduling purposes;
4. Prepare production and labor loads which reflect the proposed hours and schedule and their impact upon current firm business manloads;
5. Obtain approvals of the completed quotation to final signature of the division Director or his designate on or before the due date of the quote.

Prepare historical data records for use as a basis of analyses of future quotations.
Evaluates the impact of major design changes on Operations division direct hours and schedules.
Responsible for preparation of manload date for assembly of each segment for use in evaluation of schedule spans and the manufacturing plan.

PERSONAL DEVELOPMENT PLAN:	MEASUREMENT OF PROGRESS:
Start course in job-related educational program by October 31, 1968.	Complete course by January 31, 1969.

Figure 15. Sample Personal Development Plan.

NAME: DATE: Feb. 28, 1968

CLASSIFICATION: PROJECT SCHEDULER DEPT.: 220

JOB RESPONSIBILITIES:

Develops schedules for special products after analysis of project requirements, historical data, facilities, and related data to determine method of approach for the developments. Prepares written, graphic, and oral persentations of the schedules and presents to line organizations, coordinating line, planning and production control personnel involved to secure agreement and implementation of the operations. Tracks performance against schedule, analyzes deviations, and assists personnel involved in the development of programs for returning to and staying within schedule. Plans and conducts special scheduling studies in response to management requests, and develops proposed schedules. Guides and coordinates work of two hourly schedulers as required to prepare data and issue scheduling documents and publications. Develops statistical estimates of company exposure for precontractual work authorizations. Works with EDP programmers in machine preparation of schedule documents.

Principal contracts are with Department, Division, and Works Managers.

PERSONAL DEVELOPMENT PLAN:	MEASUREMENT OF PROGRESS:
Attend various seminars and classes having subjects pertinent or related to the task at hand.	

Figure 16. Sample Personal Development Plan.

NAME: _______________ DATE: 4-1-67

CLASSIFICATION: SALARY ADMINISTRATOR DEPT: 500

JOB RESPONSIBILITIES:

1. To provide overall direction for salary study program.
2. To act as Company Chairman, O&T Restudy Committee and to participate to extent required in precontractual activity and/or contract negotiations.
3. To formulate and direct others in formulating company compensation policies, security approval, and implementing same.
4. To provide advice and guidance, and direct others in providing advice and guidance to top, middle, and lower supervision on compensation matters within Wage and Salary function and responsibility.

PERSONAL DEVELOPMENT PLAN:	MEASUREMENT OF PROGRESS:
1. Direction of Managerial Salary Study.	Plan and direct such study to achieve completion of last division (Engineering) by October 1.
2. Prepare programs for staff to enhance their knowledge of and capability in Industrial Relations functions and activities.	Provide for such programs once each month, April through November.
3. Chair the Company-Union O & T Classification Subcommittee.	Bring work to successful conclusion by April 27.
4. Direction and preparation of rate and classification data with recommended actions for negotiations.	Complete by September 1.
5. Improve verbal communications skill.	Continue participation in and complete outside course of instruction.
6. Analyze the effectiveness of the company's salary adjustment program and, where indicated, make recommendations to improve.	Conclude by December 31.

Figure 17. Sample Personal Development Plan.

NAME: ______________________ DATE: 4-1-67

CLASSIFICATION: WAGE AND SALARY REPRESENTATIVE, SENIOR DEPT: 500

JOB RESPONSIBILITIES:

1. Direct and coordinate the completion of the Salary Study Program.
2. For assigned division, represent the Department on Managerial classification, rate and benefit actions, improve rapport and promote understanding of company's compensation policies, and maintain an updated classification structure.
3. Acquire familiarization with company's executive compensation program.

PERSONAL DEVELOPMENT PLAN:	MEASUREMENT OF PROGRESS:
1. Assure that all Managerial jobs are defined, evaluated, and presented to the Director of Engineering.	October 1, 1967
2. Develop, define, evaluate, and implement jobs in Facilities Engineering.	November 1, 1967
Accomplish a minimum of 3 contacts per week with line managers in assigned divisions to review classification actions, furnish counsel on rate and benefit actions, and maintain relationships.	Normal day-to-day review of such contacts and activity
3. Obtain orientation on executive compensation policies within WATERTITE-FLORIDA, including stock options, insurance, MIP, and the administration of same.	Review extent of exposure and familiarizations at end of September and December.
4. Appropriate university course or seminar within field of compensation.	If attendance at appropriate seminar is not possible or feasible, arrangements will be made to attend, periodically or on a rational basis, meetings of such organizations as ESWA.

Figure 18. Sample Personal Development Plan.

NAME: ______________________ DATE: 4-1-67

CLASSIFICATION: WAGE AND SALARY REPRESENTATIVE DEPT: 500

JOB RESPONSIBILITIES:

1. Participate in the completion of the Salary Study Program.
2. For assigned divisions represent the Department on Managerial classification, rate and benefit actions, develop rapport and promote understanding of company's compensation policies, and maintain an updated classification structure.
3. Analyze rate and classification data and make recommendations for contract negotiations.
4. Conduct research in selected compensation field.

PERSONAL DEVELOPMENT PLAN:	MEASUREMENT OF PROGRESS:
1. Participate in the completion of the Salary Study Program.	Contribute to team effort to insure completion of package for Division Head presentation by October 1.
2. Analysis of rate and classification date for negotiations.	Complete such analysis with recommendations by September 1, 1967.
3. Develop a specific study program, including authoritative current references in the areas of compensation and closely related fields.	By December 31, complete first phase of study program and submit written report.
4. Determine appropriate seminars offered by institutions such as FAU, AMA, etc., for attendance in latter part of the year.	Determination to be finalized by August 1.
5. Investigate potential of professional associations and attend to the extent desirable for personal development.	Arrangements will be made to attend periodically or on rotational basis meetings of such organizations as ESWA.

Figure 19. Sample Personal Development Plan.

NAME: ____ DATE: 4-1-67

CLASSIFICATION: WAGE AND SALARY REPRESENTATIVE DEPT: 500

JOB RESPONSIBILITIES:

1. Participate in the completion of the Salary Study Program.
2. For assigned divisions, represent the Department on Managerial classification, rate and benefit actions, develop rapport and promote understanding of company's compensation policies, and maintain an updated classification structure.
3. Develop a coordinated policy relative to all phases and facets of salaried field assignments--domestic, foreign, temporary, and permanent.
4. Coordinate all phases of the periodic salary adjustment program.

PERSONAL DEVELOPMENT PLAN:	MEASUREMENT OF PROGRESS:
1. Participate in the completion of the Salary Study Program.	Contribute to team effort to insure completion of package for division head presentation by October 1.
2. Become familiar with personnel and functions in assigned divisions which I did not personally cover during the Salary Study.	One such contact to be made each month and to be reviewed monthly.
3. Develop an overall field compensation and benefit policy, including participation in the review of moving and benefit practices in conjunction with Customer Service, and revision of directives to conform to present policy.	Directives to be revised and published by April 15, 1967. Comprehensive policy to be developed by December 31, 1967.
4. Become familiar with mechanics of salary adjustment program and coordinate June and December salary adjustment program.	Complete familiarization with program to be accomplished by April 15, 1967. Implementation of program to meet set deadline.
5. Resume lecturing in Personnel Administration at night school.	To resume by end of year, opportunities and conditions permitting.
6. Join and participate in a personnel group such as PIRA.	Arrangements will be made to attend periodically or on rotational basis meetings of such organizations as ESWA.
Continue improving speaking ability by participating in Toastmasters.	Now participating.

Figure 20. Sample Personal Development Plan.

MAX WHITE — RESPONSES IN A T-GROUP

Max White was the manager of an accounting division of a large manufacturing concern in Eastern Canada. He had received a B.A. in 1947 and had worked for his present employer since that time. He was responsible for three supervisors who, in turn, supervised the work of twenty men and forty women.

As part of a company-wide program of managerial and supervisory development, Mr. White and four others, each from different divisions of the company, attended a two-week management development program sponsored by a local university. One part of this program consisted of a series of ten 150-minute training groups or T-Groups. There were 12 to 14 participants in each T-Group and one faculty member designated as a trainer. The trainer explained at the first session that he was to play a nominal role in the group but that he hoped to be useful in facilitating the groups, observation of itself with a view to better understanding the behavior of small groups and the individual's relation to such groups.

The following remarks were made by Max White in T-Group sessions numbers six, seven, and eight. The frequent interactions of the group and occasional interactions of the trainer are not given.

SESSION SIX

"We are going to have our division Christmas party soon and I am going to invite our top brass; we are going to bring our wives and the executives will bring their wives; we are going to do things, but we are going to be cautious. We are going to be on our best behavior, that is what we are doing here. With a Professor sitting in we are going to be on our best behavior; we will argue a subject sure, that's what we are here for, but thinking of the party, we know darn well that if we are sitting at the head table, we are not going to start overdoing it, overplaying our part, because before very long we are going to be a marked man, and we might be called to head office, so we don't act normal at a Christmas party, nor do we act normal here. Speaking for myself, I don't drink, so I don't overplay my part because I can't blame in on alcohol. I have to be very careful, its not like sitting home.

"It is just pure respect, yes respect sums up pretty well the whole darn thing. A fellow can respect his boss right along, do what he asks when he asks, be a gentlemen even if you don't like to. ------No you should definitely not be a yes man. If your boss comes up to you and says 'Max, you do this,' and you stop to question him, and start giving your reasons why you should not do this, I think you are out of place. Why?------Because your boss has no respect for you in the first place, and all he wants from you is, 'Do this'; all he thinks of you is that you are a machine. If he comes up to you and says 'what do you think, should we do this?', then he has asked for your opinion, then I think you should give it. But only if he asks for your opinion.------No! I did not say that, I think a man should be able to give his opinion at any time.------Well that's your privilege to think this, you do what you want, but in a few years time, you look at yourself and look in the papers, and see where you are, still right at the beginning, and I'll be right up there at the top.------I don't intend to hold any floor today but I'm doing a darn good job.------Now listen------Why should you start out to question anybody, especially your superior really, remember you are inferior when talking to a superior, why whould you question him. If he says, 'What do you think? How should we turn this table? This way?' all right------he is asking your opinion, you give it, but if he says, 'You take this table and turn it this way,' you have no business in questioning that man.------So I apply the same method---Oh, by all means I would want their opinions, sometimes, but not all times. Of course, maybe if they agree with me, then I'd want their opinion; that's a point there. I would treat anybody working for me, in the opposite way to which I would like my boss to treat me. I would leave my boss in a minute---I know it is not right------I just like to drive, drive, drive. When I am driving, and I drive at whatever I am working at. And the people who are working with me, I am driving them to------With me I want it right now, business, you see. But my boss------They are working because he has set the example. They respect him. Now I couldn't do that. I don't want to take it for granted. I have got an awful feeling that if a job has to be done right, then I have got to do it myself; or else see that it is done right. Now to give you an example, you people might be criticizing this. I wouldn't let a mechanic fix my car, unless I stood around and watched him. I might be giving him a cigarette, but I usually do stand over them and look at them.

SESSION SEVEN

"I don't feel guilty about it now, I still cannot change, and I don't think I would want to change. Men are put here to work. That is all I see, is working------I would panic, I have to take things one at a time------I have to keep my desk clean; but give me one job at a time and I will hang on to it like a starving dog on a bone.------I don't want publicity, I really shun publicity------But I do want credit.

I don't want them to come up and say you have done a good job, but the next time they come up I want them to give me a bigger or better job.------No, no, money isn't everything. It has never been anything in my life,------No I never work for money. Money is the last thing in my world as far as I am concerned,------It is true------. Money is so far down the line as far as I am concerned. No I mean this. I am not acting because I don't know what it is all about. Now, should we analyze the problem and say now what has happened to me, and this is how I overcame it.

"I did pay attention this session and last session to that particular problem as I said to two or three different people I tried to study myself during the past few days, and I do have a big problem. I am still a long way from a director------I think this is part of what we are discussing here; how, when, and where, we should be diplomatic.------I think that question can be answered by us all, after all, we were taught that when we were children------But I am getting more and more------As I come to these sessions, I feel that I should have a prepared speech, now I don't know why------And I feel that this is the feeling of a lot of people right here------Have the feeling that they should have gravity, no, if we do come to this conclusion, and I think we have, by our actions I think so, then we are in a little rut,------These are my personal feelings and observations, I would never make an opinion without good observation------.

"You only have two choices, as an idiot or a brain, I mean putting it right down on the line, I am using strong words there, I don't mean that everybody is either an idiot or a brain, but I mean that you want to be considered as a brain if you are human at all. You don't want to be considered as an idiot------I know it and you know it. What we are talking about here in the discussion, is that you don't say anything if you don't know what you are talking about. What I mean is, choose your words, so that you add something to this discussion, know what you are talking about.------Because I don't feel that I can contribute too much at all. Now I may be able to contribute to an argument, to opinions, but I don't feel that I can offer any opinions or offer any argument. But if someone gets the material------but I also take this attitude, too, why should you get up and give your opinion unless you are asked------Outside this group as well as inside the group, what applies to this group applies outside------If it stayed 52 weeks of the year I would stay. I'm getting something out of this group ------I am getting a little patience, I am learning to listen a lot more than I did before------. When I am listening, I'm not just sitting quiet, I am trying to digest what he is saying; I am not just sitting quiet waiting for him to finish so that I can get a word in. Now when I first came here, the first few nights, I just sat and waited for a guy to finish so that I could jump in, I didn't know what he had said, it didn't make any difference.

"By the way, I have a very happy marriage and we don't get into arguments very much, and when we do they are only verbal we haven't come to blows yet. But the other night I said, 'I don't care what happens,' and she said 'What do you mean by that.' I am going to die tomorrow, and I am going to be happy. She took the attitude that--she said, 'You are saying that you don't want me, are you saying that you would be better off without me.' So I said, 'You haven't got the guts to go.' Of course this was early in the evening, and we still had time to cuddle up and now we're back to normal.

SESSION EIGHT

"What is your general opinion----Of how this method would work in an organization, could a company or a factory, or whatever group of people are working together, use this method that we have here. Could it be applied to a company------Do you think that this group of people here, that we could take and plan a new product introduction together? Now we would probably need a great deal of experience, say we decided to come up with something, a group of people such as this could decide to get a product on the market and go ahead and sell it.

"Is it necessary to have so many whips standing over a group of men, would it increase output, attitude to company? Would it help if you take some of the whippers off their backs, and let them work as a group------I don't know why it is unconsciously, I just happened to get us back on what we were saying last week, we wasted so much time last week, that the last hour we really went to work, the first hour to my mind we were discussing many, many topics. I surprised myself when I did bring up a topic on organization, because I did learn something. I would say that this work we are doing can definitely be applied to our everyday work. I did learn that you could be very humble, which we are being here, and honest. By using that method we could apply our work and get results unbelieved of without the necessary organization, and I do feel that you don't have to lay a man's work out in front of him, or the women. Let them think for themselves, there is organization here though, in a very democratic way, I think------But it isn't brought out right like a light.

"Now I tried this out on someone yesterday, a person I didn't think I liked. I sat and tried to listen to the man, and be very humble with the man. I certainly did find that I got results by using this method. I felt wonderful about it, I did really. I honestly felt good and clean about it inside----I was making an effort to understand the man------.

"Another thing that bothers me about these meetings is that I'll go to bed and I'll dream--not dream but nightmare about this meeting all through the night. This whole thing, it never bothered me before in my life; I don't know if its the power of hypnosis, or what------.

"Well we form our own opinions, why do we have to listen to other people's opinions for example? And this meeting is a fine example.------That book we were reading, its just too thick as far as I'm concerned------Now that was one of the things in that book------No it applies here in this group, there is no person in this group, in my opinion, remember, in my opinion--that's no one else's opinion--that wouldn't trust anyone else in this group. Mind you there are few of us who know each others' last names. But still I think they would trust each other with almost anything----Now within reason,----How many people in this group could get up and speak anywhere else without having a couple of drinks? That's a fact; that's what we are learning here, too; its to be able to speak without influence by something, without a little booster.------That you could look a man straight in the eye ----And then be able to look him in the eye again, and say something that means something. Now that is something that I can't do, that's one of my weak points."

ANALYSIS OF ERRORS MADE BY A MANAGER

Mark Leander
Management Consultant
225 Wellington Road
Houston, Texas

July 17, 1968

Mr. Jack Pascal, President
Texas Printing, Inc.
180 Hilton Avenue
Galveston, Texas

Dear Jack:

At long last I enclose three copies of my report. Portions of it might serve as topics for discussion among executives of Texas Printing.

As I told Marvin Ross in a short telephone conversation that we had yesterday, one copy of this report is for you, another for him, and the third for Sam Comens. I would be happy to discuss the findings, the recommendations, and the predictions with you, Marvin, and Sam at no additional cost.

My fee is $675. This covers interviews in my office with Sam Comens for an hour on 3/26/68, a second hour on 4/2/68, a third hour on 4/24/68, and two additional hours on 5/7/68 (i.e., five hours), with Marvin Ross for an hour on 5/22/68, and with you for an hour on 6/6/68. I devoted seven hours to the interviews, fourteen hours to the analysis of these interviews, and six hours to the preparation of the report, which is a total of twenty-seven hours at $25 per hour.

I am happy to learn from you that our interviews were helpful and hope that the report will also be useful.

Sincerely yours,

Mark

The Consultant's Report

Texas Printing is a successful, growing company that does quality work. Jack Pascal and Marvin Ross, the two top executives and (together with their wives) the owners of this firm, have an excellent working relationship. There is little conflict between these two partners. In fact, Texas Printing has an able top management team. The background and behavior of the members of that team will be discussed in the next several paragraphs.

(1) Jack Pascal, President

An alumnus of Rochester Institute, Mr. Pascal has a fine technical background. At 35 he is an effective production and finance man. He is bright, confident, calm, and fair. His partner told this writer, "Jack is a very unusual young man. . .together we've built up a hell of a good business."

(2) Marvin Ross, Executive Vice-President

After leaving the industrial real estate field, Mr. Ross was taught the printing business by his father-in-law, the founder of Texas Printing Company. During the founder's illness, and for a time after that, Mr. Ross ran the company and did so quite profitably.

Sam Comens, a manager whom we shall discuss shortly, told this writer that Ross is "a likable person, an excellent salesman, and a fine production men who pushes every element of the job in order to get it done quickly, with good quality and low cost." Customers get fine service from Marvin Ross.

Ross has said that he has everything he could want, including part ownership of a successful business. He feels that the founder and the family of the founder of Texas Printing have been very generous to him.

Although Marvin Ross ran the organization well before Jack Pascal, son of the founder, joined the company on a full-time basis, the latter now tends to be the chief executive officer. Although the two men do not argue, Jack is stronger and more sure of himself and so things frequently are done his way.

(3) Sam Comens, Production Manager

In discussing Sam Comens, Jack Pascal said, "He's the second hardest working person in our company. I'm the hardest working." Marvin Ross had the following to say of Comens: "Sam is always on time or earlier and is often the last to leave. He is out to do a good job and certainly gets a lot done."

Comens is a gentleman. He is an intelligent, pleasant, ethical man who is good with numbers and is well liked by customers. He has technical competence and is an able estimator.

When asked to prepare a description of his job, Comens wrote the following:

FUNCTION: To make sure that work brought in is processed and produced most efficiently, correctly, at the proper level of quality, for the least amount of money, and delivered on time.

OVERALL: To schedule work in plateroom and pressroom onto proper presses and in order. To adjust peak loads with farm-outs and/or overtime. To push work to fill weak spots in schedule. To assure correctness by getting proper information from salesman or customer, seeing that it's transferred all the way through--changes especially. To supervise the checking of quality in proof, plate, on press, and in finishing and packing. To provide salesmen or customers with information on status and delivery. To provide the office with all information for costing and billing. To schedule all departments for both shifts. Check out night shift. Schedule plant bindery. Check on jobs going to art department. Know about jobs. If complicated, check with press foreman, camera department, finisher, etc. Order stock. Put job in composing room or camera; avoid conflicts. Deliver proofs. Check returned proofs, schedule on presses, explain job to press foreman. Prepare for finishing operations; prepare for packing, delivery, and samples. Return art. Check presswork and binding dummy; check samples and delivery.

OFFICE: Do a certain amount of purchasing, a little estimating, talk to customers in salesman's absence. Talk to paper salesmen.

When Marvin Ross was asked to describe Comen's job he said: "Sam is the production manager. He takes an order from a salesman, buys materials, and then directs employees to see that the work is done properly and on time. This is a big job."

What, Then, Is the Problem?

Marvin Ross was asked what, if anything, Comens does that he should not do. "Nothing, except that he makes errors! I make errors. Everyone makes errors. Sam, however, does it too often. He costs us $100 a day or $25,000 a year in errors. All of us cost the company some money in errors, but not that much," was Ross's reply.

Jack Pascal also sees Comens' errors as an important problem. Four examples of Comens' errors follow. On one occasion, a book that should have been bound with an overhead cover was bound improperly after Comens sent the wrong dummy to the binder as a model. On another occasion, Comens did not mail an insert that a customer requested. A third error cost the company $100. In that case, Comens sent a collation job to a bindery that did not have collating equipment. Since they collated by hand, they charged $165 rather than the normal $65.

Finally, a wrapper that should have been scored for folding in four places was also scored in a fifth place. This made the final product less attractive and might have resulted in the rejection of the item by the customer. This would, of course, have required scrapping the finished, but imperfect, job and beginning again. Although this last error (and others, as well) may not actually have been committed by Comens, it should have been prevented or at least discovered early by him.

Explanation of Errors

There is no single cause for all Comens' errors. Different types of errors have different causes. At Texas Printing, Mr. Comens' errors appear to be the result of:

--Taking on more than can be done without making errors, although there appears to be little relationship between the volume of work in the plant and the number of errors made by Comens;
--Lack of control at strategic points in the production process;
--Inaccurate transmission (encoding and decoding) of information and improper issuance of directions;
--Comen's poor handwriting and later his difficulty in reading what he wrote earlier;
--Inadequate training of subordinates;
--Insufficient attention to and unsatisfactory handling of detail;
--Forgetting;
--Faulty analysis of the probable results of alternative course of action;
--Lack of planning (and of preparation);
--Imperfect relationship between Sam Comens and Marvin Ross. They have in the past acted as opponents rather than members of the same team. On one such occasion Ross handed Comens a written order with the comment "Even you can do it." Comens' immediate response was to "tune out." It then required will power for him to concentrate on the rest of Ross's instructions. Comens also reacted to this by wanting to follow the instructions to the letter and yet have the job fail because Ross had not planned it perfectly.
--Although Comens is good with figures and has a fine memory, when upset he will sometimes make an error in arithmetic or forget something that is right in front of him.
--Resentment against rush orders leads unconsciously to punishing the customer, the salesman, and owners through an error.
--Not voicing one's hostility means that the hostility shows up in other ways, e.g., in punishing oneself by misplacing an important paper.
--The acquisition by Texas Printing of a small printing firm for which Comens had worked led to resentment on his part. Comens had hoped for some ownership interest in that company. There the work was very much in balance with the presses fully utilized and overtime relatively rare. Also, because this small printer had serviced some customers for many years, Comens had merely to say to production people, "Do the Smith job," without having to know in detail what the Smith job was. However, because production workers at the larger Texas Printing were not familiar with the Smith job, instructions had to be given in detail.
--Since the acquisition of the small printing firm may not have been as profitable as some deals made by Pascal and Ross, at least one of them may have resented the purchase.
--When resentful or irritated by a sarcastic remark Comens has, in the past, failed to tell people things that they should know.
--When under attack Comens becomes nervous and inefficient.
--Delegations containing negative, self-fulfilling prophecies (e.g., Ross's statement "I'll probably be disappointed but I'm leaving this job entirely in your hands") lead to poor performance.
--Putting a job off until the last minute means we have to rush it and may, therefore, do it improperly.

--Spending too much time on the early stages of a job man mean that we can give the last phase of it only a "lick and a promise."
--Employing excessive pressure to get work out quickly may cause errors on rush jobs or those that follow.

There is no question that other sources of errors can be discovered and that the majority of mistakes can be eliminated. There is, however, a cost to the control of errors. We do not want to spend $200 to prevent the occurrence of an error that would cost the company $100.

Recommendations

Merely stating the causes of errors leads to methods for preventing them. Perhaps the following check list would be an appropriate way in which to present recommendations.

--Although Comens and others may be good at improvising on the spot when emergencies occur, it would be better to employ conditional planning and thus to avoid the need for hasty decision-making. During periods of relative calm we should make projections of future events and then think through difficulties and appropriate courses of action. When the predicted condition arises we should put our plans into effect. We must attempt, where possible, to avoid crash programs.
--Every person at Texas Printing should be ready to do his job. For example, Comens should not, as is often the case, be without a pen. If a pen is required, he should carry one with which to write clear, easily read reminders. Similarly, salesmen should check with Comens before making large commitments and should submit requests in writing.
--Comens has designed a "change order" form which will require that changes also be put in writing. It will make more obvious the impact of a change in one order on other orders.
--Mnemonics should be used to assist memory.
--Some errors can be prevented by checking at strategic points in the production and marketing process, e.g., look at a plate after it leaves the "prep" department and before it goes to printing. Make use of symptoms and sampling.
--Avoid getting ulcers or giving them to others by stating your position calmly and rationally.
--Recognize a job well done; accent the positive. People prefer to be praised rather than be blamed and hate to admit mistakes publicly.
--Let people know what is expected of them and how well they are doing. Also remember that they want to have some warning of changes that will affect them.
--Be patient with others. Listen carefully to salesmen and production workers. Where possible, permit people to participate in decisions that will affect them. (Delegation, however, does not mean abdication of responsibility.) People like to feel important.
--If one must be negative, criticize the behavior, not the person. Avoid sarcasm and yelling. They lead to errors.
--Tell people things they need to know in order to do a good job, e.g., Comens should be kept informed of work salesmen deliver to the "prep" department.
--Similarly, Comens might profitably use some time at the end of the day or during the lunch hour to tell salesmen and other appropriate people what is going on. The delivery man, for example, could profitably use more information.
--Everyone should make certain that cost and other data are transmitted accurately, that the communication is understood by the receiver.
--When giving instructions, also give reasons. Then ask what the person plans to do, why, and how he plans to do it.
--Employ a suggestion system for reducing errors and costs, and offer financial incentives for useful ideas. (Remember that income is important but not all-important. People are most concerned with their relative income, i.e., compared with their peers.)
--We should not demand that jobs be done our way if the outcome from our method is not likely to differ significantly from the results obtained by the use of another method.
--Employ procedures which avoid errors, e.g., asking a binder to submit a dummy that you, in turn, can send to the customer for the latter's okay.
--Ross should spend a greater proportion of his time in sales and a smaller proportion in operating departments than formerly.
--Department meetings and plant-wide meetings should reduce misdirected efforts that lead to poor quality. With few exceptions, the people at Texas Printing work hard to do good jobs.

Predictions

--Improvement in Comens' behavior with fewer errors being made. Comens learns very quickly and will apply what he has learned from our discussions. His handwriting will also improve so that Comens and others, too, will be able to read his writing long after he makes notations.

--Comens will pay more attention to the details of each job with the objective of eliminating careless errors. He will continue to grow and assume greater responsibility.

--The relationship between Ross and Comens will continue to improve because they are both mature, motivated people who are very much interested in the success of the company and, therefore, in learning to work together.

--Although Pascal might enjoy being immersed in the details of production, he will continue to fight successfully against this.

--Plant-wide and department meetings will prove beneficial to Texas Printing and to the people employed in the company. One useful question that should be discussed in those meetings: How can we help one another to do a better job, to be more effective and efficient?

Texas Printing, Inc.
180 Hilton Avenue
Galveston, Texas

July 31, 1968

Mark Leander
Management Consultant
225 Wellington Road
Houston, Texas

Mark:

Found the report quite interesting! Your check is enclosed.

After Sam gets back, I'm going to buy you a dinner and take advantage of your offer to go over the report. I'll see if I can arrange for Marvin, Sam, you and me to "break bread." I'll call you.

Jack

PLASTICS INTERNATIONAL LTD. (A)

The Attitude Survey Concept Is Introduced
Persons Central to the Case

Alton Barrow--Personnel Director, P.I.L.
William (Bill) Bauer--E.C.L. Labor Relations Director
Alan (Al) Brooke--Central Labor Relations
Dr. Harold (Hal) Gibson--American behavioral science consultant
Dr. Dietrich Hallbach--Deputy Chairman of P.I.L.
Dr. Oliver Hammond--P.I.L. Training Officer
Leland Jackson--Central Labor Relations
Dr. Charles (Chuck) Morris--American behavioral science consultant
Dr. Wolfgang Mueller--Production Director, P.I.L.
Eric Olson--Central Labor Relations
Dr. Paul Shelley--Chairman P.I.L.
Dr. Scott Starbrock--Director of R & D, P.I.L.
Wayne St. George--Central Labor Relations
Dr. Morton Wiesler--Manager of Textile Development, P.I.L. (Cologne)
Dr. Larry Wilson--Manager of Research, P.I.L. (Cologne)

Euro-Chemicals Ltd. (E.C.L.) employs some 120,000 employees in ten major divisions marketing throughout Europe. In addition there are subsidiaries in all major foreign countries. Headquarters are in Bonn, Germany. There is a good deal of mobility within the company among the management group, and significant numbers of executives are from Sweden, England, France, and Switzerland, as well as from Germany.

Plastics International Ltd. (P.I.L.) is a wholly owned division of E.C.L. The division took its present form approximately six years ago when E.C.L. decided to integrate their existing first-stage conversion plant vertically by acquiring a large company that was operating in the plastics market. As a result of the merger the research and development activities were located at two sites, Bonn and Cologne.

There were the normal problems associated with any merger. These had been coped with well--the division was expanding and, in spite of the vagaries of the plastics market, was very profitable.

Dr. Dietrich Hallbach, Deputy Chairman of P.I.L., had worked for some time with a partially owned subsidiary in the United States and had been impressed with the apparent usefulness of an attitude survey which had been used there. He talked over the idea with Alton Barrow, Personnel Director, on his return and suggested that P.I.L. might get good value from such an initiative. Alton Barrow was impressed with the report, but was aware that a number of attitudes surveys had already been "carried out in various parts of E.C.L." and, as he said, "were fascinating documents that always ended up in the bottom right-hand drawer." He wanted to be sure that the next survey would be of practical use and would form a useful pattern for the future.

Nevertheless, he talked the problem over with William (Bill) Bauer, Labor Relations Director of E.C.L. He discovered that Bauer was himself interested in the possibilities of a new form of attitude survey which an outside consultant had tried in another company. The basis of this survey was to use the questionnaire only for the purpose of focusing attention on problems and to give all the emphasis to the group meetings that would follow in order to solve the problem.

Alton Barrow saw the theoretical value of such an approach but was cautious at the prospect of "letting a whole crowd of long-haired fancy boys stop all work while they tested their latest gimmick at our expense." However, after a good deal of discussion about who would pay for the consultant, Barrow felt that it was in the division's interest to proceed, and Bauer agreed to divert all possible resources from the center to assist.

The American consultant and behavioral scientist Dr. Harold (Hal) Gibson was visiting the head office during the month of March. Although time was short Bill Bauer felt that it should be possible to achieve success, at least with a limited pilot scheme, provided adequate back-up resources were made available to Hal Gibson. He therefore wrote briefly to Hal explaining the problem and stating in broad terms what he expected from him on his arrival in Bonn.

Dr. Gibson arrived from the States knowing little about what P.I.L. might want. During a meeting at P.I.L. headquarters with Alton Barrow, it was decided to explore the possible use of the attitude questionnaire brought over from the United States by Dr. Hallbach, but to modify it based on divisional needs. (Dr. Gibson had had extensive experience in the design and use of attitude surveys, but this seemed to be reasonably well designed and had already had some acceptance in the division.)

At a subsequent meeting attended by fourteen people, including Dietrich Hallbach, Alton Barrow, two department managers and several assistant managers, possible use of the questionnaire was discussed. It developed that the assistant managers of the Textile Development Departments and the Research Departments were interested in participating in the project (the managers of those departments could not attend the meeting), but the P.I.L. Production Director, Wolfgang Mueller, withdrew from this meeting, leaving his assistant who commented "This is hard to oppose. It sounds like we are being unfashionable."

Much of the time and emphasis during those early meetings was inevitably spent on the form the questionnaire should take. Subsequently, Hal Gibson was emphatic that the necessity for workshops where action would be planned had twice been stressed. However, as will be seen, events suggested that the long process of turning replies to a questionnaire into a practical change program with action as the main criterion was not fully appreciated.

PLASTICS INTERNATIONAL LTD. (B)

The Questionnaire Is Administered

A week later, after checking out computer capability, Dr. Gibson took copies of the questionnaire, with items categorized under major subject headings, to a meeting of the original group. This group, which by now did not include representatives from Production, but continued to include the assistant managers of the two Research Departments and the two Textile Development Departments, made some revisions and additions. A small subcommittee met further that evening to finalize the revision.

Very shortly thereafter, all nine hundred employees of the four departments were assembled, approximately one hundred at a time, and requested to fill out the questionnaire. All employees participated, up to and including section heads. There were four such sessions at Cologne and five at Bonn. The employees were informed of the nature and purpose of the project, and told, "This is voluntary; you may hand it in blank, if you wish." Two questionnaires were used. The "white" version was filled out by everyone, including section heads, and was to be used for total departmental analysis. The "blue" version, much shorter, was filled out by everyone except section heads and was aimed at section analysis. (See Figure 1 for the questionnaire items and total sample responses pertaining to "Organizational Climate." Other parts of the questionnaire were "Pay and Benefits," "Relations with Other Units," "Communications," "Supervisor/Employee Relations," "Performance Counseling," "My Job," "Pressure of Work," "Management by Objectives," "Opportunities for Personnel Growth and Advancement," and "Training.")

As a next step, in a memorandum to the Central Labor Relations, Dr. Gibson outlined suggested steps in utilizing the data. (See Figure 2.)

Question No.		Organizational Climate	*	Over-all Mean	Overall Distribution % SA (1)	A (2)	U (3)	D (4)	SD (5)**
Blue	White								
39	99.	There is good cooperation and teamwork in my work group.	F	2.3	20	55	9	12	4
	90.	Employee safety is adequate in my department.	F	2.5	8	61	12	16	4
25	30.	Management side-steps or evades things which bother people on the job.	U	2.7	13	32	27	24	4
	71.	I think some practical steps for improvement may come out of filling in this questionnaire.	F	2.5	15	42	28	11	4
	40.	An excessive number of senior staff leave our department.	U	3.2	8	22	23	37	10
	86.	Staff transfers in my department are excessive.	U	3.4	5	13	23	49	10
5	8.	P.I.L. is a friendly place to work.	F	1.9	22	68	6	4	0
	58.	P.I.L. management are more concerned with productivity than people.	U	2.7	16	32	24	25	3
34	92.	The achievements of our group are not recognized at senior levels of management.	U	3.0	9	23	30	34	4
	91.	If I "stick my neck out," I am usually unpopular with management.	U	2.8	10	31	29	28	2
	9.	You "know where you stand" in P.I.L.	F	3.0	5	32	30	25	8
6	17.	We do not get the kind of backing we need from higher levels of management.	U	2.8	9	32	30	27	2
	31.	I feel I am considered to be a part of management.		3.7	2	17	17	39	25
	41.	Supervisors do not get the help they need to solve day-to-day problems.	U	3.2	4	16	40	34	5
	7.	The quality of food in the canteen is satisfactory.	F	2.8	5	48	14	26	7
	18.	P.I.L. is not yet working satisfactorily as a single company.	U	2.8	14	29	27	26	4
	19.	The external social events arranged for our department are not adequate.	U	3.0	11	27	20	35	7

*F is used to indicate that agreement is a favorable response.
U is used to indicate that agreement is an unfavorable response.

**Scores of 1, 2, 3, 4, and 5 were assigned to the responses SA, A, U, D, and SD, respectively.

Figure 1. Questionnaire items and sample responses on Organizational Climate.

Feedback and Use of Opinion Survey Results

The usefulness of the opinion survey within the Research and Textile Development Departments of P.I.L. hinges entirely on the feedback process in which results are discussed, their implications explored, and needed actions agreed upon and later carried out. The survey is justified only as it provides an intervention for change and improvement.

Now that the results of the survey questionnaires have been tabulated and made available, it is clear that there are important problems to be discussed at several levels throughout the two departments at Bonn and Cologne, and with top management. A plan for the feedback process which will make best use of the survey results is needed and this memorandum outlines my thoughts in chronological sequence.

1. 27th March — First Feedback and Planning Meeting. This meeting at Bonn attended by Directors, Department Managers and Assistant Managers from the two departments has as its purposes:
   - i) to examine a small sample of survey results and the problems they reveal.
   - ii) to discuss and agree upon plans and ground rules for subsequent feedback sessions of various kinds, and resources needed.
2. mid-April-May — Preparation of Feedback Sessions.
   - i) Further study, preparation, and organization of survey data for subsequent feedback sessions (Hammond, Jackson).
   - ii) Establish planning work-group for four feedback sessions (workshops) within Research and T.D.D. at Bonn and Cologne, and design these meetings (combined P.I.L., Central Labor Relations exercise).
3. mid-May — Summary Booklets. Publication and distribution of summary booklets on survey results by Research and Textile Development Departments.
4. mid-May-June — Departmental Feedback Workshops. Four working conferences, or workshops, are proposed for Assistant Managers and Section Heads (leaders) of the two departments at Bonn and Cologne (about 15 at each workshop). These meetings should be a minimum of three days each and should be conducted with the help of internal P.I.L. consultants and trainers (e.g., Training Section, Central Office Liaison Officers, etc.). The purpose of these workshops would be:
   - i) to review the survey results and select priority problems which could be dealt with at departmental, group, or section level;
   - ii) to begin to develop tentative action plans for solution of several problems at department level;
   - iii) to prepare Section Heads for conducting their own feedback sessions and to develop action plans with their section staff.
5. June-July — Sectional Feedback Sessions. Each of the 50 plus Section Heads or leaders should work through with his section the Blue Questionnaire material for his section on his own schedule during this period. He should have help available if desired. The purposes of these sessions are:
   - i) to discuss the section's views, to select problems for working through;
   - ii) to prepare a sectional plan-of-action steps which can be reported upward to Assistant Managers and senior management, and which represent reasonable commitment by Section Head and his section.
6. July-August — Group and Departmental Follow-up Discussion. There should be several follow-up meetings of Assistant Managers and Section Heads.
   - i) To review the action proposals by Section Heads and to integrate them where they involve group or departmental actions.
   - ii) To review the feedback process and determine what further steps might be needed to use the survey data fully as an intervention for improvement.
   - iii) To learn what training or other needs have arisen from the development of sectional action plans.
   - iv) To prepare departmental/location reports to top management on actions initiated and progress made.

Figure 2. P.I.L. Research and Textile Development Departments.

General Comments

1. As shown on the previous page, I am proposing a feedback sequence starting at the top of the organization and filtering down with some preparation of Assistant Managers and Section Heads in the process, then up again with departmental plans for action made up of the Sectional Action Plan. I do not believe there are shortcuts to this sequence if participants at each level are to be personally involved and committed to their own actions for improvement.

2. A good deal of time and careful planning of these feedback sessions is required, and I stress the importance of using all available resources from within P.I.L. and the Bonn office to ensure that these sessions are learning experiences, to demonstrate problem-solving techniques and to assist in developing action plans at several levels. The Section Head, in particular, often will be "on the spot," and need both the training during the first workshops and a supportive environment by top management.

3. Because of the interest of top management in having improvements, there will be pressure on lower levels to act. This is not unreasonable. However, top management itself may have to take some action, and at all costs a punitive attitude by superiors to subordinates must be avoided.

4. Since this kind of survey with feedback is relatively new in P.I.L. and in the company generally, it represents a pilot effort for the whole organization. P.I.L. has the opportunity to show how survey data can be used as an intervention strategy for improvements in operations and productivity. I advise making every effort to ensure that this is successful, or subsequent surveys will not be very effective.

5. I am writing a separate memorandum on the additional analysis of the survey data to help explore more fully the uses to which it can be put.

Prof. Harold Gibson
School of Management
State University

PLASTICS INTERNATIONAL LTD. (C)

Some Crunches

After some preliminary computer runs were available, Dr. Gibson developed a partial report (see Figure 3) in order to give some brief feedback to the original planning group. In addition, certain other management personnel met with the group, including Dr. Larry Wilson, Manager of Research at Bonn. Also attending was Leland Jackson, who had been involved from the beginning and had been appointed by Bill Bauer to coordinate the project and to act as liaison between the consultants and the various departments of P.I.L. who were using the questionnaire. Jackson also had been assigned the task of coordinating any workshops which might grow out of the questionnaire project.

Meanwhile, Dr. Hal Gibson, Bill Bauer, and Eric Johnson, the Assistant Labor Relations Director, conferred about who might handle any feedback sessions or workshops which might develop. Dr. Gibson had commitments in Asia and the U.S., and needed to leave after his one-month stay. At this time the name of Dr. Charles ("Chuck") Morris was mentioned and agreed upon. Dr. Morris already had been doing some work as a behavioral science consultant for the Central Labor Relations Department, was currently traveling in Europe and the Middle East, and was about to return.

Simultaneously, Leland Jackson had written a letter to Dietrick Hallbach, partially in an attempt to clarify the issue of the three-day workshops, but the letter was never answered. The matter then implicitly rested with the department heads at P.I.L. (Leland Jackson's letter is shown in Figure 4.)

As the next step, Leland Jackson, Dr. Morris, who had just returned from the Middle East, and Wayne St. George met to review the history of the project and to discuss the feasibility of meeting with each of the four department managers involved. (Dr. Gibson had left Germany just prior to Dr. Morris' return.) It became quite clear that Bill Bauer was very committed to the notion of three-day workshops, and the three-man team all felt a strong urgency to successfully "sell" the department managers on such meetings. Some of the details of the potential workshops were then discussed, including the distribution and format of the questionnaire data. For example, Dr. Morris felt strongly that section head answers to the questions be passed out in each department and be made available to the appropriate departments in the form of "% Strongly Agree," etc. The matter was resolved at a later planning meeting with the support of Alan Brooke who formed the consulting team.

Leland Jackson then arranged for half-day meetings with the managers and assistant managers of the four departments to discuss the proposed sessions, with one day to be spent at Bonn and one at Cologne. The first meeting took place in Dr. Larry Wilson's office at Bonn. In attendance were Dr. Wilson, his four assistant managers (each in charge of several section heads), Leland Jackson, Wayne St. George, and Dr. Morris. In addition, Dr. Oliver Hammond, Training Officer for P.I.L., attended. Hammond had been working with Leland Jackson on processing the data and developing the format of the various reports that might emerge.

At the beginning of the meeting in Dr. Wilson's office, Jackson briefly described the history of the project as he saw it. He then turned to Dr. Morris and asked him to describe what typically happens in meetings involving questionnaire results. Before Dr. Morris had said more than a few words about "feedback sessions" and "workshops," Dr. Wilson interrupted and stated with some heat: "I'm tired of all of the American behavioral science jargon," and then expressed his annoyance with the "jargon" he had heard at the meeting with Dr. Gibson. Dr. Wilson then asked Morris to continue. Dr. Morris, who by this time was upset and angry, stated: "This discussion makes me feel quite uncomfortable, Larry. I have the feeling that no matter what I say, you are going to attack it as American behavioral science jargon." Morris then lapsed into silence. Leland Jackson then talked for a minute about problems of semantics and terminology, and suggested to Larry Wilson that Morris should be given a chance to answer questions. Dr. Wilson appeared to be somewhat more willing to listen at this point, and Dr. Morris continued.

Later during the meeting, Larry Wilson expressed the strong opinion that his section heads absolutely could not be gone from their jobs for a period of three days. Another concern which he expressed was as follows: "We have been managing well and successfully in the past. Now we are told all of a sudden that we are not doing things properly, that we have to have an attitude survey, and then we have to go spend three days talking about it."

		Agree %	U %	Disagree %	
70. Overall, I am well satisfied with my present job.	(F)	57	18	25	(U)
52. My present job is one in which I can continually learn.	(F)	81	3	16	(U)
47. My work is interesting.	(F)	89	5	6	(U)
53. Too many people give me instructions.	(U)	13	6	81	(F)
25. I usually know whether I am doing well or badly on my job.	(F)	77	9	14	(U)
14. I feel I am often unable to use my full capabilities in the performance of my job.	(U)	59	10	31	(F)
67. I often feel that I have achieved something really worthwhile in my job.	(F)	62	14	24	(U)
68. I would put more effort into my work if other things were put right	(U)	44	17	39	(F)
73. My work is often held up by the customs and practices of the company.	(U)	42	19	39	(F)
96. My job provides sufficient opportunities for my efforts to be recognized by others.	(F)	53	16	31	(U)
46. I do not have enough say in deciding how my job is to be carried out.	(U)	29	8	63	(F)
37. It is quite possible for me to introduce new (untried) ideas on my job.	(F)	68	10	22	(U)
63. Within my department I do not get sufficient facilities and equipment to perform my job adequately.	(U)	30	10	60	(F)
95. I am frequently expected to perform tasks in my job which I consider unimportant or unnecessary.	(U)	33	10	57	(F)
15. If I had a chance to get a different job outside my department that paid as well as my present one, I would take it.	(u)	22	30	48	(F)
36. I often feel that my job is one that can be dropped.	(U)	19	9	72	(F)

Figure 3. P.I.L. Summary of my job (white questionnaire) for Research Department (n = 549).

From: Leland Jackson
Central Labor Relations Department

To: Dr. Dietrick Hallbach
P.I.L.
Bonn

Our Ref. LJ/RHM
31st March, 1969.

Following the meeting last Thursday and a further discussion I have had with Dr. Harold Gibson before he left the country, I thought it would be helpful for you to have a revised programme in addition to his paper on the Feedback and Use of the Opinion Survey Results which you already have.

1. Performance Ranking and Rating of Sections by Assistant Managers and Above.

During the week after Easter I shall be sending to Dr. Oliver Hammond for distribution to the departments concerned their Ranking and Rating of Sections and a synopsis of the factors taken into consideration when Assistant Managers and above were rating their sections' performance of High and Low.

2. Results of Opinion Survey.

(a) Towards the end of the week after Easter a condensed summary of the results of this opinion survey will be available to Assistant Managers and above. Dr. Hammond and I will be discussing the layout of this summary here tomorrow. Our objective will be to display the information in such a way that Managers can focus down on problem areas as quickly and easily as possible.
(b) Dr. Hammond and I also will be discussing the layout of Department Results for the leaflet which will be distributed to those who filled in the questionnaire. We shall be aiming to have this available for the printers during the week after Easter.

3. Feedback Workshops.

We shall be asking Dr. Hammond to arrange during the week beginning the 14th April with the Department Managers at Bonn and Cologne a meeting of about two hours (i.e., a morning with Research Department Bonn and an afternoon with T.D.D. Bonn or vice versa with a similar programme at Cologne) in order to discuss the design of the four three-day workshops. At the same time we would be wanting to fix dates for the workshops to take place as soon as possible. At last Thursday's meeting it was agreed that Managers, Assistant Managers, and Section Heads should attend the workshops. There will therefore be between 15-20 people attending each of them. For this exercise we shall be using the resources we have available here to act in a consultancy role.

Figure 4. Letter clarifying the three-day workshops.

PLASTICS INTERNATIONAL LTD. (D)

<u>Agreement on the Workshops</u>

The meeting with Dr. Wilson and his assistant managers ended with an agreement to start the session on a Thursday noon and work on through Saturday afternoon, and through Saturday evening, if necessary. The meeting ended on a reasonably friendly basis.

The luncheon which followed involved Dr. Wilson, one of his assistant managers, the consulting team, Dr. Morton Wiesler, Manager of Textile Development (Cologne), and one of his assistant managers. This luncheon partially served the purpose of briefing Dr. Wiesler on what had transpired in the morning, and as an introduction to discussions with him in the afternoon. The tone of the luncheon was friendly and jovial, and Dr. Morris and Dr. Wilson appeared to have resolved any differences between them.

The afternoon with Dr. Wiesler and one of his assistants proceeded smoothly. Dr. Wiesler agreed to a meeting involving himself, his assistant managers and the section leaders, beginning with lunch at 1:30 p.m. on a Thursday and finishing late Saturday afternoon, or early evening. During this meeting, Dr. Wiesler suggested that each section head be prepared to report about one segment of questionnaire results. This was agreed to, and section heads were to be asked to interpret the data and to discuss possible underlying causes for the questionnaire responses.

Two days later the consulting team met with the managers at the Bonn site to discuss the possibility of three-day discussions sessions. In the first meeting the two assistant managers of the T.D.D. Department were favorably predisposed toward the workshops (a manager of the group had not yet been appointed), but the meeting with the manager of the Research Department ran into some difficulties. There were concerns about what actually would happen at the meetings, what was to be the role of the outside "experts"; why was a meeting necessary, and why couldn't people from headquarters simply develop a report with recommendations? Although people seemed to be talking past each other, partly due to time pressures, a meeting with the manager, his assistant managers, and section heads was agreed upon with the stipulation that the consultants develop some kind of analysis of the data to submit to the group prior to the sessions.

As a result of these "negotiations," the following meetings were agreed upon:

a. <u>T.D.D., Cologne</u>
Thursday, 15 May, starting with lunch at 1:30 p.m. and finishing about 10 p.m. on Saturday, 17 May, at the Peterman Hotel. Consultants: Morris, St. George, Brooke, Jackson, Hammond.

b. <u>T.D.D., Bonn</u>
Sunday, 18 May, starting with coffee at 11 a.m. and finishing after lunch on Tuesday, 20 May, at the Alpen Hotel. Consultants: Brooke, Jackson.

c. <u>Research, Cologne</u>
Thursday, 5 June, starting with lunch at 1:30 p.m. and finishing about 10 p.m. on Saturday, 7 June, at the Greater Rhine Hotel. Consultants: Morris, Olson, St. George, Jackson.

d. <u>Research, Bonn</u>
Monday, 9 June, starting with lunch at 1:30 p.m. and finishing about 10 p.m. on Wednesday, 11 June, at the Schoeffle Hotel. Consultants: Morris, Brooke, St. George, Hammond.

One short, additional preparation session was held with each manager a few days before the workshop during which a number of important details were clarified. For example, in such a meeting with Dr. Wiesler, it was agreed that Wiesler would chair the meeting with the consultants acting as resource persons and facilitators and being concerned about the evolving design.

PLASTICS INTERNATIONAL LTD. (E)

The Workshops and Some Outcomes

When the T.D.D., Cologne group assembled for their three-day session, Dr. Wiesler made some opening comments in which he welcomed the group and mentioned some hoped-for outcomes. Following this, Alan Brooke made some statements on behalf of the consulting team concerning the objective which he mentioned, which the staff had agreed upon earlier, which could change the climate surrounding the attitude survey and the discussion sessions from one of a "pressure" situation to a more collaborative one. Dr. Morris then started to make a very brief overview of the survey results, but was quickly interrupted by the section heads who felt Dr. Morris was beginning to report on the areas they had been asked to analyze and report on. Although somewhat taken aback, Dr. Morris acknowledged that that would indeed be a much better procedure. He later confided to his consultant colleagues that "that was the best thing that could have happened." Subsequent planning for the meetings with the three remaining groups built that feature into the sequence as follows: (1) an introduction by the manager of the department involved, (2) a brief statement by one of the consultants as to objectives, and (3) section heads reporting on the data.

Some aspects of the questionnaire and survey were criticized by several of the section heads. The mean scores, for example, were criticized as misleading because a high percentage of "Strongly agree" plus a high percentage of "Strongly disagree" responses would result in an average score. The consultants agree that the means were much less useful than the percentages. The "Undecided" category also was attacked. When questioned as to what he thought this category means, Dr. Morris stated, "It can mean: (1) I don't have strong feelings one way or the other, (2) I'm indifferent, (3) I don't know, (4) It might be the case, or I'm not sure, or (5) The particular practice varies so much I can't say." This answer seemed to satisfy the critics, who seemed to be content, after a period of attacking the questionnaire, to move on to learn what they could from the answers.

Although the three-day workshops with each group had many different features, a number of common problems such as the above emerged, and the sequence tended to be approximately the same. The sequence and some of the content of the third workshop involving Dr. Wilson and his group were as follows:

1. Introduction
2. Objectives, Sequence, Time Blocks, and Administrative Matters.
   - A. Objectives
     - a. Identify problem areas by examining the data.
     - b. Get behind the data to specific causes.
     - c. Agree on action plans to deal with causes.
     - d. Familiarize section leaders with data in preparation for feedback and planning sessions with sections.
     - e. Move the climate of the exercise from a pressure operation to one of collaboration.
   - B. Sequence
   - C. Time Blocks and Administration

3:00 p.m. — 3. Reports from each section head based on question data and discussion.

12:00 Noon Friday — 4. "A Task-Reward-Satisfaction Model," and other behavioral science inputs.

12:30 p.m. — 5. Development of priorities--Total group discussion.

1:00-4:00 p.m. — 6. Lunch, followed by a staff meeting to categorize problem areas seen by participants as being the most important.

4:00 p.m. — 7. Team assignments (Section Heads were assigned to make teams as heterogeneous as possible).

Group A--"Job Factors"
- a. More responsibility and say about how work is carried out, and objectives.
- b. Remove customs and practices that are getting in the way.
- c. Deal with the "artificial crisis" problem.
- d. Long-term versus short-term projects.

Group B--"Personal Development and Rewards"
- a. Counseling (both the system and factors).
- b. Career planning (both pertaining to promotion and development on the job).

c. Training (on and off the job and keeping up to date).

d. Pay (information, personnel department role, the relationship between reward and performance and the role of the section heads).

Group C--"Communications--Delegation"

a. What is appropriate to communicate?

b. Why do people "feel in the dark?"

c. Communication with Bonn and other departments.

d. The role and authority of section head (including the problem of their being perceived as side-stepping problems).

Group D--(The Manager and the Assistant Managers)--"Boss-Subordinate Relationships"

a. Access (opportunities for contact across more than one level of management, and the problem of management approachability).

b. Not enough support, encouragement, praise, recognition.

c. Risks of "sticking one's neck out" and the problem of receptiveness to ideas.

d. Delegation to section heads.

4:30-6:30 p.m.	8.	General discussion of each assigned topic. (The entire group spend one-half hour on each topic exploring underlying causes.)
6:30-8:30 p.m.	9.	Cocktails and Dinner.
8:30-Midnight	10.	Teams meet separately. a. Depth discussion of causes. b. Tentative action recommendations.
9:00 a.m.	11.	Four teams report back to the total group.
Saturday		
12:30-2:00 p.m.	12.	Lunch.
2:00-4:30 p.m.	13.	Finalization of Action Plans.

During the three days the group was together, the external staff performed several functions as follows:

1. Continuous planning in response to developments and to the expressed needs and concerns of the group. Dr. Wilson was consulted several times about next steps.
2. Raising questions about some of the questionnaire data when the staff felt the group was ignoring or trying to explain away problems.
3. Serving as "process" observers, i.e., commenting on the dynamics of how the group was working together.
4. Supporting or challenging some of the assumptions underlying statements that people would make about managerial style, leadership, etc.
5. Giving brief "lecturettes" from the behavioral sciences or decision theory when appropriate.

When the session broke up late Saturday afternoon, the participants, including the consultants, expressed sentiments that the meetings had been very successful. All seemed generally very pleased at the outcome. In a few days the following resulting "Action Plan" was distributed. (See Figure 5.)

At various times during the planning sessions and workshops, the consulting staff discussed the dynamics of what was going on. One conclusion was that constantly there tended to be some common high and low points. For example, the meetings tended to start with some feeling of uncertainty, anxiety, and reluctance, but very quickly people began to feel fairly positive as the section leaders reported on their blocks of data and as discussions began to emerge. By late the second day, people tended to be somewhat discouraged, confused, and frustrated and wondering where it was all heading. However, as action planning began to emerge, the feelings again became more positive and reached a high point as consensus was obtained on action plans. Roughly, the cycle appeared to be as diagrammed in Figure 6. Illustrative of this cycle is a comment from one manager: "The first day and one-half I didn't know what was happening and wished I hadn't come. But it turned out very well and I think it was a successful exercise."

Another observation made by Dr. Morris was that all the workshops tended to take on many of the characteristics of "team-building" sessions. While the questionnaire data was based on responses from section heads and all employees below that level, probably half of the discussion and action planning focused on relationships between section heads, assistant managers, and the manager. (See Figure 5 for the Action Plans emerging from the third workshop.)

During the many planning sessions of the consulting staff prior to and during the workshop, the performance of the consulting team itself and relationships within the team were topics for regular review. This was due largely to the insistence of Dr. Morris who felt that the effectiveness of the consultants, both short- and long-range, would be a function of their own ability to model the behavior they were implicitly "selling." For example, the way the questionnaire was being used suggested norms of support, helping, openness to feedback, facing up to issues, and the expression of feelings.

During the period of time in which the workshops were being held, Leland Jackson reported to the consulting group that Dietrich Hallbach had agreed to meet for a day or two with the four managers and their superior, Dr. Starbrock, later in the year to discuss the results of the workshops and the need for any further action planning required relative to the total division. Dr. Morris was to return to the United States shortly after the four workshops, but Dr. Gibson was due back in Germany in the fall and could participate. Additional consulting help to P.I.L. section heads was to be presented through the Central Labor Relations Department.

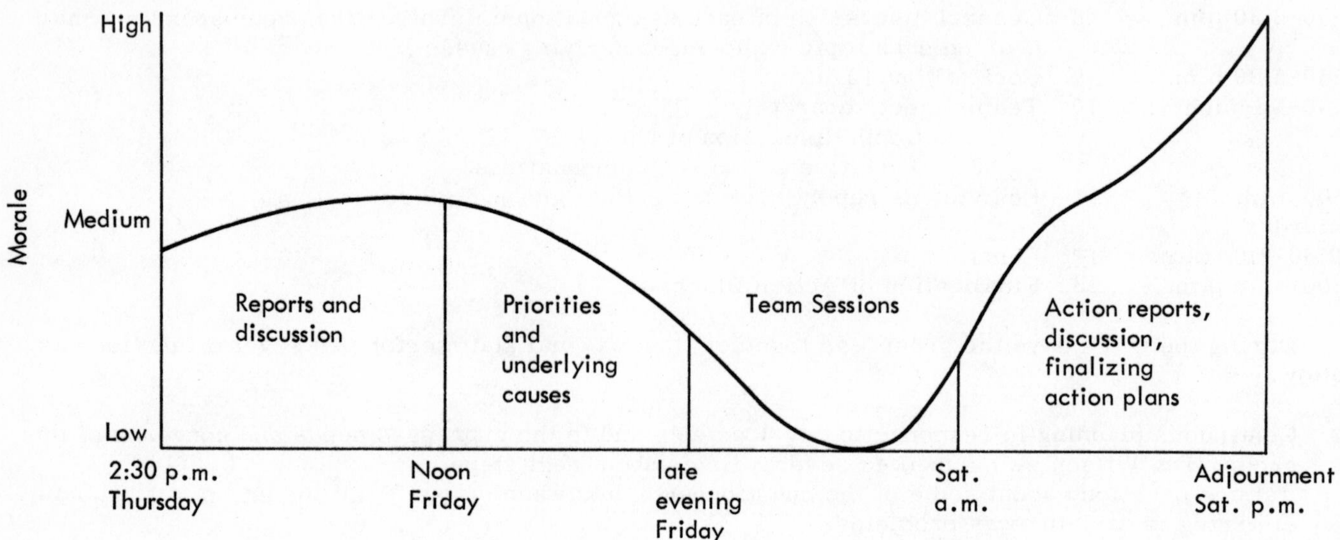

Figure 6. Cycle of response in workshop planning sessions.

	Problem	Cause	Action
MY JOB			
1.1	More Responsibility and Say in Objectives		
	Delegation of objectives downwards is lacking. Appreciation of overall departmental objectives is lacking	S.H.s have not ensured sufficient involvement at all levels. Technical dominance of juniors by seniors.	S.H.s to examine the work of junior levels in relation to work of their seniors and their objectives; they must reach agreed objectives with junior levels and give scope for increased responsibility and contribution. Junior levels to make a written contribution within their section towards the next issue of quarterly project sheets.
1.2	Customs and Practices in Research Dept., Cologne		
	Customs and practices "getting in the way."	Stores delays in Cologne Works.	A.R.M.s to re-examine immediately the system of receiving equipment through Main Plant Stores.
		Restraint of monetary sanctions.	R.M. and A.R.M.s where appropriate to anticipate sanctions in agreement with senior management.
		Paper work that "must go through Bonn."	Try and anticipate paper work by verbal agreement with Purchasing Dept. Bonn.
		Limited authorized signature list.	R.M. to make an immediate review of the authorized signature list.

Abbreviations: S.H. = Section Head
A.R.M. = Assistant Research Manager
R.M. = Research Manager

Copies: All participants
Dr. Dietrich Hallbach
Dr. Scott Starbrock

Figure 5. Research Department Cardiff action plan resulting from three-day seminar at the Greater Rhine Hotel, June 5-7, 1969.

	Problem	Cause	Action
1.3	Artificial Crises		
	Artificial crises exist in Research Dept., Cologne.	Delaying requesting reports and briefs until the last moment.	R.M. and A.R.M.s to give longest feasible notification time of requirements for reports and briefs. R.M. and A.R.M.s to issue an advance list of such reports where practicable.
		Bad planning for visitors and interviewers.	A.R.M.s to minimize delays in communication.
		Unfounded optimism in setting target conclusion date for projects and in underestimating costs.	S.H.s to investigate methods of improved estimating of project timing (possible use of network planning). Review quarterly report of objectives at end of quarter. Timing of projects, when agreed, will be adhered to by R.M. and A.R.M.s.
		Unreal emergencies from other departments.	No solution to this problem found.
1.4	Long-Term v. Short-Term Projects		
	The reconciliation of long-term projects with short-term projects.	Lack of involvement of other departmental resources (e.g., especially T.D.D.).	R.M./Textile Manager to agree on long-term objectives. S.H. to make specific recommendations to R.M. for specific allocation of T.D.D. evaluation effort for long-term research.
		No clear Company policy on the effective implementation of long-term work.	R.M. to discuss with Director of Research and Development.
SUPERVISOR/SUBORDINATE CLIMATE			
2.1	Recognition of Personal Achievement		
	Insufficient opportunities for "contact up."	Lack of personal contact.	S.H. to assist the R.M. in making personal contact by recommending discussions with personnel on specific projects so that achievements are recognized.
			All supervision to make a conscious effort to involve people at least "next but one below" in discussions.

	Problem	Cause	Action
			The R.M. to give an annual departmental review. A.R.M.s to give a 6-monthly group review. ALL staff in the department to attend these reviews. R.M. and A.R.M.s to tell secretaries not to turn people away, unless specifically instructed to do so. One S.H. from each group to monitor that there is improved "contact up." The R.M. and A.R.M.s would reconsider the departmental organization.
2.2	Receptiveness of New Ideas		
	People are reluctant to "stick their necks out." Ideas not readily accepted.	Managers chop ideas.	R.M. and A.R.M.s to make a conscious effort not to diminish people. Other members of the group could and should support an individual and his presentation of his new ideas. S.H.s to take more risks.
2.3	Delegation to Section Heads		
	Managers are short of time.	Managers do things they could delegate.	R.M. to review the authorized signature list and consult with other departments where appropriate. In particular signing for teas, cars, and advances to be done by S.H.s/Secretary as appropriate. Representation on meetings and committees to be reviewed by R.M. (e.g., S.H. might attend N.P.T.C. and New Nylons) and delegation at his discretion. A.R.M.s to authorize attendance at conference.

Problem	Cause	Action
COMMUNICATION AND DELEGATION		
3.1 Communications within R.D., Bonn.		
People feel they are "kept in the dark."	Not clear.	S.H.s must attempt to discover reasons and what people feel they are "kept in the dark" about.
	The necessary graduation of information that may be released.	S.H.s to inform staff that there is a necessary graduation of information that may be released.
	Insufficiency of personal contact.	S.H.s to hold section meetings to include technical and personnel discussions.
Communication lines cluttered within the department.	Petty chit signing.	R.M. to review authorized signature list.
Information to communicate is unclear.	Lack of directives.	R.M. to discuss with Research Director.
	Poor use of line management.	R.M. and A.R.M.s to divulge more information when given appropriate authority.
		R.M. to request Personnel Dept. to ensure simultaneous site announcements.
	Poor use of the English language.	
3.2 Communications with other Departments		
Communications with Bonn.	Delays in the telephone system.	R.M. to investigate means of improving the telephone system.
		Use telex where appropriate.
Waste of resources.	Unhealthy competition.	S.H.s to have access to and be able to put items on the agenda for R.M.s meeting when necessary.
		Bonn 3-monthly project sheets to be more widely circulated.

	Problem	Cause	Action
			Visits from Bonn Research Dept. to Cologne to be encouraged.
	Numerous contacts on a single project.	Unsatisfactory re-organization in T.D.D. Bonn.	R.M. to discuss with T.D.D. Manager.
	Part of pioneering effort is neglected in T.D.D. Bonn	Pressure of other work. Failure of communications in T.D.D.	R.M. to discuss with T.D.D. Manager (Cologne) the introduction of corresponding pioneering effort in T.D.D.
3.3	Role of Authority of Section Head		
	Evasion and side-stepping of decisions by management	Lack of clear knowledge on the role and extent of authority of S.H. and A.R.M.	R.M. and A.R.M.s to clear doubts in the area of S.H. responsibility as they arise.
PERSONAL MATTERS			
4.1	Career Planning		
	Ignorance of the existence and mechanism of career planning.	Lack of direct information.	R.M. and A.R.M.s to inform S.H.s of all permissible available information immediately. This information to be communicated as appropriate to lower levels before September, 1969.
4.2	Counseling		
	Insufficient appreciation of staff assessment factors.	Inadequate knowledge of procedure. The existence of undisclosed factors suspected.	S.H.s to explain assessment and salary adjustment procedures at next counseling interview, including the showing of the appropriate blank specimen assessment form.
		Inadequacies of counseling due to the time delay between assessment, counseling and reward.	R.M. to discuss with Personnel Dept. the telescoping of the three stages. R.M. to arrange training for counselors.
4.3	Pay		
	Lack of knowledge of salary structure.	Secretive policy. Failure to pass sufficient information via line management.	R.M. and Personnel Dept. to make appropriate arrangements before Sept. 1969 to provide information explaining the Haslam system and disclosing as appropriate Haslam levels.
	Lack of confidence in justice of the salary review.	Insufficient correlation in the relationship between merit and reward.	A.R.M.s to discuss proposed final salary adjustments with S.H.s
		Undue influence of Personnel Dept. in deciding merit raises suspected.	R.M. or A.R.M.s to sign salary letters.

Exercise

SURVEY FEEDBACK IN THE CLASSROOM

General

Survey feedback is an organization development technique in which participants complete a paper-and-pencil survey which attempts to measure various dimensions of organization climate, known or believed to be related to certain criteria of effectiveness. The data from the survey are then compiled (to insure individual anonymity) and "fed back" or reported to the participants and their group leader. The results of the survey are discussed, problem areas are identified, and programs for improvement developed. Survey feedback appears to be an effective technique of organization change because it (1) focuses on work-related issues (the content of the survey), and (2) it involves all the members of the group, both leader and subordinates, in the diagnosis and change effect (the feedback process).

Instructions

(Note: the following are general instructions. Your instructor may wish to modify them, assign different tasks to different class members, and so on.)

By most definitions of the term, your class is an organization. Survey feedback may thus be a useful technique of organizational improvement for the class.

There are two major tasks in this exercise. First, you must design the survey to be employed. This requires (1) identifying the outcomes from the classroom experience which you feel are important (establishing effectiveness criteria),[1] (2) identifying the variables you believe contribute to achievement or nonachievement of those outcomes, and (3) deciding which of those variables you wish to measure and how you can measure them through your survey. There are admittedly difficult but fundamental questions which your teacher will help you deal with.

Second, you must administer the survey, compile the results, and report back the findings to your teacher and other class members. The objective of the feedback process is to communicate accurately, but in an understandable and interesting way, the survey results, to identify problem areas, and to develop programs for improvement where needed.

Evaluation

Following are some of the many questions which arise from this exercise:

(1) What difficulties did you encounter in deciding on effectiveness criteria, and in identifying the variables which contribute to differing levels of effectiveness? Is this problem unique to the study of the classroom as an organization? If you had the time and resources, how would you go about improving on what you did in this part of the exercise?

(2) What questions arose with respect to the actual design of the survey (e.g., how questions should be worded, how responses should be scaled, the order of questions, etc.)? Does the design of the survey itself affect the survey results? How?

(3) In compiling the survey results, what measures did you decide to use? Do different statistical measures shade the meaning and bias the interpretation of results in one way or another? What techniques or devices did you employ to make the results interesting and understandable but still as "honest" as possible?

(4) How did you feel during the feedback and discussion process? Were problems highlighted? Did workable solutions emerge? Could the presence of an expert in the survey feedback techniques have been helpful to your group during the discussions?

(5) How effective or ineffective did you find survey feedback as a technique of organizational improvement? What characteristics and dynamics of the technique result in its effectiveness or ineffectiveness? How might it be improved?

---

[1]If you have already done the exercise at the end of Part I of this book ("Effectiveness Criteria for the Class as an Organization"), you may wish to use or modify the criteria identified there as a starting point for this exercise. If you have not done that exercise, you may wish to read it now since it provides a more detailed set of objectives and instructions which may be helpful in undertaking the first part of this exercise.

PART VI

INTEGRATIVE CASES

NEWCOMER-WILLSON HOSPITAL

The administrative process in a hospital is complex. There are not many organizations with such cumbersome structure which still succeed. It is neither clear, definite, nor clean cut at any time. If it were, the doctors would not want it to be. So, we have to set up an elaborate framework of communications, especially with committee structure, in order to keep things moving.

This is the typical view of how hospitals are organized and run as expressed in 1962 by Mr. William Baker, the professionally trained and experienced hospital Director (administrator) of the Newcomer-Willson Hospital.

The Hospital Business--Background and Current Status

In medieval Europe, hospitals were lodging places for travelers and were supported primarily by religious organizations. Later these places started taking care of old people and the homeless. Originally they were not institutions for the care and recovery of the sick. These charitable institutions provided for the needy, and doctors did provide some medical care mostly as a benevolence. Until about 1850 hospitals were usually very poor substitutes for home care.[1] Living standards, the evolution of modern medicine, along with many scientific and technological developments associated with the detection and treatment of illnesses, have caused hospitals to become important centers for medical care and training of doctors and nurses. Today doctors usually have a primary interest in the establishment and operation of hospitals because their chief professional interest is medical care, i.e., the same objective as that of hospital management.

According to the American Hospital Association's Guide Issue of the Journal of August 1961 there were 6,876 hospitals in the United States. These institutions employed 1.6 million people (full time), had an annual payroll of $5.6 billion, a total annual expenditure of $8.4 billion, and assets of almost $18 billion (depreciated value). There are over 1.7 million hospital beds in the United States and a daily average of nearly 1.5 million patients in all the hospitals of the nation. There is no doubt about whether hospital operation has become big business and it is growing rapidly.

The purpose of all hospitals is to provide medical care. Most hospitals provide this care on a "nonprofit" basis from an accounting point of view. However, hospitals are business organizations and must conduct their long-run activities in such a manner that total revenue from all sources equals total expenditures, i.e., they must break even.

Hospital Administration

The growth of hospitals in size and numbers during the first part of the twentieth century ushered in a new era in hospital administration. Traditionally hospital administrators were either doctors or nurses who devoted whatever time was needed to the administrative matters of the organization. In small hospitals, this was not a particularly time-consuming job especially when a full-time clerical assistant was used. The growth of hospitals (size and numbers) challenged this arrangement. Doctors and nurses were taken from their respective professional fields too much of the time, and they did not have the training or experience necessary for successful managers. In 1938 the University of Chicago established the first program designed especially for hospital administration. Since that time 17 other universities have initiated such programs while many Schools of Business Administration feel that they prepare graduates who are qualified for this type of work.

The type of academic preparation and background of hospital administrators is revealed as follows by a sample taken in the New England States in 1962 by the New England Hospital Association:

[1] Temple Burling, Edith D. Lentz, and Robert N. Wilson, The Give and Take in Hospitals (New York: G. P. Pitman's Sons, 1956), p. 4.

Number of Administrators with Degree

Size of Hospital (Beds)	Masters in Hospital Administration	Medical Degree	Bachelor Degrees in Various Fields	Only High School
Under 100	4	2	2	0
100-199	6	5	9	1
200-299	7	3	5	2
300-over	5	3	3	6
Total	22	13	19	9

The Newcomer-Willson Hospital

The Newcomer-Willson Hospital is located in a growing and prosperous suburban community. It has grown rapidly in the last 15 years, and with its recent expansion a total of 285 beds, 45 bassinets, and 700 rooms for different purposes are provided. It has a good rate (85%) of bed utilization as compared to the national average. There are 700 full-time employees, 400 medical staff members (of which 270 are courtesy members), and a nursing school of 160 students. The total budget for the coming year is a little over 3.6 million dollars.

The hospital's internal organization is depicted in Figures 1, 2, and 3.

The policies and organization of the hospital were reviewed two years ago by Cresap, McCormick and Paget, Management Consultants. The Consultant's report covered all areas of the hospital in a rather broad way. It was generally favorable. It noted that over the past several years prime attention had been given to organization for administration, but that there were some problem areas needing additional attention.

Authority Structure at Newcomer-Willson Hospital

Top Management

Figure 1 reveals the top and middle management organization at Newcomer-Willson. The top corporate body is the Board of Trustees, which is composed of about 70 Volunteers (nonmedical) from a variety of fields. Most of the trustees are local citizens of some standing in the community.

The most important body in the administrative process which deals with top level considerations and problems is the Board of Governors. This Board includes the four corporate officers from the Board of Trustees and nine elected trustees. The Board of Governors is responsible for the general administration of the organization, and it appoints all members of the Medical Staff and all other key people of the hospital.

The Medical Staff organization is headed by an Executive Committee. This committee operates within the framework of the By-laws of the Corporation and more specifically within its own By-laws which were approved by the Board of Governors in January 1962. This committee may report to either the Director, Mr. Baker, or to the Joint Trustee Medical Staff Committee, depending on a variety of situations. In the past there has been a deliberate attempt at times to override the Director because of the nature of the problems. This has not usually been achieved, however, because the Director is a member of the Joint Committee.

The medical staff is composed of doctors who have private practice in the surrounding community. They use the hospital when the need arises. They serve on committees of various types (see committees on Figure 3). These staff members are highly trained in their individual professional fields of medicine, and their primary concern is for their particular patients who are in the hospital. In fact, this concern causes some problems for Mr. Baker, the nursing staff, and others in supervisory positions because the hospital staff must think in terms of all the patients, not just one or a few.

The chief full-time administrative position is that of the Director, currently held by Mr. Baker. Mr. Baker has been with the hospital for several years. He is a Fellow[2] in hospital administration and has a great deal of administrative experience in several different positions of various organiza-

[2]This means that he has passed examinations and met the requirements of the College of Hospital Administrators, an association in this field.

tions. He has been a prime mover in establishing an improved administrative organization with the establishment of committees, by-laws for the medical staff, and written descriptions of duties and responsibilities for all managers and committees. He has an excellent rapport with both the medical staff doctors, the members of the Board of Governors, and his subordinates. He has a real sense of achievement by practicing the art and science of administration at the hospital. Although the administrative process seems to bog down at times, the network of communications through the organization and committee structure ultimately yields satisfactory results. He is a member of most of the administrative committees of the hospital and spends a great deal of time with committee meetings.

Mr. Baker emphasized the fact that the administrator's job involves many problems and believes a study made by Charles Prall[3] was reasonably representative. This study shows the percentage of administrators (by type) who reported one or more problems in several given categories. The summary report is presented in Table 1.

Table 1
Percentage of Hospital Administrators Reporting One or More Problems in Specific Categories--by Type of Administrator

	Percentage Reporting One or More Problems by Area		
Problem Areas	Laymen	Doctors	Nurses
Working with doctors	40	41	71
Improvement of Medical Care	50	63	90
Business and Finance	61	40	43
Public Relations	50	50	50
Physical Plant	33	25	50

Mr. Baker looks upon the extensive committee structure (see Figures 1 and 3) at the Trustee, Board of Governors, and top medical staff level with somewhat of a mixed feeling. On the one hand, they are release valves for troublesome issues and represent the democratic process which keeps everyone informed. On the other hand, they are very numerous, slow-acting, time-consuming, and reach few decisions which would not have been reached on a more timely basis by the Director working directly with the Executive Committee of the Medical Staff or the Board of Governors.

Middle Management Organization

The full-time operations of the hospital are organized and conducted under the supervision of 12 persons who report directly to Mr. Baker (see Figure 1).

The nursing activities are divided into two main groups; namely, Nursing Services and the School of Nursing. Figure 2 shows the internal organization for conducting these nursing activities. The School of Nursing has its own autonomy to a great extent because of its educational mission. Along with the medical staff, the Nursing Services constitute the very heart of hospital operations. The members of the Nursing staff are specialized and perform their duties on a round-the-clock basis every day of the year (by shifts) in such departments as Medicine, Surgery, Obstetrics, Pediatrics, and Operating Room. Theoretically each nurse has an immediate superior (Head Nurse) but during a normal work period she may be involved in taking instructions from several different persons. This is especially the case when dealing with the individual doctors of her various patients. Her work seems to run smoothly until "outsiders" create confusion and frustration by telling her to do things which do not constitute her job, interfere with her primary duties, or things which are against the rules or regulations of the hospital.

The Medical Staff Organization includes the doctors who are associated with the hospital. (See Figure 3 for the internal organization of the Medical staff.) In a way the hospital is a service requirement of the doctors. Its existence depends on the requirements for patient care as determined by the individual medical staff members. Sometimes the individual doctors do not fully realize the "public utility" nature of the hospital. While the doctor is concerned with his patient, the hospital personnel are concerned with all patients. This leads to some difficulties in such activities as scheduling of operating rooms, proper use of precautionary methods, and administering the rules and regulations established by the Board of Governors and outside agencies.

[3]Temple Burling, op. cit., p. 53.

Administrative and Medical Staff Conflict

Until about 15 years ago, Newcomer-Willson had a doctor administrator. After a brief experience with a layman administrator, it went back to a doctor. About nine years ago it decided again to employ a nonmedical professional administrator. Since then, strides have been made in the administrative activities of the hospital. Basic problems do arise, however, which seem to indicate the need for further improvement in the organizational arrangement and/or the administrative processes. For example, the Head (physician) of one of the full-time departments, recently demanded "individual professional status"[4] which he thought the medical staff members had and which he did not have. The problem became so serious that the physician threatened to resign if he did not get the status desired. After considerable discussions with various people and in several committee meetings, the Board of Governors decided that the current status would not be changed substantially and the issue seemed to have been settled--with no resignations. A by-product of this action was the clear evidence that the Board of Governors is the "governing" body of the hospital.

Another incident reflects the type of problems which Mr. Baker and the administrative supervisors face. Only recently a patient had been placed on "precaution"[5] by her doctor. Her physician, accompanied by several resident doctors, came into the patient's room without observing the precautionary rules. The staff nurse reported this incident immediately to her supervisor. The supervisor ordered all the doctors from the room, explaining the reasons to them. The physician took the patient off "precaution" on the spot and remained in the room. This upset the nursing staff; however, the next morning the physician placed the patient back on precaution. After discussing the problem with the Director of Nursing and the physician, Mr. Baker had to decide what must be done in this instance and also in the future to reduce or eliminate such situations.

> Mr. Baker said: "I suppose our problem is that the nature of hospital operations makes it necessary to violate some of the essential characteristics of good organization which authorities like Urwick emphasized. Maybe Emerson was right when he said poor organization is the 'hook-worm disease' of industry. It is a disease we haven't completely cured. Everyone seems to have too many bosses, but somehow we do get the job done."

Committee -
1) Better Answers
2) Slower
3) Need Good Chm.

---

[4]This means that the doctor's relationship with patients is more important than his relationship with the hospital. For example, such status would permit him to render his bills directly to the patient rather than going through the hospital organization.

[5]Precaution means that the patient either has or is likely to have a contagious disease and special clothing, gloves, and regulations are required when dealing with that patient. These regulations are established by the hospital to conform to its requirements and legislative provisions of the local, state, and federal government.

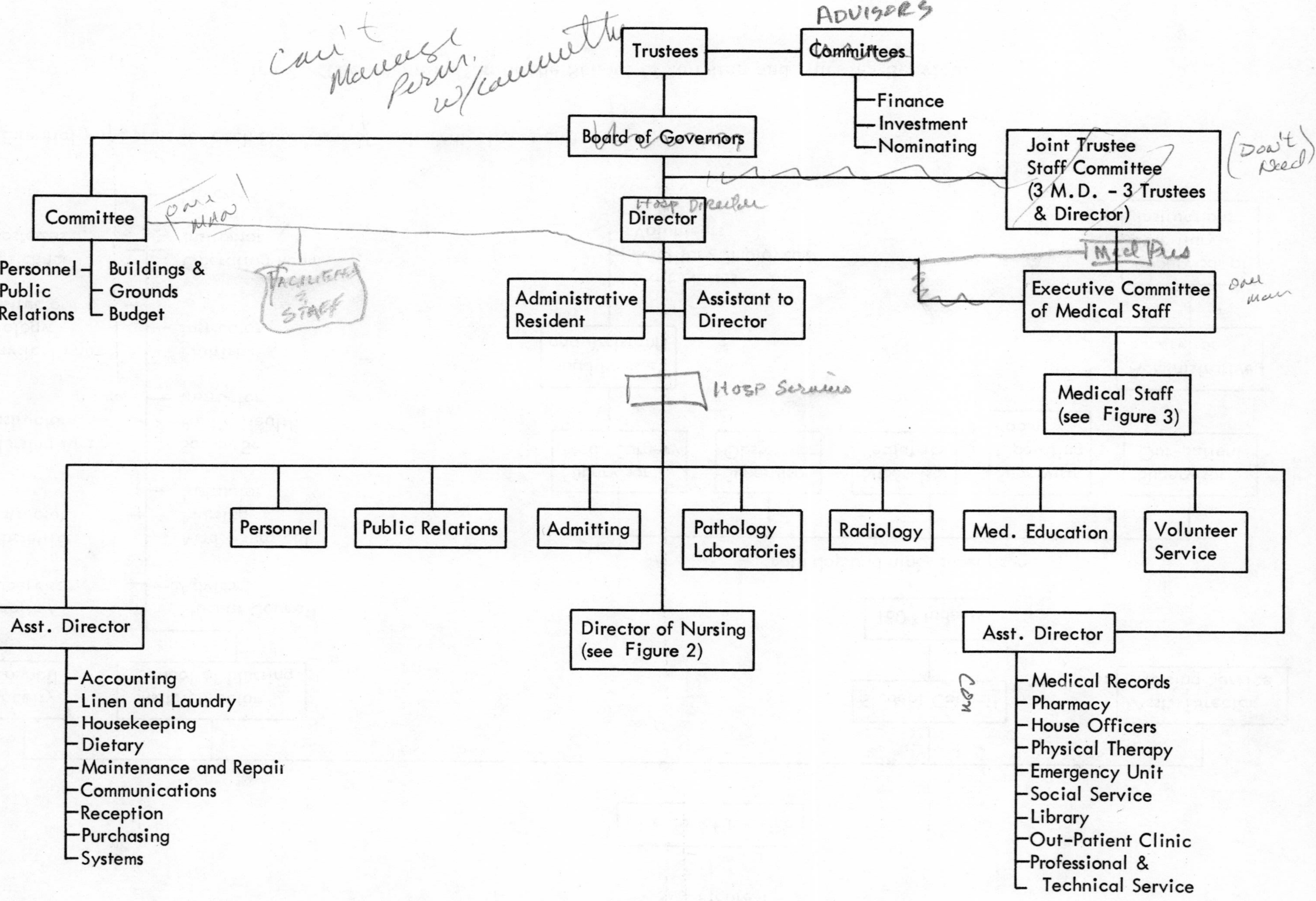

Figure 1. Basic organization of Newcomer-Willson Hospital.

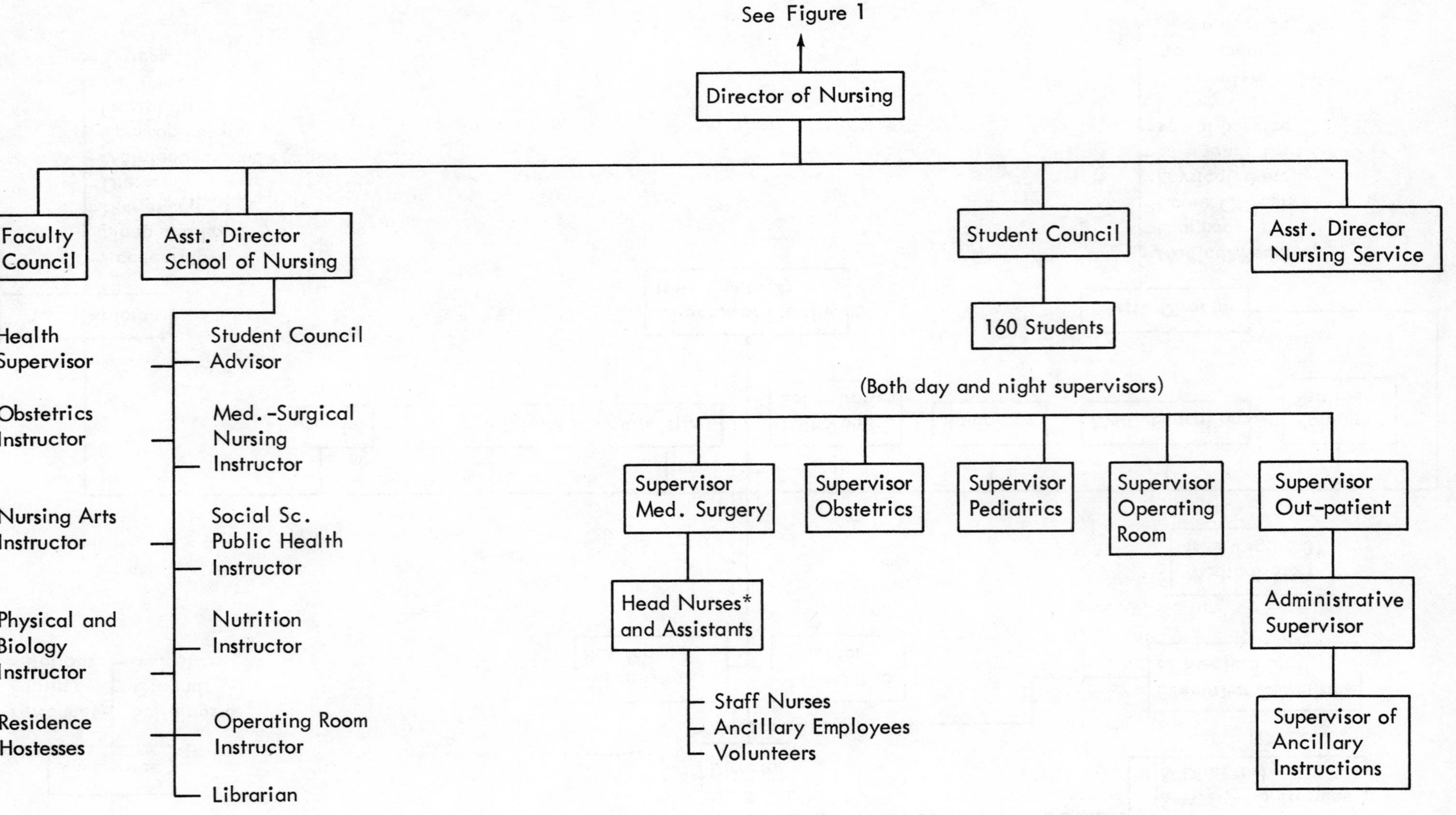

See Figure 1
Director of Nursing
Faculty Council
Asst. Director School of Nursing
Student Council
Asst. Director Nursing Service
160 Students
Health Supervisor
Student Council Advisor
Obstetrics Instructor
Med.-Surgical Nursing Instructor
Nursing Arts Instructor
Social Sc. Public Health Instructor
Physical and Biology Instructor
Nutrition Instructor
Residence Hostesses
Operating Room Instructor
Librarian
(Both day and night supervisors)
Supervisor Med. Surgery
Supervisor Obstetrics
Supervisor Pediatrics
Supervisor Operating Room
Supervisor Out-patient
Head Nurses* and Assistants
Staff Nurses
Ancillary Employees
Volunteers
Administrative Supervisor
Supervisor of Ancillary Instructions
*Essentially the same for each Supervisor of each medical care unit.

Figure 2. The organization of the School of Nursing and Nursing Service.

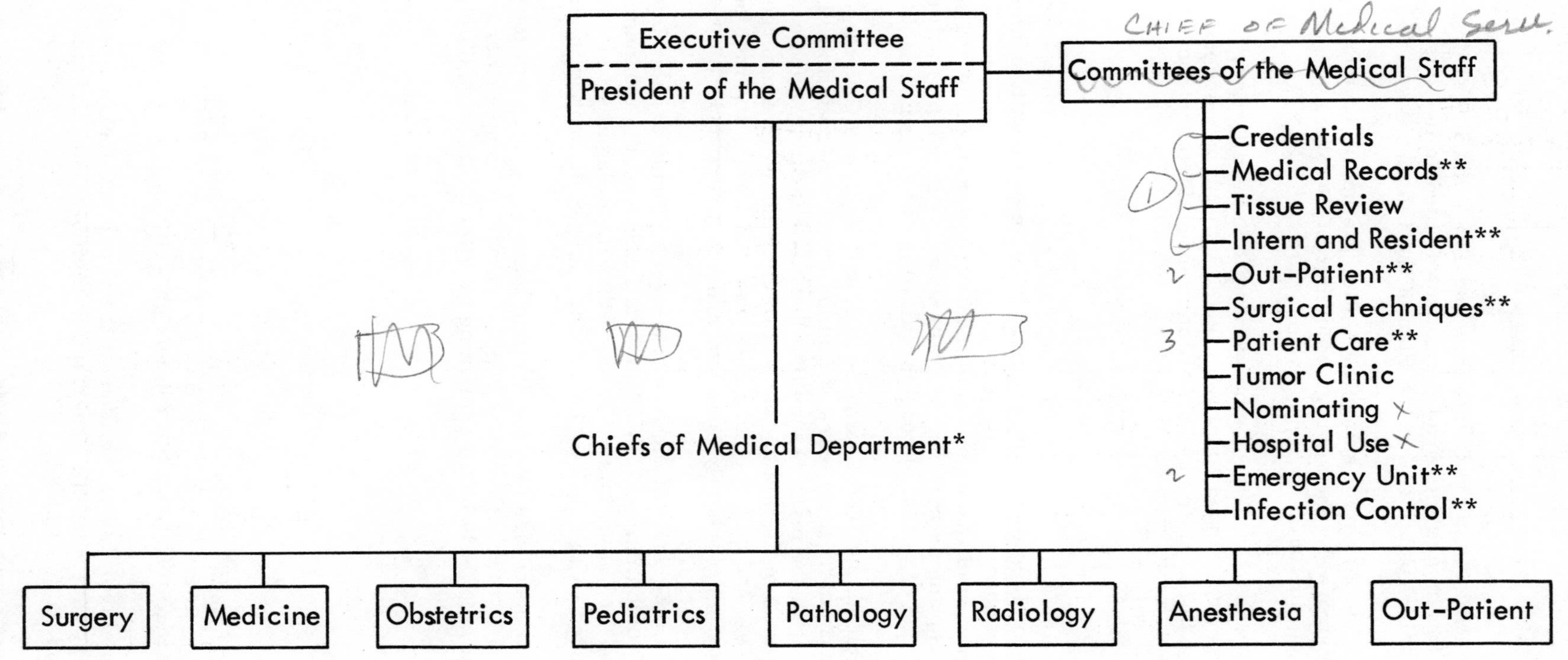

*Each medical department has several doctors.
**Administrative staff also represented on these committees.

Figure 3. The Organization of the Medical Staff of Newcomer-Willson Hospital.

UNITED METHODIST CHURCH

I. SYNOPSIS OF THE CASE

On November 11, 1966, The Methodist General Conference and The Evangelical United Brethren Conference meeting simultaneously in Chicago's Conrad Hilton Hotel voted in favor of merger of their two churches by adoption of a policy paper called the Plan of the Union.

Consummation of the Plan of the Union, establishing The United Methodist Church, required in both churches a two-thirds vote of approval by the aggregate number of members present and voting at the several Annual Conferences held in 1967.

On April 23, 1968, a formal rite was held at the Memorial Auditorium in Dallas, Texas, joining The Methodist Church and The Evangelical United Brethren Church into the new denomination which embodied 11 million members in the United States and a million more in 50 other countries around the world.

II. PURPOSE OF THE CASE

When an organization that has existed in its basic structure and philosophy for a great many years decides to alter this structure and philosophy by acquisition or merger with another organization, the impact of such a decision can create situations that introduce many problems. How management faces up to early recognition of these potential problem areas, its plans to solve or react to them, and its philosophy of accepting or rejecting certain areas as problems, will depend on the success or failure of the policy decision of growth through acquisition or merger.

The merger of The Methodist Church and The Evangelical United Brethren Church climaxed many months' preparation and approximately nine years of Methodist-EUB negotiation. During these years, the church management dealt with the many issues that had to be faced by such a merger. Out of these negotiations, and as a result of the joining of the two churches, there emerged new programs, new leadership, new structures, and new requirements directed toward the members to confront squarely a not-so-new but changing, incredibly complex, and conflict-wrecked modern society.

This writer attended the Annual Conference of the Alabama-West Florida area as lay delegate from the local church at Shalimar, Florida, during May 20 to June 2, 1967, on the campus of Huntington College in Montgomery, Alabama. It was at this conference that the delegates were required to face up to and vote on the issues needed to be resolved before the merger described in the Synopsis.

It became apparent early in the proceedings that the accomplishment of approval for merger would not be easy. Lines were clearly drawn. Emotions ran the gamut. Caucuses were the order of the day. Leaflets were passed out on a daily basis explaining or attempting to explain positions. Questions often heard were:

"Who are these people?"
"Why do we want to join up?"
"Aren't we big enough now?"

Statements added to the debate:

"I don't know any members of the EUB."
"I don't want any Negro preaching to me."
"Why should those people in Chicago tell us how to run our church?"

While there were many reactions favorable to the issues, the above comments attempt to provide the reader with the understanding that when the organization member is confronted with an issue, he will take a stand or position on that issue.

This conference, like many others across the land, did debate the issues and then voted. The result of the voting nationwide relative to the issues of the merger is the action taken on April 23 of this year at the General Conference in Dallas, Texas.

The purpose of this case is, therefore, to present to the reader some of the facts dealing with this merger of two large denominational churches and actions prompted by such a merger. Emphasis is directed toward organizational changes, particularly at the local church level, and the social impact brought about by the merger and the requirements for merger.

Grateful acknowledgment is extended to Dr. George A. Foster, pastor of Trinity Methodist Church, Tallahassee, Florida, and to Rev. George W. Gibert, pastor, Shalimar Methodist Church, Shalimar, Florida, for their helpful comments and contribution of data toward the development of this case.

III. HISTORICAL BACKGROUND

The policy paper called the Plan of the Union proposes to bring together The Methodist Church and the EUB Church, two churches that share a common historical and spiritual heritage. They hold the same fundamental doctrines of faith. Ecclesiastical organization is similar. They are Protestant churches, whose streams of philosophy came out of the Protestant Reformation of the 16th Century.

Since their beginnings, these two churches have lived and worked side by side. Their primary differences sprang from a language barrier. The Methodists worked among the English-speaking people and the Evangelical and the United Brethren worked among those speaking German. At the present time, with the language barrier gone and the goals of the two churches forming a common task, the uniting of forces seemed appropriate and timely.

To provide the reader with additional information on the background of the two churches, brief historical sketches follow to include a brief history of The Methodist Church and the Negro.

A. The Methodist Church

This is a Protestant church that had its origin within the Church of England. Its founder was John Wesley, a clergyman of that church. Wesley, educated at Oxford University, had sought in vain for religious satisfaction by strict observance of the rules of religion and the ordinances of the church. Frustration resulted in his acceptance of a philosophy at a prayer meeting in Aldersgate Street, London, on May 24, 1738, that it was not by rules and laws, nor by one's own efforts at self-perfection, but "by faith in God's mercy as it comes to us in Christ, that man may enter upon life and peace."[1] Upon such a philosophy, the Methodist Church was built.

Wesley spread his gospel throughout the British Isles. Step by step he led on until Methodism became a great movement in England. He gathered his people in groups, classes, and societies. He appointed leaders and found men he could designate as local preachers, or lay preachers--those not ordained. He called them together annually for a conference, a tradition carried on today as Methodist preachers convene once a year for their Annual Conference session.

From England, Methodism spread to Ireland and then to America. In 1766, Philip Embury, a lay preacher from Ireland, began to preach in New York City. At about the same time, Robert Strawbridge, also from Ireland, began to work in Frederick County, Maryland. In 1769, Wesley sent Richard Boardman and Joseph Pilmoor to America, and two years later Francis Asbury, who was to become the real leader of American Methodism, arrived.

Methodism was especially adopted to American life. The itinerant preacher served the people where a settled ministry was not feasible. He sought out the scattered homes, followed the tide of migration as it moved west, established "preaching places" and formed these into "circuits." Thus, by the close of the American Revolution, the Methodists numbered some 15,000 members and 80 preachers.

At the Christmas Conference, which met in Baltimore on December 24, 1784, some 60 preachers with Dr. Thomas Coke as superintendent organized the Methodist Episcopal Church in America.

In the history of Methodism, two notable divisions occurred. In 1828, one group dissatisfied with the provisions of lay representation in the church separated and became the Methodist Protestant Church. In 1844, there was another division, the cause being the question of slavery and the powers

---

[1] The Constitution for the United Methodist Church (U.S.A., The Joint Commission on Church Union of The Methodist Church and EUB, Jan., 1967), p. 1.

of the General Conference versus the powers of the espiscopacy, or the authoritarian powers of the bishops. After years of negotiation, on May 10, 1939, the Methodist Episcopal Church, the Methodist Episcopal Church, South, and the Methodist Protestant Church united to form the Methodist Church.

B. The Evangelical United Brethren Church

This church, in its present form, represents the union, consummated in 1946, of the Church of the United Brethren in Christ and the Evangelical Church.

1. Church of the United Brethren in Christ

This church was the result of the labors of William Otterbein and Martin Boehm in Pennsylvania, and George A. Geeting in Maryland, working among the Germans in America to form a new Christian society.

The first conference was held in Baltimore in 1789 with seven preachers present. A second conference was held in Paradise Township, York County, Pennsylvania in 1791.

The membership in the new society continued to increase and it included Germans who had been Presbyterians or German Reformed, Lutherans, and even Mennonites. They held a conference September 25, 1800, in Frederick County, Maryland, and there united themselves into a society called United Brethren in Christ. William Otterbein and Martin Boehm were elected Bishops.

From this time, with the society growing, preachers were appointed to travel regularly in order to cover all the "preaching places." The work soon extended into Ohio and Kentucky, necessitating the establishment of a Conference in the State of Ohio.

2. The Evangelical Church

This church was organized under the leadership of Jacob Albright in 1800 consisting of a number of persons in the State of Pennsylvania. He organized three classes, appointing a class leader for each. On November 3, 1803, there was held the first council of the denomination; the first conference was held in 1807 at what is now Kleinfeltersville, Lebanon County, Pennsylvania.

This group was first called the "Albrights," but in 1816 formally adopted the name of The Evangelical Association.

In 1891, differences arose in the church resulting in a considerable number of ministers and members organizing themselves in 1892 into a separate denomination under the name The United Evangelical Church. The two churches continued their activities side by side, growing in numbers and in missionary enterprise. At the end of the second decade of separation, the two churches decided to reunite and in 1922 The Evangelical Church was the result.

C. The Methodist Church and the Negro

When the Methodist Episcopal Church was organized at the Christmas Conference in Baltimore in 1784, 51 churches gave reports of their membership, and all but 15 reported Negro members. Negro membership in 1786 numbered 11,280; in 1811, 34,724; in 1826, 47,433; and in 1845, 150,120.

From the beginning of organized Methodism in the United States, certain powerful divisive influences were present. The two most prominent were slavery and the question of democracy in policy and administration. The two sometimes became intertwined as issues developed, and also were effective in leading to divisions.

The first separations were racial, resulting in the establishment of the African Methodist Episcopal Church in 1816 and of the African Methodist Episcopal Church Zion in 1820, centering in Philadelphia and New York City, respectively. Although Negroes were admitted into membership in Methodist societies and churches from the beginning, the facts of color and slavery resulted in discriminatory practices on the part of the majority white membership. These appeared in separate seating, order of coming to Holy Communion, and in leadership, including the privilege of preaching. Many of these Negro members were free, some quite well educated, and altogether well able to raise up a leadership to express their unhappiness. Before the turn of the century, local Negro churches of varying degrees of independence were scattered throughout the connection, mostly in northern population centers. Finally in the years indicated, 1816 and 1820, the two original, independent, national

Negro denominations were formally organized. Because of the extent of slavery throughout the South, both continued to have their membership largely in the North until after the war between the states.

A very significant separation, already mentioned earlier, came in 1844 and 1845. The particular occasion of the split of 1844 was the ownership of slaves by a bishop of the South, with the majority of the General Conference resolving to vacate his episcopal administration until he had divested himself of slave ownership.

The Methodist Episcopal Church, South, from the time of its organization until the Civil War, devoted great attention and energy to the evangelization of the Negroes in the South, most of whom were slaves. In 1860, its Negro membership was 207,766. While these held full membership in the Church, their slave status prevented full participation in its life and works as was the privilege and obligation of white members. Discrimination at many levels was maintained. In some instances, the Negroes were set apart in their own churches and circuits, while in others they were required to occupy slave galleries in the houses of worship.

After the Civil War and during the Reconstruction Period, both the African Methodist Episcopal Church and the African Methodist Episcopal Church, Zion, quickly came South. The Methodist Episcopal Church, South, rapidly lost the larger portion of its Negro membership, going down from 207,766 in 1860 to 78,742 in 1866, and to 19,636 in 1869. Most of these were lost to the two great Negro denominations. At the beginning of the war the African Methodist Episcopal Church had only 70,000 members and ten years later, around 1870, could boast 391,044 members. In eight years, 1860-1868, the Zion body jumped from 42,000 to 164,000. Obviously each was winning members among the freed slaves rather than from among former members of the Methodist Episcopal Church, South.

The General Conference of the Methodist Episcopal Church, South, met in New Orleans in 1866 and took extensive measures to regroup its ministry and its people. It gave consideration to the status of its Negro members and was controlled by the idea of setting these up in separate churches, districts, and conferences, with the possibility of eventually establishing a separate denomination. This possibility was realized in 1870 with the establishment of the Colored Methodist Episcopal Church. All but a small number of the remaining Negro members of the Methodist Episcopal Church, South, went into this new, all-Negro body.

This brief historical background of the Negro in the Methodist Church is necessary in understanding the all-Negro Central Jurisdiction which, as a part of the church organizational structure, will be dissolved as a part of the merger decision. In brief, since 1870 there have been three all-Negro denominations and a rather large Negro membership in the Methodist Church. This means there are four separate and distinct kinds of Negro Methodists in the United States of concern in the merger; however, consideration is only related to the Negro denomination known as the Central Jurisdiction, an outgrowth of the Colored Methodist Episcopal Church, who are considered to be full members of The Methodist Church.

This is a brief historical sketch of those religious organizational bodies brought together by the merger of April 23, 1968 at Dallas, Texas.

IV. REQUIREMENTS FOR APPROVAL BEFORE MERGER

In order to provide a solid foundation upon which to unite these two large organizations into one, it was necessary for the separate Annual Conferences made up of local churches with a common geographical environment, generally within a state or combination of not more than a portion of the area of two states, to approve the adoption of a number of policies.

While these policies in many areas were general in nature, dealing with establishment of boundaries, changing of names of conferences, and similar legal steps, there was one significant change required in organizational structure. This was the requirement for the elimination of the all-Negro Central Jurisdiction of The Methodist Church by September 1, 1967. The dissolution of the Central Jurisdiction would be accompanied by a transfer of their conferences to the Southeastern Jurisdiction, the all-white jurisdiction encompassing the same geographical territory as the Central Jurisdiction.

The immediate reaction to this was for the Central Jurisdiction to establish criteria which Negro conferences should insist upon before transferring, the chief of these being development of a plan of integration at the Annual Conference level. The overall plan included a 3-step process toward inclusiveness in The Methodist Church--(1) conference transfers, (2) mergers to desegregate annual conferences, and (3) interracial mergers of local churches. The Central Jurisdiction took a position of "don't take step one unless step two is assured." This was based on the feeling segregated annual conferences in regional areas are incompatible with the goal of a truly inclusive Methodist Church.

The Southeastern Jurisdiction countered by calling for Negro conferences to transfer and then to depend on the "new" jurisdiction to determine when conferences could be merged, with stress on the "one step at a time."

After a number of policy meetings addressed to a goal of resolving the issues, the Commission on Interjurisdictional Relations presented to the General Conference session of 1966 the following resolutions which were approved for presentation to each Methodist Annual and Jurisdictional Conference, and the Council of Bishops. At the convening of their respective sessions in 1967, each would be required to vote on adoption of the following provisions as recommended procedures for implementation to carry out the proposed Plan of Union of November 11, 1966:

1. Pledge to eliminate as soon as possible all forms of racial structure from the organization of The Methodist Church, and further pledge to do everything possible to develop greater understanding and brotherhood in all aspects of church life and work.
2. Authorize moving ahead in 1967 with merger movements already under way in Virginia, North Carolina, Tennessee, and Kentucky, and elsewhere if possible; approve transferring all Central Jurisdiction conferences either into the Southeastern or South Central Jurisdiction, along with the bishops in charge of them; authorize a special session of the Central Jurisdictional Conference in 1967, to make the transfers and to dissolve the Jurisdiction; agree in the Southeastern and South Central Jurisdictions that, beginning in 1968, no bishops would be assigned to an area comprised solely of former Central Jurisdictional Conferences.
3. Express a determination to do everything possible to bring about the elimination of any structural organization in The Methodist Church based on race at the earliest possible date and not later than the close of the jurisdictional conferences of 1972.[2]

In 1967, then, the Methodist annual conferences voted on two major issues. The resolution specifically regarding the Central Jurisdiction was voted upon by the 87 conferences in the United States and Cuba. The Plan of the Union including the new Constitution of the united churches was voted upon by these 87 conferences, plus the 42 active overseas conferences.

V. ORGANIZATIONAL CHANGES

The merger of the two denominations not only required major structural changes such as heretofore described, but it also resulted in other organizational changes of significance.

The new Constitution provides for the continuation of the episcopacy, the highest structural order in the church hierarchy composed of duly elected bishops. In the case of the bishops formerly elected in the EUB church, these were voted on each four years at the General Conference. Bishops elected to the episcopacy in the Methodist Church were elected for life.

Article VI of Division Three--Episcopal Supervision of the (new) Constitution reads in part:

> . . .The bishops of The Methodist Church elected by the Jurisdictions, the active bishops of The Evangelical United Brethren Church at the time of the union, and bishops elected by the jurisdictions of The United Methodist Church shall have life tenure. . . .[3]

Another organizational change occurred that is of significance to the local church. It is considered to be a more flexible organizational structure for the local churches in that it is designed to free congregations "from burdensome organizational demands so that they may spend their major resources in missions to the wider community."[4]

The former organizational structure of the local church is shown at Figure 1, page 304.

---

[2] W. H. Taylor, Ending Racial Segregation in The Methodist Church (Washington, D. C.: General Board of Christian Social Concerns of The Methodist Church, 1967), p. 16.

[3] The Constitution for The United Methodist Church, Jan. 1968.

[4] "A Union. . .And Much More" in Together (Nashville, Tenn.: The Methodist Publishing House, July, 1968), p. 7.

In the organizational chart at Figure 1, page 304, the Quarterly Conference is the connectional body which unites the local church with the Annual Conference and the General Conference.

The Official Board is the local church administrative body which has general oversight over the local church as outlined by the Methodist Discipline (the governing book of Methodism) and the Quarterly Conference. The Discipline uses a series of descriptive words and phrases:

". . .to plan and, as needed, approve."
". . .to promote."
". . .to discharge all duties and responsibilities."
". . .to take action."
". . .to have general oversight."[5]

Once policies are set, major decisions made, and the general program of the total church presented and accepted, the Official Board had the responsibility of leadership and administration of the programs.

Organizational relationships provided for a determination by the Quarterly Conference as to the amount and degree of local church participation in the overall Methodist Church programs, and the Official Board promoted interest in the work and obtained the resources to help carry out the programs. The actual local work was carried on by the commissions which were auxiliary to the board.

The new local church pattern is shown as Figure 2, page 305.

This new organization provides for a Charge Conference with functions similar to the former Methodist quarterly conference and the former EUB local conference. It is to meet annually at the call of the district superintendent. The quarterly conference met in accordance with its name.

It includes an Administrative Board, which takes over most of the housekeeping, supervisory, and policy-making functions of the former official board in Methodism. It will meet quarterly.

A new Council of Ministries is provided which will consider, initiate, develop and correlate proposals for the church's strategy for mission. Responsible to the Administrative Board, it is charged with implementation of overall local programming. Basic membership is 16 persons.

The new structure was recommended by both the Joint Methodist--EUB Commissions on Church Union and by a special study committee. Both groups recognized "insistent demands from local churches for the simplification of local church organization structures."[6]

VI. OTHER SIGNIFICANT MERGER POLICY POSITIONS

For a number of years, the two churches had recognized "twilight zones" in the relationships between churches and government. After merger, The United Methodist Church went on record with a series of policy statements in this area. The policy statements dealt with six general areas: (1) Religious liberty, (2) Social welfare, (3) Education, (4) Government chaplaincies, (5) Tax-exemption policies, and (6) Church participation in public affairs.

The new policy positions recognize that some church-related health, education, and welfare agencies may be proper channels for public programs in these fields. The policy states further, however, that government resources should not be provided to any church-related agency whose services are designed and administered to serve a sectarian purpose or which discriminate because of race, color, national origin, creed or political persuasion.

The policy statement strongly affirms United Methodist support of public education and deplores the expansion or the strengthening of private schools with public funds.

---

[5] Doctrines and Discipline of The Methodist Church (Nashville, Tenn.: The Methodist Publishing House, 1964).

[6] "A Union. . .And Much More," in Together (Nashville, Tenn.: The Methodist Publishing House, July, 1968), p. 9.

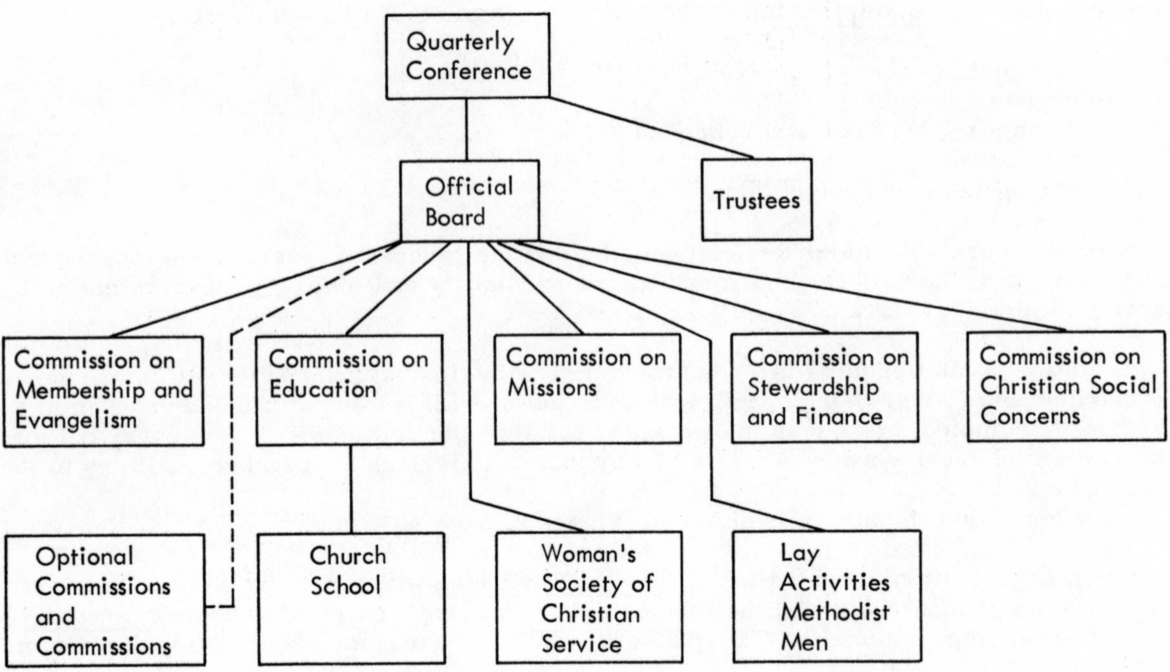

Figure 1. Organization of the local church (old).

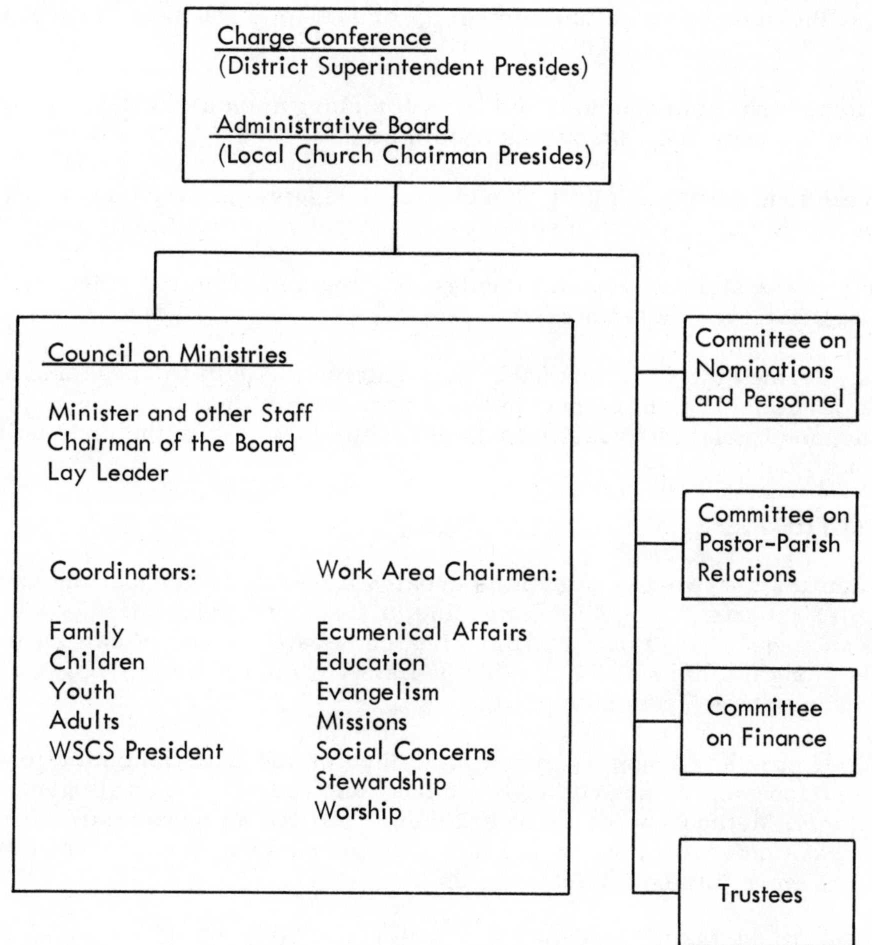

Figure 2. The local United Methodist Church.

On the question of tax exemptions granted to religious groups, the conference said that special treatment given to churches allowing exclusion of their unrelated business income from income taxation should be discontinued. With regard to property taxes, the new church's 42,000 local congregations were urged to consider making appropriate contribution, in lieu of taxes, for essential services provided by government. The statement warned of the danger that churches become so dependent upon government that they compromise their integrity or fail to exert their critical influence upon public policy.

The statement added that both special privileges for clergymen as well as all forms of discrimination against them in tax laws and regulations should be abolished.

In the area of religious liberty, Uniting Conference delegates declared support for U.S. Supreme Court decisions banning required worship services as part of a public school program.

Religious liberty, the statement added, includes the freedom of an individual to be an agnostic, a nonatheist, an atheist, or even an antiatheist.

The conference affirmed the churches have the right and the duty to speak and act corporately on those matters of public policy which involve basic moral or ethical issues and questions. Any concept of church-government relations which denies churches this role in the body politic strikes at the very core of religious liberty.[7]

VII. REACTIONS TO THE MERGER

The ceremony uniting the two denominations created a feeling of unity at the General Conference at Dallas, according to reports in Together magazine, a Methodist publication. But the uniting ceremony did not erase subsequent days of sometimes heated debate. Lines of separation, when they appeared, were rarely along the lines of former Methodists versus former EUBs, but rather between progressives and conservatives from both groups.

Far more decisive than any lingering sense of Methodist and EUB denominationalism in shaping the conference's direction was the activity of two close-knit church "renewal" groups--both on and off the conference floor. Methodists for Church Renewal (MCR), an organization formed prior to the 1964 Methodist General Conference, was represented by spokesmen in important Uniting Conference roles, and its members were influential debaters on key issues.

The second group, Black Methodists for Church Renewal (BMCR), was formed early this year, and its leaders, too, were vocal and effective, indicating for some other delegates, perhaps, what black churchmen mean when they use the phrase "black power."

MCR and BMCR, using carefully prepared strategy, affected the conference's action far out of proportion to their numbers, and few of the measures they championed were defeated. But they could not take sole credit. Their causes, it turned out, were causes which a majority of the delegates were predisposed to favor.[8]

The editors of Together made these observations relative to a "new spirit" which showed itself in many ways as a result of the unification. Among them:

1. There was more concern for action than for pronouncements, for doing rather than talking. Perhaps the best illustration was enthusiastic approval of an aggressive quadrennial program aimed at reconciliation at points of crisis. It was described as a way by which the new church could become a "dramatic sign of hope and a symbol of compassion"--in short, a way of demonstrating concern, rather than simply voicing it.
2. There was no shirking of controversy, and no holding back because of it. Time and again, delegates confronted the really hard issues of the day--but, despite strong differences of opinion on many of them, the conference pressed on through vigorous debate to majority action. Those who disagreed were heard with respect, but did not--as sometimes in the past--detour the prevailing will of the body.

---

[7] Ibid., p. 12.
[8] Ibid., p. 5.

3. There was less preoccupation with housekeeping details than many had expected. Uniting two denominations with a total membership of over 11 million is a painstakingly intricate business, and the Uniting Conference well could have bogged down in institutional details at the expense of full consideration of more basic issues. That it didn't is very significant.
4. The conference showed its intention to lead, rather than follow. In a time of crisis and change such as this, merely to stand fast is to fall behind. Delegates showed they recognized this by moving ahead on a number of fronts, even when it was apparent that some actions would not be accepted unquestioningly by rank and file United Methodists. This, of course, is a mark of leadership.
5. There was a noticeable trend to decentralization of authority and to more flexible, more democratic operation of the church. The quadrennial program again is illustrative. Bishop W. Ralph Ward, one of its principal framers, said it "reflected concerns coming up from local churches" and that local churches also were calling for more self-determination in the use of dollars. Half of the funds raised in each episcopal area for the program will be retained for local use at local discretion. Similarly, the new structure for local-church organization allows far more flexibility than in the past, so a congregation can organize itself for most effective mission. Conference endorsement of further moves toward autonomy--self-government--by overseas branches of the church was another sign of this trend.[9]

Some delegate reactions were as follows:

David M. Gotham (Chairman of Commission on Christian Social Concerns): "We are trying to understand ghetto problems, reasons why they exist, and why the response of white people has been so violent. To do this we must get involved."

William E. Thomas (Chairman, Commission on Education): "The official board cannot speak for our church, and I do not believe the church should push for open housing laws. But we should create a desire for justice in our people."

Robert F. Gilton (Official Board Chairman): "Our church ought to help every person accept every other person, even though each one has different ideas about what he is urged to do out of Christian love."

David Drewery (former member, Stewardship and Finance Commission): "I felt the church took a turn for the worse and became too liberal. I believe in human rights, but I do not favor a church pushing for laws or supporting the National Council of Churches."

Figure 3 illustrates the reaction of an element in the Southeastern jurisdictional area toward complete unification date of 1972, page 308.

VIII. INTERRELATED ACTION PROBLEMS

It is readily apparent to the reader that the formal rite of unification of The Methodist Church and The Evangelical United Brethren Church into The United Methodist Church on the evening of April 23, 1968 is just the beginning. Management, as it were, will now be required to exercise all its expertise at all levels of the organization to insure success of the operation.

As the few facts relative to this case have unfolded, managerial problem areas of a broad nature have appeared. It is believed that these broad areas can be categorized as follows:

a. Planning sociological change
b. Long-range planning
c. Designing the structure of duties and controls
d. External relationships: economic, legal, social
e. Personal leadership at the highest and lowest levels of the organization.

In the topics outlined above, some readings that are helpful to provide some insight into these areas are recommended.

---

[9] *Ibid.*, p. 17.

Figure 3. Example of a reaction to unification.

SATTERFIELD, SHELL, WILLIAMS AND BUFORD

ATTORNEYS AT LAW

JOHN C. SATTERFIELD
DAN H. SHELL
FRANK T. WILLIAMS
J. DUDLEY BUFORD
K. HAYES CALLICUTT
CARY E. BUFKIN
KENNETH G. PERRY
WALTER I. CEX, III

E.P. LOBRANDO, JR.

552 FIRST NATIONAL BANK BUILDING

TELEPHONE 948-2291 P.O. BOX 1172

JACKSON, MISSISSIPPI 39205

PLEASE REPLY TO
YAZOO CITY OFFICE
TELEPHONE 746-1252
P.O. BOX 466
YAZOO CITY, MISS. 39194

July 1, 1968

Dear Fellow-Methodists

We, the undersigned, served as the two lay delegates representing the Southeastern Jurisdiction on the Interjurisdictional Commission of The Methodist Church during the past quadrennium. We did not approve the Commission's report and recommendations to the Special Session of the General Conference of 1966, and are on record as opposing it through a minority report which we filed. The majority report included a pledge that all Annual Conferences would be merged by 1972. We are writing to ask you to act in helping defeat any attempt to have the Southeastern Jurisdictional Conference adopt such report at its meeting which begins July 24.

As has been stated many times, the Annual Conference is the basic body of The Methodist (United Methodist) Church, except for specific powers given to the General and Jurisdictional Conferences. Our main objection to the above report was and is that its adoption by the General Conference apparently calls on the Jurisdictional Conferences to ride rough-shod over their Annual Conferences.

Of the sixteen Annual Conferences in the Southeastern Jurisdiction, eight voted against adoption of the resolution for the transfer and pledge to merge with the Annual Conferences of the Central Jurisdiction, and eight voted for it by more than the two-thirds vote required. Those which voted against it are:

Conference	Against	For
Ala.-W. Fla.	267	207
Mississippi	291	127
N. Alabama	339	312
N. Carolina*	162	308
N. Georgia*	242	425
N. Mississippi	170	123
S. Carolina	434	364
S. Georgia	289	221
	2,194	2,087

*Percent in N. Carolina 65.5%, in N. Georgia 63.7%.

As you know, the transfer of the Central Jurisdiction Annual Conferences into the Southeastern Jurisdiction has been accomplished. However, the undersigned firmly believe that the Southeastern Jurisdictional Conference cannot and should not attempt to override the express wish of one-half of its Annual Conferences and/or compel them to merge with other Annual Conferences, unless and until these eight Conference vote themselves for such merger. This is in accord with the action of the General Conference of 1964 and the Southeastern Jurisdictional Conference of 1964, which determined that such merger should take place only when mutually agreeable to the Annual Conferences involved.

To do otherwise would be highhanded and dictatorial and, we think, unconstitutional. Therefore we believe it is very important that officials, ministers and members of churches in these Annual Conferences sign petitions similar to the attached and send them to the Secretary of the Southeastern Jurisdictional Council, Dr. Charles D. White, 1540 Westbrook Circle, Gastonia, North Carolina 28052.

Be sure to put name, location, and Conference on the petition when it is signed. Every petition must be sent in triplicate. They may be sent by an official board, by any organization within the Church, or by any one or more individual members of our Church. They should be sent by air mail immediately as the Southeastern Jurisdictional Conference convenes on July 24.

Our present effort is to preserve the integrity of the Annual Conferences. We believe this to be tremendously important.

Sincerely yours,

John C. Satterfield
Post Office Box 466
Yazoo City, Mississippi

Edwin L. Jones, Sr.
Post Office Box 966
Charlotte, North Carolina

Enclosure

Figure 3 (continued)

PETITION

To: MEMBERS OF THE SOUTHEASTERN JURISDICTIONAL
CONFERENCE OF THE UNITED METHODIST CHURCH

WHEREAS, only eight of the sixteen Annual Conferences in the historic Southeastern Jurisdiction adopted by a two-thirds vote the resolution recommended by the Interjurisdiction Commission of The Methodist Church to transfer and pledge to merge the Annual Conferences and the churches of the Central Jurisdiction;

WHEREAS, the vote in the eight Annual Conferences which did not thus adopt such resolution was as follows:

Conference	Against	For
Alabama-West Florida	267	207
Mississippi	291	127
N. Alabama	339	312
N. Carolina*	162	308
N. Georgia*	242	425
N. Mississippi	170	123
S. Carolina	434	364
S. Georgia	289	221
	2,194	2,087

*Percent in N. Carolina 65.5%, in N. Georgia 63.7%.

WHEREAS, such resulution has not been considered by the Southeastern Jurisdictional Conference of The Methodist Church and is contrary to the action taken by the 1964 Southeastern Jurisdictional Conference and by the 1964 General Conference, which provided for merger only when mutually agreeable to the Annual Conferences involved:

WHEREAS, the effect of such resolution is, by its own terms, limited to each of the individual and several bodies by which it is considered, the applicable wording thereof being as follows:

> 10. By the adoption of this resolution each Annual Conference, each Jurisdictional Conference, the General Conference, each College of Bishops and the Council of Bishops express their determination to do everything possible to bring about the elimination of any structural organization in The Methodist Church based on race at the earliest possible date and not later than the close of the Jurisdictional Conferences of 1972.

WHEREAS, the concentrations of former Central Jurisdiction churches and members in the above eight Annual Conferences differ in extent and degree from those in the other Annual Conferences (illustrated by the fact that in South Carolina there are approximately 340 former Central Jurisdiction organized churches compared to approximately 729 churches of the historic Southeastern Jurisdiction, and in the overlapping Mississippi Conferences there are approximately 216 former Central Jurisdiction churches compared to approximately 535 historic Southeastern Jurisdiction churches) which ratios raise questions, problems and financial difficulties entirely out of proportion and unrelated to those existing in the other Annual Conferences and in other parts of our Church, east, north, and west.

NOW, THEREFORE, BE IT RESOLVED, that the undersigned hereby memorialize the Southeastern Jurisdictional Conference of The United Methodist Church either:

To refuse to adopt the resolution recommended by the Interjurisdictional Commission of The Methodist Church and by the 1966 Special Session of the General Conference of The Methodist Church; or (in the alternative) to limit the effect of the adoption of such resolution to the Annual Conferences which adopted such resolution by the requisite two-thirds majority, i.e., Florida, Kentucky, Houston, Louisville, Memphis, Tennessee, Virginia, and Western North Carolina.

____________________ ____________________

____________________ ____________________

____________________ ____________________

CONFERENCE CHURCH CITY

A. Reference: Summer, C. E. and O'Connell, J. J. The Managerial Mind. Homewood, Ill.: Richard D. Irwin, Inc., 1968.

Readings of interest included in this reference are:

1. Leavitt. "The Volatile Organization," pp. 71-75.
2. McGrath. "The Perception of Other People," pp. 80-82.
3. Beard. "Public Policy and the General Welfare," pp. 279-80.
4. Thompson. "Modern Organization," pp. 280-83.
5. Clark. "Alternative to Serfdom," pp. 434-35.
6. Nisbet. "Community and Power," pp. 792-94.
7. Summer. "Leadership Action and the Informal Organization," pp. 640-43.

B. Two books that contain some thought-provoking ideas and concepts that are applicable to this case are:

1. Ginzberg, Eli. The Development of Human Resource. New York: McGraw-Hill Book Company, 1966.
2. Walton, C. C. Corporate Social Responsibilities. Belmont, California: Wodsworth Publishing Company, Inc., 1967.

CASE SOURCE

FIELD:

1. Attendance of Alabama-West Florida Annual Conference, Huntington College, Montgomery, Alabama, May 30--June 2, 1967.
2. Interview with Dr. George A. Foster, Pastor, Trinity Methodist Church, Tallahassee, Florida.
3. Interview with Rev. George W. Gibert, Pastor, Shalimar Methodist Church, Shalimar, Florida.

PUBLISHED MATERIAL:

1. Huff, H. S. Manual of the Official Board. Evanston, Ill.: General Board of Lay Activities, 1964.
2. Journal of the Alabama-West Florida Annual Conference. One Hundred Thirty-Ninth Session, May 20--June 2, 1967.
3. Taylor, W. H. Ending Racial Segregation in the Methodist Church. Washington, D.C.: General Board of Christian Social Concern of The Methodist Church, 1967.
4. The Constitution of The United Methodist Church. U.S.A.: The Joint Commission on Church Union of The Methodist Church and The Evangelical United Brethren Church, January, 1967.
5. Together Magazine. Nashville, Tenn.: The Methodist Publishing House, July, 1968.
6. Daily Christian Advocate. Dallas, Texas: The Methodist Publishing House.

    a. April 23, 1968.
    b. April 24, 1968.
    c. May 4, 1968.
    d. May 6, 1968.

7. Doctrines and Discipline of The Methodist Church. Nashville, Tennessee: The Methodist Publishing House, 1964.

THE CORONET INSURANCE COMPANY

In April 1958 Richard Harper, a Northwestern University case writer, visited Jeffrey Holland, president of the Coronet Insurance Company which was located in a pleasant suburb of a large West Coast city. Harper explained that the purpose of his visit was to ask permission to obtain material for a case to be used in classes of the University's School of Business.

"You see, we consider your firm outstanding in its field, and we thought a case describing the attitudes and feelings of your middle management would be helpful to students of business administration."

Holland replied, "Well, perhaps it would at that. We've certainly had our share of success, but we've had our problems, too. Tell me, how do you propose to collect your information for this case?"

"With your permission and cooperation, I would like to interview privately all available members of your middle management. (See Figure 1.) I would want to assure them that everyone's identity would be completely protected--that no one, other than myself, would know from whom I had obtained information."

"I'm sure that can be arranged. How would you actually get the information you wanted?"

"To be frank, the only information I want is what they want to give me. That is, if I can gain a man's confidence and we have enough time to talk, the things that are important to him will emerge without my seeking them out."

"Well, then, how would you arrange all of this information, their comments, criticism, etc.?"

"Well, I generally keep quite complete notes of each interview. When all of the interviewing is completed I go through the notes and try to determine which topics are mentioned with the greatest frequency and intensity. There may be anywhere from six to a dozen or more topics such as pay, working conditions, supervisions, etc., which are touched on with regularity. I try to gather together all my notes on pay for example, and write my summary on that topic from them. Then I gather all the notes on working conditions and do the same thing. So you see, the notes from the interviews really determine the organization of the information. From them I summarize and write the case, or if you will, the report."

"I see; you let the chips fall where they may."

"That's right. I try to keep my ideas of what is important, what should or should not be in the case, from influencing my interviewing and case writing. What I try to report is what the managers themselves think is important."

"Well, it sounds sensible enough to me. Now, will we be able to see this report?"

"Certainly. Of course, no names or specific identifications will be included."

"I understand. Even so, I think the report would be helpful to us. Where do you want to start."

"Before I start my interviews, I wonder if you would fill me in on some of the background of the company."

"Well, as you know, we are only thirty years old, but we're right up among the leaders in our field of fire and theft insurance. Our tremendous growth has made possible extremely rapid advancement of our personnel. This advancement has both good sides and bad, I guess, but you'll undoubtedly hear more about that in your interviews. We've always been able to show a good profit and, of course, that means that our history of bonuses has been extremely attractive to our managerial levels. Unfortunately, last year we had a profit reversal which was chiefly because of federal legislation. The whole insurance industry was hit by it and our own bonuses were hit hard. But the trouble is that our fellows don't seem to understand that the reversal was completely beyond our control--but that's something else you'll be hearing about, I'm sure."

After the interview, Mr. Holland arranged a group meeting of all managerial employees from middle management up.

The meeting was held the following week. Mr. Holland introduced Mr. Harper and explained Harper's purpose and method in collecting data for the case study. He said Harper would be assigned a private office and would have the authority to make individual interview appointments with the managers. He added, "I hope you men will avail yourselves of Mr. Harper's services and that you will feel completely free in expressing yourselves to him. Remember, he's promised anonymity, and he has the integrity of the University behind him.

"I'll make you a bargain. You express your feelings frankly to Mr. Harper, and I assure you that top management will do its utmost to strengthen what seem to be strong points and to correct our weak ones."

For the next three weeks Richard Harper conducted interviews with the 63 men of Coronet's middle management. He felt the private conferences were successful as the men seemed willing to express themselves quite candidly. When the interviewing was completed, Harper proceeded to sort his notes as described above. He then began to write his report. Three weeks later he presented the completed report to Mr. Holland. The report, which was divided into four major topics, "compensation," "advancement," "supervision," and "attitude toward job," follows:

Compensation

Pay

"Pay is adequate." Most managers feel they are well compensated for their efforts. They feel they are making more here than they would elsewhere. Many indicate they have made rapid progress and are making more money then they ever expected or thought was within reach in such a relatively short time. However, many feel that compensation at all levels, and especially at the executive level, is poorly administered. "The company is creating a lot of problems for itself by poor administration of compensation" is an expression frequently heard. "First of all, practically no one ever is fired, and raises are automatic--if you are on the payroll you get a raise almost regardless of your level of job performance." People go on to say that "this is a mechanistic system that fails to punish the poor performer and doesn't adequately reward the men with ability--while the good performer gets raises, they are formula things and, since one knows just about when, on the calendar, raises are due and what the formula raise is, you don't feel too good after you've knocked yourself out and get a formula raise; you can't feel a real satisfaction from this kind of raise--it's money, but not reward in the sense that it recognizes and compensates for real effort and accomplishment."

Employee Benefits

In the area of employee benefits, the attitude is mixed. These employees have a sincere appreciation of the value of the benefit program to them, especially the Retirement and Pension Plan. They understand the benefits, have no quarrel with the manner in which the program is administered, and feel that the company's benefits compare favorably with most other companies. They express the feeling that the plan was an indication of management's good intentions.

They do not, however, believe that their benefits are adequate, especially when compared to those offered by other insurance companies. Specifically singled out for criticism were group hospitalization, group life insurance, and vacations. They point out that other insurance companies offer more liberal benefit plans of these types. A number of employees complain about the fact that they have had to wait ten years to get three weeks' vacation. Several comment that they understand the reason for this situation--the company should "make up its mind whether it wants to be considered in the same league with other insurance businesses or just another firm here in the suburbs."

Bonuses

There is a definite concern regarding the effect this year's poor profits will have on bonuses. They remember only too well the effect of the previous year's profit reversal on their bonuses. A number of different attitudes relating to the effectiveness of management's administration are related to this problem. They know that the bonus is related to profits, but in past good profit years management has set aside a reverse which they hope will allow them to pay a bonus this year. There is, however, some doubt as to whether this will happen.

In addition, some executives are doubtful of management's ability to produce a reasonably good profit picture. They feel that in the past the company has not been very cost-conscious. (They cite as examples the great expense involved in such things as the Silver Jubilee and the cost of sending large groups of people to meetings on the East Coast.) Now that the business is less profitable, these men are doubtful that management "will be able to squeeze out a reasonably good profit picture." It appears, therefore, that much of the confidence those men have in management may be affected by this year's bonus.

Advancement

"Above everything else, the company is a place that offers opportunity to a man." "The rapid growth of the company has made it necessary for us to advance rapidly." As a result, many people feel that they have been brought along very rapidly, that this rapid rate of advancement has made them learn very rapidly, allowing for an acceleration of personal development. However, this rapid growth has not been without its problems. "The company has grown so rapidly, money has flowed in so easily, and expansion has proceeded with such vigor that a man is promoted into a job with no training--what's more, the man who occupied the position before you, probably wasn't in it long enough to have completely learned it himself, so you get no real orientation from him." Thus, "no one ever really knows what he has to do, and no one has really been prepared for his job." Then, too, "once you are in a job, you wonder how long it will be before you get out of it into another one." This results in "always looking for the next job rather than really developing the one you are in." This lack of training for a job, the lack of understanding of how an assignment should be done, and the rapid promotion of management people, have developed an almost "continuous unsureness as to what is supposed to be done, why, and how." "People have been promoted rapidly, but they haven't been developed to the state where they can function with assurance." Many people view this situation as an "inevitable part of rapid expansion" and though, to a degree, they feel it is unhealthy, they see these elements as the major contributing factors to their own rapid advancement.

In connection with advancement, a large number of people feel that "executive promotion policies are not fair," that "sparkle rather than ability is rewarded." "If a man can't make a quick five-minute hard sell, he's a dead duck with personnel," and "you've got to fit the stereotype of the high-charged personality to get promoted." In speaking of this problem, executives talked of many subordinates of real ability "who were sleepers but didn't bounce off the wall the minute someone walked in the office." These people didn't quite fit the pattern and they were passed over or had to wait a couple of years longer than they should have. Thus, while all executives feel that the company is one where nearly unlimited opportunity exists, training and development of executives for these job opportunities is almost nonexistent; the personnel practices and procedures which govern this situation of opportunities is judged to be somewhat unfair. Furthermore, the number of rapid promotions have led some men to feel that if they aren't promoted in two years, they are being forgotten. As a result, a form of insecurity appears to be developing among them.

Supervision

Identification with Company

Many men strongly identify with the company. "I've got the company's name printed on each one of my corpuscles" is the way one man expressed a feeling that was found throughout the group.

There is a very general and genuine identification with the company among these men which was especially noted among those who have been with it for a period of time and who have witnessed its growth. Many men see it as the vehicle through which they can attain many of the material goals they have set for themselves. However, a large number of men hold themselves somewhat apart from the company because of the "excessive demands it makes on your lives." It appears that "to really identify yourself with the company you have to lose yourself in it entirely."

There also is a growing problem among those who have been brought into the home office from the field. This problem seems to be one of adjustment to the parent organization. While this problem is one of identification, it is more intimately connected with the area of status and recognition which will be discussed later.

There is an especially high regard for the integrity of management which is given credit for fostering an attitude toward employees at all levels that is humane and fair. They comment about the many fine personnel policies management had developed. These employees express great confidence in the personal integrity of the president and in his sincere desire to promote good employee relations. The president is described as a "good" man, "sincere," "trying always to do what is best," "concerned with employees' welfare," and by other, similar descriptive phrases indicating the high personal regard in which he, as an individual, is held by this group. Many similar comments are made about the vice president in charge of personnel who is praised for his "integrity" and "absolute fairness," and to a somewhat lesser extent but still in a generally complimentary manner about the vice president in charge of sales and the other officers.

However, while this management group expresses the opinion that the officers are "fine" men "armed with the best in intentions," they also feel that intentions alone are not enough and that there is consequently much in the actual day-to-day administration that tends to offset this general feeling of confidence in their officers. In other words, the employees in this group do not feel that their relationship with their supervisors is everything that it should be. They do not question the technical competence of these men, but do have serious reservations about the manner in which the work of their department is administered.

In the first place, there is widespread feeling among this group that they have very little freedom of action in their jobs. They are afraid to make suggestions, to propose new ideas, to express their opinions openly. This, they say, is because management discourages their ideas and suggestions either by ignoring them or by being critical to the point where the employee expressing a new idea will be reluctant to do so again. "It is next to impossible to get anyone to consider a new idea,"--"there is so much red tape involved in getting things done,"--"management doesn't seem to be interested in our suggestions"--were expressions used by employees in this group.

Employees say that they are afraid to make independent decisions because again they feel their boss wants to make all decisions himself. Those who have acted on their own and made an independent decision have frequently been severely criticized for this.

Employees also feel reluctant to discuss problems or new ideas with people in other departments or other sections. Strict protocol requires that you "clear everything with your boss before talking to anyone else" and "since the boss is hard to get to see and, even if you see him, will frequently not give you a clear-cut, go-ahead signal, you simply don't discuss your suggestions, ideas, and problems with others."

Praise or recognition for a job well done is seldom given. "No one ever compliments you for a good job--that's expected of you; but, oh boy, if you ever slip--watch out" reflects the attitude of many members of this group. There is a feeling that "no news is good news," but many executives wish their supervisors would be more direct in letting them know where they stand. "By not knowing how you are evaluated and upon what sort of things you are judged, you can't really guide your own development."

Where friendliness of management is concerned there are two alternative reactions. The first is that management "generally is very friendly and couldn't be nicer; they are pleasant as can be and a real pleasure to work with." The other reaction agrees that all of this is true but adds that "this is a surface friendliness because 'this is the way management should act,' so people eventually become a bit cynical as to the intent of this friendliness."

Communications

There is a widespread feeling that communications--upward, downward, and laterally--are sadly lacking in the organization and as a result, this lack is seriously handicapping the overall effort of the company. More unfavorable comments are made about this subject than any other.

These employees feel, first of all, that they do not get enough information about overall company plans and thinking, or about the plans of their own department and thinking of their own department head. Some of these employees characterize their boss's reluctance to pass information on to them as "playing it close to the belt" or "he never tells us anything but the bare details we need to do our immediate job."

Secondly, employees feel that they know even less about what is going on in other departments. This is true even when two departments are working on a common project or related projects. "It's a case of the left hand not knowing what the right hand is doing." "You frequently start off in one direction only to be told after doing quite a bit of work on a project: 'weren't you at that meeting the other day? Thus and so was decided' (which was completely contrary to what you are doing)." This problem of lack of interdepartmental communication appears to be widespread with employees complaining about the embarrassment resulting from not knowing what is going on elsewhere, suggesting that departments touch base with one another more frequently, send carbon copies of communications, etc.

Employees also feel that there is almost a complete lack of upward communication. As has been discussed previously, they do not feel free to voice complaints, to express opinions, or to make suggestions to their supervisors. By and large, the monthly staff meetings are well received and most people feel they are of real value. Other than this, communications are poor. To some extent, "the company tries to communicate too much." Many people say they are "flooded with trivia," yet "they never get to the important things." Some people resent the fact that they are "close to top management, but they must learn what the company is doing from the daily newspapers rather than as an employee." Then, too, "much communication is filtered several times, even on such things as work assignments, and frequently one doesn't have sufficient background information." In some departments "routing lists have been cut down so that journals, magazines, and other literature of a professional nature are no longer available; the men are losing contact with the developments in other lines and other companies." However, most people feel that communications are poor because "the most important communicators are so busy they don't take time to do an adequate job of furnishing the organization with the kind of pertinent information that it needs." As a result, men are sometimes "without the knowledge of top management's thinking, but are expected to function as if they have this knowledge."

Attitude Toward Job

Physical Surroundings

The members of this group are well satisfied with the physical surroundings in which they work. The newness of the building, the air conditioning, and the suburban location, each came in for occasional favorable comment from members of this group. They are especially aware of the fact that proper equipment is available for their work. Its members generally feel the surroundings are quite pleasant and compare very favorably with those of other concerns. While attitudes toward working conditions are positive, there is a strong feeling among a number of the men that certain improvements are very necessary. Many feel theirs is a primary creative or "thinking" type of job, but that their places of work are not conducive to such activity. Many feel that having a door on their office would be extremely helpful. While they appreciate the "open door" policy, they feel there are times when you have to close the door to get away from distractions.

Some men indicated that at times they have gone outside the office in order to hold a meeting that would not be interrupted. While they feel very strongly about this, they did not feel upper management would be very receptive to the suggestion that doors be placed on the offices. "If a vice president hasn't got a door, I don't think I should ask for one." At the same time, they feel the vice president probably doesn't need a door because his status alone prevents undue interruptions.

Colleagues

By and large, people have a high regard for their colleagues. Most people say the executives get along well together, that there is a feeling (and this is especially true of those who have transferred into the home office) that there is a "coldness about the home office" that results, in part, from the fact that "though people are friendly, it is the smile-in-the-hall kind of pleasantness" that is lacking in real warmth and enthusiasm. In contrast to these feelings, most people say that the "employees generally are fine, of superior ability, and try to get along."

It must be pointed out, however, that although these executives have great admiration and respect for one another, the degree of cooperation among employees in this group is quite low. They do not work together, check with one another on matters where their responsibilities overlap, or help one another. While this situation is undoubtedly due in part to the fact that many of these employees are specialists (experts in their individual fields), it also appears to stem from the fact that little encouragement is given those employees to cooperate with members of their own or different departments. A number of these employees comment specifically about the lack of coordination and cooperation between individuals and departments.

Requirements

Job requirements are very heavy. Though they vary somewhat from department to department, pressures are continuous. Although they generally are accepted as "a condition of the job," the fact that "there is no let-up" has a serious influence in the lives (and some say the health) of these executives. However, one of the most important aspects of these job demands is that they are "implied rather than demanded" and "there are subtle influences that get you." First of all, the major influence is the working habits of the chief officers. These are people who are "dedicated to the company," for them "the company is a religion to which they sacrifice their family life and outside interests"--or so they are perceived by the men in this group. "The officers are the first here in the morning and the last to leave at night; they are always here Saturdays and many Sundays"--"they set the pace and, at least implicitly, it is the pace we must accept and follow"--"if you want to get ahead this is the pattern of life you, too, must accept." For many people "this is a high price to pay for success." However, there are also side issues that develop from this situation. . ."contribution tends to be judged in terms of time spent in the office, not things accomplished," and "if you want to get ahead, you come in on Saturdays regardless of whether it is necessary or not." "The cafeteria and offices are sometimes filled with visiting people who just feel they can't afford not to come in on Saturday." This combination of factors produces a pressure situation, part of which stems from the amount of work to be done, and part of which is the result of psychological forces that add to the pressures of the heavy work. They believe these pressures take a rather heavy toll on executives, for "because of the rapid expansion of the company, most men are in jobs that are new to them and are working their way into an understanding of what they are doing rather than functioning in completely mastered areas of a skill." Add to this an atmosphere of "get this done, rather than let's get in and work this out," and you have a picture of severe job pressures. Yet, as indicated previously, people tend to accept this situation; they say "we have a lot of drive here and we pay the price for it, but if we didn't have it, we would be a second-rate company."

Job Security

Most people feel little danger of losing their jobs. However, a considerable amount of general insecurity appears to run throughout the management organization. This insecurity is manifest in the uneasy feelings that (as executives) they are not holding down the duties to which they have been assigned. Advancement has frequently been so rapid that the concepts of the various jobs held have not been thoroughly grasped. Rapid advancement has not allowed for thorough integration of business knowledge and skills. To this is added the feeling that the company is frequently rudderless from a top administrative point of view. Top management does not give consistent leadership so that these executives can count upon one point of view being pursued for any consistent period of time. Thus, being uncertain about the directions they will receive, these men are reluctant to pass on actions or ideas to the people below them. Consequently, they are made to appear indecisive to subordinates. These factors, which grow from the company's administration, cause a general uneasiness among the group and unpredictability as to "what will happen next." Thus, job tenure is not in question, although feelings of job security are affected. While these people feel long service is recognized, they believe that changes on the job may not be handled fairly, that there is comparatively little security against arbitrary discharge, and that, generally, one can't count on knowing where one stands in the organization. In this connection it is well to point out that there is considerable concern over "not knowing how management evaluates one's contribution"; and the combination of "lack of credit and verbal recognition" with that of "not having an evaluation of where you stand" or the "criterion upon which you'll be evaluated" may cause people to be concerned about their job security. Many have adopted the attitude that "no news is good news," meaning that if you are not criticized by your boss this must mean you are at least doing all right. However, a few indicate that they regularly receive positive evidence of the fact that they are doing a good job.

They also state that it's not a good idea to "stick your neck out" by complaining about things. This attitude seemed to be exemplified by the fact that a number of men expressed ideas on how things could be improved or made suggestions for better organization, but none felt free to express such ideas to higher level management.

Status

These people feel they are doing work that is of importance and value--both to the company and to themselves. There is a great deal of freedom in which men can use their own judgment, and structure their assignments in ways that they feel to be most effective. However, they say that their major source of recognition is through monetary avenues; many people stated that "public or verbal reward for good work is rare." Many men feel they could perform better if they were sometimes told that they were doing well. However, others, while stating the desirability of receiving verbal recognition, are somewhat wary of such an expression, for they realize that "one can be a hero one day and a heel the next"--"one's status in the organization is not cumulative but dependent upon the last bit of work you've done." Therefore, though people like the work they are doing and feel they are rewarded for their efforts by adequate compensation, other visible and verbal reflections of their efforts are rarely forthcoming.

There also are special status problems for people transferred into the home office from the field. Formerly, these men "were people who counted"; and though "we were in a pond that was rather small, we were important elements in that pond." These transferees were high-status people in the field, but now they believe themselves to be "just like another cog in the home office." Thus, "transfer into the home offices involves a loss of esteem." Many people who come into the home office are suddenly without any of the "status symbols and privileges" that they had "slowly and laboriously earned in their previous assignments in the field." Some of these men say they are without offices, offices with doors, secretaries, or even telephones. Thus "while having been supposedly promoted to better jobs, we are demoted in terms of self-respect and prestige," and this change requires "quite an adjustment." "Going from a job that is respected to one that apparently doesn't count for much takes a great deal of adjustment." However, a more severe adjustment to make is the "drop in standard of living" that frequently comes with "promotions into the home office area where housing and other costs are much higher. In summary, the area of status and recognition is generally one of strength in this morale picture, because people feel they are doing work that is important, has value and meaning, and pays well. However, in contrast to these positive facets, people do not receive verbal or other public forms of recognition, or "overt symbols of management's appreciation" for the work they do. Transferees have a special problem in "adjusting to a demotion in prestige that is part of a promotion into the home office."

Problem

Compensation — Not Tied to Performance; Bonus Tied to Profits

Advancement — People Sparkle

Supervision — Not enough freedom on Job; Employees No F.B.

Attitude Toward Job — Status in H.O.; High Pressure attitude

1) Merit Incr.

2) Dept Meetings

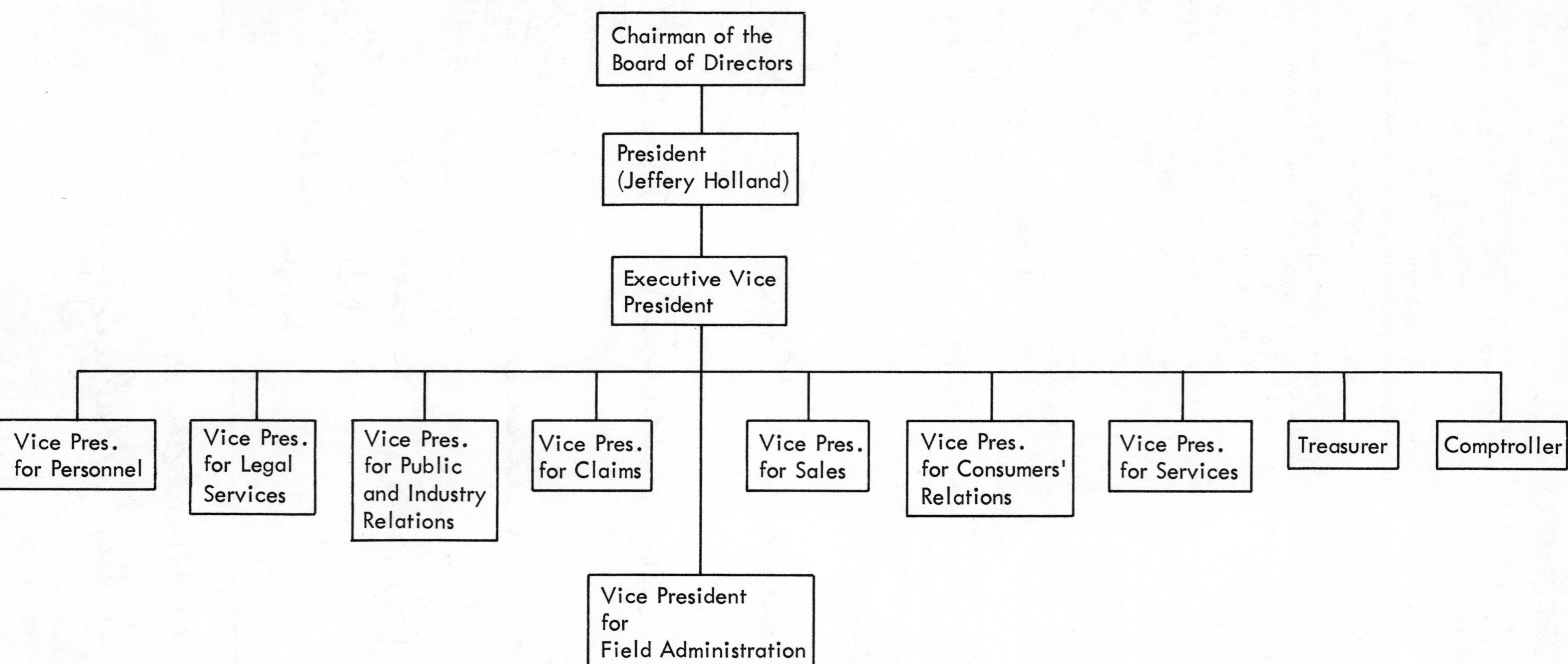

Figure.1. Partial organization chart of the headquarters management of the Coronet Insurance Company.[1]

[1]The Vice President for Field Administration had direct line authority over the territories, regions, and districts. The other departments were staff units which served the field organization in terms of their respective staff functions. For example, the Personnel Department provided the field with services related to training, wage and salary administration, etc. The "middle management" of Coronet, which Harper interviewed, consisted of headquarters personnel at the levels of management just below the Vice President level, including division directors, assistants and staff management.

MODERN FOODS, INCORPORATED

Modern Foods, Incorporated, owns and operates a chain of 15 fast-service restaurants in Midwest City. The company was started in 1952 when Mr. Martin Reese, in partnership with his father, purchased Better Burger (now known as Better Burger #1). Better Burger was a drive-in operation serving a general-type short-order menu. The following year this restaurant was converted into a specialty-type restaurant featuring charcoal-broiled hamburgers. The conversion was successful and provided the basis for operation of all subsequent Better Burgers.

The company has grown both by acquiring existing restaurants and by building new ones. Several units were subsequently closed or sold. By 1970, the company operated 6 units specializing in high-quality, premium-priced hamburgers, 1 unit specializing in high-volume, low-priced hamburgers, 5 units specializing in Kentucky Fried Chicken, 2 units offering a somewhat broader menu--breakfast, snacks, sandwiches, limited dinners--and a hamburger and frozen custard stand. Over 200 full- and part-time personnel are employed. Table 1 presents a chronological history of units opened, acquired, closed, and sold, a description of the unit, and information about each unit's current manager. All units are self-service, carry-out, and/or drive-in curb service operations. No full-service sit-down restaurants are operated at the present time.

For some time, Mr. Reese has been concerned about the present state and long-run feature of his company. For the fiscal year ending May 31, 1970, profits were down substantially. Sales volume had been on a plateau for several years and was regarded as unsatisfactory. Mr. Reese attributes the unsatisfactory profitability of fiscal 1970 in part to several nonrecurring bad decisions which he made. However, he also believes the company has been suffering from his inability to develop effective middle managers and an adequate management system and also from a slow deterioration of operating performance.

COMPANY DEVELOPMENT

Mr. Reese describes his entry into the restaurant business as follows:

> When I came home from World War II in 1946, I traveled over the state with my father, who was head of the State Restaurant Association. We visited many restaurant operators who were making $15,000 or $20,000 a year in profit who couldn't even figure a percentage. Well, I had known all my life that I wanted to be in some kind of business, but I had never known what kind. This is when I decided that the restaurant field was for me. I thought, "That is the kind of competition I want to compete against. If these guys make that kind of money, give me a college education and I can make a hell of a good living." So I went to State University on the G.I. bill and majored in restaurant management. Upon graduation, I worked for a year with a restaurant consultant and then I went into partnership with a man in Ann Arbor. He mistakenly thought I was capable of managing a brand new, general-menu-type restaurant and I, too, thought I was capable of managing it. Well, we were both dead wrong, so that partnership broke up after three months.
>
> I came back to Midwest City and sort of looked for a place I could buy. Of course, it would have to be a little bitty place because I didn't have any money and the only way I could get any money was by borrowing against my car. So I looked around and I found the Better Burger and I found that I could buy it for $3,200 plus $900 for the inventory. I bought the Better Burger in partnership with my father, but it became clear to me that we couldn't work together. So after about six months, I bought him out, again borrowing against my car. From then on, I was on my own.

At this time the Better Burger was a run-of-the-mill drive-in, not significantly differentiated from many other drive-ins in Midwest City. The charcoal-broiled hamburger was introduced in 1953. As Mr. Reese tells it:

> My father would come into Better Burger and eat a hamburger and on the way out he would say, "Son, that was a good hamburger, but it wasn't as good as Gump's." This Gump's was some outfit up in Milwaukee that had charcoal-broiled hamburgers--whatever that meant. I heard that about a dozen times. So one night when he was walking out and said, "That was a good cheeseburger, son, but it is not as good as Gump's," I had had about enough of that. So I told him, "Wait a minute, I am going to Milwaukee and I am going to eat every God-damned hamburger that man turns out. If they are not the best hamburgers I ever ate in my

life, I don't ever want to hear that word spoken around here again." He said, "Go ahead and you'll see." So I caught the flight to Milwaukee the next morning. I got to Gump's at 9:30 a.m. and left at 5:30 p.m. and I ate all or part of every hamburger or hot dog on that man's menu. They were clearly the best I had ever eaten anywhere. So I came back here and started looking for a place to open up and put in charcoal-broiled hamburgers. I rented a beer joint that had gone broke [the Burger Bin on Table 1] and opened it. I borrowed $1,800 from the girl I later married to get it open. It wasn't second class or third class. It was about seventh class. But it was good enough to get by with originally, and it had by far the best dad-gummed hamburgers this town had ever seen.

From this humble beginning, the charcoal-broiled hamburger[1] was introduced into the original Better Burger and has become the mainstay and distinguishing characteristic of the entire Better Burger chain which was subsequently developed. As shown in Table 1, Better Burgers were added in 1955, 1957, 1961, 1964, 1965, and 1968. All units include a self-service dining room. Three units also have drive-in curb service. All feature a short menu based on the charcoal-broiled hamburger and its variations, plus french fries, cole slaw, potato salad, soft drinks, malts, and so on. There is some variation in menus from unit to unit. Some units serve onion rings, for example. Two units serve fried chicken. Three units serve beer. The Better Burgers try to compete by offering a superior hamburger (at a premium price), quick service, and a clean, attractive place to eat. Company executives regard the Better Burger hamburger as the Cadillac of hamburgers and their hamburger is, indeed, widely regarded as a superior product in Midwest City. Random sampling in five of the six units showed that in three of these units the average time required to put out an order during the noon rush period varied from 1 1/2 to 2 1/2 minutes. The average times in the other two units were about 4 minutes. Cleanliness and attractiveness vary somewhat from unit to unit.

During 1963, Reese attempted to diversify for the first time:

I became aware that Kentucky Fried Chicken was a solid business and that it was going to go places. I decided Northern City (a large metropolitan area) was a marvelous market for Kentucky Fried Chicken. [Mr. Reese's father already had the exclusive franchise for the Midwest City area.] I visited the Colonel and he gave me the Northern City market at no charge at all. I opened up three stores there. Two were excellent locations and one was a strong location, yet I could hardly give away the product. It became apparent that either I had to invest a bunch more money and pour some massive advertising to it and open up two or three more stores to take advantage of the advertising or else I had to go back home.

Mr. Reese had moved his family to Northern City. At about the same time that it became apparent that he would have to plow in much more capital to turn the marginally profitable stores into worthwhile ventures, Mrs. Reese commented that "I would rather be poor in Midwest City than rich in Northern City." Upon reflection, Mr. Reese believed that he, too, preferred to live in Midwest City, except that the believed, "We can be rich in Midwest City and not worry about Northern City." So the decision was made to sell the Northern City Kentucky Fried Chicken stores. Within a week, the stores were sold and the Reeses had moved back to Midwest City.

The second opportunity to diversify came within two years, in 1965. Martin Reese's father and mother operated a 3-unit food business in Midwest City, a combined low-priced hamburger (Jolly Jack) and Kentucky Fried Chicken unit and two Kentucky Fried Chicken carry-out stores. The low-priced hamburger operation competes with outlets such as MacDonalds, Burger Chef, and the like. There were other fried chicken outlets in Midwest City, but the Reeses had the exclusive franchise for Kentucky Fried Chicken. The franchise was especially desirable since it was one of the earliest contracts and was less restrictive than franchises now available. The elder Reeses wished to retire in 1965 and sold their three stores to their son, Martin. Two more Kentucky Fried Chicken carry-outs were opened in 1966 and in 1969. In addition, the combined hamburger/chicken unit was replaced by two separate stores in 1970 (this decision is discussed in more detail below).

The Better Burger units and the Jolly Jack/Kentucky Fried Chicken units are the mainstays of Modern Foods, Inc. The headquarters management system is built primarily around the operation of these two groups of stores. However, as Mr. Reese says:

---

[1]Although charcoal-broiled hamburgers are sold through many outlets in other cities--and therefore would not be a distinctive product in those cities--Better Burger has a near monopoly on these hamburgers in Midwest City.

> You can't have 30 Better Burgers in Midwest City. And you can't have 30 Kentucky Fried Chicken units. So I have been wanting to diversify. One of my objectives has been to experiment with a broader menu, a menu with some platter orders. I wanted to kind of get my feet wet toward the day when we might go in for some different type operation.

Since 1967, Modern Foods has acquired three units that do not fit the pattern of the older units. The Cavern, acquired in 1967, is a university-area restaurant which is open from early morning throughout the day and which does a strong business all day long on coffee and soft drinks. It serves not only hamburgers, but also breakfast, doughnuts, sweet rolls, snacks, and plate lunches. Reese believes this unit has the best location of any food operation in Midwest City. Another university-area restaurant, University View, was acquired in 1969. The menu is similar to The Cavern's. The location is somewhat less prime, however, and the unit must overcome a less than favorable reputation derived from earlier poor management. Finally, a small carry-out stand serving hamburgers and frozen custard was acquired in 1968. This operation was acquired primarily for its location, but Mr. Reese now believes it may be possible to use this unit as a prototype for a chain of similar units.

Upon reflection, Reese was able to articulate three factors which he believes have been the primary determinants of his rate of expansion:

> Number one, the pleasure I get in negotiating and working on a new project as well as anticipating the return on it. I have always wanted to grow more and I get more of a challenge and a thrill out of growing than I do in actually operating. Number two, Dr. Smith [a professor at the university where Mr. Reese obtained his degree] told me years ago, "There is no shortage of money, locations, equipment, buildings. You can expand only as fast as you can attract, train, motivate and retain fine people, good men." Well, I've tried to do that. When we end up with one or more strong men trained and ready to step into a job of managing and we have no job opening for them, then that builds a pressure within me because these men have spent the time and effort to get to where they are ready and you can't keep men like that forever. Once a man really gets ripe, within six months to a year at the outside, you have to get him a spot. If you have people who are doing a good job in all of the present jobs, you either have to expand or lose him, one or the other. And then, number three, whenever we get money built up in our reserve above a certain point, then it starts burning a hole in my pocket.

It is this combination of internal pressures which stimulates Mr. Reese to begin searching the city for opportunities. Simultaneously with the search for opportunities, Reese would begin discussing any necessary loan with his banker. Mr. Reese has always managed to obtain needed financing. Location is the most important factor that determines whether Reese will try to acquire a particular unit. He is less concerned with the present profitability of a business or with how well it has been operated. A good location is described as,

> where a whole lot of people have to drive by often whether they want to or not and where you have good circulation into and out of the particular piece of property you are interested in. Hopefully, there is also a lot of visibility to the traffic. It is a curious thing. You can trace the profitability of our businesses in direct proportion to the amount of rent that they have to pay. The highest spot rent-wise is our most profitable store, the next highest is our next most profitable, and so on right down the line with very little deviation.

Mr. Reese says there has been no specific plan or strategy behind his expansion, but says he has always had a built-in desire to expand. In the past, he has favored self-service, limited-menu units because they were easier to operate profitably. However, he has been thinking recently of diversifying. He believes the city offers room for strings of two other types of restaurants which he does not wish to talk about at this time. And he is looking for opportunities to do "something new" in the food business. He is not actively seeking opportunities outside of the food service business at the present time because he believes this would distract his attention from his food operations to an undesirable degree. About the future of the company, Martin Reese says:

> We have a marvelous opportunity here in Midwest City. We can end up with some 50 to 75 restaurants right here in Midwest City, with all the benefits of being localized and the advantages of scale and quantity buying and use of management talent. We can do that if we get after it, but we can't do it doing just exactly as we have done before, because that isn't good enough. Our standards have been slipping. We have to get our standards back strong and get ourselves better organized.

Table 1
MODERN FOODS, INCORPORATED
Operating Units

Date Acquired/Opened	Unit[1]	Description	Manager[2]
1952*	(16) Better Burger #1	Drive-in operation, general short-order type menu. Converted to limited high-quality hamburger menu in 1953. Completely rebuilt in 1959 with inside seating as well as drive-in facilities. Busy cross-town street near downtown.	Roger Jacobs; 30-12-6; manager and assistant manager of other units, hourly employee; high school graduate.
1953	Burger Bin	High-quality charcoal-broiled hamburger first introduced in this unit. Closed 1957 when lease expired.	
1955	(12) Better Burger #2	Self-service dining room only. Limited high-quality hamburger menu. University area.	Mike Monroni; 29-2-4; supervisor, hourly employee; high school graduate.
1957	Better Burger #3	Self-service dining room only. Limited high-quality hamburger menu. University area. Closed 1967 when university acquired the property for expansion.	
1961	(13) Better Burger #4	Self-service dining room and drive-in. Limited high-quality hamburger menu. Busy commercial street. On edge of small shopping center. Some office buildings near by. Near low-income residential area.	Allen Long; 21-5-1; assistant manager, hourly employee, no previous employment; high school graduate.
1963	M.R. Inc.	Opened 3 franchised Kentucky Fried Chicken units in Northern City. Sold in 1964.	
1964	(14) Better Burger #5	Self-service dining room and drive-in. Limited high-quality hamburger menu. On very busy commercial street in middle-income neighborhood.	Karl Duran; 28-13-1/2; area supervisor, assistant manager of other unit; 1/2 year of college.
1965*	(11) Better Burger #6	Converted from a cafeteria. Self-service dining room only. Limited high-quality hamburger menu and fried chicken (not Kentucky Fried). In upper middle-income residential area.	Charles Jiles; 60-1-1; no other jobs in company; owner and manager of other restaurants; 1/2 year of college.

Table 1 (continued)

Date Acquired/Opened	Unit[1]	Description	Manager[2]
1965*	(27) Jolly Jack	Acquired from Mr. Reese's father. Jolly Jack provides self-service dining room and carry-out facilities. Limited high-volume, low-priced hamburger menu.	Louis Jamison, 27-9-3; manager of other units, hourly employee; Coke truck driver; high school graduate.
1965*	(1) Kentucky Fried Chicken #1	Carry-out facilities only. On busy commercial street.	Leslie Lorimer; 25-2-2; Assistant manager of different unit; previous employment unknown; high school graduate.
1965*	(12) Kentucky Fried Chicken #2	Carry-out facilities only. On busy commercial street.	Kay Cramer; 39-11-7; assistant manager of different unit; manager of food service in a variety store; 10th grade.
1965*	(8) Kentucky Fried Chicken #3	Carry-out facilities only. On busy commercial street.	Steve Zanetos; 28-9-2; assistant manager of different unit; no previous employment; 2 years of college.
1966	(8) Kentucky Fried Chicken #4	Carry-out only. On busy commercial street near a university.	George Rivoli; 29-7-4; hourly employee; previous employment unknown; business school.
1967*	(20) The Cavern	Self-service dining room only.	Ronald Lubicek; 29-11-3; area manager, manager and assistant manager of different unit, hourly employee; high school graduate
1968*	(4) The Short Stop	Carry-out only. Hamburgers and frozen custard. Busy cross-town street near downtown.	Carol Jordan; 27-4-4; No other company experience; previous employment unknown; high school graduate.
1968*	(14) Better Burger #3 (New)	Full-service sit-down fried chicken restaurant when acquired, converted to self-service dining room. Limited high-quality hamburger menu and fried chicken (not Kentucky Fried). On busy commercial street near university.	Morris Hlavka; 25-5-1; assistant manager, hourly employee; food service work with other company; 3 1/2 years of college.

Table 1 (continued)

Date Acquired/Opened	Unit[1]	Description	Manager[2]
1969	(6) Kentucky Fried Chicken #5	Carry-out only. On very busy commercial street in middle-income neighborhood.	Basil Tokar; 30-1-1; no other company experience; previous employment unknown; high school graduate.
1969*	(9) University View	Drugstore and snack bar converted to self-service dining room. Menu similar to The Cavern above. In university area.	Kevin McLeod; 25-4-1; assistant manager; parole officer; B.A.

*Indicates unit acquired rather than opening of new establishment.

[1] Number in parentheses represents number of employees. For most units approximately 1/3 of all employees are full time, but in several units this number approaches 1/2.

[2] Information shown in sequence: manager's name, age, number of years with company, number of years in present job, previous full time employment with the company, previous full time employment elsewhere, educational level attained.

MARKETING

Modern Foods operates only in Midwest City at the present time. Midwest City is a sprawling city with a population of about 300,000. It is the home of a large state university, a smaller private university, and several small colleges. Quite a number of corporate and government offices are located in Midwest City. Manufacturing is not important but it is the trading center for several surrounding counties. The city is predominantly Anglo-Saxon, but about one third of the population consists of Blacks and ethnic groups from Eastern and Southern Europe. These groups are concentrated, for the most part, on the city's west side.

Modern Foods restaurants are located throughout the city as shown in Figure 1. Four of the units are clustered around State University. Three of these units are on the same very busy street. The other unit is located on a street with little through traffic between the university and a student residential area. Three units are clustered just north of the downtown shopping and office district and just south of a lower-middle and lower-income residential area on a busy cross-town street. Two pairs of units are located on well-traveled arteries near middle-income residential areas. Another pair of units is located on a busy highway near lower-middle and low-income residential areas. One unit is on a lightly traveled street in an upper-middle-class residential area. Mr. Reese believes that the most important factor in locating a restaurant is to find a spot where many people have to pass by "whether they want to or not." All but two of the Modern Foods locations would clearly satisfy this criterion. Mr. Reese does not believe the clustered units compete with each other:

> The hamburger business is like the automobile business. You have people who like Chevrolets, you have people who like Buicks, and you have people who like Cadillacs. Well, a Jolly Jack burger is down here in the Chevrolet end of the spectrum. A Better Burger is the Cadillac. When the Jolly Jack customers are in the market for that product, either because of money or shortage of time, they are not in the market for a Better Burger and vice versa. When you are hungry for chicken you are not going to eat a hamburger. When you are hungry for a hamburger, you are not going to eat chicken. They don't compete toe to toe.

Most company officials believe not only that the several types of Modern Foods restaurants do not compete in a significant way with each other, but that these units have little head-on competition from other food service operations in Midwest City. Midwest City had an abundance of sit-down restaurants of all varieties and in recent years has experienced an influx of franchised, fast-service food outlets featuring such items as hamburgers, chicken, roast beef sandwiches, hot dogs, and Mexican foods. Some company executives believe these outlets are beginning to cut into Modern Foods' volume. One executive commented that "anybody that serves food is a potential competitor of ours if he can satisfy someone's hunger before he gets to us, so we can't pass up anybody as a potential competitor." However, this is not the dominant attitude in the company.

Modern Foods tries to sell quality food, fast service, and clean and attractive surroundings. Advertising campaigns are designed to attract customers into the restaurants. It is the job of the restaurant manager and his crew to provide the kind of food, service, and surroundings that will result in repeat business and word-of-mouth promotion. The company normally tries to spend about 4 percent of revenue on advertising. Advertising campaigns are handled by an outside account executive and vary somewhat depending on the type of unit being promoted.

In the case of the Kentucky Fried Chicken units, 1 percent of sales revenue is paid to the franchiser who in turn provides television advertising and also provides some aids for other types of advertising efforts. The primary market for chicken is believed to be young marrieds and the company attempts to find media that appeal to this population group. The basic promotion effort is built around radio spots and newspaper ads. The company runs spots several times a day on each of four radio stations. Newspaper advertising is built around a weekly special for a slow day of the week. One ad is run on the theatre page of the local newspaper. All radio spots also mention the special on that day. Whatever money is left over in the advertising budget after the radio spots and the newspaper ads are taken care of goes for TV coverage. Weekend coverage is used, according to the account executive, because "this is the time when people tend to go out to eat and tend to buy our type of food." As volume builds, radio and newspaper promotion are not increased, but TV promotion is. Kentucky Fried Chicken is primarily a dinner item and the radio spots are designed especially to be heard by people driving home from work.

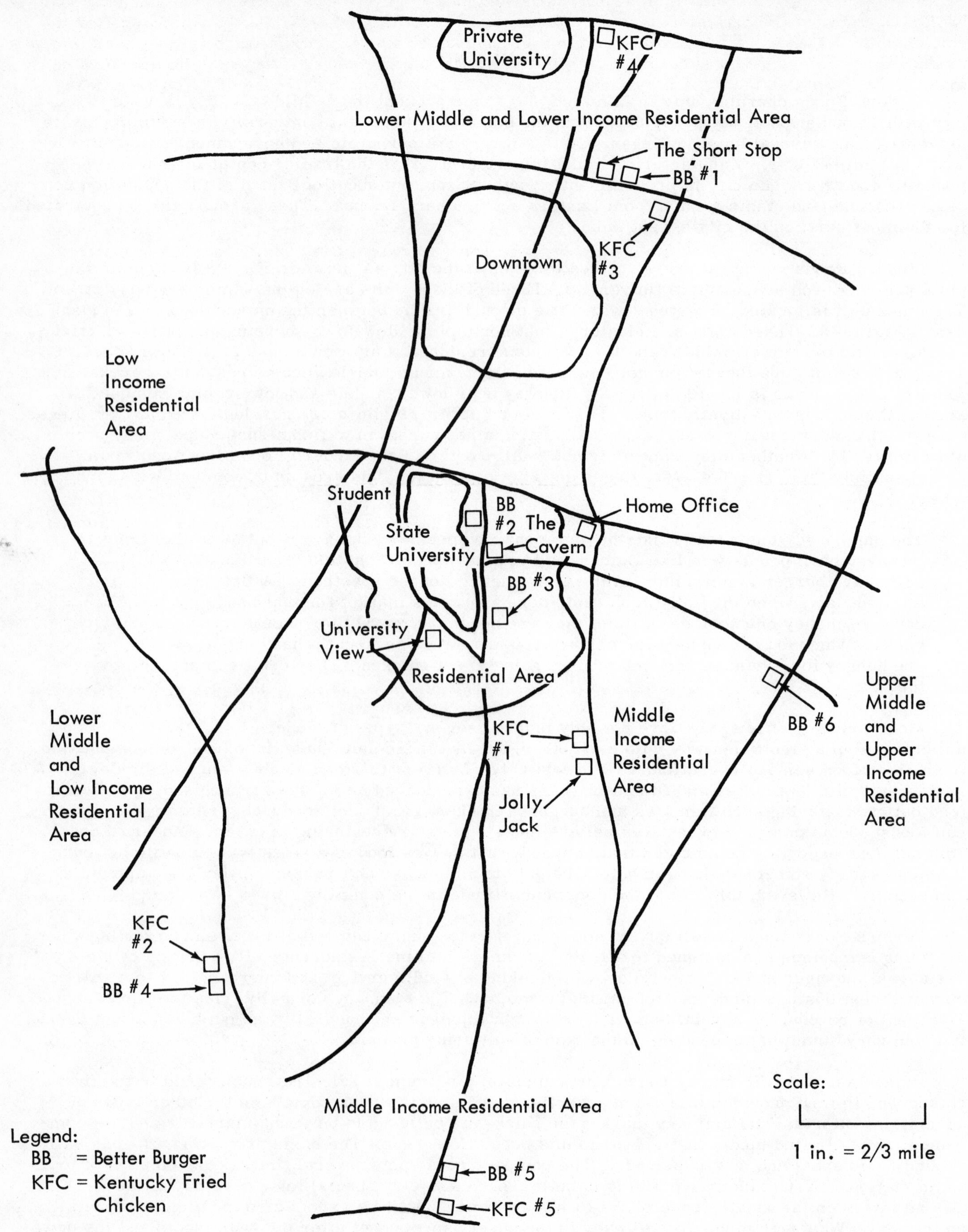

Figure 1. Modern Foods locations.

The Better Burger business is heavily lunch-oriented. Advertising stresses a quality charcoal-broiled hamburger and the campaigns use the media in about the same way as the campaigns for the chicken units. The account executive believes the market is less well defined, however. In an effort to build the evening business for the Better Burger units, the company refurbished the interiors of many of its outlets so that they have some unique advertisable feature. These features have been used to promote the restaurants as interesting places for the evening family meal, according to the account executive. Fried chicken has also been added to the menu of two Better Burger units in order to see if this will increase their attractiveness as places to have dinner.

The one-location restaurants--Jolly Jack, The Cavern, University View, and The Short Stop--are problems from a promotion standpoint because it is difficult to justify spending much money on any one of them--4 percent of the revenue of one unit is much smaller than 4 percent of the revenue of five or six units. Jolly Jack's has always been promoted primarily to children. The unit itself features a small playground and some kiddy chairs in the dining room. The promotion budget is spent largely on TV kiddy programs. Children also are encouraged to sign up to receive a birthday card and a free food item on their birthdays. A child receives a card and the offer of a birthday gift for 12 years after he signs up and is encouraged to have birthday parties at Jolly Jack's. However, Jolly Jack's does not have a very distinctive product (its hamburger was described by its manager as "kind of bland--not something that you'd remember") and it has been difficult to build up a large adult clientele. As the case was being prepared, building Jolly Jack's volume was regarded by company executives as a major problem to be solved. On the recommendation of an outside consultant, Jolly Jack's was recently rebuilt to support a doubled volume which has not been forthcoming.

University View is promoted primarily in the State University daily newspaper, in football programs, and the like. It does not receive city-wide media coverage. The Short Stop receives no promotion other than an occasional newspaper ad promoting a special. The Cavern is not advertised because of its location: "People just fall into it."

According to the account executive, continuous advertising compaigns are important. Volume declines when they are dropped. As this case was being prepared, the company had no continuing advertising programs in effect and had not had any for about six months. A direct mail campaign was tried as recommended by a restaurant consultant, but this proved to be a failure.

Unit managers tend to be critical about both the quantity and quality of advertising for their units. Some comments from the unit managers:

> We have very little advertising. When we had it, it was bad advertising. It was childish. We seem to be married to one advertising man that Martin has had for some years. I didn't really notice any difference in sales when the advertising was dropped, but then I don't think it was good advertising, either.
>
> They made mistakes. They would advertise, "Come and enjoy the onion rings at your local Better Burger." Well, not all Better Burgers sell onion rings. Or they would say something about chicken. Well, only two Better Burgers have chicken but all of them would have people coming in asking for chicken. Many mistakes like this were made. We managers would bring them to top management's attention when we heard them, but it seemed to take forever to get these things off the air.
>
> I have specific things in my unit that could be pushed, but they have not been advertised one bit. If they advertised the unique things each unit has, think about how many people would come in. But who knows about them? [This statement directly contradicts the statement of the advertising account executive about the use of unique features in promotion.]
>
> They only spend $(X) per month (much less than 4 percent of sales) on advertising for us. Isn't that wonderful?

FINANCIAL STATEMENTS

The financial statements for Modern Foods for the years 1966 through 1970 are shown in Table 2. Each unit manager receives a monthly statement of income and expenses which shows his profit for the current period and for the year-to-date. Monthly financial reports for Jolly Jack and Kentucky Fried Chicken #1 for May, 1970, are shown in Tables 3 and 3A. (NOTE: The restaurant consultant's fee was charged to the Jolly Jack unit; consequently, the net income for this unit was affected by this expense during the 1970 fiscal year. Also, the Jolly Jack unit was not in operation for over four months due to the construction of new facilities.)

UNIT MANAGEMENT

Each operating unit has a resident unit manager who is responsible for day-to-day operation of the unit. Each unit also has an assistant manager (salaried) and/or a supervisor (hourly employee) whose function is to provide supervision in the unit during the absence of the unit manager. Assistant managers are also regarded as potential managers. Whether a unit has an assistant manager, a supervisor, or both is a function of the size and complexity of the unit. Unit managers recruit, hire, train and schedule hourly employees. They are responsible for the quality of food, the quality and speed of service, and for the sanitation of the unit. They are expected to control the cost of food, payroll, paper and other consumables. In general, the manager is responsible for staffing and maintaining his physical plant and for daily supervision toward the end that quality food and service can be provided profitably.

The unit manager's job is by no means trivial. At the same time, he is not an independent entrepreneur. He is provided with many resources and operates within many company-imposed constraints. He does not raise either capital or operating funds. He is provided with a physical plant including furniture and equipment. He is given a fixed menu, standard recipes, and fixed prices. His store hours are set for him. Promotion and advertising are handled centrally. Meats, sauces, salads and, in the case of Kentucky Fried Chicken units, paper goods are purchased centrally. Units then order these items from a central commissary. Other food items, paper goods, cleaning supplies, etc., are purchased by unit managers from approved purveyors and from an approved list of brands. Wage rates for hourly employees must conform to an approved schedule and raises must be approved. A 33-page operating manual specified detailed rules and procedures for handling such items as purchasing, inventories, customer complaints, accidents, lines and uniforms, personnel records, vacations and holidays, working hours, jury duty, insurance, wage and salary advances, collections and donations, sick leave, food discounts for employees, grievances, suggestions, discharges and disciplinary action, smoking, personal appearance, leaves of absence, use of telephones and bulletin boards, lost and found items, sanitation and cleaning, cash disbursements, check cashing, cash register errors, preparation of daily sales reports, processing of guest checks, and permits and licenses. The manual also includes a four-page description for the unit manager.

The typical unit manager started as an hourly employee. As can be seen from Table 1, many unit managers have been with the company since they were teenagers; some started as part-time employees while in high school, others after graduating or dropping out of high school. While only two managers are over thirty, it is common for managers to have many years of service. Unit managers in the past have been hired by Mr. Reese, usually after consultation with the area supervisor. When asked what he looks for in a potential unit manager and how he finds them, Mr. Reese replied:

> I always believed that most businesses underestimated the capability of young men. I have always tried to pick young guys who were kind of hungry and ambitious and then I try to fan that fire of ambition. The main thing I always tried to do with my managers was to point out to them how successful they could be with this company if they would learn how to do their jobs and then work hard at it. Those who have, have done well. If you can show a guy how he can get what he wants and then if he has the manhood to sweat for it, you can have yourself a whale of a good manager. One of the best managers I ever had in all the years I've been in business was 18 years old when he became manager and he did an outstanding job for us. He now has his own business and is doing very well.
>
> You discover potential managers by observing how employees handle themselves and by talking with them and seeing what their ambitions are. Most men are ambitious to the point of wanting things. But if you really put your mind and your antennae to it, when you listen to the men talk, you can tell which ones are willing to pay a price for it and which ones aren't. When you spot those who are willing to pay a price, the next thing you do is make them start paying it. And then you find out whether they were sincere or not. Those that pay the price and pay it with a good attitude and keep trying even harder are the ones you want to clear out the obstacles for and give them oxygen and let them run, because there is an old saying that when a man is on fire let him burn. Well, boy, when you get one that is ambitious and willing to pay for the opportunities, give him the opportunities. If I have to go out and spend $100,000 for a store for that kind of man, I will do it because it is a helluva good investment. But you have to have the horse for any new store. If you don't have, you are just whistling in the dark. You're betting that you can get a man by the time the store is ready. Well, that is a foolish bet. The biggest thing that I can do in the case of such a man is to let him know that I am aware of him, that I am aware of the

job he has done in the past and that I have confidence that he can do a hell of a lot bigger and better job in the future. I don't do this from the standpoint of trying to goose him into helping the company more but from the standpoint of letting him know that what he has done has been recognized and that opportunity will be given to him to show that he can do more. If we succeed in that, the company always benefits.

One of the operating vice presidents comments further on the qualities required of a good unit manager:

> Top management does not actually run the stores. They can set policies, organize, plan for the future, negotiate, open up stores and so on, but they have to have somebody in that store running it like it was his own. This is going to make you successful. Industriousness is the big thing in running one of these stores. The manager has to be willing to put in the time. Most managers come in on the line. They come in on production work, washing dishes, or cleaning tables. I think they need to know every aspect of that business, especially of that store. They need to know how to cook the meat and how to assemble a hamburger, how to put it on the counter, how to work the fountain. They need to be able to see the overall picture, also. If they can do this well and have the ability to tell a man how to do it, to teach a man how to to it, and can see if he does it right or wrong and can correct it, these will usually make your managers. They have to see the overall picture. They have to know when the dining room needs cleaning. They have to know when that neon sign needs to be turned on, when that trash needs to be picked up on the outside. They have to be able to tell when a certain piece of equipment isn't working right by the way it sounds. Some can administer better than others. Some can put things down in writing better than others. The food service business is getting more technical and more professional. It is going to necessitate more administrative abilities in the man running the store. We need a more proficient, a more professional manager as we go along. Ten years ago you didn't have to worry much about figuring out percentages and the technical end of the operation. Now you do.

The company has never had any formalized training programs for store managers. Potential managers pick up many of the repetitive operations and procedures while serving as hourly employees. The on-the-job training continues when they become store managers as they are coached by their supervisors. One top management executive comments:

> For these routine, repetitive-type jobs in the stores, you can best train on the job. The people we get to be store managers will not absorb written information or classroom instruction nearly as easily as if you show them, tell them, and follow up and correct them right there on the job.

All top managers are in agreement that the kind of on-the-job rote learning that took place in the past is not entirely satisfactory. The managers are limited in their abilities to handle nonroutine situations and to problem solve. One executive comments: "When the P & L statement comes in at the end of the month, they look at it. If they made money, fine. If they didn't, they cry about it and wonder why. That is not really their fault. They just don't know."

Unit managers are salaried. Until recently, the company had no formalized salary schedule. Salaries and raises in salary were handled informally, usually on an annual basis. Although there were not explicit criteria used, most managers believe that length of service was the most important determinant of salary. In general, raises came faster for managers with good profit and loss statements. Salary schedules have now been formulated for Better Burger managers and are being formulated for Kentucky Fried Chicken managers. Salaries in these schedules are tied to length of service in the food business and in the company. In addition, each manager is on a bonus system. The bonus is expressed as a percentage of sales volume. A manager earns one third of his bonus by meeting a food cost standard, another one third if he meets a payroll cost standard, another one sixth if he meets a standard for other controllables such as fuel, cleaning supplies, linens, kitchen supplies, etc., and another one sixth if he passes his monthly sanitation inspection. Bonuses are paid monthly. In addition, the manager receives an extra bonus if he meets the standards for a three-month period. All hourly and salaried employees also participate in a profit-sharing plan. The company makes a maximum contribution of 15 percent of salary or wages or a minimum contribution of 10 percent of net profits into a profit-sharing trust. It is company policy to make the maximum contribution if at all possible. This has been done in all years except one. Each employee's share becomes partially vested after four years of service. The vesting percentage increases yearly until

100 percent vesting is reached after 12 years. Top management believes that unit managers make more money with the company than they could in other jobs. Some unit managers made the same observation. Others think they could do as well somewhere else. No one, however, complained about compensation and manager turnover has been low.

Unit managers must staff their own stores. They recruit employees by running ads in newspapers, using employment agencies, posting signs in windows, and asking present employees to recommend friends and relatives. Most managers say they have a difficult time recruiting and retaining qualified employees. Wage rates for hourly employees are believed to be somewhat above those paid by most other restaurants in Midwest City. However, one manager points out:

> If you compare us with any other kind of company in town, you find that our pay scale is below theirs. We are only able to attract dropouts who are in need of work and those who come from poor families. I think our pay scale needs to be increased heavily to get it comparable with other jobs. Then we can attract the family man who is attracted by any other kind of company. We haven't been able to keep people with the company. Employee turnover has been heavy.

The operating units employ many part-time persons--one half to two thirds of total employment is part time, depending on the store. Part-time persons are employed because it would be uneconomical to staff with full-time personnel to handle peak periods at lunch and/or dinner. Heavy reliance on part-time employees creates additional problems for the unit manager:

> You can tell the difference in any part-time person who knows his job is part time and that he is only going to be here temporarily. When you're right there, then he's very conscientious. But when you're off somewhere in the afternoon, that's something else. When you deal with part-time people, you are going to have a lot who come through here to make a dollar today who will be gone tomorrow. You have to keep closer tabs on them because they're the kind that are going to say "Well, this pickle hanging outside of this hamburger isn't going to hurt a thing this time."

Unit managers regard training of hourly employees as a major part of their jobs. One unit manager estimated that he spent 25 percent of his time in training. A top executive believes unit managers should spend 70 percent or 80 percent of their time training employees.

Unit managers believe they can affect the sales volume of their units primarily by training and supervising their employees to produce good food, give good service, and keep the physical facilities clean. This induces repeat business and word-of-mouth advertising. Some managers also make a point of suggestive selling at point of sale. Others do not emphasize this. Menu planning and pricing as well as promotion and advertising are entirely out of their hands. Most of the managers interviewed believe that advertising is an important determinant of their sales volume. Managers are not responsible for meeting a target sales volume. However, "If our volume is down, the first thing they come to is management, regardless of whether my food is bad, the advertising is bad, or economic conditions are bad." In addition, it is difficult to meet the payroll cost standard when volume is below expectations. Therefore, the manager has an incentive to do what he can to promote volume.

Managers control food costs primarily through portion control, control of waste, theft, and employee food consumption, and through judicious purchasing of those items which they buy directly from purveyors. Payroll costs are influenced by work scheduling, the number of employees used, and wage rates (the manager has a range of rates which he can pay for cashiers, boardmen, carhops, etc.). Each manager must learn to balance off service against payroll costs. Managers vary in their ability to do this.

All unit managers interviewed were questioned at length about their relationships with top management--about what top management did for them, about how often they saw top management, about how top management controlled their operations, about what top management was really interested in at the store level, and about top management deficiencies. Responses to these questions varied from manager to manager. Except for the responses of one manager who believed he had very good relations with top management and that top management generally did an excellent job for the stores, the usual responses to these questions tended to be unflattering to central management.

Table 2

MODERN FOODS, INCORPORATED

Statements of Income and Expense--Years Ended May 31, 1966-70

(Cents Omitted)

	1970	1969	1968	1967	1966
Sales	$3,115,213	$2,913,244	$2,414,425	$2,064,696	$1,506,938
Cost of Goods Sold	1,355,623	1,259,314	1,060,928	926,187	668,720
Gross Profit	$1,759,590	$1,653,930	$1,353,497	$1,138,509	$ 838,218
Expenses					
Amortization		10,000	8,000		
Depreciation	132,928	93,869	69,812	82,029	62,342
Interest	23,978	28,742	18,448	13,941	11,000
Officer's Salaries	120,890	87,795	67,936	65,262	74,667
Operating Franchise	29,041	12,042	10,431	10,398	9,983
Profit-Sharing Contributions	88,235	78,304	63,153	74,582	47,967
*Other	1,515,245	1,323,875	1,095,129	937,250	688,993
Total Expense	$1,910,317	$1,634,627	$1,332,909	$1,183,462	$ 894,952
Operating Profit	(150,727)	19,303	20,588	(44,953)	(56,734)
Other Income					
Coin Machines	5,179	6,586	4,575	3,631	2,907
Other	193,971	197,127	149,889	135,960	99,337
Total Other Income	$ 199,150	$ 203,713	$ 154,464	$ 139,591	$ 102,244
Net Income before Federal Tax	48,423	223,016	175,052	94,638	45,510
Federal Taxes on Income	25,578	76,301	64,177	24,732	15,082
Net Income	$ 22,845	$ 146,715	$ 110,875	$ 69,906	$ 30,428

*Salaries and wages other than officers' salaries are included in this figure.

Table 2 (continued)
MODERN FOODS, INCORPORATED
Balance Sheets 1966-1970 as of May 31
(Cents Omitted)

	1970	1969	1968	1967	1966
Assets					
Current Assets					
Cash on Hand	$ 3,740	$ 7,602	$ 6,997	$ 3,947	$ 3,711
Cash in Bank	266,998	317,396	321,190	216,511	154,128
Notes and Loan Receivable	13,421	7,197	4,740	10,530	28,865
Accounts Receivable	47,513	34,338	5,995	1,969	6,369
Advances to Employees	1,345	1,429	1,785	1,169	132
Inventory	43,750	40,329	32,888	24,696	20,237
Prepaid Expenses	34,555	33,735	22,540	18,329	22,218
Total Current Assets	$ 411,322	$ 442,026	$ 396,135	$277,151	$235,660
Fixed Assets					
Land	52,500	52,500	3,602	3,602	3,602
Leasehold	22,521	24,221			
Recipes	5,000	5,000			
Covenant	31,021	6,354			
Agreement (Autos)	12,920	58,528	52,579	15,599	11,772
Franchise	81,000	81,000	81,000	81,000	81,000
Furniture and Equipment	644,144	559,759	407,388	369,945	333,400
Leasehold Improvement	415,945	338,512	238,082	226,399	220,260
Accumulated Depreciation	-510,557	-521,232	-434,776	-368,532	-291,250
Total Fixed Assets	754,494	604,642	347,875	328,103	358,784
Other Assets					
Investments	96,661	78,692	271,729	49,000	44,700
Unamortized Organization Costs		30	80	194	307
Deposits	175	83	52	52	305
Total Other Assets	$1,262,652	$1,125,473	$1,015,871	$654,410	$639,756

Table 2 (continued)
MODERN FOODS, INCORPORATED

	1970	1969	1968	1967	1966
Liabilities and Net Worth					
Current Liabilities					
Accounts Payable	$ 228,801	$ 153,150	$ 96,401	$ 82,611	$ 70,305
Withheld Tax Payable	4,735	2,970	644	5,562	7,433
Accrued Expenses	30,164	33,600	23,245	15,679	22,672
Sales Tax Payable	-4,771	-8,184	-4,021	-2,426	-2,125
Federal Income Tax Payable	18,400	61	34,046	17,743	10,781
Total Current Liabilities	$ 250,071	$ 181,597	$ 150,315	$119,169	$109,066
Long-Term Liabilities Notes	399,720	353,862	422,257	204,346	274,898
Net Worth					
Capital Stock	41,230	41,230	41,230	39,700	34,500
Paid in Surplus	3,000	3,000	3,000	3,000	3,000
Retained Earnings	545,785	399,070	288,195	218,289	187,861
Net Profit or Loss	22,845	146,715	110,875	69,906	30,428
	$ 612,860	$ 590,015	$ 443,300	$330,895	$255,789
Total Liabilities and Capital	$1,262,651	$1,125,474	$1,015,872	$654,410	$639,753

Table 3
JOLLY JACK STATEMENT OF INCOME AND EXPENSES--UNAUDITED--MAY 31, 1970

	CURRENT PERIOD		YEAR TO DATE	
Sales	$22,975.63		$253,208.42	
Total Sales	22,975.63	100.0	253,208.42	100.0
Cost of Sales:				
Food Costs	9,108.88	38.3	96,952.35	38.3
Paper Costs	968.13	4.2	14,781.56	5.8
Total Cost of Sales	$ 9,987.01	43.5	$111,733.91	44.1
Gross Profit	$12,988.62	56.5	$141,474.51	55.9
Expenses:				
Salaries Executive	$ 1,012.80	4.4	$ 14,791.12	5.8
Salaries and Wages	6,564.95	28.6	65,915.50	26.0
Advertising	501.07	2.2	12,818.81	5.1
Administrative Charge	778.04	3.4	12,710.21	5.0
Bank Credit Card Charge		.0	64.12	.0
Cash Over and Short	11.03	.0	35.45	.0
Contributions		.0	368.42	.1
Depreciation and Amortization	1,432.17	6.2	9,775.30	3.9
Education and Research	250.00	1.1	10,690.79	4.2
Employees Relations		.0	120.92	.0
Insurance Other	162.25	.7	2,660.18	1.1
Insurance Group	61.71	.3	918.61	.4
Insurance Officer Life	12.62	.1	132.70	.1
Insurance Workman's Compensation	131.87	.6	731.84	.3
Interest	461.11	2.0	1,606.34	.6
Janitor and Cleaning Supplies	27.93	.1	518.39	.2
Kitchen Supplies		.0	397.61	.2
Laundry	237.42	1.0	1,100.20	.4
Legal and Accounting		.0	503.54	.2
Managers' Bonus		.0	894.47	.4
Miscellaneous Expense	125.59	.5	4,415.86	1.7
Office Supply, Post, etc.	.31	.0	139.42	.1
Franchise Fees		.0	1,276.80	.5
Purchased Services	115.60	.5	2,319.72	.9
Profit-Sharing Contribution	1,160.36	5.1	12,138.98	4.8
Rent	500.00	2.2	8,250.00	3.3
Repair and Maintenance	4.14	.0	3,169.75	1.3
Taxes and Licenses	146.56	.6	1,959.45	.8
Taxes Payroll	287.00	1.2	3,327.16	1.3
Telephone and Telegraph	20.96	.1	391.18	.2
Travel	25.53	.1	257.93	.1
Utilities	627.06	2.7	4,417.64	1.7
Total Expenses	$14,658.08	63.8	$178,818.43	70.6
Net Operating Income	(1,669.46)	(7.3)	(37,343.92)	(14.7)
Other Income:				
Coin Machine Receipts	35.64	.2	247.20	.1
Interest Income		.0	28.43	.0
Miscellaneous Income	60.84	.3	759.07	.3
Sale of Assets		.0	(15,122.06)	(6.0)
Divided Income		.0	175.00	.1
Total Other Income	$ 96.48	.4	$ (13,912.36)	5.5
Net Profit or Loss	$ (1,572.98)	(6.8)	$ (51,256.28)	(20.2)

Table 3A

KFC#1[1] STATEMENT OF INCOME AND EXPENSES--UNAUDITED--MAY 31, 1970

	CURRENT PERIOD		YEAR TO DATE	
Sales	$21,840.09		$239,736.23	
Total Sales	21,840.09	100.0	239,736.23	100.0
Cost of Sales:				
Food Costs	$ 9,090.16	41.6	$ 94,747.66	39.5
Paper Costs	1,160.65	5.3	12,653.01	5.3
Total Cost of Sales	$10,250.81	46.9	$107,400.67	44.8
Gross Profit	$11,589.28	53.1	$132,335.56	55.2
Expenses:				
Salaries Executive	$ 972.00	4.5	$ 14,008.98	5.8
Salaries and Wages	2,978.79	13.6	40,214.69	16.8
Advertising	797.89	3.7	12,548.81	5.2
Administrative Charge	791.23	3.6	9,248.49	3.9
Bank Credit Card Charge	9.60	.0	114.46	.0
Cash Over and Short	(17.11)	(.1)	(62.02)	(.0)
Contributions		.0	339.43	.1
Depreciation and Amortization	804.68	3.7	7,341.39	3.1
Education and Research		.0	324.30	.1
Insurance Other	55.42	.3	812.15	.3
Insurance Group	18.78	.1	639.68	.3
Insurance Office Life	10.65	.0	146.06	.1
Insurance Workman's Compensation	62.23	.3	484.87	.2
Interest	69.16	.3	687.11	.3
Janitor and Cleaning Supplies	21.56	.1	901.87	.4
Kitchen Supplies	21.69	.1	487.19	.2
Laundry	29.74	.1	595.02	.2
Legal and Accounting		.0	284.09	.1
Managers' Bonus	345.27	1.6	3,622.38	1.5
Miscellaneous Expense	4.00	.0	60.79	.0
Office Supply, Post, etc.	1.02	.0	67.89	.0
Franchise Fees	374.45	1.7	4,110.85	1.7
Purchased Services	78.20	.4	1,110.87	.5
Profit-Sharing Contribution	587.88	2.7	8,128.79	3.4
Rent	150.00	.7	1,800.00	.3
Equipment Rent	634.35	2.9	1,144.01	.5
Repair and Maintenance	94.82	.4	2,235.93	.9
Taxes and Licenses	81.32	.4	1,161.57	.5
Taxes Payroll	161.09	.7	2,350.67	1.0
Telephone and Telegraph	18.70	.1	225.45	.1
Travel		.0	282.67	.1
Utilities	339.93	1.6	3,274.27	1.4
Total Expenses	$ 9,497.43	43.5	$118,692.71	49.5
Net Operating Income	2,091.85	9.6	13,642.85	5.7
Other Income:				
Coin Machine Receipts	19.91	.1	129.98	.1
Miscellaneous Income	14.52	.1	351.77	.1
Sale of Assets		.0	(36.93)	(.0)
Total Other Income	$ 34.43	.2	$ 444.82	.2
Net Profit or Loss	$ 2,126.28	9.7	$ 14,087.67	5.9

[1] Kentucky Fried Chicken #1.

All managers interviewed except one believed that performance evaluation was based largely or entirely on profit and loss statements. When asked about the importance of conforming to the rules and regulations in the operating manual, the manager typically responded as follows:

> If everything was plus on the bottom line, well old Joe was a good old boy. The manual wouldn't be there if they weren't interested in it. But I would say that, in the past, if the store is running a beautiful statement, the central office will spend very little time at your store. And in all seriousness, I don't think they would be aware if you were conforming to the do's and don'ts or not. I would say raises have been based strictly on the statements for the past 12 months.
>
> Providing that your bottom line is in order and you are breaking these operational rules, I don't think they will get on you as much as they would if your bottom line is zero. You can break some of these rules or change or bend the rule and get away with it provided that you are doing an outstanding job. Up to a point, the rules are for the bad manager.

Another manager answered the question with "What manual?" When the interviewer had explained what he meant, the response was "Oh, I saw one of those several years ago. I haven't seen one recently. It is probably all out of date anyway." One manager did believe that more was expected than just earning a good profit:

> Just because you have a good P & L doesn't mean that you are doing good. I believe that most places are only interested in a good P & L. This is one of the most important things here, but this doesn't insure your job. We still have do's and don'ts. You have to make money, but you are supposed to do the things in the manual at the same time because they keep close tabs on it.

This comment was from the only manager who believed that his performance was significantly impeded by top management-imposed constraints. Managers point out that in addition to the P & L statement, top management learned about their store's operations from the reports submitted daily, weekly, and monthly. Daily records were kept on sales volume, payroll percentage, cash shortages and overages, cash disbursements for the day, and a daily inventory of meat and buns. Weekly food cost records were kept and a complete inventory was taken monthly. In addition, all members of top management periodically visited the stores. Because these visits were infrequent, usually of short duration, and observations were unsystematic, the managers were usually critical of them:

> My supervisor will come in and stay for about 10 minutes and leave. A lot of times he will just sit and observe. Or he will look around the kitchen. Other times he will have something on his mind and he will tell me. Too many times, I think, they harp on little things. If he or Martin come in, they evaluate the situation the way they see it when they come in. Maybe all the tables are dirty. You might have been busier than hell. But they don't see that and they don't ask why. Or they see a man who is sweaty and dirty without his hat and tie on. Well, you might have had him working in the storeroom where it is about 120 degrees, but they don't see that. They will tell you to get rid of him because he is a dirty person. Why should they be the ones to decide how good an employee is when they are not around him working all the time? They base their opinion on what they have seen by coming here only once a week. I work with that man six or seven days a week. Yet my supervisor decides if that man is worth a nickel raise or not.
>
> I'll tell you one thing about this company that I don't like. If a store has a bad statement one month, well, this is kind of like sending an invitation to the office because I guarantee you they'll all spend a lot of time there the next month and most of the things that they do are not corrective. They're more picky than they are corrective. I can sit right here and see that this grille beside us has some dust on it. Now a customer eating at this table doesn't train himself to look at grilles. He will probably never see it. I'll bet you didn't see it.[The interviewer had not seen it.] It's definitely dusty. Well, if, say, my payroll is out of line, people from the central office will be coming out here and instead of saying "Let's find the real problem, let's see how we can get your payroll down," they will come and say "See that dusty grille. That probably offended 20 customers today and they won't be back." Now these things are important. But I don't want anybody coming into my store being picky about little petty things like that. That isn't going to get my payroll down if that's my problem. They'll do it with employees. I may have a damn good employee that I think is doing a hell of a good job and maybe this fellow does something wrong just when

> this person from the central office walks through. Well, automatically he isn't worth keeping on the payroll. This isn't an occasional thing. This happens often. All the time.

The one manager who did not have similar complaints was a manager who said he saw at least one person from headquarters, usually his supervisor, every day. Other managers said they were visited twice a week or once a week or less. One supervisor estimates that in the past, when his job involved much more than supervision of the units, he spent about 25 percent of his time in the stores. He expects to spend more time there now. The other supervisor estimates that he spends 50 percent of his time in the stores and that this will go up. One store manager, however, took the amount of time his supervisor spends in his store weekly and multiplied it by the number of stores that supervisor is in charge of and then wondered aloud what the supervisor did with the other four and one half days of the week. Not only do most of the managers believe that top management gets a biased and unsystematic picture of their operation from these casual visits, but most of them complain that they get nothing helpful from a top management visit:

> I asked my boss how to handle that. He said to do whatever I wanted. That was no help at all.
>
> I think it would be good to have a visit from my supervisor or from Nathan or Martin where they come out and say "I have your statement here. Let's look at it. You have a bunch of things that are out of line. Here's what you need to do to correct them." But nobody does that. Instead they come out here and look for things that really don't exist and that have nothing to do with the statement.
>
> I don't think they understand my store. I can talk to them about my problems and I get the feeling they don't know what I'm talking about.

Managers are critical of vertical communications in the organization, of the information they receive from top management, and of the slow response rate of upper management to problems in the stores:

> I have to have their ideas. If I don't have their ideas, I can't run the store the way they want it. We have lagged in communication. There might be a little slowness in getting for the unit what the unit needs. Or if I recommend something, they are going to be a little slower than I think they should be.
>
> I would like to have information comparing my store with other units. I would like to know how much we are spending on advertising. I haven't seen my profit and loss statement for several months. All I see is what I control. I disagree with this.
>
> You might make a suggestion or something to your boss, and supposedly it is to go to Martin. But you may never hear anything else about it. Our communications have been very bad in the past. An idea or a problem that we have sometimes gets lost. Supposedly since Nathan came, this will change.
>
> Our malt machine has a leak in it. It is pretty dilapidated. We should have had a new machine in this unit three or four months ago. This is only handicapping the people in the unit and the customer is not getting the right product. When they react slowly to the crying need of a particular unit, it is not helping anybody.

At the time when materials for the case were collected, morale was rather low in the operating units. According to one manager, the abyss was reached a couple of months earlier and morale had started to improve:

> Morale was mainly low when Charles Jiles, Jr. was fired. People couldn't understand why he was fired. He had been with the company nine years and he was fired very suddenly. People had a lot of bad thoughts about this. I felt very uncomfortable about it. Also Martin made a lot of bad business decisions. A lot of money was thrown out the window. And there was this consultant that Martin hired. Martin paid him a lot of money and we got virtually nothing out of him. I think a lot of people disagreed with that.

Managers also were upset about the demotion of Sam Russell and the acquisition of a new executive vice president (to be described below). The consultant referred to above was described by several managers as rude and arrogant as well as uninformed. One manager commented, "I used to enjoy coming to work in the morning. I was very loyal to this company. It was my life. Now the only reason I'm staying is because I couldn't make as much anywhere else."

CENTRAL MANAGEMENT

1952-1970

Central management consisted solely of Martin Reese until 1961 when Mr. Reese realized he needed help with the day-to-day supervision of the three Better Burgers if he was to have time to perform administrative and entrepreneurial functions. Mr. Sam Russell was brought to the central office at this time from his post as manager of Better Burger #2.

Sam Russell, 39, had worked for Modern Foods since 1955. He began as an hourly employee while a student at the State University. Prior to this time, Mr. Russell had worked part time in a grocery store and had done office work while he was a high school student. He also spent four years in the Air Force during the Korean conflict. He earned a B.B.A. from State University while working for Modern Foods. Russell became a store manager several months after he was hired in 1955. He believes he was the first official manager Reese ever had. Russell was brought to the central office as general manager. "I was responsible for three or four stores at that time and did some administrative work, but primarily I still worked out in the field with the stores." Mr. Russell has continued as the general manager of the Better Burger units since that time.

Mr. Russell shares many strengths and weaknesses with Reese. Both are intuitive managers. Both have a deep knowledge of Better Burger operations and a strong loyalty to Better Burger. (Jolly Jack/Kentucky Fried Chicken managers feel they are stepchildren because of their loyalty. They believe Mr. Reese and Mr. Russell neither understand nor have a deep interest in their part of the company.) Both are field-oriented rather than office-oriented. Russell was the developer of most paperwork systems. Both are disposed toward an informal mode of operations, although Mr. Russell is personally a much more reserved and less outgoing individual. Sam Russell's subordinates respect his knowledge of their operations. They do not always like him. When he moved into the position of general manager of Better Burger, he spread his very considerable knowledge of how to run a Better Burger restaurant from one restaurant to three. He became a kind of supermanager, coaching and showing the Better Burger managers what he had already learned. His responsibilities broadened in terms of number of units, but functionally his role was not enlarged a great deal. Something of Mr. Russell's approach to store management is conveyed in the following:

> You measure effectiveness largely by the P & L. Observation is another big factor. We spend a lot of time in the stores. I always go to eat in the stores. You get a picture of how they are functioning at busy times. I feel I know pretty much what is going on in each store --what the problems are, where they need help, and so forth. You learn this through visitation and through the reporting system--mostly through visitation, through talking with the manager and with the employees.
>
> If the manager is doing a good job, you know it. If you walk into a store and have no difficulty locating the manager, if he is always on the job when he is supposed to be there, and if he has a good attitude and his crew is happy and he seems to be producing and business is good, I think he deserves a pat on the back. It is obvious that the man is doing a good job. If you have one that is goofing off, it is quite obvious. I ran a store for six years. I know what he is supposed to be doing. You know how much time it is going to take to do a good job in a particular store, and they are all different.
>
> We have always had an estimated figure of what I think the sales should be for that particular unit for that year and the manager usually was aware of it. But I wouldn't say it was a definite figure, that you have to reach this sales figure. A lot of things could affect it. We gave them a percentage to shoot at on labor, a percentage on food costs, and a figure on charcoal, cleaning supplies, and kitchen supplies. That is about the only budget that I felt you could realistically have for the stores.

Mr. Reese and Mr. Russell shared the top management responsibilities until 1965 when the Jolly Jack/Kentucky Fried Chicken units were acquired. Mr. Frank Drake had been working for Martin Reese's father as general manager of these units. He continued in this position when Martin Reese purchased the units. Frank Drake, 34, joined the Jolly Jack organization in 1955 while a student at State University. He earned a degree in chemical engineering while working at Jolly Jack's. At Jolly

Jack's, he became successively manager of the original store and then general manager in charge of all the chicken units as they were added. Despite several changes in title, Drake has essentially continued in the position of general manager of Jolly Jack/Kentucky Fried Chicken to the present time. He is an easy-going, affable person. His managers respect his operating knowledge. Not everyone believes he works as hard as he might ("I suppose he does something. He's always tired.") He is disposed to be more systematic and more numbers-oriented than Mr. Russell. He describes his operating philosophy:

> I take the attitude that as the supervisor I am not there to stand over the manager and wait for him to make a mistake and point out to him what the mistake is. I am there to help him and to develop him to be a good manager. I look at it more as helping the guy than of being critical of him when he does something wrong. A manager's real job is to train the people. In a restaurant it is to train the people to prepare the food the way it should be prepared, to sell it the way it should be sold, and to keep the store clean. I feel that my job is to help the manager get his tasks organized. When you have several units that all operate the same, then you learn from one and put this into effect in another. For example, I go around and check work schedules every week. Here is a manager who has learned a little trick to cut his payroll. I will learn that and take it to the other stores. Then they will learn the same thing. Then I help them on their controls. Also, there is a certain amount of looking over the shoulder to keep them honest, to keep them on their toes doing their jobs. Where I fit in is in training the manager to train his people, standardize jobs, keep them on their toes, help them with their controls. If they start getting stale, boost them up. If they get their costs out of line, show them where they are out of line and what to do about it. It is much easier for someone who is not directly involved in a store minute by minute to see some of these things. If a manager has been around 10 or 12 years, he doesn't need someone coming around and picking at him. But they slip up occasionally. They need help more than criticism. Occasionally they need criticism, too.
>
> I am responsible for costs and teaching the managers to keep their costs in line. We have gone farther in developing controls than Better Burger. I am a stickler for rules. I think the rules are there to be followed, occasionally to be broken. I like to enforce the rules. I think this is important. I try to get by each store every day. If a manager is running a good P & L, I will be in his store more to try to learn how he is doing it so I can teach the others the same thing.
>
> I can't spend an hour a day in each store doing the manager's job for him. What time I do spend has to be effective time. That is why I like written daily check lists. I go into a store and make notes and give them to the manager. He may be busy when I go in and not be able to talk to me. But if I see something that he needs to be working on, I give it to him in writing so that when he has time, he can look at it.

In 1965 when the Jolly Jack/Kentucky Fried Chicken units were acquired, they were at first run separately by their own general manager, Mr. Drake. But in 1966 Mr. Reese decided that there should be one manager for the entire company. Mr. Russell was placed in that position and given the title of president. Russell became Drake's superior. In addition, two unit managers, Charles Jiles, Jr., and Ronald Lubicek, were elevated to new positions of "area manager" for the Better Burger units. Mr. Jiles was in charge of the drive-in units and Mr. Lubicek supervised the other units. These two men reported to Mr. Russell. Mr. Russell also was responsible for the office, the commissary, and for maintenance. Figure 2 shows this organizational arrangement which prevailed from August 1966 through August 1967. The arrangement proved unworkable for the managers concerned, and so the two groups of operating units were once again placed under general managers reporting directly to Mr. Reese. Since their roles were judged to be unnecessary, Jiles and Lubicek were returned to positions of unit manager. Russell continued to supervise the office and commissary as well as the operating units. One person commented on the abandoned arrangement: "Sam only knew the hamburger business and Frank knew the chicken business. And personalities were involved." Mr. Russell commented that he exercised very little supervision over the Jolly Jack/Kentucky Fried Chicken operation because Drake knew that business much better than he did. The organization that prevailed from September of 1967 through August of 1969 is shown in Figure 3.

In September 1969, Mr. Reese again reshuffled the headquarters management system. He wished to be able to withdraw somewhat from the operation of the company to pursue other interests. Mr. Russell was again named president of the company. Reese's title became chairman of the board, although the company had (and still has) no board of directors. Russell reported directly to Reese, as he had always done. He now had three operating subordinates--Drake, who supervised the Jolly Jack/ Kentucky Fried Chicken units as he had always done and two area managers who were once again introduced to manage the Better Burger units as well as the recently acquired The Cavern, University View and Short Stop. Mr. Charles Jiles, Jr. became an area manager for the second time and Mr. Karl Duran was elevated from unit manager to fill the other area manager position. (Ronald Lubicek, who had been an area manager earlier, continues to work for Modern Foods as manager of The Cavern.) The organization as it was from September 1969 to the Spring of 1970 is shown in Figure 4. During the late Spring of 1970, Mr. Reese decided that this arrangement was not producing the results that he had hoped for and initiated further changes in the headquarters management. These changes and the events that led up to them will be described below. One executive comments on the series of administrative changes:

> You know, we changed the lines of authority, but nothing really changed. We were operating just like we were before. I feel that Martin was fighting this thing of getting big. We really all just dealt with operations. We didn't know how to structure ourselves up here and I think Martin was playing this chess game for about four years of trying to find something that would work. So we have gone through several stages of reshuffling, of reorganizing. It doesn't affect the job which you actually do so much as it affects who you are responsible to. I think Martin was playing a game where you have to decide where to put the pieces so that it will function smoothly. This is the stage we are in now. This is another stage we're going through. Hopefully it will work.

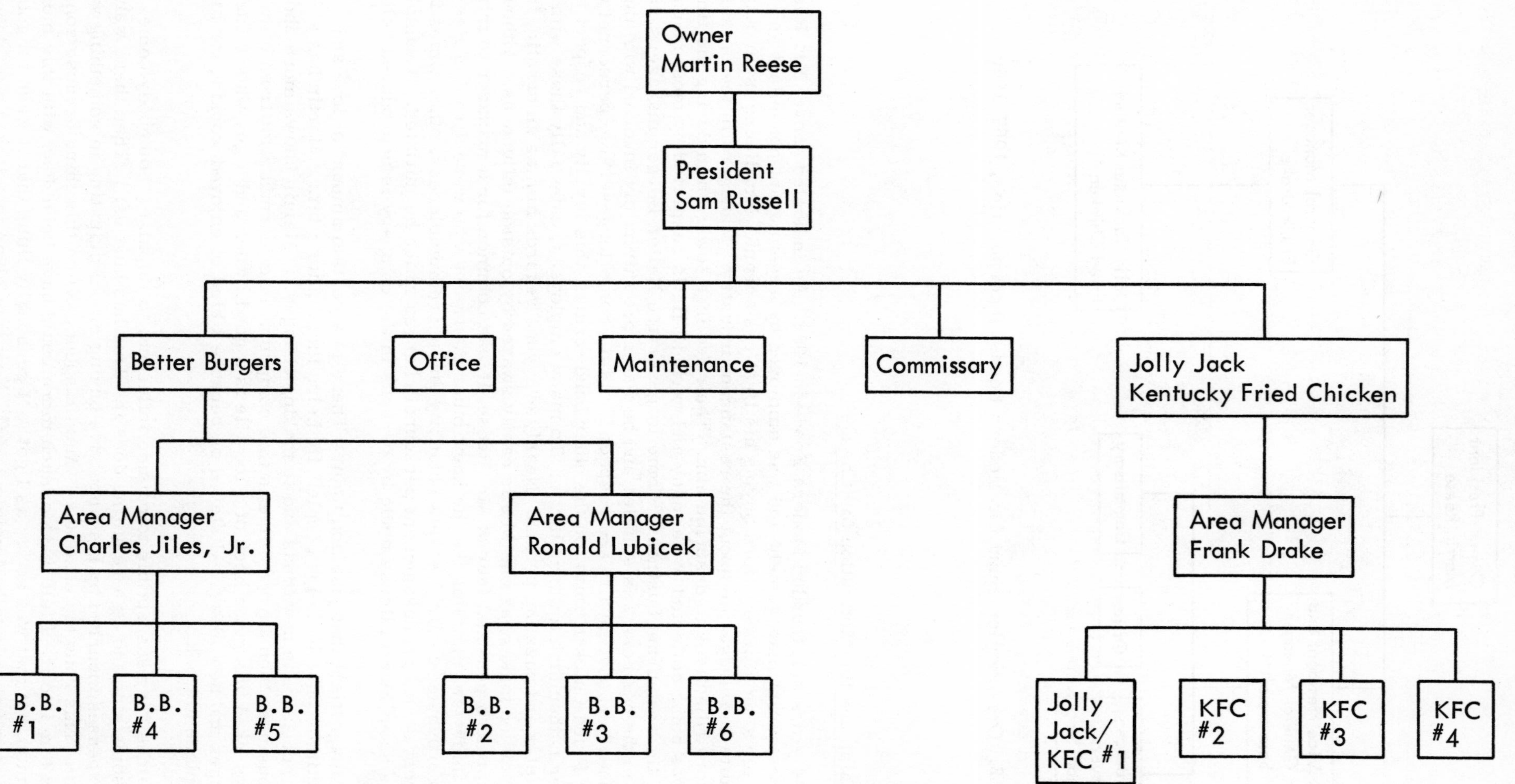

Figure 2. Organization chart for Modern Foods, Incorporated, 1966-1967.

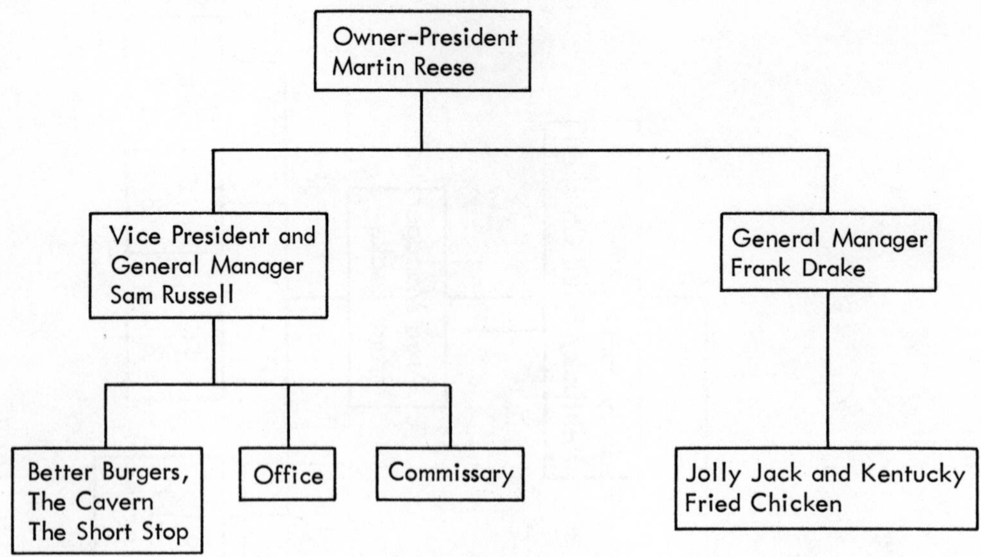

Figure 3. Organization chart for Modern Foods, Incorporation, 1967-1969.

Martin Reese--The Man and the Motivation for Change

Martin Reese, 44 years old, founded Modern Foods in 1952. As indicated above, Mr. Reese earned a degree in restaurant management and was employed by a restaurant consultant and as a restaurant manager for a short time before buying his first restaurant. Mr. Reese is an outgoing, likable individual, quite knowledgeable about the restaurant industry. Managers in the organization use many contradictory adjectives to describe him. Their feelings toward him during the time material for the case was being collected were many and varied. He is respected by most managers for his knowledge of the restaurant business. Some long-service Better Burger managers, those who worked with him when the business was smaller and he was more intimately involved with the operating units, have a deep personal loyalty and respect for him. Some long-service personnel in the Jolly Jack/Kentucky Fried Chicken units, on the other hand, exhibit this loyalty and respect toward his mother and father rather than toward Martin. To many employees, especially those with shorter service, he is a complex and puzzling person. Nearly everyone regards him as an erratic, inconsistent, impulsive decision maker, as one who is easily swayed by outside influences. Although most managers did not express a personal fear of Mr. Reese, it was common for a manager to introduce this topic during an interview, claiming that he knew other managers who were afraid of Reese. This fear was sometimes attributed to Mr. Reese's volatility and unpredictableness; other times it was attributed to the recent series of management personnel changes which he initiated. A sampling of the varied comments about Martin Reese made by persons in the company is reproduced below:

> This man has a magnetism that just won't quit. There is a certain amount of love and respect for Martin because he helps people. He helps them quite a bit. . .Martin has always been very receptive to new ideas and to making changes. . .Martin knows more about the restaurant business than anybody else in this company. I've learned a lot from him . . .I have always liked this guy a heck of a lot. He is a good owner and a guy who is susceptible to changes and new ideas. . .I stayed on because I kind of enjoyed working for him. This was a fun place to work.

> Martin was at times very susceptible to outside influence, to impulse. Somebody comes in and says to do something and as a result he does it. This has hurt us. . .Then there were the additional expenses incurred by his impulsive buying or participating in something we weren't aware of. This runs the costs up. . .Martin spent $(X) on this thing because some salesman talked him into it. I felt that so much more could have been done with this money. I voiced my opinion, but that was as far as I got. . .I personally think that it wasn't a good investment, but I wasn't able to talk Martin out of it. Now it is clear that it was a mistake.

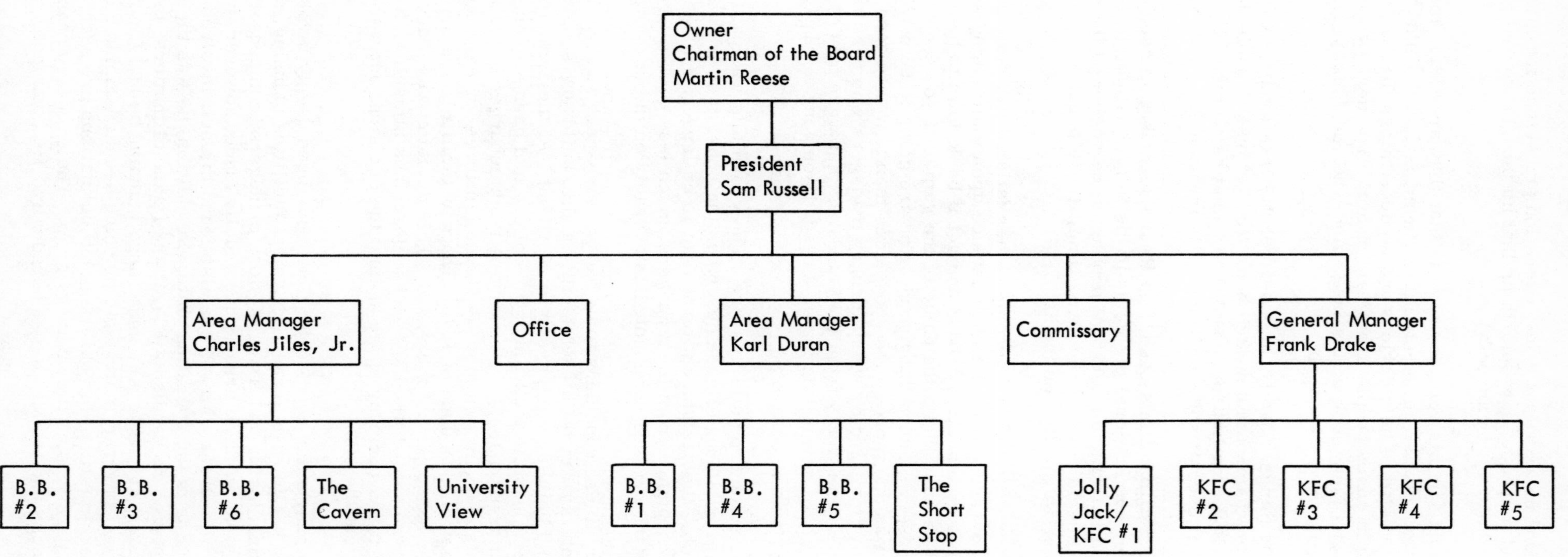

Figure 4. Organization chart for Modern Foods, Incorporated, September 1969 - Spring 1970.

Sam or Frank may have a good idea and put it into operation and before it really gets on its feet, Martin comes along and maybe he saw something that he thought worked good, too, and so he goes and changes it without telling anybody.

One problem that a lot of people in this company have is that they are afraid to talk to Martin. I am leary of Martin, too, because he is sometimes inconsistent. . .I like Martin. I think most people do. But sometimes he's devious and he does things that are unfair, that hurt people. That's why I think many people are afraid of him. You never know when you're going to be next. . .He gets this funny look on his face. And when he does, you know he means business. Something is going to happen.

Martin sometimes does funny things. Lately, he's been pretty irrational. . .Of course, Martin's thinking gets a little wham-bam now and then. You get questionable decisions. That has been a problem. . .It seems like he doesn't know what he's doing. He keeps making change after change, but it doesn't solve anything. It's irrational.

During the year prior to the writing of this case, Mr. Reese describes himself as having been emotionally upset due to some serious personal problems in his family. He believes that due to this upset condition and his preoccupation with his personal problems, he neglected the business and also made an abnormal number of bad decisions. At the same time, Reese became aware that his company was beginning to slip in other ways. He comments:

I was aware that over a period of time I had become rather fat and lazy personally. I had lost a lot of the hunger to grow and I lost a lot of insistence upon maintaining standards. I knew that I needed to turn this organization around and get it back down to bedrock as far as standards are concerned because that's the name of the game. If you can't perform for your customers, you don't deserve a darn thing good. You are going to be out. A lot of the money we had been making was due more to the good times than it was to good, tight operations. We had individual units managed by sharp, hungry managers who performed brilliantly, but overall we were slipping away from the standards that were needed. I felt like my people had gone deaf to what I was telling them. I needed someone to really build a fire back underneath my organization.

Mr. Reese hired a restaurant consultant to build this fire. The consultant was paid $30,000 to visit "at least once a month" for a year. Although Reese describes the consultant as "a good man, a sharp man who did his best to do his job," the assignment turned out to be largely a waste of money. The consultant was not able to win acceptance from the managers, much less build a fire under them. Without exception, all managers interviewed commented unfavorably on the consultant.

A second decision which Mr. Reese considers to be bad in retrospect was the decision to demolish the combined Jolly Jack/Kentucky Fried Chicken facility and to build new, separate facilities for each of those operations. The old building was physically worn out. At the same time, the chicken business had been growing in volume while the hamburger volume had been slipping steadily in volume. Reese believed that the chicken business was carrying the hamburger operation and that it would be desirable for each to stand on its own feet. Separate facilities for each operation, geared for a much larger volume, were opened in June of 1970. The new facilities are much more expensive to operate. Volume, on the other hand, has not increased. This decision was made at the urging of the restaurant consultant during the period when Mr. Reese describes himself as having been emotionally upset. Other managers in the company spoke against the decision, but were unable to dissuade Mr. Reese from carrying out the plan.

Throughout most of the company's history, Martin Reese has been deeply involved in operations. He was the principal decision maker in such areas as physical facilities planning, menu planning and pricing, promotion and advertising, hiring and firing of store managers, compensation, and formulation of operating policies. Decisions in these areas were usually made, however, with the advice and consultation of Mr. Russell and Mr. Drake. Mr. Reese also found himself involved in the day-to-day troubleshooting and problem solving in the operating units. In addition, he was the organization's chief mediator with the environment. He handled all legal and financial matters, the planning and acquisition of new operating units, and did whatever long-range planning he had time for, which was little. He found himself neglecting long-range strategic planning because so much of his time was taken up with operations. At the same time, his abilities and inclinations are such that he was increasingly unable to cope with operations as the business grew. The existing arrangements were unsatisfactory both for the business and for Mr. Reese personally. He comments:

I don't really get my kicks any more from operations as such. I would rather be out here hunting new opportunities and what have you. I have no desire to retire. I am not at the retirement stage, but I want time to take fresh looks at what is happening in our business and what I think is going to happen, and how we can blend in with that and take advantage of it and profit from it. And I want time for my own personal life.

The reorganization of September 1969 was intended as a means to take Mr. Reese out of operations to a considerable extent, and it introduced more manpower into the ranks of central management to cope with the increasing load. By the Spring of 1970, Mr. Reese was beginning to doubt the wisdom of his move and to fear that the company was slowly deteriorating in terms of operating performance. The organization remained quite informal, training programs were not developed, planning of operations was minimal, budgets were nonexistent, reporting and paperwork systems in general were rudimentary and unsystematic. Consequently, the operation depended heavily on personal daily supervision to function. Not only was Reese unsuccessful in developing the mechanisms that would have reduced the burden of personal supervision, but he also felt that he had not developed his subordinates so that they might share significantly this burden of personal supervision. He has been disappointed that his immediate subordinates have not developed the initiative to take on much of the operational decision making. He is also disappointed that they have not been as conscientious in day-to-day supervision as he would like them to be.

The Reorganization of 1970

During the late Spring of 1970, Mr. Reese moved back into the position of chief operating officer of the company. He took the title of president. Mr. Russell was named senior vice president and general manager in charge of the Better Burgers, University View, The Cavern, the central office and the commissary. Mr. Drake's title was changed to vice president in charge of Jolly Jack's, Kentucky Fried Chicken, and The Short Stop and he reported directly to Mr. Reese once again. The positions of the two area managers were abolished. Mr. Duran was returned to a position of unit manager and Mr. Jiles was fired because Reese believed he had been neglecting his responsibilities. The organization took the form shown in Figure 5. This arrangement required most of Reese's attention to be focused on operations, which he says he is no longer particularly interested in, and he believed that much more needed to be done:

I have seen within the last two or three years that the old way of operating just wasn't going to be able to cut it in the future and so my choices were clear--either tool up and get capable enough to handle future ways of operating or else trim back down to a fighting weight with the outstanding locations we have and then get rid of the rest of them. I can make a grand living on that basis, but there is no feeling of accomplishment in going backwards. We're going to go forward.

I am not really good at organizing. I've built this organization about as far as I think it can be built on a casual, amateurish basis. If we are going to get bigger, we have got the framework, the formal organization and communication. I am a very poor man at details. I don't enjoy detail work. I am not really good at it and I have a relatively poor memory for details. When it came to budgeting, formal reporting, and things like that, I was really not interested. I never saw the need for it until recently. We are going to be more formalized. People are going to be forced to organize themselves and plan their activities better and communicate in both directions better. We will suffer the disadvantages of this as well as reap the advantages. There may not be as personal a relationship between a lot of the people and myself. But we are going to build in opportunities for people. Right now we have about run out of them under this personalized way of operating.

I haven't really known how to build a successful formal training program. Also, our expansion has been at such a leisurely rate that there was no real need for it in my opinion. Now, I am about to come full circle on that. I think that we do need a continuing training program that is more formalized, but always in combination with on-the-job training. I don't think either one by itself is ideal at all. We are not today in a position to take advantage of the opportunities, partially because we don't have the formal organized training program to be able to quickly teach people to uphold our standards or our systems or what have you. We need a formalized training program, especially if over the next five years we want to acquire or open, say, ten more units.

Most managers in the company believe with Mr. Reese that the company has outgrown its present management system. However, many of them do not believe that Mr. Reese can bring himself to withdraw from the operating end of the business. They believe that he has an inclination to have his finger in all of the pies and that this has caused many of the company's difficulties. Because he felt the need to be involved and make decisions personally while at the same time he was too busy and too poorly informed, he often made bad decisions. Some managers believe that Mr. Reese's immediate subordinates have not developed more initiative largely because they felt the need to second guess him, because they felt the need to look over their shoulders to see what he wanted them to do, because if they were going to have their decisions reversed anyway, they might as well wait and let Mr. Reese make the decisions in the first place. Some managers believe that Mr. Reese is really an operating man, that he never expressed any interest in strategic planning and corporate development until a consultant told him that he should be concerned with these things. They believe that despite what he says, he will continue in the same old role.

Nevertheless, on August 1, 1970, Mr. Reese made a dramatic move. He brought a new, high-level executive into the organization from the outside. Mr. Nathan Carter was named executive vice president and became the immediate superior of Mr. Russell and Mr. Drake. Russell and Drake were given new titles of vice presidents for operations. The organization chart adopted on August 1, 1970 is shown in Figure 6. The role of operating vice president is described in detail in Figure 7, "Responsibilities for Supervisors," a document prepared by Mr. Carter (Carter always refers to the operating vice presidents as supervisors).

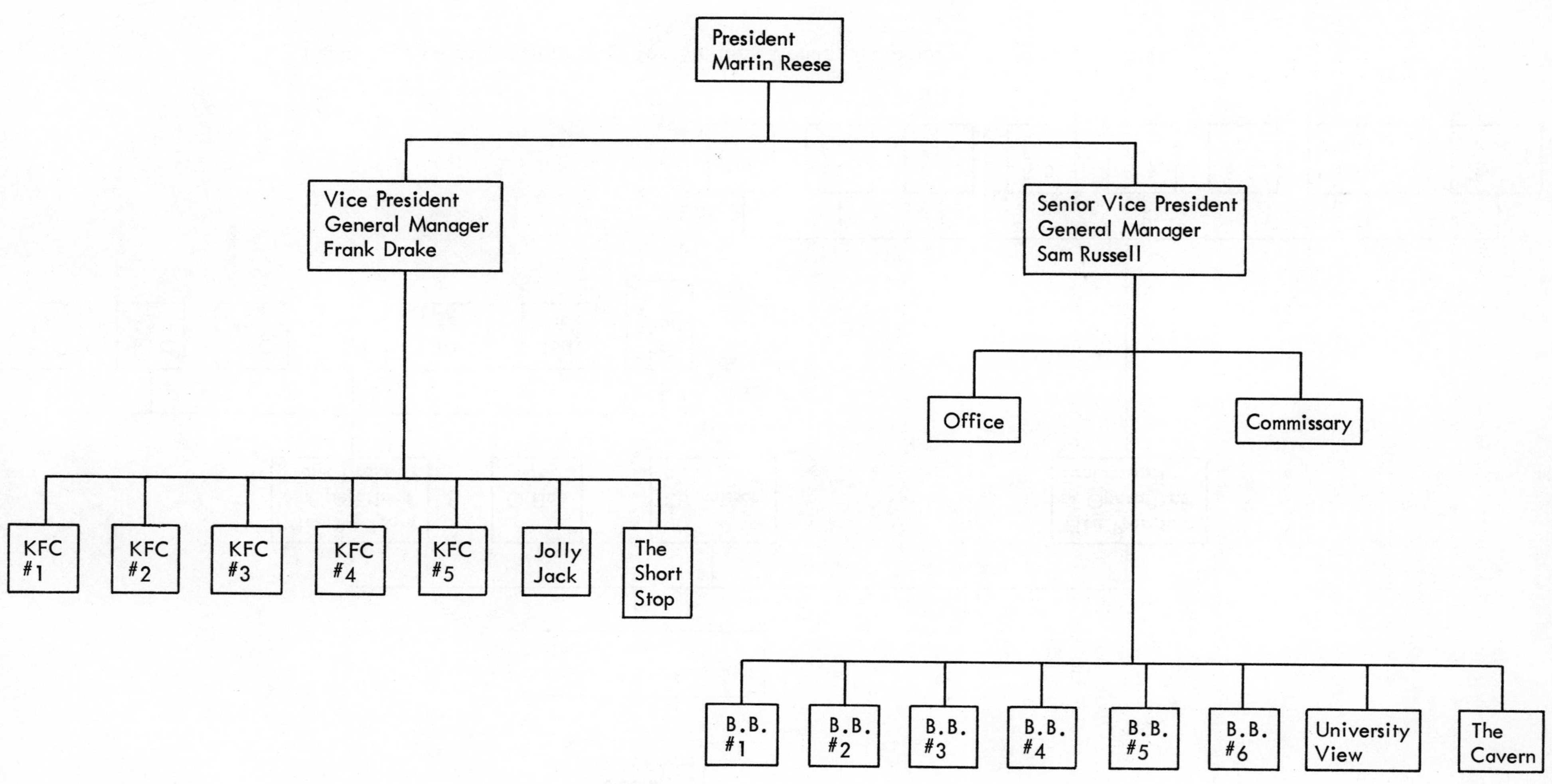

Figure 5. Organization chart for Modern Foods, Incorporated, Summer 1970.

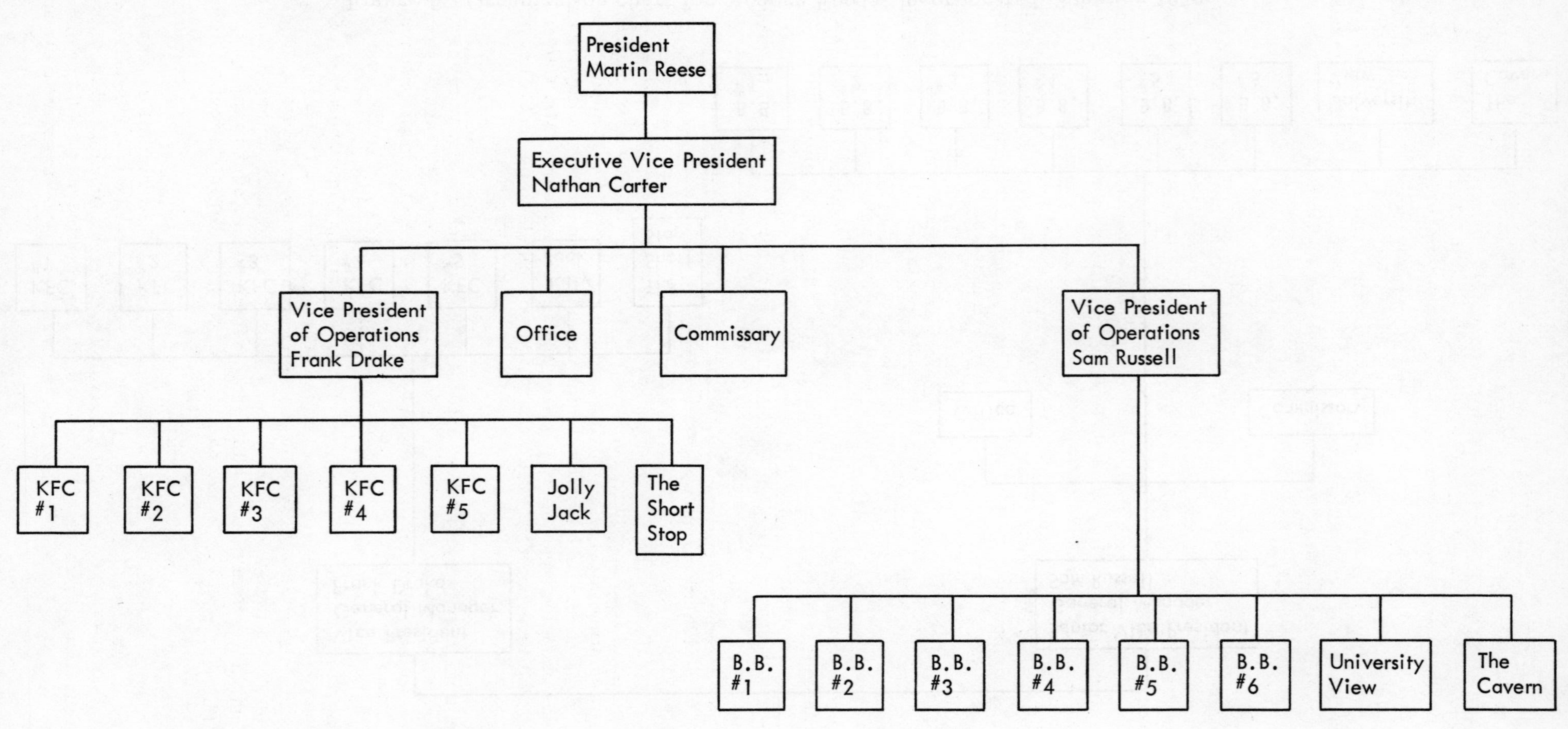

Figure 6. Organization chart for Modern Foods, Incorporated, August 1, 1970.

As can be seen from Figure 7, this position is not intended to be a policy-making one. It is a role of implementation, of day-to-day training, overseeing, problem-solving, and evaluation in the operating units. It is difficult to say precisely how drastic the role change will be for Mr. Russell and Mr. Drake because responsibilities were never very clearly defined in Modern Foods central management in the past. However, it is probably accurate to say that both Russell and Drake, especially the former, did participate in policy making with Mr. Reese, even though final decisions were made by Reese. Even final decisions about such operating matters as advertising campaigns for the various groups of units, physical facilities planning, and the hiring and compensation of unit managers were usually made by Mr. Reese. Frank Drake's responsibilities have probably not been changed in a major way. However, there is no question that Sam Russell's position in the company is now markedly different. The scope of his responsibilities has been much reduced, both in terms of operating units and functions.

As mentioned above, Nathan Carter, 44, joined the company in his present position on August 1, 1970. Although he had been working with Mr. Reese for the past year on another food service venture (a venture which, for a variety of reasons, has been shelved), Mr. Carter had never been an employee of Modern Foods per se before stepping into his present job. He is the only headquarter executive who did not make his way up from the ranks. In fact, he is one of the very few managers in the entire organization who did not begin as an hourly employee in one of the stores. He and Mr. Reese, however, have known each other since high school days.

Mr. Carter holds a B.B.A. degree from State University. He also completed much of the work toward an M.B.A. in transportation as well as toward a law degree from the same university. He regards organization as his strong area.

Carter first went to work for a construction company but shortly thereafter entered the food business when he was hired to work in a food distribution venture operated by a conglomerate built by another State University graduate. Mr. Carter remained in this company for some years, during which time he had the experience of managing a number of restaurants and of developing a franchise program for a string of specialty restaurants. In 1968, he joined another company which operated a string of specialty restaurants in order to develop a franchise program for them.

Because the organizational shakeup of August, 1970 is potentially the most far-reaching change that has been introduced into this company in years, we will let Mr. Carter describe his plans at length and we will also report the reactions of others to the change at some length.

It is the expressed intention of Mr. Reese that Nathan Carter will become the chief operating officer of the company. The operating vice presidents will report to him, he will be responsible for the overall effectiveness of food operations, for cost analysis, for testing new equipment, food, and menu items, and for assisting in problem solving in general. He will develop policies, prepare budgets, develop a reporting system, develop a training program, handle day-to-day correspondence and administrative affairs and supervise the main office and the commissary. Mr. Carter has some very definite ideas about what is wrong with the company and what needs to be done. Let us listen as he talks about the company and some of the things he intends to accomplish:

> They have done a tremendous job, a beautiful job in this company. But in order for us to be able to expand and get bigger, we have to organize ourselves. We have to get good management in here so that when we start expanding we can run the company properly. This is basically what I hope to accomplish.
>
> We will set down the policies that need to be formulated and put into operation. Policies and changes won't be made just for the sake of changing. There will be a purpose. It will be timely and well organized before we make policies and changes. I will be developing company policies, accounting, and so on. I will also be developing Sam and Frank in this new organization and they, in turn, are the prophets who will go back to the operating units and put it into effect. I won't go to the operating units and put it into effect. It is their job to do that.
>
> For the remainder of 1970 what I want operations to do is to clean up all the units. Soap, water, and muscle are cheap, you know. I want them to get out there and really clean them up--inside, outside, and personnel. Then I want to build up confidence and the morale factor in this organization. I want the supervisors for the remainder of 1970 to work on this and get it done. [Mr. Carter always uses the term "supervisors" to refer to the operating

vice presidents. He refers to unit managers as "managers."] Then for 1971 we are going to launch a lot of these plans that I am coming in with, like preparing an effective statistical reporting system. Right now we don't have one. We have sort of a half-way deal, but we are going to get a good one. This reporting system has to be presented for review by October 1, 1970. Then we will develop an operations budget. Something that this company has never really had is a budget. And, of course, I believe in them very much. Then we need to analyze our present profit and loss statements, to see what we don't like about them, to see how they can be changed, what the flaws are, what value we get from them. If we get no value from these monthly statements, then we need to change them.

Every place I have worked, we have always had a weekly report. The unit managers will send a report to their supervisors, these supervisors will send a report to me, and then I will work with it and send a report back to the supervisors and to Martin. I will write down what I have found from the supervisor's weekly report and I will send this back to the supervisor and he reads what I have found from his report about his operating units and he should go out and correct things. We will do this each and every week. To me, this is a very, very useful tool. Reports, as far as I am concerned, have two basic benefits. They inform the top level management executives in a quick concise nutshell what has gone on and what is going on. But just as important, maybe more important, this is a beautiful means for the unit managers, the supervisors, and for me to develop ourselves, to coordinate ourselves, to organize ourselves. If you have this and you know what you are going to to next week, you don't get up in the morning, scratch your head and say "Now, what am I going to do today?" It is all right here. It gives you a lot of real valuable information on sales, food costs, labor costs, etc. If you interpret it correctly and study it properly, it can give you all kinds of advance information.

The supervisors were not trained properly to be supervisors. They were not organized themselves, so how could they go out and organize somebody else? I want to develop duties and responsibilities for the supervisors from an operational standpoint. I want them to plan, to schedule themselves on a week-to-week, month-to-month program, to know each day in advance what they are to accomplish the next day. I want them to set up a continuous training program for each unit under their supervision. I want them to develop the same high standards of quality and service in all units. I want them to work with unit managers on purchasing techniques and standards. Portion control in our business means money. Yet in our five Kentucky Fried Chicken units, three different sizes of containers are being used for cole slaw. This is wrong. Each supervisor will see that all control and statistical reports are prepared at each unit daily, weekly, or monthly, as the case may be. These reports are to be carefully scrutinized and analyzed by the supervisors and if any items need action, such action must be taken within twenty-four hours. The supervisors will keep the necessary reports, paper work, and general administrative work current. There is a definite need for a training program. We will develop the training topics and the supervisors will then conduct the training for their managers who will take this information back to the units and train their people.

We are setting up a preventive maintenance program. Right now it is only corrective. When something breaks down, we fix it. But I contend that if we practice preventive maintenance, we can reduce our maintenance costs drastically. We can prolong the life of our equipment. We are going to reduce those costly surprises. There are a lot of existing facilities that need to be repaired. We will budget this systematically month by month instead of just going down there sometime and putting on a new roof. We will tie this in with our cash position in our planning and this will allow us to have a systematic maintenance program.

There is a certain amount of administrative work that the unit managers have to do and there are a lot of things that they have to control. These controls are a real important thing on their part and these are some of the things that we are going to tighten up. You don't just come in every morning and turn on the lights and turn them off at night. You look at your equipment and you do preventive maintenance. You don't buy the product from the first vendor that comes into the store in the morning. You learn to purchase, when to purchase, how to take advantage of prices.

General: The supervisors are the key personnel through whom policy and procedures are effected. They directly represent management to the restaurant employees. Supervisors should be aware of the objectives of the company and of the manner in which their jobs are related to those objectives. The supervisor is the operations and communications link between management and operating units. He reports to the executive vice president.

Specific: Maintain proper cost percentages in all units supervised. Make prescribed number of visits to units. Provide unit manager with help and advice in problem solving. Maintain satisfactory relationship with managers. Keep managers informed of new information, changes, promotions, policies, laws, etc. Provide the manager with an accurate and definite evaluation of his operation. Help the manager improve his unit or correct his problems by setting up an action plan with the manager. Provide executive vice president with complete, accurate, and detailed evaluation of each unit and copy of action plan for solving problems. Keep informed of all complaints, compliments, and problems of assigned units.

Planning: Fill out an evaluation of own work every three months. Set objectives and target dates for completion of objectives every three months. Set up action plan for all problem areas and for self improvement. Initiate operations budgets for units.

Reporting:
Daily Reports - Obtain daily sales by unit and others as directed.
Weekly Reports - Complete progress report for past week and show schedule for next week. Turn in to executive vice president each Tuesday.
Monthly Reports - Make monthly statistical reports. Complete inventories, P & L statements, analyze, interpret, and make adjustments.

Figure 7. Responsibilities of supervisors in Modern Foods, Incorporated.

You don't come in and just overstock your refrigerators and shelves with products. You have to learn how to control your inventory for a smooth inventory turnover and you have to balance inventory with sales. These are the kinds of things where training comes in. And training comes into how the cashier meets the public, how she grooms herself, how she handles cash, and so on. I don't want to be derogatory about how these things were handled, but we are going to improve on all of this and sharpen up some.

We also have to develop a good communication system here. This has been lacking in many respects. A lot of the managers have good ideas because they work there each and every day. They know the flow, they know how things should be handled. Too often they have suggestions for changes or they made recommendations and then the person they made it to used it as his original idea. Well, they quit making suggestions. The supervisors wanted all suggestions from the units to seem like "Man, I thought of that." So they put a stopper on communications upwards from the units. Communications were not getting up to the central control point where help could be initiated. This was something of deep concern to the managers. They had lapsed into an attitude of "Well, shoot, I have a problem but there is no one I can turn to, so why say anything about it." And so the problems continued to exist. Problems don't solve themselves. They just get worse. I knew we had this problem-solving problem, that no one was getting satisfaction. So I developed a problem-solving technique where we will have this form for the units to indicate their problems and their recommendations for dealing with them. This will be sent to the main office. I promised that all problems either would be solved within a 24-hour period or would conscientiously be worked on within that period of time. We will put a date on this when the supervisor started action on it, and we will follow up on it. I will look at these things every morning to see if these problems are being solved. If they are not, then the supervisor and I have a few words.

There was a certain fear that had developed among the managers because of lack of recognition, because we changed three supervisors and got rid of one, because we hired a consultant that some of them didn't get along too well with, and because I came on the scene. There is an unrest. I can understand that. What I am trying to tell them is that so long as they do their jobs and do them right, so long as they use these tools that we are going to be giving them, they have nothing to fear. I am trying to dispel this fear. I am trying to set the stage so that I am accepted by them.

The comments above cover, in a general way, the kinds of things Nathan Carter has in store for the organization. Several additional comments are reproduced below which convey somewhat better the way in which he operates, his managerial style:

I have this little notebook and I will put down in one-two-three-four fashion the things I have to do that day. As I do these things, I mark them off. Anything that I have left from today's schedule that I was unable to accomplish becomes Number 1 tomorrow. I am trying to get my subordinates to do the same thing.

I am a firm believer that when things are approved, they should be dated and signed. Too many things go out unsigned or unapproved and then people have a tendency to forget or don't accept it. The signing shows authority.

I must apologize for this report. It is the first one. When I had a secretary, I had her trained. She thought like me and everything else. She knew how to label something like this. I guess I have to train myself to train them how to do this right.

You know, if you are going to develop your managers into professionals, you have to be set up like professionals and not be giving your president handwritten forms. I think there is a certain amount of communicating that needs to be done and I think we are restricted in this because we don't have a secretary that I or Martin or the supervisors can give a letter to and get it out.

Right now the supervisors can sign any amount on a check. We just redid a unit and the supervisor signed a $19,000 check. To me it is just good business that you set a limit. I put this limit at $500. Anything above $500 will have a double signature. I know we don't have thieves, but it is just sound business. This is not something that really worries me because these are honest, reputable people that we have, but I want to keep them that way.

I would like an operating manual and then a policy manual. An operating manual is to show you how to operate and you can give it to people. But a policy manual has some privileged information and it should be kept separate. Here these are lumped together and we are going to have to separate these things out.

Martin Reese believes that he has found in Nathan Carter the man who can do the things that he was neither able to do nor interested in doing.

Nathan should do a better job from the standpoint of operating than I can because of his better feeling for detail, for organization, for communication. I will do the blue sky if he can take care of those operations. He showed me that he was both a self-starter and that he had good judgment. And that is why when I made up my mind that I had to either get a strong man underneath me or replace my two key men, I decided to give it to Nathan.

But at the same time Mr. Reese makes it clear that Carter must prove himself, that he is on trial. He points out that Carter is not receiving a particularly high salary during this trial period and that he intends to keep an eye on things. As he says:

I am going to have to make sure that Nathan is a strong enough man and competent enough to keep going not only with what we have but to keep it growing before I would feel free to take my mind off the food business. He will have to show me before I will ever be tempted to do so.

Other managers in the company are cautious in commenting on Mr. Carter. As one said, "I'm not going to jeopardize my future by making rash comments about Nathan Carter." Because less than half of the unit managers were interviewed, it is difficult to determine how many of the managers are responding positively and how many are responding negatively. Far more positive than negative comments were made during the interviews. This may reflect the true attitudes of the managers, it may reflect a reluctance to comment negatively to the interviewer, or it may be due to a fluke of sampling. Two managers who were believed by others to be particularly hostile were not interviewed. With only one exception, all persons interviewed believed there were serious deficiencies in the top management of the company that needed to be corrected. Even persons who are not favorably disposed toward Nathan Carter believed something needed to be done:

I am not sure Nathan is the answer. I know that there is definitely a need for somebody in his position. Whether he is the right man for the job, I don't know. He hasn't been here long enough to really prove himself. I think I know what needs to be done. It just takes the manpower and the putting of it all together to get it done.

A number of other people not only saw a need to do something but believe that Mr. Carter may be the man to do it:

This company has overpowered Martin in a way because he has been the sole manager over so many people and didn't allow himself to get someone to handle this for him. Now he has a man who is capable and able. Things we have suggested for several years are now being put into effect and, I am sure, will bear fruition within a very short period of time. It is going to be a completely different picture, I think, six months from now because of the realization that we need this individual that can be top dog over the others. We've sort of had the "Peter Principle" [the Peter Principle states that managers tend to rise to their level of incompetence] operating in this organization. We tried to get by with individuals from within the organization in that position. They were good managers, but they have been unable to operate in that position. It just hasn't worked.

Nathan Carter is the kind of individual who has had a great deal of experience in supervision and I think he is going to demand and get more. We will have a cleaner Better Burger. We will have a Better Burger which is always in first-class order in terms of equipment. We will have a report on what these units do each month. Each month we will get it and we will be able to know where we stand and how much we spent, how much we took in, and what we are doing. Now we will have some standards. We will have some criteria. The best thing probably is that we have one man who won't be trying to do it himself but will be delegating authority to do these various things and requiring that certain things be done and records will be kept that never have been kept before. I think we will have a more orderly growth than we have had. It won't be quite so impulsive. There will be some planning and thinking before it's done. I think if we don't do another thing, we will earn money by just the educational program with the people who work in the restaurants, getting them to do suggestive selling. We will have better organization, a delegation of authority and better communications between individuals so that when something is wrong in your particular restaurant you know who to go to. You don't just go through a bunch of people. You go to Nathan and you say "This is what I need." The proper use of authority has been lacking. I don't think you can lay this at the feet of Sam or Frank or Martin. The authority was just not clearly defined. It almost had to be a man brought in from the outside. Sam and Frank are capable people, but I'm not sure either one of them could take the job that Nathan Carter has. I think possibly they are capable of doing such a job, but not in this organization. They are too close to the rest of the people in the company.

I think Nathan is a good addition. I think they finally got somebody in the top management who is going to really organize all the units toward one goal as one company. I've always felt in the past that Jolly Jack/Kentucky Fried Chicken was kind of secondary to the Better Burgers because the top men, Sam and Martin, were Better Burger men. Over a period of time, Martin learned that we could make more money than those Better Burgers could, so he changed his feeling. But Sam never did. I think Nathan is unbiased. We need to have all the stores doing things the sam way so that whether I work at this store or I work at that store, I know what I'm doing. Also the office is going to have more information about the unit. And you are going to know on the 31st how your store did, not in the middle of next month when you have another month behind you and you're still in the same shape you were in last month. I expect my job to be more organized, more uniform, and I expect to know more what is expected of me and what kind of goals I'm supposed to reach. Nathan is the type of guy who is definitely interested in his job. I feel that if I don't do well here, there is no way for Nathan to do well. If I'm doing bad, well, Nathan's doing bad, too. I couldn't feel that way about Sam because all the time that he was in that position, he never said one thing to me about the store or what his operations ideals or views on management were or anything. I feel if my store ain't doing well, I can go to Nathan and say, "Look here, my store ain't doing well, what are we going to do about it," and, from what he told me, he'll do something about it.

I feel if Nathan doesn't do a good job, Martin is going to get rid of him and if he does a good job, it is for our good. Possibly then the company will expand and there will be more opportunities for people who are ready to take them. I think I will be better off with Nathan here. I think that communication will improve. I think there will be a standardization in book work and this is good. Nathan knows a lot about training. Sam has been just with Better Burgers but Nathan has been around a lot. I feel that there is a lot that I can learn from the man that I couldn't learn from Sam. Of course, Nathan is what I call a "paper manager." He is going to manage from his desk. He isn't going to spend much time out here, so maybe I won't have much chance to learn from him. The company hasn't gone anywhere in a couple of years. Hopefully with Nathan it will.

Despite the hopefulness and the optimism reflected in the remarks presented above, Mr. Carter has some obstacles to overcome. Nearly everyone in the organization was upset by the way the recent changes were introduced and many people believe that Sam Russell was treated in a very unfair and shoddy manner. Although whatever hostility has developed on these accounts is directed primarily toward Martin Reese rather than toward Nathan Carter, the hostility nonetheless colors the climate of the company at this time and some of it can't help but rub off on Mr. Carter:

Morale may be low in a few stores now because a lot of people seem to object to Nathan Carter. I don't. A lot of people object to him because he is new, because he wasn't brought up with the company, because he doesn't know a lot about our operations, because he was put in a position where Sam was at one time. Sam has been around a long time. A lot of people are loyal to him.

What Martin did to Sam shouldn't happen to anybody. Sam was the president of this company at one time. Now he's just a supervisor. It will take a long time for us to forget that this was done.

When you see a top man like Sam demoted, you get the feeling that maybe you could be demoted, too. This is where the fear comes that there is going to be a lot of turnover. Of course, I think Nathan is a smart man. He isn't going to go out there and cut off his nose to spite his face. He is not going to come in and make snap decisions. He is going to discuss them. I don't know of any manager in any unit who has decided to quit because of Nathan Carter. I think if any guy is going to quit, he is going to quit strictly over the way it was handled. If a guy quits over that, of course, that's pretty petty.

I think morale has come down considerably since this change was made. The reason wasn't explained enough to each manager. There has to be a reason, whatever it was. I don't know the reason for the change. The reason we were given is that he might train Sam and Frank. But in my mind, they have all the training they need. Maybe they don't know all there is to know about running an office, but who cares about that? It is the unit that you worry about. So I have this uncertain feeling because I can't see Martin's reason. And Sam has a depressed feeling which brought morale down. He lacks the enthusiasm that keeps your unit trying. The change was a surprise to most people. Martin just went in and did it and then he came around and explained or tried to explain why. It was never talked over with anybody. If he had done that it would have been better. You need to promote an idea. If you aren't promoting it, the buyer is not going to buy it. It is not so much the change itself as the way the change was made. There was not enough talking it over. I don't know the guy very well, I haven't had many dealings with him and I don't know his background. I don't even know enough about him to be scared. He might come up with one or two good ideas, but we are going to go through a period of twenty bad ones to get to those one or two good ideas. It will be disruptive for awhile. We have gone through efficiency experts and people like that. They come up with ten ideas and maybe one is suitable for our business.

In addition, Nathan Carter has a managerial style and some personnel mannerisms that have predisposed many people not to like him, regardless of whether they value his abilities or not. He believes that there is one best way, his way, of doing things. The managers believe he is hard-nosed and inflexible. He is not very sensitive to interpersonal relations. He is not always aware of the impact he is making on other people. He is described as a "paper man," a "paperwork manager." All of these things connote a managerial style quite different from that which people in this organizatiom have experienced in the past. There have been many ways of doing things, management demands have not been rigorous and often were not met anyway, interpersonal relationships have been quite informal and, for the most part, positive and warm, there has been a relative absence of paperwork systems and certainly of "paper managers." Although he has visited some of the units hardly at all, when he does visit he tends to make comments and suggestions about very specific things. The managers believe he does not understand their operations very well at this point and, therefore, should not be making such comments. Since the disliked management consultant who had been working in the organization tended to to the same thing, some of the managers have begun to associate Mr. Carter with the consultant. Some of the managers believe he thinks too well of himself and too little of them:

Nathan says "I" a lot--"_I_ will accomplish this," "_I_ will accomplish that." Well, if he isn't careful we're all going to sit back and say "OK, big shot, _you_ accomplish this and _you_ accomplish that. _We_ aren't helping."

This feeling was very much enhanced by a formal speech Mr. Carter prepared to deliver to the employees when he stepped into his job. This has not been a speech-making company. In addition, many people found the speech to be pompous and patronizing:

I think if Nathan will be himself he can do a hell of a job. If he will be himself he will get through to people. But he started off by writing a speech and reading it to all the employees. He must have looked up all those big words in the dictionary. That was bad. He wasn't being himself at all.

In the meeting, Nathan read from a piece of paper. This man does not sell me. He had better stand up and give me his own thoughts rather than what is written down on paper. I will get a better idea of what he has in mind. If you are going to speak to me, speak to me person to person, not from a piece of paper. The guy did not sell himself. He hurt himself this first go-around. I have used papers in meetings but not constantly read from them word for word. I try to talk to my people.

One manager pointed out that the company has a long history of talking about grand programs that might be beneficial. But somehow these programs seldom get implemented, there has been very little follow-through. Time will tell whether this program will be implemented.

Mr. Russell says, "I think bridging the gap between goals and performance is the thing to work on now. The goals have been reevaluated and some new ones established. I think in some areas there is quite a gap between these goals and actual performance, for example in equipment, sanitation, proficiency of personnel, and profits. Mainly profits." Mr. Drake believes "We are going to have to get more professional and get things down to routine. I think it is amazing that we have gotten this far by being as informal as we have. And Mr. Reese was quoted earlier: ". . .there is no feeling of accomplishment going backwards. We're going to go go forward."

1) Adv. Manager Out of Date – Touch

2) Oper. Mgrs Man Part of Plans

3) Need to Eval Organ. & settle on One Set (Quit Changing)

4) Russell Pres Hip Pocket Not a Planner.